Sport and Migration

From Major League Baseball to English soccer's Premier League, all successful contemporary professional sports leagues include a wide diversity of nationalities and ethnicities within their playing and coaching rosters. The international migration of sporting talent and labour, encouraged and facilitated by the social and economic undercurrents of globalization, means that world sport is now an important case study for any student or researcher with an interest in international labour flows, economic migration, global demography or the interdependent world economy.

In this dazzling collection of chapters, leading international sport studies scholars chart the patterns, policies and personal experiences of labour migration within and around sport, and in doing so cast important new light both on the forces shaping modern sport and on the role that sport plays in shaping the world economy and global society. Presenting original case studies of sports from European and African soccer to Japanese baseball to rugby union in New Zealand, the book makes an important contribution to our understanding of a wide range of issues within contemporary social science, such as national identity politics, economic structure and organization, north–south relations, imperial legacies and gender relations.

This book is invaluable reading for students and researchers working in sport studies, human geography, economics or international business.

Joseph Maguire is Professor in Sociology of Sport in the School of Sport, Exercise and Health Sciences at the University of Loughborough, UK. He is a past President of the International Sociology of Sport Association and an executive board member of the International Council for Sports Science and Physical Education.

Mark Falcous is Senior Lecturer in the Sociology of Sport in the School of Physical Education at the University of Otago, New Zealand. He is an editorial board member for the *Sociology of Sport Journal*.

Sport and Migration

Borders, boundaries and crossings

Edited by
Joseph Maguire and Mark Falcous

Routledge
Taylor & Francis Group

LONDON AND NEW YORK

First published 2011
by Routledge
2 Park Square, Milton Park, Abingdon, Oxon OX14 4RN

Simultaneously published in the USA and Canada
by Routledge
270 Madison Avenue, New York, NY 10016

Routledge is an imprint of the Taylor & Francis Group, an informa business

Typeset in Baskerville by
Book Now Ltd, London
Printed and bound in Great Britain by
CPI Antony Rowe, Chippenham, Wiltshire

British Library Cataloguing in Publication Data
A catalogue record for this book is available from the British Library

Library of Congress Cataloguing in Publication Data
Sport and migration: borders, boundaries and crossings / edited by
Joseph Maguire and Mark Falcous.
    p. cm.
1. Sports—Sociological aspects. 2. Emigration and immigration.
3. Sports—Cross-cultural studies. 4. Athletes—Relocation.
I. Maguire, Joseph. II. Falcous, Mark.
GV706.8.S646 2010
306.4'83—dc22   2010013224

ISBN13: 978–0–415–49833–3 (hbk)
ISBN13: 978–0–415–49834–0 (pbk)
ISBN13: 978–0–203–87731–9 (ebk)

To Jennifer, Thomas, Ruaidhri and Tiernan
J.M.

To Rosie and Lily
ki āku tamāhine ataahua, e whakaako ana i ahua ia ra ia ra.
M.A.F.

Contents

Illustrations

Contributors

Sine Agergaard was trained as a social anthropologist at the University of Aarhus, Denmark, and Brunel University, United Kingdom. After finishing her PhD in 2004, she was employed as Assistant Professor in the Department of Sport Science at Aarhus University. She now holds the position of Associate Professor in the Department of Exercise and Sport Sciences, University of Copenhagen. Her research has focused on sporting landscapes and more recently on migration and integration issues in sports.

Wladimir Andreff is Professor Emeritus at the University Paris 1 Panthéon Sorbonne, France, and former President of the International Association of Sport Economists, the French Economic Association and the European Association for Comparative Economic Studies. He sits on 15 scientific journal editorial boards and is a peer-reviewer with 32 scientific journals. He is the editor of the book series 'New Horizons in the Economics of Sport' with Edward Elgar. He is the author of 10 books and 347 scientific articles and the editor of 12 books, including *Handbook on the Economics of Sport* (edited with Stefan Szymanski), Edward Elgar, 2006.

Terry Austrin teaches sociology at the University of Canterbury, New Zealand. He has research interests in the fields of historical sociology, work, gambling, new media, sport and ethnography. He has published widely in international journals including *Historical Sociology, Work, Employment and Society, Qualitative Research, Convergence: The International Journal of Research into New Media Technologies* and *New Media and Society*.

Roger Besson is a geographer and he graduated from the University of Neuchâtel, Switzerland. He is writing a PhD on the role of football stadiums in the fostering of social integration. He is employed as a scientific collaborator by the International Centre of Sport Studies and also works as Lecturer at the Institute of Geography of the University of Neuchâtel, the same university. Since 2008, he has been a key member of the Professional Football Players' Observatory.

Vera Botelho has a PhD in Social Anthropology from University College London and is currently Research Fellow at the University of Southern Denmark. Her research interests include migratory movements in the Brazilian Amazon

Region, Canada and Denmark. She has lectured on migration and environment at the University of British Columbia and Simon Fraser University, Vancouver. At the moment her research focus is on sports migration.

Toni Bruce is Senior Lecturer in the Department of Sport and Leisure Studies at the University of Waikato, Hamilton, New Zealand. She is interested in how issues of gender, race and national identity play out in the sports media, both locally and globally. Her current research explores the meaning of rugby in New Zealand. Her work is published in a range of journals and she is co-editor of a forthcoming book, *Sportswomen at the Olympics: A Global Comparison of Newspaper Coverage*, which includes analyses of the Olympic Games from researchers in 18 countries.

Paul Darby is Senior Lecturer in Sport and Exercise at the University of Ulster, UK. He is the author of *Gaelic Games and the Irish Diaspora in the United States* (2009) and *Africa, Football and FIFA: Politics, Colonialism and Resistance* (2002) and joint editor of *Emigrant Players: Sport and the Irish Diaspora* (with David Hassan, 2008) and *Soccer and Disaster: International Perspectives* (with Gavin Mellor and Martin Johnes, 2005). He sits on the editorial board of *Soccer and Society* and *Impumelelo: The interdisciplinary electronic journal of African sport.*

Richard Elliott is Senior Lecturer in Sport and Director of the Lawrie McMenemy Centre for Football Research at Southampton Solent University, UK. His expertise lies in the area of athletic migration where he has examined various dimensions of the migration process in a number of professional sports. Richard has published and presented his work internationally and is regularly consulted by the professional football industry.

Andrew Grainger is Senior Lecturer at Liverpool Hope University, UK. Broadly interested in the relationship between globalization, immigration and identity, Andrew's recent work examines the cultural politics of race and nation as played out through physical culture and the sport of rugby in particular. Despite the nature of this research, and in a classic case of Orwellian doublethink, he remains a fan of the New Zealand All Blacks rugby team.

John Horne is Professor of Sport and Sociology at the University of Central Lancashire, UK. He has published many articles and book chapters on sport in Japan and is the author of *Sport in Consumer Culture* (Palgrave, 2006) and co-editor (with Wolfram Manzenreiter) of *Japan, Korea and the 2002 World Cup* (Routledge, 2002), *Football Goes East* (Routledge, 2004) and *Sports Mega-Events* (Blackwell, 2006).

Alan Klein is Professor of Anthropology at Northeastern University, USA. He has examined Dominican baseball as both a transnational phenomenon as well as in terms of globalization. He is the author of *Sugarball: The American Game, the Dominican Dream* (Yale University Press, 1991), *Baseball on the Border: A Tale of Two Laredos* (Princeton University Press, 1997)and *Growing the Game: Globalization and*

Major League Baseball (Yale University Press, 2006). He is currently working on his newest book, *New Pride, Old Prejudice: The Second Coming of Dominican Baseball.*

Geoffrey Lawrence is Professor of Sociology and Head of the School of Social Science at the University of Queensland, Brisbane, Australia. His areas of research include global and local relations, the restructuring of agri-food industries and the sociology of sport. In relation to the latter, his co-authored and co-edited books include *Globalization and Sport: Playing the World* (Sage, 2001) and *Tourism, Leisure, Sport: Critical Perspectives* (Hodder, 1998). He is Fellow of the Academy of Social Sciences in Australia.

Toby Miller is Chair of the Department of Media and Cultural Studies at the University of California, Riverside. He is the author and editor of over 20 books and hundreds of book chapters and journal articles, most of which lie seemingly unnoticed. His latest books are *Makeover Nation: The United States of Reinvention* (2008) and *The Contemporary Hollywood Reader* (2009). His new book, *Television Studies: The Basics,* appeared in 2010.

Gyozo Molnar is Senior Lecturer in the Institute of Sport and Exercise Science at the University of Worcester, UK. He completed his doctorate in Sociology of Sport at Loughborough University, was the co-ordinator for the Centre for Olympic Studies and Research and has taught modules in the areas of sociology and politics of sports and exercise. His current publications revolve around migration, football, globalization, national identity, the Olympics and sport-related role exit.

Camilla Obel teaches sociology at the University of Canterbury, New Zealand. Her research interests currently include sport media technologies, sport fans and sport and indigeneity. She has published on the politics of race, ethnicity and nationalisms, embodiment, disability, gender, sport and recreation facilities. Her work has featured in international journals including *Sociology of Sport,* the *International Review for the Sociology of Sport, Sporting Traditions* and the *International Journal of Sport Management and Marketing.*

Raffaele Poli, a Geographer and Sociologist by training, is Junior Professor Assistant at the Institute of Sport Sciences of the University of Lausanne, Switzerland. He is also employed as a scientific collaborator by the International Centre of Sport Studies of the University of Neuchâtel, Switzerland. He is Co-founder and Director of the Professional Football Players' Observatory. He works on issues related to the themes of migration, the labour market, globalization, social networks, identity and geopolitics of sport, in particular football.

David Rowe is with the Centre for Cultural Research, University of Western Sydney, Australia, of which he was Director (2006–9). He has published in many academic journals, including *Media, Culture & Society, International Journal of Sport Communication, Journalism, Social Text, Journal of Sport & Social Issues, International Review for the Sociology of Sport, Social Semiotics* and *Sociology of Sport Journal.* His books include *Popular Cultures: Rock Music, Sport and the Politics of Pleasure* (London: Sage, 1995) and *Sport, Culture and the Media: The Unruly Trinity* (second edition, Maidenhead, United Kingdom: Open University Press, 2004). His work has been translated into several languages, including Chinese, Italian, Arabic, French and Turkish.

Yoshio Takahashi is Associate Professor in the Graduate School of Sport and Health Promotion at Tsukuba University, Japan. He has worked for several sport-related organizations and has published widely on many aspects of sport, including 'Japanese football players and the sport talent migration business' (with John Horne) in W. Manzenreiter and J. Horne (eds), *Football Goes East* (Routledge, 2004) and 'Soccer spectators and fans in Japan' in E. Dunning *et al.* (eds), *Fighting Fans* (University College Dublin Press, 2002).

Holly Thorpe is Lecturer at the University of Waikato, New Zealand. Her research interests include social theory, physical youth culture, gender and extreme sports, and she is currently writing a book titled *Snowboarding Bodies in Theory and Practice*. Her latest research project, titled 'Transnational Youth Cultures: Travel, Lifestyle and Extreme Sport', is a longitudinal study of the experiences of lifestyle sport migrants in transnational physical cultural 'hot spots' in Australia, Canada, Indonesia, France, Japan, and New Zealand.

Ricardo Trumper is Associate Professor of Sociology in the Irving K. Barber School of Arts and Sciences at the University of British Columbia Okanagan. He received his PhD in Social and Political Thought from York University. His present research includes migration, mobility and neoliberalism. He is currently working on mobility, fear and sports in Chile and on the repercussions of migration and neoliberalism on the Okanagan Valley in Canada.

Jason Tuck is Head of the Department of Sports Studies and Principal Lecturer in the Sociology of Sport at the University of Winchester, UK. Having completed his doctoral research at Loughborough University, which examined rugby union and national identity, much of his post-doctoral research has focused on further developing a figurational sociological framework through which to explore national identity. Jason is also Fellow of the Higher Education Academy.

Belinda Wheaton is Senior Research Fellow at the Chelsea School, the University of Brighton, UK, where she teaches Sport Studies and Sport Journalism. Belinda's research on lifestyle sport, the politics of identity and consumer culture has been widely published in books and journals. She is the editor of several books including *Understanding Lifestyle Sports: Consumption, Identity and Difference* (2004) and *On the Edge: Representations of Adventure Sports* (2009, with Joan Ormrod).

Lloyd L. Wong is Associate Professor of Sociology at the University of Calgary, Canada, and Research Affiliate and Domain Leader at the Prairie Metropolis Centre – one of the five Canadian Centres of Excellence for Research on Immigration, Integration and Diversity. His research interests include ethnicity, racism, immigration, transnationalism and citizenship.

Acknowledgements

We would like to thank family, friends and colleagues for the support and advice throughout the long process of completing this book. In addition, we are grateful to the numerous colleagues who have contributed to this collection in both direct and more indirect ways over an extended period. For computing and technical support thanks are also due to Hamish Gould and Chris Sullivan (University of Otago). Finally, to Simon Whitmore and his colleagues at Taylor & Francis – thank you for your patience.

Introduction

Borders, boundaries and crossings: sport, migration and identities

Joseph Maguire and Mark Falcous

> So far we lack not only an overall study of the course and structure of the long class conflict between the nobility and the bourgeoisie in European (or other) societies; we also lack studies of many individual aspects of the social tensions that concern us here. Mozart's life illustrates one of these aspects in a truly paradigmatic way – the fate of a bourgeois person in court service towards the end of the period when, almost everywhere in Europe, the taste of the court nobility set the standard for artists of all social origins, in keeping with the general distribution of power. This applied especially to music and architecture.
>
> (Elias, 1994, p. 12)

While Norbert Elias was writing about the life of Wolfgang Amadeus Mozart and his moves around the various courts of Europe, his insights into the conflicts, tensions and costs associated with Mozart's career – his personal creativity and the tastes of the societies that sought to control it – are also applicable to the study of the highly skilled of today, including sport migrants. This area of research has received some attention over the past two decades or so. Since the 1994 publication of *The Global Sports Arena: Athletic Talent Migration in an Interdependent World* edited by John Bale and Joseph Maguire research into sports labour migration has developed along several lines. These include, first, which sports are most involved, why have they been so affected and what structural or cultural changes have thus occurred in those sports and in the societies in which they are located?; second, what are the patterns of global movement and how and why have they developed in this manner?; third, what has been the impact of and on fans in their own migration as 'tourists' or as part of a diaspora, and their perception of the sports they consume? fourth, what has been the impact on 'host' and 'donor' countries more broadly?; fifth, why do 'professional' athletes become labour migrants, how is this process contoured and shaped and what do they experience along their journey? sixth, in what ways does such migration reflect the movement of highly skilled workers more generally? and seventh, what implications are there for sport policy and for the domestic and foreign policies of nation-states more broadly?

Building on these research trends it is also possible to focus on migration to ask questions about the impact of global sport more broadly. That is, does sport extend some degree of emotional identification between members of different societies and civilizations – whether as migrants or the consumers of migrant labour? With the flow of athletic talent across the globe and with the holding of world-wide contests played out in front of people from different nations, and watched by billions via the media sport complex, has an array of more cosmopolitan emotions developed within and between the peoples of different nations? Or, conversely, have globalization processes been accompanied by a more powerful decivilizing counter thrust, in which groups, within and between societies and civilizations, have reacted aggressively to the encroachment of foreign people, values and cultural products? Despite the research so far conducted, firm conclusions regarding these issues are yet to be reached.

The themes identified do not exhaust the possible areas of enquiry. Research of this kind has attracted the attention of economists, geographers, historians, sociologists and political scientists. Each draws upon their disciplinary expertise, utilizing a range of concepts and informed by a variety of approaches. In some senses, the collection of papers contained in *The Global Sports Arena* reflected this diversity. Given that it is over 15 years since it was published it is timely both to reflect on the book and offer an overview of how the field developed, what recent work there is and what new lines of enquiry are emerging. That, at least, lies behind the selection of papers in this collection. Let us first consider how the original collection viewed migration and how it has been received.

Reviewing *The Global Sports Arena* Matthew Taylor, a historian, noted, in a paper examining the association of football, migration and globalization since the 1930s, that 'Footballers, then, are not "on the move" as Bale and Maguire suggested: they have in fact always been moving' (Taylor, 2006, p. 13). This is misleading. These words are part of Bale and Maguire's opening sentence. Bale and Maguire argued that 'Athletes are on the move' (Bale and Maguire, 1994, p. 1) and went on to note that 'in some ways…these migration patterns are nothing new. It appears, however, that the process is speeding up' (Bale and Maguire, 1994, p. 5). Far from being insensitive to the need for examining 'patterns of flow over time' (Taylor, 2006, p. 9) what Bale and Maguire (1994, pp. 5–6) argued is worthy of quoting at some length:

> Sports labour migration is arguably gathering momentum and appears to be closely interwoven with the broader process of global sports development taking place in the late twentieth century. In turn, this sports development is interwoven with a process of accelerated globalization which has been unfolding at least since the late nineteenth century…Several aspects of sports development highlight the interconnections between this migration and globalization. The last century and a half has, for example, witnessed the emergence and diffusion of sport, the establishment of international sport organizations, the global standardization of rules governing sports, the growth of competition among individuals and club teams from different countries and among the national sides of such countries and the establishment of global competitions such as the Olympic Games, soccer's World Cup tournament and the athletics world championships.

The Global Sports Arena also contained a section entitled 'Sports migration: tradition and change'. The section included 5 papers out of a total of 15 – 3 of which focused on football. One paper was by Pierre Lanfranchi, later to be co-author with Taylor in the work *Moving with the Ball: The Migration of Professional Footballers* (2001) and on which Taylor draws much of his argument for the 2006 paper. There is much of note and interest in this account of male footballers but which Taylor himself acknowledges is a 'brief overview of the history of the migration of footballers and its relationship to broader patterns of migration and notions of globalization'. Other papers in *The Global Sports Arena* also had a 'historical' or 'processual' perspective, including work by Simon Genast, Kalevi Olin and Matti Penttilä and Maguire.

Bale and Maguire went on to consider different aspects of globalization and argued that

> the number, length, density and strength of the chains of interdependence which individual people form with others in a time-space continuum is an extremely fruitful way of understanding both sports labour migration and the broader process of globalization within which it is enmeshed.
>
> (Bale and Maguire, 1994, p. 9)

In this regard they advocated that an overall grasp of sports labour migration would be better placed if it drew from human geography and historical sociology. Bale and Maguire should have made the case for drawing on the social sciences as a whole and that is certainly the position that underpins this collection. But, the essential point remains, no one discipline alone, history or any other, explains all aspects of the phenomena. Instead of denigrating or misrepresenting any one approach a dialogue between advocates of different disciplines is required.

As part of his 2006 paper Taylor also argued that Maguire's analysis of football migration was 'largely based on quantitative analysis': yet this overlooks the interviews conducted with Scandinavian players and the archival work conducted at Fédération Internationale de Football Association (FIFA). In addition, Maguire's work on global sport (1999, 2005) and on migration in particular rests on an approach that is 'developmental' or 'historical sociological' and which eschews giving priority to an economic analysis and advocates a long-term perspective in dealing with globalization processes. The work by Maguire and Stead (1998a) on cricket, for example, attempts to provide both insight into the long-term involvement of migrants in the game, the changing nature of regulation and how this past informs the contemporary experience of migration.

Taylor broadens his narrative to take in sociology/social science as a whole and appears critical of the use of the concept of globalization that 'explains little if not used carefully' and goes on to argue that 'much of the writing on football migration has tended to employ "globalization" uncritically', that 'some sociologists of sport…may well have embraced the concept too readily and enthusiastically' and that 'a significant flaw in much of the literature on sport and globalization, and globalization more generally, has been its insensitivity to historical change'

(Taylor, 2006, pp. 10–11). These are significant charges to make but no evidence is provided to substantiate the points made. Here, we argue, consistent with the observations made in *The Global Sports Arena*, that a sensitivity to *continuity* and *change*, across time and space, is required.

Such observations are also consistent with the general debate with regard to globalization. Throughout the 1990s and into this century, attention has been paid to globalization and, increasingly, to inter-civilizational relations (Albrow, 1996; Beynon and Dunkerley, 2000; Held, 2000; Held and McGrew, 2000; Therborn, 2000; Hoogvelt, 2001). The study of globalization is characterized by a diversity of perspectives and competing concepts and ideas. However, some degree of consensus has been reached with regard to the fact that globalization has undoubtedly changed the relationship between time and space, and that the globe is a more compressed space. In addition, there appears greater agreement that terms and concepts like interdependency, networks, multicausality, multidirectionality and glocality enhance the ability of researchers to grasp the dynamics of globalization. Indeed, Held *et al.* go so far as to conclude that 'contemporary globalization is not reducible to a single, causal process, but involves a complex configuration of causal logics' (1999, p. 11). Cultural globalization, of which global sport is a part, can thus be viewed as unifying, universalizing, progressive and liberating, or as divisive, fragmenting, constraining and destructive, of local cultures. There appears to be evidence for both.

That is, on the one hand, a world market for capital, commodities, labour and communications has developed, which is dominated by, and differentially favours, (over)developed countries in general and the 'civilization' of the west in particular. Materially, people, at an everyday level, and nations, at a geopolitical level, are bound up in the matrix of global financial transactions (the hosting of the Olympic Games and the International Olympic Committee's (IOC) The Olympic Programme Sponsors (TOPS) programme for major sponsors being examples of these processes at work); culturally, global brands structure the availability of and meanings associated with products consumed at a local level (consider the tennis and golf products provided by Nike and Callaway); personally, the media supplies us with images of far-off places and superstars who act as cultural icons, thereby sensitizing the individual to the need to be globally aware and to think globally (the hosting of the FIFA World Cup in South Africa in 2010 and the celebrity status of soccer stars being indicative of this).

On the other hand, people, nations and civilizations appear adept at reacting differently to similar-mediated experiences of the global and of global sport. Globalization has sparked 'anti-globalization' movements whose members not only wish to resist the processes described, but also seek to promote, reinvigorate and/or establish local organizations with roots in the community and based on notions of autonomy and democracy (Guest, 2009). Further, these movements, and others linked to environmentalism, are composed of people who share a 'globe-oriented perspective' (Robertson, 1990). Such a perspective recognizes what humans share in common, while respecting difference. In addition, while globalization may involve the development of transnational groupings, such as the European Union, such centripetal forces have also, simultaneously, been matched by the acceleration of centrifugal forces, as witnessed by a surge in demands for self-government and autonomy for regions and nations and such tensions also surface in a sporting context. Finally, while still highly asymmetrical, the current phase of globalization is less dominated by the west – a changing balance of power is evident in this new global order – especially evident post 'credit crunch'. The power shift in global cricket to the Indian sub-continent and the movement of elite cricketers to India is a case in point. The tendencies identified are not as mutually exclusive as some of their more ardent exponents claim. This conclusion holds true for studies of sport (Maguire, 1999, 2005) and assessments regarding cultural globalization more generally (Waters, 1995, p. 40). Global sport, of which sport migration is a part, is a highly contested, structured process that is contoured by power dynamics that enable and constrain and provide both opportunities for social advancement and the reinforcement of exploitation and inequality.

Given the complexity of the phenomena under investigation denigrating or misrepresenting any one approach is unfruitful: a dialogue between advocates of different disciplines and perspectives, as noted, is required. Recent work by Elliott and Maguire (2008) continues this theme and draws on work from human geography that considers skilled migrants more broadly. The migration of athletes and others involved in the 'sports industry' occurs at three levels: within nations, between nations located within the same continent and between nations located in different continents and hemispheres. A complex and shifting set of interdependencies contour the migrant trails of world sport. These interdependencies are multilayered and incorporate not only economic but also political, historical, geographical, social and cultural factors. Thus, in seeking to explain global labour migration, a broad approach must be taken, involving an examination of wider societal processes – not a priori, focusing on one aspect of the sports industrial complex (Maguire, 2005). Questions concerning broader issues such as not only power and established-outsider relations but also more specific matters relating to, for example, 'talent pipelines', stereotyping and the ascribing of qualities to athletes from different countries and ethnic groups are also part of the migration process. How, then, to understand the current state of sport migration?

Migration and sport: some inconvenient truths

To migrate as part of the broader global sports process is often portrayed as something to celebrate, reflecting the individual's right to move, or viewed in unproblematic terms. However, sports migration is bound up in a sports industrial complex that is itself embedded in a series of power struggles that characterize the global sports system. Migration is marked by a series of political, cultural, economic and geographical issues and pressures of which, in the migrant figuration, owners, administrators, agents, officials and media personnel play a prominent part in structuring the migrant's life. These issues and pressures vary between sports played in different continents and countries. Since the early writing on sport migration there has been significant changes in the transnational labour market and comparisons can be drawn between the 'highly skilled' whose finesse moves in advertising, accountancy, banking, law and IT and elite sport migrants.

Over the past three decades their 'flexibility' in the transnational labour market has grown. This, in part, stems from the intensification of globalization processes, one aspect of which being the deregulation of the financial markets – with all its recent side effects. Aligned to these changes has been a global restructuring of business practices, reinforced by developments in information technology and transport/communication systems. With this growth in chains of 'glocal' interdependency, and the formation of what Castells (2000), among others, has called network society, formal/informal translocal communities have developed and traditional 'bridgeheads' that migrants have used have become enhanced and realigned. In this connection there has been, in particular countries and sectors of the employment market, a shift from traditional settler migration to the more transient migration of the highly skilled. This latter process has also been fuelled by the demands of Trans National Corporations (TNCs) to brand and market themselves as 'world firms' in an increasingly flexible and globalized service community – sport clubs such as Manchester United and the New York Knicks and local/global associations such as FIFA and the National Basketball Association (NBA) have adopted similar strategies.

The movement of highly skilled human capital has thus increased significantly in terms of scale, pattern and composition.[1] Elite sport migrants are another example of the highly skilled – enmeshed in local, national, global technological, political and economic state, transnational and TNC policies and whose movement is reflective of and reinforcing the changes realigning the nation state. The debate about this movement of the highly skilled has moved on from simply a discussion of a 'brain drain', to a consideration of 'brain exchange' and 'brain circulation' as well. With elite sport migrants 'brawn' as well as 'brain' is involved. That is, the exchange and circulation of sports migrants has involved performers, coaches, scientists, administrators and educators. This broader process involves both 'sport development' and 'development through sport' with all the attendant rhetoric of building a better world and all the associated reality of consumption and exploitation (Maguire, 2006).

In examining whether the recruitment of foreign migrants is 'good' or 'bad' questions concerning power, culture and control of sport arise. What counts as good or bad depends on who decides and by what criteria – whoever defines what counts as 'success' succeeds in the contested process of player migration. This conflict has involved struggles between those promoting the commercial success of the clubs or the prestige associated with the national team; between entrepreneurs striving for short-term viability or officials concerned with long-term development; and between those who market the creation of a spectacle that can be sold to the media and those who advocate local identity and player development. These tensions have arisen in a range of sports.[2] The debate in male English and European football can serve to illustrate the struggles involved. The advantages are perceived to lie in the better quality of performance – with foreign players improving the standards of existing players and also acting as a role model for younger players. The disadvantages are seen to stem from the lack of opportunities for indigenous players and the concomitant lack of investment in good quality talent identification and development by clubs.

By employing 'too many' foreign players the club, the league and eventually the national team are seen to enter a phase of 'dependent development'. These disadvantages are even more pronounced with those leagues, such as the English, when indigenous player emigration is limited: few elite English players are employed by other European clubs. On the other hand, with this influx of migrant players it is not uncommon for some Premier League clubs to have only one or two English players in the starting line-up. This imbalance between the import of foreign players and the export of English players exacerbates the problem. While this clearly restricts opportunities for current senior or aspiring players, the impact these processes are having on youth development is claimed to be even greater.

With the growing commodification of European football as part of the wider sports industrial complex the rewards for success and the cost of failure are so great that managers cannot afford the promise of longer-term youth development. Managers go, instead, for ready made, experienced foreign players who offer a greater chance of instant success. The response to these issues has been contradictory. Increasingly, national federations express concern that the combined effects of a rapid influx of foreign players and the absence of youth development policies equates to a decline in national playing standards. In some instances youth or reserve teams have been abandoned and 'nursery' club links established in less developed, usually African, soccer nations (see also Cornelissen and Solberg, 2007). The resistance to these processes has been matched by a concern with the development of national teams. The presence of overseas players denies indigenous players access to teams and leads, in some instances, to personal and national under-development. Several papers in this collection seek to address these issues and others that characterize the sports labour migration process. These, at least, are some of the inconvenient truths regarding migration and sport.

Borders, boundaries and crossings: overview of contents

The editorial style adopted in this collection has been to allow contributors some freedom in their approaches. That is, rather than impose rigid requirements in terms of structure, methods and/or analysis we have chosen to allow contributors to structure their work in the way they best see fit. Contributions, consequently, reflect the diversity of work in the sport migration area, drawing upon disciplinary traditions from economics, sociology, anthropology, cultural studies and geography. In turn, contributors' questions, methods and analysis are diverse, reflecting this broad disciplinary mix. This diversity within the field inevitably features opposing paradigmatic approaches and the attendant conceptual tensions. We have, however, pushed authors to make connections with broader theoretical debates in the sport migration area and pressed them to write in an accessible way for international audiences. This is particularly pertinent given the wide range of local/national contexts of the case studies within the book. As a result there is variety in the collection. Some chapters are heavily empirical and some more expressly theorized. The hope is that collectively they reflect, and indeed contribute to, the breadth of understanding in the sport migration field.

The book is structured around five themes: *Patterns*; *Bridgeheads*; *Experiences*; *Identities*; and *Impacts*. Although these sections thematize sports migration issues in an apparently discrete way, we would urge readers to see the intersections between, and as well as within, these sections; and indeed, to read the collection as a whole. In this way, it acts as an overview of the current status of the research field complete with varied approaches – in terms of discipline, theory and methods.

In Part I, entitled 'Patterns of migration and sport', four chapters, drawing on diverse case study examples, both map migratory patterns and interrogate their wider resonance in the context of shifting regulatory and economic contexts. Raffaele Poli and Roger Besson compare patterns of football labour movement from Africa and Latin America to European clubs. Their quantitative analysis teases out the simultaneous diversification of migration patterns *and* the enduring history of colonial linkages in player movements. Key differences in the relative professionalization of the two zones mean players migrate with differing economic prospects, at varying points in their careers, to differing levels of the game and with differing stereotypes (relating to playing position) attached. Also focusing on the economic determinants of migration, Wladimir Andreff's chapter then highlights the problems associated with the international transfer of teenage players in world football. The merits of a model of international player transfer taxation, specifically geared towards hindering teenage transfers (the 'Coubertobin tax'), are then explored as a regulatory control mechanism.

Shifting the focus to Japanese baseball, Yoshio Takahashi and John Horne chart the wider shifts that have re-formulated – and consequently re-configured – labour movement patterns over a 20-year span. In particular, they note the acceleration in movements of Japanese players to Major League Baseball (MLB) in North America and to Korean leagues. Such trends, they note, have reshaped consumption surrounding baseball; for example, lifting interest and stimulating economic activity around Japanese MLB migrants. For example, they chart new patterns of Japanese investment in MLB sponsorships and fan tours to North America. They also note the institutional tensions between United States and Japanese baseball in struggles over legitimacy and control of talent. Such institutional responses to dynamic economic conditions they argue are critical in patterning migration.

Shifting migratory patterns are also evident in Gyozo Molnar's work. He explores migration in and out of Hungarian men's football within the context of the shifts from the Communist era to one defined by the new – although not unfettered – modes of fluidity and opportunity associated with EU membership. Specifically, Molnar details the shifting patterns of migration both within Europe and beyond the Hungarian game which are rooted in a complex combination of shifting economic opportunities, geographic proximity, ethno-cultural links and cultural similarities, agent networks and 'camaraderie networks'.

Part II, 'Bridgeheads in migration and sport', draws together research which sheds light on processes of recruitment, talent 'production' and intermediaries in sports migration processes. First, Joseph Maguire revisits aspects of his work originally published in *Sociological Review* in 1994. The work is included here to identify what the state of knowledge development was like over a decade ago and also signal what directions sport migration was thought to be moving in. In the paper the nature and extent of the global and local processes at work were identified and several key issues connected with sport migration outlined. On this basis, one specific case study – the role of, and the resistance to, American sports labour migrants in the commodification of English basketball during the 1980s and early 1990s – was outlined. The paper concluded by drawing together some of the strands of sports migration and the global development of sport. Given the range of work finding expression in this collection it is useful to assess the degree to which the original observations are borne out.

Drawing on a 'Global Value Chain' (GVC) model Alan Klein explores the institutional arrangements involved in the production of baseball labour from the Dominican Republic; from being talented amateurs, to professionals who, subsequently, are promoted to play in the United States. Consisting of relations that are both formal and official, as well as informal and loosely consented to, Klein reveals the various 'links' in the chain connecting the buscón – Dominican brokers/intermediaries who house, train and mentor players as young as 12; the (US) major league academies who hone talent in the Dominican Republic; and the ever-present disciplinary demands of MLB franchises overseas. Most critically, Klein forces the analysis of sports labour migration to explore the place of 'exception' from the neoliberal labour model (i.e. unskilled, infinite and low-paid) to account for the unique economies – and intermediaries that emerge in these contexts – surrounding sporting labour.

Richard Elliott and Joseph Maguire's chapter focuses on making sense of the informal interdependencies that are used to facilitate recruitment of Canadian migrants in English ice hockey. They reveal the significance of the informal networks of recruitment, and specifically the role of 'bridgeheads' in forging migrant pathways and facilitating future player movements. In doing so, they make a case for informal as well as formal mechanisms to be a site of interest for scholars. Holly Thorpe then explores the transnational flows of youth cultural products, images, values and ideas and participants, via the case of the global snowboarding culture. In the context of this collection this chapter is of value in shedding light on some of the aspects of non-elite sporting migrations. Advocating for a 'global ethnography approach', Thorpe reveals how snowboarders' transnational mobility facilitates the communication of cultural values and styles across borders, and how these global connections are negotiated in particular local spaces and places in contingent ways.

Part III, 'Experiences of migration and sport', shifts the focus to both the reception in 'host' cultures and the experiences of migrants themselves. Andrew

Grainger explores the origins, consequences and legacies of players moving from the 'less-developed' rugby union nations of the Pacific to the New Zealand game. He powerfully reveals the economic and political imbalances and inequities in the exchange of Fijian, Tongan, Samoan and New Zealand rugby labour. Any gains in the freedom of movement of Pacific players, he cautions, must be set against those actions of state agencies, transnational corporations and sport associations that seek to manage migration in a way that ultimately reinforces the dominance of those holding the levers of administrative and economic power within world rugby. Significantly, Grainger's work highlights the contradictory processes of economic openness, regulation and power and territorial closure within the global sport labour market.

Joseph Maguire's paper on Canadian 'blade runners' was originally published in 1996 and sought to examine issues that frame both 'migrants' and 'host' experiences of British ice hockey. He captures how the issues, problems and tensions associated with migrants, who have both intended and unintended features, involve issues of recruitment, retention and release, adjustment, dislocation and foreign sojourn. Questions of labour rights, work permits and salary caps also impinge on the migrant experience. The case study proved an important source of comparison for other scholars and signalled new directions which the study of migration could take.

As several scholars in the field have noted, sporting mobilities are certainly gendered in powerful ways. Research in the area has frequently reflected the imbalance, focusing on male migrations, contexts and experiences. In presenting a case study of immigration into Danish women's football Sine Agergaard and Vera Botelho offer steps towards a remedy. Drawing on questionnaire and interview data, they explore the growing professionalization of clubs since the early 1990s; the motivations for the recruitment of foreign players; and players' motives and experiences of the process. The motive of obtaining social mobility as a sport migrant, Agergaard and Botelho argue, takes a specific form in female football migration. Because there is little possibility for obtaining economic advancement, they note, the opportunity of obtaining social capital by spending a period abroad and gaining experience as a professional is critical. In particular, they call for close analysis of recruitment strategies which moves the focus towards the specific processes of recruitment and retention as a significant feature of migrations.

Part IV, 'Identities in migration and sport', brings together research that explores the varying significations of migrant flows. Mark Falcous and Joseph Maguire use a case study of English basketball to reflect on the intersection of local fans with the presence of 'globetrotters' – North American migrants – in the constructions of local identities. The case study shows reactions to be complex and nuanced, intersecting identity politics in pragmatic ways. In this way, basketball migrants are revealed as both 'globetrotters' and 'local heroes' with local fans simultaneously resisting and embracing migrants within the context of local leisure lives and identities.

Toni Bruce and Belinda Wheaton then explore the utility of the notion of diaspora as a means of understanding sporting migrations which retain a range of ties – economic, familial, symbolic – to the original place of departure.

Analysing newspaper discourses in England and New Zealand they explore the case of sailor and environmentalist Sir Peter Blake. While emphasizing different aspects of Blake's fluid and overlapping identities, the coverage, they note, ultimately embraced dual conceptions of 'home' rather than a separation of self from nation. Such identifications hold resonance, they note, within the context of a specifically racialized construction of migrants belonging to (post)colonial networks within white-settler nations.

Jason Tuck then explores national sporting representatives as highly visible 'patriots at play'. He explores how international rugby union players as actors can negotiate, define, reflect, protect and fuel the 'national character' of nations. Drawing upon Elias's work, Tuck explores the nationalistic we-images and fantasy group charismas to shed light on the interlocking themes of globalization, national identity politics (i.e. competing national discourses) and national habitus (i.e. the 'second nature' of belonging to the nation).

In Part V, 'Impacts of migration on sports and societies', Toby Miller, David Rowe and Geoffrey Lawrence evaluate the movement of sporting labour through the concept of the 'New International Division of Cultural Labour'. Miller and colleagues locate sporting migrants within the context of an aggressively globalizing (sporting) capitalism that seeks comparatively cheap labour in countries that can provide skilled workers to supplement costly local labour. That is, 'production' is increasingly 'outsourced' (as is consumption) while control over content remains at the 'centre'. The resulting 'system' they reveal is one of imbalance and profound inequity.

Focusing on the significance of particular migrant athletes as embodiments of shifting identities associated with intensified globalization, Ricardo Trumper and Lloyd L. Wong explore case studies of Chilean Iván Zamorano (fútbol) and Canadian Wayne Gretzky (ice hockey). In doing so, they are able to tease out the tension between how these migrant athletes – both working outside their home nations – embody transnational cultural and capitalist business practices while *also* willingly serving as national cultural icons that reaffirm particular versions of national identities. Paradoxically, Zamorano represented and symbolized an emergent neoliberalized Chileanness and, in Canada, Gretzky operated (and still does) as a symbol of both mobility and a selective 'true' Canadianness. Both cases reveal elite athletes navigating the fluid and ostensibly contradictory social relations between both national and transnational spaces.

Examining the historical shifts in the transit of African footballers to Europe, Paul Darby demonstrates the ways in which these patterns have been underpinned by broader colonial legacies and subsequent developments within the political economy of world football. Specifically, he details the dramatic expansion in the numbers of Africans who earn their living in the European football market. Most significantly, Darby closes with propositions for future theorizations using a 'Global Commodity Chain' (GCC) model as well as its theoretical successor, 'GVC' analysis, as a more satisfactory model than neo-Marxist variants such as dependency theory and World Systems Models. Such models, he argues, promise to account for the complexities of resistances *alongside* highlighting extractive processes, rather than monolithic conceptualizations of power.

Camilla Obel and Terry Austrin, exploring the case of New Zealand rugby union, argue that regulation of team and player mobilities has always been central to the configurations, of the national union and local clubs, that have sought to stabilize the game. Specifically, they contrast this regulation in the amateur (1892–1995) and professional periods (1995 onwards) and show how it has always privileged the national team, over local clubs. The capacity of national governing bodies to constrain player mobility they reveal has been challenged by recent shifts in the rugby labour market, but remains a key site of struggle for power and legitimacy in control of the game.

As noted above, the hope is that readers will read the collection as a whole – as a reflection of the collective stock of knowledge on the movements of athletes, administrators, fans and ancillary staff – drawing on papers published over the past two decades and appearing here collectively for the first time. Our contributors approach their topic from varying positions, at points cohering and at points opposing. The diversity of approaches within the book, reflected in the variety of theoretical, methodological and paradigmatic approaches, will provide challenges. Readers, then, are charged with making sense of the field and evaluating the diversity of approaches and what they offer as a collective.

Notes

1 See Beaverstock, 'Transnational elites in the city: British highly skilled inter-company transferees in New York City's financial district'; Castells, *The Rise of the Network Society: Vol. 1: The Information Economy, Society and Culture*; Dezalay, 'The big bang and the law: The internationalization and restructuration of the legal system'; Iredale, 'The migration of professionals: Theories and typologies'.
2 For discussion of how this relates to national identity see Maguire and Tuck 'National identity, rugby union and notions of Ireland and the Irish'. For discussion of Irish migration see Cronin, 'Which nation? Which flag? Boxing and national identities in Ireland'; McGovern, 'The Irish brawn drain: English league clubs and Irish footballers, 1946–95'. See also Giulianotti and Robertson, 'Glocalization, globalization and migration: The case of Scottish football supporters in North America'.

Part I

Patterns of migration and sport

1　From the South to Europe

A comparative analysis of African and Latin American football migration

Raffaele Poli and Roger Besson

The history of the migration of footballers to Europe and within this continent is not something new (Lanfranchi and Taylor, 2001; Taylor, 2006). From the outset, the worldwide diffusion of football has been the work of a transnational elite expatriated within the context of the expansion of capitalism (Lanfranchi, 2002) and the development of a 'world economy' (Wallerstein, 2006). Quotas limiting the presence of foreign players were first introduced in the 1920s as a result of the interwar geopolitical tensions (Poli, 2006a). For several decades, legal constraints have drastically limited expatriate presence in European clubs. Up until 1995, the percentage of expatriates in the five major European leagues[1] had never risen above 10 per cent (Poli and Ravanel, 2009).

At the end of the 1980s, regulations were eased and foreign presence started to increase. With the advent of the 'Bosman' law, decreed in 1995 by the European Court of Justice (Dubey, 2000), this progression increased markedly. In obliging the federation of EU countries to review their regulations and to free up the circulation of EU players, this ruling has allowed clubs to take advantage of new recruitment possibilities. In just five seasons, between 1995 and 2000, the percentage of expatriates taking part in the big-five leagues has increased from 18.6 per cent to 35.6 per cent. While it has slowed down thereafter, this augmentation has continued without interruption to the present day. During the season 2008/2009, the percentage of expatriates in the five top European leagues has reached a record level of 42.6 per cent (Poli *et al.*, 2009).

The increase of international flows following the liberalisation of the football transfer market takes place as much between EU member countries as it does between non-EU ones. Between 1995 and 2005, the percentage of extra European players in the five principal leagues has gone up from 6.4 per cent to 19.2 per cent. During the 2005/2006 season, extra-European footballers made up half of the total of expatriates, instead of one-third ten seasons previously. The augmentation of non-EU players is due to the fact that they benefit from the places left vacant by citizens of countries that are no longer taken into account by quotas. From this point of view, the 'Bosman' ruling has particularly favoured Latin American footballers, a majority of whom are also in possession of EU passports (especially Spanish, Italian or Portuguese).

The strategies for global recruitment elaborated by European clubs reflect the development of a new international division of labour in the 'production' of footballers. Powerful transnational transfer networks made up of players' agents, private investors, club managers and trainers henceforth take charge of the setting up of the relation between supply and demand on a global level (Poli, 2007a, 2008). With this in mind, certain countries such as Brazil and Nigeria have become progressively specialised in the training of footballers and their exportation to Europe or Asia, continents where football generates higher revenues. The increase in international flows and the development of new recruitment strategies form part of the framework of the globalisation of the labour market of sporting personnel (Bale and Maguire, 1994a; Maguire and Stead, 1998; Poli and Ravenel, 2005b). Considered from a transformationist's perspective (Held *et al.*, 1999), this process implies the functional integration of spaces on a vast geographical scale (Dicken, 2007).

Today Africa and Latin America constitute preferred recruitment areas for European clubs. The objective of this article is to comparatively analyse the presence of players of these two zones of origin within the principal European championships so as to bring out similarities and differences. The data on which we base our analysis comes from a census carried out between September and October 2008 by the Professional Football Players' Observatory (PFPO)[2] based on a sample of 30 top division leagues in countries belonging to Union of European Football Associations (UEFA) (Figure 1.1). This census, undertaken by cross-referencing the data from different sources (official club websites, federations and electronic databases), has allowed the enumeration of 11,015 active footballers[3] including information on their origin as well as certain characteristics such as position, height or age. Our goal being to measure the international flows directly linked to football, independently of the nationality of players, the notion of expatriate is preferred to that of foreigner. An expatriate is a footballer playing outside of the country where he grew up in, from where he departed following recruitment by a club abroad.

Spatial logics of international recruitment and diversification of migration routes

In total, the 456 European clubs taken into account by the census employed 3,923 expatriates or 35.6 per cent of the total number of footballers. The Latin American players, numbering 979, represented a quarter of expatriates (25.0 per cent). Less numerous, players recruited in Africa (531) constituted 13.5 per cent of the total number of expatriate footballers (Table 1.1).

It is interesting to note that, from a geographical point of view, the 'production' of players in Africa is concentrated primarily in the western part of the continent (Figure 1.2). On a national level, Brazil is by far the country that exports the greatest number of players to Europe. Numbering 551, Brazilians make up the biggest contingent of expatriate players. Brazil's role in the training and exportation of players is not limited to Europe. In 2004 alone, the Brazilian Football Confederation recorded the departure of 846 players seeking to capitalise on their talent worldwide, 60 per cent of them elsewhere than in Europe (Théry, 2006).

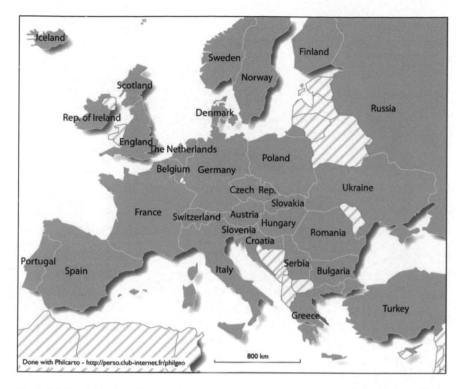

Figure 1.1 Spatial logics of international recruitment and diversification of migration routes

Table 1.1 Number and percentage of expatriate players by zone of origin

	Players	*% of players*	*% of expatriates*
Western Europe	1,195	10.8	30.5
Eastern Europe	1,083	9.8	27.6
Other	135	1.2	3.4
Latin America	979	8.9	25.0
Africa	531	4.8	13.5
Total expatriates	3,923	35.6	100.0
Non-expatriates	7,092	64.4	
Total players	11,015	100.0	

While numerous European countries also export players to other European nations (particularly France), the flows from Asia and North America remain limited. The worldwide geography of football differs in this way from that of international trade where Asia and North America occupy a central position. Conversely, Africa and Latin America, two continents somewhat on the fringes of

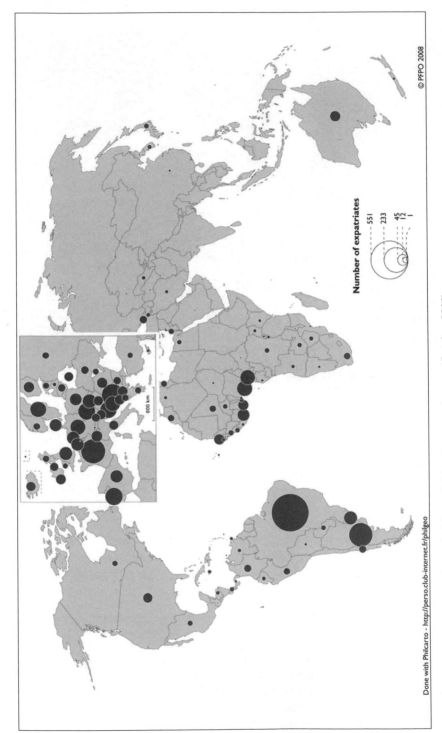

Number of expatriates

551
233
45
12
1

800 km

Done with Philcarto - http://perso.club-internet.fr/philgeo

Figure 1.2 Origin of expatriate players in 30 top division European leagues (October 2008)

major international commercial flows, play an essential role in the worldwide market for footballers.

The process of globalisation is often understood from an aspatial perspective (Massey, 2005) that deems that there are no longer any borders and that the world has become a homogenous space of action for all individuals. This vision had been strongly criticised in that it does not take into account the permanence of social factors linked to history of relations between territories in the geographical configuration of flows. Incidentally, Meyer proposes a connectionist approach and reminds us that 'people are not moving in a vacuum between supply and demand. They are actors whose movements, constructed through and resulting from collective action, can be traced and described accurately instead of being left to external and elusive macro-determinations.' Accordingly, for Meyer, migrants are not made up of 'a volatile population of separate units in a fluid environment but rather a set of connective entities that are always evolving through networks, along sticky branches' (2001, p. 96).

The importance of networks in the migration of sportsmen has also been highlighted by Maguire and Pearton, for whom

> it is evident that it would be impossible to explain élite talent migration in football by recourse solely to an economic theory. Although economics play a crucial part in determining the patterns of football migration, they are by no means the only factor involved. Rather, a set of interdependencies contour and shape the global sports migration.
>
> (2000a, pp. 187–8)

In the case of English football, McGovern (2002) has also insisted upon the permanence of spatial logics inherited from the history of territories in the structuring of flows. In a more recent article, Maguire and Elliott (2008) underline the importance of going beyond the sole analysis of the motivations of sporting migrants, so as to also study the structure and mechanisms of recruitment.

On the basis of these observations, it is not surprising to notice that the presence of Latin Americans among the expatriates in the 30 leagues is quite contrasted. It is particularly strong in Portugal (79.6 per cent), Italy (51.0 per cent) and Spain (47.8 per cent), countries with which relations are historically important. In nine other leagues, Latin American footballers make up more than one-fifth of the expatriates. In contrast, championships such as the Scottish (2.5 per cent) or Irish (1.5 per cent) ones hardly have any. Generally speaking, the percentage of Latin American players decreases relative to a South–North gradient (Figure 1.3).

Though the ratio of players having grown up in Africa also varies according to country, the differences are less important. The country in which they are the most present among expatriates is France (37.0 per cent). Contrary to Latin American players, the championships of Northern Europe such as Finland (35.9 per cent), Sweden (23.5 per cent) or Norway (18.7 per cent) figure among those where the proportion of African footballers is higher than the European average. African players are also relatively numerous in Central Europe (Switzerland,

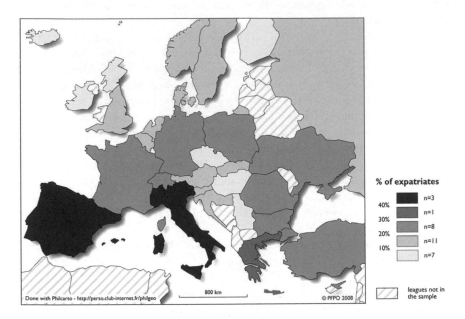

Figure 1.3 Percentage of Latin American players among expatriates

Belgium) and in certain Eastern European leagues (Serbia, Hungary, Turkey, Romania, Ukraine). In contrast, no African footballer is playing in Iceland. Among the countries where Africans are not numerous we also find Scotland (3.3 per cent) and Ireland (3.0 per cent), which have already stood out in the case of Latin American footballers (Figure 1.4).

The analysis of the distribution of Latin American and African players brings to light a double logic. On the one hand, with the exception of the English championship, where international recruitment is much more orientated towards neighbouring countries, the old colonial powers such as France, Portugal and Spain continue to amply draw from the reservoir of talent of the previously colonised countries (Ivory Coast, Cameroon, Senegal, Mali, Brazil, Argentina and Uruguay notably). On the other hand, the migratory routes tend to diversify, which reflects the functional integration of spaces taking place in the context of the globalisation of the footballers' labour market.

This confirms the analysis carried out by Maguire and Stead (1998a), who have highlighted that 'sports labour migration is, in part, a reflection of pre-existing social, political and economic power arrangements in sport. It can also be an indicator of, and a factor in, bringing about change' (p. 60). The tension between continuity and change has been expressed by these authors in terms of 'centrifugal and centripetal forces' (p. 72), which are simultaneously at work in the context of the international labour market of footballers.

The diachronic analysis of the concentration of expatriate players according to their origin allows us to measure the relative weight of these two types

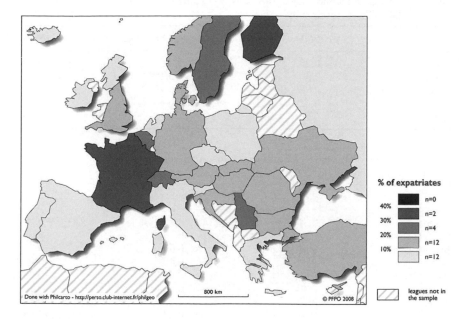

Figure 1.4 Percentage of African players among expatriates

of forces in the last few years. The index of dissimilarity[4] is an index of segregation that has long been used in the social sciences (Rhein, 1994; Apparicio, 2000; Voas and Williamson, 2000). It measures the proportion of a given population that must change spatial unit so that its distribution between the different units is identical to that of another population. When applied to the case of footballers, this index permits the comparison of the distribution of players having a certain origin in comparison to other expatriates. If all the expatriate players coming from a given country take part in the same championship and if the latter only has players from this origin, the dissimilarity is maximal (index value of 1). Inversely, if players of the same origin are distributed exactly in the same manner between the different championships as those of other origins, the dissimilarity is minimal (index value of 0).

In 2008, Africa constituted the zone of origin for which the distribution within the 30 championships was the most balanced (0.28). The degree of specialisation of the distribution of Latin Americans (0.35) is similar to that of expatriates from Western Europe (0.36) and those from the category 'Others' (0.36), which includes North American, Asian and Oceanic footballers. Eastern Europeans, particularly over-represented in the east of the continent due to a logic of proximity, are those who show the greatest dissimilarity (0.42) (Table 1.2).

A comparison with the situation in the 30 leagues in 2002/2003 indicates a reduction in the specificity of the distribution of expatriates according to origin. This result confirms the existence of a process of diversification of migration

Table 1.2 Change in the index of dissimilarity according to zone of origin
(2002/2003–2008/2009)

	2008/2009	2002/2003	Change
Africa	0.28	0.37	−0.09
Latin America	0.36	0.40	−0.05
Western Europe	0.36	0.45	−0.09
Eastern Europe	0.42	0.46	−0.04
Other	0.35	0.29	0.06

Table 1.3 Change in the index of dissimilarity according to nationality
(2002/2003–2008/2009)

	2008/2009	2002/2003	Change
Ghana	0.31	0.40	−0.09
Cameroon	0.31	0.36	−0.05
Brazil	0.31	0.39	−0.08
Nigeria	0.32	0.40	−0.08
Ivory Coast	0.40	0.63	−0.23
Senegal	0.40	0.50	−0.10
Argentina	0.43	0.53	−0.10
Uruguay	0.51	0.54	−0.03

channels. With the exception of the category 'Others', of which the numbers are few (123 players in 2003), all the zones of origin have seen their index of dissimilarity decrease in 2008. The drop is particularly noticeable for Africans (−0.09), even though they already had the least specific distribution in 2003 (0.37). By comparison, the dissimilarity of Latin Americans dropped only half as quickly (−0.04).

While the differences in the index of dissimilarity between zones of origin are relatively low, the contrasts are more marked when one takes into account national origins separately. Between the eight main African and Latin American producers (which represented at least 40 expatriate players in the 30 leagues in 2008), Ghana, Cameroon, Brazil (0.31) and Nigeria (0.32) stand out due to a high level of dissimilarity. For these origins, the spatial logics of recruitment appear to be more universal and less influenced by historic factors. Senegal and the Ivory Coast (0.40), however, are characterised by a more specific distribution of expatriates. Indeed, players from these countries are particularly well represented in France. About 22 per cent of Senegalese and 17 per cent of Ivorians present in the 30 leagues play in French clubs. As for Latin Americans, the Argentinians (0.43) and the Uruguayans (0.51) account for the highest concentration in a small number of countries. Despite their high total number (222 players), nearly half of the former play in Spain, Italy and Greece (49.1 per cent). In the case of Uruguayans, the concentration in these three countries is even more important (57.7 per cent). Consequently, 14 leagues have no player of this origin (Table 1.3).

Table 1.4 Index of dissimilarity according to zone of origin and by age group

	Africa	Latin America	Western Europe	Eastern Europe	Others
<21 years old	0.54	0.37	0.47	0.45	0.53
22–26 years old	0.27	0.35	0.36	0.39	0.44
>27 years old	0.31	0.42	0.38	0.48	0.43

The emergence of a diversification in migration routes is also noticeable on a nationwide level. In the case of Africa and Latin America, no national origin of a certain importance has seen its index of dissimilarity rise between 2002 and 2008. The process of diversification is particularly marked for players from the Ivory Coast (–0.23). While in 2002/2003 almost three-quarters of Ivorian footballers played in France (27.5 per cent) and Belgium (45.0 per cent), this proportion had dropped to one-quarter (24.4 per cent) six seasons later.

Our analysis therefore confirms the tendency towards a diversification of migration channels. However, this process does not mark a complete break with the past, but occurs in a context that still remains influenced by spatial structures that are the result of the history of relations among territories. This is particularly the case of Latin American footballers, with the exception of Brazilians. Generally speaking, however, African players are distributed more equitably among different countries. Today, Ghanaian, Cameroonian and Nigerian footballers make up a truly transnational labour force comparable with that of their Brazilian counterparts. However, these findings must be nuanced if we take into account the criterion of age.

The concentration of expatriate players according to their zone of origin is generally stronger at the start of their career. For all categories (Table 1.4), the index of dissimilarity diminishes for the 22- to 26-year-old age group in comparison with the under 21s group, before stabilising or slightly increasing for those over 27 years of age. This change can be seen particularly in young African players, whose index is divided by two between the age group of the under 21s (0.54) and that of the 22- to 26-year-olds (0.27). Young African footballers have a tendency to migrate to lesser number of leagues (notably France, Norway, Denmark) and to disperse afterwards to other countries, once are already present on the European market. By comparison, the evolution recorded for Latin Americans is clearly less marked. The relative stability of their index of dissimilarity tends to show that clubs of a large number of countries directly recruit these players. This result reflects the greater diversity of recruitment networks used by European clubs to hire footballers in South America than in Africa.

Sporting level and economic logics of recruitment

The level of expatriate players varies strongly according to the sporting level of championships. A statistically significant correlation was measured between the UEFA league coefficient[5] and the number of expatriate footballers playing there (Figure 1.5).

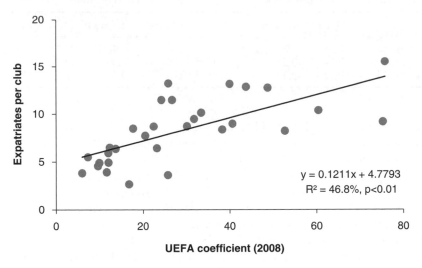

Figure 1.5   Correlation between the number of expatriates per club and the UEFA association coefficient

The graph clearly illustrates that the more successful a league is, the more clubs will tend to recruit players abroad. If one distinguishes expatriates according to their zone of origin, this also holds for Latin American footballers (Figure 1.6). However, there is no significant statistical correlation between the presence of African players and league level (Figure 1.7).

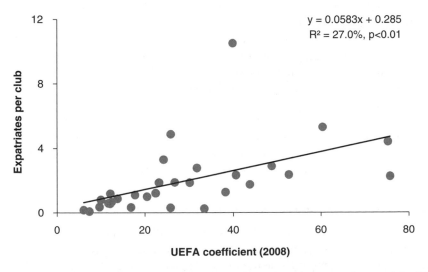

Figure 1.6   Correlation between the number of Latin American expatriates and the UEFA association coefficient

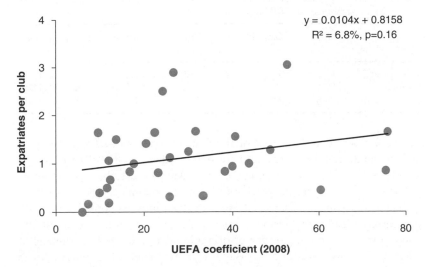

Figure 1.7 Correlation between the number of African expatriates per club and the UEFA association coefficient

The result recorded in the case of Africans shows that, by comparison with Latin American expatriates, players of this origin are relatively more present in less well-performing leagues. In so far as the sporting hierarchy generally reflects an economic one,[6] this suggests that footballers recruited in Africa constitute a cheaper labour force (Poli, 2006b) in comparison with South American players. The analysis of the distribution of expatriate players according to origin and league level, measured in relation to the place occupied in the UEFA rankings (Table 1.5), allows us to bolster this hypothesis.

The proportion of Western European and Latin American players among expatriates decreases as the level of clubs diminishes. This is not the case for African and Eastern European footballers.[7] Their presence is relatively higher in the less successful championships. The five major leagues have proportionally three times as many players of Latin American origin (30.8 per cent) than those ranked between the 20th and 37th place in the UEFA rankings (11.7 per cent). Conversely, the proportion of Africans is slightly higher in the countries of the

Table 1.5 Distribution of expatriate players according to zone of origin and league level (30 countries, October 2008)

UEFA country ranking	Africa (%)	Latin America (%)	Western Europe (%)	Eastern Europe (%)	Other (%)	Total (%)
Rk 1–5 (level 1)	13.0	30.8	35.3	16.0	4.8	100
Rk 6–19 (level 2)	13.6	26.7	29.5	27.4	2.9	100
Rk 20–37 (level 3)	14.2	11.7	26.1	45.1	2.9	100
Total	13.5	25.0	30.5	27.6	3.4	100

Table 1.6 Distribution of expatriate players according to zone of origin and ranking of clubs (five leagues, 2007/2008 season)

	Africa	Latin America	Western Europe	Eastern Europe	Others	Total
1 (first five places)	11.2	37.1	37.6	11.3	2.8	100
2 (mid-ranking)	16.4	27.9	33.1	16.8	5.8	100
3 (last five places)	15.6	24.3	34.1	17.6	8.4	100

third level (14.2 per cent) than those of the first (13.0 per cent). Thus, while the relation between the number of Latin American footballers and that of African players is clearly favourable to the former in the top ranking leagues, the latter are more numerous in the championships whose sporting and economic levels are weaker.

A similar result can be observed if we only take into account the five best European leagues (England, Germany, Spain, France, Italy) and observe the distribution of players according to zone of origin in relation to the final ranking of clubs during the season 2007/2008. While the proportion of Latin American players tends to diminish as the level of the clubs decreases, that of African footballers tends to increase (Table 1.6). This result shows that the status of Latin American players in the European footballers' labour market is very different to that of Africans. Contrary to the latter, Latin American expatriates are over-represented in the top leagues and in the best clubs within these championships.

The age of the first international migration also differs appreciably between Latin American and African footballers. The former depart abroad much later than the latter, generally after already having had a professional experience in their country of origin. This situation does not often occur in Africa where, with the exception of Maghreb and South Africa, professionalism only concerns a limited number of clubs and players. During the 2008/2009 season, African footballers playing in the top five European leagues left their country on average at 18.9 years of age, as opposed to 22.1 years of age for Latin Americans (Poli *et al.*, 2009).

This situation affects the transfer sums that European clubs are prepared to invest to sign players. While the employment of footballers from Latin America can cost more than 20 million euro (Sergio Agüero, Javier Saviola, Walter Samuel, Alexandre Pato, etc.), transfers carried out from sub-Saharan Africa rarely attain more than one million euro, even for the most promising players. For example, in January 2009, ASEC Mimosas of Abidjan sold Cyriac Gohi Bi, a great hope of Ivorian football and top scorer in 2008, to Standard Liège for less than one million euro. In comparison to sub-Saharan Africa, the greater level of development in professionalism in Latin America encourages the promotion of players and their transfer to the most ambitious clubs, which are ready to pay out higher transfer fees. On the contrary, African clubs suffer from the breakdown of local football structures (Poli and Dietschy, 2006) and often find themselves obliged to quickly give up their most promising talents to less ambitious clubs who recruit them in exchange for much lower sums.

The average age of expatriates counted in the 30 leagues is another element that reflects the precocious departure abroad of Africans. Generally speaking,

Table 1.7 Average age of expatriates by zone of origin (30 leagues, October 2008)

	Average age
Africa	24.7
Latin America	25.8
Western Europe	26.0
Other origins	26.1
Eastern Europe	26.6
All expatriates	25.9

Table 1.8 Average age of expatriate players by zone of origin, according to level of competition

UEFA country ranking	Africa	Latin America	Western Europe	Eastern Europe	Other	Total
Rk 1–5 (level 1)	25.13	25.89	26.28	26.52	26.70	26.07
Rk 6–19 (level 2)	24.82	25.66	25.70	26.53	26.18	25.81
Rk 20–37 (level 3)	23.82	25.89	26.25	26.88	24.64	26.10
Total	24.70	25.76	25.98	26.64	26.13	25.94

while expatriate players are older (25.9 years of age) than footballers playing in the country in which they grew up (25.3 years of age), Africans are younger (24.7 years of age). The average age of Latin Americans is, on the other hand, very close to the average of expatriates (Table 1.7).

The average age of expatriate footballers is generally lower in clubs ranked between the 6th and 19th place in the UEFA rankings. This holds for all origins with the exception of African footballers. For the latter, age decreases in a linear manner as the sporting level of leagues diminishes. The variations in the average age of Latin American footballers correspond, however, to the general model (Table 1.8).

The young age of African footballers playing in the least performing leagues supports the hypothesis according to which clubs of these countries recruit youths 'cheaply' in Africa with, above all, a speculative logic in mind, with a view of selling them on in future to clubs with more means at their disposal. Independently of its effectiveness, this strategy involves the constant replacement of players recruited in Africa with ever-younger new talents offering better transfer possibilities. This contributes to keeping the average age of footballers at a very low level.

Cultural logics and homogenisation of players' characteristics

The discourse on globalisation is often accompanied by cultural considerations on the homogenisation of the world which, within the context of the development of

Table 1.9 Distribution of players by zone of origin and position (30 leagues, October 2008)

	Africa	Latin America	Western Europe	Eastern Europe
Goalkeepers	3.4	5.0	8.0	11.6
Defenders	23.9	28.9	34.3	32.0
Midfielders	35.4	36.9	33.4	34.5
Forwards	37.3	29.2	24.3	21.9
Total	100	100	100	100

capitalism, leads to the emergence of a global consumer culture symbolised by the term 'McDonaldisation' (Ritzer, 2004). From this perspective, worldwide economic integration would inevitably lead to a loss of local particularities. Even though nowadays it is strongly challenged, this vision continues to permeate the manner in which media and researchers deal with the question of styles of football, especially regarding national teams. These would differentiate less and less from each other. Among the factors summoned to explain this process is that of the strong presence of African and Latin American players in European clubs. Players of these origins are supposed to have been formatted to fit a particular style of play and thus lose their specific characteristics within the framework of a process of acculturation.

While it is not possible to arrive at a definite answer to this question, the analysis of positions occupied on the field by African and Latin American players in comparison to their colleagues of other origins indicates that important differences remain. Indeed, recruitment carried out by European clubs in Africa and Latin America continues to focus on attacking players (Table 1.9).

The over-representation of forwards is particularly strong for African players, and, to a lesser extent, for Latin Americans. More than 70 per cent of African footballers play in midfield or forward positions. For Latin Americans (66.1 per cent), this percentage is greater than that of Western European (57.7 per cent) and Eastern European (56.4 per cent) expatriate players. This situation is even more marked if we count national footballers, who tend to occupy more defensive positions in comparison to expatriates. The distribution of players by position thus indicates that the globalisation of the football players' labour market reflects the European clubs' need for a labour force, which brings together qualities that allow an offensive style of play. The over-representation of expatriate players, and, more particularly, Africans and Latin Americans, in offensive positions thus tends to suggest that, independently of existence of a process of standardisation, footballers of these origins continue to possess specific characteristics that set them apart from national players or, more generally, European ones.

Significant differences in the characteristics of expatriate footballers in relation to their zone of origin also exist in terms of height. On average, Latin American and African players are shorter than the others. Their over-representation in forward positions only partially explains this difference (Table 1.10).

Latin American migrants 'with the ball' (Lanfranchi and Taylor, 2001) are, on average, two or three centimetres shorter than their expatriate European counterparts.

Table 1.10 Average height of expatriate players by
zone of origin

	Average height
Latin America	180.1
Africa	180.9
Western Europe	182.2
Other origins	182.4
Eastern Europe	183.4
All expatriates	181.3

The difference is less for African players, whose average height is nevertheless also shorter. Given this information, we can posit that the relative physical deficit of players recruited in South America and Africa is compensated by an exceptional technique. Of course, this remains more a hypothesis partially derived from stereotypical representations, both from the clubs' officials (Maguire and Stead, 1998) and authors' side, than a fact that has been scientifically proven. The next step would be to carry out an analysis of variance on performances on the pitch (dribbles, passes, touches, drops, etc.) between players by position according to their origin. If the hypothesis of exceptional technique of Africans and Latin Americans holds true, it would go against the theory that, within the context of globalisation, all the players, whatever their origin, would have the same characteristics.

Conclusion

In the 30 leagues that have been the subject of our study, African and Latin American players represent 38.5 per cent of expatriate footballers and 13.7 per cent of the total number present. The players recruited in South America, numbering 979, are relatively more numerous than their colleagues transferred from Africa (531).

Important differences in the circulatory models exist between these two populations, whose migrations do not reflect the same stakes. Africans tend to have a more precarious integration in the European football labour market. This can be directly linked to less developed professional football south of the Sahara. This situation results in a younger departure age and a relative over-representation in clubs of a weaker level. From an economic point of view, the consequences can be measured in terms of the lower transfer fees and lower earnings that African players are subjected to (Poli, 2004, 2006b).

The spatial logics of flows towards Europe are also partially distinctive. Latin Americans continue to be strongly over-represented in Portugal, Italy and Spain, while Africans are relatively more numerous in France. At the same time, there is a tendency towards the geographical diversification of the network channels. As the evolution in the index of dissimilarity shows, this process affects players from all countries. The continent where players are distributed more equitably between the different European championships is Africa, particularly for players over 21 years of age. For the younger players, the concentration is higher. While Latin American footballers come directly to a large number of European countries, African players are in a first instance recruited by clubs situated in a restrained circle of nations, and then subsequently leave for other championships. From the point of view of single nationalities, the most well-distributed players are Ghanaians, Cameroonians and Brazilians.

African and Latin American players are strongly over-represented in midfield and, especially, forward positions. Despite the generalised discourse positing that globalisation leads to a formatting of players from around the world, our analysis tends to show that European clubs continue to look first in Africa and South America for attacking players, which seem to be more difficult to find at home. This difference is also apparent regarding the morphology of players. Latin American and African expatriates are indeed shorter in height than their European counterparts. From this point of view, the case of footballers from the 'South' is quite comparable. Generally speaking, however, the differences are greater than the similitudes.

Notes

1 Comprising the English Premier League, the Spanish Primera Liga, Italian Serie A, the German Bundesliga and French Ligue 1. For the 2007/2008 season, these championships generated 53 per cent of the total turnover of European football (14.6 billion euro) (Deloitte, 2009).

2 Founded in 2005, the Professional Football Players' Observatory is a research group bringing together researchers from the Institute of Sport Science of the University of Lausanne, the International Centre for Sports Studies of the University of Neuchâtel and the Centre of Study and Research on Sport and Territorial Observation of the University of Franche-Comté (see www.eurofootplayers.org).

3 The criterion for the census of a player is to have participated in at least one championship match since the start of the season, or, if this condition has not been fulfilled, to have taken part in professional matches during the two preceding seasons. Given their particular profile, substitute goalkeepers who are part of the A-team have been taken into account up to a total of three.

4 The index of dissimilarity (Duncan and Duncan, 1955) is calculated using the following formula:

$$ID = \frac{1}{2} x \sum \left(\frac{x_1}{X} - \frac{y_1}{Y} \right)$$

5 This coefficient is measured each year according to results obtained by the clubs in European competitions (Champions League and UEFA Europa League).

6 The coefficient of determination between the average income of clubs in top division leagues according to country and the UEFA association coefficients for 2008/2009 was 77 per cent.

7 In this instance it must be noted that most of the championships ranked in level 3 are situated in the eastern part of the continent, which goes a long way in explaining the clear over-representation of Eastern European players measured in the lowest echelons.

2 Why tax international athlete migration?

The 'Coubertobin' tax in a context of financial crisis

Wladimir Andreff

International athlete migration is not a new economic fact. English football spread to France in the late nineteenth century and British players moved to Paris and created a football club there, the so-called Racing Club. As early as the 1950s, the Argentine football player Di Stefano, the Hungarian Puskas and the French Kopa were playing together in the Real Madrid squad. More recently, the growth of international athlete migration has increased significantly in the past 15 years due to economic globalisation and a change in regulation of European professional sports (Andreff, 2006a).

Globalisation has affected the sports economy in its various dimensions (Andreff, 2008). The global market for all sporting goods and services, in 2004, was assessed to be in the range of €550–600 billion. The global market for football is valued at €250 billion. The market for all sporting goods is valued at about €150 billion. The value of broadcasting rights related to sport events is estimated at €60 billion, although the global market for sports sponsorship is nearly €18 billion. In 2006, the global market for doping was assessed at €6 billion. Even if these figures are not exact, the trend towards globalisation of sport business is crystal clear. By the same token, the market for high-level sporting talents has also globalised. It is a labour market in which professional players and other highly talented athletes are internationally transferred – from a club in one country to a club located abroad. International transfers of football players skyrocketed in this global labour market since it was entirely deregulated in 1995. Then, this deregulation has affected international labour market in other professional sports and, finally, in all high-level sport. Recently football has become the most investigated global market in the sports economy, giving rise to serious concerns with regards to transfer of teenage players below the age of 18. In the face of a teenage trade sometimes compared to trafficking of human beings or even new (international) slavery, some recipes have been suggested to supervise and regulate international athlete migration, including the design of a specific taxation. In the new context of financial crisis and global economic recession it is as yet unclear if this is likely to put a brake on such migration or to boost it.

This chapter is structured as follows. First, some empirical evidence is provided as regards to the magnitude of international athlete migration, including the international transfer of teenage athletes or players. Then, the focus is on the economic determinants of such migration and some of its outcomes. A model of international player transfer taxation more specifically geared towards hindering teenage transfers is elaborated on, whose strengths and weaknesses are compared to former and existing (FIFA) regulation in football. Did the whole picture change with the emergence of the current financial and economic crisis? Since the latter is not over and an economic analysis of its consequences is not stabilised yet, only some hints about its impact on international athlete migration will be sketched in the conclusion.

Empirical evidence of international athlete migration

The first significant international player transfers in football can be traced back to the 1950s. In the same decade, an outflow of baseball players from the Dominican Republic towards North American baseball leagues started to become more significant. However, it is globalisation of the labour market for talents that has really boosted athlete international migration, sometimes coined a 'feet drain' or, better, a 'muscle drain' (Andreff, 2001) by analogy with the long-lasting brain drain in the global economy. Such globalisation was triggered by the Bosman (1995) case in football. A similar jurisprudence was extended to different sports and citizens of Central Eastern Europe and CIS countries by the Malaja, Kolpak and Simutenkov cases (Andreff, 2006b). Then, in 2000, a Cotonou agreement signed by the European Union with 77 African, Caribbean and Pacific countries allowed athlete transfers from the latter area under the qualification of 'assimilated Europeans', which means under the same conditions as those players who could claim benefiting from Bosman, Malaja, Kolpak and Simutenkov jurisprudences. The outcome is a global labour market for player talents.

After 1995, the international mobility of football players grew and the percentage of foreign players in European football leagues was on average more than twice higher in 2008 compared with 1996. In particular, an increasing percentage shows up in the five major European football leagues. According to data collected by Loïc Ravenel and Raffaele Poli (Table 2.1) regarding the five major European football leagues, 38.7 per cent of all players involved in 2006 were foreign, that is, 277 players, of which 50.2 per cent had migrated from other European countries. We basically witness a North–North international migration in European football. The English Premier League is the most internationalised labour market in European football. Such evidence has triggered the publication of the *Meltdown Report* in the United Kingdom in December 2007, that is, a report attempting to understand why the English national squad had not been able to qualify for the Euro 2008 final stage. The major reason put forward is that, in 2007–8, only 196 players in operation in the English Premier championship were *not* foreign while foreigners originated from 66 different countries. This was compared with 23 foreigners playing in the Premier League when it was created in 1992.

Table 2.2 provides a snapshot of the global market for football players with regards to the 30 major exporting (home) and 30 major importing (host) countries. It is to be noticed that major European leagues are both exporting and

Table 2.1 Share of foreign players in professional football, pre- and post-Bosman (%)

First division championship	1995	1996	1999	2005	2006
England	34	34	37	56	55
France	18	18	22	36	36
Germany	19	27	39	50	41
Italy	14	17	33	31	31
Spain	20	29	40	28	32

Source: CIES data base (Poli, 2008).

Table 2.2 Migrant football players in 2008: 30 major leagues

Home country league	Number of migrant football players	Host country league	Average number of foreign players per club
Brazil	551	England	15.6
France	233	Greece	13.3
Argentina	222	Portugal	13.2
Serbia	192	Russia	12.9
Portugal	121	Germany	12.8
Czech Republic	113	Switzerland	11.5
Croatia	109	Belgium	11.5
Nigeria	94	Italy	10.4
Sweden	94	Scotland	10.2
Germany	92	Romania	9.9
Bosnia and Herzegovina	91	Turkey	9.5
Cameroon	87	Spain	9.2
Slovakia	76	Ukraine	8.8
Uruguay	71	Norway	8.7
England	70	Austria	8.5
Netherlands	66	Netherlands	8.4
Belgium	64	France	8.3
Spain	62	Denmark	7.8
Denmark	60	Slovakia	6.5
Ivory Coast	59	Bulgaria	6.4
Poland	59	Sweden	6.4
Switzerland	49	Hungary	5.9
Finland	46	Ireland	5.5
Austria	45	Poland	4.9
Senegal	45	Slovenia	4.9
Ghana	44	Finland	4.6
Romania	44	Croatia	3.9
Ireland	41	Iceland	3.8
Macedonia	41	Czech Republic	3.6
USA	38	Serbia	2.7

Source: CIES data base (Poli, 2008).

importing, which means that two-way trans-border flows are a characteristic of international athlete migration across major developed market economies. The only dividing line among European countries is that some countries are net

Table 2.3 Transfers of Brazilian players abroad

	2002		2003		2004	
Total	654		787		857	
Moving to:	NB	%	NB	%	NB	%
Europe	365	55.8	454	57.7	435	50.8
Portugal (first destination)	141	21.6	141	17.9	132	15.4
Asia	94	14.4	128	16.3	169	19.7
South America	80	12.2	71	9.0	95	11.1
Africa	53	8.1	65	8.3	79	9.2
North–Central America	60	9.2	67	8.5	68	7.9
Oceania	2	0.3	2	0.3	11	1.3

importers of foreign players (England, Greece, Germany, Italy, Spain) whereas some others are net exporters (France, Belgium, Portugal, Denmark).

On the other hand, outside Western Europe, some countries appear to be net exporters, first of all Brazil, Argentina and Serbia, but also the Czech Republic, Croatia, Nigeria, Bosnia and Herzegovina, Cameroon, Slovakia, Uruguay, Ivory Coast, Senegal, Ghana and Macedonia, that is, in a nutshell Latin American, Central Eastern European and African countries. Thus, South–North athlete mobility is a crucial facet of international athlete migration, even more so than North–North player transfers. Nearly half of foreign players operating in the five major European football leagues are originating from developing countries. The percentage is even higher if we look at second rank leagues like Belgium or Portugal and second and third division clubs of the big five European football countries. For example, in the French professional football league (*Ligue du Football Professionnel*), 50 per cent of foreign players are from African countries. Southern (and Eastern European) countries usually are net exporters and Northern countries are net importers in player trade with the South (and Eastern Europe). France is a typical case in point: 13 out of 45 foreign players who entered the French *Ligue 1* in 2007–8 were from developing countries whereas 3 out of 54 players who moved abroad have left for a developing country. The balance is a net import of 10 players from developing countries. Seen from the South, a similar orientation is witnessed. From 1989 to 1997, over 2,000 Brazilian players migrated to European football clubs, and there were still 654 to move in 2002 and 857 in 2004 (Table 2.3). Their major host country is Portugal, then other European countries. Hundreds of African and other Latin American football players are transferred to European clubs every year.

The same sort of South–North international athlete migration is observed from developing countries to North America. A total of 1,300 players in the Major and Minor Baseball Leagues are citizens from the Dominican Republic, a

Table 2.4 Geographic distribution of domestic team affiliation, African 2002 World Cup players

Domestic team affiliation	Cameroon	Nigeria	Senegal	South Africa	Tunisia	Total
Home country	—	2	1	7	14	24
Africa	—	—	1	—	—	1
England	4	4	—	3	—	11
France	7	3	20	—	2	32
Germany	1	—	—	2	1	4
Italy	3	—	—	1	3	7
Spain	4	1	—	—	—	5
Other European	3	11	1	10	3	28
Rest of World	1	2	—	—	—	3
Total	23	23	23	23	23	115

Source: Gerrard (2002).

number of African and Latin American players operate in the National Basketball Association and Czech and Russian superstar players are often hired by National Hockey League teams.

Since the late 1980s, post-communist transition economies from Central Eastern Europe and the former Soviet Union became significant net exporters of athletes so that they could compare – and indeed compete – with developing countries on the global labour market for sporting talents. For example, from 1990 to 1997, over 600 professional football players, 520 ice hockey players, 300 handball and volleyball players, 100 ice skaters and 20 coaches moved abroad from the former USSR (Andreff and Poupaux, 2007). With economic recovery in Russia, nowadays a reverse flow has emerged of importing foreign players in the most performing Russian clubs, like the 2008 UEFA Cup winner, that is, Zenit St Petersburg.

The other side of the coin is the selection of players enrolled abroad in an increasing number of national squads. During the 2006 football World Cup, the overall number of players selected in national squads was 736, out of which 392 (53 per cent) were playing abroad. The 2006 French football squad encompassed 13 players registered abroad. National squads of developing (and transition) countries now comprise of many players whose club affiliations are outside their home domestic league. This is even more clearly exhibited with African national squads participating in the football World Cup final stage (Table 2.4). For the five African squads that qualified in 2002, only 21 per cent of players were affiliated to their home domestic league. The same observation is made at each football African Cup of Nations. The extreme case was the Ivory Coast team in which all the players were registered in foreign leagues and clubs.

International teenage player transfer is the most contentious, and possibly illegal, international migration business, since FIFA rules adopted in 2001 absolutely forbid transferring from abroad football players below the age of 18. Indeed, such transfers emerged in the late 1980s, but importing teenage players from developing countries was boosted by liberalisation and resulting globalisation of the football labour market after 1995. Many clubs increasingly looked for a substitute to more mobile European superstar players in recruiting new young and cheap talents in the Third World.

During the 1990s, 4,809 foreign players, aged from 6 to 16, originating from Latin American and African countries, were found in Italian football clubs. In the Netherlands, 33 football clubs had been sued by the immigration office for illicit importation of Latin American and African players. Belgian football clubs were – and still are – utilised as 'nursery hubs' for training African players before their transfer to major European leagues. In 2000, 15 young African players lodged a complaint in the Belgian court against professional clubs and players' agents, complaining about the 'trade and trafficking of human beings'. And eventually they won (Tshimanga Bakadiababu, 2001).

Often spotted by players' agents at the African Cup of Nations – which is nicknamed the 'cattle fair' – teenage players are invited to be tested in European clubs and recruited when the test is successful. When it is not, they are abandoned by both clubs and players' agents without a labour contract and return airplane ticket to their home country. Thus, they are left *de facto* in a position of being illegal migrant workers and, sometimes, cracked down on by the police. Some cases were so outrageous in France that the French Minister for Sports, Ms Buffet, ordered a report (Donzel, 1999) that confirmed the existing extremely bad practices of clubs and players' agents as regards to African teenage players. After a decade of such devastating teenage transfers, the Fédération Internationale de Football Association (FIFA) reacted in 2001 with a new regulation article 19 that stated that 'international transfer is allowed only if the player is at least eighteen'. However, three exceptions left the door open to regulation being circumvented: teenage transfers are allowed when their parents move abroad for reasons that are not linked to football, when it is a transfer across EU countries, and when a teenage player is living close to the border of a foreign country. As a consequence, teenage muscle drain has not vanished even though it is clearly illegal. One can still find some cases reported by the press. For example, in 2002, Isa Mohammed (Nigeria) was transferred to a Polish first division nursery club, and his transfer was supposed to develop his international career in a major European football league. Unfortunately, he was injured, excluded from the team, and eventually abandoned by the club.

A small, though rapidly increasing, share in international migration of sporting talents comes when an athlete or player changes his or her citizenship (naturalisation), which is the most visible and sometimes contentious part of muscle drain. The number of naturalised citizens in national squads competing at the Athens Olympics in 2004 and the Beijing Olympics in 2008 was far from negligible (Andreff, 2006b). A forthcoming issue resulting from increasingly numerous naturalisations, which has urgently to be dealt with, is what will be the meaning, status and recognition of national squads in the future. The Qatari strategy of naturalising African and Latin American athletes is of particular concern.

Economic determinants of international athlete migration

Some determinants of international athlete migration are not economic; for instance, when an athlete simply follows his or her parents' international relocation for non-sport motives or looks for the opportunity of better training conditions abroad or is willing to practise in a country with better weather and so on. In economic terms and with reference to North–North international athlete migration, a major determinant is wage differentials across different sports and differently developed market economies. If one compares average monthly wages in different sports in a same country, money distribution appears to be very much uneven. In 2007, the average individual wage was €44,000 per year in French Football *Ligue 1*, €11,000 in *Ligue 2*, €12,500 in cycling Pro Tour, €7,000 in basketball A (first division), €6,500 in rugby Top 14 and €1,500 in athletics *Ligue Pro* (about 30 times less than in football's first league). It is crystal clear that the French labour market for sporting talents is unevenly attractive to migrant athletes depending on the sport discipline. Available data also provides an insight into the impact of wage differentials in the same sport across developed market economies. For instance, the average wage in English football's Premier League was €145,000 in 2007 (three times higher than in the French league) and €45,500 in the second division (four times higher than in the French second division). This obviously explains why so many French football players move to English clubs and so few (if any) English players are hired by French clubs.

A comprehensive explanation of wage differentials between English and French football leagues would lead us into an economic theory of professional sports leagues (Andreff, 2009a) and variants of league regulation in European football (Andreff and Bourg, 2006) that is beyond the limits of this chapter. In a nutshell, wage differentials are resulting from club revenue differentials relying on different club attractiveness and access to gate receipts, sponsorship money, TV rights revenues, merchandising and naming.[1] In this respect, English football clubs' attractiveness is stronger than French clubs'. Chelsea could afford a €190 million payroll in 2007–8, that is, 70 per cent of overall payroll for the whole French *Ligue 1* (€268 million). Seen from transferred player revenues, wage differentials trigger their decision to move from French to English clubs.

A second determinant is league regulation and its impact on a more or less balanced contest, the so-called competitive balance. The more unbalanced a championship, the more a player's move to a top club of this unbalanced league will translate into a substantial wage increase. French players often migrate from the more balanced French *Ligue 1* to the less balanced Italian *Lega Calcio*, Spanish *Liga de Fútbol* and English Premier League in view of significant wage gains. A more unbalanced domestic championship raises the probability of its top clubs qualifing for (or even win) the Champions League and then increases revenue expectations for players (including bonuses, sponsorship contracts, etc.). Playing in a successful club such as a Champions League winner, finalist or semi-finalist will increase the value of a player's human capital which would materialise in a more profitable international transfer fee afterwards. In South–North athlete migration, again the wage gap is obviously the most effective determinant. In the Brazilian first division football league in 2007, the average wage was €12,000, whereas in the African leagues it was below €2,000 in different countries and seldom over €5,000 anywhere in Africa. English and French football wages are extremely appealing, even if paid below average, to any Latin American or African player.

A third determinant is economic underdevelopment of the Third World – and to some extent transition – countries (Andreff, 2001). Developing countries are usually plagued with a shortage of sport teachers and coaches, a low domestic sports financing, limited sport facilities and equipment, and fewer world-level sport performances than in developed countries, namely few Olympic medals, since the number of medals is markedly determined by GDP per capita and population of participating countries (Bernard and Busse, 2004; Andreff *et al.*, 2008). These countries are not capable of hosting more than a few mega sport events; they suffer from widespread corruption in sport and embezzlements and wage arrears in professional clubs. Therefore, for a domestic athlete, moving to the North means that he or she will find better training conditions, better technologies in sport equipment and medical care, better expectations to win at the world level and more competitive athletes to compete with. In addition, he or she can access a better standard of living and purchasing power in a developed market economy. The same determinants obviously apply to teenage muscle drain from developing countries. An additional one is the 'dream of a personal achievement as a future superstar player' in the North with all its associated benefits, a dream continuously fuelled by unscrupulous players' agents painting an enticing – though fallacious – picture of assumed advantages.

Major outcomes of international athlete migration may be sketched as follows. For athletes, when a transfer is successful, a major effect is a higher wage and revenues, and consequently, a better way of life. When unsuccessful, the player is left aside by the host club or resold on the labour market or simply abandoned in the case of teenagers. If unsuccessful, a player has to drift towards another club, usually in a lower division, or find a way to return home. For host clubs, they become 'multi-national companies' (Andreff, 2009b) sampling players and coaches from different countries. They offer sport shows and events of a better quality due to their recruitment of the best players/athletes abroad and they increase their probability to win on the pitch. Consequently, they attract more money from fans, sponsors and TV channels. Since they earn more money, host clubs for foreign players are more capable in recruiting international superstars which can prolong their capacity to win, to earn more money and so on, in a sort of winners' 'virtuous circle'.

With regards to professional sports leagues, the impact depends on whether a host country is a net importer of players or not. For instance, despite a significant number of French football players enrolled abroad, French *Ligue 1* had a deficit transfer balance in the early 2000s, which jeopardised the league's financial equilibrium, due to even more significant imports of players from European and developing countries. When it comes to the economic impact of importing foreign athletes on the host country's economy overall, an obvious gain consists in having higher quality domestic sport contests without having financed the cost for education and training foreign players/athletes involved in the domestic championship. With superstar foreign players, host countries' teams may enjoy winning prestigious (and profitable) international contests like the European football Champions League. However, a possible 'windfall cost' may happen with regard to the host country's national squad, as has been witnessed with the English football squad being unable to qualify for the final stage of Euro 2008.

For developing countries that basically are net exporters of sporting talents, the main issue is that the home country and the nursery club are not compensated – or are not enough – for educational and training costs they have covered before their players have been transferred. An absent or limited compensation deepens the gap between the sports economy of a developing home country and a developed host country and undermines the sporting substance of developing countries as well as their expectations and probability of winning international contests or Olympic medals. Developing countries' national squads are often weakened by European or American clubs' reluctance to release their Third World players, which erodes the home country's capacity to field its most talented athletes in international contests. And when players are released, the national squad of a home country is less and less national in some sense insofar as most of its players are expatriate workers. Since they are not compensated enough for transferred players, professional clubs and leagues in developing countries remain poor and are unable to keep their best players or to get a reasonably high price (transfer fee) for them on the global market.

Regarding the role of players' and athletes' agents, the more they transfer players, the bigger their revenues since they levy a percentage on each transfer fee and/or initial wage. Transfers of teenage players are illegal and undertaken under outrageous and infamous conditions offered to young players. Increasing turnover in the labour force and growing international athlete mobility still occur and destabilise the manpower of many sport teams, with the exception of the richest. Such consequences of free movement in a global market call for the introduction of more regulation. Another outcome is the emergence of an underground (black) market for teenage players after the introduction of new FIFA regulations released in 2001. These regulations prohibit the transfer of players below the age of 18. With player transfers from developing countries, players' agents often cheat on player birth dates in order to either 'rejuvenate' rather old players or give the appearance that a minor player is older than 18. This 'trade' is run by unregistered players' agents unsupervised by FIFA-outlaw agents. For instance, nearly 80 per cent of agents in operation in the French football league are unregistered. Hence, there is a high risk of fuelling the 'bung' culture of bribes, embezzlements and so on, as pointed out by Lord Stevens' (2006) report in the United Kingdom. Sometimes, a conflict of interest emerges when there are tight links between host club managers and players' agents. All in all, developing countries are losers in the athlete migration business. An issue to be solved is one of losers' compensation by winners basically located in developed host countries: clubs, leagues and players' agents. This has not been tackled yet since sport globalisation has emerged.

A model of international player transfer taxation: the Coubertobin tax

In the face of similar issues with excess international mobility of short-term capital on global financial markets, James Tobin, a Nobel Prize winner in Economics, suggested 'throw[ing] sand in the wheels of international finance' and designed a 1 per cent Tobin tax to put a brake on short-term capital movements (Tobin, 1978). Such a tax has not been implemented so far, but with the current financial crisis partly resulting from too much free capital movements through banks, financial markets, fiscal paradises and so on, the Tobin tax may come back to the fore in the coming months and years.

Thus, it is recommended here to design and introduce what I call a 'Coubertobin' tax on international player transfers (Andreff, 2004) with the four following objectives:

1   The tax is to extensively cover educational and training costs of teenage athletes in their home countries.
2   The tax is likely to slow down international athlete migration from developing countries to professional players' markets in developed countries.
3   The tax should provide a strong disincentive to transferring teenage players or even children.
4   Tax revenues would accrue to a fund for sport development in developing home countries and could finance sport facilities' building and maintenance, training, sports at school and sport for all.

The idea is to levy the Coubertobin tax at a 1 per cent rate on all transfer fees and initial wages agreed on in each labour contract signed by players moving from developing countries with foreign partners in developed host countries (for the technicalities of the tax, see Table 2.5). Regarding transfers of teenage and very young talents, a graduated surcharge would be added to the 1 per cent tax itself; the younger the player, the higher the rate of surcharge.

The Coubertobin tax obviously is not designed to be a panacea. A number of issues would have to be resolved if one wants such a tax to be enforced. Which would be the accurate body to levy the tax and take over tax administration? It could be a World Bank or UN department or an international body specifically created to manage the tax. An international agreement is necessary between host and home countries and sport federations; otherwise the tax will not be implemented on a global scale, the only relevant scale. Political willingness seems to be missing so far in favour of such a tax. The current financial crisis with its impact on professional finance and a hardened budget constraint on wages and transfer fees might well create a window of opportunity for those convinced that the global market for sporting talents must be regulated.

When it comes to regulating international athlete migration, there are at least two other options than the Coubertobin tax. A first option is the one adopted in the 2001 FIFA rules. First, teenager transfers are prohibited. The problem is that

Table 2.5 A model of a Coubertobin tax

$$FR = (P_i - r.V_1).T, \text{ if } a > a_1 \qquad (1)$$
$$FR = (P_i - r.V_1).[T + s_1(a - a_1)], \text{ if } a_1 < a < a_2 \quad (2)$$
$$FR = (P_i - r.V_1).[T + s_2(a - a_2)], \text{ if } a_2 < a < a_3 \quad (3)$$
$$FR = (P_i - r.V_1).(T + s_3), \text{ if } a < a_3 \qquad (4)$$

FR: revenues rose through taxation for home developing countries

P_i: international transfer price (fee) + initial annual wage of transferred player

V_1: player's value on home country market

r: exchange rate between domestic currency and the hard currency of host country

T: Coubertobin tax at a uniform rate of 1% for all transferred players

s: tax surcharge for players under 18

a: player's age at the date of transfer

a_1: first age threshold below which a tax surcharge is to be paid

a_2: second age threshold below which a tax surcharge must be deterrent

a_3: third age threshold below which the tax is prohibitive on transfers of extremely young players

Example: $a_1 = 18$ years, $a_2 = 14$ years and $a_3 = 10$ years

If $a_1 < a < a_2$, the tax surcharge $s_1 = 2\%$ more for each month under the age of 18 at the date of transfer; transferring a player of 16 would cost a 48% surcharge

If $a_2 < a < a_3$, the surcharge $s_2 = 10\%$ more for each month below the age of 14 at the date of transfer; transferring a player of 12 would cost a 240% surcharge

If $a < a_3$, the surcharge $s_3 = 1000\%$ lump sum tax

prohibition usually creates very strong incentives to either find some excuse that triggers an exception status or develop an international black market for teenage players, which already exists. Second, FIFA rules establish training cost compensation for players transferred over 23 with a 5 per cent solidarity mechanism which distributes compensation on a *pro rata* basis among all nursery clubs involved in a player's training from the age of 12 to 23. In a nutshell, the comparison between FIFA rules and the Coubertobin tax (details in Andreff, 2001, 2002; Gerrard, 2002) comes out with FIFA rules being more profitable for players of age over 23 and much less below 18. A main limitation of FIFA rules, comparatively to the tax, is that they are restricted to football whereas the Coubertobin tax targets all sports. On the other hand, FIFA rules have been adopted while the tax is still in prospect. In some sense, FIFA rules are a step in the right direction, but it is not in tackling the less desirable effects of international athlete migration.

A third option is to revert to the pre-Bosman quotas system of domestic players, such as the 6 + 5 rule, which would compel any football club to field at least six domestic ('national') players, and no more than five foreign players, in each match that counts for a contest. This rule is strongly supported by Sepp Blatter, and more recently he has been joined by the former French State Secretary for Sports,

Bernard Laporte. The incumbent UEFA president, Michel Platini, is apparently less in favour of quotas. Nevertheless, the number of 'locally trained' players who must be fielded in UEFA contests has been increased from four to six and then to eight players since 2007–8. In the Italian *Lega Calcio*, the quota is now of at least 50 per cent Italian players. A quota of locally trained players is also discussed in the French rugby Top 14. The concept of a locally trained player is rather blurred and must be further clarified in the near future, otherwise it could be considered as an attempt at breaching the Bosman ruling and the Treaty of Rome article which guarantees international labour mobility to all EU citizens. Finally, the Andrew Webster case at the Sport Arbitration Court seems to be a recent U-turn compared with the Bosman case, since it allows a player – considered as a free agent – who breaches their labour contract before the deadline, to obtain compensation though not higher than cumulative wages until the end of the contract. This sounds similar to the previous transfer fee system that had been abolished by the Bosman case. If player quotas based on citizenship were to be re-introduced, they would be subject to criticism by the European Court of Justice.

The most urgent regulation of international athlete migration may well be a quite tighter supervision of players' agent businesses. According to FIFA rules those who start up a players' agent business must exhibit a clean police record, must not be an attorney, must pass an interview with his or her domestic football federation and must open a bank deposit in Swiss francs. A number of agents do operate without fulfilling these rules. This regulation should be more tightly supervised, to say the least. Another option would be to forbid affiliated clubs (affiliated to sport federations) to deal with outlawed players' agents and to fine those who do not align to such a rule. Some doubt may be raised about the efficiency of supervision as long as players' agents and host clubs have converging, confusing or merged interests. Creating an international association of players' agents on the model of the Bar (association of barristers) has also been suggested (Tshimanga Bakadiababu, 2001) that would define and supervise honorariums and fees, and rule the whole agents business. Here again, like for the Coubertobin tax, such reform requires political willingness which is missing so far. What is urgently needed is to build up an exhaustive data collection process about all international transfers (in all sports and not only for football as suggested in Poli and Ravenel, 2006) and incurred transfer fee amounts. The latter is absolutely unknown and is only publicised through estimates and speculation by journalists or through acquaintances with some players.

International athlete migration and regulation in times of crisis

The development of the sub-prime bubble and its propagation into a global financial crisis that subsequently triggered a global economic recession may provide new support to economic regulation at the world level. Perhaps the time is ripe for implementing such a thing as a Coubertobin tax on international labour migration. There are several reasons to consider this.

First, what is the impact of financial and economic crises on sport? Based on first observations regarding sport financing in Europe (Amnyos, 2008; Andreff, 2009c; Andreff *et al.*, 2009a, 2009b), major channels for crisis transmission to sports are household and local authority sport expenditures, then government sport budget and private money flowing into sports through sponsorship and the media. The global crisis affects household revenues downwards and thus, through a decreasing purchasing power, it shrinks household sport consumption expenditures. Let us imagine a 5 per cent cut in household expenditures. If sports products and services are normal goods, considered as a usual part of the European way of life, the decrease of sport expenditures would be about 5 per cent on average since it is the expected fall in European GDP in 2009. Deep national disparities will occur around the average, depending on how hard each domestic economy will be hit by the crisis – for instance harder on the new EU members (Andreff, 2009d). The crisis may have a *substitution effect* in household expenditures between sport practice (and paying ticketed sport events) on the one hand and, on the other hand, sport events that can be watched for free or at a reasonably low price (sport TV broadcasts). In fact, sales of sport goods have dropped after September 2008. Adidas sales worldwide have dropped by 6 per cent in the first trimester of 2009 and its profit by 97 per cent (Puma's profit fell by 94 per cent); Nike's global sales have decreased by 2 per cent in the same trimester and the company has cut 1,400 of its 35,000 jobs. Shrinking household purchasing power is also a threat for professional sports clubs. Stadium attendance has dropped in various sports in the past months but not that much in European football where attendances have still increased in the English Premier League and the German *Bundesliga* while they are stagnating in French *Ligue 1* and decreasing in the Italian *Lega Calcio*. Another crisis index is that specialised sports newspapers, such as *L'Equipe* in France, are facing a fall in their sales.

In most EU member countries, local authorities have financed local clubs, athletes and infrastructures on the basis of money borrowing from the banking system. As a result, a number of local authorities are now indebted to banks which has negative implications for sport finance. Local authorities will not be able to maintain existing amounts of sport finance or, at least, will select the most significant clubs, athletes, sport events and infrastructures. The global economic crisis has obviously an impact on governments' budgets. The great bulk of fiscal deficit is simply due to the recession crisis itself which lowers tax receipts while it increases public expenditures (unemployment, social protection) and debt. Increased public debt will have to be reimbursed soon and this will trigger an austerity fiscal policy as soon as the deepest part of the recession is over. With 0.01 per cent to 0.88 per cent of government budget in European countries, sports ministries will suffer more than other ministries from budgetary cuts because of their low priority.

Except in a few industries, a number of industrial and commercial enterprises have been seriously hit by economic recession since the last trimester of 2008, and some of them have gone bankrupt. Since their sales and profits are down they reduce their 'less useful' expenditures, including sport sponsorship. Sponsors are changing their strategy towards sports since the crisis. Some simply quit sport sponsorship. A number of cases have been witnessed since September 2008: Honda, ING Royal Bank of Scotland and Crédit Suisse have left Formula 1, Kawasaki has abandoned its Moto GP team, banks have left the golf PGA Tour, Kodak has given up Nascar, Nomura the Japan Olympic team, and Vodafone has withdrawn from UK cricket and horse racing and breached Tiger Woods' sponsorship contract one year in advance.

A second strategy is simply to reduce the amount of sport sponsorship without giving up all sport support (AIG, Northern Rock, XL charter, Fortis, Dexia). Sponsors also diminish wages of sponsored athletes. Rossignol is bargaining on limiting by half its previous wage agreements with skiers.

Other sport sponsors – like Lacoste for example – prefer to concentrate their reduced finance on a few very high profile professional athletes and clubs and on sport mega-events. This means that amateur sport clubs and events that previously benefited from sponsorship will suffer more from financial shortages than professional sports. However, even some professional football clubs have found it difficult to attract a sponsor for 2008–9 like, for example, Aston Villa, Sheffield Wednesday and Leicester City.

In the case of media (TV channels) that basically finance sport through broadcasting rights, the crisis impact is less crystal clear. Recession affects advertising budgets of numerous enterprises downwards, and this would reduce the revenues offered for broadcasting sport events, in general. A countervailing tendency may be the following: if the viewing figures were to increase during the crisis, the audience rates of TV channels would increase and its attraction for advertisers would increase since, in a period of crisis, enterprises need to reach more potential consumers for their products (in order to maintain sales). On the other hand, the number of (sport) TV viewers might well increase during the crisis due to reduced purchasing power available for paying for leisure and sport. Moreover, the number of sport TV viewers would increase if the previously mentioned substitution effect of free sport TV broadcasts to sport practice and paid sport shows materialised. A number of broadcasting contracts between TV channels and different sports, including football, have already been revised downwards in Europe.

In the current model of professional sport finance,[2] professional clubs can afford to push wages and transfer fees up to acquire superstar players, and do it in a sort of arms race (Andreff, 2009a), as long as nobody imposes a hard budget constraint and good corporate governance on them. This applies even in the French and German cases where football clubs are more tightly supervised by auditing bodies than elsewhere in Europe (Andreff, 2007a). Clubs are often stuck in a vicious circle between increasing broadcasting rights negotiated with TV channels in order to cover their wage and transfer fee increases, which in turn requires a new negotiation for higher TV rights later on and so on (Andreff, 2007b); such a vicious cycle derails into pandemic clubs' deficits. Thus, the creeping financial crisis which affects European football (Lago *et al.*, 2006), and other professional sports to a lesser extent, is going to deepen with the global financial crisis and recession. The English Premier League deficit has reached €3.8 billion overall in October 2008, with Arsenal, Chelsea, Liverpool and Manchester United being accountable for two-thirds of it. The deficit of the Spanish *Liga de Fútbol* was up to €2.8 billion in December 2008, with Real Madrid, FC Barcelona, Atletico Madrid and Valencia being the most substantially in the red. As a consequence of such financial woes in European football clubs, the *mercato*[3] transfer market collapsed in winter 2008–9 due to a sponsorship shortage in French *Ligue 1*, the German *Bundesliga*, the Italian *Lega Calcio* and to a lesser degree in the Spanish *Liga de Fútbol*. Again, the exception to this was the English Premier League. Finally, the summer 2009 market for international transfers has also slowed down in the English Premier League. For the first time in many years, Manchester United, Liverpool, Chelsea and Arsenal have spent much less on foreign players than clubs such as Lyon, Marseille and Bordeaux. This downward trend is tightly linked to the crisis since it is triggered by the sterling pound depreciation in terms of the euro and a more stringent English tax system (in reaction to the crisis) which hits higher revenue earners, which include football players. To compensate for their loss of players, English clubs will have to increase wages and transfer fees, which few of them can afford.

It might be that the crisis, by itself, will put a brake on international athlete migration in a sort of market 'self-regulation'. Does it mean that there is no longer any need for a Coubertobin tax? A slowdown in international athlete transfers does not resolve at all the issue of outlawed teenage players' transfers. There is still significant room for regulation in particular when this global crisis ends and international athlete migration gains further momentum.

Notes

1 Naming refers to an increasing number of professional sport teams that have sold the naming rights for their facilities to private firms.
2 Primarily based on media finance (TV broadcasting rights), then on corporate finance, merchandising, labour market (players' transfers) and capital market (flotation of clubs' shares at the stock exchange); see Andreff and Staudohar (2000).
3 *Mercato* is the annual re-opening of the transfer market during the season's winter break.

3 Moving with the bat and the ball

The migration of Japanese baseball labour, 1912–2009

Yoshio Takahashi and John Horne

Research interest in the movement of elite athletes within and between nations has grown in the past 25 years as this collection and other articles (e.g. Maguire, 2004) testify. Although sports geographers were the first to monitor the geographical variations in migratory flows of athletes (Bale, 1984, 1991), sociologists and social historians, amongst others, have been quick to take up the challenge of considering the implications of athletic talent migration for various sports (e.g. Bale and Maguire, 1994a, 1994b; Maguire, 1999; Lanfranchi and Taylor, 2001; Obel, 2001b; Magee and Sugden, 2002).

Research has focused on three themes: first, the impact of athletic talent migration on both host countries and donor countries, on the role of intermediaries such as sports agents, and the effect on sports fans and the athletes themselves; second, the responses of nationally based governing bodies of sport and sports associations to athletic talent migration; third, the implications of athletic talent migration for conceptions of identity in regions and nations. These developments have been affected by changes in the regulatory frameworks within which professional and elite level sport is conducted and within which elite athletes function (Gardiner and Welch, 2000). For example, in 1995 the Belgian football player Jean-Marc Bosman won a court case confirming that players were free to work anywhere in Europe when their contract with a club expired. The European Union was attempting to abolish transfer fees as part of its effort to remove all obstacles to the freedom of movement of labour in European member state countries. Many European football clubs have depended on transfer fees as compensation for the scouting, training and development of junior players. Some are also concerned that now 'star' players will have even more bargaining power, and local loyalties will diminish even further in importance for players. Nationally developed players may no longer represent the route to success for teams, and there are also implications for coaching, training and national sides. Similar concerns have been expressed about the growth in the number of Japanese baseball players in Major League Baseball (MLB) since Nomo Hideo joined the Los Angeles Dodgers in 1995 (see Hirai, 2001).

Much of the research on sports-talent migration focuses on the cultural rather than the economic significance of labour mobility. An overwhelming interest in identities has developed in such a way as to occlude attention to the economic and organisational dynamics of labour mobility. A further shortcoming in the sport migration literature is methodological – the data used in some analyses have appeared to be derived, somewhat uncritically, from the print or other mass media. In addition, to date, there has been less sustained academic analysis of the mobility of non-western sports stars, including those from Asia and Africa. In the case of Africa, work by Bale (2004), Bale and Sang (1996) and Darby (2000, 2001) has contributed to our understanding of the migration of football players and athletes. In Australasia, Hall (2000) has discussed the impact of the sports 'brawn drain' on football in Australia, and Obel (2001) has considered the response of the NZ Rugby Football Union (NZRFU) to player migration. With a few exceptions (e.g. Klein, 1994; Chiba, 2004) academic interest in sports-labour migration among professional baseball leagues in the Pacific-Rim countries has been quite limited. Specific interest in Japanese player migration into MLB has largely been the preserve of journalism, and this has been marked by attempts to frame developments within certain pre-existing stereotypes, especially the idea of 'Samurai Baseball'. Hence the hard cover edition of Robert Whiting's book about Suzuki Ichiro, published in 2004, was re-titled with this in mind for the paperback edition (Whiting, 2005). This chapter offers more systematic, whilst still preliminary, reflections on the recent migration patterns of Japanese professional athletes, with particular emphasis on the migration of Japanese baseball labour.

The migration of Japanese sports labour

Takahashi and Horne (2004) have analysed the history of the migration of Japanese football players. Using Internet searches, and especially Japanese language databases, players' web pages, autobiographies and biographies, they found that over the past 20 years shifts have taken place in the geographical spread of Japanese football talent, corresponding to new opportunities, both in Japan and internationally, for football labour. South America has given way to diverse regions, including Europe. Both socio-cultural and structural–institutional factors were used to explain these developments with respect to Japanese football players. Takahashi and Horne concluded that since 1993 (and the formation of the professional football 'J. League') Japanese football players have increasingly begun to follow Japanese capital (sponsors) to European and South American league clubs and likewise Japanese capital has begun to follow players (through the emergent sports tourism business for example). Increasingly football clubs in mature soccer cultures have recognised the economic benefits that Japanese (and in a few cases Chinese and Korean) players can bring. But it is notable that most Japanese and other football players from East Asia are hired on loan rather than full registration contracts. European football clubs operate risk-averse strategies. Rather than providing evidence of a global labour market in football therefore, Takahashi and Horne found confirmation that it was primarily employer strategies in national, though internationalised, football labour markets that largely continue to determine who is recruited by which clubs and why (cf. McGovern, 2002).[1]

Analyses of the migration of Japanese baseball players to MLB in the United States, and to other countries, provide an instructive comparison. Baseball has been the leading Japanese spectator sport – with a different history, tradition and centre of gravity in the world of sport than football.[2] Yet academic and popular attention in the English-speaking world has often focused on the supposedly unique idiosyncrasies of Japanese baseball (cf. Kelly, 2009). As we have noted, this approach has been stimulated and sustained by the writings of journalist Robert Whiting (1977, 1989, 2004, 2005; and see also Cromartie and Whiting, 1991), and it can also be detected in other reviews of Japanese baseball conducted by Japanese scholars in English, such as Hirai (1996, 2001). The following reflections on the migration of Japanese baseball players over the past 20 years provide one possible start in reassessing the relationship between Japanese sports labour migration and economic, rather than socio-cultural, power and influence.[3]

Methodological comments

Preliminary data about migrant Japanese baseball players were collected from websites and print media (newspapers, magazines and books), mainly published in Japanese. This material has been supplemented by data collected from the library in the Baseball Hall of Fame and Museum (Yakyu Taiiku Hakubutsukan) in Tokyo. Several websites that deal with Japanese baseball players who played in other countries were also accessed. These data were corroborated by checking other websites, such as those written by a player or about players. These data were used to establish the number of Japanese players contracted with foreign professional baseball teams, including professionals but also those belonging to high school teams, university teams, amateur baseball teams and company teams in other countries. If a player moved to another club in the same country they were only counted once. A limitation of the data is that it was difficult to identify the nationality of players simply from their names. Although it was possible to exclude those with foreign (non-Japanese) sounding names, some players have Japanese-sounding names but do not have Japanese nationality. These include Korean players living in Japan who have in the past been forced to take Japanese names. This survey thus counts the number of players whose name is Japanese-sounding, and only further detailed research will be able to ascertain the number of those who are Korean.

The labour market for baseball in the United States and Japan

The size of the labour market is fixed by the organisational structures of professional baseball in each country. MLB in North America currently consists of two leagues and 30 teams (with one based in a Canadian city). US Minor League Baseball, organised into AAA, AA and A or Rookie divisions, is also professional and linked to MLB and consisted of 19 leagues and 243 teams in 2009 (http://web.minorleaguebaseball.com/milb/stats/). In addition to the minor leagues, there are Independent Leagues, so-called because they include teams that are not directly affiliated to MLB teams. Like MLB, Minor League Baseball is also transnational, featuring teams that play in countries outside the United States. As a result of this there are many more opportunities to become a professional baseball player in North America than anywhere else. MLB is now ethnically diversified and has expanded its scouting of players internationally. According to Whiting (2004, p. xv), 'As of Opening day of the 2004 MLB season, players born outside the United States and Canada constituted more than a quarter of all big league rosters (and the percentage in the minor leagues was nearly half).' By the start of the 2009 season out of 818 players in MLB 28 per cent were non-US nationals, including over 10 per cent from the Dominican Republic, 6.4 per cent from Venezuela and 1.6 per cent from Japan.[4]

In Japan, where professional baseball (Nippon Professional Baseball or NPB) began in 1936, there are six teams in both the Central League (CL) and the Pacific League (PL). Since 2007 the leagues have played 144 games per season, compared with MLB currently playing a 162-game season. In the first nine years of the twenty-first century, the Japanese professional baseball market has been changing rapidly. Because of the long-term recession in the Japanese economy, one of the Japanese professional teams, Osaka Kintetsu Buffaloes, was dissolved in 2004, and a rising information technology (IT) company formed a new team, Rakuten Golden Eagles, to replace it. Mobile phone company SoftBank also purchased the Daiei Hawks in 2005. For the same economic reason, many company baseball teams have been disbanded and the professional baseball labour market in Japan has shrunk. There were 148 company teams in 1994, but in 2009 there were only 85 company teams (http://www.jaba.or.jp/team/clubteam/suii. pdf). Increasingly, top-level players have sought work outside Japan. A related development has been the establishment since 2005 of new local independent professional leagues within Japan sponsored by local companies (copying in some respects the successful formula adopted by the J. League – see Horne with Bleakley, 2002). One of the reasons for restructuring is that an increasing number of foreign investors in global Japanese companies demand a financial dividend, a capital gain, and are reluctant to meet the expense of managing a company baseball team for marketing purposes.

In the past 15 years three other developments have emerged to challenge the foundations of Japanese baseball. First, there have been changes in labour relations and attitudes towards work on the part of baseball players (as well as on the part of many others in the Japanese workforce) leading to the growth of free agency (FA) and the appearance of player agents (McDonald *et al.*, 2001, pp. 49–50). The FA system in Japanese baseball was introduced in 1993 and revised again in 1998. Currently players can move to foreign teams after nine seasons (this compares with six seasons in MLB). Second, the pull and push of different employer strategies both within and outside Japan have been altering the nature of Japanese sport. In baseball there has been a pull from US sources and a (initially reluctant) push from Japanese sources. Miller *et al.* (2003) argue that there has been a dual strategy in US sports in recent years – expanding to create markets in the First World, and recruiting cheap labour (athletic talent) from the Third World, although the case of Japanese athletes suggests that talent may be sought wherever it is available. By recruiting Japanese athletes, MLB has been able to stimulate audiences for its product, including the TV rights, in Japan and encourage the growth of new sports tourism businesses.[5] Third, the relationship between the mass media and business opportunities also influences migration between Japan and the rest of the world of sport. Both new media (satellite, digital and cable TV, Internet, mobile telephony, etc.) and new forms of tourism find that sport is a 'killer content' to attract new customers.

Trends in Japanese baseball player migration

The signing of Nomo Hideo to the Los Angeles Dodgers in 1995 marked a new relationship between Japanese and US baseball. Hirai (2001, p. 188) describes Nomo as 'the proto-typical transpacific sports star' whose transfer marked a transition in Japanese taste for baseball. Hirai argues that understood as *yakyu* – the Japanese national game – administrators, coaches, players and fans alike were satisfied with baseball the way it was in Japan before the 1990s. The acceptance of baseball as a full Olympic event in 1992 helped to hasten its internationalisation, and developments in mass communications technology also helped to bring the wider world of baseball into Japan. In 1989 Japanese national public TV broadcaster NHK (Japan Broadcasting Corporation) started the live televising of MLB through satellite. Japanese fans as well as players have been attracted to baseball leagues in other countries, especially MLB. Less prosaically, Nomo's transfer was facilitated when his agent – Dan Nomura – identified a loophole in the US–Japan Working Agreement reached after the 'Murakami affair' (Whiting, 2004, pp. 96–117). This meant that Japanese players at the end of their contracts with NPB teams could elect to negotiate freely outside of Japan, with MLB teams for example (Whiting, 1999, p. 41).

According to our findings, since Nomo in 1995, 41 other Japanese players have joined Major League teams and over 90 have joined minor league or independent sides in North America. Table 3.1 shows a total of 261 instances of Japanese baseball player *outward* migration since 1912. Whilst we counted all cases of migration we found that 23 players were double or triple counted, and in the case of veteran pitcher Maeda Katsuhiro, counted four times. Hence our data actually relate to the experiences of 228 different players. These trends up to 2009 remained consistent with our findings published in the original journal article in 2006. The migration is still very much US-centred: 38.7 per cent have been to US MLB or Minor Leagues. If US-based Independent and Canadian Leagues are included, the proportion that has migrated to North America is 52.9 per cent. As professional opportunities have developed in East Asia migrations too have increased: since the launch of the Korea Baseball Organization (KBO) in 1982 and the launch of the Chinese Professional Baseball League in 1990, 41.5 per cent of migrations have been to East Asian neighbours (South Korea, Taiwan and the PRC).

Before the start of the Korean professional baseball league, only eight instances of Japanese baseball labour migration were identified. In a second phase, from

Table 3.1 Trends in Japanese baseball player migration*

League	Before 1982	1982– 1994#	1995– 1998##	1999– 2002###	2003– 2006	2007– 2009	Total	%
US MLB	1	0	5	9	11	17	43	16.5
US Minor League	6	1	19	13	8	11	58	22.2
US Independent League	1	3	7	24	1	§	36	13.8
Korean	0	28	0	2	6	2	38	14.6
Chinese/ Taiwan	0	6	9	28	16	9	68	26.1
Chinese/ PRC	0	0	0	0	2	0	2	0.8
Canadian	0	0	0	0	1	0	1	0.4
Mexican/ Central American	0	1	0	2	2	3	8	3.1
European	0	0	0	3	3	0	6	2.3
Australian	0	0	0	0	1	0	1	0.4
Total	8	39	40	81	51	42	261	100.0

Sources: Japanese language websites and publications listed in references.

Notes

*The table lists the total number of migration movements, including 23 players who are double, triple and, in the case of veteran pitcher Maeda Katsuhiro, counted four times. In total the table identifies 228 different players. The table is a substantially revised version of that published in the original article and includes four additional players identified as migrating before 1982.

#The Korea Baseball Organization (KBO), the Korean professional baseball league, was started in 1982.

##Nomo Hideo migrated to MLB in 1995. From 1997 to 2002 there were two professional baseball leagues in Taiwan. In 2003 the leagues merged.

###In December 1998 a new Posting System was introduced that enabled MLB teams to bid blindly for available NPB players.

§Information from the US-based Independent Leagues is not reliable for the period 2007–2009 and is thus omitted. Since 2005 several Independent baseball leagues have also started in Japan, but for obvious reasons these are not counted in this table of Japanese baseball player *outward* migration.

1982 to 1994 (before Nomo), 28 players went to South Korea, 6 to Taiwan, 4 to minor or independent leagues in the United States and 1 to Mexico. All the migrants to Korea had either Korean nationality or parents who were Korean.[6] The start of South Korean and Taiwanese professional baseball has thus greatly influenced Japan-based baseball player's migration, although not necessarily that of *ethnically Japanese* players. It is only since Nomo went to MLB in 1995 that the number of cases of migration to the United States has increased significantly.

Many of the Japanese players who have joined MLB since 1995, including Nomo, Hasegawa, Ishi and Suzuki (who registered his given name, Ichiro, to NPB), have remarked that the experience of playing with a US-based team was their major incentive for joining MLB (Nomo, 1995, p. 29; Komatsu, 2002, p. 110; Hasegawa, 2003, pp. 16–18; Ishi, 2003, p. 39). In 2000 Sasaki Kazuhiro joined the Seattle Mariners, Suzuki Ichiro followed him a year later and in 2003 Matsui Hideki left the Yomiuri Giants for the New York Yankees (the latter prompting Beach (2004) to write a book entitled *Godzilla Takes the Bronx* after Matsui's nickname).

Internationalisation and the impact on Japanese baseball

In terms of live attendances and television viewing figures, NPB has been the most popular sport in Japan. However, recently, there has been a decline in live and television audiences. As the number of talented and popular Japanese players migrating to MLB has increased, and live broadcasts of MLB games became available in Japan, Japanese baseball fans have become more interested in the activities of Japanese players in MLB rather than the implied 'second-class' games in NPB. In the Japanese mass media Suzuki Ichiro's record-breaking season in MLB in 2004 received more coverage than the amazing performance of Matsunaka Nobuhiko (Daiei Hawks) in NPB – he achieved the triple crown for having the most home runs, runs batted in (RBIs)[7] and holding the highest batting average for the season. If one impact of the migration of Japanese players has been to increase the number of Japanese baseball fans who were well informed about MLB, it is also possible that the success of Japanese players in MLB may begin to challenge American prejudices about Japanese players (see Sherwin, 2002). It is too early to tell if these views will be revised, since as we have seen the US media still plays a major role in the framing of Japanese (and other foreign) baseball players through narrow, reified, stereotypes (see Mayeda, 1999; Nakamura, 2005; Kelly, 2009).

However, Japanese players in MLB bring profits to both Japanese and US companies. By the time Matsui had arrived in the United States a market had been developed. R&C Tours organised trips to see the Yankees' opening games in Toronto in March and April 2003 at a cost of 89,800 yen (at the time, approximately US$9,000) per person per game. Similar tours have been organised for some years to watch Japanese players with the Seattle Mariners. Kobayashi (2004, pp. 21–2) noted that the number of Japanese spectators at Safeco Field (Seattle Mariners) grew from 100,000 in 2000 to 130,000 in 2004. The Mariners thus agreed a new advertising contract with Nissan and increased the amount of money they received from their sponsors, Nintendo. In New York the number of Japanese spectators attending the Yankees Stadium increased from 1,000 per game in 2002 to 6,000 per game in 2004. The Yankees sold stadium sign boards to Japanese companies, including Canon, Sharp, Ajinomoto, Komatsu, Fuji Film and the Yomiuri Newspaper group. MLB increased its TV rights contract with NHK from 7.8 billion yen for a four-year deal to 30 billion yen for a six-year deal. NHK currently broadcasts about 250 live MLB games per season, and in 2007 began to broadcast all matches of the MLB World Series; especially notable was the fact that it was the first time in their history that Japanese players were involved in both the competing teams, including Daisuke Matsuzaka ('Dice-K') of the Boston Red Sox.

When the most popular home run hitter in Japan, Matsui Hideki of the Yomiuri Giants, joined the New York Yankees in 2003 its significance lay in the move from the core team in NPB to one of the core teams of MLB. However, the deal Yomiuri Giants made with MLB concerned not only the size of Matsui's transfer fee but also the agreements about future business opportunities. The following year, in March and April 2004, the New York Yankees played opening games in Japan, sponsored by Yomiuri Shinbun. The development of the World Baseball Classic (WBC) competition – which Japan has won both times it has been staged, in 2006 and 2009 – also owed a lot to the business relationship developed between MLB and Yomiuri. With these and other developments MLB Japan's office has tripled its business since 2003, amounting to 60–70 per cent of MLB's international revenue (Robinson and Corbett, 2008).

These developments have not been without controversy, in Japan and in the United States (see Kelly, 2007 for a more detailed discussion). In the United States the posting system was criticised after the Boston Red Sox signed pitcher Daisuke Matsuzaka from Seibu Lions in 2007. The posting system operates according to a blind bidding procedure, which can lead to inflated transfer fees. The Red Sox paid approximately US\$103.1 million in total, including the transfer fee and contract, to acquire the pitcher. The amount was considerably more than any other Japanese player has been signed for. As in other professional leagues, one of the arguments is that smaller teams cannot afford to compete with large-market teams for the rights to negotiate with some posted Japanese players. At the time of writing, discussions about the posting system, among other things, were ongoing.

Another controversy developed in 2009 connected to Boston Red Sox, over the transfer of pitcher Tazawa Junichi. He was considered the best amateur player in Japanese company baseball, but he refused his selection to the NPB draft and made a contract instead with the MLB team. NPB then took steps to deal with this movement; NPB teams are now forbidden from making a contract with any player who moves to a foreign team without experience of the NPB draft for two years should they want to return to NPB. This regulation is clearly designed to make talented young players' direct moves to MLB teams less palatable, and in this way NPB seeks to protect its human resource market.

These and other developments have signified that the Japanese market is considered important for the business of both teams and national leagues in the United States and Japan. They are another sign that some US and Japanese professional baseball teams now seek to gain profits not only from their local/national markets but also by reaching out to international markets beyond their national boundaries.

Conclusions

Most researchers agree that athletic talent migration involves the study of processes that are evolving and developing. Athletic labour migration is a dynamic subject involving national sports organisations, clubs/teams and athletes in a complex chain of negotiations over rights and responsibilities. Whether it is correct to portray it as an example of heightened globalisation, regionalisation or internationalisation continues to be debated.

What is clear from our preliminary research, however, is that at the basis of player migration are institutional responses to economic crises and opportunities. By adopting strategies of both domestic and transnational expansion both MLB, and, to a lesser extent, teams in NPB, have sought mutual profit. Outside of North America and Japan unequal exchange relationships (e.g. with Latin America) continue to shape the development of the sport. Of course, in baseball as in other sports, economic power does not automatically translate into sports supremacy. Nonetheless it is apparent that sport labour migration, and those who are fortunate enough to engage in it, is an important reflection of prevailing economic relations.

Klein (1994, p. 200) argued that Japanese involvement in Latin American baseball, and investment in North American teams, saw Japanese capital 'further ensconced in the web of North American baseball and ever more dependent'. Developments since 1994, and further incursions of Japanese capital and labour into MLB and elsewhere in the world of baseball, suggest that a revision of Klein's view may be required. Our data suggest that Japanese baseball player migration in the past two decades, while continuing involvement with MLB, has also helped to boost professional baseball in the Republic of Korea (South Korea), Taiwan and the People's Republic of China.[8]

It would appear therefore that both MLB and NPB (and possibly Japanese capital) are finding that contemporary developments are to their mutual advantage. Japanese capital and baseball labour are finding new opportunities in East Asia as well as North America. This is not an argument for the economic determination of cultural activities but rather a reminder that economics underpins the movements of workers, including transnational sports migrants. Further research is needed to continue to clarify and better understand the impacts, responses and implications of sports labour migration from and to East Asian societies.

Notes

1 As Rowe and Gilmour (2008) note, such players have sometimes been dismissively referred to as 'T-shirts' for the merchandise revenue stream they attract.
2 Compared with football, with 207 national football associations affiliated to the Federation Internationale de Football Association (FIFA), only 112 associations, including three 'provisional members', are affiliated to the International Baseball Federation (IBAF; http://www.ibaf.org/). The number of professional baseball leagues in the world is even smaller. Only a small number of leagues, such as Japanese professional baseball (The Professional Baseball Organization of Japan or Nippon Professional Baseball – NPB) and Major League Baseball (MLB) in North America, have any real gravitational attraction for the players in the world. As Kelly (2007) argues, the dominance of MLB in the sport makes it more of an international rather than truly global sport.

3 Although we focus mainly on players who migrated in the past 20 years, it is possible, as historians of baseball have shown, to identify earlier periods when Japanese players were involved in baseball in the United States (Dreifort, 2001; Reaves, 2002). A Japanese student began playing professional baseball in one of the American 'coloured' independent leagues in 1914. Hence arguably Mikami Goro, nicknamed 'Jap Mikado' by Americans, was the first Japanese baseball player to play in competitive matches in the United States (Sayama, 1996). Furthermore, the first Japanese baseball player to formally join a professional MLB team was Murakami Masanori, who joined the roster of the San Francisco Giants in 1964. Disagreement between the Giants and the Nankai Hawks (his previous NPB team in Japan) over his contract led to the suspension of relationships between the MLB and NPB. Eventually it was agreed that he belonged to the San Francisco Giants, but the following season he returned to Japan. In 1967 a US–Japan baseball player concordat or 'Working Agreement' was reached, according to which players could not move to another team without the agreement of both parties.

4 The data source is from a press release by MLB on the opening day of the 2009 series, 4th April 2009 (http://mlb.mlb.com/news/press_releases/press_release.jsp?ymd=20090406&content_id=4139614&vkey=pr_mlb&fext=.jsp&c_id=mlb).

5 In 1998 a new agreement was reached between Japan and the United States (and South Korea in 2001) over the signing of baseball players. A posting system was introduced between the countries so that when a Japanese or Korean professional player wished to play in the United States, they could be posted to the 30 MLB teams with the highest blind bidding MLB team being able to negotiate a contract.

6 During the Japanese colonisation of Korea between 1910 and 1945, a sizeable Korean minority ethnic community was established in Japan. Whilst most of the 'Korean-Japanese' today are second, third or fourth generation residents for whom Japanese is their first language, they retain foreigner status, which requires them to take part in 'alien registration' procedures. In 2004 about 460,000 Koreans were so registered. Japanese professional baseball regulations however permit 'Korean-Japanese' students, who have studied for more than three years at a junior high, high or special school that is affiliated to the Japanese High School Baseball Federation, to be exempt from 'foreign player' status. Because most of the 'Korean-Japanese' professional baseball players have risen through the ranks in this way, they are registered with NPB the same as other ethnically Japanese players.

7 When a player is credited with runs being scored by other team members as a result of their own batting performance.

8 For an excellent historical background to baseball in East Asia that also notes the twin influence of the United States and Japan on the spread of the game see Reaves (2002).

4 From the Soviet Bloc to the European Community

Migrating professional footballers in and out of Hungary

Gyozo Molnar

Hungary has undergone fundamental social and political changes in the last 20 years. The country rid itself of Soviet communist oppression and moved from a one-party to a multi-party (political pluralism) system. This generated extensive transitions affecting all aspects of Hungarian society. Although after some initial turmoil the political system slowly began to consolidate, Hungary's economy did not develop with the desired velocity. Financial instability was present in all areas of the country in the 1990s (Meusburger, 2001) as the communist regime left Hungary with obsolete economic and social conditions. According to a survey carried out in 2000, 82 per cent of the respondents lived better during the old regime than in the new democracy (FRIDE, 2002). Gyula Horn, Prime Minister of Hungary between 1994 and 1998, expressed the difficulty of economic transition as follows:

> During the first year of transformations, 1.5 million Hungarians lost their jobs; we did not reach the production figures of 1989 until the year 2000; we had to wait until 2002 to regain the standard of living we had in 1989, even though it was not especially high.
>
> (2002, p. 16)

Hungarian sporting life and Hungary itself had to be recreated to survive post-communist conditions and to preserve long-established national traditions (Crampton, 2004). This constant struggle of residual and emerging socio-political practices and conditions created new and unpredicted social and footballing circumstances, football migrations *inter alia*, that, partially because of the lack of proactive behaviour on the part of Hungarian football clubs and the regional economic, political and social conditions, came as a surprise to most involved.

Many Hungarians, including leading politicians, were expecting Hungary's accession to the European Union (EU) to turn this snail-paced economic and social growth around and to provide a higher, core-like economic status. Although there have been improvements (see Index of Economic Freedom, 2009), the much-awaited EU enlargement, which happened on 1st May 2004 with Hungary along with seven other post-communist countries (A8) joining the European community, has not produced the anticipated economic boost. According to Eurostat (2009),

Hungary now belongs to the group of countries whose Gross Domestic Product per capita was between 30 and 50 per cent lower than the EU average in 2008. In other words, Hungary has not yet become one of the core economies and remains one of those countries that are on the (semi)periphery. Nevertheless, as a consequence of EU enlargement, Hungary and its citizens found themselves in the second phase of post-communist transition leading to new opportunities as well as uncertainties.

One of these opportunities was/is the free movement of labour force within the European community (see Edgar *et al.*, 2004) which was expected to influence Hungary's socio-economic life. With regard to migration, in general, and the migration of athletes (Molnar, 2006), in particular, it was anticipated that there might be a significant surge towards Western European countries in the form of economic migration (Wallace and Stola, 2001; Glenn, 2003), leading to the regional movement of target earners. This prediction is embedded in the idea of 'factor price equalisation', which means that goods, people and capital moving across national borders tend to equalise prices between countries (Stalker, 2000). That is, as Stalker explains, 'labour should travel from low-wage to high-wage economies and capital should move in the other direction' (2000, p. 11). Observations, in line with Stalker's idea of labour movement, have been made with regard to sports. For instance, Bale (2003) observed that sport clubs have undergone significant geographic readjustments that, in part, manifested in extending their radius of recruitment in the hope of finding 'cheap' talent, thereby exploiting the financial gap between the economic core and periphery. Maguire *et al.* (2002, p. 27) also noted that 'after the people's revolutions of 1989 and the subsequent "opening up" of Eastern Europe, Hungarians, Czechs, Slovakians and Romanians moved west'. Consequently, to predict that there would be newly emerging migration patterns, triggered by both financial and cultural gaps, from the East (periphery) to the West (core) (cf. Grečić, 1993), appeared to be logical given the border policies of the A8 (Accession 8) countries during the communist era.

The border policies of the Eastern Communist Bloc were isolationist, hence Hungary could become fully part of European migration processes only after the collapse of the communist regime. In fact, the migratory limitations of the communist regime fundamentally reshaped general migration patterns in Central and Eastern Europe, in general, and in Hungary, in particular (Dovenyi and Vukovich, 1994), and, thus, general and sport-related migrations drastically declined. 'When the communists took over at the end of the Second World War, emigration was generally prohibited on political and economic grounds' (Grečić, 1993, p. 139). Hence, the communist era, in terms of migrations, appeared virtually irrelevant in Hungary. Dovenyi and Vukovich (1994, p. 194) explain that:

> The Communist regime regarded the desire to live outside the country as a manifestation of anti-Communist views. On the other hand, those who were authorised to cross the border were not trusted to be willing to return; consequently individuals or families who were granted passports and exit visas

normally had to leave 'hostages' behind to ensure their return. Those who did manage to cross the border illegally, or who crossed legally but did not return, were tried as criminals, sentenced to prison terms . . . and their property confiscated.

Although it has been observed that border regulations became less restrictive during the 1980s (Öberg and Boubnova, 1993), the first wave of general immigrants arrived in Hungary between 1989 and 1991 (Dovenyi and Vukovich, 1994). As Grečić (1993, p. 139) puts it: 'population movement began in earnest on that day in May 1989 when the first Hungarian border guard cut away the first piece of the Iron Curtain'. Ever since, hundreds of thousands of people have been moving from Eastern and Central Europe to the West, in search of richer pastures in the global core economy. Thus, it can be argued that a new era and patterns of general and sport migrations occurred after 1989 and were induced primarily by cultural, economic and political changes and gaps of the 1980s (Wallace and Stola, 2001).

The tumult of transition did not cease with the ossification of democracy and market economy and a new wave of change due to Hungary's EU accession emerged. Glenn (2003) indicates that enlargement-related anxieties often feature worries about massive waves of immigrants coming from the newly joining countries of lesser economic status. However, post-enlargement reports suggest that 'fears of mass migration are unlikely to materialise' (Glenn, 2003, p. 222). Glenn (2003) notes that predicted vast migration waves with regard to Spain's and Portugal's joining of the European Union simply did not happen. Over five years after the A8 enlargement, it is now possible to look at some preliminary evidence and tendencies of the initial effects EU membership has had on migration patterns associated with the A8 countries.

Consequently, in this chapter, I discuss Hungary-related migrations in football, focusing on pre- and post-EU accession eras, and map the migration patterns of elite footballers in relation to Hungary, both as a donor and host country.[1] The aim is to explain these patterns considering fundamental networks and push and pull factors that exist between countries of the core and of the periphery in relation to intermingled economic, political, social and cultural factors. The observations presented here are based on a quantitative data set, covering 16 years of Hungary's post-communism and EU enlargement-related transitions. This data set represents the emigration of professional Hungarian footballers to the professional leagues of UEFA countries and the immigration of foreign footballers to the Hungarian professional football league.

Hungary-related football immigrations

During the post-communist/pre-EU era footballers migrated to Hungary from almost all the football confederations to play in the professional league and there were a few talent pipelines emerging, for example, between Hungary and Brazil and some of the countries of the African continent (see Molnar, 2006), but

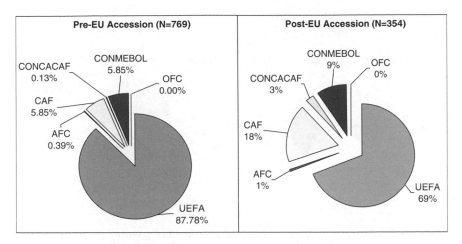

Figure 4.1 Percentage of foreign pro-footballers in Hungary from donor confederations

research also indicated that the most significant donor confederation was UEFA (Molnar, 2006). Statistically, over 87 per cent of migrant footballers playing in the professional league in the given years arrived from UEFA countries (see Figure 4.1). In fact, an average of 56 players representing various UEFA countries played in the Hungarian professional football league. The number of footballers from UEFA countries has been continuously increasing between 1991 and 2003 and by the 2002/2003 season the number of foreign footballers from UEFA increased to 72.

Although UEFA remained the most significant donor confederation after Hungary's EU accession, the number of players from the countries of this confederation was slightly reduced to an average of 61 players per year. On the other hand, the Confederation of African Football (CAF) has become a more considerable provider of migrant players (see Figure 4.1). This is due to the fact that Hungary has had various relationships with some of the countries of CAF. For example, Hungarian higher education has been attracting students from some of the CAF countries (e.g. Liberia and Nigeria) for years (Molnar, 2006). Also, the ever-increasing agent networks (see Poli, 2005a) would facilitate the cross-continental movement of footballers. Poli (2005a, p. 218) explains that there is a 'growing recruitment of players from less well-off continents, such [as] Africa or South America'. This 'recruitment' takes place via transnational socio-economic networks created by top- and middle-range football clubs (Poli, 2005a; see also Bale, 2003). Besides, Hungary's current political status and the free movement of labour within the European Union would make the country a desirable destination or transit state for footballers, and perhaps for other migrants too, who would want to make their way to other European countries and leagues, that is, wish to move from rags to riches.

Although UEFA has become somewhat less significant in providing footballers for the Hungarian professional league post 2004, there is still a distinctly high

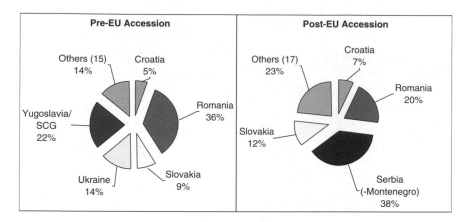

Figure 4.2 Percentage of foreign male pro-footballers in Hungary from UEFA countries

number of players from this confederation. This is due to geographic proximity, fewer cultural differences, analogous football development and well-functioning agent networks in Europe. Furthermore, the migration of footballers within Europe is not a novel phenomenon. It has been detected that football-related migrations (pioneers) existed prior to the First World War in Europe (see Fox, 2003). Thus, football migration routes have a much longer history in Europe than on any other continents. Since UEFA is still the most significant supplier of foreign footballers in the Hungarian professional football league, a deeper analysis is provided as to which countries of UEFA have sent the largest number of foreign players to Hungary.

Countries of UEFA

Previous research indicated that the main providers of footballers for the Hungarian professional league between 1991 and 2003 were Slovakia, Croatia, Romania, Ukraine and the Federal Republic of Yugoslavia[2] (Molnar, 2006). Most of these countries retained well-functioning migration pipelines with Hungary after 2004, except for Ukraine (see Figure 4.2). The fact that Ukraine ceased to be one of the relevant suppliers of footballers to the professional league is not surprising, and is probably due to the lapsing of agent networks between the countries, as the number of Ukrainian migrant players was gradually declining between 1991 and 2003 (Molnar, 2006). This decrease is indicated by the fact that the sum of players from Ukraine was 99 between 1991 and 2003 whereas in the EU accession era this number is only 3. Even though the examined transition periods are not equal in length, the change in migration pattern is significant and indicates the decline of the Hungary–Ukraine migratory pipeline.

The data also indicate that there has been a continuous and significant inflow of Slovakian, Romanian, Croatian and Serbian players to the Hungarian professional football league before and after Hungary's EU accession. The existence of these migratory pipelines can be explained by three main factors. First, there is an obvious geographic proximity that facilitates the migration of these footballers to Hungary. There is also an economic push factor driving footballers towards Hungary, which represents higher economic standards than Romania, Croatia and Serbia (see database of worldbank.org, which also indicates that in terms of Gross National Income Slovakia has overtaken Hungary, which has eradicated the previously existing economic push factor). Finally, these countries have mutual historical roots. Some of the current territories of these countries used to be a part of Hungary, but after the Trianon Peace Treaty (1920) they were detached, along with a large number of Hungarians living there. A large number of those Hungarians migrated back to the 'remains' of Hungary or fled to the United States, Canada or South America, after the World Wars. Nevertheless, not all ethnic Hungarians left these countries. A significant number of Hungarians still live along the border and have managed to maintain their Hungarianness.[3]

The case of Slovakia and some of the football migrants from this country could shed some further light on the existing migratory pipelines. Because of the long historical connections between Hungary and Slovakia, some Slovakian football migrants have Hungarian names, speak the Magyar language and sometimes perceive themselves to be Hungarians and the bearers of Hungarian culture in Slovakia. That is, Slovakians and Hungarians have been living together for centuries and have impacted upon the cultural development of each other. Hence, moving to Hungary for a Slovakian footballer, who belongs to the Hungarian minority, is usually not as demanding a task as it might be for a non-Central European. On the other hand, it must be noted that simply being a Slovak-Hungarian does not necessarily dissolve all the problems a football migrant may face while in Hungary. Slovakian footballers only have a higher potential to accommodate to a Hungarian way of life and can visit their country of origin more easily and more often than, for example, a non-Central European player. Although, it complicates the matter of assimilation and the making of generalisation further that some of the Slovakian players with Hungarian-sounding names do not speak the Magyar language at all, whereas some with Slovak-sounding names consider themselves part of the Hungarian community.[4] For instance, Szilárd Németh, a Middlesbrough player between 2001 and 2005, has a perfectly Hungarian-sounding name despite the fact that he is Slovakian, and without specific knowledge about his personal views, it is only speculative to make claims about his cultural belongingness and the experiences he would have as a migrant player in Hungary. Nevertheless, it seems that Slovakia possesses a certain constellation of features that facilitates the migration of professional footballers to Hungary, which are geographic proximity, a less-developed economy in the pre-EU era and similar economic conditions in the post-EU era, bridgeable cultural differences and a significant Hungarian minority.

Romania, Croatia and Serbia (-Montenegro) possess characteristics similar to Slovakia. Moreover, these countries have less-developed economies in comparison to Hungary both in the pre- and post-EU accession eras, leading to an economic push factor. For instance, the United Nations Economic Commission for Europe statistics demonstrate that, among these countries, Hungary has the highest purchasing power that reinforces the existence of an economic pull factor towards the country.[5] In addition, all of the three countries share borders with Hungary, underlining the importance of geographic proximity as a secondary facilitator of migration in general. Furthermore, all of these nation-states have a considerable Hungarian minority living within their territories. For instance, according to the statistics of the Hungarian Ministry of Foreign Affairs,[6] Romania had approximately 1.6 million in 1992; and Serbia (-Montenegro) had some 341,000 in 1991. The high number of Hungarians is inevitably an important factor in initiating and maintaining football migratory pipelines in a similar way to that which has already been described in the case of Slovakia.

In addition, the role of agent networks must be mentioned. Romania and Slovakia were member countries of the Eastern Bloc.[7] Beyond sharing an ideological belief system, the sovietisation of Central and Eastern European countries was designed to develop a comradely network among those countries. It can be argued that this network did not completely vanish with the collapse of the communist bloc and residual forms have helped to create a type of 'post-communist football camaraderie' amongst the above-mentioned countries through which footballers could be channelled to Hungary. The importance of networks, migratory meso-structures, is acknowledged in migration studies as people often rely on them for assistance for both moving and settling in the host country (see Tilly, 1990). For instance, Mike Hammond (1995, p. 525) observes that the excellent business connections of József Stadler, owner of Stadler FC, with Romania and other post-communist states 'have brought many players from these countries'.

Croatia and Serbia (-Montenegro), successor states of Yugoslavia, constitute a different scenario since Yugoslavia distanced itself from the Soviet Union and built its own way to socialism, under the strong political leadership of Josip Broz Tito. The country criticised both Eastern and Western blocs and, along with other countries, began the Non-Aligned Movement in 1961, which remained the official policy of the country until it dissolved. Nonetheless, there were extensive football connections between Hungary and Yugoslavia. Indeed, an interview with a Hungarian ex-football agent revealed some of these post-communist comradely networks between Croatia/Serbia (-Montenegro) and Hungary. According to the interviewee, these networks were created during communism, facilitated by geographic proximity and remained active after the collapse of the iron curtain (Molnar, 2005).

The significance of 'post-communist camaraderie networks' is reinforced by the fact that hardly any players moved to Hungary from Western Europe (see Molnar, 2006) as communist countries in general had underdeveloped diplomatic and business relations with the West. This situation began to change only after the collapse of the communist bloc and then was fundamentally transformed by Hungary's EU accession. Regardless of these geo-political transitions, Hungary's football status has not changed since the 1980s and Hungary's reputation, earned in the 1950s and 1960s, as a 'great football nation' has never been re-erected

(Molnar, 2007). In other words, the country is not part of the footballing (and economic) core and, hence, not a highly desired destination for talented athletes of both west and east. In fact, for migrant footballers, Hungary often represents a place of retirement where disposed players, branded 'second class' by Western football networks, come with already declining abilities (see Molnar, 2005). It can be observed that, both in the pre- and post-EU accession periods, Hungary heavily relied on 'post-communist camaraderie networks', which were revitalised in the 1990s and remained functional and relevant in terms of supplying the Hungarian pro-league with (mostly second class) migrant players even after Hungary's EU accession.

It is not only the low quality of Hungarian football but also the country's economic circumstances that contribute to preventing foreign athletes' migration from countries of the core economy. There were approximately 30 players (3 per cent of migrant footballers) from Western core countries in the Hungarian pro-league between 1991 and 2008. The low number of foreign players from core economies can be explained through an international division of labour, a bipolar system that is structured around central versus peripheral economies (Wallerstein, 1974). Accordingly, labour is divided among functionally defined and geographically distinct parts arranged in an economic hierarchy, thereby differentiating core and peripheral countries. It is essentially a structuralist approach to the international division of labour (Harvey and Saint-Germain, 2001) which indicates that the core or First World countries have kept the periphery in an economically (and, perhaps, politically) dependent position. This, in effect, means that lesser developed countries are in a disadvantaged situation because the surplus and talent they produce is siphoned off by core or, occasionally, semi-peripheral countries (see Klein, 1991b). Consequently, migratory pipelines from countries of peripheral economic status to Hungary, which assumes semi-peripheral economic standing, can be clearly identified (see Molnar, 2006). On the other hand, it can also be observed that football-related migrations from core countries to Hungary are virtually non-existent. However, this approach, embedded in Marxist political economy and world-system theory (Castles and Miller, 2003), has its limitation as migrants are viewed as passive reactors manipulated by and reacting to the global economy (Brettell, 2000). Although in the case of migrant Hungarian footballers there is a relatively high degree of passivity when selecting host countries (see Molnar and Maguire, 2008), other factors influencing migration patterns and potential must also be considered such as agent networks, culture and geographic proximity. These factors, creating a migratory blend of motivational and demotivational forces (Molnar and Maguire, 2008), have affected not only immigration patterns but also the movements of Hungarian players in the countries of UEFA, which will be discussed later.

Emigration of Hungarian pro-footballers

This section will illustrate general migration patterns of Hungarian professional male footballers within the region of UEFA, the core football confederation

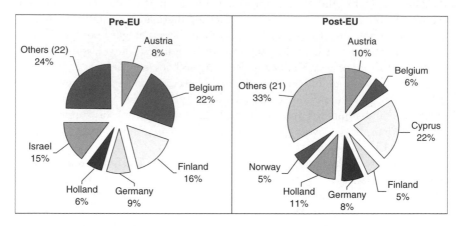

Figure 4.3 The most significant UEFA host countries for Hungarian football migrants

(Sugden and Tomlinson, 2000). As has already been observed by Maguire and Pearton (2000c), UEFA attracts the most players from other confederations and also has the most movement within the confederation itself. By virtue of this, it can be argued that UEFA players in general, and Hungarian players in particular, tend to stay within their confederation as that is the most economically powerful and the professionally most challenging one. It may also be perceived by players of other confederations as the 'finishing school of football'.[8] The importance of this confederation in the migration of Hungarian footballers was always visible, but it has grown since 2004. This expansion is indicated by the fact that the average number of Hungarian players in UEFA leagues was 36 in the pre-EU era and increased to 54 in the post-EU accession era. The following will shed some light on emerging and existing migration patterns with regard to Hungary as a donor country.

Host countries of UEFA

The data clearly indicate that the major host countries were Western European countries both in the pre- and post-EU eras. These countries included and include Finland, Belgium, Holland, Austria, Germany and Norway (see Figure 4.3). These countries possess a constellation of pull factors that make them attractive to Hungarian and, perhaps, to other Central European athletes.

Networks of Hungarian football emigrants

Hungarian footballers tend to move towards economically more advanced nation-states, that is, Western Europe (see Figure 4.3), because those countries possess certain general features – successful and stable economies, well-implemented employment rights and higher levels of football – that attract them. Thus, the

importance of economics as part of migratory movements of Hungarian footballers must be considered, along with other potential pull factors.

Most of the Western European countries can simply seem attractive as they
represent a higher quality of football and have more prestigious and challenging
leagues (Maguire *et al.*, 2002). For instance, the German Bundes Liga is one of the
richest leagues in Europe, making it an attractive destination. Moreover, the financial benefits of playing in Western European countries are undeniable. First, footballers have higher financial security in Western European countries that was not
always the case in Hungary during the post-communist period (see Meusburger,
2001). For instance, in the 1991/1992 season, Siófok, one of the first division football clubs at that time, experienced a total financial collapse as its sponsor, a
German businessman, Andre Ritter, withdrew his funds (see Hammond, 1992).
Players' wages were delayed and some players even had to be sold as a consequence of this financial hardship. Moreover, in the 1998/1999 season, as
Hammond (1999, p. 509) observes, 'virtually all the clubs were operating in debt,
and many players had to make do with reduced salaries or, in some cases, no
money at all'. Regardless of Hungary's EU accession, Hungary's general economy
is still struggling and there remains a significant economic gap between Central
and Western European countries. Economic insecurities have had a fundamental
destabilising effect on all aspects of social life, including sports. These insecurities
can be a central push factor for migrants and, in this particular case, are partially
responsible for the movement of Hungarian footballers towards Western core
economies. The existence and significance of this financial gap support the migratory aspect of World-system theory, which explains that within the world economy
'there is a division of labour and hence significant internal exchange of basic or
essential goods as well as flows of capital and labour' (Wallerstein, 2004, p. 23). As
part of the World-system-generated labour flow, Hungarian footballers move predominantly to countries of higher economic status and, thus, financial security.

It is then evident that football players earn significantly more in Western
European countries than in Hungary. In expressing the differences in earning
potentials, Bocsák and Imre (2003) publicised the wages of some of the top
Hungarian footballers. According to their figures, Hungarian footballers working
in Western European leagues have the potential to earn at least seven times more
than domestic Hungarian footballers, supposedly of the same skills. To put it differently, Hungarian footballers playing abroad can earn an average of HUF 250
million (£674,000) per annum in Western European football leagues, whereas
Hungarian footballers in Hungary have an average earning potential of HUF 34
million (£91,600). Hence, it is not an exaggeration to say that the difference
between earning potential in Hungary and abroad is significant, and can be perceived as a strong pull factor.

Although Western Europe is a desired destination for Hungarian footballers, not
all the countries of this region have significant migratory pipelines with Hungary.
Figure 4.3 illustrates that the most significant host countries of this region are
Austria, Germany, Finland, Belgium, Holland, Finland and Norway (post-EU).[9]
The relatively high number of Hungarian footballers in these countries can be

mostly attributed to the role of agent and sport personnel networks on which some light will be cast later.

The Austria–Hungary pipeline is partially the result of geographic proximity and, on the other hand, of well-developed football connections between these countries (cf. Duke, 1994). In fact, Austria represents a unique case as it borders Hungary, which helps facilitate the migration of Hungarian footballers. Regardless of geographic proximity, Austria's first division football teams receive less Hungarian footballers than one would expect. However, it must be mentioned that Austrian football leagues per se host many more footballers from Hungary than shown in Figure 4.3, but those players sign for the lower divisions and thus are excluded from the sample. Other research has shed light on this migratory movement from Hungary to Austria which is mostly based on geographic proximity and economic differentials (see Duke, 1994). For example, during the early 1990s it was a common practice for first division Hungarian footballers to sign for lower division Austrian teams (often called 'weekend contracts') where they could earn significantly more. Therefore, similar to Hungarians of other professions, footballers worked in Austria and lived in Hungary. As a result, they earned more than an average Hungarian footballer did but had similar expenses as they remained resident in Hungary (see Duke, 1994). It is safe to say that after 2004, with the opening of European borders, this practice emerging in the 1990s could spread even more without border and work permit restrictions and, thus, could help reinforce this migratory trend. The Austria–Hungary pipeline is also perpetuated by football networks, the building blocks of which are often difficult to trace but have existed both in the pre- and post-EU eras (see Molnar, 2006).

The Germany–Hungary pipeline has also been shaped by migratory networks. Some of these are based on German investment in Hungarian football clubs. Hammond (1992) pointed out that, in the 1991/1992 season, Siófok was sponsored (if not owned) by Andre Ritter, a German businessman. Furthermore, one of the sponsors of Békéscsaba has been *uhlsport*, which is a German company that provides a range of football equipment. Ferencváros has been supported by *T-Mobile*, a German mobile phone company, and Zalaegerszeg has been sponsored by *E.ON*, a German electricity supplier.[10] It would be an overstatement to say that these business connections are solely responsible for the Germany–Hungary football pipeline, but they are obviously part of it.

The presence of Hungarian football agents in Germany can be traced back to around the 1970s. They were (and are) involved in many European football transfers. For example, in his autobiography, Tony Woodcock acknowledges an agent network that organised his transfer to Cologne, the head of which was a Hungarian, Gyula Pásztor, who had also facilitated Kevin Keegan's move to Hamburg SV (Woodcock and Ball, 1985). The contract of Hungarian footballer Zoltán Varga with Hertha BSC was also facilitated by a Hungarian agent named Miklós Berger in 1968 (Bartus, 2000). Varga used to play for Hertha BSC, Olympique Marseille, Ajax and FC Aberdeen and lived in Germany when he was offered an opportunity to coach Ferencváros in the 1996/1997 season (Hammond, 1997). He certainly had the opportunity to develop football connections throughout Europe and become part of football migratory meso-structures.[11] Hence, it can be suggested that Hungarians were involved, mostly as agents, in the European migratory movements of footballers as early as the 1970s. These networks, that probably continued to exist in the 1980s, were reinstated in Hungary after the collapse of the communist regime and are responsible for the transfer of Hungarian players not only to Germany but also to other Western European countries (see Molnar, 2006).

The Finland–Hungary, Belgium–Hungary and Norway–Hungary channels are mostly built on football connections similar to the ones described earlier. For example, Kispest-Honvéd had a Belgian owner, Louise De Vries, in the 1992/1993 and 1993/1994 seasons who hired a Finnish coach, Martti Kuuslea, to strengthen the team in the 1992/1993 season (see Hammond, 1993). Besides, Belgium is often perceived as the depot for migrant footballers (Poli, 2005a). Interviews with migrant Hungarian footballers (Molnar, 2005) reinforced this argument in stating that Belgium is a major reservoir of migrant footballers for Europe, which, in turn, explains the existence of the Hungary–Belgium pipeline.

On the basis of the earlier developments, the relatively high number of Hungarian players in Western European countries can be attributed to well-developed football migratory networks that are usually created and perpetuated by migrant or ex-migrant football personnel. The importance of network-mediated migration (Wilson, 1994 cited in Brettell, 2000) is of relevance here as football migrants are recruited and channelled by agent networks. Migratory networks are facilitative, making the migration experience safer and, hence, have the potential to cushion the encounter with the new and unknown. However, in the case of athletes, agents not only make the actual migration safer (cf. Poli, 2005a), but negotiate with clubs on behalf of the players. In other words, 'certain individuals, groups or institutions [meso-structures] may take on the role of mediating between migrants [micro-structures] and political or economic institutes [macro-structures]' (Castles and Miller, 2003, p. 28). Individuals built into migratory meso-structures can be both helpers and exploiters of people embarking on foreign sojourns. Agents may exploit players' lack of social and cultural capital (see Poli, 2005a) and may be reducing the number of theoretically available destination countries (see Molnar and Maguire, 2008). However, regardless of how meso-structures treat migrants, the complexity of migration and of formulation of migratory pipelines cannot be fully understood without considering all levels (micro, meso and macro) of migration and the constant, ever-changing interplay between them. As Castles and Miller suggest: 'Macro-, meso- and micro-structures are intertwined in the migratory process, and there are no clear dividing lines between them. No single cause is ever sufficient to explain why people decided to leave their country and settle in another' (2003, p. 28). In search of multi-causality and providing coherent interpretations of migrations and migrants' experiences, Brettell and Hollifield (2000) suggest 'talking across disciplines' and eradicating disciplinary silos to study this extraordinarily complex phenomenon. In line with this proposal, both world-system and push and pull factor theories have been employed in this chapter to interpret the migration patterns of Hungarian footballers between 1991 and 2008.

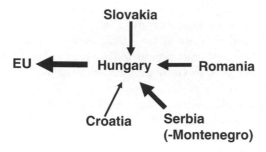

Figure 4.4 Major migration patterns of pro-male footballers in and out of Hungary between 2004 and 2008

Summary

In terms of football migrations, Hungary is both a host and a donor country with positive net migration of professional male footballers. Most of the foreign footballers tend to arrive from UEFA countries whereas other football confederations do not supply Hungary with significant numbers of professional football players. However, CAF may become a more relevant provider in the future due to continuously growing agent networks (see Poli, 2005a). UEFA is the core donor confederation because of geographic proximity, less cultural difference, analogous football developments and pre-existing migration routes in Europe. Within UEFA, four chief donor countries have been identified in the pre-EU era: Slovakia, Ukraine, Romania and Serbia (-Montenegro). Except for Ukraine, all the other countries have remained significant providers of foreign players for the Hungarian professional football league. In the post-EU accession period, Croatia emerged as a significant new donor country, replacing Ukraine and indicating changing political and economic conditions and agent networks affecting migratory pipelines. Figure 4.4 illustrates migration patterns that remained and emerged after 2004.

The migration of Hungarian professional male footballers tends to involve the countries of Western Europe. This does not represent a new trend as it was the dominant direction before Hungary's EU accession. These countries form part of the global core economy and have the same pull factors as they did before 2004 such as higher levels of football and economic standards. Some minor changes in migration patterns can, however, be detected. For instance, the number of EU countries hosting Hungarian players has increased and a few new host countries appeared. There are some Hungarian footballers in the English and Scottish leagues, which was unprecedented prior to Hungary's EU accession. Although there are signs of Hungarian footballers playing in a number of countries in Western Europe, they do not represent a considerable labour force as Hungarian footballers are not a sought-after commodity (Molnar, 2005, 2006; Molnar and Maguire, 2008). Molnar and Maguire (2008) observed that Hungarian footballers are often at the mercy of agent networks and have limited control over selecting their destination countries. Therefore, the presence and distribution of Hungarian footballers in Western Europe are both the result of migratory meso-structures and, to a lesser extent, of the chiefly economic pull factors of those countries. Besides, Hungarian players seem to have a relatively low-migration potential as they usually struggle with the cultural and professional challenges they face in the host environment (see Molnar, 2010). Consequently, they, with a few exceptions, tend to stay abroad for a few years with the ultimate desire of returning to their home country (Molnar and Maguire, 2008).

By virtue of the above, when interpreting the migrations of people in general and professional Hungarian footballers in particular, the demand for foreign imports, the role of agent networks and individual migration incentives have to be taken into consideration in conjunction with both local and global/regional migration conditions. These components shape and perpetuate the migration patterns, which create a dense and complex ever-changing lattice-work. The chief reasons why migrants are often tightly bound to these networks seem to be connected to the fact that Hungarian football and footballers do not represent an outstanding quality on the international domain, that is, they are rarely in the public 'football' eye, and they do not represent a globally acknowledged 'trade mark' (Molnar and Maguire, 2008). This lack of interest in employing Hungarian footballers in the professional leagues of UEFA countries has had a considerable effect on the migration-related opportunities and destinations for Hungarian footballers. Therefore, the expected surge of Hungarian footballers in Western leagues has not (yet) manifested.

Notes

1 To indicate the massive increase in football migration in general, the BBC Sport website observes that, in the 1989–90 season, leading clubs like Arsenal and Manchester United featured one or two regular first-team players from outside the United Kingdom. Now, Premier League teams have, on average, 13 foreign-born stars within their clubs (see http://news.bbc.co.uk/sport1/hi/football/eng_prem/8182090.stm).

2 The Federal Republic of Yugoslavia (FRY) existed between 1992 and 2003. In 2003, the FRY was reconstituted as the State Union of Serbia and Montenegro, which broke up in 2006 due to a referendum on full independence in Montenegro. Consequently, on 5th June 2006 the independent Republic of Serbia was declared. After the split, it became obvious that migrant footballers to Hungary predominantly arrived from Serbia.

3 According to the Hungarian Ministry of Foreign Affairs, the number of Hungarians living in Slovakia was 521,000 in 2001 (see www.kulugyminiszterium.hu).

4 For an illustration of the complexity of the dynamics between Hungary and Hungarian minorities see Jon Fox (2003).

5 UNECE. *Economic Survey of Europe 2004 No. 1* [website]. Economic Analysis Division, 10/06/2004 [cited 04/07/2004]. Available from www.unece.org.

6 Data were retrieved from www.kulugyminiszterium.hu.

7 Slovakia was a part of Czechoslovakia and Ukraine was annexed by the USSR.

8 Maguire and Stead (1996) made a similar observation concerning the global significance of English cricket.
9 In this chapter I exclusively focus on Western European host countries as other UEFA countries generally do not attract a large number of Hungarian footballers. There are only two exceptions to this observation. In the pre-EU era, Israel was a significant host country but the Hungary–Israel migratory pipeline ceased to exist in 2000 due to Israel's changing domestic political situation (Molnar, 2006). The other non-Western European country attracting Hungarian players is Cyprus. It has been argued that Hungarian footballers tend to move to Cyprus for financial benefits and for lower professional demands. Moreover, they may be a desirable commodity there as they can strengthen the quality of the national leagues, which they often fail to achieve in some of the Western European leagues (see Molnar, 2006).
10 Siófok, Békéscsaba, Ferencváros and Zalaegerszeg are professional football clubs.
11 For a detailed description of migratory meso-structures, see Tilly's (1990) 'Transplanted networks'.

Part II

Bridgeheads in migration and sport

5 Preliminary observations on globalisation and the migration of sport labour

Joseph Maguire

Initially, several dimensions of sports labour migration and a range of sports in different societies and across continents will be considered. In this way, in preliminary form, the nature and extent of the global and local processes at work will be identified. In doing so, several key issues connected with sport migration will be outlined. This discussion precedes the main substantive section which focuses on one specific case study: the role of, and the resistance to, American sports labour migrants in the commodification of English basketball during the 1980s and early 1990s. The paper concludes by drawing together some of the strands of sports migration and the global development of sport.[1]

Whereas artists, musicians, poets and scholars have long moved around European royal courts, salons and universities today, the migration of sports talent as athletic labour is a pronounced feature of Europe; and indeed, a global cultural interchange. This labour process is interwoven with the commodification of sports within the capitalist world economy. It is not usual for sports devotees to think of these sportspeople as workers. They are, however, not unlike other sectors of the workforce who, for various reasons, have to ply their trade in various national, continental or trans-continental locations. Again, not only unlike their counterparts in other occupations, elite athletes as a group experience varying degrees of exploitation and dislocation, but also enjoy some personal gains. Whatever advantages there are, they appear to flow along gender lines. For the global migration of sports labour predominantly, though not exclusively, involves men. Their ability to move over time and across space is based on a patriarchal structure that ensures that it is usually women who perform the domestic labour, whether in the company of their travelling partners or waiting 'at home'.

Such sports labour migration occurs within nation-states, between nation-states located within the same continent and between nation-states located within different continents. Specific examples can be used to capture the complexity of this global movement of sports labour. A socially and geographically mobile workforce is a feature of most modern industrial societies. The movement of athletes from their hometown to their place of initial recruitment to elite or professional sports clubs is part of this process. There are discernible patterns to the recruitment and subsequent retention of people in sports such as American football, baseball, basketball, ice hockey, track and field and soccer (Bale, 1991).

Focusing on 'British' sport reveals several quite specific and more general features of sports labour migration. That is, although Britain, or more properly, the United Kingdom of Great Britain and Northern Ireland, is composed of England, Scotland, Wales and Northern Ireland, these 'nations' have, for example, soccer leagues that contain varying levels of 'indigenous' labour and labour from other 'nations' within the United Kingdom. Movement of Welsh rugby union players to English rugby league also occurs. It was also possible, at least until recently, to point to the former Soviet Union and now former Yugoslavia as countries where similar processes were at work. That is, sports performers from different republics, such as the Ukraine, Georgia, Croatia and Bosnia, moved within these former nation-states, to ply their athletic labour for sports teams such as Moscow Dynamo and Red Star Belgrade.

Sports labour migration also occurs between countries located within the same continent. If one considers the 'states' within the United States, inter-state migration of sports talent is extremely widespread and is not without controversy (Bale and Maguire, 1994). Also witness the involvement of citizens of the United States in Canadian baseball teams and athletes from the Dominican Republic in 'American' baseball teams. In Europe this sports labour migration takes place in several sports including, among others, soccer, ice hockey, rugby and basketball. This process is arguably most pronounced in soccer where professional players regularly criss-cross the continent of Europe. In this case, elite soccer talent is purchased above all by the national leagues of Italy and Spain. This labour stems from 'donor' countries spread across Europe, including Germany, the Netherlands, the United Kingdom, the Commonwealth of Independent States and the Balkan and Scandinavian countries. However, Italy and Spain are not the only 'host' countries in this regard.

Soccer labour flows across the continent with the more economically powerful leagues in these two countries attracting a standard of player commensurate to their ability to pay transfer fees and the salaries of the players concerned. Even in countries where the outflow of talent is most evident, for example the Scandinavian countries, players from abroad and less talented players from home are recruited. The opening up of Eastern Europe, with Hungarian, Czechoslovakian and Romanian players to the fore, will further complicate this movement of athletic labour, a process that will largely involve the outflow of talent from Eastern Europe in the first instance. This trend was a precursor of a broader pattern of migration from Eastern and Central Europe to Western Europe. For example, over 50 top Romanian rugby union players were playing in France in the early 1990s.

A similar trend was also evident on a trans-continental level. Movement of sports labour occurs between North America and Europe in sports such as basketball, American football and ice hockey. More than 400 Americans played in Europe's professional men's basketball leagues in the early 1990s, with the higher calibre players 'residing' in Italy and Spain. Issues of ancestral links to specific countries and the imposition of quotas on 'foreign' players by particular national sports organisations further complicated the situation. That is, some American citizens claimed dual nationality and resided in and, in specific instances, played for the European country from which his or her ancestors came. Anglo-Canadians and French-Canadians displayed their ice hockey skills in Britain, Germany, France and Switzerland. At the World Ice Hockey Championship held in Italy in April 1994, apart from the Canadians appearing for their national team, more than 50 were playing for other teams as dual nationals (*The Guardian*, 30th April 1994, p. 17). There was also a flow of sports labour in the opposite direction. North American ice hockey clubs recruited Scandinavian players. American universities actively recruited European men and women in sports such as track and field, soccer, rugby, basketball and swimming (Bale, 1991). This trend was also the subject of critical debate within the United States with a quota of non-US athletes being proposed (*USA Today*, 2nd January 1992). In the early 1990s a campaign was launched to keep baseball American and 'say no to foreign owners' (*Sports Illustrated*, March 1992).

The movement of sports labour on a trans-continental level also occurs between Europe and Africa. Africans are prominent in the English, French, Belgian, Portuguese and Dutch soccer leagues (Maguire, 1991b). Issues of first and second generation migration patterns emerge. Sport can provide a means of integration into the host society, exemplified by the continuous stream of foreign footballers into France. As Pooley (1981) discovered, however, sport does not necessarily aid in the cultural assimilation of ethnic groups. Rather, in specific instances sport can serve as a symbol of identification with the cultural heritage of the group to which the individual belongs.

The migration of labour in general and of sports labour in particular on a trans-continental level is also evident in the involvement of first and second generation Afro-Caribbeans in English soccer (Maguire, 1988, 1991b). That is, with regard to English and mainland European soccer, several players were the sons of migrants who had settled in the country that was formerly their colonial overlord. African track and field talent was also part of the American university scholarship programme. Australian, Afro-Caribbean, South Asian and South African players figured prominently in English cricket, and had done so for many decades.

Sports labour tends to be 'hired' by a specific club or organisation and individuals reside in the host country for a limited period. However, this is not always the case. Some athletes stay on and make the host country their 'home'. This occurs either through marriage to a citizen of that country or by having stayed attached to a specific country for a sufficient length of time to qualify for nationality status. Take, for example, Chen Xinhua, a former citizen of the People's Republic of China, who played for Britain at table tennis in the early 1990s. Also consider Sydney Maree, a South African runner, who became a naturalised American citizen to run in international competitions. Sometimes, such as in European basketball, individuals begin to play for the country in which they have become resident and for whom they subsequently claim 'nationality'.

In certain sports, such as cricket and rugby league, migration has a seasonal pattern. The northern and southern hemispheres offer in specific sports such as cricket what amounts, in effect, to two seasons of continuous play. Other sports migrants experience a transitory form of migration. Take, for example, the experience of European, American and African athletes on the European track and field Grand Prix circuit or European and American skiers on the World Cup Alpine skiing circuit. Other examples include cycling and motor racing ranging from Formula One to motor cycling. Sometimes, seasonal and transitory migration patterns interweave. Here we can recognise the global travels of golf and tennis players. Golf and tennis players are arguably the nomads of the sports labour migration pattern with a seemingly constantly shifting workplace and place of residence. Though both men and women have their global circuits, the enabling and constraining features of this experience may be markedly different.

Four main issues can be identified that should arguably form the core of a research agenda in this area. First, questions of labour rights arise. The rights enjoyed by sport migrants, and indeed indigenous sports workers, vary considerably between sports and across continents, and may also have changed considerably over time. The employment rights achieved by players in team sports such as European soccer are minimal compared to the freedoms gained by sportspeople in individual sports, particularly in tennis and golf. Boris Becker, Steffi Graf, Nick Faldo and Lotta Neumann all enjoy greater control over the production and exploitation of their sports talent than do soccer players of comparable ability such as Marco Van Basten or Paul Gascoigne. Not all participants in individual sports enjoy the advantages of tennis players or golfers, of course. Track and field athletes initially pressed the International Amateur Athletic Federation (IAAF) to pay prize money at the 1993 World Championships. In response to the athletes' threat to boycott the championships, the then IAAF President, Primo Nebiolo, threatened to withdraw recognition of boycotters, thus preventing them from competing at the Atlanta Olympic Games.

Within team sports, employment rights also vary across sports played in different continents. Although North American athletes in sports such as American/Canadian football, ice hockey, basketball and baseball have unionised, conducted negotiations with owners based on collective bargaining and have taken strike action, they have not been that successful in gaining greater employment rights (Beamish, 1982, 1988). The draft, in which college athletes are assigned to specific teams, still operates in North American sport. In comparison, the free movement of labour is now part of European Union law. Individuals are technically free to ply their athletic labour where they wish within the European Union (EU). Employment protection legislation also applies to migrant labour. Despite the existing and proposed social protocols, the European soccer transfer system was described by Euro MPs as a 'slave' system. Its legality was challenged in the Belgian courts in an action brought by Jean-Marc Bosman against the European Football Association (UEFA). It was subsequently successful and significant change in both European football and sport more generally flowed from this judgement.

Indeed, the very rights which Bosman sought enforcement for are still not applicable to all players. Individuals from countries outside the EU were and some are still subject to visa regulations. Sport migrants have to prove international status in their respective sports. Further, as with migrants more generally, exploitative labour practices also take place. No detailed substantive research on the experience of migrants from less developed countries, for example African and East European soccer players, existed at the time of the original study though (see the work of Darby in this collection and in his earlier work). Questions regarding whether they receive wages comparable with their EU counterparts would need to form part of any enquiry. Sport labour migration is not, then, a uniform experience. It has its own highly differentiated political economy.

This movement of athletic talent involves, in specific instances, the deskilling of donor countries and this issue should arguably form part of a second broad area of enquiry. Latin and Central American countries, for example, regularly experience the loss of baseball stars and soccer players to the United States and Europe. Here, less developed countries have invested in the production of athletic talent. Once this talent reaches maturity, more economically developed leagues, such as Major League Baseball, cream off the best available talent (Klein, 1991a). Not only is the native audience denied direct access to the talent nurtured and developed in their country, but, in some cases, such as with African national soccer teams, sports lose some of their quality players when the demands of European clubs clash with international matches. The central issues here are of under-development and of dependent development.

Questions regarding the impact of sport labour migration on the 'host' culture could form part of a third research area. The social–psychological problems of adjustment and dislocation need consideration. King's (1990) work on design professionals in areas such as architecture and advertising highlights how this new band of specialists work outside the traditional professional and organisational cultures of the nation-state; they also experience the problems of inter-cultural communication. Further, the constant moving back and forth between different cultures requires that such groups develop new types of flexible personal controls, dispositions and means of orientation. In developing this new type of habitus, such people do not infrequently work in and inhabit a specific type of urban space, the redeveloped inner city areas.

Problems of inter-cultural communication also arise for sport migrants. Witness the 'babel-like' quality of global sports festivals or tournaments. For sport migrants such a social milieu involves a multi-layered form of inter-cultural communication centring on interaction with fellow players, coaches, officials, crowd and media personnel. In the world of European soccer, Swedes, Norwegians, Dutchmen and Germans appear adept at deploying flexible personal controls and often communicate with ease in several different languages. While some migrants may find the move from one culture to another relatively free of culture shock, this may not always be the case. The burn-out of young women tennis players may, in part, be connected to the processes under discussion. Further, the movement of Eastern European ice hockey and basketball players to North America may also bring problems of adjustment to free market economic processes. Some elite sport migrants, in a manner not dissimilar to design professionals and lawyers, also work in and inhabit a specific type of urban space. Think of the redeveloped city areas now occupied by sport-work places such as the Skydome in Toronto, the Globe in Stockholm and the Palais Omnisports in Paris. As yet, we have (and some 15 years later, still do not have) little systematic, research-based knowledge about this experience.

This labour migration also engendered hostility in some host countries. Sport labour unions, such as those in European soccer, have sought to protect indigenous workers by arguing for quotas and qualification thresholds to be applied to potential migrants. During 1993, the English Professional Footballers Association (PFA) called for tighter controls and checks on the playing credentials of foreign players (*The Mail on Sunday*, 14th January 1993, p. 95). An attempt by FIFA, the world governing body of soccer, to remove restrictions on foreign players in European leagues was met with the threat of a Europe-wide strike by professional players (*The Guardian*, 25th November 1992, p. 16). Following a meeting held in February 1993 between the PFA, the football authorities and the Department of Employment, tighter restrictions were imposed on non-EU foreign players – however, since then the growth in foreign migrants has increased significantly (*The Guardian*, 27th February 1993, p. 16). This resistance was matched by those concerned with the development of national teams.

The presence of overseas players was viewed as denying indigenous players access to teams and thus leading to personal and national under-development. Cesare Maldini, the Italian under-21 national coach, highlighted this issue in the early 1990s when he noted that, at youth level, 'our football is getting worse. We don't have the players any more. The increasing number of foreigners in our game means the opportunities for the youngsters are vanishing' (*Daily Mail*, 1st March 1993, p. 47). In contrast to these sentiments, major European soccer club owners seek to strengthen their position at every opportunity. The ascendancy of AC Milan in this period exemplified this process. Its owner, Silvio Berlusconi, argued for no restrictions on sport migration. As part of this process Berlusconi concluded that 'the concept of the national team will, gradually, become less and less important. It is the clubs with which the fans associate' (*World Soccer*, April 1992, p. 10). Given this approach the fortunes of the national team becomes secondary. Corporate success is what counts: over the past decade the competing interests of clubs and country have become more evident.

Reference to the impact on the success of national teams relates to the fourth area that could form part of a research agenda examining sport labour migration and globalisation. Questions of attachment to place, notions of self-identity and allegiance to a specific country are significant in this connection. Reference to the de-monopolisation of economic structures in the world economy shows that such processes led to the concomitant deregulation and globalisation of markets, trade and labour. The globalisation of capital has also entailed the globalisation of the market in services for finance, commerce and industry (Dezalay, 1990). Crucially, this led to a new category of professionals. These professionals included international lawyers, corporate tax accountants, financial advisers and management consultants. This group emerged as transnational corporations charted and formalised the newly globalised economic arena. While the experience of these professionals was not the same as for all sport migrants, in certain respects some elite sport labour migrants did appear to embody the characteristics of this new breed of entrepreneurs.

For Dezalay, deregulation and the globalisation of the market for legal and financial services have led to an emphasis in the professional craft of those involved that centres on technical competence, aggressive tactics and a merito-cratic ethos. Gone are the quasi-aristocratic 'fair play' values of an older genera-tion of lawyers and advisers. These new professionals present themselves as sweeping away archaic practices, replacing them with modern and highly rational decision-making. The prototype of this new regime is the corporate law firm of the United States. A re-modelling of legal culture has occurred and can be said to involve a process of Americanisation.

Though there is no systematic research available on the details of these issues as far as sport is concerned, from the evidence so far to hand some tentative parallels can be highlighted. The introduction of competition and market imperatives similar to those in the world of law has also been a more pronounced feature of the sports world during the late 1980s and early 1990s. The quasi-aristocratic notions of the legal profession and the amateur ideology of elite sports administrators were superseded by the need to compete in the market-place. The globalisation of the market for sports services parallels the globalisa-tion of the market for legal services. A new generation of agents and organisations, such as Mark McCormack and his International Marketing Group, and media–sport production executives have created sport spectacles by employing elite sport migrants to perform exhibition bouts or contests – the equivalent of Dezalay's 'hired guns' in North American law firms. As with the globalisation of legal services, so too, regarding sport, elements of an Americanisation process are evident. The pervasiveness of this American practice in sports such as American football, basketball and baseball has forced a range of sports to align themselves to this model if they wish to survive in the global media marketplace (Maguire, 1990).

The new generation of sport migrants such as tennis star Ivan Lendl, the Romanian middle distance runner Doina Melinte or the Americans plying their trade in the World League of American Football appeared to have little sense of attachment to a specific space or community. Observe the phenomenon in the 1980s and 1990s of South Africans such as Zola Budd and Alan Lamb represent-ing Great Britain in athletics and England in cricket, respectively. Highly rational and technical criteria determine their status and market value. Just as the new generation of lawyers stress technical competence, aggressive tactics and a meri-tocratic ethos, sport migrants embrace the ethos of hard work, differential rewards and a win at all costs approach. Aggressive and violent tactics character-ise the occupational subculture of some elite sport migrants, in ice hockey for example (Smith, 1983). Lawyers who adopt such practices are said to be 'perfect auxiliaries to the new breed of corporate raiders' (Dezalay, 1990). The 'rebel' cricket and rugby union tours to South Africa highlight how sport migrants can likewise act as mercenaries for big business. Sometimes, the link between corpo-rate raiders and sport migrants is only too clear. Take, for example, the World

Series Cricket organised by Kerry Packer or the activities of Alan Bond with the America's Cup sailing competition.

The fact that Canadian ice hockey players represent Britain is not an isolated example. As the case of English basketball reveals, American players have represented Great Britain and a range of other European countries in Olympic qualifying tournaments. While not underestimating the pull of national traditions, they are not necessarily always as fixed as they sometimes appear (Hall, 1992). Questions of national and cultural identity also relate to the process of globalisation. It is, therefore, appropriate to outline how sports migration in particular, and sports development in general, fit in as parts of this broader process.

English basketball, American sport labour migrants and globalisation

The English Amateur Basketball Association was formed in 1936 and, up to the late 1960s, the game remained amateur, tied to voluntary organisations and university teams, and was supported by only a small band of devotees. Mostly, it was played, controlled and administered by the same group of British nationals. Created in 1971, the National Basketball League (NBL) was composed of six teams. Though teams were mostly unsponsored, and 'amateur' in outlook, on occasions officials would recruit overseas players who 'happened' to be living, working or studying in the local community. A sense of continuity with the past was evident.

In the following 20 years a transformation occurred in English basketball. Between 1971 and 1988, the league expanded from six teams to 52 teams, 45 of them defined as 'senior' (Maguire, 1988). Elite participants shifted from being amateur, 'home based' players to achievement-oriented migrants and 'indigenous' workers. The game became a commodity competing in the media and sponsorship marketplace. As part of this process of competing with other sport forms, the cultural meaning of the game shifted in the direction of 'spectacle'. Dovetailing with this commodification process, 'Americanisation' involved the recruitment of American sport migrants as players and coaches, the 'adoption' of American-style marketing strategies and media coverage and a change in the ideological messages underpinning the game centring on American spectacle and entertainment. Centrally, these processes were marked by conflicts between the desire of a new breed of club owners and their auxiliaries, the American sport migrants, to provide an instant commercial product to 'display' to spectators, and the aspiration of more established officials of the English Basketball Association (EBBA) to build the foundations for the long-term playing success of 'English' basketball.

Increasingly, the game became subject to market pressures, its success tied to its market value. That is, the viability of clubs became more and more dependent on income derived from spectators, sponsors and the media. The new owners of clubs actively encouraged this process and proposed structural changes to the league that would accelerate this commodification process. In turn, the commodification of the game allowed the recruitment of American sport migrants to become a formal strategy of the clubs who tended to couch their arguments in terms of the advantages gained regarding playing standards, entertainment value and increased attendances (Maguire, 1988). The utilisation of American imports was initially promoted by most groups connected with the game. The hope was that the 'entertainment' they would provide would produce several benefits, but above all more sponsorship and media coverage, increased attendance figures, greater participation rates and improved playing standards. With regard to these factors, quite a degree of success was achieved. However, issues relating to the defensive reaction of native Britons to this migration soon arose.

In 1972, the year in which the NBL was founded, only two sport migrants were registered with the English Basketball Association. However, between 1981 and 1986 American sport migrants accounted for some 20.5 per cent of the total number of players. When players designated as 'dual nationals' or 'English acquired' are combined with 'Americans', that is to say, players who grew up and learned their basketball in North America, the trend towards Americanisation was further established. Taking these categories into account the involvement of 'American' sports migrants in English basketball between 1982 and 1986 averaged 30 per cent each year. This trend continued into the early 1990s. English players, moreover, tended increasingly to occupy supporting positions. This process was subject to debate within the game. Take, for example, the comments of Miles Aitken, an American who had played basketball in Europe, and who during the early 1980s commented on the game for Channel 4. His subject was the possible conflict between indigenous, dual national and naturalised players competing for team positions:

> There's no conflict. That's how all the major basketball powers have developed . . . The dual national or naturalised player allows the country, or the club team, to compete immediately. Without the dual nationals it could take 15 years to build a team of indigenous players who are able to compete.
>
> (*Basketball Monthly*, Autumn 1982)

While Aitken was keen to downplay the potential conflict, of greater importance is the suggestion that the pattern highlighted was followed by other countries in this period. This phenomenon is thus of interest to a wider study of sports labour migration, raising issues of sports 'development' or 'under-development'. For English basketball during the 1970s, the continued recruitment of American players was seen as essential to attracting publicity that would lead to greater sponsorship. The strongest sides were those who combined the recruitment of top Americans with significant sponsorship from large transnational corporations. Despite some internal dissension, the EBBA publicly welcomed this commercialisation and, in their annual reports of 1977–8 and 1978–9, praised the increased media attention and growth in sponsorship.

During 1978, however, the influx of American sport migrants began to cause concern to the National Executive Committee of the EBBA. At a meeting in April 1977, while they agreed that two 'foreign' migrants per club would continue to be permitted, they also expressed reservations regarding this influx. In the same month, Ian Day, a leading English player, critically reviewed the trends towards the commodification of the game and the recruitment of overseas migrants. He concluded that 'Basketball has become a commercial enterprise where the Americans are viewed in terms of financial investment' (*Basketball Monthly*, April 1977).

The recruitment of American migrant labour stemmed from the perceived need to compete with other sport forms in marketing the game to the media–sport production complex. Writing later in the same year, an anonymous author made several observations that confirmed this: 'Dare our sport, on the point of a major breakthrough into TV, risk losing the crowds, the media and with them the sponsors? [The] Americans are needed to retain spectator interest and with it the sponsors' (*Basketball Monthly*, Summer 1977).

Such observations not only highlight the commodification and 'spectacularisation' of the game but also illustrate the struggle for ascendancy in basketball. Fear of the commercial consequences of the removal of the American sport migrants from the league, and a relative loss of power to the increasingly commercially oriented clubs, resulted in English players, coaches and the EBBA becoming marginalised. While the number of Americans allowed per club remained at two, some officials within the EBBA, however, did seek to limit even further the recruitment of sport migrants by the clubs. The Coaching Sub-Committee of the EBBA recommended, for example, the restriction of American players to one per club. A writer in *Basketball Monthly* (Summer 1977) noted that the proposal 'faces a predictably rough passage' at the hands of those 'concerned to attract spectators to the game'. Officials and coaches concerned with the development of native English players were losing ground to those who advocated the need to recruit American players to provide an entertainment package that would attract spectators, media coverage and sponsorship.

This import of American players, television coverage and sponsorship was part of a general commodification process. The following comment by Mel Welch, a leading figure in the EBBA, illustrates the extent to which American marketing models were dependent upon access to the media–sport production complex:

> Ten years ago, basketball in Britain was a sport for enthusiastic players. There was little spectator following and virtually no media coverage. Then came sponsorship, and basketball is now on the verge of being regarded as a major sport in this country. But sponsorship, basketball and television are now inextricably linked, and sponsorship of basketball will continue to increase as TV coverage increases.
>
> (*Basketball Monthly*, February 1980)

The recruitment of American sport migrants paralleled these developments. Whereas in the early stages of the NBL concern was expressed regarding the number of American imports, towards the end of the 1970s and in the early 1980s criticism of the number of 'dual nationals' began to rise. At issue was the fact that, while a particular team could have two 'foreign' players on its roster, it could also add Americans to its squad if the latter could claim British nationality. Given the rationale underpinning the commodification of basketball, it is not surprising that clubs sought to exploit this loophole.

By the early 1980s, the question of dual nationals had become, according to Richard Taylor, 'the most contentious issue in English basketball' (*Basketball Monthly*, January 1981). In the preceding month, the National League Committee recommended that teams should be allowed only three spots for non-English players. Taylor subsequently suggested that 'legal action and withdrawal from the league were mentioned as possible outcomes if this proposal was accepted by the National Executive'. The fact that the National Executive did not endorse the recommendation arguably showed the erosion of EBBA power in the wake of commodification. Within ten months, the EBBA were issuing temporary English licences to Americans who had not yet received British passports. The growth in the number of migrants designated as 'dual nationals' and 'English acquired' – players who had served a minimum residence period – continued. Not content to frustrate these recommendations, the clubs sought to increase their power. In *Basketball Monthly* in December 1981, it was noted that:

> Division One Men's clubs are moving towards the formation of a new body to represent their views within the spectrum of English basketball . . . The old NBL Committee was itself formed at the wishes of the clubs, but pressure began building against it after a number of recommendations were poorly received, particularly one concerning the eligibility of foreign and dual national players.
>
> (*Basketball Monthly*, December 1981)

The recommendations centred on limiting the number of American migrants but the clubs' dissatisfaction with the governing body also involved the distribution of the income derived from sponsorship. The clubs began to demand the formation of an independent league. This, coupled with the influx of Americans and the distribution of the wealth coming into the game, prompted several criticisms. Dave West, coach of Stockport Thoroglaze Belgrade, writing in 1981, called on the EBBA to 'enforce regulations to safeguard the future of England's juniors'. He argued that:

> We sacrifice the future of the game for the Americans. Since the majority of First Division teams have two foreign and one dual national player, this can absorb up to 75% of a club's annual budget. We must have the only national team in European basketball that speaks with an American accent. The introduction of the foreign player has helped to popularise the game. But their numbers must be controlled to create opportunities for our own players to develop. The destiny of the game lies with the Association. They must be responsible for its future development.
>
> (*Basketball Monthly*, December 1981)

Although West suggested that the English national team was the only one in Europe to 'speak with an American accent', the processes in question were occurring to varying degrees throughout Europe (Olin, 1984). Such comments, however, vividly highlight the contested nature of the recruitment of sport migrants and the commodification and shift of the game towards spectacle. In addition, while West argued that the 'future of the game lies with the Association', he overlooked the extent to which the power of the EBBA had declined. The growing power of Basketball Marketing Limited, the company set up by the EBBA and the clubs, and the growing ownership of clubs by entrepreneurs not hitherto connected with the sport were indicative of this.

The struggle over the import of American migrants continued throughout the 1980s. In commenting on an alternative to the BOA's policy, Bill Beswick, the national coach, argued that, if elected to the National Executive Committee, he would align himself 'with those concerned with the development and progress of our sport as a healthy, exciting and wholesome game – basketball is not owned by anyone' (*Basketball Monthly*, February 1984). With the rise of the BOA, it would appear that the position of those with whom Beswick sought to align himself had been further eroded. At the start of the 1984–5 season, however, the game went into recession: TV coverage declined, several sponsors withdrew and recriminations followed. The struggle between those seeking to develop the sport as TV entertainment and those who sought to promote it as a participant game has continued to mark English basketball up to today (Falcous and Maguire, 2006). As this conflict has taken place, the concomitant Americanisation of the game has accelerated. By January 1985, Beswick appears to have felt that this process had gone too far:

> Basketball in this country without a well-thought out, properly organised structure and not governed with imagination and firmness by those elected to lead will deny national teams their rightful place, will fragment and alienate the various areas of development, and will leave the N.B.L. an over-commercialised, over-Americanised entertainment package with little or no relationship to the real game in this country.
>
> (*Phillips World Basketball Series programme*, January 1985)

Since this period the power balance within the game has shifted even further in the direction of the owners and away from the EBBA. It was not surprising that the owners have been resistant to any changes that would be detrimental to their position. In fact, the leading First Division clubs decided in April 1986 to form a breakaway league under the owners' control. In the power struggle that followed, the EBBA, urged by their National League Council not to recognise the breakaway league, opposed the move. In June 1986, the Sports Council, acting as arbiters, broke the impasse. Under the agreement they negotiated, the clubs would take over the responsibility for the administration and management of Division One, renamed the Carlsberg League, from the 1987 to 1988 season. By the end of the 1980s, the entrepreneurs had gained a greater degree of autonomy, but were faced with the commodification of the game reaching a plateau.

Globalisation and sport migration: some tentative conclusions

One dominant, but by no means exclusive, theme of global sports development in the late twentieth century has been Americanisation. It is also legitimate, however, to talk of competing cultural flows including Japanisation, Europeanisation, Asiaticisation, Africanisation and Hispanisation which have, so far, been weaker. In such a context, the very notion of 'sport', as well as that of 'development', becomes problematic. The present analysis is not, however, arguing a case for homogenisation and integration as those who support the cruder forms of Americanisation thesis do. The broad cultural processes identified in this paper arguably interweave and commingle along the sorts of cultural flow lines specified. The twin process – sociological concepts of diminishing contrasts and increasing varieties – arguably helps avoid the excesses of research that stress that homogenisation has occurred as a result of either modernisation or cultural imperialism.

In short, cultural processes involve interdependencies and out of this something emerges that was neither planned nor intended that both reflects and contributes to broader globalisation processes. At the time of writing the original paper I had in mind the image of global culture that Robertson (1990) referred. Two further points were made. Although sport migrants, officials and consumers are no less caught up in this unfolding globalisation process, they do have the capacity to reinterpret cultural products and experiences into something distinct. Furthermore, the receptivity of national popular cultures to non-indigenous cultural wares can be both active and heterogeneous. These are areas in which much more work needs to be done: this analysis remains the case. Because of this interweaving and the possibly emergent 'decentring' of the West, sport migrants will be likely to increasingly come from non-Western, as well as Western, countries. The effect on their labour rights and sense of cultural identity is a question yet to be explored: much further work remains to be undertaken.

While it is important to probe the existence of relatively autonomous transnational practices, this should not lead the analyst to overlook that national and transnational agencies, including sports organisations such as the National Basketball Association (NBA) in Britain and the National Football League (NFL) in the United States, will attempt to manipulate and control such processes. It is also worthwhile to note that, although criticisms have been advanced here regarding aspects of the Americanisation thesis, this is not to deny that processes of commodification and Americanisation occurred. These can take several forms: the global migration of American sports personnel, the global spread of American sports forms and the global adoption of the marketing of sports along American lines. Usually, such developments mutually reinforce each other, though they have developed to varying degrees in different countries and continents. Because the media–sport production complex markets diversity as well as sameness (Maguire, 1993a), American football, basketball and baseball appear ready to become global sports. As such, American sport migrants would appear likely, for the time being, to be one of the dominant groups traversing the globe. With the marketing of soccer and rugby union as global sports, the significant presence within these global flows of Europeans, South Americans and Antipodeans should not, however, be overlooked. What consequences this will have for the donor and host cultures is, as yet, and remains, relatively unexplored.

The conscious strategies adopted by officials of particular sports organisations led to the predominance of American sport migrants in specific sports. This can be highlighted if reference is again made to basketball. Over 400 Americans were playing at an elite level in West European basketball leagues by the late 1980s (FIBA, 1989). Those leagues that have undergone the most intensive commercialisation processes – many Italian and Spanish clubs are closely connected to transnational corporations – tend to recruit higher quality American migrants. The English case is not an isolated example. Further, just as English officials looked across the Atlantic for marketing models to follow, European basketball officials were reported as considering:

> Their own version of the NBA . . . creating a league of top clubs from across the continent [and that] plans also are under way for creation of a world club championship tournament that would be an expanded version of the four-nation McDonald's Open.
>
> (*USA Today*, 14th November 1990)

Teams such as the Denver Nuggets, the Boston Celtics and the New York Knicks competed in the McDonald's Open tournament. As in the English case, some American migrants began to 'settle' in specific European countries. Americanisation involved not simply the quick raising of playing standards, but also the transformation of the structure and meaning of the game in Europe. In several respects these developments mirror that launched by the NFL in its marketing of American football both in specific countries and with regard to the formation of the World League of American Football (Maguire, 1990, 1991b). Though located in Barcelona, Frankfurt and London, the vast majority of gridiron football players within this league were American. Little sign of resistance to such American migration was evident. These processes are not confined to England or to Europe, but were at work to greater or lesser degrees on a global basis. The 1990–1 NBA season's opening matches were held in Tokyo with the series being seen as 'a giant marketing test for the NBA'. Games were reported as having 'had an undeniable NBA stamp' (*Sports Illustrated*, 16th November 1990). This marketing image included official NBA clocks, baskets and floor, and the whole operation was supported by official NBA entertainment. The NBA Commissioner, David Stern, was reported as seeing the world as one big NBA supermarket and Charles Grantham, the executive director of the NBA Players Association, though conscious of the demands being increasingly made on American players, concluded: 'just think of this global picture as a big pie. The bigger the pie gets, the bigger the piece for the players' (*Sports Illustrated*, 16th November 1990). The squeezing out of indigenous players was, not surprisingly, overlooked by Grantham.

In some ways, the operations of the NFL and the NBA correspond to the marketing strategies of other large transnationals including The Disney Corporation and MacDonalds. While the globalisation of sport is, in part, powered by the intended ideological and economic practices of specific groups of people from particular countries, its pattern and development cannot be explained solely with reference to these ideological practices. The interdependency chains and time/space compression that characterise globalisation processes have intended and unintended dimensions. Evidence of resistance to and reinterpretation of these processes is also evident. Nevertheless, it is along the lines of these cultural, economic, ideological and technological global flows that the speed, scale and volume of existing and future sports labour migration will be contoured.

Note

1 This chapter is a revised and edited version of the paper 'Preliminary observations of globalisation and the migration of sport labour', *The Sociological Review*, 1994, 42(3): 452–80.

6 Sport labour migration as a global value chain

The Dominican case

Alan Klein

Major League Baseball (MLB) has experienced a dramatic rise in the number of foreign athletes in its ranks. Over the past two decades, the percentage of foreign players on Major League rosters has risen from 2 per cent to 29.2 per cent (see MLB.com, August 12th 2009, for subsequent figures as well). Even more impressive, however, are the number of foreign Minor Leaguers (those playing their way up to the Major Leagues in one of the many Minor Leagues in North America) which, as of 2009, has mushroomed to 47.8 per cent of all players (3,356 of 7,021). The small island nation of the Dominican Republic (DR) dominates this foreign infusion of players. In 2008, 98 Dominicans (11.4 per cent of all players) played on one of the 30 Major League teams. The next closest nation represented in MLB is Venezuela with 52 players. Further underscoring the growing importance of the Dominican Republic: 29 of 30 Major League teams operate new, costly, state-of-the-art player development academies there; and the MLB Commissioner's Office established its only office outside of the United States in the Dominican capital of Santo Domingo.

The following study uses a 'Global Value Chain' (GVC) model to forge a look at global distribution of baseball players from the Dominican Republic. In doing so, the emphasis shifts to fuse the ways in which multinational professional teams attempt to craft athletes with their production. The latter is not thought of simply as a matter of athlete migration but, as will be argued: (a) production of international-calibre athletes is transnational, moving through multiple nation states; (b) production and distribution are linked economically and politically; and (c) sport represents a unique form of production in which labour is not only involved in the act of production, but also is the commodity being produced. Hence, understanding the role of production in athlete migration necessitates an understanding of transnational links of an economic, social and political nature for which GVCs constitute a heuristic model. The GVC model also provides a fresh insight into the specific ways in which the relation between MLB and the Dominican Republic has been moving away from neocolonialism towards something that approaches (but stops short of) globalization. In the past, these kinds of relations have been described in terms of Dependency Theory (Frank, 1969) and World Systems Theory (Wallerstein, 1984; Mintz, 1985): both are systems built around the extraction of commodities from developing nations (the periphery) by industrial giants (core nations), and contain a number of assumptions about the core's structural capacity to both govern and reproduce features that enable its dominance. MLB's globalizing effort has, to an extent, followed these trajectories; that is, multinational corporations that secure and manufacture key resources (talent) abroad. The modernized industry of baseball, then, sits between a neocolonial view of power relations and a neoliberal economic climate that demands access to markets, flexible production and a malleable workforce.

When, however, the commodity produced is of the sort of human labour required in professional sport, an unstable factor enters the equation which can change the overall calculus. Most critically, professional baseball talent deviates from the neoliberal labour model (i.e. unskilled, infinite and low-paid) by being highly skilled, rare and highly paid; a climate that can favour the Dominicans and insists that we explore the place of 'exception' within our model (Klein, n.d.).

Within sport sociology, virtually all of the discussion of the international athlete has focused on global flows and, to a slightly lesser degree, on the social psychology involved (e.g. motivations and identity). Joseph Maguire has been at the forefront of these studies. By himself (Maguire, 1994a, 1996, 1999) and with others (Bale and Maguire, 1994; Maguire and Stead, 1996; Maguire and Pearton, 2002) Maguire has examined athletic migrations *vis-à-vis* nationalist responses to foreign labour as well as the factors driving these flows. Other sports scholars have added their voices to these discussions as well (Bairner, 2001; Magee and Sugden, 2002; Darby, 2007b). Sport sociology has failed to keep abreast of contemporary developments in globalization, missing the opportunity to view transnational production of commodities as a single encompassing system rather than a grouping of disparate functions in multiple settings.

Global value chains

In a seminal 1986 article examining pre-nineteenth-century international trade and capital flows as 'a *network* of labor and production processes whose end result is a finished commodity', Hopkins and Wallerstein (1986) coined the term 'Global Commodity Chains' as an economic dimension of World Systems Theory. This framing of commodity production facilitated thinking about transnational production and exchange. Dependency theorists quickly linked this to their views of political economy so that commodities emanating in the periphery reflected core–periphery power relations.

By the mid-1990s, sociologists Gereffi and Korceniewicz (1994) redirected the discussion of global commodity chains towards mainstream sociology via models borrowed from development sociology. Eventually, these chains came to be termed 'Global Value Chains' (GVCs) emphasizing the value-added component to the process. The Gereffi and Korceniewicz model and the vast majority of work that their model influenced tends to be bereft of any critical orientation, approaching globalization from the top-down – emphasizing 'chain governance' or possibilities for 'upgrading' by faithfully aping successful neoliberal practices, as opposed to the potential for change and control that can be generated from the bottom-up (see Barrientos *et al.*, 2003; Gibbon, 2003; Ponte, 2003; Humphrey and Schmitz, 2004; Gereffi *et al.*, 2005).

The variables most widely cited as central to the assessment of GVCs are the following:

- *Governance*: The manner in which the industry and/or firms control the process, that is, how power is wielded in the chain. This includes the firm's decision-making apparatus; corporate dominance; as well as industry policy.
- *Institutional relations*: The structural arrangements between the firm's operatives and operations, and governmental agencies, and the various layers within the chain. It also includes consumers as active agents in the process of production and distribution.
- *Geography*: Where it touches down geographically and why (political geography of the chain).
- *Input–output relations*: What a firm spends to bring a commodity to fruition – the sale price reflecting total inputs versus what the market bears (i.e. profit).

In its insistence on integrating non-production factors (e.g. regulatory policy, marketing, consumers) into its analysis, GVC research also offers a view beyond mere production. Hence, the GVC model is also capable of looking at factors that go into both the distribution and consumption of commodities; creating a cyclic feedback loop that has the potential of allowing us a view of globalization as more multifaceted and multidirectional. In the context of the present case, I would argue that, because labour is the commodity being produced, social and cultural factors are also at work at the root of the manufacturing process.

More immediately, the present study will seek to inject an element of critical thinking into the GVC model. Because political and economic asymmetry are key in North–South relations, we have to be prepared to look, not only at hegemony by global forces, but also at ways in which local institutions and actors push back against the efforts to 'govern' them by controlling the commodity chains.

Studying the Dominican global value chain

Following a 12-year hiatus, I began a new round of Dominican research in 2002. The goal has been two-to-three fieldtrips per year, each lasting between one and three weeks. The primary purpose has been to create a political–economic map of the transnational relationship between MLB and the Dominican Republic. To flesh out this social geography, I worked with several teams. A combination of interviews and observations is being carried out in a multisited format. I chose a small market team (Tampa Bay) and two large market teams (New York Mets and Boston Red Sox). I had access to their Dominican operations and personnel and visited them at least every other trip. I also had access to several buscónes (who train the players before they sign) and their operations which allowed me to see how players entered this commodity chain and how they were groomed for a career in baseball. Finally, I also examined the MLB Commissioner's Office in Santo Domingo which oversees the academies.

The GVC that characterizes MLB's relationship to the Dominican Republic is a lengthy one that centres on the production of professional baseball players. It begins with identifying and securing crude resources (i.e. young unrefined talent), and ends with the player having ended his career. This movement is transnational and reciprocal – that is, players move repeatedly between nations and organizations grow increasingly dependent upon that movement as well (Figure 6.1).

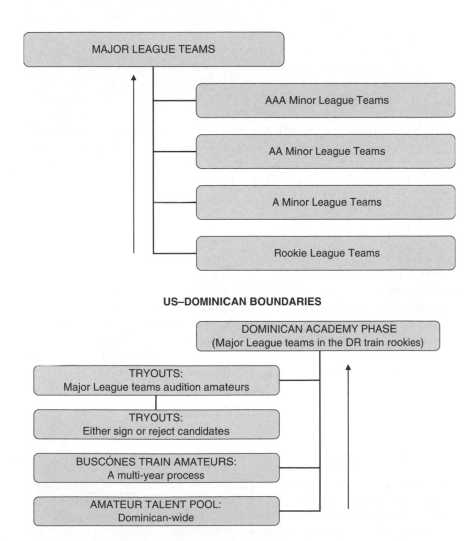

Figure 6.1 Dominican–US baseball GVC

This study primarily focuses on the Dominican base of this chain: that part of the process by which a player (raw commodity form) goes from being a talented amateur, to a professional, and then to being promoted to minor league play in the United States. Some discussion will also look at the earliest phase of transitioning to the United States. Once in the US Minor League system, players are evaluated and promoted or demoted on grounds of merit (their playing statistics). It is only upon entering the United States that most foreign players begin to be noticed in any serious way by key figures (and the media) in the baseball world. But, the actual production of that athlete has already gone through major development by then – out of sight and mind. Even in terms of migration, the production of Dominican players has already included a certain amount of migration within their own country. Hence, it is imperative that we see athlete migration as linked to production and as multisited.

The Dominican end of this chain consists of transnational relations between MLB and Dominican agencies. While the value chain differs from sport to sport, all sport labour production includes the capacity of the 'lead firm' (sport franchise) to govern the production of labour. This paper specifically examines Major League Baseball's capacity to control or govern the production of players, a situation that is effected by the significantly longer gestation period for the formation of baseball players relative to, for instance, soccer and basketball players. The description cited for the Dominican Republic draws upon both new and previously published research over a 20-year period (see Klein, 1988, 1989, 1991b, 1995, 1999, 2000, 2006a, 2007, 2008).

The slightest familiarity with the Dominican Republic includes an acute awareness of the level of poverty that exists there. It is a country where 42 per cent of the population lives below the national poverty line (World Bank, 2006). Dominican desperation is often attested to by the extremes to which people will go in trying to escape it. Boatloads of Dominicans lose their lives each year in attempts to illegally migrate to Puerto Rico and Florida. Within this context, Dominicans have long considered baseball as a viable escape from a life of poverty.

An International Scouting Director I was interviewing at a Dominican academy stood up, stretched his arms out from his sides looking around in all directions and exclaimed, 'Show me another country where we (baseball) get all of the best athletes!' (Klein, 2006a, p. 114). The dominance of baseball in this country ensures that the most talented are funnelled into MLB's quarters. But how that talent is shaped, how it moves transnationally and where it ends up is in large part determined at the base of the chain.

Institutional relations

The institutional arrangements involved in the production of the modern Dominican player consist of a set of relations that are both formal and official, as well as informal and loosely consented to. Within the Dominican Republic, the most important institutional component of the chain – the hub of modern baseball – is the Dominican baseball academy. Each Major League team operates its own Dominican academy which roughly parallels similar operations that they have in the United States. Since its inception in the 1970s, the Dominican academy has evolved from being merely the most convenient place for Major League teams to conduct whatever operations it deemed desirable, to become absolutely essential: a uniformly regulated, complete and insular environment within which prospective players are signed and refined before being shipped ('promoted') to the United States to continue their careers (Klein, 1991b, 2006a, 2008).

The Buscón

A conventional structural assessment of player development would have us examining player development from the 'top', which is to say from the outside. In MLB that would register once the players enter the North American baseball system. The present examination, by contrast, begins at the base, with the academy. But even in doing this we miss an equally critical, but less visible, stage in the creation of the player: the buscón (Klein, 2006a, 2008). Not a part of the formal process of player development, the buscón has emerged over the past decade as the most essential institutional feature of the commodity chain. By virtue of his placement at the very origins of the chain – finding and training young players before they are of the age at which they can sign a professional contract – the buscón is an essential piece of the chain.

The formal signing of a prospect to a professional contract is, then, preceded by a lengthy period in which he is discovered, signed and cultivated in an informal and purely Dominican context – an apprenticeship if you will, taking place outside of officially sanctioned contexts. There are no criteria for who may become a buscón. He may or may not have any baseball experience; and he may or may not be honest. It is simply a matter of a person being able to convince a young player (sometimes as young as 12 or 13 years of age) and his parents of his capacity to get that youngster a tryout with a Major League team. In an impoverished country like the Dominican Republic that promise made is as risky as any street-level relationship; hence, while most buscónes are honest, there exists the potential for exploitation.

The buscón takes over the young player's life. He trains him daily, feeding him and providing him with equipment. If he is a successful buscón, he may have a staff that oversees training and even houses the players. In their operations, the more established buscónes essentially replicate the operations of the formal Major League academies only at an earlier stage – that is, they develop the player to be developed! While they may carry a number of players, only a small fraction will ever be impressive enough to sign with a Major League team. Because of the pervasive losses sustained by buscónes, if and when his players do sign, their agreement typically involves a commission be paid to the latter by the player for somewhere between 25 per cent and 50 per cent of the signing bonus.[1]

The buscón–player relation is directed towards getting the player a tryout with a Major League team. This results in the player being signed to a contract; rejected; or kept at the academy for further consideration (an additional 30 days before a final decision is made). Signed players immediately enter the ranks of baseball professionals as 'rookies' (as do their counterparts in the United States). Once signed to a contract the young player effectively leaves his relationship with the buscón and enters his second apprenticeship with his team.

The academy

Dominican rookies are immersed in an environment where they are constantly trained and evaluated by coaches from their Major League employers. These Dominican rookies follow team regimens for conditioning and practice; and they play in the Dominican Summer League where they are constantly monitored and assessed. In-house coaches work with them while the team's US personnel regularly fly down to confer on the steady stream of evaluations. By 1990, the number of academies in the Dominican Republic had climbed to a dozen, but with the exception of a few, they remained partial facilities: housing players in pensions with a pieced-together meal plan. Beginning in the mid-1990s, a series of changes took place that altered the landscape of Dominican baseball. The number of Dominicans making an impact at the Major League level rose to the point where they couldn't be ignored. As a labour pool, Dominican talent was cost effective and the quality was excellent. This served to bring more and more teams into the country in search of talent and as they arrived they too set up shop, that is, created some sort of academy.

By the turn of the century the academy system had grown to become the dominant baseball institution in the country – eclipsing even the Dominican professional league in importance. Major League teams began to invest heavily in their academies, transforming them into state-of-the-art facilities that are either owned or leased by 29 of the 30 Major League teams. They, likewise, competed more intensely for labour which fuelled a meteoric rise in signing bonuses paid to young players ($5,000 was average in 1990, whereas today it is anywhere from $50,000 to $100,000, with more and more being signed for seven figures). Not only did the academy become the most impressive structure in the industry, it also developed a venue for the game that also showcased excellence.

The Dominican Summer League (DSL)

Begun in 1987 as an informal arrangement among several teams to play against each other, the Dominican Summer League has evolved into a premier rookie league. This league is now an official part of MLB's Minor League system, which means that the players are unionized and integrated into the North American structure of the sport. The DSL's reputation has grown steadily and is now considered to be roughly on par with the Florida Gulf Coast league (the official rookie league for signed players in the north). The level of competition is so fierce here that it is referred to by players as 'Vietnam', a highly combative proving ground.

The Professional Baseball Players' Union which represents all professionally signed players also played a very important role in the formation of the MLB–DR value chain. The Union's role is to safeguard players by securing the best playing conditions and salary in regular negotiations with MLB. For the Dominicans (and other foreign players) this has resulted in greatly improved work conditions (see Darby, 2007b for comparative data). Pressure to overcome subpar living conditions in many academies was furthered by the unions, as were the guarantees that their signing bonuses and salaries come into line with those of US players. The result has been that, as MLB became more involved in signing Dominicans, the latter experienced a sharp improvement in the quality of their odyssey into North American baseball. The modern GVC has significantly benefited Dominicans.

Features of the chain

Geography

Why the chain is centred in the Dominican Republic as opposed to other locations is important in determining baseball's current political economic significance. Until 1960, Cuba was the most advanced baseball-playing country after the United States. Cubans took the game to heart shortly after bringing it back from the United States in the 1860s (Pérez, 1994). Cubans also introduced the game to the Dominican Republic in the 1890s (Klein, 1991b). Dominican excellence in baseball is traced to the early decades of the twentieth century when a level of local competition combined with periodic competition against strong foreign teams helped raise the calibre of play. In the United States, the first half of the twentieth century was defined by race segregation resulting in an insularity of the game in Latin America. Within that racist climate, Dominican baseball was able to develop a vibrant local identity independent of foreign influences.

By the 1950s, with racial segregation abolished, MLB had begun looking to the Caribbean for players. The onset of formal relations between Dominican and North American baseball operatives centred on the 'working relationship': a loose set of ties that clearly fostered governance of an incipient value chain. The relationship was almost completely skewed towards MLB's interests. Eager to gain acceptance by MLB, Dominican teams and operatives were more than willing to do whatever was asked of them: specifically, changing their playing season from summer to the winter months so as not to conflict with MLB's season. Additionally, Dominican teams were encouraged to identify and pass along information on promising players and, when asked, teams would hold on to players that their North American partners expressed interest in. In return, American teams would send scouts and coaches to the Dominican Republic to help develop whatever talent they were tipped off to. The San Francisco Giants developed the first Dominicans to get to the Major Leagues (Klein, 1991b; Ruck, 1991). Ozzie Virgil was the first in 1956, followed quickly by the three Alou brothers and Juan Marichal. The genie had been let out of the bottle.

It was the Cuban Revolution of 1959, however, that changed the way MLB looked at Dominican baseball. The political and economic embargo of Cuba by the United States, begun shortly after the revolution, resulted in the drying up of the rich flow of talent from Cuba. In an effort to continue to find foreign talent, Major League scouts began turning to the Dominican Republic. What began as a trickle resulted in a torrent of Dominicans getting to the Major Leagues. In the decade of the 1950s, two Dominicans broke into the Major Leagues; 22 did so in the 1960s; 38 in the 1970s; 65 in the 1980s; and 143 in the 1990s (Klein, 2006a). By contrast, on the opening day of the 2007 season – just a single season – there would be 98 Dominicans on Major League rosters, 36 more than appeared in the first three decades.

Initially, Dominican talent was viewed as something to be haphazardly gathered by the occasional Major League team. Getting a report of a potential player of interest, scouts swept into and out of the Capital in a 'hit-and-run' fashion, generally staying only long enough to have someone they knew on the ground arrange a tryout for them and make determinations (Klein, 1991b).

With the modern Dominican academy having grown in size and ability to handle a large number of players, the institution has matured into a complex and complete facility for the processing of elite players. It has also become the contemporary embodiment of baseball as an officially recognized industry. Like other 'Free Trade Zones' (concentrated international industrial complexes) in the country, academies have, over the past decade, become concentrated into one small area to the east of the Capital of Santo Domingo. This makes for an ease of access by administrators from the United States (and Canada), who because of it visit the academies more regularly. It also confirms the increased importance of these academies to the overall health of the franchise. The facilities are intentionally remote in order to keep distractions or hazards to a minimum.

Chain governance

This is the most important component of the GVC model. Dolan and Humphrey have pointed out that 'governance requirements increase when developing country producers have difficulty meeting the requirements of developed country markets' (Dolan and Humphrey, 2000). This 'difficulty' is present in the Dominican–MLB GVC. The gap between the raw talent found in the Dominican Republic and the player that eventually plays in the United States is wide both in terms of skill as well as cultural preparedness for achieving in another cultural setting. The player that is eventually watched and 'consumed' by fans in North America cannot be understood outside of the attempts to manufacture him in the Dominican Republic and this consists in large measure of the Major League attempts to control that process. It is also noteworthy that governance by outsiders is part of the larger historic context for this country. As any history of the region points out, the Dominican Republic has been formally or informally governed by outsiders for virtually its entire existence (Black, 1986).

Academy as 'discipline'

The manner by which teams attempt to carry out governance brings to mind Foucault's notions of 'discipline', the ways dominant institutions go about forging conformity of both body and mind (Foucault, 1991). Academies are intentionally located at some distance from cities and towns. This allows teams to better 'control the rookie environment'; minimize distractions to the players; and conversely to intensify the resocialization process. In the case of baseball, the academies run by Major League franchises are more than simply sites for the development of players' skills. The academy is a complex mélange of socialization, mentoring, testing, monitoring and evaluating one's readiness to be promoted to the next phase of their baseball careers. For up to three years, players are intensively trained and compete – individually and collectively – against others. This period is composed of constant mentoring, monitoring and evaluation of every aspect of the player. Despite being highly skilled labourers, baseball players must, nevertheless, be ready to fit into the mould of the organization if they are to progress up the chain.

As baseball players, they receive daily instruction from coaches in the academy, as well as a regular stream that come in from the United States. Each day comprises baseball routines of some sort as the players seek to play according to these newly taught skill sets and drills. The coaches confer with each other weekly and carefully monitor each player's performance. Performance creates objective criteria of worthiness: player statistics. But non-playing variables are also important. For instance, 'coachability', which refers to how well they internalize the instruction received and also how open they are to input from coaches, is highly valued as a tool to evaluate worthiness. Written evaluations regularly refer to their 'character', a trait that expands beyond the physical capabilities of the athlete to include his willingness to alter his makeup so as to become more like the kind of player the team demands.

With reference to the objective criteria of worthiness, playing in the Dominican Summer League (DSL) is the most critical element. The DSL marks the first time that these players produce playing statistics – the first line in creating a Dominican player's resume and used to argue for his promotion or demotion. This is the closest to a purely rational system in which the skills manifest under real game conditions can assist the player's effort to move up the chain. Through a 72-game season, Major League teams have their Dominican academies compete as teams. It is a lengthy enough season to allow maximum exposure of a player to the organization's scrutiny. In contrast to North American (Canada and United States) players, this is the first time that Dominicans get their play empirically evaluated. Because this represents the beginning of a 'paper trail', the initiation of his professional career dovetails with the attempt to govern – to 'domesticate' – the Dominican ball player.

The immensely talented player can easily move through such a system and in only a few years is well on his way to becoming a Major League player; but most are not so easily characterized as exceptional, 'can't miss' prospects. For them, additional factors have to work in tandem to enable them to move up the chain. Since most players come from impoverished backgrounds, they require a good deal of cultural remediation; 'We have to teach them about their own culture even before we teach them about life in the US' is the way that one academy director put it (Avila, 2007). Many of these young players have grown up on the streets where life's lessons are based on survival instincts of the basest kind. Family life is often minimal and responsibility is defined narrowly. This includes learning about personal hygiene; structuring the day; following directions, among other things. In going to play in the United States, a player will have to learn how to behave off the field as well as on it: how to avoid risky behaviour that could undermine his career both in the Dominican Republic and the United States. Every Major League team has a long list of players who, despite a wealth of skills, were unable to make the cultural transition to North America, ending up being released by the organization.

Language and culture are most fundamental in negotiating the passage to the US Minor League system. This involves such matters as the importance of tending to injuries before they sideline the player unnecessarily, dealing with figures of authority in the United States, and fiscal responsibility. Along these lines he must also understand what it means for a player to date women, eat at restaurants and avoid issues that might provoke charges of sexual aggression in a foreign culture. Language is critical to functioning in these contexts, so he must learn English (as well as in some cases how to express himself properly in Spanish). Such programmes are mandatory and offered by all academies, albeit the range and quality of such programmes can vary greatly.

In this environment all of a player's time is accounted for and monitored. Each hour of the day is parcelled out among a range of activities. Players get up early (6:30 am) to begin the day with breakfast and a string of routines. They are to dress and arrive on time and ready to participate (whether it is a drill, workout or game). They all receive language training (and some teams make attending high school classes compulsory). The strict regimen is designed to counter the often lax life these young men had before baseball. Ralph Avila, retired Dodger Vice President of Latin American Scouting and founder of the academy system, wanted a heavily structured environment to counter 'their (the boys') life in the streets. These "tigres" (literally, tigers) never had to listen to anyone, and that won't help them get to the Major Leagues' (Avila, 2007). As with all sport, the failure rate in baseball is predictably high, but particularly so for Latin players who must navigate not only the playing field but culture as well.

The MLB Commissioner's Dominican Office

In the case of Major League Baseball, the industry has been able to physically imbed its practices and policies into the Dominican end of the chain. From the autumn of 2000, when MLB opened its office in Santo Domingo, the Commissioner's Office began to centralize control by making all academies adhere to a uniform set of standards and practices. Academies would have to abide by rules and policies developed through the MLB Commissioner's Office in all matters pertaining to player development. The most problematic area has been in signing players to professional contracts, an area rife with corruption and fraud. Under the watchful eye of the Commissioner's Office, all players' identities and documents would have to be verified. Additionally, all monetary transactions would have to be conducted at the Commissioner's Office and witnessed.

The Commissioner's Office has made significant headway in regulating the general functioning of Major League teams on the island; but despite their successes complete governance of this end of the chain remains beyond MLB's capacity. Protecting young players from exploitation by unscrupulous agents within and outside the game has been one of the Commissioner's Office's greatest accomplishments, but much remains to be done.

Resistance to governance

While the overt mechanism for getting promoted to play in the United States is merit-based, a good bit of the struggle to successfully migrate has nothing to do with the game on the field. The most significant thing that hampers the elite athletes' chances of playing to their fullest potential is being unable to bridge the cultural divide that separates them from their North American teammates and from a sense of belonging. This concept applies equally to Nigerians playing their way to Chelsea; Russians playing their way to the National Hockey League; or Indians playing in English cricket. The GVC model should include cultural variables in its analysis to provide insight into these cultural areas. Language acquisition is routinely the most immediate and powerful barrier to cultural competence. The inability to do the most simple of things, such as ordering food at a restaurant or negotiating simple exchanges, can make day-to-day existence, in a host country, quite alienating. The stories told by players are uniform in this regard. Latin American players will order the same dish for months on end because it is the only one that they can make sense of. So, too, are the accounts of players who look dumbly at police officers or clerks who ask them the most simple of questions. Team efforts to teach players English have met with somewhat limited success because of the overall low level of education attained by most players. With little schooling, most young Dominican players find that they are in need not only of learning about American life, but their own culture as well. Sadly, it also serves to diminish their effectiveness on the field as well. Clearly, being able to communicate with your teammates is vital especially at certain positions (e.g. catcher and pitcher).

Language barriers can also impact players more directly. Reporting and treating injuries are very important, and can seriously set back players if they do not deal with it in a timely manner. Yet, language barriers can derail this effort. One player, in trying to communicate to his coach that he could not pitch because he was injured, actually repeated that he did not want to pitch. [Coach] 'Can you pitch today?' [Player] 'I don't want to' (Klein, 2009). The manager interpreted his not wanting to pitch as a negative attitude, the kind that finds its way into reports on the general character of a player.

Culture shock may be so severe as to result in an almost virtual shutdown on the part of the player. One young man was so unnerved in his early months that he was too frightened to use the bathroom in his boarding house. He took to urinating out of the window on the second floor, an act that, in short order, brought the local police around to investigate. Some of the behaviours of young players are quite rational, but get misinterpreted. For instance, in the case of one team, coaches found that their youngest Minor League players from the Dominican Republic took the money that the team gave them for their daily meal and sent most of it home to their families. The young players began losing weight and their productivity dropped off, predictably. When it was later discovered what they were doing the team unsuccessfully tried to get them to understand that that meal money was not to be treated as remittance. Eventually, they solved the matter by eliminating meal money and instituting a buffet for their Latin players.

Conclusion

Globally tracking the movement of players makes more sense if it is embedded in the system that produces them. Where the commodity is elite talent, the system of production should include social–cultural factors as much as it does structural ones. It is vital that we find a model that envisions this as a single global entity and the GVC can provide us with a workable model. In the case of MLB we can see that the teams (both individually and collectively) operate on a transnational model in which structure, agency and policy move between nations. Some organizations are more sophisticated in their globalization strategies than others, but all must be flexible enough to function in multiple national settings.

In generating labour for Major League rosters, teams have adopted an aggressiveness: setting up production sites in other countries (in this case, the Dominican Republic); and fashioning policies that are designed to operate in multiple settings. Some, like the New York Mets, are cutting edge in their chain production. The Mets are transnational from top to bottom. Their General Manager (top administrator) is Dominican born, and they have assembled a staff that is stacked with Latinos and/or bilingual people. Their administrators are able to function in both Latin American settings and in the United States. The Mets have invested heavily in the Dominican Republic, building a state-of-the-art facility and instituting innovative programmes that are impressively culturally sensitive. From a structural perspective, Mets policy has the advantage of looking as if it was created in the Dominican Republic as much as having originated in the United States. Hence, they have made it mandatory for their players in the Dominican Republic to attend school while at the academies, even though it may not directly advance players – it was fashioned, as one administrator put it, 'because it was the right thing to do; not because it was baseball-driven' (Klein, 2007). Similarly, they instituted a programme whereby their North American players would be sent to the Dominican Republic for a few weeks to gain an appreciation of where their Dominican teammates have come from. While most teams do not approach the Mets in terms of the breadth of their transnationalism, Dominican players are now protected by their union membership; MLB regulations having been extended to them in the Dominican Republic; and the modernization of facilities in that country. By way of comparison, football clubs in the European Union are light years away from operating in Africa along the lines outlined here (Darby, 2007b). FIFA may make sensitive public statements about the mishandling of

African players, but they have done little to regulate clubs or partner with local African governmental groups.

Cultural issues play a significant role in the production and migration of foreign athletes, especially from impoverished developing nations. Again, where the commodity produced is labour, we have seen that cultural variables loom large in how far and how fast the athlete can move up the chain. Because the GVC model represents a single entity operating transnationally, it demands that we look at the ways in which the enterprise is aided or hampered in its attempts to produce a commodity. In this case, MLB's ability to manage the production process, while substantial, is not without its failures. GVCs allow for microexamination (especially ethnographic) which can highlight the ways in which 'unintended consequences' can enter the production process (e.g. buscónes). To the extent that the 'lead firm' (i.e. the Major League team) is invested in the area, these unforeseen factors have a dual effect: it may introduce a local agency as an active partner in the process and it may also reveal how atavistic or 'globalized' that firm really is. Insofar as an industry is capable of operating in a mixed setting in which local actors are taken on as partners, that industry is more globalized. To the extent that the industry resists the possibility of playing on a more level playing field that admits local influences, it bespeaks of more atavistic operating impulses, 'testicular globalization'. At present, MLB operates in a fashion that suggests an affinity for top-down or 'testicular' versions of globalization (Klein, 2006a).

Note

1 The bonus is considered excessive by 5 per cent of North American agents. The North American agent, however, only represents his client, while the Dominican agent/buscón has raised his client for years. He is recouping his investment and covering losses incurred by the many players that he carries but who don't sign.

7 'Net-gains'

Informal recruiting, Canadian players and British professional ice hockey

Richard Elliott and Joseph Maguire

The migrations of athletes have become a prominent feature of global sports worlds (Maguire, 1999; Maguire *et al.*, 2002). In many sports, athletes are migrating within nation states, between nation states on the same continent and beyond their own continents. Contemporary sporting culture is marked by athletic labour flows that increasingly traverse geographical, political, cultural, ethnic and economic boundaries. This chapter revisits research that has been conducted in the sociology of sport. More importantly, however, attention is given to the increasingly dynamic area of highly skilled migration. By drawing on concepts derived from the sociology of highly skilled migration, it can be argued that an understanding of the global migrations of athletic workers is enhanced. A synthesis is developed on the understanding that, whilst athletic and highly skilled workers are not totally equivalent, highly skilled migration increasingly involves the movements of workers from a range of fields, including athletic workers, who are increasingly employed as highly skilled 'specialty labour' (Castells, 2000, p. 130).

The majority of researchers who have examined the movement of athletic workers have done so within the confines of the athletic sphere. That is to say that few sociologists of sport have broadened their vision to include concepts derived from those studies examining the movement of other non-athletic but highly skilled workers. Equally, those writers examining the migrations of the highly skilled have restricted their focus to those professionals based in various sectors of international business, such as information technology (Khadria, 2001), finance, banking, accounting (Beaverstock, 1991, 1996, 2005) or law (Dezalay, 1990; Beaverstock, 2004). Arguably, much can be learnt by developing a synthesis that draws on concepts derived from research that has examined the movements of highly skilled workers *and* research that has analysed the migrations of athletic workers. However, to this point, Maguire (1996), Miller *et al.* (2001) and Elliott and Maguire (2008) are the only writers to make use of research located beyond the sociology of sport.

In providing a conceptual synthesis which draws on research located within the sociology of sport and the sociology of highly skilled migration, and in capturing how some athletic migrations actually occur, this chapter is based on a critical case study. Here, then, we examine the mechanisms through which Canadian ice hockey players are recruited to teams in Britain's professional ice hockey league:

the Elite Ice Hockey League (EIHL). For these athletic workers, mutually beneficial recruitments are facilitated using similar mechanisms to those identified in
research examining the movement of highly skilled workers. For both types of
workers, recruitments do not always occur through more formal channels where
agents or consultants are employed. Rather, they are facilitated by informal communicative channels maintained by networks of interdependent relationships.

To show how migrations can be facilitated using interdependent networks of
relationships specific attention is given to two studies which have examined the
processes by which migrant workers can be recruited. In the first part of the
chapter Bale's (1991) 'friends-of-friends' networks are examined in the context of
athletic recruitment, whilst Meyer's (2001) concept of the 'bridgehead' is considered in the context of highly skilled recruitment. In the second part of the chapter
a 'developmental' (Maguire, 2005) account helps to contextualise the 'place' of
British ice hockey both in a global and local sense. Such a contextualisation is
important when comprehending how recruiting practices have developed in the
way that they have for workers in the EIHL. Following this contextualisation, the
specific responses of EIHL players, coaches, managers, team owners and agents
are examined. These responses show how the recruitments of migrant labourers
in the EIHL are facilitated using informal mechanisms.

Conceptualising recruiting mechanisms

Relative to other areas of the migration experience, little research has been conducted which has sought to analyse the mechanisms through which athletic
migrants are recruited. Whilst Klein's (1989, 1991a, 1991b) analyses of Dominican
baseball and research by Darby et al. (2007) into African soccer have sought to
make sense of more formal mechanisms, research by Bale (1991) and Elliott and
Maguire (2008) has sought to make sense of the informal mechanisms that are
used to facilitate migrant recruitments (see also chapters by Klein and Darby in
this collection). With respect to informal recruitments Bale's work deserves particular attention.

Bale (1991) argued that athletic recruitments could be facilitated using networks comprising two contact groups: either through coaching colleagues, or
through current or former players. With respect to the former group, Bale argued
that coaches could call a coaching colleague in another country to enquire about
particular athletes, or that they could recommend athletes to other coaches, in the
hope that the athlete might be recruited. With respect to the latter group, Bale
argued that coaches could facilitate additional migrations, from a given location,
following an initial movement. Accordingly, athletes, who were either currently
plying their trade in a given location, or who had been recruited to a particular
location in the past, could help to provide a vital link between the host location
and potential migrants situated in the original donor location.

In contact frameworks which were facilitated either by colleagues of the
recruiting coach, or by current or former players, Bale argued that recruitment
was facilitated through a series of 'friends-of-friends' networks (1991, p. 106). In

these networks, information about particular migratory destinations, or about potential employment opportunities, would be passed through informal channels of communication. In a similar manner, research examining the recruitments of highly skilled workers such as that by Yeoh and Willis (2005), Conradson and Latham (2005), Voigt-Graf (2005), Beaverstock (2005) and Meyer (2001) has focused on the significance of friendship networks in the mobilisation of highly skilled workers. In particular, Meyer identified how 'bridgeheads' could be seen to circulate knowledge with respect to potential employment opportunities and, thus, facilitate mutually beneficial recruitments for highly skilled workers.

Bridgeheads, Meyer argued, were migrants who had already experienced the migration process and who could mobilise additional migrations within similar interdependent networks to their own. Similar to Bale's (1991) work, Meyer observed how migrations could be facilitated through a network of contacts, be they friends or colleagues, who could facilitate a flow of information to the recruiter, in terms of establishing the possibility of movement for a potential migrant, or to the potential migrant themselves, in terms of the practicalities of any movement. The central contention that should be observed here is that bridgeheads, whether they are friends or colleagues, have the capacity to mobilise migrations using interdependent networks and, thus, prove vital in creating networks of relationships which might not otherwise exist.

Research examining the recruitment of migrant workers shows that recruitment need not always be mediated by a formal third party. In this respect, recruitment specialists, be they agents or consultants, are not always involved in the securing of employment opportunities for migrant workers. Instead, in a more informal manner, friends or colleagues can assume the role of intermediary, circulating knowledge with respect to potential employees and potential employers within a series of interdependent communicative networks. This is not to underplay the role that agents do play (see chapters by Darby and Andreff in this collection). Our point here is that in specific instances, such as the movement of Canadian migrant workers into the EIHL, it is these more informal mechanisms which also facilitate this movement. Our contention is that attention, therefore, needs to be given to both the formal and informal mechanisms which are at work. Before it is possible to establish exactly how recruitments are facilitated in an informal manner it is important to consider the 'place' of the EIHL and ice hockey in Britain more broadly.

'Skating on thin ice': professional ice hockey in Britain

To understand the manner in which labour migration is facilitated in the EIHL it is important to appreciate that the migratory movements being made are bound within the broader social, political and economic power geometries which exist within the sport globally (Maguire, 1996). Ice hockey, at the global level, is enmeshed in a complex and interdependent series of power struggles where governing bodies, commercial investors, sponsors and consumers vie for attention in the broader sports industrial complex (Maguire, 2005). Within this complex enmeshment of power struggles, the migration of athletic labourers is a distinct component, with the majority of these workers migrating along determinable 'talent pipelines' (Maguire *et al.*, 2002) which flow to various global markets, but which originate, most commonly, in Canada.

Canada serves as the core locale for ice hockey labour production. The best Canadian players are recruited, via the 'draft' system, by the teams of the league at the economic and cultural core of global ice hockey, the North American National Hockey League (NHL). However, given the extent of overproduction in Canada (Miller *et al.*, 2003), routinely those players who do not secure NHL contracts seek employment in the global network of leagues (Maguire, 1996). The best players not recruited to the NHL may be recruited to the NHL's 'feeder' league, the American Hockey League (AHL). Alternatively, these players may seek employment in one of the *established* European economies (e.g. Sweden, Czech Republic or Slovakia). For those players unable to secure employment either in the NHL, the AHL or one of the better quality European leagues, the search for professional employment is, on occasion, directed towards those leagues located outside of the sport's more established economies, the EIHL for example.

The EIHL sits as an *outsider* to the established European ice hockey economies for a number of reasons. One of the most significant reasons, however, is the manner in which the sport has developed in Britain. Ice hockey is perceived in Britain as an 'import' sport, one which offers few ties to the country's history or culture (Crawford, 2002). As a consequence of the manner in which it is perceived, ice hockey has struggled, throughout most of its existence in Britain, to break into the popular sporting consciousness. It is little known, for example, that Great Britain were Olympic, World and European champions in 1936 and that large crowds gathered at games in the post-World War II era.

Given these problems, the development of ice hockey in Britain has been, at best, sporadic and haphazard. The fragility of the sport's place in Britain is evident in the number of governing bodies which have been launched, and then liquidated, organised and reorganised; the number of different professional leagues which have been created, only to subsequently fold, or be forced to change structure; and the number of teams which have been formed, and then disbanded, only to re-form, and then disband again. Indeed, it would appear that one of the only consistencies which can be observed during the sport's development in Britain is the recruitment of Canadian migrant workers.

Canadian migrant workers have been consistently recruited to British ice hockey teams throughout the history of the sport in Britain. Whilst the numbers of migrant workers permitted may have fluctuated at different points during the sport's development, the reality is that professional ice hockey in Britain has been built, almost entirely, on Canadian players (Kivinen *et al.*, 2001). Such a reliance is much in evidence in the EIHL, where Canadian migrants make up the bulk of the playing personnel.

The playing facilities available to the teams of the EIHL vary considerably. Whilst some teams enjoy the space and the amenities offered by purpose-built arenas, and a dedicated spectating environment, the majority of the teams in the league are located either in leisure parks where the facility is also used recreationally by fee-paying members of the public, or in local authority run ice centres where practices and games have to be scheduled to fit around public skating sessions. The level of disparity in facilities in the EIHL means that audience numbers fluctuate considerably across the teams. Whilst the 'big arena clubs' are able to accommodate greater numbers of fans, usually averaging approximately 3,000, some of the teams in the league have a maximum seating capacity of 900. Most commonly, fan groups are drawn from areas where specific pockets of interest for the sport exist, usually in the cities where EIHL teams are based. Beyond these small groups, little national interest exists in the sport either at the professional or participatory-recreational level.

The apparent disinterest in ice hockey in Britain is evident in the amount of national media coverage which is dedicated to the sport. Like the spectator following, the media coverage of EIHL games is reserved for the local media in the cities where EIHL teams are located. Whilst some games are televised via BSkyB, the UK satellite broadcaster, little national coverage is dedicated to the sport either in the press or on terrestrial television. As a consequence of the lack of national media interest, EIHL teams often have to operate within very tight budgetary boundaries. The salaries that can be paid to players are, therefore, limited. This has a direct effect on the type of migrant players that EIHL teams can afford to recruit, and, arguably, the processes by which these players are recruited. EIHL teams are not able to entice those players who might ordinarily be recruited to the NHL, or elect to play in the more established European economies. Rather, the players employed by EIHL teams are predominantly recruited, towards the ends of their careers, from the North American minor leagues; on some occasions the AHL, but most commonly from the less prestigious East Coast Hockey League (ECHL). In essence, ice hockey in the United Kingdom, despite the hype provided by owners and promoters, is marked by acute instability.

Whilst the quality of the players recruited to the EIHL may be limited, this is not to assume that these players cannot still be categorised as highly skilled workers, however. Whilst they may not represent the *most* highly skilled workers in their field, these athletic labourers are still employed as highly skilled speciality labour (Castells, 2000). Therefore, whilst highly skilled migration involves the movement of financial analysts, scientists, engineers and computer programmers, it also involves the movement of 'artists, designers, performers, *sports stars* [emphasis added], spiritual gurus, political consultants, and professional criminals' (Castells, 2000, p. 130). Accordingly, the employment profile of EIHL migrants should be seen to fit with definitions of what constitutes a highly skilled worker. Iredale, for example, argues that workers occupying this category have 'intensive or extensive experience in a given field' (1999, p. 90). To show how the similarities between athletic and highly skilled migrants extend beyond definition, the case study, which is based on a series of interviews conducted with EIHL team owners, managers, players and agents, examines the manner in which Canadian migrant workers are recruited to EIHL teams.

'It's all about who you know': recruiting through the network

It became clear from discussions concerning the manner in which Canadian migrant workers were recruited to EIHL teams that the majority of movements were facilitated through informal networks of communication, and not through the intervention of agents. Indeed, all of the players interviewed had been recruited in this manner. For the players, the intent to facilitate their own movements, without the intervention of an agent, appeared to be both a conscious decision, in an attempt to save the money that they would have to pay to an agent, and a reflection of how recruitment in the league was generally facilitated. For example, when asked why he didn't have an agent to help facilitate his move to an EIHL team, one of the Canadian players, Peter, suggested that:

> To be honest with you, to get over here, it's all about who you know, so it's all about if you have a friend over here, and if you can be recommended. So I really didn't feel that I needed an agent.

This was a position that was reiterated by Mike, another Canadian player who had facilitated his own move. When asked, like Peter, why he didn't have an agent, he commented: 'After you've played for a few years, you get to know the hockey world is a very small world, so with the contacts that I've made, I didn't need one.' Similar remarks were offered by other Canadian migrants. Simon, for example, discussed how he had been contacted directly by a former coach under whom he had played in North America. Given this direct form of contact, he made it clear that there 'wasn't a need for an agent'. Wayne had also been contacted directly by a former coach who had relocated to the EIHL. When asked how this affected his decision whether or not to use an agent, he replied: 'I had to pay my agent, so when the opportunity came along to work out a contract by myself, I got rid of him.'

For the players identified here, and for others interviewed, it appeared that using an informal contact to facilitate a migratory movement was the preferred method of securing professional employment in the EIHL. This method permitted players to navigate a path to a professional contract, without incurring the expense associated with agents' fees. From the coaches' perspective, being able to navigate this path was also both useful, and indeed desirable, given that clubs would also be responsible for paying a fee to an agent. One of the EIHL coaches, Henry, identified that this was the case, remarking: 'I think the clubs are trying to kind of bypass the agents, obviously because of fees and budgets.' A similar position was identified by another coach, Carl, who remarked:

> I'm not a big believer in agents . . . I think that some agents take advantage of players, they cost them jobs in-the-fact that they ask too much money for them . . . The number of players I went for through agents this year is zero.

Thus, whilst being able to take advantage of relational networks was significant for EIHL players, so too were these methods desirable for EIHL coaches whose recruiting decisions were bound, very much, by the limited financial position of their clubs.

For the players and coaches interviewed, the ability to be able to avoid the expense associated with the employment of an agent by facilitating their own movements using informal networks was both possible and desirable. The agents themselves, however, were not oblivious to the fact that recruitments in the EIHL were facilitated, for the most part, through networks of informal relationships, and not through more formal mediation. One of the EIHL player agents, James, recognised that the use of informal networks in the recruitment of players was common. In this respect, he was pragmatic about such practices, commenting: 'Once the players know everybody then yeah, if they're going to stay in the league, then they don't need my services.' Another agent, Gavin, made a similar observation. When asked why some players didn't have agents, he remarked: 'Some players are able to get the job through friends, sometimes the manager or coaches call a player directly in order to avoid using an agent.' Thus, it was accepted that recruitments could be conducted in this manner, and that interdependent relational networks were used by migrant workers and coaches as a mechanism to sidestep the expense associated with the employment of an agent.

Whilst being able to sidestep the expense associated with the payment of agents was clearly a tangible benefit to be enjoyed by those players and coaches who facilitated their own migratory movements, it became apparent that, for the coaches interviewed, being able to recruit players through informal networks was as much about being able to recruit the best players available for the EIHL level of competition, as it was an opportunity to manipulate their limited financial position. Like the coaches identified in Bale's (1991) work, for whom knowledge networks were highly significant, the ability to be able to recruit the best players available lay, for the EIHL coaches, in the manner in which they manipulated specific networks of relationships. As one of the coaches, Henry, put it: 'You exploit every contact you have to find out about a player, you phone some of the players that he might have played with, you phone his coach.' These networks appeared to operate in a similar manner to those identified in Bale's research. Coaches sought to gain knowledge about and recruit migrant players using networks comprising either coaching colleagues or current or former players. In this respect, and reflecting the relative state of development of British ice hockey, such recruitment processes stand in contrast to the much more formal mechanisms revealed by Klein in reference to Major League Baseball in the Dominican Republic.

For those coaches who elected to make use of the network of other coaches when seeking to gain knowledge about migrant workers, the key to successful recruitments lay in the ways in which knowledge could be circulated by other coaching colleagues. John was one coach who used the coaching network. In his case the coaching network was used to reduce the risk associated with the recruitment of migrant workers, many of whom coaches would have had little contact with prior to recruitment. In this respect, he commented: 'I'm more comfortable bringing in a player whom I might have known his coach.' Other EIHL coaches also approached the network in a similar manner, seeking to take advantage of the knowledge available from their coaching colleagues. Henry, for example, commented how gaining knowledge about potential migrant recruits was 'all about getting scouting reports on the players through coaches that have coached the player, and coaches that have coached against the player'.

For the coaches who sought to take advantage of the relationships developed in the players' network, the success of recruitments lay in the manner in which current and former players could be used to provide the information necessary to make recruiting decisions about potential migrants. One coach who chose to adopt this framework was Carl. When commenting with regard to the manner in which he recruited migrant players to the EIHL team he coached, he observed:

> It's a sport of connections; your players are your biggest recruiters, players that you coached, players that you've played with. So if you're a good person, and people respect you, your name will get passed on quite a bit.

One of the EIHL team owners, Roger, also recognised the importance of players in the circulation of knowledge with respect to employment opportunities. As he put it: 'You have to know players . . . You have to build up your contacts . . . It's just communication, you have to be in the network of people who talk.'

Tapping into the players' network was important for coaches, as they felt that taking advantage of this source would not only facilitate a flow of information about potential recruits, but that current and former players could also be used to act as bridgeheads in the same ways that Meyer (2001) had previously identified in his research. In this respect, bridgehead players could be seen to be providing vital links between the club, and the potential recruit, given that the circulation of knowledge in the players' network was often facilitated by groups of friends, many of whom had already experienced the migration process. The use of bridgeheads in the recruitment of potential migrant workers was observed by John, who remarked: 'Most guys who come over here will already have friends in the league, so it helps if somebody can pass your name on to a coach.' Ian also made reference to the manner in which bridgeheads could be used to facilitate recruitments, using an example that had occurred at his club:

> Once you get one guy, for example we got Mark, he was good friends with Jim, so we signed Jim, and Jim said: 'Hey this guy's a good player, similar style, probably what you're looking for, give him a call.'

As this example shows, bridgeheads could be identified as a resource through which appropriate knowledge was circulated to the potential migrant, and through which the suitability of the potential migrant could be established for the recruiter.

The significance of networking: an evaluation

An examination of recruiting processes in the EIHL shows that the gaining of knowledge about, and the recruiting of, migrant workers does not appear to involve the intervention of a professional employment consultant, such as an agent. Instead, the movement of migrant workers is facilitated by informal communications, maintained by distinct contact groups, in a series of informal networks of social relationships. Networks of contacts are used as a resource through which links to potential migrants can be developed, and through which information valuable both to the potential migrant, and the potential employer, can be circulated. The form of these networks may differ; however, the result, for the most part, is the same: players acquire their employment via a series of interdependent connections. Thus, social relationships can be seen to constitute the most effective means towards mutually beneficial recruitments.

For the EIHL coaches interviewed, the contact structure utilised to gain knowledge about and recruit migrant workers would appear to differ little from the framework proposed by Bale (1991) in his work. EIHL coaches placed their trust either in their coaching colleagues situated in the worldwide network of leagues, or in current or former players. Being able to gain access to the circulations of knowledge in these networks was vital for coaches who were not able to see prospective migrant recruits play. Given the limited financial positions of their clubs, coaches were not able to make recruiting trips to North America to scout potential recruits, nor, of course, to establish formal links with clubs. Therefore, being able to secure as much information as possible about a player from a trusted coaching colleague or player proved vital in establishing the player's suitability for recruitment. Moreover, recruiting players using such mechanisms also strengthened the financial position of EIHL clubs, given that the money which would have to be paid in agents' fees could be directed elsewhere.

Whilst interdependent networks proved vital for EIHL coaches in terms of establishing the suitability of migrant workers for recruitment, and in strengthening the financial position of EIHL clubs, current and former migrant players were particularly useful in establishing links between the club and potential migrants. Whilst coaching colleagues could be used to provide the information necessary for coaches to make informed decisions about whether or not to recruit a particular migrant, EIHL coaches had still to convince players to play for their team in the EIHL. When using players as bridgeheads to potential migrants the need to convince players was lessened given that the knowledge in the players' network often flowed between groups of friends. EIHL coaches could rely, therefore, on players to perform the recruiting function in a more informal manner. Some coaches relied on players to provide a vital link, and to facilitate a flow of information to the migrant, in terms of the practicalities of migration to a foreign culture, and to the coach, in terms of the players' suitability for employment with the team. These are processes which have been seen to be significant in research tracing the recruitments of highly skilled workers where the ability to be able to take advantage of human mediation has been seen to be highly significant. As Meyer (2001, p. 94) put it:

The pre-existing relationship between the (future) employee and the employer, through the intermediary of an individual known by both, not only provides the employee with information about the job but also guarantees the employer that she/he is, to a certain extent, appropriate for the vacant post.

Meyer's research shows, therefore, that highly skilled employees required some sort of bridge to facilitate their encounters with potential employers, and that this vital link need not always be provided by a formal mediator such as a recruitment consultant or agent. Meyer's research shows that highly skilled workers are more likely to take advantage of diverse and extensive networks consisting mostly of colleagues to facilitate their movements.

Conclusion

A study of recruiting mechanisms in the EIHL draws attention to the significance of interdependence in the recruiting process. What it also does, however, is draw attention to the increasing flexibility of the global labour market (Beaverstock, 2005). With greater regularity workers, in a number of fields, including athletes, are traversing the globe in search of the best possible employment opportunities. With fewer national regulations for migrant workers (Iredale and Appleyard, 2001), and a more global approach to the workplace, highly skilled labourers can search for employment on a global, rather than local, level. Canadian ice hockey players are not restricted to an immediate geographical locality. Indeed, given their 'over-production', employment in the domestic or North American market is saturated and necessitates movement. Therefore, many professional ice hockey players seek employment in Britain. This group of workers use a series of interdependent bonds to search out employment opportunities, and to make themselves available in a global rather than local market place. In that sense, they are both symptomatic of, and responding to, the global restructuring of ice hockey and sport more generally.

By traversing the globe in search of the best employment opportunities, and by taking advantage of a series of interdependent bonds by which to do so, Canadian migrants entering the EIHL show that they share the characteristics of movement previously identified for workers in the highly skilled sphere. In this respect, the data presented in this chapter should be seen to have value both for studies in the sociology of sport and the sociology of highly skilled migration.

By developing a conceptual synthesis it is possible to show that the migrations that are occurring for some athletic workers are, indeed, similar to the movements that have been identified for workers in the highly skilled sphere. It is possible, therefore, to conclude that the similarities between athletic and highly skilled migrants extend beyond definitional comparisons when considering the area of movement mechanism. Further research adopting this synthesis of conceptual approaches will be required to establish if the similarities which have been identified in this study exist between workers in other sports and occupational groups in the migration process.

8 'Have board, will travel'

Global physical youth cultures and trans-national mobility[1]

Holly Thorpe

Global media cultures and patterns of consumption are changing contemporary youth cultural formations. Attempting to understand and explain these changes, researchers are increasingly moving from intensely focused ethnographic studies of youth within locally bound spaces, to more broadly based investigations of complex, fluid and globally connected youth groupings in and across local, national and international fields (e.g. Horak, 2003; Huq, 2003; Nayak, 2003; Nayak and Kehily, 2008; Pilkington and Johnson, 2003; Robertson and Williams, 2004; Skelton and Valentine, 1998; Wiles, 2008). Building upon this research, this chapter explores the trans-national flows of youth cultural product, images, values and ideas and participants, via the case of a global snowboarding culture. Developing in a historically unique conjuncture of trans-national mass communications and corporate sponsors, entertainment industries and a growing affluent and young population, snowboarding has spread around the world at a phenomenal rate and far faster than many established sports and physical cultures. In a little over three decades, it has gone from a marginal activity for a few aficionados to an Olympic sport and global culture with mass appeal.[2] Attracting an influx of participants from around the world, and from different social classes and age groups, snowboarding has seen a 385 per cent increase in participation between 1988 and 2003; there are currently more than 18.5 million snowboarders worldwide ('Fastest growing sports', n.d.).

Despite changing cultural demographics, it is important to note that the majority of snowboarders are still from the middle and upper classes (see NGSA Newsletter, 2001). Approaching the sport from a position of privilege, many snowboarders travel internationally in pursuit of new terrain and fresh snow. In the words of *Transworld Snowboarding* journalist Sherowski (2004), 'when it comes to seeing the world, snowboarders are lucky':

> . . . we don't have to vacantly watch it pass by outside the tour-bus window or through the camcorder scope like most people. Nope, the emptiness of 'tourism' is not for us, because we belong to a *planet-wide culture* that makes journeying to the remotest places the equivalent of visiting a pack of friends for a day of slashing it. You shred a place, you live it, you know it – you don't just buy the postcard at the airport. (p. 106; emphasis added)

Glossing over local, regional and national differences, as well as the logistical complexities and privileged nature of such travel opportunities, Sherowski (2004, p. 106) continues to wax lyrical: snowboarding is a 'global culture' that 'transcends borders and language barriers'.[3] In this chapter I examine snowboarders' trans-national mobility to illustrate how cultural values and styles are being communicated across borders, and how these global forces and connections are negotiated in local spaces and places.[4] In so doing, I reveal fresh insights into the lived trans-nationalism and global migration of contemporary youth facilitated by the 'extreme' or 'alternative' sports economy (Wheaton, 2004a).[5]

Researching trans-national physical culture: towards global ethnography

The value of traditionally defined ethnography – as an 'intensively-focused-upon single site of ethnographic observation and participation' (Marcus, 1995, p. 96) – has recently been called into question. In light of fundamental transformations of space, place and time, anthropologists and sociologists are increasingly calling for more broad-based research strategies, or what some are calling 'globalizing methods' (Stoller, 1997), 'mobile ethnography' (Marcus, 1995), multi-site 'transnational fieldwork' (Knowles, 1999) and 'global ethnography' (Burawoy *et al.*, 2000; Hendry, 2003).[6] Here, I am particularly interested in the potential of global ethnographic methods for studying contemporary youth cultural formations. Where many traditional ethnographies of youth cultures have focused on a particular site in one moment in time (e.g. the punk scene in London during the 1970s; a local skateboarding subculture in Southern California in the early 1990s), global ethnography provides us with new tools to examine the flows of youth cultural commodities, images, discourses, power and populations across local, national and international fields, and helps us understand how young people are negotiating these global transformations in and across local spaces (Canniford, 2005; Muggleton and Weinzierl, 2003; Nayak and Kehily, 2008).[7] Of course, there is a plethora of ways in which globally sensitive ethnographies of contemporary youth cultures may transpire. To illustrate the potential of such an approach, I offer a brief description of the global ethnographic methods I employed to reveal some of the complexities of contemporary snowboarding culture.

Understanding trans-national snowboarding culture: a global ethnographic approach

My research on global snowboarding culture *officially* began in 2004. Prior to commencing this study, however, I had already spent approximately 600 days snowboarding on more than 30 mountains in New Zealand, Canada and the United States. Between 1999 and 2004, I held many roles in the snowboarding culture (i.e. novice, weekend warrior, core boarder and athlete) and industry (i.e. semi-professional athlete, snowboard instructor, event organizer, terrain-park employee and journalist).[8] During this time, I lived, worked, trained, competed, travelled and socialized with snowboarders from various nationalities. Despite many languages and countries of origin, we seemed to 'share a discourse, a kind of global discourse' (Hendry, 2003, p. 499). I was fascinated by the extent to which snowboarders seemed to form a global network, and how these connections were being experienced in and across different locations. As a seasonal 'lifestyle migrant' (Knowles, 2005) chasing the winter between hemispheres, I was embedded in the 'time-space rhythms' and global processes of snowboarding culture (Burawoy, 2000, p. 4). But my knowledge and understanding of trans-national cultural flows was initially tacit rather than clearly articulated or theoretical. Thus, driven by an innate sense of curiosity in my immediate world, I set out to gain a deeper understanding of the global–local nexus in snowboarding culture via a multi-site 'global ethnographic' study.

With the goal of further examining the values, practices and interactions unique to local snowboarding cultures, as well as regional, national and global flows of people, objects, value systems, information and images within and across these places, I conducted 14 'ethnographic visits' – ranging from one week to one month – in an array of snowboarding communities and ski resorts in Canada, France, Italy, New Zealand, Switzerland and the United States between 2004 and 2009. Each field was unique in its social, cultural, political and natural geography, and offered different insights into the local, regional, national and trans-national flows and connections in the global snowboarding culture.[9]

Attempting to understand how the 'global forces, connections and imaginations' (Burawoy *et al.*, 2000) were being experienced in (and across) these local snowboarding fields, observations were made in natural settings both on and off the snow (including lift lines, chairlifts, resort lodges, snowboard competitions, prize-giving events, video premieres, bars, cafes, local hangouts, snowboard shops, bus-shelters, train stations, airports). During this fieldwork, I observed, listened, engaged in analysis and made mental notes, switching from traveller to snowboarder to researcher depending on the requirements of the situation. For Burawoy (2000, p. 4), global ethnographers should become 'the living embodiment' of the processes they are studying by 'continually switching places, moving among sites within the field'. Indeed, my multi-sited ethnographic approach offered new opportunities for experiencing, observing and sharing the bodily and social pleasures, as well as pains and frustrations, inherent in snowboarding and snow-related travel. My ethnographic observations were developed in dialogue with 54 participants (28 females and 26 males) from an array of countries, including Australia, Canada, Europe, France, Great Britain, New Zealand, South Africa, Switzerland and the United States.[10] In conjunction with my multi-sited trans-national fieldwork and interviews, I also gathered evidence from cultural sources, such as magazines, films and websites,[11] to help deepen my understanding of cultural complexities of the global–local nexus in snowboarding.[12]

Each of the locations visited for this project posed different opportunities *and* challenges (e.g. language, localism, cultural access, accommodation, pre-existing contacts in the field, funding), as well as pleasures *and* perils.[13] According to Stoller (1997, p. 91), the key to doing research in complex trans-national spaces is 'suppleness of imagination', which may be learned from our research participants who are often 'exceedingly creative' in negotiating space within complex fields. Inspired by the 'epistemological suppleness' (Stoller, 1997, p. 91) of trans-national snowboarding migrants, I attempted to respond and adapt flexibly to social circumstances as they arose in the field, and remain open to a wide variety of different types of relationships and interactions (e.g. on chairlifts, in snowboard shops, on buses, in youth hostels, etc.).[14]

My 'suppleness of imagination' in the trans-national snowboarding field – that is, my ability to access (and respond to) an array of culturally insightful 'circumstances' – was greatly facilitated by my past experiences as a travelling snowboarder. But, as Amit (2000, p. 7) points out, the 'melding of personal and professional roles in ethnographic fieldwork makes for a "messy qualitative experience" which cannot readily or usefully be compartmentalized from other experiences and periods in our lives'. Thus, throughout my trans-national fieldwork, I self-consciously reflected on my constantly shifting positions as an (increasingly less) active snowboarder and a young, white, heterosexual, middle-class female researcher and academic from New Zealand, and how these roles influenced the theoretical and empirical development of the study (also see Wheaton, 2002). While the focus of the remainder of this chapter is the trans-nationalism of 'others' in the snowboarding culture, it is important to note that my own privileged trans-national experiences – as a snowboarder and researcher – influenced every phase of this study. Indeed, as Knowles (1999, p. 62) argues, 'the autobiography of the transnational researcher contains many insights into the lived interior of transnational mobility'.

Snow border crossings: a case of global physical culture and mobility

As a number of physical youth cultural scholars have explained, contemporary 'alternative', 'lifestyle' or 'extreme' sport cultures are highly fragmented (e.g. Booth and Thorpe, 2007; Ford and Brown, 2006; Rinehart and Sydnor, 2003; Wheaton, 2004b). Cultural participants include professional athletes, devoted or 'lifestyle' participants, less-committed newcomers and novices, marginal participants (e.g. poseurs, weekend warriors) and various subgroups. While many of the early participants in these studies were young, white, heterosexual males from Western countries, today alternative or extreme sports are attracting participants from different social classes, age groups, genders, sexualities and racial and ethnic groups (see, e.g., Thorpe, 2008a; Wheaton, 2004b). With such cultural diversity, it is not surprising that the travel patterns facilitated by the 'alternative' or 'extreme' sports economy vary considerably, ranging from budget to luxury national and international holidays (e.g. marginal participants, ex-core participants or retired athletes), to cyclic seasonal migration between the hemispheres (e.g. core participants working in the sport or tourism industry), to brief international adventures to remote and exotic destinations for competitions, events or as part of media or contractual obligations (e.g. professional athletes). Here I build upon existing research on youth and travel more broadly (e.g. Deforges, 1997; Skelton *et al.*, 1997; Vogt, 1976) to offer one of the first in-depth examinations of trans-national mobility in contemporary physical youth culture via a discussion of the migratory practices of snowboarding tourists, professionals and core participants, respectively.

Snowboarding tourism: from hitchhikers to helicopters

For many years, snow-related travel was an expensive and privileged activity limited to upper-class skiers (Coleman, 2004). Recent changes in the ski industry and international travel, however, have contributed to shifts in the social demographics of snow-sport tourists. During the 1990s and early 2000s, ski-fields and mountain resort destinations recognized snowboarding as offering the industry a new youth market and potential for ongoing economic prosperity (Thorpe, 2007). Attempting to further attract regional, national and international snowboarding patrons, many (not all) resort destinations began offering cheaper travel and accommodation options for the typically younger and less affluent (though still privileged) snowboarder, as well as developing unique events for niche groups (e.g. snowboarding competitions for university students, women's snowboarding clinics, gay ski and snowboard weeks). Many travel companies also realized the economic potential in snowboarding tourism and began offering a wide range of snow-sport travel options (e.g. budget or backpacker specials, long-weekend student deals, all-inclusive family packages).[15] Some airlines also re-tooled to better service the influx of snow-sport tourists. For example, in 2007 low-cost carrier Ryanair announced a new winter schedule 'designed with skiers and snowboarders in mind' (cited in 'Ski tourism on the rise', 2007, p. 5). Nonetheless, while international snow-related travel has become more accessible to (some) families, younger participants and budget travellers, other experiences (e.g. helicopter snowboarding) and locations (e.g. Aspen, Colorado) remain remote, costly and exclusive.[16] At the time of writing this chapter, however, international winter sport tourism was experiencing a considerable downturn.[17] The irony here, of course, is that despite growing diversity in the cultural demographics of snow-sport tourists over the past decade, in the current socio-economic climate, snow sports may once again become activities afforded by only the most privileged.

Professional snowboarders: 'living the dream'

The life of the contemporary professional snowboarder is indeed a privileged one, typically consisting of extensive national and international travels for competitions and events. Not dissimilar from professional golfers or tennis players, competitive snowboarders following the International Ski Federation (FIS) Snowboard World Cup circuit compete at ski resorts around the world. Not all professional snowboarders, however, follow a strict international competition circuit. Some make a living from sponsorships with snowboarding companies who pay salaries based primarily on niche media coverage (e.g. interviews and photos in snowboarding magazines and websites, segments in snowboard videos). Some of these athletes are paid to travel to the most exotic and remote locations to pioneer new spaces and places (e.g. Alaska, Japan, New Zealand); their exploits are then covered in snowboard magazines, films and websites. The representations of idyllic trans-national lifestyles (i.e. travel to exotic snowboarding destinations, financial independence, partying) of professional male (and some female) snowboarders, promoted by snowboarding companies and media (e.g. advertisements and videos), then work to create a compelling mythology for many cultural participants (also see Frohlick, 2005; Kay and Laberge, 2003). According to Chris Sanders, CEO of Avalanche Snowboards,

> The dream is basically what the kids see when they look in the magazines and see Damian [Sanders] or Terje [Haakonsen]. They are great lifestyle icons. They have it great. It looks like their lives are 24-hour-a-day adventure. You get handed these plane tickets, you hang out with cool photographers, dye your hair however you want to, and you're making money so your parents have no say in your life. It's all sex, action and glamour. To an 18-year-old snowboarder, this is the dream.
>
> (cited in Howe, 1998, p. 68)

Simply put, snowboarding companies and media invest heavily in the transnational flow of professional snowboarders because it enhances global connections and promotes youth cultural consumption of discourses, images, product and travel.

Most professional snowboarders embrace the travel opportunities afforded them in this market-structured snowboard economy. But, for some, snowboarding travel assumes the same relations as the workplace. Professional snowboarder Mike Basich reveals the risks, pains and frustrations associated with his 'job':

> A lot of people say I'm lucky for what I do for a living. Sure, maybe that's true. I get to travel the world and not have a nine-to-five job. But when I get to work, my worries are not about giving a report to my boss or something. I worry about making it through the day without breaking a bone or getting stuck in an avalanche (knock, knock). Your body takes a beating. You're never home. Lots of lag time at the airports.
>
> (cited in Baccigaluppi et al., 2001, p. 95)

It might be argued that professional snowboarders experience a form of 'alienation' when they travel to remote destinations, and confront serious injury and even death in order to 'get the shot', and thus 'earn' a wage (Rigauer, 1981 [1969]). But, professional snowboarding consists of opportunities and constraints, and therefore cannot be explained solely by the concepts of alienation and exploitation that neglect snowboarders' critical faculties and interpretive capacities. It is important to note, however, that not all professional snowboarders receive the same levels of support from their sponsors; some struggle for many years to subsidize their own trans-national snowboarding lifestyle. Thus, while the media and snowboarding companies work hard to (re)create the 'dream' of the trans-national snowboarding lifestyle via extensive coverage and sponsorship of travelling professionals, in reality such opportunities are only afforded to a select few. In pursuit of this 'dream' lifestyle, however, many others (e.g. core boarders, semi-professional snowboarders) invest heavily (i.e. financially, physically, time) in their own snowboarding journeys, and in doing so, support the global snowboarding economy.

Core snowboarders as 'lifestyle sport migrants'

As previously mentioned, the cultural demographics of participants at the *margins* of the snowboarding culture (e.g. weekend warriors, novices) are shifting. However, with more than 75 per cent of snowboarders still under the age of 24, and the majority being white (89 per cent) and from the middle and upper classes (see NGSA Newsletter, 2001; Thorpe, 2009), it is inevitable that young, white, privileged men and women continue to constitute a dominant force at the *core* of the snowboarding culture. In their late teens and early twenties, many core participants have yet to take on adult responsibilities (e.g. marriage, children, mortgages, long-term employment, etc.), and their commitment to snowboarding is such that it organizes their whole lives (see Wheaton and Tomlinson, 1998). Many core snowboarders are nomadic, travelling nationally and internationally to experience new terrain, meet new people or 'live the dream' of the endless winter. A recent online survey of more than 2,000 snowboarders from around the world, for example, showed approximately 43 per cent of correspondents had snowboarded at least once in a foreign country ('Poll results', 2006).

At the end of high school or tertiary education (or during a leave of absence from education or the workforce), many committed snowboarders migrate to mountain towns where they find accommodation and employment, and spend several months to many years practising, playing and performing in the various physical (e.g. mountains) and social (e.g. bars, cafes, shops) spaces and places. Core snowboarders typically begin their lifestyle migration by moving to snowy destinations within their country of origin. For example, many Canadian snowboarders living on the east coast relocate to larger resorts in Alberta (e.g. Banff) and British Columbia (e.g. Whistler); and passionate New Zealand snowboarders living in the North Island often move to mountain towns in the South Island (e.g. Queenstown, Wanaka) which host thriving international snowboarding scenes during the winter months. Observing the lifestyle migration of core snowboarders, Sherowski (2005, p. 160) writes:

> Not everyone who rides a snowboard is a snowboarder but for those who do bear this illustrious title, it's an undeniable *way of life*. High school ends, and the road starts calling – off to mountain towns and the assimilation into weird, transient tribes full of people who work night jobs cleaning toilets or handing you your coffee in the early mornings, all so they can shove a fistful of tips in their pocket and ride, their real motives betrayed by goggle tans or chins scuffed by Gore-Tex. In this world, people don't ask what you 'do',

they ask you where you work – knowing that what you do is snowboard, just like them, and any job you might have is simply a means for it.

Some of the more fervent snowboarders follow the winter between hemispheres, thus becoming what Maguire (1996, p. 339) termed 'nomadic cosmopolitans' and I refer to as 'seasonal lifestyle sport migrants'. To facilitate (and prolong) their trans-national snowboarding lifestyles, many pursue further training and education to obtain skilled employment in the snow-sport industry (e.g. instructor, coach, journalist, photographer, judge). It is important to reiterate, however, that despite the highly skilled nature of many of these jobs, the majority are not high paying; they tend to be held by passionate snowboarders committed to the lifestyle rather than the economic rewards. In the words of top snowboarding photographer Trevor Graves: 'If you're shooting to maintain the lifestyle, it's worth it. That's all you can do with the time constraints anyway. It's not a huge cash-maker, like fashion or rock photography. It's really about travelling the world and living snowboarding' (cited in Howe, 1998, p. 107).

While committed snowboarders are travelling within and across many Western – and some Eastern (e.g. China, Japan, Taiwan and South Korea) – countries, the trans-national flows of youth cultural participants are stronger in some directions than others. Some salient flows of seasonal lifestyle sport migrants observed during my fieldwork include Australian, British, New Zealand and Japanese snowboarders to Canada – particularly Alberta (e.g. Banff) and British Columbia (e.g. Whistler) – and the United States – particularly California (e.g. Mammoth), Colorado (e.g. Breckenridge) and Utah (e.g. Salt Lake City); American, Australian, British, Canadian, European and Japanese snowboarders to New Zealand (e.g. Queenstown, Wanaka); and British snowboarders to France (e.g. Chamonix). Importantly, the trans-national mobility of snowboarding 'lifestyle migrants' is facilitated (and constrained) by various factors, including work and travel visas, travel and accommodation costs, employment opportunities and wages, languages and exchange rates. For example, the availability of temporary youth work visas among the Commonwealth countries facilitates the mobility of Australian, British, Canadian and New Zealand snowboarders, and J1 Visas enable tertiary students from an array of countries to spend five months working in ski towns in the United States during their university holidays.[18] In contrast, a recent quota on the number of H2B visas (which permit internationals with the support of a US sponsor to work temporarily in the United States) has significantly impacted the seasonal migration of skilled ski industry employees.[19] Indeed, thousands of committed Australasian, European, South American and South African skiers and snowboarders – many of whom have invested heavily in their 'careers' in the sport and industry (e.g. instructors, rental technicians) and the establishment of long-standing relationships with host resorts in the United States – have been forced to reconsider their travel, employment and lifestyle options.

Of course, many snowboarding seasonal migrants are from privileged backgrounds. However, it would be remiss to ignore the considerable social, financial and emotional investments they make in pursuit of the trans-national snowboarding lifestyle. As *New Zealand Snowboarder* magazine editor Butt (2006) explains:

The effort that goes into organizing an overseas mission is pretty huge. The long hours of work to save enough money . . . The calls, emails and random hook-ups through friends of friends . . . Dragging bags off planes onto trains and buses, through cities, small towns and villages . . .

(p. 16)

A conversation with Erin and Lisa (pseudonyms) – two highly esteemed New Zealand snowboard instructors who have been doing consecutive winters between New Zealand and North America since the early 2000s – revealed some of the difficulties experienced by female lifestyle sport migrants:

It is quite hard to stay in the industry for a long time, whether it's because you're sick of travelling, or sick of being broke, or you're ready to settle down. While doing back-to-back winters is awesome, it can take a lot out of you; you are always living out of a bag . . . you definitely can't have 15 pairs of shoes like city girls [laughing].

(Erin, personal communication, 2008)

Another big thing with doing lots of back-to-back winters would be six-month friendships. You meet the coolest, like-minded people who have travelled and love, love, love snowboarding [and] you have these intense friendships. [But] at the end of the winter you all go your [separate] ways. It can be really hard, emotionally, sometimes.

(Lisa, personal communication, 2008)

Pamela also describes the financial and physical difficulties and personal sacrifices she made as a semi-professional athlete and lifestyle sport migrant during the 1990s:

'Living the lifestyle' meant a small bag, not many possessions, all funds funnelled into travelling to the next competition. I used to come home and think I could have had a street lined with cars, but I'd spent all that money on snowboarding, and I guess, my 'life education'. . . I was riding up to 200 days a year; I had chill-blains, constant aches and pains, and colds and flus that would last for months. My body never got to recover or get strong between seasons.

(Pamela, personal communication, 2008)

Continuing, however, Pamela proclaimed that through her trans-national snowboarding experiences she developed 'a sense of confidence – that is priceless': 'I now know,' she adds, 'that I can do things that other people think are impossible' (personal communication, February 2005).

Despite the physical, social, emotional and financial demands of seasonal lifestyle sport migration, many core snowboarders highly value the opportunities for personal development and self-growth facilitated by their trans-national experiences:

Travelling is an integral part of snowboarding for me. Stepping off the beaten track and leaving familiarity behind can add an entirely different dimension to a snowboard trip. Experiencing new environments and differ-ent ways of living brings rewards all of its own. The most important thing that snowboarding has given me has been the opportunity to expand my horizons.

(James McPhail, snowboarding photographer, cited in Barr *et al.*, 2006, p. 92)

Interestingly, committed New Zealand snowboarder Mel attributes her snow-boarding travel experiences with helping her critically reflect upon her privileged upbringing and position in society:

[Snowboarding] helped me push myself to places there's no way I would've gone otherwise, and I'm not just talking about cliff drops, rails and jumps. I'm talking about people, places, and major attitude adjustments. I grew up on the Northshore, sheltered as, basically a snob. But through the places snowboarding's taken me, here and overseas, the people I've met, it's made me a much more open and accepting person.

(personal correspondence, 2005)

Unfortunately, it is beyond the scope of this chapter to further explore how the trans-national migration of snowboarders may, in some cases, lead to greater reflexivity, or even identity transformation (see Noy, 2004). Future research seek-ing to better understand youth cultural mobility and reflexivity, however, might fruitfully draw upon Bourdieu's (1998) habitus–field complex. Arguably, for some privileged lifestyle sport migrants, crossing local, national and global 'fields' with different values, norms and rules may lead to moments of dissonance and tension, and thus a 'more reflexive account of one's location and habitus' (Kenway and McLeod, 2004, p. 525; Thorpe, forthcoming).

Thus far, I have focused on the going 'away' experiences of core snowboarders, yet coming 'home' (either temporarily or permanently) can also prompt the lifestyle sport migrant to 'renegotiate their entwined understandings of place and subjectiv-ity' (McKay, 2005, p. 75; Knowles, 1999). As the following comments reveal, 'returning' from a snowboarding journey can be a highly affective experience:

There's nothing quite like returning to New Zealand after a winter overseas, and on the plane home emotions can be mixed. You might be dreading com-ing back after living it up in North America or Europe and having what can only be described as the 'best time of your life'. On the other hand you're probably looking forward to getting back to good food, friends and family. . . . You may be returning home battered and bruised, dosed up on codeine with a broken wrist, tweaked shoulder or torn ACL, and facing the daunting task of rehab before the next season. Whatever the case . . . you can't help but feel some kinda 'butterflies in the stomach' when you look down and see the Southern Alps, Mt Ruapehu or Mt Taranaki.

(Westcot, 2006, p. 18)

The careers of many lifestyle sport migrants are short-lived and, whatever the cause of physical youth cultural 'retirement' (e.g. injury, social pressures to 'grow up and get a real job' or adoption of more social responsibilities such as marriage, children and mortgage), re-emplacement can be an emotional experience. Indeed, some lifestyle sport migrants describe experiencing physiological and socio-psychological difficulties transitioning out of the trans-national snowboarding lifestyle:

> When I stopped snowboarding it was really hard, but it was less the snowboarding and more the people I missed the most. . . . Going back to university after snowboarding more than 200 days per year for seven years was incredibly difficult. I was always looking for a window to open. I couldn't handle being inside all day, every day . . . I had horrendous headaches.
>
> (Paula, personal communication, 2005)

> Everything I did was for snowboarding, whether it was saving money to head south for winter, or organizing university papers. . . . Snowboarding was my whole life and everything I owned fit into my car. . . . In later years, this was a really tough mind-set to break. I felt really uncomfortable buying a bed or furniture because, in my mind, I couldn't take it with me. Settling down, and even staying in one place for more than a few months, was really difficult at the beginning.
>
> (Nick, personal communication, 2008)

Similarly, Pamela, who currently works as an architect in a large urban metropolis, describes how, ten years after her transition from semi-professional athlete to 'weekend warrior', she still experiences physiological cravings for snowboarding: 'If I read a snowboarding magazine or think about the snow, my heart races, my blood pulses and I am overtaken by a desire to be back on the mountain' (personal correspondence, 2008). While older or injured participants may no longer be able, or willing, to organize their lives around the trans-national snowboarding lifestyle, memories and stories of places travelled and experiences shared with close friends often remain in heavy circulation, and continue to influence their sense of identity and personal history for many years (see Robertson *et al.*, 1994). Moreover, many continue to enjoy regular family holidays to national and international ski resorts, or save up for short luxury snowboarding adventures with groups of friends (e.g. a helicopter-accessed snowboarding trip).

In sum, snowboarders do not constitute a homogenous group; participants approach the activity with different motives and values depending on an array of factors including style of participation (e.g. freestyle, alpine, half-pipe, backcountry), level of commitment, skill level, age, sexuality, race, class, gender, nationality and so forth. Moreover, individuals' goals and styles of participation change during their lifetime. In this highly fragmented and dynamic culture, participants' travel patterns vary considerably, ranging from short road-trips to the local ski resort, to budget international holiday packages, to luxury snowboarding adventures to exotic and remote locations, to working holidays and seasonal lifestyle migration between the hemispheres. The mobilities in contemporary snowboarding culture are diverse, and ski resorts and mountain destinations, once the exclusive domain of upper-class skiers, are increasingly being shared by skiers and snowboarders from the middle *and* upper classes, and various nationalities and age groups, and from different positions within these physical cultures (e.g. professional athletes, core cultural participants, tourists, novices and poseurs). As a result, the interactions between individuals and groups in ski towns are becoming increasingly complex. This is particularly true for some key locations (e.g. Chamonix, France; Queenstown, New Zealand; Whistler, Canada) which host such strong flows of physical cultural enthusiasts (e.g. skiers, snowboarders, climbers, mountain-bikers, kayakers, skateboarders, sky-divers, hang-gliders) that they have become, what I refer to as, 'transnational physical cultural hot spots'. Unfortunately, it is beyond the scope of this chapter to offer a detailed discussion of the complex dynamics and interactions between physical cultural participants in various natural spaces (e.g. mountains) and social places (e.g. car parks, gas stations, bus stops, bars, cafes, sport-specific shops, sports events) in these mountain towns. In a concurrent research project, however, I am exploring how cultural hierarchies are contested, negotiated and reinforced in different spaces and places within these trans-national physical cultural fields. In other words, I am exploring how lifestyle sport migrants *and* local participants establish notions of self and the group, and a sense of belonging, and demarcate who belongs and who is excluded in 'transnational physical cultural hot spots'.

Conclusion

There has always been movement between countries, yet an increasingly mobile global labour force, as well as European and Commonwealth legislation, has enabled young people with the financial means (or a strong desire) to move more freely between nations. While scholars have offered insightful theoretical and discursive analyses of the trans-national flows of youth cultural discourses, products and images, few have explored the voluntary migration of youth cultural participants themselves. Adopting an interdisciplinary approach (e.g. youth cultural studies, social and cultural geography, tourism studies, critical sport sociology) and employing global ethnographic methods, this chapter offered an examination of the travel, lifestyle and sporting experiences of contemporary physical cultural participants via a discussion of snowboarding mobilities. Future research that builds upon this case study and further explores the lived trans-nationalism and global migration of physical cultural participants could certainly make important contributions to understandings of sport and youth cultures in the early twenty-first century.

Notes

1 The title of this chapter is a direct reference to a glossy, non-academic, cultural history of surfing, skateboarding and snowboarding: *Have Board, Will Travel: The Definitive History of Surf, Skate, and Snow* (Brisick, 2004).

2 While it is beyond the scope of this chapter to explain all the major forces and constraints, events, human agencies and convergences and contingencies contributing to the globalization of the snowboarding culture (see Thorpe, 2006), some brief comments about the snowboarding industry help reveal the trans-national connectedness of the contemporary culture. Since the 1970s, the snowboarding market has flourished, rapidly developing from a medley of backyard businesses to a global industry worth US$2.28 billion per annum ('Select snow brands to show at ASR', 2004). Burton Snowboards, which holds approximately 40 per cent of this market (Chester, 2004), is an excellent example of a successful 'transnational company' (Pries, 2001). From their offices in Innsbruck and Tokyo, and headquarters in Burlington (Vermont), Burton Snowboards distributes to speciality retailers in 36 countries ('Fact sheet: Burton Snowboards', 2003). The company sponsors over 100 snowboarders worldwide and, in 2006, established the Burton Global Open Series. Not only are the events in this series attended by athletes, coaches, judges, photographers, journalists and enthusiasts from around the world, they are also consumed by local, national and international audiences via various forms of mass (i.e. newspapers, magazines, television, You Tube), niche (i.e. local, regional, national and international snowboarding magazines, films and websites) and micro media (i.e. blogs) (Thorpe, 2008b).

3 Of course, globalization is not solely a co-opting force in snowboarding. Some boarders embrace local, regional and national differences; others are active agents who resist and negotiate the images and meanings circulated in and by global consumer culture (see Thorpe, 2006; Wheaton, 2004a).

4 Unfortunately it is outside the limits of this chapter to critically reflect on social justice implications of snowboarding travel or snow-sport tourism more broadly. However, for an insightful discussion of social justice and surf tourism in the Mentawai Islands, see Ponting *et al.* (2005).

5 Much of the contemporary research on youth and mobility has focused on the involuntary movement and forced displacement in some young people's lives (e.g. Stanley, 2001). This chapter, however, explores the lesser studied phenomenon of the voluntary migration of privileged, middle- and upper-class youth in the early twenty-first century.

6 Of course, anthropologists have long studied nomadic people, travellers and transhumant populations (Hendry, 2003). The recent emergence of 'multi-sited fieldwork' or 'global ethnography', however, is located within 'new spheres of interdisciplinary work', including media studies, science and technology studies, cultural and social geography and cultural studies broadly (Marcus, 1995, p. 95; also see Burawoy, 2001; Gille, 2001).

7 For an interesting discussion of the possibilities (and problems) associated with doing ethnography in the 'touristic global surfing subculture' see Canniford (2005).

8 My most intense period of involvement was between 2000 and 2003, when I completed eight consecutive, 'back-to-back' winters, training and competing in snowboard events in Queenstown (New Zealand), and working as a snowboard instructor and supervisor of a children's ski and snowboard school at Mt Hood Meadows (Oregon, USA).

9 Most of this fieldwork was self-funded (with the exception of two small research grants) and thus conducted on a shoe-string budget. However, I am very grateful for the finan-

cial assistance provided by a New Zealand Postgraduate Study Abroad Award (2005) and a University of Waikato Research Grant (2007). Approaching this study from a position of privilege, particularly in relation to my previous snowboarding and travel experiences, and cultural knowledge and connections, certainly helped make this longitudinal and multi-sited research feasible within tight time and fiscal constraints.

10 Participants ranged from 18 to 56 years of age, and included novice snowboarders, weekend warriors, core boarders, professional athletes, an Olympic judge, snowboarding journalists, photographers, film-makers, magazine editors, snowboard company owners, snowboard shop employees and owners, snowboard instructors and coaches and event organizers and judges. To accommodate the nomadic existence of many snowboarders, I also distributed follow-up interviews via email to 35 participants living or travelling in various countries. In this chapter, I reference interviews conducted in-person as 'personal communication', and email interviews as 'personal correspondence'.

11 According to Williams and Copes (2005) 'regardless of the subculture they participate in, many of today's youths use the Internet to develop new relationships and to gain insights into how their peers perform subcultural selves' (p. 68). This is certainly true for many snowboarders who, according to *Transworld Snowboarding*, spend on average 22 hours per week on the Internet ('Hard numbers', 2005, p. 58).

12 Some of these sources (e.g. guidebooks, travel stories in snowboard magazines and websites, films) also proved useful for my understanding of regions in which snowboarding is practised but I am yet to visit (e.g. China, Japan, South Korea).

13 As Knowles (1999) explains, 'fieldwork offers the transnational researcher the prospect of reconnection with a former life or the prospect of escape; it sustains the possibility of alternate sense of belonging and self, deftly busied in conceptions of work and intellectual enterprise' (p. 60). While I certainly enjoyed moments of escapism, nostalgia, adrenalin and joy during my fieldwork, the practice of global ethnography should not be romanticized. Global ethnography has the potential to be 'humiliating, belittling, at times dull, boring and downright exhausting' (Silk, 2005, p. 75), as well as dangerous (see Thorpe, 2009).

14 Language barriers in France, Italy and Switzerland, for example, made participant observations and interviews considerably more difficult. Responding to this situation, however, while conducting observations in social spaces (e.g. lift lines, resort cafes) I became more attuned to the interactions and movements of snowboarding bodies, as well as the tone and inflections of voices.

15 In 2009, Ski New Zealand offered Australian snow-sport enthusiasts an array of all-inclusive packages ranging from 'luxury holidays' to 'backpacker specials' (i.e. five nights' accommodation in a multi-share room in a hostel in Queenstown, four-day lift pass and rental equipment for NZ$595). Similarly, British snowboarders can choose from a variety of 'inclusive packages' (e.g. a three-day trip to Courchevel, France, including flights, lift passes, chalet board, rental, flights and three days' packed lunch, for just £465). As noted by Prof. John Sugden, many of these packages are cheaper than the prices paid by working-class football fans attending 'away' matches (personal communication, 2007).

16 Indeed, lift-pass prices at some resorts have sky-rocketed in recent years. During the 2009 winter season, a one-day lift pass at Treble Cone (Wanaka, New Zealand) and Vail (Colorado, USA) was NZ$99.00 and US$97.00, respectively. During the same year, five helicopter-accessed runs in the Southern Alps (New Zealand) cost NZ$1,245.00 per person, and a week of helicopter-accessed snowboarding in Valdez (Alaska) costs

US$7,640 per person (including accommodation and food). An even more exclusive week-long 'private package' for eight persons in Valdez costs over US$67,000!

17 As Ralf Garrison, author of the Mountain Travel Research report, explains: 'economic conditions had a significant impact on the long-distance, multi-day visitor' (cited in Lewis, 2009: para. 3). Colin Chedore, president of the Canadian Ski Council, also observed many Canadian resorts gearing their promotions to local – 'rubber tire' – visitors, as opposed to 'international travellers who stayed home, scared off by the impact of the global recession' (cited in Bouw, 2009: para. 7). Due to the rising cost of jet fuel, many airlines are also imposing baggage charges which are directly impacting snow-travellers' 'decisions of where to travel and what to bring' (Lewis, 2008: para. 4).

18 A plethora of commercial services have been established to cater to the growing number of middle- and upper-class youth wanting to experience an international 'working holiday' at a ski resort. Prior to commencing my post-graduate studies, I worked for IEP (International Exchange Program) – a non-profit organization that offers an array of student travel programmes (i.e. Work USA, Work Canada, Work France, Colorado Mountain Express). My experiences of working for IEP in New Zealand, and working for a ski resort in the United States with many other students also holding J1 visas, serendipitously informs my understandings of the temporary trans-national migration of student snowboarders.

19 In light of government concerns about US unemployment, the law was amended such that only 66,000 visas are available to 'alien' workers per year. Visas are spread out over 12 months and excluded from the cap workers who were employed in the United States during the previous three years. Prior to this law, the ski industry accounted for approximately one-third of all H2B visas issued each year ('H2B visa information', 2009). Recognizing the detrimental effects of this quota on the US snow sports industry, the National Ski Areas Association (NSAA) continues to actively lobby Congress to reconsider this law.

Part III

Experiences of migration and sport

9 Migrants, mercenaries and overstayers

Talent migration in Pacific Island rugby

Andrew Grainger

It has become something of a truism in New Zealand rugby circles that the local game has become increasingly 'browner' in recent years. A popular reference to Pacific peoples[1] (see Anae, 2002, 2004, 2006), 'brown' has been taken up as the descriptor *du jour* for the new ethnic make up of New Zealand rugby, from schoolboys to the national side, the All Blacks. In the words of the former All Black and race-relations conciliator Chris Laidlaw, Pacific peoples are 'transforming' the New Zealand game. 'A page in New Zealand's sporting evolution is being rapidly turned,' he writes. 'The 21st century will be an age in which [rugby] will be dominated by young Polynesians [*sic*]' (Laidlaw, 1999, p. 183). Certainly, the number of Pacific peoples playing top-level rugby in New Zealand has increased significantly since the 1970s, and, while little more than ten years ago there were 25 players of Pacific Island descent contracted to play for New Zealand's professional Super 12 franchises, 50 of the 162 contracted players in the expanded Super 14 competition could trace their roots to either Fiji, Samoa or Tonga by 2007 (Paul, 2007b). Such is the 'growing dominance' of 'Polynesian athletes' that the rugby writer Gregor Paul suggests it to be 'not inconceivable that come the 2011 World Cup, New Zealand, as hosts, kick-off the first game with a match-day 22 that consists solely of players who come from a Pacific Island background' (Paul, 2007b, p. 1).

In part, rugby merely reflects demographic change. During the most recent census in 2006, those identifying with the 'Pacific peoples' ethnic group numbered 265,974, up some 14.7 per cent from 2001. Moreover, the Pacific population is projected to grow by some 59 per cent, rising from 6 per cent to 9 per cent of all New Zealanders by 2021 (Statistics New Zealand, 2008). It is scarcely surprising, then, that rugby in New Zealand should in some way reflect this shifting social milieu. For some critics, however, the 'Polynesianization' of New Zealand rugby has less to do with population statistics than the work of avaricious administrators picking off and naturalizing the rugby talents of New Zealand's Pacific neighbours. While the English press have been the most vociferous proponents of such arguments (see, e.g., Butler, 2005; Gallagher, 2005; Morgan, 2005; Salmon, 2005; Slot, 2005), local journalists have at times been equally critical of the manner by which Pacific players have been recruited and assimilated into the New Zealand rugby system. One of the more striking examples is the prominent Pacific-based journalist Michael Field who likens the recruitment of Pacific schoolboy rugby players to the erstwhile practice of 'blackbirding', the slave-trading that occurred in the Pacific from the mid-1800s through to the early 1900s. As Field describes it:

> Blackbirders used to slip into harbours and lagoons with promises of good things over the horizon . . . [they] would lure people aboard ships, seize them and sail them off into a life of slavery. These days the techniques are different, but the outcome is the same: white men are grabbing Pacific Islanders, not for the sugar cane fields of Queensland, or the mines of Peru, but for the rugby grounds of the old colonialists.
>
> (Field, 2003, p. 1)

While the analogy may be a little overstated, Field is somewhat more accurate in recognizing the imbalance of power within South Pacific rugby. The degree may be open to question, but the 'host' nations of Australia and New Zealand have undoubtedly benefited in drawing from a larger Pacific-wide talent pool. Conversely, sentiment in the Islands echoes Arbena's description of Latin America wherein the recruitment of local players has contributed to 'a sense of loss, a feeling that the home country is being robbed of its own human and recreational resources' (Arbena, 1994, p. 103). For the Pacific Islands the migration of talent also raises the issue as to whether these outflows precipitate a 'de-skilling' of Islands' rugby, and, in turn, asks questions about the labour and recruiting practices involved. Are they magnanimous, in fostering personal and national 'development', or exploitative, in contributing to 'underdevelopment' or 'dependence'? Brought up, too, are interesting questions about notions of attachment to place and locality, of self-identity and allegiance and of the internal and external identity politics at play within and between host and 'donor' nations.

In this chapter I thus explore the origins, consequences and legacies of players moving from the 'less-developed' rugby nations of the Pacific to one of rugby's 'core economies' (Maguire, 2008, p. 449). I am interested, in particular, in the actors and institutions that contour the migrant trails of Pacific athletes. The ascension and affirmation of a neo-liberal model of free enterprise within the global sports system may, on the one hand, have opened up the labour market, producing, in turn, sports workers of high 'flexibility'. However, any gains in the freedom of movement must be set against those actions of key actors, including state agencies, trans-national corporations and sport associations, that seek to manage migration, that give rise to exploitative labour practices, and, ultimately, serve to reinforce the already-existing dominance of those holding the levers of power within global sport. As Maguire (2008, p. 451) has rightly noted, 'sport migration has its own highly differentiated political economy', and, thus, the progressive integration of the global sporting economy must not distract us from the persistent structural processes that underlie the production and reproduction of a global sporting labour reserve. Using the 'talent pipelines' (Falcous and Maguire, 2005, p. 141) of South Pacific rugby, I highlight these contradictory processes of economic openness, regulation and power and territorial closure within the global sport labour market.

Beyond subjective assessments of the impact of player migration on the field of play, I begin the chapter by first considering the 'impoverishment' of Pacific rugby in light of the imbalance of power within international rugby's current administrative and political structures. I suggest that the nature of the interactions between rugby's 'core' and its Pacific 'periphery' can only be understood in light of the way in which the undertones of imperialism, neo-imperialism and colonialism still resonate within the global development and regulation of rugby. The significant economic and political disparities between the Pacific and rugby's more powerful economies are, I contend, part of a wider historical process rooted in imperialist and neo-imperialist economic exploitation. As such, I consider how the traces of colonialism, particularly new forms of (bodily) colonization, operate in the present as a means by which to more fully understand rugby's Pacific labour market. Given that such markets are, in Maguire's (2008, p. 447) terms, 'multi-layered', in that they are constituted not merely by economic but also by political, historical, geographical, social and cultural factors, as an example below I assess the extent to which the relationship between New Zealand rugby and the game in its former Pacific 'colonies' can be explained in terms of cultural imperialism, colonial and neo-colonial exploitation and dependency. In order to demonstrate the present role of representations and ideologies rooted in colonial and neo-colonial encounters, I also consider how debates surrounding the flow of Pacific rugby labour are instances by which to highlight the constitutive role of the processes of racialized and ethnicized 'othering' in New Zealand. To borrow from Gilroy (2005, p. 21), it could be said that, with regard to how Pacific migrants are understood, rugby in New Zealand is an 'important site on which the limits of the nation as well as its character are routinely established'.

Exports, economics and eligibility: Pacific Island rugby's shrinking player pool

Writing on the eve of the opening test between Samoa and England in 2005, *The Independent* journalist Chris Hewett aptly suggested of Pacific Islands rugby that, while 'they may be talent-rich', they are 'cash-poor, [they] have no economic muscle' (Hewett, 2005). The disparity between rugby's powers and the Pacific was particularly stark at the most recent Rugby World Cup (RWC) in 2007. The All Blacks' campaign was estimated to have cost around NZ$50 million. The players flew to France first class, took charters to games in Scotland and Wales, stayed at a luxury hotel in Marseille's most salubrious suburb, and got to enjoy the beaches of Corsica during a stop-over en route. Samoa, on the other hand, arrived in Paris a week prior to kick-off without the money to pay their players' expenses. They were saved only when residents from Haute de Seine volunteered to take care of them, taking players to restaurants, paying for their drinks and arranging post-training outings to the city's famous landmarks. Though it seems an extraordinary episode for a national sporting side, Samoa's experience in France was hardly atypical for teams from the Pacific. Money is, of course, the most obvious root. In

2005, for instance, the Fijian Rugby Union (FRU) was approximately F$4 million short of its budget, even after a six-figure injection from the Fijian government. Tonga, A$300,000 in the red, was forced to take out a A$150,000 bank loan after exhausting its annual budget on World Cup qualifiers and participation in the International Rugby Board's (IRB) World Sevens Series. Meanwhile, in Samoa, the secretary of the Samoan Rugby Football Union (SRFU) described the organization as 'barely in the black' (Gregory, 2004).

As well as lacking the professional infrastructure and financial resources to pay players salaries that might encourage them to remain at home, other matters have made it increasingly difficult for Pacific unions to put together cohesive, well-prepared, successful national squads. Since rugby went professional in 1995, for instance, there have been a growing number of 'club-versus-country' disputes involving players eligible to represent Pacific Island nations. Many such players are now frequently opting to 'remain with overseas club sides for financial reasons' ('IRB admits club problem', 2003) – further diluting an already weakened talent pool. It is difficult, if not impossible, to be critical of such decisions when one considers the case in point of the Samoan national squad that was once rumoured to be paying players £12-a-day while on tour. To be fair, the IRB has recently instigated a series of measures designed to ensure 'that every country is able to select their best team, that they are not forced to leave players behind because those players may be threatened with the loss of their contract' ('ARU wants to stop club pressure', 2003). In many instances, however, the measures seem to have had little effect. Most notably, though clubs in member unions of the IRB are 'duty bound' to release players for the RWC, they are not obliged to carry on paying them. The result is that players from poorer Pacific unions often 'feel trapped between taking a pay cut or playing in the World Cup' ('Raiwalui rejects Fiji appeal', 2003). As an example, at the 2003 RWC, Samoa, Fiji and Georgia were all 'hit by players opting to stay with their clubs rather than play in Australia' ('IRB should pay players', 2003). Most affected were Samoa who lost key forwards Trevor Leota and Henry Tuilagi. As Leota explained it, pulling out was a matter of simple economics:

> I worked out that I would lose more than $NZ70,270 in earnings if I went to Australia [to play in the RWC] . . . All the Samoan players get is $NZ561 a week when the competition starts and that did not begin to compare with what Wasps pay me. I had to think of my wife and kids, and they will always come first.
>
> (quoted in 'Raiwalui rejects Fiji appeal', 2003)

Ostensibly, Pacific players are protected by Articles 9.1 and 9.2 of the IRB's 'Regulations of the Game' that afford national unions with 'first and last call upon the availability of a Player' and prevent any 'Union, Association, Rugby Body or Club whether by contract or otherwise' from 'inhibit[ing], prevent[ing] or render[ing] unavailable any player from selection, attendance and appearance in a National Representative Team or National Squad'. While laudable in intent, such rules have only ever been loosely enforced – particularly in the case of Pacific players. By way of illustration, former coach Pat Lam has described how he had to fight 'tooth and nail' (quoted in 'European clubs pressured Islanders players', 2006) to get European clubs to release players for the Pacific Islanders 2006 tour of Wales, Scotland and Ireland. The lack of willingness on the part of both Australasian and European clubs to release their players was also highlighted by the revised start date for Pacific Six Nations (PSN) in 2007. With the IRB pulling the start forward to 19 May, the PSN clashed with the Super 14 and European club games, with the first two rounds of the competition also falling outside the IRB 'test window'. According to a number of Pacific players, British clubs threatened to impose severe financial penalties or terminate contracts if they chose to play for their country over their club (Paul, 2007c). Considered to be 'critical preparation time of the World Cup' (Paul, 2007c), the tournament consequently started without its best players.

Pacific unions have been further hampered in their access to top players by changes to the IRB's national eligibility rules. The impact of these laws on Pacific players has long been a talking point in world rugby, and they become particularly troublesome in and around the quadrennial cycle of the RWC. In 2003, for instance, the then Samoan coach Michael Jones frequently used press conferences to highlight what he described as 'the very real issues' facing Pacific Islands rugby (quoted in 'Iceman highlights Pacific plight', 2003). He has been particularly critical of the new eligibility regulations which essentially bar players from representing more than one country during their careers:

> A Player who has played for the senior fifteen-a-side National Representative Team or the next senior fifteen-a-side National Representative Team or the senior National Representative Sevens Team of a Union is not eligible to play for the senior fifteen-a-side National Representative Team or the next senior fifteen-a-side National Representative Team or the senior National Representative Sevens Team of another Union.
>
> (Section 8.2 from the IRB's *Regulation 8: Eligibility to Play for National Representative Teams*)

While the code was only amended in the wake of the 'Grannygate Affair' surrounding former All Black Shane Howarth later turning out for Wales (see Hewett, 2000), it has arguably had more effect in 'impacting negatively on weaker rugby nations such as the Pacific Islands' ('Former All Blacks challenge IRB', 2002, p. 25). The most obvious example is the way in which young Pacific Island migrants have been 'captured' within the New Zealand system as a result of the new laws. As Souster (2001: paras 5–6) explains:

> Talented players head to New Zealand at an early age to chase the All Black dream and the Kiwi dollar . . . When their dreams collapse they find themselves in international limbo for the rest of their careers. Players who might have played only ten minutes for the New Zealand Sevens side but who will never become regulars are effectively stymied.

Similarly, Jones has argued of Samoa that:

> There are Samoan players who could play a vital role for us, but because they've played 30 minutes in a New Zealand jersey, even if it's New Zealand A or even a sevens team, we can't touch them. . . . These guys are left floundering, playing provincial rugby for the rest of their lives when they could be playing in a World Cup for Samoa, the ultimate.
>
> (quoted in Woollard, 2001: paras 11–12)

The nature of professional contracts in New Zealand has further exacerbated the issue. In the first instance, anyone seeking a Super 14 contract must first commit his international future to the All Blacks. The New Zealand Rugby Union's (NZRU) justification is that having too many players ineligible to play for New Zealand 'will limit selection choices for the All Blacks . . . which is the NZRU's number one priority' (Logan and Rees, 2006, p. 15). However, there have been a growing number of cases testament to Jones' claim that '[the NZRU] deliberately selected Samoan players to represent a sevens team, or the New Zealand A team, thus disqualifying them from ever representing their country of origin' ('Jones hits NZRFU over "abuses"', 2003). Jones' contention is echoed by other Pacific-based administrators who believe one reason why the All Blacks and New Zealand age-group selectors pick so many Pacific players is to ensure they are eligible to play exclusively for the All Blacks (see Gregory, 2004; Hewett, 2005). While this may increase the playing depth in New Zealand, Pacific nations have had to watch on as players 'no longer required for the All Blacks, are unable to finish their careers playing for the nation they were born in' ('Helping out Samoa', 2003, p. 8). Notably, a proposal to relax the eligibility rules so that players who represent 'Tier One' nations such as New Zealand could later play for 'Tier Two' nations such as Samoa, Tonga or Fiji was also rejected at a recent IRB Full Council meeting.

That the IRB has failed to address the more pressing issues facing Pacific rugby is perhaps hardly surprising, given the enormous power gap within the organization. Of the 20 teams that played in the 2007 RWC, eight were non-voting members of the IRB, and while 95 unions are affiliated, only 13 of them have voting powers on the IRB Council, the eight founding unions of the IRB having two votes each. With regard to the Pacific, while Fiji, Tonga and Samoa attend the Council's meetings, they do so only as 'observers'. As the former Pacific Islanders Rugby Alliance (PIRA) chief executive Charlie Charters has suggested, '[The IRB] has become a pretty exclusive lot, and the sad thing is, there's no sign of this changing' (quoted in Pareti, 2004). Paternalism on the IRB's behalf is perhaps not unexpected in light of the undertones of 'imperialism' that seem to readily resonate in their intercourse with Pacific rugby. Arguably, the body is still underpinned by an ethnocentric view of 'development' in which economic and cultural hegemony is centred in the European core. There are other areas, too, in which what Maguire *et al.* (2002, p. 34) describe as the 'residual impact of colonial links' are apparent. Samoa is, again, a useful illustration. Despite the fact that the country gained independence in 1962, the exodus of Samoan players continues to follow a pattern which mirrors imperial connections. In addition, there is room to suggest that Samoan talent migration to New Zealand can likewise be interpreted as a form of cultural (neo)imperialism. New Zealand's exploitation of labour power and material resources is perhaps clear. But, New Zealand rugby could also be charged with producing a malignant *cultural* effect. There appears, in particular, to be a growing 'devaluation' of Samoan rugby. Competing for New Zealand, or now even a professional club side, has increasingly become more important than representing one's own country. In a recent piece on the present difficulties faced by Samoan rugby, *The New Zealand Herald* quotes one New Zealand-bound schoolboy player as admitting that 'of course' he would rather play for the All Blacks than Manu Samoa (quoted in Gregory, 2004).

Nations, knowledge and perceptions of Pacific rugby migrants

The examples immediately above are a useful introduction to how the paternalistic treatment of Pacific rugby relies on practices built on particular representations of the Pacific and Pacific Islanders, and that are ultimately implicated in the production of meanings and identities. It is important in this regard to consider how the Pacific, Pacific Islanders and Pacific peoples have been discursively represented by administrators, policy-makers and journalists. Thinking in terms of representational practices calls our attention, for instance, to an economy of abstract binary oppositions that are routinely drawn upon to describe the status and development of Pacific rugby in relation to the IRB's elite. Developed/underdeveloped, Tier One/Tier Two, advanced/behind, modern/traditional and superior/inferior are just a few that readily come to mind. Such discursive constructions are arguably 'crucial to the sustainability of particular relations of power and subordination' (Slater, 2004, p. 19). The liberal international economic order of the global sporting system and the unequal relations that result are affirmed and perpetuated by a neo-colonialist ideology that views the Northern and Southern Hemisphere powers as 'rightly' and 'naturally' dominant over those, such as the Pacific Island unions, who, in turn, lack the same economic and political strength. As much as the Pacific's subordinate position within international rugby results from a set of unequal relationships of dependency and power, it is the production of knowledge and identities, and of representations, that in many ways make these various courses of action possible.

It is perhaps illustrative to consider one of the more striking features of discursive practices as they relate to rugby in the Pacific: the denial of effective agency to the Pacific Islands and Islanders themselves. In particular, the representation of the Pacific Other within world rugby reflects historically dominant forms of enframing non-Western others that tie race and geography to cultural, political and economic traits deemed inferior to those from more, so-called, developed nations. Most notable is the symbolic significance of the Pacific body, and in this regard it is important to consider the way in which Western culture has long commodified and traded in images of Pacific Otherness (see Brislin, 2003; Edmond, 1997). Young

Pacific rugby players have in many ways been similarly commodified, becoming, to quote Bale and Maguire (1994, p. 16), 'the equivalent of the cash crops which they sell in other sectors of the world economy'. In essence, the young Pacific player is reduced to a body, the body to a commodity, and as such the player becomes dehumanized, quantifiable, absorbed into the world of markets of productive exchange (Bale and Maguire, 1994; Maguire, 1999). In rugby, like the South Pacific labour market generally, the Pacific body is a source of physical labour, a commodity to be bought and sold to the highest, or most prestigious, bidder.

Bringing together the ideas of latent Eurocentric imperialism and the way in which forms of representation and their production are linked to power relations, there seems to be an obvious analogy between talent migration in rugby and the history of broader labour migration from the Pacific to New Zealand. What is perhaps most salient to the present analysis is the complex combination of race and belonging that has informed migration policy and understandings of citizenship and national identity in New Zealand. These wider attitudes and responses to Pacific Island labourers in many ways provide a telling context for understanding the migration of Pacific rugby players to New Zealand, their recruitment and exploitation, and, in turn, the consequent under-development of Pacific rugby. In brief, while New Zealand's relationship with the Pacific Islands dates back to the era of British imperialism, the mass migration of Pacific Islanders to New Zealand began in the 1960s. Emigration from this time was a function of population growth, limited resources and the lack of economic opportunities at home, as well as the growing demand for labour within New Zealand's rapidly expanding economy. The New Zealand government also coveted the Pacific Islands as a source of cheap, 'unskilled' labour. By the 1970s, however, as the country faced an economic downturn, New Zealanders became increasingly nervous at the number of immigrants arriving from the Pacific Islands. Rising unemployment and the budding recession led to accusations that migrants were inflating unemployment figures or taking the jobs of poorly qualified 'native' New Zealanders. As economic conditions deteriorated, Pacific Islanders, 'being more visible than other groups, became a convenient scapegoat for some of the economic problems facing the country' (Krishnan *et al.*, 1994, p. 78).

An initial response was the introduction of stricter controls over entry and a crackdown on so-called 'overstayers'. In both instances, and as Bedford (2003) has identified, it became 'much easier to focus attention on potential "brown" overstayers from the Cook Islands, Fiji, Niue, Samoa and Tonga than to try to find "white" overstayers from the UK and Europe'. Certainly, the racially biased implementation of immigration regulations was apparent in the dawn raids on homes of people belonging to Pacific Island communities and in random street checks of people who appeared to belong to a Pacific Island ethnic group (Spoonley, 1990). Paul Gilroy has noted how, in Britain during the 1970s, '"immigrant" became synonymous with the word "black"'. In similar fashion in New Zealand during this same period, 'immigrant' became synonymous with 'Pacific Islander' (Gilroy, 1987, p. 46). Irrespective of citizenship or residency status, as Mitchell (2003, p. 139) argues, 'there was an implicit assumption of what a New Zealander was and that Pacific Islanders in New Zealand collectively fell outside of this definition'.

Even today some of the social stigma of being once undesirable immigrants clearly persists in the discursive framing of Pacific peoples. Though they are clearly at 'home' in New Zealand, given that migration from the Pacific peaked many years ago and that some 60 per cent of the Pacific population were born in New Zealand, one of the identifiable and recurring themes of 'dominant discourse' (see McCreanor, 2005) is continued allusions to Pacific peoples as 'foreign', as Others. References to Pacific people as 'overstayers', 'coconuts', 'bungas' or 'FOBs' ('fresh off the boat') may not be as common as during the 1970s perhaps, yet as Loto *et al.* (2006, p. 100) have found, 'the legacy of a domineering relationship between the Palagi [people of European descent] majority group and Pacific minorities that is captured by such derogatory terms is still evident in public forums'. Put simply, citizenship has not been sufficient for Pacific peoples to transcend the prejudices of race. Even Pacific All Blacks – generally the emblematic national icon – are not necessarily immune to this 'perpetual foreigner syndrome' (Wu, 2002, p. 79). In one telling example after the All Black team for the 2003 World Cup was named, a caller to a local talk back show aporetically asked, 'Why in a country where we have so much rugby talent do we have to select four Samoans in the All Blacks?' (quoted in Romanos, 2002).

Historically and materially, then, Pacific peoples have played a crucial role in building and sustaining New Zealand identity. In particular, as 'immigrants' they have been 'fundamental to the construction of the nation as a simulacrum of inclusiveness' (Lowe, 1996, p. 5). Yet this project of imagining the nation is haunted by the fact that Pacific peoples are still seen as 'the foreigner within', even when born in New Zealand and the descendants of past generation New Zealanders (Lowe, 1996).

Conclusion: national thinking, trans-national reality

As Paul Darby has noted in his analyses of African football, it is difficult to assess the true impact of sports migration on 'donor' countries (Darby, 2000, 2002, 2005, 2007). This could be an equally accurate description of the consequences of migration for Pacific Islands' rugby. However, it is nonetheless apparent that Pacific unions are increasingly hamstrung by the fragile economic and political conditions which confront them and to which the talent exodus has been an obvious contributing factor. In addition, while rugby certainly provides a small number of young Pacific Islanders with the opportunity to further their education or careers through scholarships or professional contracts, they seldom return to the Islands, often choosing instead to declare themselves eligible for the country – frequently New Zealand – in which they ply their trade. As the Samoan-based journalist Peter Rees suggests, Pacific Island unions have seemingly of late become 'no more than feeders for the Wallabies and All Blacks, a production line guaranteed to keep them strong' (Rees, 2005). There is cause to wonder too about the inflexibility of the IRB on the matter of eligibility laws as they relate to so-called Tier Two nations. Arguably, relaxing these laws for players from, or eligible to play for, Pacific Island nations would do more for the strength of Pacific rugby than their current strategy of cash-injections and development programmes. While the IRB deserves praise for implementing its 'three-year global strategic investment programme aimed at driving the competitiveness of the global game' (Federation of Oceania Rugby Unions, 2008), one wonders whether Pacific nations may improve even quicker if they were accorded greater flexibility and power in choosing qualified players.

Also problematic is the narrow sense in which organizations such as the IRB and NZRU define citizenship and determine national eligibility, both of which, ultimately, have had counterproductive effects for Pacific Island unions. These regulations largely assume a taken-for-granted way of looking at citizenship and migration from the point of view of the nation-state; in essence, the nation is taken as the point of departure, with the measure of residence requiring renunciation of one's previous national identity or loyalty. This is perhaps unsurprising given how migration has long been popularly and politically conceived. As Lie (2001, p. 355) argues, traditional views of migration have 'presumed a particular imaginary of population movement' in which the sojourn is seen as singular and irreversible: migration becomes a passage wherein 'people uproot themselves from their country of origin and restake themselves in the land of destination'. In short, Lie rightly identifies how the language of migration has privileged permanence rather than transience. As historically and popularly understood, 'true' migration has been seen to involve 'settling into a routine in a particular locale as opposed to acting as a temporary visitor' (Block, 2005, p. 8). Residence and citizenship, too, have historically been defined in terms of a connection between the individual and the nation-state wherein 'the dominant understanding of citizenship in modern times has . . . been shaped by conceptions of nationality' (Delanty, 1995, p. 160). For a growing number of migrants, generally and within the world of sport, however, the tenets of unilineal assimilation are becoming less relevant. Increasingly, 'migrants' maintain, build and reinforce multiple linkages with their countries of origin and destination and travel in circuits rather than in a route from 'origin' to 'destination'. Given that, as Sua'rez-Orozco (2001, p. 187) argues, 'the old straight-line model of thinking about assimilation and national cultures is, in some ways, being bypassed by the globalized, trans-nationalized strategies that the new immigrants deploy', there is at least some basis for arguing that governing bodies need to come up with new eligibility criteria that are not based solely on nationality or citizenship given how problematic eligibility issues are likely to become in the future.

Such issues have particular pertinence for Pacific peoples, given their migratory traditions and their tendency to live as part of what Macpherson (1997, p. 96) refers to as 'meta-societies' – trans-national societies that are formed to encompass highly dynamic systems of free movement of people, ideas and practices between various localities. As the eminent Tongan sociologist Epeli Hau'ofa suggests in a description that has both historical and contemporary relevance for understanding contemporary mobility in the South Pacific, 'so much of the welfare of ordinary people in Oceania depends on an informal movement along ancient routes drawn in bloodlines invisible to the enforcers of the laws of confinement and regulated mobility' (Hau'ofa, 1993, p. 11). In his seminal and by now universally quoted article, 'Our Sea of Islands', Hau'ofa has argued that those in the West misunderstand the Pacific by consistently envisioning the ocean in terms of 'islands in a far sea' (Hau'ofa, 1993, p. 7). In Hau'ofa's view, however, Pacific peoples have always existed in a world of blurred boundaries, of connections between Islanders beyond and within nation-states. An obvious criticism of policy-making within world rugby, then, is that it takes no account of such indigenous knowledge.

As much as Hau'ofa provides a corrective of history, his argument resonates with not only the long-term migration patterns of the past but also present-day lifeworlds. In particular, there is growing evidence of an emergent 'diasporic Pacific' well captured in the increasing use of terms such as Tagata Pasifika – a designation inclusive of multiple Pacific subjects, citizens and identities. Generally used to describe 'the people from the various nations who make up the range of Pacific people's communities in New Zealand' (Community–Government Relationship Steering Group, 2002, p. 34), the use of Tagata Pasifika, or sometimes merely Pasifika, in reference to a collective identity, has become increasingly common in both political practice and popular culture. Pasifika could be described as an emergent form of 'diasporic nationalism' (Lie, 2001) that 'transforms ethnicity' and 'locate[s] migrants and diasporic subjects within global rather than national landscapes' (Madan, 2000, pp. 24–35). In this way, Tagata Pasifika is a trans-national affiliation which provides a means for 'contestation over local discourses of power and race' (Fernandes, 2003, p. 576).

Ironically, in this light rugby within Pacific communities may offer a potentially crucial site for the political mobilization of identity categories such as Tagata Pasifika. A prime example is the Pacific Islanders rugby team which, although it faces many of the same economic and political hurdles outlined above, may lead to greater economic and sporting autonomy, while simultaneously promoting new diasporic affiliations between disparate Pacific Island communities and nations. Granted test status by the IRB in 2004, the Islanders are a combined side made up of players from the three member unions of the Pacific Islanders Rugby Alliance (PIRA) – Samoa, Tonga and Fiji. Arguably, in drawing players from dispersed Pacific populations, this Pasifika side both problematizes IRB criteria of citizenship and further questions historical conceptions of national eligibility and inclusiveness. Given that the coalitional politics of post-nationalism, trans-nationalism and nationalism are dependent on situational context (see Hall, 1990; Madan, 2000), Pacific rugby players, and perhaps even the All Blacks themselves, may offer a means by which to undermine identities such as 'Samoan', 'Tongan', 'Fijian' or 'New Zealander'. The diasporic culture being articulated through, and negotiated within, rugby may offer new trajectories, names and labels to which Pacific peoples may identify. While there is certainly a need for both the IRB and the Pacific unions to work towards creating the financial incentives and development routes that might persuade elite Pacific players that their future lies in the Pacific, it is nonetheless possible that increasing migratory flows may actually be culturally and politically empowering for the wider Pacific community. Just as

Madan (2000, pp. 28–9) has noted of cricket within the diasporic Indian communities of the Commonwealth, rugby for Pacific peoples similarly serves as

> a place, space, and discourse through which collectives located outside the national sphere can negotiate the postcolonial ideologies of race and nation that define their subjectivity and identity . . . [Rugby is] a situational context or space in which diasporic agendas and coalitional politics are articulated.

However, while rugby may provide a space for the performance of new Pacific identity practices and for the expression of diasporic discourses, the way in which organizations such as the IRB and NZRU continue to discipline, control and regulate both the movement and 'citizenship' of Pacific peoples suggests that the discursive boundaries of diasporic subjecthood continue to be defined by transnational political structures. Thus, while identifying oneself as Pasifika may involve identifying with a widely dispersed emigrant population, a global – or even regional – community which increasingly recognizes each Pacific Island nation's place within a wider Pacific diaspora, the arrangements and organizations of both the nation-state and global sporting capitalism still provide the context within which such an identity is both structured and negotiated. However much rugby offers a symbolic space for Pacific peoples to challenge dominant projections of community, nationality and citizenship, it would be a utopian take on global talent migration that sees a levelling out of inequality resulting from players and populations becoming more mobile or communities more flexible. We need to acknowledge the continuing salience of nationally and internationally structured power relations and the ways in which such power relations inhibit or facilitate the migration choices of Pacific peoples. In particular, if the trade in Pacific players is to be properly regulated then the cooperation of organizations such as the IRB and NZRU as well as clubs in both Europe and Australasia remains crucial. Sadly, in a context where both clubs and nations are seeking to both improve their success on the field and maximize their profits off it, it is highly likely that those from rugby's more powerful, core nations will continue in their pro-active drive to seek out cheap, talented recruits from the Pacific. Furthermore, so long as the connections between relations of power and modes of representation and knowledge remain unexamined in world rugby, talent migration will only continue to form part of the unequal relationship between rugby's power-brokers and those facing an uncertain future on the Pacific periphery.

Note

1 'Pacific peoples' is the official term used by the state sector to describe those people residing in New Zealand who identify as being migrants or descendants of migrants from the Pacific Islands. In popular usage, and particularly within the media, Pacific peoples is often used interchangeably with 'Polynesian' or 'Pacific Islanders', a tendency I try to avoid here given these latter terms problematically gloss over the diversity in languages and cultures that exists between Polynesian, Melanesian and Micronesian communities.

10 Blade runners

Canadian migrants and European ice hockey

Joseph Maguire

Focusing on Canadian 'blade runners' this chapter examines several interconnected issues that frame both the migrants and people from the host culture's experiences of ice hockey in the global sports arena. These issues, which have both intended and unintended features, involve issues of recruitment, retention and release and are closely connected to problems of motivation, adjustment, dislocation and foreign sojourn. Questions of labour rights, work permits and salary caps also impinge on the migrant experience. It is intended here to examine the broad pattern of Canadian male ice hockey labour migration and then to focus on the experience of these migrants in one country, Great Britain (GB). Developments in British ice hockey are used as a 'critical case' to highlight the issues, problems and tensions associated with migrants in global sport processes.[1] For further discussion of British ice hockey see Elliott and Maguire (2008).

Canadian ice hockey players as part of global labour migration

The migration of talented athletes as athletic labour currently is a pronounced feature of global flows that contour and shape global sportization processes that include not only the flow of people with different habitus and identities but also the flow of technologies, media images and finance. This labour process is interwoven with the commodification of sports within the capitalist world economy. Migrants are not unlike other sectors of the workforce who, for several reasons, have to ply their trade in various locations. Elite athletes as a group experience varying degrees of exploitation and dislocation, but they also enjoy some personal gains (Maguire and Stead, 1996). Whatever advantages there are, they appear to flow along gender lines, given that the global migration of sports labour predominantly, although not exclusively, involves men. In some sports such as golf, tennis, track and field and, to a lesser extent, basketball, women are travelling more frequently and in increasing numbers. Despite this, the dominant trend of men moving more freely and in greater numbers over time and across space is based on a patriarchal structure that ensures that it is usually women who perform domestic and reproductive labour, whether in the company of their travelling partners or waiting 'at home' (Massey, 1994). Although it is important to explore

the lived migrant experience to understand how the individual interprets relocation, dislocation and the sense of being an outsider in an established culture, it is
also necessary to use a conceptual framework that avoids separating this experience from 'glocal' (i.e. local and global, interconnected) cultural processes. The
ethnographic description must be placed on a wider conceptual canvas. In a
similar vein, in discussing how the life of Mozart must be understood as part of
an analysis of court society, Elias (1994, p. 14) outlined the approach that underpins the present investigation:

> One needs to be able to draw a clear picture of the social pressures acting
> on the individual. Such a study is not a historical narrative but the elabora-
> tion of a verifiable model of the figuration which a person – in this case an
> eighteenth-century artist – formed through his interdependence with other
> social figures of his time.

In examining court society more broadly, Elias also observed that neither the
development of Louis XIV as an individual nor his actions as a king can be
understood adequately without reference to a sociological model of court society
and without knowledge of the development of his social position within its structure (Elias, 1983). In keeping with this approach, in this section I locate labour
migration as part of wider 'glocal' sport processes. In this way, I try to map the
main features of a sociological model within which to locate the individual
Canadian ice hockey migrant.

Discernible national patterns can be identified in the recruitment and subsequent retention of people in sports such as American football, baseball, basketball, cricket, ice hockey, track and field and soccer (Bale and Maguire, 1994).
Sports labour migration also occurs between countries located within the same
continent. Witness the involvement of citizens of the United States in 'Canadian'
baseball teams and of athletes from the Dominican Republic in 'American' baseball teams (Klein, 1991). A similar trend is also evident on a transcontinental level.
Movement of sports labour occurs between North America and Europe in sports
such as American football, basketball and ice hockey (Genest, 1994; Maguire,
1990, 1994a). Sports labourers tend to be 'hired' by a specific club or organization, and individuals reside in the host country for a limited period of time. Some
athletes also stay on and make the host country their 'home'. This occurs either
through marriage to a citizen of that country or by having established residence
in a specific country for a sufficient length of time to qualify for nationality status.
Sometimes, such as in European basketball, individuals begin to play for the
country in which they have become resident and from which they subsequently
claim 'nationality' (Maguire, 1994b). From the evidence at hand, these issues
repeatedly surface and permeate the lives of elite labour migrants (Bale and
Maguire, 1994).

In certain sports, such as cricket and rugby league, migration has a seasonal
pattern. The northern and southern hemispheres offer, in specific sports such
as cricket, two seasons of continuous play. Other sports migrants experience a

transitory form of migration. Sometimes a seasonal and a transitory migration pattern interweave, as with golf and tennis players (Bale and Maguire, 1994). Golf and tennis players are arguably *the* nomads of the sports labour migration process, with constantly shifting workplaces and places of residence. Although both men and women have their global circuits, the enabling and constraining features of this experience may be markedly different. To frame more effectively what follows, a preliminary typology of sport labour migration was identified but the point was also made that the categories identified are not rigid and that, in the lived experience of migrants, these dimensions overlap and shade together in different combinations (Maguire, 1999).

Those migrants identified as sport 'pioneers' possess an almost evangelical zeal in extolling the virtues of their respective sports (Bromberger, 1994). Their words and actions can be seen as a form of proselytizing by which they seek to convert the natives to their body habitus and sports culture. Similarly, some migrants can be identified as 'settlers' who not only bring their sports with them but are sports migrants who subsequently stay and settle in the society where they ply their labour (Lanfranchi, 1994). Other migrants can be viewed as 'mercenaries' who are motivated more by short-term gains and are employed as 'hired guns' (Maguire, 1993). These migrants have little or no attachment to the local, no sense of *Heimat* in relation to the place where they currently reside or do their body work. By contrast, some migrants are 'nomads' who are more motivated by a cosmopolitan engagement with migration. They use their sports careers to journey; they embark on quests in which they seek the experience of the 'other' and indeed of being the other; that is, in Simmel's terms, of being, for example, a stranger in a foreign metropolitan culture (Maguire and Stead, 1996). In English soccer, overseas players such as Eric Cantona and Jurgen Klinsmann typify the cosmopolitan stranger. But the stranger may also seek to journey away from the city. Surfers, snowboarders and participants in 'extreme' sports all share the desire to explore the experience of difference and diversity. Yet some cosmopolitans, along with pioneers, mercenaries and even long-term settlers, act as returnees in the global process. The lure of home soil can prove too strong. Although this typology required, and still requires, further investigation, in this context the typology was used to map out the pattern of Canadian migration as part of global ice hockey competition.

Canadian players as part of the global ice hockey circuit

Whereas the economic core of ice hockey can be located in North America and with the National Hockey League (NHL) in particular, the sport also flourishes in Europe and in parts of Asia. With the exception of the NHL, global ice hockey is under the jurisdiction of the International Ice Hockey Federation (IIHF). Transfers between federations have to be recorded with the governing body. Examining data drawn from the files located at the Zurich headquarters of the IIHF, a quite discernible pattern to the import and export of players across the globe is evident. The main exporters of ice hockey players during the 1990s have been Canada and the former Soviet Union (Maguire, 1996). The migration of former Soviet citizens is, in part, accountable to the collapse of that state and the consequent 'internal' migration between former Soviet republics. In addition, however, Russians and Ukrainians in particular have been flooding to the West. This movement parallels a similar process that has occurred in soccer (Duke, 1994). The main importer was the unified German Republic. Note, too, that clubs in Great Britain were also major recruiters. If attention is given to the 1994–5 season, 34 per cent of migrants come from Canada, whereas Germany and Great Britain import some 40 per cent and 12 per cent, respectively, of the total number of migrants (Maguire, 1996). Of the 433 Canadians who migrated abroad during the 1994–5 season, Germany (31 per cent) and Great Britain (26 per cent) take the lion's share of these player transfers (Maguire, 1996). During the 1990s, Canadians made up, on average, 33 per cent of the total number of migrants on the global ice hockey circuit (Maguire, 1996).

It is impossible to determine, on the basis of this data, why these migrants moved. It is feasible to speculate that the main motivation of those players who moved from the former Eastern bloc involved either a desire to relocate and settle in the West or to earn as much 'hard currency' as they could in a short period of time and then return home. In terms of the migrant types identified, former Eastern bloc citizens act as settlers or as mercenaries. The pattern of Canadian migration reflects a blend of economic, cultural, ethnic and political factors and involves a combination of all five types of migrants identified (Maguire, 1999). Monocausal explanations do not capture the complexity of what is involved. A series of seemingly contradictory dynamics appear to be taking place. For example, the more economically powerful ice hockey leagues of mainland Europe (Germany, Switzerland and Italy) attract a higher calibre migrant player who may be motivated more by short-term economic gains. Yet this pattern is also contoured by cultural factors. French Canadians tend to travel along talent flow lines whose destinations are French-speaking areas of Europe. Here a more cosmopolitan style may be at work. There is also a process of differential recruitment and perception by the potential host cultures. Italy actively recruits Canadians for both the domestic game and the national team. The Swedes, by contrast, appear to be more protective of their 'national game'; and the degree of recruitment of Canadians is less than it is in other top Western European countries. Until recently, only one foreign migrant was allowed per team.

Largely on account of the demise of the Soviet Union and the Eastern bloc, ice hockey clubs in Russia, the Czech Republic and the Ukraine simply did not have the economic or cultural capital available to recruit Western European or Canadian migrants. The recruitment patterns were dominated by Western European countries. Despite the SM-*Liiga* in Finland and the *Elitserien* in Sweden being regarded as the premier leagues in terms of standards of play, it is to Germany and Great Britain that the vast majority of Canadians travelled. In Great Britain in particular, where a lower standard of play was evident and where the sport continues to have marginal status, the migrant can seek and play the role of pioneer, promoting the virtues of ice hockey. The flow of Canadian migrants across the Atlantic is not, then, simply an economic affair. Migration is also contoured in the case of France, Great Britain, Italy and the Nordic countries, to cite just these examples, along lines of ethnic heritage. By claiming cultural affinity and nationality status, migrants are able to navigate a route through the thicket of eligibility regulations and quotas developed by sports organizations, national governments and the European Union (EU). In considering this overall movement, Jan-Ake Edvinsson, IIHF general secretary, observed:

> It's a problem for the sport itself . . . Then if a new player comes to a new country and plays for a team, he takes the place of one junior. And we like to develop ice hockey from as many countries as we can . . . There should not be such a big movement.
> (Interview with the author, Zurich, March 1995)

This issue of dependent development is particularly evident in Great Britain. Canadian migrants were also joined in British ice hockey by a growing number of East Europeans. This prompted a quite defensive ethnic response from Canadian migrants. In addition, very few Western Europeans, Swedes, Finns, Germans or Swiss have ever played in British ice hockey; it is basically a Canadian preserve and this situation has not changed (Elliott and Maguire, 2008). Given this, it is appropriate to note that, in a perhaps not unrelated development, the number of Canadians playing in the NHL has declined from 97 per cent in 1967 to 75 per cent in 1988. By the 1993 season, some 17 per cent of the NHL players were now European and the number of Canadians had fallen to some 66 per cent (MacGregor, 1993, p. 48).

It is also important to observe that, during the 1994 NHL lockout, many European players, acting as returnees, sought to return home and play for their former clubs on a temporary basis. The IIHF, which recently signed an agreement with the NHL in which the latter agreed to support the development of ice hockey outside North America, sanctioned this return migration. Given the Swedish desire to protect their home players and their correlative reluctance to recruit Canadian migrants, it is perhaps less surprising that the Swedish Ice Hockey Association refused to allow former Swedish-based players to return and play on a temporary basis. Given both this sociological model of labour migration and the general substantive background outlined, attention is now given to one specific case study to bring the various tensions and issues that surround labour migration in general, and ice hockey players in particular, into sharper relief.

Canadian players as part of British ice hockey subculture

Canadians have had a long involvement in British ice hockey. For example, British-born players who learned their ice hockey in Canada had a significant impact during 1935–6 when Great Britain became the first team to win the Triple

Crown of Olympic, World and European Championships (Drackett, 1987). This success was to assist in the launch of a postwar British ice hockey boom that would last through to the late 1950s. During this phase, Canadian-born players made an increasingly important contribution. By contrast, from the late 1950s through to the early 1980s, British ice hockey experienced long-term decline. From this point on, however, and in a series of moves that have several parallels with developments then occurring in British basketball (Maguire, 1988), ice hockey exponents sought to establish its place among other marginal sports in the 'glocal' marketplace. In tackling phenomena of this kind, we need ideally to trace how the present ice hockey formation is connected to the structured processes that have characterized its development during this century. More broadly, we need to do for British ice hockey what Kidd (1981), Gruneau and Whitson (1993) and Aldskogius (1993) have done on the developments in Canada and Sweden.

For present purposes, however, consideration is given to the post-1990 period of British ice hockey. During this period, the British team unexpectedly gained promotion from Pool C to Pool A of world ice hockey. Subsequently, the team was relegated to Pool B. In addition, unusual success in qualification tournaments brought the national side to the final elimination stage for gaining a place at the 1994 Winter Olympics in Lillehammer, Norway. Further, the domestic game underwent restructuring with the formation of a premier league. Finally, during the same period, the NHL arranged preseason exhibition games involving major league teams in Great Britain (e.g. the Toronto Maple Leafs), and moves were under way for closer links between the NHL and the IIHF (e.g. negotiations to include NHL/professional players in Olympic ice hockey in Nagano, Japan, in 1998). In each of these areas, the roles of media coverage, sponsorship revenue and the involvement of overseas migrants figured prominently. Using these events, the issues, problems and tensions associated with migrants in global sport processes can be highlighted. In considering Canadian ice hockey migration, an examination of the occupational subculture that considers coaching strategies, playing styles and instrumental forms of violence is also required. The problematic nationality status of Canadian migrants in British ice hockey is also a powerful feature of the figuration in question. Simply put, the result of this long-term process is that GB players increasingly 'ride the pine' while the 'Canucks' dominate the ice time.

The Canucks: desires, dreams and reliving 'glory days'

The recruitment of Canadians was interwoven with the commodification and restructuring of the game that occurred during the 1980s and early 1990s. The reasons offered for the recruitment of Canadians into British ice hockey are, as noted, similar to the sentiments expressed about the involvement of Americans in British basketball during the same period (Maguire, 1988). Exponents argue that their presence will provide a better product to sell to a live audience, media networks and potential sponsors. In addition, Canadians are seen as providing a powerful role model and as acting as a spur to the development of indigenous talent. Given that the GB team was languishing in the bottom division of world hockey, the recruitment of foreign migrants came to be seen as desirable by key figures within the ice hockey federation and the club owners' association.

The motivation and mode of migration of the Canadians who play in British ice hockey reflect the ideal types in sport labour migration outlined. Those who settle and make Great Britain their home – at least for a limited period – express an almost missionary zeal with regard to spreading a positive message about the attractions of the game. Canadians cast themselves in the roles of pioneers and proselytizers. If only the 'Brits' would 'get the message' and 'see the light' (or the puck), their appreciation of and standard of playing the game would improve. For the majority of Britons, however, the significance of the 'blue line' remains a mystery. Some 7,500 players were registered with the British Ice Hockey Association (BIHA), of which 3,000 were seniors playing in the men's leagues (Roberts, 1994).

For some Canadians, British ice hockey is but another port of call. This rapid turnover appears to stem from two main factors. It may flow from the 'mercenary' desire of the migrant to 'make a fast buck' and skate swiftly to another rink in the same or a different society. Alternatively, the migrant may wish to experience different cultures and to 'do the European tour'. For example, Gary Yaremchuk, currently playing in Great Britain, played in five different European countries between 1987 and 1993. This temporary residence sometimes results from the inevitable downward spiral as a player ages and seeks more comfortable rinks in which to ply his craft. On the other hand, the pattern of migration may be the result of some miscalculated agent-inspired move. In the case of more talented players, the lure of money usually ensured that their involvement in British ice hockey was a temporary affair. They were, and arguably remain, the 'hired mercenary guns' of European ice hockey.

In some instances, departures by migrants can be rather conflict ridden, such as when players simply walk out on clubs. The Fife Flyers, a Scottish-based team, had one such experience in January 1995 when an American import, Tony Szabo, hastily departed Heathrow Airport in London bound for the United States. The Flyers' Canadian coach commented:

> When we got to his flat, it was empty and even his car was gone . . . By the time we contacted Heathrow authorities, we had missed him by 20 minutes. Thank God he's American, a fellow Canadian wouldn't do that to me.
>
> ('Flyers floored by Szabo's walkout', 1995, p. 32)

Yet, for some Canadian migrants, including former NHL players such as Doug Smail, there are other features of British ice hockey that outweigh the attractions of Zurich, Paris, Munich or indeed their home countries. The close overlap between the Canadian and English versions of the English language avoids some of the problems associated with adjustment, relocation and foreign sojourn in a linguistically different country (although the Durham dialect sometimes is impenetrable even to fellow Britons!). The attractions of a nomadic lifestyle are not for them. Besides, as players come to the end of their playing careers, the desire to give back something to the game dovetails well with the role of pioneer in British ice hockey. In addition, being local heroes rekindles memories of 'glory days'.

The added advantage of British ice hockey is that it is dominated by a Canadian ethos, coaching strategy and playing style. Europeans see British club and national teams as rough, violent clones of the Canadian game. Canadian migrants, by contrast, are welcomed into the fold, slide easily into the playing patterns, and are assimilated smoothly into the Canadian network as smoothly as the British upper classes were into the Singapore cricket club during the days of the Raj. Canadians can adopt the role of the pioneer, feel safe in the company of fellow Canucks, settle for a while, almost feel at home, yet also feel secure in the knowledge that the option to return to their roots is still available.

Migrants, national identity and the restructuring of ice hockey

Looking over the longer term, it is clear that the eligibility regulations and quotas regarding Canadian migrants have changed considerably. In the immediate post-World War II period, few restrictions were applied and, as a result, Canadians dominated the British game. The tensions between those who wished to use the migrants to gain a better position in the global ice hockey marketplace and those who were more concerned to promote local talent and the long-term development of the British game were all too evident. Until the mid-1990s, four foreign players were allowed per team including three imports and one dual national. This, however, underestimates the presence and influence of Canadians. Over time, several Canadians have stayed and made or remade Great Britain their home, be it temporary or permanent. As residents, they qualified as GB players. Teams actively recruited this category of player and, indeed, they, along with the dual nationals who hold British passports, were eligible to play for the national team. Canadians still use the United Kingdom as a staging post, waiting for a move to a more high status and financially rewarding league (Elliott and Maguire, 2008).

The methods by which migrants entered Great Britain can, however, vary considerably. Although some clearly use official channels and their clubs apply for work permits, other methods were also employed. In the following comments, made by a reporter for *Ice Hockey News Review*, some of the methods used by Canadian migrants, as well as the perceptions of them, are evident:

> I can vouch for the fact that many a Canuck was told that on entry to the mother country he was to tell the immigration officials that he was of course just visiting and on vacation. And that under no circumstances should he be seen to be carrying ice hockey sticks as hand luggage with his skates dangling round his neck. Needless to say, from time to time some

Canucks from the backwoods managed not to obey this simple instruction and found themselves being turned straight around and shipped out on the next flight.

('More than just work permits to fuss about', 1993, p. 9)

If the success of the GB team in the mid-1990s is considered, then it is also clear that the team's promotion from Pool C to Pool A and reaching the final qualification stage for the Lillehammer Olympics was heavily dependent on dual nationals. Between 1993 and 1996 the number of dual nationals continued to grow. In the 1995 Pool A World Championship tournament, 15 of 23 GB players were Canadian dual nationals. Even this underestimates their impact, for the team tended to operate a two-line game plan that is made up almost exclusively of Canadians. As with the domestic game, so with the national side, the Brits are left with goaltending duties and with 'riding the pine'. Defending this development, David Frame, chief executive of the BIHA, commented:

I think we're quietly confident of staying in Pool A and it's important for the sport's profile that we do so. People criticize dual nationals, but they're the only way we can compete at the top until we've brought our youngsters on. Countries like Italy and Germany have taken the same route as us and prospered.

('Frame inherits bleak scene', 1994, p. 34)

Significantly, Frame referred to the fact that the use of dual nationals also occurred in Italy and Germany. However, it was not confined to these countries. In the World Championships to which he referred, some 51 Canadian-born players, and players developed through Canadian local and provincial ice hockey programmes, were playing for other national sides. In the 1995 World Championships, the success of France was heavily dependent on the role of French Canadians. Blade runners, then, have a significant impact at both the club and the international levels. Here the players are hired mercenaries, plying their craft for other nations. Yet, although economics plays a part, their representing other countries appears to stem more from a desire to test their skills against the very best. In this regard, ice hockey players are not unlike elite cricket migrants who also perform for countries other than their places of birth (Maguire and Stead, 1996).

Local heroes? Pioneers, mercenary labour and 'Brits with Canadian accents'

How did the various groups who interact in the 'glocal' ice hockey subculture view these developments? If groups from the host culture are considered, a variety of responses were evident. The owners of British ice hockey clubs welcomed the involvement of the Canadians. Some of the elite clubs also welcomed the predicted development of a European super league in which Canadians would play a prominent part. This view was not shared by all. One writer in *Ice Hockey News Review*, Norman de Mesquita, remarked:

> Some overseas players do not give value for money, something we can iden
> tify with. We have all seen a few imports who fell into that category and
> who were just here to feather a financial nest and have a paid holiday. Then
> there is the feeling in cricket that too many native-bred players are being
> kept out of the first class game by foreigners. Isn't that familiar too? How
> many highly talented British-born players can you name who should, by
> now, be an integral part of the GB set-up if only we had included fewer
> mediocre veteran Canadians? It also applies to most clubs in our game and
> is the result of short-sighted management attitudes and the mistaken belief
> that short-term success is all that matters. [This is] exactly what killed off
> the game in the sixties.
>
> ('The good . . . the bad . . . and the nuts', 1994, p. 5)

Criticisms of this kind centred on issues such as the over-reliance on foreign stars, problems of financial instability, the lack of opportunity for British players, the lack of European players, regimented coaching and the adoption of a violent playing style, and the presence in the GB team of 'Brits with Canadian accents' ('The good . . . the bad . . . and the nuts', 1994, p. 10). Discontent resulting from these features of the game manifests itself in several ways. British under-21 and B international players become disillusioned and refuse to make themselves available for selection. Although some Canadians see themselves as pioneers whose aim is to promote the good of the game, British players see them as mercenaries who settle and take over British ice hockey. Take the following remarks made by Tony Hand, a player for the Sheffield Steelers:

> I've nothing against imported players. I think they've been good for the
> game – to a certain extent. But obviously now there's too many, and that's
> got to be to the detriment of the British player . . . It's going to take an
> exceptional British player to come through, to actually get the ice time
> they're going to need to develop. There's a lot of good British talent about,
> and teams should realize that all they need is a little bit of development.
> But a lot of teams won't develop players.
>
> ('Hand strikes for the home-grown', 1995, p. 16)

Such resentment about the underdevelopment of indigenous talent was not confined to verbal criticism. Some British players target Canadian players to ensure that they retaliate and then end up off ice in the penalty box ('Permit problems hit imports', 1993). Such criticism of Canadian players, and their presence as dual nationals in the GB team, was held in check by advocates of their use, but only for as long as the team was successful. Relegation from Pool A and the failure to qualify for Lillehammer prompted critics of Canadian migrants to pose the question, 'How British is British?' ('How British is British?', 1994, p. 3). The editor of *Ice Hockey News Review* concluded:

> The BIHA should forget about artificially importing players eligible to play for GB because that has undoubtedly been a factor in the development of what I believe is currently a most unhealthy situation for British youth. If we must have unlimited Canadians with British passports, then so be it. But the genuine imports must pay the price of that 'freedom'.
>
> ('How British is British?', 1994, p. 5)

In contrast to these sentiments, and not surprisingly, the Canadian-born coach of the Great Britain side defended the decision to rely on dual nationals. Arguing that Great Britain could not compete without their involvement, Alex Dampier suggested that their presence provided a powerful role model and that the long-term strategy was to develop and play more British-born players. For the players, representing another nation does not call into question their sense of being Canadian. They aspire to be and to play against the best. Representing another nation involves playing for a 'flag of convenience'. Peter Johnson, England's ice hockey coach, was prompted by the presence in the Scottish team of a Canadian who then held a British passport to comment on this issue of national identity:

> It's still England against Scotland, no matter who's playing, but the rivalry is born into the British lads. The Canadians tell you they're British when they get a British passport. That might be so, but it doesn't make them English or Scottish.
>
> ('Conway holds key', 1993, p. 15)

Although the advocates of the use of dual nationals appeared to be in the ascendancy regarding the national team, they did not hold total control over the domestic game. Significantly, those groups within the BIHA arguing for a more protectionist strategy were able to ensure that even those dual nationals who had played for the British team would be subject to the 'four-foreigner rule' in the domestic game. That is, although they held British passports and had played for Great Britain, they were classified as foreign and therefore subject to the club quotas and eligibility regulations applied to other foreign players. This issue, combined with wage-capping schemes developed by the BIHA and the club owners, prompted the players, both Canadian and British, to form a players' association in late 1993 and early 1994, a move that provoked two responses. One of the instigators of the move, Kevin King, had to defend the launch, protesting that it would not be an organization run by and for imports ('Join us brothers . . . Brit or import', 1994). The British players had to be won over. In addition, the BIHA and the club owners were fiercely critical and rejected the notion that the players could have any role to play in the governing of the game. Significantly, one of the first actions of the Ice Hockey Players' Association (IHPA) was to begin conducting discussions with Department of Employment (DOE) officials. Their meetings focused on the issuing of work permits for foreign players, chiefly Canadian but other non-EU players as well. This prompted the BIHA secretary, David Pickles, to observe:

> We could not accept a situation where the IHPA has a right to veto work permit applications. We are asking the DOE to retract all of this and we have informed them, both verbally and in writing, that we will take it to the Home Office.
>
> (BIHA, 1994, p. 5)

Labour rights: European law and on-ice enforcers

Questions of labour rights were not confined to ice hockey players (Bale and Maguire, 1994). Athletes in several sports face similar problems. In soccer, problems over freedom of contract and the right to reside in and play for clubs within the European Union forced a Belgian player, Jean-Marc Bosman, to take the Belgium Football Association and the European Union of Football Associations to the European Court. In a landmark provisional judgement, the advocate general in September 1995 found in favour of the players' right to move, and concluded that quotas covering EU citizens were illegal and constituted a restraint of trade. This judgement was confirmed by the court in December 1995. In discussing the issue of European legislation prior to this judgement, Edvinsson, the IIHF general secretary, observed, 'Even if we are not happy about it, we have to follow it. If it's the law, then also the sport must follow it' (interview with the author, Zurich, March 1995).

Significantly, although the case and the publicity that surrounded it centred on Bosman, Tim Cranston, a Canadian-born dual national currently playing for the Sheffield Steelers, was also named as part of the court action. Despite being a British passport holder and also playing for Great Britain, he had been designated by the BIHA as an import. As a result of this designation, his transfer to a top German club fell through; the foreign quota was full. On hearing the advocate general's provisional judgement, Cranston commented, 'When I heard about Bosman, I contacted his legal team and became part of the ruling. The only question now is who will be liable for the money I'm owed' ('Cranston now looking for cash', 1995, p. 43). Senior soccer officials had to face up to the implications of this judgement, but ice hockey, with its dependence on foreign-born talent, was also particularly affected. Indeed, subsequent to the judgement, the BIHA held meetings with officials of the Canadian High Commission regarding the citizenship status of up to 20 players currently playing in Great Britain ('Illegal import turmoil', 1995, p. 20). In May 1995, the BIHA decided to abolish virtually every restriction on clubs signing foreign-born British passport holders. Following the Bosman judgement, restrictions regarding EU citizens also had to be abandoned. Although these changes strengthened the position of Canadian migrants, non-EU players from the former Soviet Union stood to gain little. Internal sport migration within the European Union had been seen to be subject to European legislation. The external controls remained in place. Hence the BIHA held meetings with officials of the Canadian High Commission to establish the players' nationality status.

Canadian migrants also adopted less formal strategies to deal with issues of labour rights and the problems arising from or threats to their migrant position. Although preceded by defections by players from the Eastern bloc, since the people's revolutions of the late 1980s, top-flight Eastern Europeans flowed across the Atlantic in greater numbers to be recruited to the ranks of the NHL. A similar process, albeit at a different standard, occurred in mainland Europe and Great Britain. For club owners seeking to impose wage capping, the recruitment of Eastern Europeans strengthened their negotiating position and allowed them to drive down wage costs even further because citizens from depressed Eastern economies are prepared to play for lower wages. Any Canadian who holds out for too long in salary negotiations risks being told to 'hit the highway'. Little wonder, then, that the Canadians viewed the flood from the East as a threat to their livelihoods. During the 1994–5 season, some 31 per cent of the total number of transfers recorded by the IIHF were from those countries that made up the former Soviet Union and Czechoslovakia (IIHF archives). Whereas some migrants felt that the newly formed players' association might be able to influence the decisions of the DOE regarding the regulation of this inflow, the reaction of other Canadians in British ice hockey was more brutal and immediate. Following the recruitment of Ukrainian players to the Humberside Hawks club, the coach, Peter Johnson, observed that the Eastern Europeans in general 'just get clobbered every game' ('Dorion shines as Hawks' plan to look to the East goes West', 1994, p. 15). Referring to his own Ukrainian players, Johnson concluded:

> There is no question both he [Alexei Kuznetsov] and Alexander Kulikov have seen big threats and physical attention because Canadians see them as a threat to their jobs. I had a go at Durham's Chris Norton because he was hitting them so hard it was embarrassing. I told him that he should treat all players the same.
>
> ('Brothers Johnson dropped by father', 1993, p. 30)

The use of violent play was not confined to threats posed by Eastern Europeans in the domestic game. The use of rough, violent play in international matches gained the GB team the reputation of adhering to a Canadian style. A report in the Swiss ice hockey magazine discussing British ice hockey highlighted these issues clearly:

> What the Panthers and Beavers exhibit is 'bush hockey' – good old Canadian style. First the man, then the puck. The harder the check, the harder the thud against the board, the louder the jubilation from the crowd. Of European playing culture there is not a trace . . .
>
> ('How others see us?', 1994, p. 10)

There is, perhaps, a certain irony in this criticism. Canadian commentator Don Cherry repeatedly denigrated European players for their alleged lack of a tough masculine style. Cherry also criticized European involvement in the NHL per se, arguing that these foreigners are taking the jobs of 'good Canadian boys' (Gillett *et al.*, 1995, p. 15). This trend did not go unnoticed by other commentators. As MacGregor (1993) stated:

> By 1992–93, however, there could be no dismissing the Europeans as a fad. In all, 88 Europeans had been drafted the previous June, with the most dramatic exodus coming from Russia. By the time the season ended, 49 Russians had skated with NHL teams and another 48 had played in the minor leagues or in junior [leagues] . . . When NHL expansion began in 1967, Canadians held 96 percent of the available slots. By the time the 1993 playoffs opened, that figure had fallen to 66.2 percent – slightly below two thirds. Don Cherry's response: 'There should be quotas.'
>
> (pp. 47–8)

Despite Cherry's comments, the logic of the global expansion plans of the NHL, and the unrestricted recruitment of labour by a dominant cartel, ensured that top Europeans continued to cross the Atlantic. Equally, the 'overproduction' of young Canadian men who dream of making the pros, or of older veterans who seek new rinks to relive glory days, also resulted in them continuing to follow well-worn European migrant trails (Elliott and Maguire, 2008). The irony is that they then hold down team positions that EU and Eastern European citizens could occupy. Cherry overlooked the extent to which ice hockey labour was part of a global marketplace.

The Canadian migrants were aware that the migrant labour was a trade in pain. Young Britons would provoke the Canucks and get them off the ice. On occasions, quite serious free fights occurred. In October 1994, a Canadian migrant was subject to a systematic attack while on ice. Playing for the Durham Wasps, Richard Little, a forward, sustained severe facial injuries. Subsequent to the game, the local police were called in to view the video evidence. The Wasps' general manager, Paul Smith, commented on the case to the national press:

> He's been back [to the hospital] this morning, but they don't think it's fractured [cheekbone]. But it was terrible. You get the physical side to it, but that was just callous. [The video] clearly shows it was a sucker punch from behind. After that, the whole of Richard's body went limp; he just could not defend himself. As he went down, he got another four or five very heavy blows to the face. We had to end the period around two minutes early just to get the blood off the ice.
>
> ('Durham call in police for Little', 1994, p. 23)

Given Cherry's comments about how Europeans should be treated in Canada, it is somewhat ironic that a violent reception also awaited Canadians in Europe.

Conclusion: blade runners and 'glocal' ice hockey

The involvement of Canadian migrants in British ice hockey raised a series of issues and questions. It is clear that Canadian migrants to Great Britain were faced with a series of problems regarding labour rights, work permits and salary caps. The actions of the BIHA and the judgement of the European Court contoured and shaped the experience of these players. Yet the players were not passive victims of these processes. The formation of a players' union and the actions of individuals such as Cranston demonstrated that migrants actively sought to improve their material conditions. The case study also highlighted the complex and, at times, seemingly contradictory nature of both recruitment strategies and the desire of migrants to move. There was no single motivation driving Canadians around Europe or beyond. Elements of the pioneer spirit, settler role, mercenary style and cosmopolitan desire all are evident. To explore this further, more detailed fieldwork-based accounts of players doing their body work, and also office experiences highlighting the nature of their lives between games, have to be done. It is also clear from the evidence that Canadians played for their adopted countries out of a wish to play at the highest level possible rather than from a desire to represent the nation. They appear, like elite cricket migrants, less interested in patriot games (Maguire and Stead, 1996).

Canadian migrants accordingly highlighted several features of a general model of labour migration and shared a number of experiences and problems faced by fellow migrants in other sports. What appears to be significantly different from the majority of sporting migrants, however, is that this experience involved the exercise of a violent masculine style. Located within a subculture where violent norms are tolerated and encouraged, Canadian migrant labour involves a trade in pain. Again, more fieldwork-based investigation of this feature is required.

This migration was also part of the broader development of ice hockey and of global sportization processes. The IIHL was keen to establish a European Super League, and the NHL was actively supporting this strategy, funding IIHF developments to the tune of some £6 million. Although the IIHF had rejected these overtures for some time, they seemingly were forced into a compromise agreement. Plans by the US-based International Hockey League (IHL) to expand into Europe by 1995–6 effectively forced the IIHF into the agreement during June 1994. These moves by the IHL prompted Rene Fasel, the IIHF president, to observe: 'We are looking forward to working with the NHL instead of the IHL. If they [IHL] want to fight, we are ready. They need our cooperation; if they think they can work without us, that would be a mistake' ('Rival plans for new leagues in Europe raise British hackles', 1995, p. 19).

In turn, such migration, and the strategies of the NHL and the IIHF, is part of a global sportization process that has both short-term features and longer-term unintended dimensions. Analyses must explore the interdependencies that contour relations between, as in this case, insider/established countries as well as those between such countries and the outsider nations that lie at the edge of the global sport action. Both the strategies of multinational corporations and the unplanned features of global sportization processes need to be better traced and understood. Given that the NHL had a five-year, $210 million television contract with the Fox network, and given that its merchandising sales since 1992 nearly doubled to more than $1 billion annually, its global impact could not be underestimated at that time (Deacon, 1995, p. 64). It was clear that the NHL was intent on emulating the National Football League's global expansion strategy (Maguire, 1990). One of the keys to this was working out an agreement with the IIHF, the International Olympic Committee and the NHL players' association to enable these players to compete in the 1998 Winter Olympic Games. In addition, given that Europe remains the main target for licensing and merchandising expansion, it is no surprise that the NHL would have liked to have established a Pan-European league. As part of this process, the NHL held exhibition games in England to promote the game. Yet this prompted contradictory reactions. When BIHA President Freddie Meredith rejected NHL overtures and argued that the BIHA 'doesn't need or want the NHL to help promote the sport in Britain', he was described as 'uppity' in the Canadian media (*Toronto Sun*, 9 September 1993, p. 56). Given the subsequent compromise agreement reached between the NHL and the IIHF to fend off the challenge of the IHL, Meredith was forced to change his position. Yet, although the BIHA once proclaimed it did not need the NHL, the BIHA, along with officials of ice hockey federations across the globe, now are locked into a political economy structured by their agreement with the NHL and that their mutually dependent development remains based on a continuing reliance on the overproduction and consumption of Canadian blade runners.

Note

1 This chapter first appeared in 1996: 'Blade runners: Canadian migrants, ice hockey, and the global sports process', *Journal of Sport and Social Issues*, 23: 335–60.

11 Female football migration

Motivational factors for early migratory processes

Sine Agergaard and Vera Botelho

In 1994 Joseph Maguire and John Bale, both pioneers of the study of sport migration, noted that the migration of sports labour was gathering pace and occurring over a widespread geographical area and within an increasing number of sports subcultures (Bale and Maguire, 1994, p. 5). Two years later, Maguire also commented on the growing number of female athletes who were becoming sports migrants (Maguire, 1996, p. 336). Despite this recognition even today there is little literature on migration for those sports disciplines which enjoy little international publicity and female migrants. This is well illustrated by the case of women's football.

In recent years women's football has enjoyed a boom in participation and it is now the fastest growing women's sport worldwide. The number of registered players has more than doubled since 2000 and there are now over 30 million females playing football (FIFA, 2007; Harris, 2007). In some countries, such as England, Norway and the United States, football is already the favourite sport among girls (Skogvang, 2006; Williams, 2007). Besides its increasing popularity the game has also experienced a growth in economic support and coaching, the expansion of well-organized and professional leagues in several countries and, though thin, increasing media coverage (Weigelt and Knanoh, 2006; FIFA, 2007).

Alongside its development, new dimensions of the game have been emerging, such as the international migration of players. Though lacking literature, media coverage suggests that this international flux of women footballers has been increasing substantially in recent years, expanding beyond traditional geographic limits and assuming globalized characteristics. Very little, however, is known about how the migration of female footballers has developed and what drives this migratory process.

This chapter presents a case study of immigration into Danish women's football that attempts to provide a foundation upon which an international debate on this topic can develop. A study of female football migration can give insight into the early stages of migratory processes and help us to understand what drives sports clubs to start recruiting foreign players and sports migrants to leave their home country. For that, we describe first of all the historical development of immigration into Danish women's football since the early 1990s. Second, we analyse the motivating and de-motivating factors with respect to the clubs' recruitment of foreign players. And, finally, we analyse the players' motives for migrating and their experiences of the process. Our approach is mainly qualitative and data are drawn from a questionnaire survey sent to all the clubs in Denmark's premier league for women's football and from 15 interviews we conducted with foreign players and their coaches and managers in three of the clubs.

Reviewing football migration research

Preceding studies of female footballers as migrants are few if any. Skogvang (2008) and Eliasson (2009) give a glimpse of some of the issues surrounding the exporting and recruitment of women footballers in Norway and Sweden, respectively. Inversely, there is a relatively large literature on the international migration of male football players (Maguire and Stead, 1998; Maguire and Pearton, 2000a, 2000b; Stead and Maguire, 2000a, 2000b; Lanfranchi and Taylor, 2001; Magee and Sugden, 2002; McGovern, 2002; Poli and Ravanel, 2005a; Dietschy, 2006; Molnar, 2006; Poli, 2006b; Taylor, 2006; Cornellisen and Solberg, 2007; Darby, 2007a, 2007b; Darby *et al.*, 2007; Tiesler and Coelho, 2007; Molnar and Maguire, 2008). We are, however, aware that female football migration might be a quite different phenomenon not only for its more recent development, but, according to our preliminary enquiries, it also has much less money involved and different geographical routes. At the same time, we expect that there are similarities between the processes that make athletes migrate, so studies of male athletes' migration are used here as a starting point for our enquiries into motives for sports clubs' and migrants' engagement in female football migration.

To date, there has been relatively little research into the recruitment mechanisms that bring migrant players to their new sports clubs (Elliott and Maguire, 2008a, p. 160). But in one of the early studies in this sparse literature Maguire (1988) did describe how English elite basketball clubs recruited American players to attract publicity and thereby greater sponsorship; so outlining possible economic motives for engaging in migration. Furthermore, McGovern (2002) has described hiring practices in England's football premier league between 1946 and 1995 and one noteworthy observation from this study was a tendency for clubs to conduct homo-social reproduction; that is, selecting players with a similar language, football style, culture and so forth from countries with which England has historical ties or colonial links. In this respect, Denmark is quite different from England, and as we shall see the foreign players in Danish women's football represent quite diverse nationalities, and their differences in language, football playing style and culture are all issues that the recruiting clubs must address.

There are a number of studies that have contributed to the development of a typology of athletes' motives for migrating (Maguire, 1996; Stead and Maguire, 2000b; Magee and Sugden, 2002). Maguire (1996) presents a preliminary typology for migrants, which is based on studies of various sports disciplines and emphasizes the combination of different aspects of the migrants' motives. This typology identifies five categories of migrants: *pioneers*, who are motivated by an almost evangelical zeal to expand their sports; *settlers*, who are interested in subsequently staying in the host country; *mercenaries*, who are motivated by short-term gains; *nomadic cosmopolitans*, who use their sports to travel and experience other cultures and cities; and *returnees*, who aim to return home, for example, to finish their career.

Subsequently, Magee and Sugden developed the model further by looking specifically at football and adding three new categories including one that refined sporting ambition as a motive split into three subtypes.[1] First of all, there are the *ambitionists* who migrate to fulfil dreams of a professional career; second, those who migrate to play in a particular country and a particular club; and finally the migrants who seek to be signed by a club with the highest possible sporting level. The other categories of sports migrants added by Magee and Sugden are the *exile*, who for sport-related, personal or political reasons leaves home voluntarily, and the *expelled*, who has been forced to leave home through a combination of behavioural problems and media exposure. As Maguire has pointed out, these are overlapping categories that will be defined more closely through further studies (Maguire, 2004). In other words we understand Maguire's and Magee and Sugden's typologies as ideal types to explain general motives for sports migrants that must be combined and elaborated further in specific case studies. So, our job is to examine these general traits together with more open-ended questions about what drives the specific clubs and players in our study to engage in female football migration.

Examining this complex set of clubs' and migrants' motives for engaging in migration, we are theoretically in line with Molnar and Maguire's description of the complex and dynamic nature of migratory processes as 'migration figurations' (Molnar and Maguire, 2008, p. 75). Molnar and Maguire (2008) also describe a so-called first phase in migratory processes. In their case, the focus is on the first football migrants who left Hungary for different countries where male football migration is already widespread. In our case, the migratory process is only just beginning for club leaders, coaches and the players alike. Here, we seek to understand sports clubs' as well as migrants' motives for engaging initially in migration.

Previous analyses of push and pull factors for migration have explained macro-structural aspects such as the centre and periphery in the international flux of players and different migration patterns (Poli, 2006b; Taylor, 2006; Darby, 2007a, 2007b). This study applies a more micro-sociological perspective on the agency of migrants, club leaders and coaches as persons that act and reflect upon the current opportunities and barriers in sports labour migration (Stead and Maguire, 2000b; Falcous and Maguire, 2005; Elliott and Maguire, 2008a). So we must turn our attention to the ways in which motivating and de-motivating factors are present in our informants' everyday life.

Female football migration: an empirical account

Initially, we contacted all clubs in the Danish women's premier football league and asked them to list the players who had come to Denmark to play football. In other words, this excluded ethnic minority youngsters and foreigners who happen to be in Denmark for other reasons. We were interested in the foreign players who had moved to follow their chosen sport and enjoyed professional conditions as players.[2] The clubs were asked to list information about the foreign players' numbers, nationality, birth year, period of stay, position, salary and so on, with the understanding that they may be reticent to give details of the latter. This information gave us a preliminary overview of the immigration in Danish women's football, the characteristics of the migrants and their conditions in the clubs.

Further, we focused on three clubs in the Danish women's premier football league, which all have years of experience with recruiting foreign players.[3] Moreover, they illustrate the wide diversity of clubs in the league (in terms of history, economic conditions and administration) and in their approaches to migration. FC Women is a football club funded and led by women, with a long successful history and a good economic standing due to income-generating activities. FC City is a football club situated in a large Danish city that has a women's section, but which has limited economic resources. FC Sport is an up-and-coming sports club where women's football is arranged as part of a larger sporting enterprise of elite sports teams. Like the first club, this enterprise is situated in a provincial city.[4]

To gain more insight into the clubs' and migrants' motives for engaging in football migration we conducted semi-structured interviews with the clubs' main coaches and their chairperson or sports director, depending on who was more knowledgeable about the club's recruitment and integration of foreign players. Moreover, we interviewed all foreign players who played in the three clubs in the spring of 2009.[5] The nine foreign players interviewed were between 22 and 29 years old and had been in Denmark for a period ranging from six months to almost seven years. For six of the players it was their first move as migrants, while the rest had been playing in another club and country before coming to Denmark. Only one of the migrants is a world top class player, while four players have been selected for their national teams for shorter or longer periods. The players were drawn from nations in North America, Africa and South America,[6] so representing some of the major sending countries and new migrant groups in Danish women's football, as we shall see below.

Immigration into Danish women's football

Despite the fact that Danish female footballers were quite successful in the early 1970s it was only after the Union of European Football Associations (UEFA) urged their national members to take over the organization of women's football in 1971 that the Danish FA (DBU) included women's football in 1972 (Brus and Trangbæk, 2003, p. 106; Grønkjær and Olesen, 2007, p. 156). Accordingly, the national team was abolished for two years when UEFA had not organized any international tournaments, and in the same period there was no national tournament.

The recruitment of foreign players to Danish women's football can be traced back to around 1990 when FC Women recruited three international players. The club had developed (and recruited staff) on the strength of its involvement in the organization of an international tournament which had been running since the early 1980s. The first foreign players were mainly from Australia, the United States and other Nordic countries. In the early 1990s there were no or few precedents for having foreign players in the club, and they were employed as amateurs and often only stayed for short periods.

The Bosman ruling in 1995, ensuring the free mobility of players within the European Union, is described as an event of major importance for the international flux of male football players (Maguire and Stead, 1998; Frick, 2009). It does not seem, however, to have had that big an effect on the international flux of female footballers. In Denmark, at least, national legislation has been more important in giving, among other things, the first licence for a women's football club to contract players in 1997. Other clubs followed in subsequent years.[7]

By around 2004 three Danish clubs in the women's premier league had recruited foreign players. In 2008 the number had grown to 15 foreigners in these three clubs (see Figure 11.1). In the present season, migration into Danish women's football is, however, marked by a decrease in the number of players primarily as a result of the financial crisis. During the past decade the origin of the foreign players has also become more diverse in the sense that South American and African players were recruited by FC Women and FC City, while players from New Zealand came into FC Sport. In general, the foreign players who have played in the Danish women's league represent quite a wide variety of nationalities (see Figure 11.2).

Though our material is limited, the general picture is that the primary groups of foreign players have come from quite distant countries such as the United States, Australia, New Zealand and Canada, which are regarded as familiar countries in terms of language and football culture. The presence of the Africans and South Americans may be explained by their achieved as well as ascribed status as nations with brilliant football skills.

In general, there have been few professional foreign players from the other Nordic countries. This might be due to the fact that Norwegian and Swedish women's football clubs have better economic conditions. In Sweden, in particular,

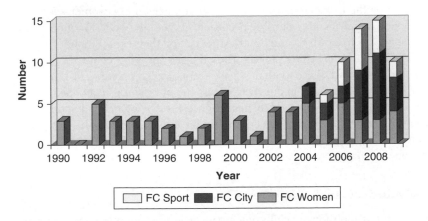

Figure 11.1 Numbers of foreign players in the three selected clubs, 1990–2009

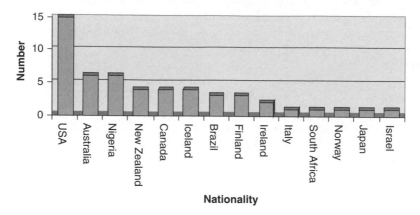

Figure 11.2 Nationality of foreign players in the Danish women's premier football league, 1990–2009

there is a high level of professionalism and many Swedish players tend to stay in their country along with the foreign players that are recruited (Eliasson, 2009). Thus the flux of migration rather points the other way with the best Danish players going to these neighbouring countries to play as professionals. The one exception to this general picture concerns the cooperation agreements whereby a Copenhagen-based premier league club paid the expenses for seven young Swedish players from Malmö to play in their club as amateurs.

In this case study migration seems not to be governed by cultural alliances and colonial links as has been described for male football migration (Lanfranchi and Taylor, 2001; McGovern, 2002; Poli, 2006b). Rather, as Maguire has observed, it seems to be a complex set of political, economical, historical, geographic, social and cultural factors that influence the flow of sports labour migration (Maguire and Guttmann, 2009). Given our limited material we can only speculate on the significance of the lack of political power and organization of women's football in the donor countries, the clubs' expectation of getting 'value for money' by recruiting players from Africa and South America and their expectations of better social integration by choosing players from English-speaking countries or their cultural ascription of skills to football players from, for example, Brazil. The variety of nationalities observed in our specific case might be simply explained by the fact that the routes of female football migration are still being defined at this early stage in the migratory process. To enquire further into what drives the first phase of female football migration we need to take a closer look at the clubs' motives for recruiting foreign players.

Clubs' motives and side effects

A possible motivation for the clubs' engagement in migration is economic gain. FC City found that recruitment of a world top class player attracted sponsorship interest and media coverage. As Maguire (1988) has pointed out, the import of foreign players can contribute to publicity and thereby economic gains for elite sports clubs. Yet, the money in women's football is modest, and the possible profit therefore small, suggesting other motives are more important. Probably the most important common motive for the women's clubs is sporting ambition. All three clubs started recruiting foreign players with the aim of getting to or remaining at the top of the Danish women's league. Particularly, the club leader at FC Women refers to their geographical location in a provincial city as a challenge for recruiting and keeping the best Danish players:

> So sometimes it might be easier to get a player from Africa to travel to here rather than getting a Dane [from a major city] moving. It is probably the reason why we have been forced to reinforce us in this way.

It is a fundamental premise for sports clubs that they, as employers, are often bound to a geographical location, while players can decide to move or not to move between the clubs (McGovern, 2002, p. 24).

Even if sporting ambitions have been a primary motive for recruiting foreign players, the interviews with club leaders and coaches disclose a number of other motivating or de-motivating side effects of the migratory process. The coaches in all three clubs emphasize that the foreign players have brought professional attitudes to the clubs, are very competitive and, in one club leader's description, they have a 'gene for winning'. The migrant players' approach to football therefore appears not only to contribute to the team's performance, but also to the football socialization of the indigenous players. The clubs thereby experience a possible side effect of migration.

However, the presence of migrant players, as well as young Danish talents, has also become a challenge for the clubs. In particular, FC City has been criticized in the media, and by parents, for hindering the development of young Danish talents through its recruitment of foreign players. The public debate about foreign athletes' 'invasion' of Danish sports has mainly dealt with the rapid increase of foreign players in female handball (Agergaard, 2008). The number of foreign athletes is still very small in Danish women's football but there are already indications of xenophobia, for instance amongst Danish parents who want to see their young daughter playing. This seems to have made some of the clubs aware that, if they recruit foreign players, they must have an indisputable sporting level and adapt to the local surroundings. This situation may also be influenced by the general debate of immigration into Danish society that through the last ten years has been influenced by an anti-immigrant discourse and a growing concern about immigrants' adaptation to so-called Danish values and norms (Wren, 2001; Østergaard-Nielsen, 2003; Rydgren, 2004).

FC Sport has used its foreign players not only in the football club but also at local schools and meetings to talk about their home country's politics and history. The club emphasizes international exchange as a motive for recruiting foreign players. Besides the obvious merits of this motive, the international players also contribute to the branding of the club as a multi-cultural sporting enterprise that can attract young players from distant places.

However, club officials also note that the presence of foreign players can be a time-consuming activity. In FC Sport there is a voluntary mentor following the players that are not local. Generally, it is a challenge for the clubs to support the foreign players through the day-to-day immigratory process, getting them accommodated, sorting out their papers, talking about their challenges, inviting them out to prevent loneliness and so on. It is an extra challenge for the clubs that have no professional administration and are almost entirely dependent on volunteers. A lack of administrative and economic resources is one of the arguments why FC City is considering not recruiting more foreign players. Another argument is the challenge posed by the players' adaptation.

The adaptation challenge

All of the club leaders and coaches indicated that encouraging the foreign players to adapt to their football style is a challenge as much as helping them adapt to the team and the club. The explanation is often made in cultural rather than structural terms. That is, the difficulties in the players' adaptation are described with references to cultural differences between them and us. For instance, as one of the club leaders observes: 'They definitely don't think in the same way as we do.' Only a few of the club leaders and coaches refer to structural differences between the foreign players' isolated everyday life compared to the Danish players' engagement in education and jobs and the structural conditions for female football migration.

Despite this adaptation challenge, none of the clubs had developed an explicit strategy for the recruitment and integration of migrant players. Still, we found a diversity of more implicit strategies in use. FC Women aim to have two players with a similar background at the same time, so that they can live together and speak their language together. According to the coach the foreigners tend to remain a segregated group. FC City emphasizes the foreign players' adaptation including eating the same food as the Danish players and drinking alcohol with them. According to the coach it is important for the team performance to become a close-knit group. Further, he describes the club's strategy of assimilation as the Danish way: 'That is speaking Danish. Of course, if it gets too detailed we have to explain things in English, but we should make a serious attempt to implement a Danish tone.'

The coach describes his thoughts about implementing a Danish tone on the entire team not only as a matter of teaching the foreign players the Danish language but also as an attempt to make all of the players adapt to a Danish way of talking and behaving. In comparison, FC Sport is focused on developing a multi-cultural sports milieu and does not seem particularly pre-occupied with cultural adaptation. This integration strategy is supported by the fact that their players are all from western countries and they are accommodated together with young Danish talents and migrants in other sports disciplines.

Recruiting players from geographically distant countries is a risky business. One of the club leaders describes how budgetary constraints mean that they can seldom bring players from abroad over for a try-out and that they spend a lot of time in the preparation phase, selecting and informing the players: 'We use a lot of time beforehand because neither the players nor we can afford a mistake.' A similar situation is described for the migration of Canadian players into British ice hockey, where the financial position of the clubs is also limited, and so the coaches are not able to make recruiting trips to North America (Elliott and Maguire, 2008a). In these circumstances, being able to secure information is crucial.

For the clubs to successfully recruit foreign players they must know the quality of the football players and their ability to cope with the club's adaptation expectations. Two of the Danish women's football clubs have had foreign players that had their contracts brought to an end prematurely. Only one of the nine players we interviewed was recruited through a player's agent. The rest have been players that the club leaders and coaches have met and watched playing at international tournaments, or players who have come to the club by way of personal recommendations and social networking. As Bale (1991) noted in his pioneer study of the recruitment of track and field athletes to American universities, networks are used to facilitate contact in two ways: through coaching colleagues or current or former players. Elliott and Maguire (2008a) have also pointed to Meyer's concept of the 'bridgehead' to describe the significance of friendship networks in the mobilization of highly skilled workers.

McGovern draws attention to the fact that the employer (club) cannot predict how a footballer will manage; the uncertainty is high: '. . . employers prefer to engage in repeated transactions with reliable or known sources as a means of reducing the uncertainty that characterizes labour as a commodity' (McGovern, 2002, p. 24). A football player is different from other kinds of commodities (even if they, at times, are treated as such; Poli, 2005b) by the fact that his or her labour cannot be divided from the social characteristics of the owner. For the clubs it is important to ensure that the migrant will perform well as a player, but also as a social person. Our analysis of the motivating and de-motivating factors for the clubs therefore shows that it is not only sporting ambitions that are important. The clubs are also motivated to develop and expand a social network in which former players can help them in their further recruitment of players that will suit the clubs' expectations. Now we will consider the migrants' motives.

Motivating and de-motivating factors for migrant players

When analysing the foreign players' motives for migrating, our starting point is, as mentioned earlier, Maguire's and Magee and Sugden's typologies. However, a fundamental problem occurs in the description of the first type – the category of the mercenary – since the money in female football differs greatly from that in male football.[8] The money is not at all a motivation for the North American female players, but for the African and South American players the salary can be remitted back to their families. One of the African players, Cathy, says that the money is not important but it does help her and her family. We read this explanation as a reminder of the fact that the players' motives may be diverse.

Besides low salaries, many of the first migrants also experienced rather poor employment and labour rights, staying for short periods, often not on a professional contract. In one case the club did not have a licence to make contracts with professional players, so the foreign players were employed as au pairs and later enrolled in a folk high school so that they were able to get a residence permit. This particular case was examined by the Danish police and proved to be a difficult time for the players and club alike since basic things such as health insurance for the players were not resolved either. But what is interesting is that, in spite of low salaries, poor employment and labour rights, players still choose to come to and stay at Danish football clubs. But why?

A primary motive for all of the players is sporting ambition. Magee and Sugden's description of the types that fulfil their ambitions by migrating to clubs with the highest sporting level or by playing in a particular club or country where they have always wanted to play is not the case here. Instead, it appears that finding an appropriate place to have a full-time career as a footballer may explain why the migrant players choose Danish clubs. The North American players often cannot get a position in their own world-leading league and so come to Denmark after finishing university in order to be able to continue their career. South American and African players, meanwhile, come to develop their careers under better conditions. The ambition to have full-time careers as footballers is related to a motive that we suggest is best described as the football experience.

The football experience

Several of the players stress that migration is their opportunity to gain international experience within football and thereby improve themselves. Cathy says: 'It's playing the game, it's for the game.' Patricia, Mary and several of the players also refer to their 'love of the game' and 'passion for football'. When asked to further elaborate on what they mean, the players talk about feelings of satisfaction in the activity itself; of the excitement of being physical, its challenges and the connection/bonding it provides them. They enjoy their strong bodies and see football as providing a safe space for sharing that joy. A sense of self-determination emerges in their discourses suggesting that it is this pleasure (or love of the game) that motivates them to face the sacrifices of living abroad. So the migration period can be seen as a challenge that they have to go through in order to become more experienced footballers, a rite de passage (Stead and Maguire, 2000b). Moreover, their explanations suggest that the football experience is important for their future life. Patricia and Kate say that 'football is my life', and 'I don't see football just as a job, I see it as part of me'. Through the interviews it becomes clear that almost all of the players want to continue working with football in some way or other, coaching or conducting projects to engage girls or socially deprived groups in football.

The players focus on football to such an extent that the experience of moving to another country becomes less important. In other words, the category of the nomadic cosmopolitans is not that relevant here. First of all, the players don't change clubs that often, and second, they seldom come to experience the country as such. They rather come to get 'a different taste' about how football is played and organized in another country. So their focus is not so much on the experience of being in another country and cultural context as such, but rather on the football experience.

Rebecca expresses difficulties in understanding her club's emphasis on her cultural adaptation:

> I don't understand why people are always concerned about my adaptation . . . I'm here to work, not to do tourism or be on holiday; of course I want to know something about the culture, but to be honest I'm not so concerned with that.

The migrant players do refer to cultural differences between themselves and the Danish players; among other things they talk about communication problems. These problems are particularly acute for those migrants who do not speak the Danish language and are unfamiliar with the body language. As Maguire (1999) has pointed out, it is both on and off the field that the players face the issue of adjustment, and problems of dislocation and retention. In this case, the players seem not that worried about their adaptation off the field compared to their adaptation to the football game, which is played with another style, training routine and coaching strategy.

In talking about their experiences as players in Denmark in general, a de-motivating factor that emerges early in the interviews is the differences in the style of the game in comparison with their home country. Some players see Danish women's football as faster and more physical, and with different tactics. A primary difference for particularly the African and South American players is the collective style of game. 'Here it's much more, how do you say, it is collective. Back home we do a lot of skills you know, the dribbling; make fun out of football.' Cathy describes how she has learned to 'play off and on the ball' and several of the other players, such as Lana and Lilly, also describe how passing the ball to their team mates and running into position seems to be a crucial part of the Danish playing style. Another common challenge for some of the foreign players has been to play less vigorously so that they don't receive yellow and red cards. The football adaptation process requires a period of learning, often longer than the players had expected, and the whole process is de-motivating at times. Rebecca describes her adaptation to the playing style in her club and, at the same time, longing for the kind of football she grew up with:

> I'm playing like them now, but not all the time; if I have an opportunity I like to show some skills, to make the game more beautiful . . . yes, I miss the beauty of the game.

According to the players, the difficulty in adapting to a new style of playing football explains the generally poor performances of some foreign players in their initial period in a foreign club and the reason why several players have decided to return to their home countries prematurely.

Additional motives for the players

The players who have gone through a long period of adaptation may become motivated to settle in their host country as Maguire (1996) originally described. One of the long-term-staying players in our study, Cathy, has established relationships with a Danish family that she calls her 'family'. She has also found a church with members that she describes as 'like family'. The feeling of attachment to these people and a specific locality might partially explain her reasons for rejecting other clubs' offers and her plan to apply for Danish citizenship. On the other hand, she says that there is not one Danish person that she can call her friend, and she knows that she will be going home some day. The feeling of dislocation from home is described both by the players who have been in Denmark for a short period and several of the other players who have spent longer in the country but continue to feel like outsiders particularly off the field. As Maguire and Stead (1996) pointed out, the sense of being an outsider has several dimensions depending both on the extent to which the migrant is integrated into the sporting subculture and specific team, and the ways in which the migrant is treated (and not least perceives herself) as an outsider or insider in the host community as such.

One of the North American players, Catharina, expresses her interest in settling in Denmark. She describes herself as well integrated, she almost speaks the language, she has a job as a coach and she intends to start the course for talent coaches run by the Danish FA. When asked about the feeling of being dislocated from her home and from her family, she says that she feels at home in Denmark, but she would like to bring her family over. In other words, the players keep facing the prospect of dislocation when settling for a longer period. In our case, settlement has not been an initial motive for the players.

An initial motivation, on the contrary, is having a personal recommendation or personal contact in Danish women's football before making the decision to migrate. As Catharina says, 'the biggest consideration is the connections'. Moreover, Kate describes how she came to Denmark (rather than Greece where she could get a higher salary), because she could stay at a club with a player from the same nationality. It would appear that social relationships are very important for the football migrants not only when deciding whether to migrate but also in their choice of a specific club. In other words, there is a social network of female football migrants developing that is related to the social network through which the clubs recruit their players and reduce the uncertainty in engaging in migration.

Gendered motives?

So far we have not seen big differences between the motives in this preliminary study of female football migration compared to the earlier studies of male football migration, except that money seems to be a less dominant motive for clubs and players alike. When looking at de-motivating factors it seems that female football migrants experience quite a few disadvantages in terms of poor salary and employment rights, adaptation challenges and the continuous feeling of dislocation. As Maguire *et al.* (2002, p. 37) state: 'There may be specific features of these processes that reflect broader gender inequalities that differentially hamper and constrain women: the gendered nature of these processes requires consideration.'

In addition, the disadvantages of the migratory processes due to gendered aspects may be inter-related with the present state of women's football. Magee and Sugden's category of the exile or expelled may be developed to cover gendered aspects of female footballers' migration. The players are not necessarily avoiding persecution in their home country, nor are they fleeing their country for political reasons. Rather, some of the players' migration seems to have more to do with a feeling of exclusion due to, among other things, the debated image of women's football in their home countries (Harris, 2007; Scraton *et al.*, 2008). The South American and African players, in particular, have been motivated to move away from their home country because of a feeling of disrespect for their chosen profession and the poor organization of women's football. On the other hand, the players from the United States come from a setting where football is primarily an activity for girls, and they experience a lack of respect in Denmark.

Moreover, female football players are motivated to migrate not only to leave possible disrespect and poor organization behind but also to come to obtain higher social status. The dream of social mobility seems to be important for some female footballers and it appears to have specific characteristics. The dream of gaining social respect and acknowledgement as a footballer has, in the literature, been related to low socio-economic conditions and ethnic minority status, where a career in sports is seen as the only 'way out' to obtain economic resources and social status (Carrington, 1986; Maguire, 1991a; Eitle and Eitle, 2002; Bourke, 2003; Collins and Buller, 2003). In women's football the prospects for economic gain are poor, but there is still the opportunity to enhance your social status through the act of migrating.

Poli (2006b) has described how, in sub-Saharan African countries, football is considered a means to achieve the migratory dream, departing to the countries where the rest of the population dream of going. Kate describes football as 'the people's hope' in her home country. Another African player, Patricia, describes her football career as her chance: 'My [football] career was a way out, and it was probably too late for me to go back to school.' This quotation illustrates one of the central points made in the literature about athletes' possibilities for establishing themselves in a sports career, namely that a gamble on your physical skills also means that you become dependent on having a sports career (Eitle and Eitle, 2002). Cathy, who came to Denmark at a very young age and could not get into upper secondary school here, is worried about not having an education:

> . . . it bothers me a lot because I really want to move forward with my education and I can't really do that here, that's one of the reasons why I sometimes feel like I should leave . . . I could feel like I'm losing my brain . . .

The stakes are high for migrants who have left their home country at a young age to play football abroad. As a professional footballer you come to acquire physical capital and not academic capital that can ensure your future social position. In other words, a football career is a temporary and often risky venture based on your bodily skills (Agergaard and Sørensen, 2009).

Still Cathy describes it as a dream, being able to have a football career in another country. 'I feel blessed because I know the players [other African players] and it's a dream for them but they haven't had the opportunity you know.' This quotation draws attention to the fact that the dream of social mobility is widespread among female footballers from some of the migrants' home countries. Sally points out that her social status will have changed when she returns home: 'I will have more prestige at home, if I play abroad.' For our informants the opportunity of enhancing their status is related to having undergone the football experience and adaptation challenges, rather than having gained economic wealth per se. What general observations can be made from what we have described?

Conclusion: what do we know now and not yet?

The Danish case indicates that the immigration of foreign players has developed since the 1990s, particularly since the introduction of the clubs' licence to contract foreign players, and with the growing professionalization and organization in the clubs. Though our data is limited, we see indications that female football migration is part of a growing internationalization developing from social connections between individuals who have met at international tournaments or somehow are connected around female football. As Elliott and Maguire (2008a) have described, recruiting networks are developed in interdependence between migrants and clubs and draw attention to the fact that workers and employers use a series of bonds to search out employment possibilities outside their local setting.

There are several driving forces underpinning the early stages of this migratory process. First, there are few financial incentives for either the clubs or the players (although some of the African and South American players do use their salary to send remittances home). Instead, a primary motive seems to be sporting ambitions, for the clubs which are looking to improve their sporting results and for the players who hope to establish a full-time career as footballers. Related to this is the players' motive to enhance their football experience and the clubs' realization of a possible side effect in terms of football socialization of their young Danish talents. A contentious factor among the clubs and players is the adaptation question. The concepts of assimilation and integration are used to describe the clubs' diverse strategies for the foreign players' adaptation not only to football but also their specific expectations regarding cultural adaptation. Moreover, it has been pointed out that the players are mainly focused on adapting to a new football playing style on the field, but less interested in the adaptation to the cultural context and country as such. Some of the players signify a new generation of skilled workers (Botelho, 1999). They are professionals and migrate to fulfil a specific job under the given conditions. As Stead and Maguire (2000b, p. 55) note, the new migrants adjust to, but do not want to become assimilated into, the local culture. It is the discipline (football) itself that keeps them motivated and they keep in touch with family and friends at home or internationally through the use of technology such as Skype and Facebook.

Further, we have discussed whether gendered aspects can be found in the analysis of the motives for female football migration. Re-interpreting Magee and Sugden's categories of the exile and expelled we point to respect or disrespect to women's football as contributory factors for the migratory flows. Moreover, we suggest that the motive of obtaining social mobility as a sport migrant takes a specific form in female football migration. There is little possibility for obtaining economic advancement, which means that the opportunity of obtaining social status is almost solely linked to the act of migration, that is, having spent a period abroad and having gained experience as a professional footballer.

Our analysis indicates that female football migration is not a globally uniform process but that local clubs develop different strategies for engaging in the process and realizing different side effects during the migratory process that might become new motives for them. In other words, a combination of factors creates a motivational blend that varies through the course of the migration process and for the individual (Molnar and Maguire, 2008, p. 79). The implication of these findings is that we need to consider the individual athlete and club much more seriously in our analysis of the driving forces of sports labour migration. And it is necessary to develop concepts that can help to differentiate between the clubs' and players' various levels of engagement in the migratory process.

Further studies are to be done to evaluate the importance of the different driving forces and the future perspectives for female football migration. Although our focus in this chapter has been motivational factors for clubs and migrants, they are not solely responsible for the development of female football migration. Studies are yet to be done on the macro-sociological dimensions in female football migration. What are the patterns and main trends in the international flux of female football migrants? What roles do football governing bodies and players' agents hold in the development of female football migration? To what extent is the migratory process global with respect to the global economy, and transfer of players on a global market? What are the push and pull factors in the various origin and destination countries, and what influence does the emigration and immigration of football players have on, for instance, Danish women's football?

There are also a number of micro-sociological issues that require further enquiry in order to understand crucial issues and problems for female football migrants. How does, for instance, the image of women's football affect the migrants, and how do they cope with this image? Are there particular disadvantages for female athletes (and coaches) as migrants? We also need further knowledge of the ways in which different club strategies for recruiting and integrating foreign players influence the migrant experience. Several studies are waiting to be done on female athletic migration in not only football, but also other sports disciplines where migration is gathering pace or just beginning.

Notes

1 Sporting ambition was also identified in Stead and Maguire's (2000a, 2000b) studies of football migration as an important motivational factor for sports labour migration.
2 We found that several players also migrate to Danish women's football to play football as amateurs.
3 Other clubs in the league have rented foreign players for shorter periods or received young players who have commuted back and forth to their home in other Nordic countries.
4 The clubs are given alias names.
5 One player was not interviewed, since she was injured and back in her home country for surgery.
6 To enhance the anonymity of our informants we will not mention the specific country of the players but refer to them as North American, African or South American players and under alias names. Also we are careful to not give too much information about specifics; for instance, a player's age, club and period of stay.
7 The clubs can apply for a licence by documenting that they can fulfil some minimal economic requirements regarding capital and salary expenses, and provide relevant information about their youth football organization (Cirkulære nr. 45, § 6.2. http://www.dbu.dk/page.aspx?id=1407, accessed 13 July 2009).
8 The information collected from the clubs can serve as a starting point for knowing which amounts we talk about. The third club has informed us that their players' salaries are between 5,000 and 12,500 DKK (670–1,680€) a month. The second club tells us that their foreign players are given around the minimum wage for employees from outside the European Union, namely 8,500 DKK (1,149€). In the first club we got the impression that the salary is a bit higher but still very modest.

Part IV
Identities in migration and sport

12 Globetrotters in local contexts

Basketball migrants, fans and local identities

Mark Falcous and Joseph Maguire

As Robins (1997) notes, 'with mobility comes encounter' (p. 18). The movement of sporting migrants precipitates such 'encounters', raising questions surrounding: labour rights and barriers; recruitment and integration; and cultural adjustment and dislocation. The strength of interrelated attachments to place, space and identities inherent to many sporting contexts is notable in evoking a range of emotive encounters surrounding sporting mobility. This chapter explores some of the questions surrounding the 'encounters' of sports labour migrants with host cultures.[1]

A host of case studies (Olin, 1984; Klein 1988, 1989, 1991a; Maguire, 1988, 1994a, 1994b, 1996; Lanfranchi, 1994; Maguire and Stead, 1996, 1998a, 1998b; Moorhouse, 1999; Maguire and Pearton, 2000a, 2000b; McGovern, 2000, 2002; Chiba *et al.*, 2001; Lanfranchi and Taylor, 2001; Kudo *et al.*, 2003; Falcous and Maguire, 2005) have revealed contestation and resistance across varying national and sporting contexts. Common themes in this work highlight the threat of 'deskilling' concerns regarding national team performances and the underdevelopment of indigenous talent. Such fears concerning the effects of migration have resulted in protectionist labour barriers, including quotas, residency clauses, selection limitations and eligibility thresholds to assuage local concerns. In some cases, however, migrants are courted, actively recruited and embraced by locals. Hence, there is the potential for widely varying responses to sporting migrants in local contexts. Such patterns highlight the paradoxes and ambiguities in the responses to flows of sports migrants around the globe and, indeed, globalisation processes more generally.

Theoretically, there is a clear need to understand the entanglement of migration with the commodification of global sport. Within the sports literature insights drawing upon elements of neo-Marxist-inspired variants of dependency theory (Klein, 1989) and world systems theory (Bale, 1994; Bale and Sang, 1996) have been critical in highlighting the economic dynamics by which core states dominate and control the exploitation of resources and production – common across numerous sports and locales. Yet the economic dimensions of labour migration are entwined with identity politics, where issues of attachment to place, identity and allegiances are as significant in the emerging global system.

Subsequently, Miller *et al.* (2001, 2003) have sought to evaluate the movement of sporting labour through the concept of the 'New International Division of

Cultural Labour'. Miller *et al.* locate sporting migrants within the context of an aggressively globalising (sporting) capitalism that seeks comparatively cheap labour in countries that can provide skilled workers to supplement costly local labour. That is, 'production' is increasingly 'outsourced' (as is consumption), whilst control over content remains at the 'centre'. Yet, the commitment of such an approach to a cultural imperialism thesis and its centre–periphery model points to the ongoing need to comprehend the interplay of the economic and cultural dimensions of migration. This chapter, in focussing on the reception of migrants by local audiences, reinforces the need to understand labour migration as entangled with wider interdependencies associated with globalisation. Hence, consideration of political–economic features is complemented with a broader analysis of zones of prestige, established–outsider relations drawn from a process with a sociological perspective (Maguire, 2005). We use a case study of the presence of labour migrants in English basketball to explore these conceptual issues (Falcous and Maguire, 2005).

Exploring migrants in 'the local': research setting and method

The data presented in this chapter emerged from a two-year multi-method ethnographic case study that sheds light on the juncture between local 'basketball identities' of fans of an elite men's team – the Leicester Riders – and the presence of migrant players. For these purposes we draw upon participant observations, 12 individual interviews and three focus group meetings in which six, six and four fans were involved – a total of 16 further fans. In this way, alongside numerous field encounters, a total of 28 individual fans were encompassed directly within in-depth data collection.

The research setting was Leicester (population: 279,921 – 2001 Census), one of the biggest cities in the English East Midlands and the tenth largest in England.[2] The sportscape of the city is dominated by professional men's sports of football, rugby union and cricket, with basketball peripheral to the sporting hierarchy of the city.[3] As well as the men's professional team, the club operates coaching initiatives within local schools to coach basketball. Migrant players are prominent within these initiatives, taking on roles in association with their playing contracts. Whilst this study explores the local presence, we now turn to the wider political–economic terrain which patterns basketball migrants' presence in Leicester.

The political economy of global basketball and labour migration

Understanding basketball labour migration in local contexts requires an awareness of the global contours of social, political and economic power arrangements within global basketball, characterised by differing interest groups at the global, regional and national levels. In terms of global governance, the Munich-based

International Basketball Federation (FIBA) has over 200 national governing bodies affiliated. Both between and within locales asymmetrical power relationships exist. The contested field of global basketball features struggles for commercial dominance and expansion, administrative influence, power and sovereignty.

A distinctive component of global basketball interdependence is wide-scale labour migration characterised by multi-directional, if imbalanced, 'talent pipelines'.[4] The movement of overwhelmingly male players is shaped by a range of restrictions including quotas, nationality restrictions and thresholds. The US functions as a 'core' area of talent production 'exporting' players around the globe. The US high school and collegiate system produces players who 'feed' the NBA labour market. The scale of 'overproduction', however, sees those not securing NBA contracts seeking employment in the worldwide network of leagues (see Olin, 1984; Maguire, 1988; Miller *et al.*, 2003). Consequently, the NBA acts as the apex of the hierarchy of global men's basketball leagues, overwhelmingly recruiting from the US college system, but also increasingly taking talent from 'donor' countries. Other national competitions are the recipient of surplus players from the collegiate system, and also suffer 'deskilling' due to their best players gravitating to the NBA.

In 1996, the European Union (EU) granted the same freedom of movement of labour to athletes as are enjoyed by other workers (see Maguire and Stead, 1998a; Moorhouse, 1999). This had a dramatic effect on sport in general – basketball was not immune. Notably, the collapse of internal barriers – in the form of foreign nationality quotas – saw players able to play in any European country as an EU national (rather than as a 'foreign' player). The consequence has been heightened migration within Europe, characterised by the concentration of the better players in the commercially dominant leagues.

Subsequently, in December 1998, FIBA agreed in principle to the free movement of players worldwide. Despite, in theory, permitting ten foreign players per team, the ruling allowed national competitions to establish their own quotas. Most mainland European leagues opted for two, whilst in Britain it was set at *five*. The outcome of this 'free market' increased the number of migrant players within the British game during the late 1990s. We now turn attention to this context.

The contested terrain of migrant players in British basketball[5]

Debates surrounding foreign player recruitment have been recurrent in British basketball since the mid-1970s (see Maguire, 1988). Concerns regarding the marginalisation and development of local players and the welfare of the national team have been countered by team-owning entrepreneurs who advocate North American (primarily from the United States) 'star' players as central to the emerging commercial viability of the game during the 1970s and 1980s. These processes, Maguire (1988) notes, meshed with issues of 'race' in significant ways by precipitating 'a shift away from a game played, by and large, by "respectable" white Britons, to one where the involvement of black Americans and black

Britons has increased significantly' (p. 308). Illustrating this, Chappell *et al.* (1996, p. 308) document the 'striking numerical increase' of 'Black involvement' in the National Basketball League competition between 1977 and 1994. Two related factors underpin these dynamics. First, migration centrally involved African American US players plying their talents in Britain. The presence, and indeed predominance, of these players was a significant factor in transforming the 'racial' make-up of the English game. Second, the influx of US migrants was matched by a rapid increase in the presence of Black Britons in the elite game.[6] From a total of only 8.8 per cent in 1977, the percentage of Black Britons within the total number of British players in the league increased to 58.9 per cent by 1994 (Chappell *et al.*, 1996). This timescale intersects with the commercial take-off and cultural redefining of the sport. Accordingly, processes of migration contoured along 'racial' lines have impacted upon the cultural significations and meanings of the game in Britain.

The high levels of foreign players during the late 1970s and 1980s were extended throughout the 1990s with teams permitted up to five foreign players who monopolise playing time, scoring, rebounding and assisting statistics and constitute the 'starting five' of most teams (see Falcous and Maguire, 2005). Further to this, coaching roles are dominated by 'imports' predisposing themselves towards further recruitment of migrants, with British players stereotyped as the 'back up'.

A salary cap alongside a foreign player quota allowing teams up to five non-EU players mediates labour movement. Whilst players seek the most favourable working conditions, clubs apply highly rational criteria to recruitment. Symptomatic of the global labour hierarchy noted earlier, the best British players migrate to the higher status professional leagues in Europe, with the elite appearing in the NBA.

Following the introduction of EU freedom of movement legislation in 1996, greater numbers of elite indigenous *English* players have migrated to the higher status leagues of southern Europe. A further trend is the movement of US migrants, having played in Britain for the requisite number of years, to higher profile leagues in Europe. Having qualified for a British passport these players are not subject to labour restrictions as US nationals. In this way the British league fulfils a function as 'stepping stone' for migrants who wait out their time to circumvent labour regulations to more lucrative career opportunities.

Continuing the pattern detailed by Maguire (1988), clashes between EBBA officials and elite club owners (operating under the title British Basketball League – BBL) have been recurrent. Long-time England coach Laszlo Nemeth was outspoken in his criticisms of the marginalisation of local talent, resulting from the dominance of foreign players, and problems of availability for the national team due to commercial pressures.[7] This marginalisation has recently been consolidated with the hosting of the London 2012 Olympics and the desire of UK Sport and basketball officials to have a 'competitive' team. The 'solution' has been to search for 'qualified' Americans. Such conflicts are the wider contextual terrain of the presence of labour migrants in British basketball. Yet, their reception within the national 'host' culture is also contoured by the specific local contexts of the consumption of basketball. This chapter grounds the broader political–economic analysis in the substantive *lived* reception and cultural experiences, attachments and identities of local consumers. In exploring the complex interplay of wider political–economic tensions the local consumption of basketball is revealed.

Theorising local responses: fandom, identity and consumption

To understand responses to migrant players, the social and cultural environment of fans – the fandom – is significant (Fiske, 1992; Harris, 1998). As Fiske notes, fandom emerges as 'popular audiences engage in varying degrees of semiotic productivity, producing meanings and pleasures that pertain to their social situation out of the products of the culture industries' (p. 30). In the case of Leicester basketball fans this 'meaning making' centres on the juncture between the consumption of commercial basketball and interpretive understandings of local leisure lives and identities. These lives and identities are, in turn, grounded in national, local and civic identities, themselves patterned along dynamic intersections of class-based, ethnicised and gendered lives. These structural components of identities inform specific interpretations of the pleasures and meanings associated with attendance.

The basketball audience is dominated by white, middle class, family groupings – the established group within Leicester – despite the sizeable presence of South Asian Britons noted above.[8] Differing emphases are evident in the central attractions, meanings and pleasures of attendance for fans. Some attendees' consumption centred on loyalty and 'support' of the Riders. Such affiliations are strongly entwined with parochial local identities and civic pride in Leicester – that is, they draw upon established local identities. For others, the 'family friendly' entertainment values, desires for spectacle and senses of identification with players were emphasised. Significantly, these interpretive variations are not necessarily mutually exclusive. Alternatively, fandom is characterised by multi-faceted identification and consumption of Riders games which, in conjunction with wider political–economic tensions within basketball, shape interpretations of foreign players.

The 'meaning making' of basketball fans is embedded in the way in which the individual generates meaning and social identity. In this regard Elias's (1965/1994) established–outsider relations framework sheds light on the linkage between power, basketball fandom, identities and 'readings' of migrants. Elias argued (from a case study based on a suburb of Leicester) that within power relations the 'special charisma', or qualities, attributed to established groups are mobilised as a means to reinforce 'we-identities', and simultaneously stigmatise outsider groups. Basketball is an arena where established *civic* identities are frequently mobilised in rivalry with 'outsider' teams and fans. The 'encounter' of local fandom and migrant players also stimulates the mobilisation of established *national* identities, which too draw upon the 'fantasy shield' of 'we-images' that protect the status of dominant English identities. Hence, basketball acts as a site where multi-layered established–outsider identities inform the meaning making of fandom.

Interpreting migrant players: identity and consumption in 'the local'

Fans' interpretations of labour migrants reflected the wider tensions of the debates surrounding British basketball operating in conjunction with varying facets of local consumption noted above. Thus, wider tensions were subject to interpretations grounded in the specific place of basketball in local lives, resulting in complex and, at times, competing interpretations. Several key themes of fans' reactions, illustrating the nuanced nature of the local–global interplay, can be identified. These draw upon several considerations: the role of migrants in team success; the desire for 'committed' players in the context of local civic pride; the marginalisation of local players; and the desire for spectacle and entertainment, which are detailed below.

Team success and spectacle

This desire for a winning team was entwined with conceptions of local pride and civic identity. Subsequently, there was an emphasis on the need to recruit and retain the most talented players. There was widespread acknowledgement amongst fans of the superior playing abilities of North Americans compared to their local counterparts. As Christian[9] reinforced: 'the Americans are obviously a lot superior to home players' (focus group, 01/04/00). As a consequence, many fans acknowledged migrant players as instrumental in the success of the team. Capturing this, David suggested: '. . . it's the only way you're gonna win, or do well at all in this league, if you've got a coach who's got contacts in America and he can get good players from colleges over to play for you' (focus group, 15/03/00). Consequently, he saw the recruitment of US players as pivotal to club success – indeed, as 'the only way'. In this light, numerous fans viewed the presence of migrants as essential.

Fans' interpretations were further shaped by perceptions of US players providing more *excitement* than their English counterparts. Phil, for example, emphasised the 'better spectacle' they offered:

> I think they can only do good for British basketball, because they improve the players that are already here; okay it probably reduces the chances of a local guy getting in your team . . . but I think *it makes the game a better spectacle* if you've got better players.
>
> (interview, 04/03/00, our emphasis)

Phil's opinion was clearly linked to a taste preference that games should provide 'spectacle', which he associated with the 'better' US players. Specifically, he viewed this as an acceptable trade-off, despite the fact that it 'reduces the chances of a local guy getting in your team'. Several fans emphasised US players' contributions to their enjoyment of Riders games: '. . . I think it's great that you've got the Americans for the flair and skill' (Harry, focus group, 01/04/00). Similarly,

Delia emphasised: 'I think watching the Americans play is exciting' (focus group, 24/03/00). In this way several fans viewed US players positively, premised on the style, entertainment and spectacle they associated with them compared to local players. Yet these perceptions were countered by a range of competing issues.

Migrants, commitment and local pride

Acknowledgement of the importance of Americans in team success and entertainment was countered by questions regarding their sense of attachment to the local community. Several fans questioned US players' loyalty to the city of Leicester, and consequently to the Riders. The following dialogue between a husband and wife, Alan and Denise, captures perceptions of migrants' ability to identify with the city:

ALAN: . . . a lot of import players, *they don't associate with the local community.*
DENISE: There's no pride in wearing that shirt is there . . . ?
ALAN: Yeah, because *they don't identify with Leicester, they've probably never heard of Leicester before.*
DENISE: . . . Hilroy [a local player] always had pride to wear that shirt, he always wanted to wear a Leicester Riders shirt . . .

(interview, 19/09/00, our emphasis)

In this extract the efforts of 'import' players (who 'don't associate with the local community') are contrasted with a Leicester-born player (Hilroy Thomas). Hence, compared to locally born players, they perceive a problem with imports lacking 'local pride'. Denise continued: 'I have a tendency to think the English players actually have a greater pride in wearing the Leicester jersey than the imports' (interview, 19/09/00). Similarly, Christian argued: 'British lads, they tend to work harder, maybe it's just a cultural thing' (focus group, 01/04/00). This comment reinforces perceptions of migrants' lack of identification with club and city as grounded in cultural stereotypes – as 'a cultural thing'.

David also questioned American players' commitment to the club. He reasoned:

> . . . *the Americans, you just never get the feeling . . . that they really care, and they really want the team to win and they want to play for the Riders* . . . you just feel sorry for them, like 'Oh you're just all the rejects that didn't quite make the NBA, or get good contracts in Europe, and you've had to come to this'.

(focus group, 15/03/00, our emphasis)

This quotation demonstrates David's acute awareness of the global basketball labour hierarchy which renders Leicester a low-status career option for players from the United States. Of note is David's (and others') scepticism of how this contextualises migrants' commitment to the Riders.

The comments of these fans are symptomatic of a disjuncture between the global movement of basketball players as 'mercenary' labourers and local fans' sense of loyalty and commitment to the locality the Riders represent. Here, there are clear tensions between fans' affiliation to the local community and the highly rational *economic* criteria which pattern migrant flows. These perceptions draw upon generalisations of the personal and professional characteristics of US players – their 'ascribed status' (Maguire *et al.*, 2002, p. 35) as financially motivated mercenaries with flair, yet lacking in 'work ethic' or attachment to the city or club. These contrasted with fans' observations on the status of local players.

The marginalisation of 'local lads'

Insights into perceptions of migrant players emerged as fans reflected on the marginalisation of local players. The ascribed status of US players, noted above, continued to be prominent, particularly with regard to senses of attachment to the local community. For example, fans (referring to the import quota having increased from two foreign players to five) lamented the marginalisation of less skilled, but more committed, 'English lads'. As Steve noted:

> There used to be only two foreign players allowed in each team . . . and *we used to get a lot of good young English lads come up, who were giving everything . . .* and now we've got five overseas players allowed, and there's very little scope for the British players . . . *I think it would be far better if we developed the youth we've got* and bringing in a couple of quality Americans.
>
> (Steve, focus group, 15/03/00, our emphasis)

Here, it is clear Steve expresses a desire to invest in local youth development, with more minimal American migration. This sentiment was echoed by Terry who argued:

> You might as well just have two American players, like we used to have in the 'good old days', and then *have the rest of the squad built up from basic English lads* who might not be the best of basketball players, but I used to enjoy them going on, because *there was a good rapport with those players, you felt that they were really playing for the club.*
>
> (Terry, focus group, 15/03/00, our emphasis)

Hence, Terry preferred the high levels of commitment and effort from English players than US 'mercenaries'[10] who, despite being better players, were perceived to be less loyal. Notable in both Terry and Steve's desire to see more English players is the perceived level of commitment of local personnel to the club (also reflected in fans' perspectives given above) and a sense of identification with fans.

These extracts demonstrate that fans' preferences for local players are underpinned by their perceptions of greater commitment to the club and rapport with fans compared to imports. These perceptions draw upon cultural stereotypes of 'mercenary' migrants who lack the passion and commitment to the local 'cause'. Clearly, such observations provide tension with the observations noted above on desires for team success and spectacle, to which migrants were integral. Subsequent findings revealed that issues of ascribed status operated in negotiation with the observations regarding the superior playing ability of migrants. The result was a series of nuanced views on migrants which are detailed below.

The paradox of migrants: 'It doesn't matter whether you're English!'

Viewing fans as simply 'anti-American' obscures the complexity of how the interplay between local identities and consumption shapes encounters with migrant players. As noted, US migrants were acknowledged as pivotal to team success which informed fans' pride and identification with the team. This factor, alongside the experience of 'committed' imports, complicated fans' interpretations of migrants. For example, Terry (having already expressed how he favoured 'English lads') questioned the distinction between migrant players' lack of identification with the club compared to 'committed' English players. He noted: 'I think it depends on the personality, that's the critical thing, because we've had Americans who give everything' (focus group, 15/03/00). Similarly, Alan responded: 'It doesn't matter whether you're English, you know, you can have English quitters, as well as you can have American quitters, it's about individual mettle' (interview, 29/09/00). Such observations complicated the picture of resistance and scepticism towards US players detailed above.

Despite a general preference towards local players, due to their apparent attachment to the club and community, fans acknowledged that migrants were also capable of the commitment and effort they sought, and could thus be viewed, sometimes, favourably. Perspectives on Americans, despite the pre-disposition for scepticism, were subsequently contextualised and subject to some 'negotiation'. Subsequently, several fans emphasised the effort and commitment of players, rather than national origins, as the key to how they viewed them. Capturing this, Christine explained: 'It doesn't matter where they come from, if it's America fine, let's have American quality, but equally if we've got a Brit that can do the job, let's have him' (focus group, 15/03/00). Significantly, Christine reinforced the acceptance of migrants on the basis of their offering 'quality', whilst also tacitly reflecting concerns that locals should not be marginalised. This example suggests that, amongst supporters, a simplistic pro-British, anti-US stance is not necessarily evident. This is despite the pre-disposition of several fans to favour English players on the basis of cultural stereotypes regarding 'work ethic' and allegiances to Leicester. The results are complex and suggest the presence of multi-layered fans' perspectives on US migrants representing Leicester.

Local players: development or underdevelopment?

The resistance towards migrant players noted above reflected wider tensions regarding the development and underdevelopment which have characterised English basketball over the past 20 years. As these data demonstrate, fans' perceptions are complicated by the desire for spectacle, entertainment and a winning team. Indeed, despite concerns about the presence of migrants, there were also views which perceived them as contributing, in a wider sense, to the British game. Perceptions of prominent migrants as acting to 'develop' local players were consistent. Davina, for example, suggested: 'Because it's an American-based game, I think they can bring that knowledge to Britain, and educate, like, local-based players as well' (Davina, focus group, 24/03/00). Likewise, Sherry noted: '. . . I think they've had a strong influence on, erm, the Riders and basketball in the UK, particularly in schools . . . I think they've inspired a lot of youngsters into basketball most definitely' (focus group, 24/03/00). Similarly, Leslie suggested: '. . . the game's not big in England . . . if children see American players then it might give them an interest' (focus group, 15/03/00). These comments illustrate perceptions of the positive impact of, most notably, US migrants on the indigenous game and the prestige they carry relative to their British counterparts – whatever the 'real' consequences of such recruitment. These impacts were seen in terms of generating interest, inspiring youngsters and 'educating' British players. Such perceptions are similar to the justifications offered by those in the game who advocated their introduction over 30 years ago.

These data reinforce the complexity of the encounter between English basketball fans and migrants showing how perspectives draw on, at times competing, considerations. For example, several fans who acknowledged the entertainment value of US imports expressed a simultaneous desire for more local personnel. Notably, they did not link the presence of migrants with the marginalisation of British players. Katie, for instance, suggested: 'I think they [US players] bring a lot more of the skills into the game . . . it's just a shame that there aren't more British players who are as good' (focus group, 01/04/00). In this way, Katie demonstrates competing desires. Simultaneously, she lamented the lack of English players, considered migrants to assist local player development, *and* yet valued the skills migrants brought to the game. Yet, the recruitment of US players and the development of locals are, in reality, contradictory – the former ensures that British basketball remains in a state of dependent development.

This example shows how perspectives are characterised by competing concerns within fans' identities and consumption. Thus, perceptions may include contradiction and are not necessarily politicised within the contexts of wider global political–economic tensions. Alternatively, the reception of migrants is shaped by established identities which draw upon local and national stereotypes and expectations, basketball's place in local pride and civic identities, and desires for entertainment and spectacle. These specifically local allegiances and understandings render a nuanced engagement within the wider political–economic flows and tensions of global basketball. The result is fans holding varying and complex perceptions of migrants.

Conclusion: global processes through the local lens

In considering the interplay between labour migrants, the consumption of English basketball and local fandom this chapter highlights the complexity of the local–global nexus. Local consumption was informed by: civic pride and loyalty; rivalry with teams; desires for club success and for spectacle and entertainment; and a sense of rapport with players. Broader concerns regarding the welfare of the 'national' game and fears of 'Americanisation' operate largely in 'negotiation' with the immediate realities of local meaning and leisure identities. The backdrops to this local consumption are established–outsider identities that contour reactions to migrants in several ways.

Fans' views of migrants featured variation and paradox. On one hand, engagement was informed by the playing superiority of migrants, leading them to be valued for their contribution to team performances. Notwithstanding this, numerous fans viewed British 'lads' most favourably, associating them with 'commitment', 'work ethic' and a sense of identification with the city of Leicester. This contrasted with the ascribed status of US migrants, which led fans to question their commitment and loyalty to the city and team. Thus, desires for a team victory and spectacle, to which migrants were seen as pivotal, were countered with pre-dispositions to favour 'local lads' on the basis of civic and national allegiances, and cultural stereotypes. Hence, 'conditional acceptance' of migrants in the context of local identities and civic pride was evident.

Wider concerns regarding US domination and the marginalisation of local players were subject to 'negotiation' according to fans' identities and leisure concerns. Where resistance and scepticism towards migrants was evident these surfaced largely in the context of concerns about the commitment and passion that non-locals may lack. Thus, concerns reflected fears that migrants may lack commitment in upholding local pride through winning results, rather than necessarily denying local players or threatening the English national team. In this way, wider discourses of brash, uncouth or mercenary 'Americans' in Britain are interpreted (and negotiated) through the specifically local lens of community and consumption through basketball fandom.

Our findings also reveal how the intersection of local established identities and 'race' can be complex within the context of the local–global sports nexus. As noted above, in conjunction with commercialisation processes commencing in the 1970s, labour migration transformed the 'racial' and ethnic compositions of the British game on the court. Subsequently, it is predominantly (but not exclusively) 'Black' North Americans, and Black British players, who are watched by predominantly white, middle class, family audiences (by the mid-1990s, 60.2 per cent of players were 'black' [Chappell *et al.*, 1996][11]). The way in which established English identities mesh intimately with conceptions of 'race' – that is, 'whiteness' – has widely been demonstrated within the wider literature (Gilroy, 1987; Hebdige, 1996; Solomos, 2003). Accordingly, the ways in which dominant constructions of the 'sporting nation' are entwined with constructions of race has also been demonstrated (Carrington and McDonald, 2001; Gilroy, 2001).

These issues are significant within the context of wider discourses of labour (im)migration in Britain, the cultural politics of which have been intimately entwined with 'race'. Specifically, as Solomos (2003) demonstrates, the politics of immigration, refugees and moral panics surrounding asylum seekers, fuelled by right-wing media and politicians, has centrally concerned threats to 'Britishness', to which 'race' is a central component. Our observations in this regard are revealing. Specifically, racialised subtexts of tension between 'local lads' versus Americans are complicated by the fact that it is frequently Black Britons who are the 'local lads'. In turn, a proportion of migrants are white. That is, whilst national identifications were a point of tension, the specifically racialised component of local and national identities was complicated, and indeed at points inverted. Furthermore, as we have detailed, the utility of migrants in upholding established local identities was significant.

In this sense, the wider discourses of 'threatening' economic migration, grounded in 'racialised' visions of nation (and in turn locality), are complicated in the (sporting) case we have observed.[12] Accordingly, we might tentatively speculate that sport may be perceived by some fans to occupy a cultural space beyond 'normal' social relations. Accordingly, as Back *et al.* (2001) observe in the case of English football, Black players 'wearing the [local] shirt' may somehow, however temporarily or ephemerally, dissolve racial difference in fans' interpretations. The 'hero status' of some African American basketball migrants amongst locals in Leicester is premised upon his upholding local pride and established identities. Such acceptance and indeed adulation of labour migrants is unlikely to be emulated beyond the sporting realm.

Though preliminary in scope, the observations of this case study warrant some discussion in the context of the dynamics of the local–global nexus. Theoretically, we have employed the conception of established and outsider groups (Elias, 1965/1994) to reveal the multi-layered identity politics that characterises local–global dynamics. The stigmatisation of US players as 'mercenaries', lacking commitment, effort and identification with local values, is symptomatic of the 'collective fantasy' which reaffirms established national (English) and local (Leicester) identities. In turn the ascribed status of Americans is countered by idealised 'we-image' visions of local players' sense of civic allegiance, effort and rapport with the local audience. These dynamics are pivotal in the local consumption and impact of migrants.

Yet, the encounter demonstrates the complex nature of established–outsider relations at the local–global nexus. For example, the collective utility of migrant players to established/dominant Leicester community identities and local leisure lives means they can be accepted on 'negotiated terms'. These relations arise from within a global political economy of basketball which sees US migrants themselves as the established group in terms of labour within English basketball. English players, the former established group at a local level, are pushed to the outsider role in the global division of labour. The consequence is a nuanced interplay between local and global stimulated by the presence of migrants. There is, then, simultaneous retrenchment and reconfiguration of power relations as local established identities are forced to reconcile the presence of 'outsider' labour migrants.

These observations afford scope to evaluate conceptualisations of the globalisation debates, both with regard to sport and more widely, that we have sought to address. Our approach has been to draw upon elements of cultural studies, critical political economy and figurational sociology to explore the encounters of sports migration. In doing so, a more nuanced analysis of local–global dynamics than explications which emphasise solely global capitalism is possible. In this regard the established–outsider concept offers a means to reveal the nature of local–global identity politics within the contexts of wider political, economic and cultural structuring. Specifically, a more nuanced analysis of local consumption, meanings and identities is thus possible in preference to those using an econo-centric analysis (e.g. Takahashi and Horne, 2006). Clearly, our approach is not the only way, but it does afford ways of conceiving the multi-faceted nature of global sport development as a means to conduct further work and avoids the reification associated with strictly economic accounts.

Substantively, this work highlights the complexity of the local consumption of global sports contoured by local identities and affiliations, yet operating within wider political, economic and cultural dynamics. In the case examined, local cultural affiliations are clearly significant in sports consumption and 'encounters' with sports labour migrants. The game is a source of meaning and identity within the everyday lives of English basketball fans. Central to affiliations in this case were issues of local pride, collective representation and place identity, always relative to other local East Midland, regional and national identities. As noted, global flows – in the form of migrants – albeit with caveats, become active constituents within local discourses of civic pride, rivalry and entertainment. Thus, whilst local consumption and identities are pivotal in the reception of global sports flows, in turn these flows actively inform local cultures. For example, US migrants were at the forefront of upholding local civic pride in fiercely contested matches against local rivals Birmingham Bullets or Derby Storm. These local Midlands towns, characterised by successive waves of migration more generally, likewise have labour migrants at the forefront of fans' civic pride as experienced through basketball (as well as in association with football, cricket and rugby).

Such observations have resonance with previous work (Andrews *et al.*, 1996; Jackson and Andrews, 1999) that posits the 'reinvigoration' of local cultures resulting from the circulation of global sports flows. Yet, caution is required in heralding the significance of the interpretive potential of 'the local'. Both the political–economic dynamics of sport, and the broader civilising struggles that characterise globalisation processes, highlight the interpretive limits that confront local sporting identities. As Maguire notes, 'a sensitivity to local responses to global flows has to be stressed. But so does the balance of power between the groups involved' (1999, p. 149). What is at stake is the power geometry between established–outsider groups, at a series of nodal points or levels, within the migrant and wider global figuration. Hence, local affiliations to British basketball are contextualised by deeper global interdependences that, arguably, actively *underdevelop* the British game relative to US influences in political, economic and cultural terms. Understanding power geometries then is crucial in contextualising the significance and limits of local interpretation.

Notes

1 This chapter is based on Falcous, M. and Maguire, J. (2005) 'Globetrotters and local heroes? Labour migration, basketball and local identities', *Sociology of Sport Journal*, 2: 137–57.

2 Large-scale immigration during the late 1960s and 1970s altered the city's cultural diversity substantially. About one-third (29.9 per cent) of the population identify as Asian or Asian British and a much smaller percentage (3.08 per cent) as Black or Black British (2001 Census). The largest single ethnic minority community group in the city are of Indian origin – 25.7 per cent (72,000). Accordingly, one of Leicester's distinguishing characteristics is ethnic diversity in population terms.

3 The club started as the Loughborough All-Stars located at Loughborough University, 13 miles north of Leicester. Concurrent with commercial shifts within the game, the club moved to Leicester in 1977, and was a founder member of the National Basketball League in 1986. In 2001 the club returned to play at Loughborough University following the loss of their home arena.

4 We use the word 'pipelines' to denote 'the structures and processes through which athletes are identified and nurtured' (Stead and Maguire, 1997, p. 70).

5 We use the term British here as the league operates as the British Basketball League (BBL). Teams are predominantly drawn from England with only one featuring outside it – from Edinburgh, Scotland. The competition is distinctly Anglo-centric. The case used in this paper is English, making the findings nationally specific.

6 Of note is the marginal cultural status of basketball within Britain. Accordingly, no high school and 'college' feeder-system of playing talent exists as it does in the United States.

7 Notably, Nemeth himself is a Hungarian national. As a 'settler' migrant himself, his 'championing' of the British game demonstrates the contradictions and paradoxes within the global sport system, characterised by complex migratory patterns and allegiances.

8 Questionnaire data suggested that the basketball audience does not mirror that of the wider city. In particular, the ethnic minority profile of the basketball audience (6 per cent) shows an under-representation of the city's ethnic population which stands at 36 per cent (2001 Census). In particular the large Asian and British Asian population are under-represented.

9 Pseudonyms are used to protect the anonymity of fans.

10 The term 'mercenary' is taken from Maguire (1996). It refers to those migrants who are motivated more by short-term gain, with little or no attachment to the locality within which they 'ply their trade'.

11 The data of Chappell *et al.* (1996) are taken from the 1993/1994 season.

12 In the context of this case study, attempting to gauge the role of 'race' in the explicit reception of migrants is challenging. Specifically, the political sensitivity of enquiries presents methodological difficulties. Overt questioning of white consumers regarding perceptions on the basis of race is likely to evoke 'socially desirable' responses. Throughout participant observations during this time it did not emerge as an expressed factor among the fans we engaged. It is only even longer-term ethnographic work which may gain closer entrée to the linkages between race and consumption.

13 Diaspora and global sports migration

A case study in the English and New Zealand contexts[1]

Toni Bruce and Belinda Wheaton

In an increasingly globalised world, athletic migration becomes an important vector through which to understand issues related to citizenship, nationalism and identity. The intensification of such sports-related migration has spurred research into how sporting migrants are understood, and understand themselves, in relation to concepts such as nationalism, transnationalism, globalisation and cosmopolitanism.[2] Indeed, our analysis begins from the position that sport is an important site for exploring 'the complex interplay between ethnicity, "race", nation, culture and identity' (Ansari, 2004, p. 209). Sport researchers clearly identify the continuing importance of sport to nationalism (e.g. Bairner, 2001; Maguire, 1999; Rowe, 2003; Silk *et al.*, 2005). At the same time, social commentators make a broader case that the decentring of the state has led to multiple narratives and new identities including diasporic forms of identity and citizenship (see Appadurai, 1996; Billig, 1995; Cohen, 1997; Urry, 2003). As a result, analyses of internationally mobile athletes can provide insights into wider processes of cultural globalisation, raising questions about identity, place and allegiance in the context of a 'pluralization of national identities' (Maguire and Bale, 1994, pp. 283–4).

What is surprising is the relatively late entry of the concept of diaspora into the theorisation of sporting migration, especially given its salience in describing wide-ranging forms of transnational migration and settlement.

Diaspora broadly refers to the movement of peoples who travel across borders, most often of nation-states, to form communities which retain a range of ties – such as economic, familial and symbolic – to the original place of departure (see Anthias, 1998; Brah, 1996; Brubaker, 2005; Clifford, 1994; Reis, 2004). Diaspora, therefore, 'denotes transnational movement and ties in with debates about non-nation based solidarities' (Anthias, 1998, p. 557). More recently, theories of diaspora have expanded beyond the original focus on traumatic, forced dispersal to include voluntary forms of movement which appear more relevant to the sporting context. Our analysis is grounded in versions of diaspora which are variously termed as postmodern (Anthias, 1998), cultural (Cohen, 1997) or contemporary (Reis, 2004). Most relevant are the versions that stem from debates around the ways in which 'race' and ethnic boundaries are re-configured in the context of global transformations (e.g. Brah, 1996; Cohen, 1997; Gilroy, 1991, 1993; Hall, 2001). Here, questions about the cultural politics of 'home' and 'belonging' – of 'roots' and 'routes'

(Brah, 1996, p. 192) – in contemporary transnational migration have been interrogated. In such diasporic movements, people may retain multiple affiliations that transcend the nation-state, such as the 'double consciousness' negotiated by 'black' people who adopt African and western identities which Gilroy (1993) so ably illustrates in *The Black Atlantic*. We suggest that, despite the need for conceptual clarification, diasporas in transnational settings offer 'an alternative paradigm for national (or multinational, transnational, and even postnational) identification' (Braziel and Mannur, 2003, p. 8). Most importantly for our analysis here, diasporic identities offer increasing challenges to the 'notion that a national community is necessarily bounded by its geographic borders' (Braziel and Mannur, 2003, p. 15).

Diaspora and sporting migration

In the sporting migration literature, a series of illuminating studies have recently emerged that critically examine diaspora in the context of understanding the racialisation and globalisation of sporting culture and identities (see Andersson, 2007; Burdsey, 2004, 2006; Carrington *et al.*, 2001; Grainger, 2006; Joseph, 2009; Madan, 2000; Spracklen and Spracklen, 2008), the majority of which explore the experiences of and reactions to non-dominant racial groups within predominantly 'white' nations. Carrington *et al.*, for example, find that black British males may embrace non-British 'black' athletes such as basketball star Michael Jordan as significant resources for defining their own black identity and conclude that 'the sports arena thus operates as an important symbolic space in the struggles of black people against the ideologies and practices of white supremacy' (2001, p. 205). Madan also argues that, for populations who are 'other' within a particular nation, sport becomes 'a space through which national, ethnic and diasporic identities are articulated and played out' (2000, p. 28).

Such studies help us understand how migrants may refuse to adopt single identities but instead embrace multiple allegiances; for example, Englishness/Asianness (Burdsey, 2006), Englishness/Irishness (Darby and Hassan, 2008; Hickman *et al.*, 2005), Englishness/New Zealandness (Bruce and Wheaton, 2009) or Australianness/ Indianness (Madan, 2000). From this growing body of work comes an understanding of how diasporic identities may expand to embrace other groups perceived to share a similar status such as 'black' or 'Asian' (Andersson, 2007; Carrington *et al.*, 2001; Madan, 2000). For example, Madan (2000, p. 30) finds that World Series Cricket grounds are transformed into places of 'diasporic consciousness' that are activated on a racial binary of white/non-white. Thus, Australian 'Indians' embrace other non-white teams (such as Pakistan, Sri Lanka and West Indies) as part of a broader diasporic understanding of being 'similarly "sort of different" from mainstream Australian society' (Madan, 2000, p. 31). These studies and other work on British Asian and black sporting identifications (e.g. Burdsey, 2006; Carrington *et al.*, 2001) illustrate that, although sport is a prime arena in which minority ethnic groups are physically and symbolically excluded from the national collectivity, at the same time they use their sporting affiliations to perform a range of diasporic identities. Indeed, some British Asians perform 'multifaceted, fragmented' identities such as supporting English teams in football but Indian subcontinent teams in cricket, enabling them 'to emphasize both their cultural traditions and the permanency of South Asian settlement in Britain' (Burdsey, 2006, p. 11).

Mirroring the diasporic research more generally, what is generally absent from the sporting diaspora literature is consideration of what Gamlen calls the experience of 'middling' transnationalism, especially in relation to former British territories such as New Zealand, Canada, Australia and South Africa 'that occupy what might be thought of as the "middle-class suburbs" of the global system' (2005, p. 32; see, however, Maguire and Stead, 1996, in relation to English cricket).

A case study of the death of Sir Peter Blake

In this chapter, we expand the focus to include a group which is conceived of as 'the same' as the host nation rather than racially or culturally different. We do this via a case study of media coverage of the death of world-renowned sailor and environmentalist Sir Peter Blake in New Zealand and English[3] broadsheet newspapers.[4] Our analysis is based on more than 180 articles and photographs (150 in New Zealand, 32 in England) collected in the two weeks following his death, as well as a visit to his grave in England. We conceptualise the coverage as a series of texts that 'offer especially rich opportunities to observe the cultural construction of meaning . . . where we can see the social production of ideas and values happening before our eyes' (Turner, 1997, p. 326), and ground our analysis in the belief that, although media representations do not tell us what to think, they set the boundaries for what we can think about (Hall, 1984).

Our focus on diaspora emerged as we tried to make sense of the apparently unproblematic representations of Blake as a transnational and cosmopolitan citizen *and* as a signifier of New Zealand nationalism (Bruce and Wheaton, 2009). Briefly, Blake was a white New Zealander who moved to England as a young man to pursue his sailing dreams. His international reputation grew from winning two of yachting's greatest events, the America's Cup and the round-the-world yacht race, for New Zealand syndicates. Blake's unexpected and violent death during a bungled robbery in Brazil while on an environmental mission in 2001 led to widespread media coverage in many countries. However, it was in New Zealand (where he was born and for which he sailed) and Great Britain (where he married, had children and lived for most of his adult life) that the majority of the coverage appeared. In brief, our analysis revealed that Blake's death was reported in overlapping but slightly different ways in both countries. The New Zealand coverage virtually ignored his lived transnationalism; instead, it highlighted Blake as an internationally successful Kiwi who brought glory to his nation. The public embrace of Blake should not be underestimated: the largest crowd in New Zealand history attended the 1995 America's Cup parade and there was an outpouring of national grief after his death (see Cosgrove and Bruce, 2005). In contrast, the UK coverage was multi-dimensional and able to acknowledge Blake as a New Zealander while simultaneously recognising his English connections. In both countries a taken-for-granted diasporic fluidity in Blake's identity was apparent; as in the lack of contradiction in the reporting of his achievements as *New Zealand* Sportsman of the Year and *British* Yachtsman of the Year ('Blake killed in Amazon shootout', 2001; Gorman, 2001).

Elsewhere, we have examined the multiplicity of representations of Blake in terms of racial, transnational, national and cosmopolitan identities (see Bruce and Wheaton, 2009; Cosgrove and Bruce, 2005). While the concept of diaspora has informed our previous work, in this chapter we attempt to excavate in more detail the ways in which the coverage was underpinned by a particular understanding of New Zealand identity; one that encompasses a taken-for-granted Kiwi diaspora and is grounded in dual conceptions of 'home' in both New Zealand and English contexts. We explore the ways in which Blake occupies a different 'space' from members of the sporting diasporas discussed above, by virtue of his race, class and birthplace. Rather than the hostility, ambivalence or conditional acceptance experienced by members of non-white diasporas, we argue that Blake was fully accepted in both national contexts; an acceptance that intersects with current debates about race and the nation in both countries and derives from and re-forges a particular historical empire–colony relationship.[5] In the remainder of the chapter, we weave together theorising about diasporic identities and the empirical evidence as we explore how British and New Zealand media represented Blake's death.

Contextualising British–New Zealand relations

While many categorisations of diaspora, including those investigated in sporting contexts, emphasise forced migration, marginalised ethnic groups and a (post-colonial) 'politics of oppression' (Alexander and Knowles, 2005, p. 8), the New Zealand diaspora fits more comfortably within definitions that acknowledge the increasing complexity and variety of diasporic formations (Anthias, 1998; Cohen, 1997; Reis, 2004). Blake's life and media representations of it reinforce Braziel and Mannur's (2003) contention that theories of diaspora increasingly challenge the belief that national communities are bounded by fixed geographic borders. Furthermore, they point out that defining nations by such geopolitical boundaries 'is inherently reductive, exclusionary and problematic' (Braziel and Mannur, 2003, p. 15). In Blake's case, he left New Zealand as a young man, reportedly seeking opportunities to challenge himself as a sailor that were not available in New Zealand. In this, his motivation was not dissimilar to other young[6] New Zealanders for whom a period living in the United Kingdom is a 'well-recognised rite of passage' (Bedford, 2005, p. 14; Conradson and Latham, 2005; Wiles, 2008). As Conradson and Latham argue, 'this is a group for whom a period of living and working abroad has come to be viewed as an almost central part of reaching adulthood' (2005, p. 289). It is 'taken-for-granted' and viewed as '"natural" . . . "usual" . . . "unexceptional"' (Conradson and Latham, 2005, p. 298). The unexceptional nature of such migration is grounded historically: not only have many New Zealanders, especially those of British ancestry, been 'comfortable with a dual identity embracing twin conceptions of "Home"' but both nations have also been comfortable imagining a subject-hood that was simultaneously British and New Zealand (Pearson, 2006, p. 6; Spoonley *et al.*, 2003; Wiles, 2008). Indeed, it was not until 1949, the year after Blake was born, that New Zealanders ceased to be British subjects and legally became New Zealand citizens. As Belich argues, 'between the 1880s and the 1950s at least, most people living in [New Zealand] had no doubt that they were both New Zealanders and Britons' (2007, p. 5). This sentiment still has currency: it emerged at the recent unveiling of a war memorial in London which recognised the 'enduring nature' of England as a place for New Zealanders to call 'home' (BBC News, 11 November 2006). Thus, it is not surprising that the history of back-and-forth movement has resulted in the development of flexible, fluid, pluralistic and multi-layered identities (Pearson, 2006).

This shared history has led to a sizable transnational offshore population in London, many of whom continue to imagine themselves as Kiwis despite some-times decades of living overseas (Wiles, 2008). By the 1970s when Blake first migrated to England, he was among the first generation which 'did not go "Home" with a capital H' (James, 2007, p. 3), and his initial travels reflect recent findings that many New Zealanders do not intend to live in the United Kingdom permanently. Instead, like Blake – who met his wife at an English sailing club, married, had two children, and made England his base of operations – the fact that 'their lives become entangled in a more enduring capacity . . . generally emerges in an unplanned fashion' (Conradson and Latham, 2005, p. 297).

The comfort in dual conceptions of home is concretely reflected in the fact that Britain constitutes the second largest population base, after Australia, for the esti-mated 20–25 per cent of New Zealanders living abroad (Bedford, 2001, 2005). The movement of people between New Zealand and Britain therefore exemplifies a long-term but constantly evolving relationship – entailing migration in both directions – that involves informal and formal ties to both countries (Pearson, 2006; Wiles, 2008). Indeed, mobility has taken on an important cultural significance – becoming 'an important . . . aspect of being a New Zealander' (Conradson and Latham, 2005, p. 299). However, like Blake who identified himself as a New Zealander throughout his life, many young New Zealanders who travel today in the opposite direction to their ancestors – the British expansion and settler diaspora that colonised New Zealand – have no wish to identify Britain as 'home', construct-ing instead their identity, activities and relationships 'around the idea of a shared collective imaginary of "home"' being New Zealand (Wiles, 2008, p. 134). It is clear that many do evince a 'diasporic consciousness with a foot in two or more locations' (Cohen, 1997, p. 164) – living and socialising together with other New Zealanders (Conradson and Latham, 2005).

Yet, surprisingly, public and government framing of this movement as a diaspora is relatively recent. In New Zealand, public discussion of a Kiwi diaspora emerged in the mid-1990s in response to concerns about the 'brain drain'; that is, as an explicit strategy to renegotiate the terms of how New Zealanders abroad were understood (Bedford, 2001; Conradson and Latham, 2005; Gamlen, 2005; Larner, 2007; Wiles, 2008). New Zealand has a particularly large diaspora in relation to its population size; it is second only to Ireland in the proportion of its population living overseas according to a recent OECD estimate (Bedford, 2005; Wiles, 2008). However, although recent New Zealand research explores the explicit emergence of government diaspora strategies which involve 'a new geographic imaginary [and] the active constitution of new spaces and subjects' (Larner, 2007, p. 332), it is clear that implicit knowledge of the New Zealand diaspora has existed for a long time and in much broader terms than the relatively narrow, exclusionary, male, success story, Northern hemisphere and economic orientation of recent government discourses (Larner, 2007).

Blake the (diasporic) Kiwi

However, explicit reference to the diasporic nature of Blake's identity was virtually invisible in the British and New Zealand coverage, and references to it emerged only rarely. For example, some British coverage alluded to it, such as describing Blake as 'a man who brought both national pride and identity to a community of less than four million people, many of them at the opposite ends of the world to where they have their roots' (Alexander, 2001, p. 6). A New Zealand story quoted Blake's Emsworth-based business partner: 'Apart from their lengthy spells in New Zealand for campaigns, this is his home. He is always a New Zealander . . . but his roots are also here' (Potter, 2001, p. 2). In New Zealand coverage Blake's links to New Zealand were emphasised in terms of patriotism rather than physical location. The fact that he *identified as* a New Zealander, sailed *for* New Zealand syndicates and won international recognition *for the nation*, including spearheading the push to develop the Auckland waterfront for the successful America's Cup defence in 2000, far outweighed the facts of his physical location: 'Blakey's only agenda was to do stuff for New Zealand. He always put New Zealand first' (Pepperell, 2001, p. 15). In this discourse, *being* a New Zealander was not restricted to those who lived in the country (see also Cosgrove and Bruce, 2005). It recognised that New Zealandness was more about an imagined sense of identity than actual location within the physical boundaries of the nation. Thus, if only implicitly, this framing recognised the existence of a Kiwi diaspora.

Indeed, the New Zealand media refused the chance to highlight Blake's diasporic identity; seldom acknowledging the length of time he had lived in England, and avoiding any articulation of Blake's identity to Britishness. Few identified Emsworth or England as his home and most represented his burial in a small seaside village near Emsworth as a choice made by his English wife for their English children. In contrast, the British media were able to acknowledge Blake as a New Zealander and to apparently unproblematically suggest Blake's Britishness or Englishness.[7] Blake's English home was referenced in almost all articles, suggesting that, despite being born in New Zealand, England was where Blake had chosen to be: 'Blake's body has been flown *home* to Britain' (Pelly, 2001) 'where he and his English wife, Pippa, brought up their children' (Jeffery, 2001, p. 19). That Blake was buried in England was depicted as natural and obvious.

However, while Britishness or a particular regional Englishness was inscribed in the English articles, the English media did not claim Blake as 'our' hero. He was constructed as either a Kiwi hero or ascribed some sort of global citizenship – a hero of an elite international sailing world, albeit one in which Britain was assumed to play an important role. Rather than his living in the United Kingdom and calling it 'home' signifying a distancing from his Kiwiness, British coverage illustrated the ways Blake was able to exist as a more flexible citizen. In this sense, Blake transcended his national context; he was represented as a transnational cosmopolitan citizen, able to inhabit different places and spaces without contradiction (Bruce and Wheaton, 2009). Indeed Blake's gravestone appears to explicitly acknowledge his transnationalism in the naming of both his 'homes' (of New Zealand and Emsworth), and cosmopolitanism in the inclusion of the words 'adventurer' as well as 'yachtsman' (Bruce and Wheaton, 2009). We argue that these words, the offerings left by New Zealanders on his grave (New Zealand and silver fern flags, letters, stuffed toys dressed in New Zealand colours) and the media coverage which articulated him to New Zealand national identity despite his residence and burial in England are strongly linked to a diasporic Kiwi identity which renders these potential contradictions unproblematic. Therefore, while on one level appearing to embrace both transnational and cosmopolitan identities, the gravestone is a physical manifestation of a taken-for-granted diasporic Kiwi identity that underpinned, without being overtly acknowledged, the ways in which Blake's life was represented.

Discourses of diaspora and race in the British–New Zealand context

Another key aspect of media coverage was the almost complete erasure of Blake's racial identity; a finding that led us to consider how discourses of race and (im)migration might intersect in both countries to create the space for Blake to be unproblematically embraced as both Kiwi and British (or English). In both countries, the publicly and politically mediated rhetoric and practices of inclusion and exclusion in relation to immigration have revolved around 'non-white' populations. In addition, around the time of Blake's death there was an intensification of cultural racism in both countries based on an assumed incompatibility of cultural traditions between large immigrant groups and an assumed authentic white ethnicity or identity (see Anthias *et al.*, 1992).

New Zealand was in the grip of another cycle of backlash against non-white immigration; this time in the form of xenophobic media coverage of immigrants from a range of 'Asian' countries such as China and South Korea. This coverage is dramatically different from the discursive construction of white sportsmen such as Blake (and later rally driver Possum Bourne and mountaineer Sir Edmund Hillary) as national heroes whose character is articulated to historical imaginings of masculine whiteness (Bruce, 2004; Cosgrove and Bruce, 2005). This bifurcated, racially driven discourse is revealing of the ways in which whiteness has long been used to signify difference between 'us' and 'them' (Pearson, 2008); where groups constituting 'them' have included Chinese and Indians in the late 1800s and Pacific Islanders in the 1970s (Ballara, 1986; Spoonley *et al.*, 2003).

In the UK immigration has become synonymous with blackness and concern about the inversion of imperial domination, as the former colonies of the Caribbean and Indian subcontinent are perceived to be colonising the coloniser (Gilroy, 1991; Hall, 2001). The reporting of Blake's murder took place in a social-political climate – only months after the World Trade Center bombings and during a period of extensive unrest in 'Asian' communities in the North of England (see Bagguley and Hussain, 2005) – in which British Asian, predominantly Muslim, men were increasingly being treated with 'suspicion and hostility', constructed as 'the enemy within' and their loyalty to the British state questioned (Burdsey, 2007, p. 615).

In stark contrast to the concern with immigrant 'others' in both countries, however, New Zealand and British (or 'English') values and lifestyles are seen to be compatible. The New Zealand community living in England tends to be well educated, wealthier and significantly more visibly *white* and *middle class* than the population in New Zealand in general[8] (Wiles, 2008), and many have left secure, well-paid professional jobs, tempted to London 'as much by what it offers them in lifestyle and personal experience terms as by any narrow economic calculus' (Conradson and Latham, 2005, p. 290). As a result, members of the New Zealand diaspora occupy a privileged position in British discourses – seen to be desirable immigrants (Wiles, 2008) and likely to become productive citizens contributing to the well-being of the nation (Conradson and Latham, 2005). As members of white settler nations, they are 'privileged by being perceived and acted towards as intimate, close kin' (Pearson, 2006, p. 10). Thus, whiteness clearly played a central part in British 'fondness' and New Zealand articulations of Blake to nationalism (Cosgrove and Bruce, 2005).

The context of relatively free movement of people between both countries and the location of New Zealanders within a 'community of Britishness' (Pearson, 2006, p. 10) may help explain why the British media showed no need to claim Blake as a *British* hero but instead positioned him as an icon of old-fashioned, non-commercialised sporting heroism that transcended his nationhood, and as a specifically *white* gentile man from the former colonies; a man who could be seen as 'one of us'. His representation echoed an historic, nostalgic archetype of heroic masculinity that could be linked in Britain to the characteristics of white English football stars of the 1950s such as 'ordinariness, restraint, team work and understatement' (Holt, 1996, p. 44), and in New Zealand to idealised forms of Pākehā[9] masculinity which include attributes such as modesty, determination and self-sacrifice (Cosgrove and Bruce, 2005). Embracing Blake can therefore be read as a nostalgic desire in both countries for a mythical 'golden age', in which the culturally hegemonic position of white males as the 'embodiments and arbiters of normality was not properly challenged' (Maguire, 1994b, p. 409).

Conclusions

Cohen argues for a more relaxed definition of diaspora which is now being used 'in a variety of new, but interesting and suggestive contexts' (1997, p. 21): we suggest that the New Zealand diaspora, and Blake as representative of it, is one such example. Like other diasporas, many New Zealanders living in the United Kingdom are 'both inside and outside' (Cohen, 1997, p. 168) British society and retain a strong sense of identity as New Zealanders: their voluntary, and often non-permanent, migration does not preclude a potent 'collective identity in a place of settlement' (Cohen, 1997, p. 25).

What is also evident is that athletes who, like Blake, embody transnationalism and cosmopolitanism in terms of their physical location and professional careers do not necessarily adopt a post-national imaginary in the cultural realm (Appadurai, 1996). Instead, by competing *for* the nation and publicly identifying as *citizens of* the nation, they actively contribute to the symbolic, 'imagined' national community to which they have pledged their identity. As one member of the public was reported to have said: 'He will always be a son of New Zealand regardless of where his resting place is' ('Blake's death leaves Viaduct crowd in sombre mood', 2001, para. 18). The British and New Zealand coverage of Blake clearly reinforces the challenge that diasporic identities pose to the 'notion that a national community is necessarily bounded by its geographic borders' (Braziel and Mannur, 2003, p. 15).

By way of a caveat, however, we draw attention to the British and New Zealand reaction to Blake's heir-apparent, white New Zealander Sir Russell Coutts, who defeated New Zealand in the 2003 America's Cup as skipper of Swiss consortium Team Alinghi. By sailing 'against' New Zealand, he was negatively represented in both countries as a defector who deserted his nation; his decision to leave team New Zealand almost immediately after the win in 2000 'seen as the act of a traitor, by a man who valued love of money above love of country' (Cosgrove and Bruce, 2005; Gilchrist, 2005; Phillips, 2000, p. 324). As one New Zealand sailor put it, 'many people feel he committed treason' (Wise and St John, 2003, para. 5). As this reaction to Coutts makes clear, it is the adopting of a diasporic positioning that is *for* the country of birth which is important. Thus, Blake's ability to simultaneously reinforce both transnational and national identities is not available to all diasporic citizens. Another revealing corollary to the acceptance of Blake, a wealthy *white* New Zealander, is the ways in which 'brown' Samoan-born rugby players playing for New Zealand's celebrated men's national rugby team are still excluded; treated not as citizens but as immigrant others (Grainger, 2006). In this case, as Andersson also illustrates, sport provides a graphic illustration of how 'racial and ethnic minorities in western nation-states historically and in the present are excluded from the imagined community of the nation' (2007, p. 67).

The existence of a recognisable and welcome white Kiwi diaspora in Britain which is understood and understands itself as similar to the host nation creates a context in which Blake could simultaneously, and relatively unproblematically, be represented as transnational, cosmopolitan, British and Kiwi in the English media, and as a national hero in the New Zealand media. Diasporic identities are 'at once local and global', always 'plural' and 'in process', even when – like Blake's representation in New Zealand – they are primarily represented as fixed (see also Grainger, 2006). Thus, although media coverage obscured Blake's diasporic identity, we suggest that the widespread understanding that living overseas is not a barrier to retaining a primary identification with New Zealand is central to the coverage in both countries. More particularly, without this taken-for-granted understanding, the New Zealand media's glorification of Blake – a man who lived beyond New Zealand's borders for most of his adult life – as national hero would make no sense. Finally, we conclude, in line with Pearson's (2006) arguments, that media coverage in both countries, while emphasising different aspects of Blake's fluid and overlapping identities, ultimately produced a set of discourses that reinforce the diasporic ability to embrace dual conceptions of 'home' rather than a separation of self from nation.

Notes

1   An earlier version of parts of this chapter has been published in Bruce and Wheaton (2009).
2   Space precludes discussion of the sporting migration literature more generally; our focus is limited to the emerging work on sport and diaspora.
3   While in the United Kingdom we tend to refer to the *British* press, broadsheet papers are produced regionally and often have some regional variation, particularly in sports coverage. For example, the *Guardian* has three sites – in Stratford (London), Manchester and Scotland – and the *Times* and *Daily Telegraph* both have separate Scottish and Welsh editions, although the Welsh one tends to be very similar to the English version. So it is more accurate here to use the term *English* newspapers, while recognising that the content of the other regional/national variations was likely to be similar, particularly for a story like Blake's death which tended to be situated in the world news sections of the papers. Indeed the differing uses of the terms British and English reflect the complex nature of British and English identity more widely, with Britishness often assumed to be cognate with Englishness (see also footnote 7 below).
4   Our focus on broadsheet newspapers reflected the lack of tabloid newspapers in New Zealand and allowed us to provide a comparable sample of coverage. This included articles from the six major New Zealand broadsheets and largest-circulation Sunday newspaper (the *New Zealand Herald, Waikato Times, Evening Post, Dominion, Christchurch Press, Otago Daily Times* and *Sunday Star Times*), and from five major English broadsheets and four Sunday newspapers, including the *Guardian, Times, Sunday Times, Independent, Independent on Sunday, Observer, Financial Times* and *Daily Telegraph*. In both cases, the articles came from a variety of sources including online databases (InfoTrac Power Search, Thomson Gale and Newztext), the newspapers' own web pages, and original print editions.
5   Maguire and Stead (1996) also discuss the influence of empire on migration in English cricket.
6   'Young' in this instance tends to incorporate New Zealanders aged in their twenties and thirties, such as Conradson and Latham's (2005) sample of London-based New Zealanders who ranged from 27 to 33.
7   As noted above, the use of both terms reflects the complex nature of British and English identity and the coverage reflected the tendency noted by commentators for Englishness to stand in for the broader whole (Maguire, 1994b; Whannel, 2002). For example, although Blake tended to be referred to as a *British* rather than *English* sailor, discussions of his home, family, wife and funeral referred to them being in England, Hampshire or as English.

8 We note that Australian emigration follows a similar pattern, being 'highly selective of young, educated, high-income, skilled so-called "urban professionals"' (Hugo, 2006, p. 110).

9 Pākehā generally describes people who are not Māori and, more particularly, those with a white European heritage whose cultural values and practices reflect their location as members of the dominant group within New Zealand (Bell, 2004; Hokowhitu, 2007).

14 Tries for the nation?

International rugby players' perspectives on national identity

Jason Tuck

In his article on sport, globalization, migration and the reconfiguration of the nation-state, Maguire (2008) illustrates the multi-directionality of global flows by observing how people and nations appear to react differently to similar experiences of global sport. In addition, Dyreson (2003) notes that the globalization of modern sport, rather than developing a singular global culture, has paradoxically fuelled a diversity of national interests. The challenge of this work is to further investigate the complex inter-relationships that bind together sport, globalization processes and national identity.[1] National identity has been identified as one of the main causes of problems encountered by sporting migrants as they flow through 'talent migratory pipelines' between host and donor countries (Molnar and Maguire, 2008). The particular focus here is on viewing national identities through the eyes of elite rugby players from the British Isles as national representatives in a 'world in union'.[2]

A figurational, or process-sociological, approach can provide a useful lens through which to both make sense of sportspeople's views and develop a more refined approach to the investigation of the ways in which (sporting) nations are in process. Such an approach to national identity connects well with the seminal works on nationalism as provided by, among others, Anderson (1983), Hobsbawm (1990) and Smith (1991, 1995). For example, Norbert Elias's introduction to *The Established and the Outsiders* (Elias and Scotson, 1994) helps contextualize the dynamics of the nation as somewhat more than an 'imagined community' built on 'invented traditions' by considering the formation of national 'we-images' grown from historically rooted national 'we-ideals' which are grounded in both emotive fantasy and real events. For Elias, these we-ideals contribute to a nation's 'special charisma' (i.e. national character) which is, in turn, protected in times of change by a 'fantasy shield of imagined charisma'.

This work seeks to explore the context of international rugby union as a figuration of specific we-images and fantasy group charisma to flesh out Elias's work and further consider the interlocking themes of globalization, national identity politics (i.e. competing national discourses) and national habitus (i.e. the 'second nature' of belonging to the nation). Sport has long played a significant role in both nation building and globalization processes (Maguire, 2005; Miller *et al.*, 2001). Maguire (1999) suggests that international sport provides a global arena for 'patriot games'. Individuals representing their countries can thus become highly visible embodiments of national sporting dreams. In their world these 'patriots at play' are significant actors who can define, reflect, protect and fuel the special charisma of nations.

Sport, national habitus and 'British' identity politics

'National identity describes that condition in which a mass of people have made the same identification with national symbols – [and] have internalised the symbols of the nation . . .' (Bloom, 1990, p. 52). National identities, through their ability to transmute between the political and the cultural, remain powerful forces in today's 'global era' (Smith, 1995). In a similar vein, Elias (1996) describes nationalism as 'durable' and receiving impetus from changing power ratios between nations. This suggests the possibility of 'increased varieties' of national cultures through reinvigorated nations as one of several responses to homogenizing globalization processes (Maguire, 1994b). In conjunction with this, nations remain in process as 'survival units' that continue to provide individuals with one of their main sources of self-identity and we-attachment. Elias observed that:

> In the present day world, nations . . . appear to have become the dominant and most powerful of all . . . supra-individual influences on people's feelings of meaning and value . . . . [People] are coming to recognize more and more clearly the functions of nations or national groups as the guarantors, guardians, embodiments or symbols of a great part of that which they perceive as of lasting value in their individual existence.
>
> (Elias, 1996, p. 352)

Interlinked with these views are a range of figurational concepts that include: the multi-layered nature of personal identity and the role of national habitus; the concept of established–outsider relations; the use of personal pronoun pairings as a means of establishing I/we and us/them images; and the place of identity politics within the context of globalization processes.[3] In Elias's work on established–outsider relations some of the processes at work in the relations between established (the 'we' element) and outsider ('they') groups are explored. These observations are connected more explicitly to national 'character' by Elias (1996) in his work on the Germans where he observed that the fortunes of the nation become sedimented, over many years, into the habitus of its citizens – individuals and the nation become interlinked in a we–I balance. This 'strong and vivid bond' (Elias, 1991) between individual and nation is described by Elias (1996) as a type of 'self-love' concretized through '"sleeping memories" which tend to crystallise and become organised around common symbols – national sports teams being one example . . .' (Maguire and Poulton, 1999, p. 19). This rich collection of expressive symbols and shared memories form the soil for the growth of national we-ideals. National communities are more than imaginary, notional collectives – they are not simply the products of 'discursive consciousness' (Giddens, 1984). Through the reproduction and circulation of symbolic national images (i.e. habitus codes) and the practical actions of social groups the nation can be evoked, or 'flagged', as something more than just invented or imagined (Schrag, 2009). As Goudsblom points out: 'Social actions are often legitimated as having been performed in the service of a symbolic "it" – a creed or a flag, . . . or the glory of a nation . . . their symbolic appeal is not to be underestimated' (Goudsblom, 1977, p. 180).

The contention here is that despite (and, in some cases, because of) changes in the face of globalization/denationalization processes the nation remains a touchstone for strong I/we feelings and national character endures as a meaningful layer of social habitus which is embedded deep in the personality of the individual. This is most obvious when established 'we' groups are confronted by outsiders and:

> . . . when national habitus codes are stimulated . . . it is possible to see a reflexive process [whereby] the individual can feel they 'become' the . . . nation and the social group represented by the nation 'becomes' that individual.
>
> (Maguire and Tuck, 2005, p. 499)

This is a particularly interesting historical moment to be studying 'British' national culture and identity. As globalization processes intensify, the British Isles are facing an identity crisis (as originally outlined by Nairn in 1977). This 'crisis' has been coloured by dreams of an imperial past; migration processes that have stimulated multiculturalism; the devolution of the United Kingdom and the rise of the 'Celtic fringe' (i.e. Ireland, Scotland and Wales); and Europeanization processes. External processes of globalization (such as Europeanization), and internal politico-cultural processes, may work in multiple directions to either weaken, strengthen or pluralize a dominant national habitus.[4]

Sport is frequently a 'container' for nationalist sentiment and it has, historically, contributed to the formation of identities and invented traditions (Bairner, 2001; Maguire, 1999). Poli (2007b) contends that sports federations have played a key part in preserving the primacy of nations within global sport. International sport forms one of the most significant arenas where the local and the cosmopolitan mix, and nations become/remain visible. Particular sports can also symbolize the nation – a process which dates back to the third phase of sportization in the late nineteenth century (Maguire, 1994b). The close bind of sport with national identifications has made sport an important vehicle for popular consciousness (to bond 'us') and collective resentment (of 'them'). Nations are, in many ways, dependent on international sport for their own validation (Morgan, 1997).

Within the British Isles, the Celtic nations have employed sport in various ways as a means of asserting their own identities. In the late nineteenth century, Irish cultural nationalists rejected 'British' sports and established their own Gaelic games under the auspices of the Gaelic Athletic Association (formed in 1884).[5] In contrast, the Welsh and the Scottish have used traditional 'British' sports to challenge the political and economic dominance of England by trying to beat them at their own game(s). For example, in rugby union the Calcutta Cup is played annually between Scotland and the 'Auld Enemy'. Indeed, rugby union also provides one of the main sources of 'I/we' identity politics by which the English identify the Welsh and the Welsh identify themselves. As the BBC put it in their promotional previews of the 2009 Six Nations Championships: 'You don't play the team – you play the nation.'

Rugby union in the British Isles represents a unique arena for the construction, reproduction and contestation of national identities. This arena has stimulated a range of multidimensional transnational sport labour migration trails that fit with Maguire's (1999) typology of sport labour migration with each national team including some pioneers, settlers, returnees, mercenaries and nomadic cosmopolitans. In addition to recent de-amatuerization and professionalization processes, rugby also provides a series of national cultural paradoxes which include: juxtaposing the Anglo-Saxon English against the Celtic nations in the annual Six Nations Championship, whilst also uniting the best players from the Home Unions as British and Irish 'Lions' every four years; and appearing to unite the people of a politically divided nation – Ireland.[6]

Rugby special: rugby union and the making of nations

The role of international rugby players as 'patriots at play' in the context of the British Isles was explored in a series of interviews with male international rugby union players (who represented either England, Ireland, Scotland or Wales) and whose international rugby careers spanned two decades from 1987 to 2007.[7] Many of the players regarded rugby union as a central part of their particular national culture. Of course, one reason for this perceived importance of rugby could be that, during this period of time, the national rugby union sides of the British Isles have, arguably, been the most successful wielders of their respective national sporting fantasy shields. The English players were well aware that as a result of recent failures in other 'national' sports the rugby team had become the chief source for English sporting pride and patriotism (Tuck, 2003b). Indeed, even before England won the 2003 Rugby World Cup, Charles viewed rugby union as England's sporting saviour and potential provider of a nation-wide group charisma:

> I think as a nation we need something really . . . I think it would be beyond everyone's wildest dreams, as a nation, to have [us as] World Champion . . . It would just be the biggest thing since 1966 . . . I just really hope it does something for the country . . . We haven't had anything to shout about recently and it would be nice . . . to say we were . . . World Champions . . .

The strong tie between rugby union and the English nation was emphasized by Jack who declared that:

> . . . it has this 'national' sort of thing with the fact that it has got so well supported it has generated a 'feel-good factor' on a Monday, Tuesday and Wednesday the following week. Everyone's talking about it . . .

This 'feel-good factor', frequently associated with a sporting triumph, is often accompanied by a reawakening of national habitus that can provide a powerful, albeit temporary, panacea to a nation's ills (Tuck, 2003b).

The importance of rugby to the nation was also commented on by the Scottish players. Hamish stated that rugby is '. . . highly regarded in Scotland and the people are very passionate'. Gordon further commented on the impact of a successful Scottish rugby team on the morale of the Scottish public: 'We need the [Scottish] people to feel that they're part of a winning nation . . . thus giving themselves more pride and confidence.' Ewan referred to the importance of Scottish rugby to the nation as being somewhat less significant (and, to a degree, transient) as a result of the combination of patriotism and pessimism that he perceived to exist amongst the Scottish people: '. . . as a country we are patriotic, and sporting success does lift morale; but there does seem to be a feeling that we are bound to fail soon after achieving success'. This links with the work of Jarvie and Walker (1994) who explore the notion of the Scottish as 'ninety minute patriots'.[8]

The long tradition of Welsh international rugby, coupled with the extraordinary dominance of the Welsh in the 1970s, has ensured that rugby union has become firmly embedded within Welsh national culture as one of the chief signifiers of 'Welshness' and, more recently, 'Cool Cymru' (Harris, 2006).[9] This was typified in the acknowledgement of the history and 'special' tradition which lies behind playing rugby for Wales and the feeling that rugby was truly '. . . *the* national game of Wales' (Rhodri). Bryn, indicating the unique position of the sport to Wales, stated that: 'We have something other countries don't have – the Welsh heritage and the place the sport of rugby holds in the Welsh nation. [Representing Wales is] . . . something special that every Welshman wants to accomplish.'

However, the players also found that this tended to create a sense of false expectancy amongst sections of the Welsh public who, perhaps reflecting a sense of wilful nostalgia (Maguire, 1994b), demand that the Welsh recreate the domination of the sport which they enjoyed in the 'good old days' of the 1970s. Alun commented that:

> . . . the nation does expect . . . [and] playing for Wales, with . . . all the tradition . . . [and] history, the Welsh public has expectations which are far higher than . . . many other publics.

Rhodri spoke of the importance of rugby to the fanatical Welsh public:

> . . . everybody responds to a winning team but it's a big fault in Wales that when the national side loses everyone's head goes down . . . [and] everyone's in a massive state of depression [for] three or four months.

This reinforces the work of Harris (2008) who notes that Welsh rugby tends to either stimulate celebration or crisis in the Principality.

Rugby union also occupies a special place within Irish national identity politics – the sport is perceived to have a unique ability in Ireland to transcend both political and religious divisions (Hassan, 2003; Maguire and Tuck, 2005; Tuck, 2003a).

Rugby union provides one of the few sports in which a united (albeit invented) 'All-Ireland' can compete on a world stage against other nations. This is important as the traditional Gaelic sports, whilst still very popular in the Republic, do not give the Irish this opportunity to compete internationally on a regular basis. Sean commented that:

> . . . rugby is one of the only sports in Ireland where you have guys from the North and South [of Ireland] playing under the same title with the same colour jersey. . . . So having a successful rugby team is important, not only for rugby, but for the country as a whole.

When victorious, the Irish team was seen by the players to generate a sense of national pride across both Northern Ireland and the Republic. This role as 'pioneers' of a united Irish identity was powerfully infused in some of the players' experiences. Additionally, even during the darkest moments in North–South relations, the players could not recall the troubles ever materializing in a rugby context. When probed about the effect of the political situation on rugby in Ireland, Patrick (from Northern Ireland) remarked that:

> I don't want to get too controversial about the Northern Ireland/Republic of Ireland thing. . . . We have just got to accept that there are two different countries – but in rugby terms we are one. . . . Nobody has ever made a political issue out of it and they never will because rugby is bigger than that.

Such observations not only illustrate a romantic denial of the politics surrounding the sport, but also reaffirm how the two Irelands can be as one in a player's rugby world. In contrast, few of the other players made such explicit references towards a truly united Ireland. Indeed, on closer inspection, it is evident that there is still a degree of a 'them and us' feeling (as illustrated in the previous statement by Patrick) between the Northern Irish (often given the misnomer of 'Ulstermen') and those from the Republic. This division in the island is perhaps most apparent in terms of language (the Southern Irish mainly speaking English but having a Gaelic language as well whilst the majority Protestant North speak only English). This creates an interesting series of Irish we-images among the 'Ulster British' which are discussed in further detail by Bairner (2003) and Hassan (2003).

Eighty-minute patriots

This section investigates both what it means to the players to be representatives of 'their' nation and how they perceived other countries' national traits. Through these findings it is possible to shed more light on the concepts of 'Englishness', 'Irishness', 'Scottishness' and 'Welshness'. It was not surprising, given their responses to the centrality of rugby union to Wales, that the Welsh players also displayed the strongest sense of national identity, pride and patriotism. Alun offered a typical response when he said that he was unequivocally '100 per cent Welsh' whilst Bryn stated that 'Because I was born and bred in Wales (and especially down in West Wales) . . . I think rugby is half of Wales. . . . I'd rather be Welsh than English, Scottish or Irish, definitely.' In addition, the Welsh players also saw themselves as the most 'British' of the representatives of the Home Nations – a feeling that has been evident since the early 1900s (Andrews, 1991; Williams, 1991). When asked about his patriotism, Bryn declared as follows:

> I think . . . when I'm in Wales I am Welsh but when I travel outside Wales . . . to other countries, maybe when I'm representing Wales . . . in a foreign country, it seems to me I'm Welsh *and* British.

Such views link neatly to Balsom's (1985) notion of a 'British Wales'.

This conflict between national identities in the British context provides some indication of the multiple layers of self-identity. These layers were also evident amongst the Scottish players. When asked how Scottish he felt, Ewan replied: 'I know a lot about Scottish history and I am proud to be Scottish. I live there and consider myself Scottish first and British second.' These comments demonstrate, albeit simplistically, that personal identity (and indeed national identity) is a complex phenomenon which can operate on more than one level at any one time in different environments (Jarvie and Walker, 1994; Maguire, 1994b). It does appear that when a British identification is present it tends to reside in a layer beneath that of the individual's primary national identity. Thus 'Britishness' can be said to be acting at a 'supra-national' level.

Strong sentiments of national pride were espoused by the majority of the Scottish players. This included two dual nationals who qualified to play for Scotland through Scottish grandparents and had become 'settlers' (Maguire, 1999). Angus epitomized the players' patriotic attitude when he said:

> I am very proud to say I'm Scottish. I am always a great supporter of Scottish sports people who I feel succeed 'despite the system'. But I don't know enough about the political aspects to comment on, for example, devolution. I am always keen to say what a great country Scotland is and how much I enjoy living there.

Here a player refers to wider political dimensions of national identity – namely Scottish nationalism. Whilst it is apparent, from his comments, that he has an awareness of a relationship between sport and identity politics, this particular Scottish player does not actively link the two.

Several of the Irish players had connections with England. Sean explained his dual nationality:

> Being born in England, having an English accent and having been educated in England . . . [and to then] go up to an Irish person and say I'm Irish – they'd probably laugh at me because of the way I speak. But deep down I feel Irish and I feel proud to say to anyone 'I'm Irish'.

Sean's decision to choose Ireland over England was a mix of family leanings and opportunities for success. As such, this particular migrant dual national had been driven by a combination of 'returnee' and 'mercenary' tendencies (Maguire, 1999). His experiences illustrate how complex the I/we-image of dual nationals can be and how a migrant dual national, experiencing a range of pushing and pulling motivations, may find it hard to be anything more than an 'eighty-minute patriot'.

The English players tended to be more muted about their national identity. Harry stated that:

> I'm not patriotic in a Falklands flag-waving way. . . . I'm proud of a lot of things in this country but they're not things like the World Cup or two World Wars. Really it's things like the English civilized way of life, . . . the sense of justice and the sense of humour which I think is . . . the best in the world.

This illustrates the traditionally understated (and mainly middle-class) style of nationalism which has tended to underpin the expression 'Englishness'. Although this identity appears to be more reserved, Englishness has traditionally had close links with race, class and gender. This can mean that the English national habitus is both hard to define and frequently misunderstood. Harry reinforced this in his comments on English identity where he neatly exposed one of the double binds of Englishness – understated patriotism and aggressive imperialism. He stated that:

> There's a huge sense of pride and patriotism . . . [but] I think . . . there's been a lack of that passion in the past . . . it's not necessarily in the English nature to be too boastful or overt about . . . national pride. I think far too many people confuse national pride with jingoism.

The 'abuse' of nationalist sentiment was also commented on by Jack (a dual national born outside England): 'One element of nationalism that I'm not happy about is the way our victories are used by an element of people that are supporting England . . . to further their egos and . . . [their] nationality trip.' These comments refer both to the journalists who tend to amplify nationalism (as seen in the xenophobic representations of 'outsiders' used in tabloid newspapers) and the politicians who tend to jump on the bandwagon of successful sporting teams and use sporting victories for their own personal/political ends (Tuck, 2003b).

Jack went on to say: 'I'm not an archetypal Englishman . . . I have a cosmopolitan background. . . . I'm not a fervent Union Jack wearer or flyer of the flag, but I am proud to represent England.' Charles, another dual national, commented that:

> . . . I've a Welsh mother and an English father . . . and I've never disinherited my Welsh-hood. But it wasn't a choice between England and Wales,

[only] England gave me that chance to play . . . [and now] every time I pull that [England] shirt on I couldn't feel any more proud [like] a sort of a reborn-again Englishman.

Malcolm (2009) provides a means of making some sense of these comments by drawing on the work of Edmunds and Turner (2001) who suggest that recent changes in English national identity have actually created different models of Englishness ranging from the 'malign' (closed, insular and reactive) to the 'benign' (open, cosmopolitan and creative and more 'civilized').

It may be possible to extend such thinking to reflect further on Maguire's (1999) typology of sport labour migration as a way of understanding how the experiences and behaviours of sport labour migrants can impact longitudinally on the broader 'map' of national identities, particularly in host countries. This could allow for deeper consideration of the role of sport labour migrants as key players in utilizing, challenging and developing an increasing variety of (benign and malign) national identities over time.

National anthems and patriotic conversions

From the perceptions of the players it became apparent that feelings of national pride tended to flow more openly during the build-up to the game and especially during the playing of the national anthems. The anthems, especially in a sporting context, provide habitus codes of common cultural collective symbols through which to celebrate self-love and love for the nation (Elias, 1996; Maguire and Poulton, 1999). From an English perspective, George encapsulated the significance of the anthem:

It can be quite stirring. . . . It can actually focus your mind . . . and . . . it reminds you of what you're there for. . . . I . . . sing [the anthem] because I am quite nationalistic. I'm proud of my country and . . . the Royal Family . . .

Harry remarked that the anthem was important as a 'psychological tool' which the players could latch on to. Clearly *God Save the Queen*, the *British* national anthem used by the English for sporting occasions, is imbued with reverence for the monarchy. Some of the players argued that they could not identify with the anthem and that this particular song was no longer representative of today's England. Jack was among several players who suggested that *Jerusalem* would be a more appropriate song for the English team to sing before a match.[10]

All the Scottish players cited the playing of *Flower of Scotland* before a match as an emotional experience which, as Hamish put it, '. . . puts a lump in my throat [and] moistens my eyes'.[11] Stuart described that 'it stirs the passions in the belly, and Scots can relate to it historically'. These views are brought together by the views of Ewan who said: 'The history and background of the words [to *Flower of Scotland*] are emotionally recalled. Also the fact that 60,000-plus supporters are singing with you makes you stand taller and makes the . . . hairs stand up on the back of your neck.' The contrast between *God Save the Queen* (a rather dour cele-bration of the British monarchy) and the more passionate nationalistic *Flower of Scotland* mirrors the wider social awakening of a Celtic nation with a desire from sections of the nation for political independence from England.

Issues surrounding the pre-match anthems received their strongest expressions amongst the Irish team. The existence of two Irish nations (with two different languages) outside of rugby union has made both the selection and rendition of the 'Irish' national anthem problematic in the context of rugby internationals. This is, in Elias's (1991) words, a habitus problem *par excellence*. Up until the 1995 World Cup, the official anthem sung by the Irish rugby team was, in most instances, *The Soldier's Song* (or *Amhrán na bhFiann*) which, sung in Gaelic, is the anthem of the Republic of Ireland (where Ireland's home grounds are located). However, the national anthem for players from Northern Ireland, part of the United Kingdom, is *God Save the Queen*. Patrick stated in this connection that 'I can't sing the anthem [*The Soldier's Song*] because I don't know the words. . . . Me being from the North, it's not my anthem so I don't sing it. I respect it, I stand still for it . . . but it's in Gaelic . . . so I don't know it.'

The players from Northern Ireland, feeling some outsider emotions, all com-mented on how difficult it was for them to sing the traditional Gaelic anthem. Most of them simply could not identify with it; others had backgrounds that con-flicted with the anthem's nationalist sentiments. Some of the Ulster-based players spoke of the coaching they had received in the past from the other players who had attempted to teach them suitable replacement lyrics in English so that they could sing along (albeit in meaningless terms) to *The Soldier's Song* and keep their mouths in time with the others. Callum, from Northern Ireland, declared that:

> The anthem [*The Soldier's Song*] is officially played because the game is played in Dublin, not because it's the team anthem. . . . But they've brought in *Ireland's Call* . . . to give the team a sense of identity so that all the mem-bers of the team could associate themselves with this song, with Ireland, with Irish pride . . .

The words of *Ireland's Call* mirror the provincial nature of rugby union in Ireland and how the players perceive it. As some of them mentioned, in Irish rugby there is no real North–South divide – everything is organized on a provincial basis. It just so happens that one of the provinces, Ulster, which is composed of nine counties, is frequently assimilated to Northern Ireland, which has only six of Ulster's nine coun-ties inside its border. This adoption of a new sporting national anthem demonstrates some of the complexities of 'Irishness', the problem of national symbolism and contemporary Irish identity politics in a sporting context.[12]

The rendition of the Welsh anthem *Land of My Fathers* (or *Hen Wlad Fy Nhadau*) before international matches is perhaps one of the most famous features of Welsh rugby. During the anthem two great Welsh we-ideals, rugby and song, are united in a mass celebration of Welshness that serves to awaken the nation. All the Welsh players perceived their anthem as having the ability to lift the team and 'switch them on' to the occasion. Alun commented that '. . . knowing that the anthem is just played for you representing Wales is absolutely outstanding'.

As with the Irish, the Welsh anthem is not sung in English. This has raised questions related to the Welsh language debate and another national divide with rugby often perceived to belong more to South Wales (Harris, 2006). Whilst being able to speak Welsh was seen as being advantageous and, as Rhodri remarked, 'something pretty special', not all Welsh players speak Welsh. Rhodri offered assurances that there were no Welsh-speaking cliques within the team and that everyone, irrespective of whether or not they could speak Welsh (or indeed were born in Wales), was united. He stated: 'It would be good if we could all speak Welsh but the thing is [for] the boys who can't, it's not their fault . . . they just try their best to sing the anthem, that's the good thing.' That said, the different languages spoken by the Welsh team did suggest that a type of intra-national transient migration might be required to be undertaken by some – even if it was just for the duration of the anthem.

It appears that the pre-match national anthems have become a specific focal point for an international rugby team's identity and the building of we-images (Maguire and Tuck, 2005). Amongst the Irish and Welsh players in particular, whose anthems were sung in a 'mother' tongue, it was clear that the team rallied together during the anthem to ensure that outsiders in the team were not ostracized. In addition, the employment of *Flower of Scotland* by the Scottish Rugby Union, which explicitly recounts the defeating of the English in battle, provides the players with a passionate pre-match reminder of the Scottish fighting heritage and demonstrates what can be achieved if all the clans can unite.

Them and us: Celtic cousins and the English enemy

When players spoke about the other British national rugby teams and nations (i.e. 'they-images'), a clear schism was identified between the English and the other Celtic nations. Whereas the representatives of all the Celtic countries saw themselves as 'cousins', the English were seen as 'the enemy' and feelings of anti-Englishness were frequently expressed. Interestingly, one of the Irish players commented that this dislike of the English was 'tradition' and bordered on hatred. For some of the players of the Celtic nations, beating the 'established' English was seemingly their main *raison d'être*.

The English players were very clear that other national teams saw England as *the* team to beat. Some reasoned this was due to the relatively successful period (between 1991 and 2003) the English team had enjoyed as the most successful of the Home Nations. Jack gave an alternative explanation for why England remains the chief target of others and how the feelings of anti-Englishness arise; he said:

> . . . [it is] because we are seen to be of the stoic 'rule the waves' mentality and . . . are viewed as the arrogant upstarts . . . who expect to win and expect to be the best – which provides [the other teams with] a . . . natural enemy . . .

The role of 'the enemy' had been experienced by Charles:

> I don't particularly like the Scots. . . . [When] we were up there for the [1991 World Cup] semi-final [against Scotland] . . . , the actual anti-English feeling . . . really got home to you. It was just oppressive, from children to grandmother[s] all gesticulating. . . . You think, hold on a minute, I mean obviously [there is] the history that has gone on before, but this is a sport. . . . It's just tradition I think. It's whatever England did in history, whatever England has passed down – it's someone [for the Scots] to have a go at.

Many of the Scottish players also expressed a range of aversions to the English in keeping with the symbolism evoked by *Flower of Scotland*. As Elias (1994, p. 23) observed: '. . . symbols have attained a very high degree of adequacy to reality, it is often difficult . . . for people to distinguish between symbol and reality'. For example, Gregor commented on the fact that 'England are the team you want to beat because . . . they are the Auld Enemy' whilst Stuart remarked that the English players '. . . have an arrogance which gets up your nose'. In contrast, other Scottish players perceived that the game against England was more to do with the public and with a media-driven tradition of defeating the Auld Enemy, and that anti-English feelings were more applicable to the Scottish players of yesteryear. Angus remarked: 'At the end of the day rugby is only a game and it is not important in the bigger picture of life. . . . I am totally against fighting old battles on the rugby pitch . . .' These views, although in the minority, appear to point towards a more 'benign' sporting we-image that is developing parallel with the professionalization of the game and is coloured by the civilizing effects of lengthening chains of interdependence (White, 2004).

The majority of the Scottish players denoted a close affinity with the Irish. This was encapsulated by Ewan who, commenting on the Irish, said that 'they are a good-natured people, the country is lovely and I know a few players and get on with them well'. Angus added to this by revealing he possessed 'an affinity to the Irish because they have a similar style of rugby to the Scots and are very similar in nature. Both also have similar resources and constraints in playing terms.' All the Irish players, reciprocating Scottish views, expressed an affinity to, and saw some similarities with, the Scots (in terms of playing styles, approach to life and also in terms of the broader national identities). The matches between the Irish and the Scots were seen by each side as fierce but the after-match celebrations were the wildest and most enjoyable. John said this was because they were 'fairly close land masses . . . and Celtic cousins . . .'.

In contrast, England were perceived as the enemy to the Irish and Patrick articulated this aversion by stating that:

> Everybody hates the English – it's tradition. . . . I think it's because of their personalities. We tend, as Irish people, to . . . like to be underdogs – I think it's because we always have been. . . . Whereas the English . . . [are] confident, it comes from their history. They're used to ruling the world . . . so they walk

about with this . . . attitude and everyone dislikes them for it. They have supreme confidence in their own ability, which is fine, you can be arrogant but you don't have to be impolite with it.

The Welsh players, and public alike, are sensitive to certain 'traditions' within rugby union which put further emphasis on the annual 'must-win' game against the English. This was reinforced to some extent by the comments of Bryn:

> . . . everyone wants to beat the English . . . they have such self-confidence . . . and they think they're better than the other countries. So I think . . . that's the big game . . . [and] if we only beat England it would be . . . not a disastrous season.

This provides another good example of the use of personal pronouns to identify both established and outsiders in everyday speech (Elias, 1991). In this instance, Bryn refers to the English as 'they' which clearly implies that the English are perceived as outsiders and, therefore, as an enemy. In contrast the use of 'we' in talking about the Welsh implies a bond which binds the people of the Welsh nation together. However, this general level of 'anti-Englishness' did not apply equally to all the Welsh players. Alun, whilst appreciating that a lot of Welsh people have this all-consuming animosity towards the English, seemed quite frustrated by the level of parochialism in Wales which he saw as holding back the development of Welsh rugby. Rhodri stated that:

> I don't think Wales–England is anything special. A lot of people do think it is but . . . it's just another game. . . . Say last year if we had beaten all the other teams [but] . . . not beaten England then a lot of the Welsh public would have said it's been a bad season because we lost to England.

This evidence points towards the presence of multiple national identities made up of competing discourses (Maguire, 1999). Members of the Celtic teams appear to have formed a supra-national we-identity which is juxtaposed against the dominant Anglo-Saxon English ('them'). These shared national (and sporting) characteristics can act as strong identity markers in the development of, what Elias might call, a shared Celtic group charisma. This would appear to have ramifications for the cohesion of any British and Irish Lions team and yet the evidence suggests the contrary. By means of an example, former England international and Lion Jerry Guscott clarifies that 'The Lions concept breaks down barriers and preconceptions between individuals and nationalities like nothing else' (cited in Westgate, 2009 [online]).

Conclusion

This work has attempted to provide some insight into the complex relationship between sport, globalization and the nation by using figurational sociology as a 'learned fund of knowledge' (Elias, 1994). In general terms, sport is clearly one of the nation's most prominent 'fantasy shields' and, being deeply interconnected with the (global) fortunes of the nation, offers a valuable site for the study of national identity politics and national habitus. As an arena in which the nation can awaken, sport provides an important crucible for representations of 'national character' – particularly when considering the role of international sporting migrants.

From what has been highlighted it is clear that a series of interdependent relationships exist between rugby union, national habitus and those who play 'for' the nation. The players are embodiments of the nation – at least for eighty minutes. In the players' eyes, rugby is an important source of national pride and a central part of national culture. The players highlighted that *the* principal moment that forged a national group charisma was the playing/singing of the national anthem as the final part of the pre-match build-up to an international match. This was especially evident among the players from the Celtic countries who tended to display more overt we-images in their language. In addition, the Celtic players distanced themselves from the common English 'enemy' using a range of I/we and us/them sentiments which nurtured a common Celtic group charisma. This symbolic we-image was furthered with the creation of a Celtic League for Scottish, Irish and Welsh teams in 2001.

This study of identity politics at play within the sport of rugby union has provided no more than a snapshot of the complex and dynamic nature of the interlinkages between sport, globalization and the nation. Recent developments, within what White (2004) refers to as the sixth phase of sportization of the sport, also pose interesting questions relating to the relationship of rugby union to national habitus in the British Isles.[13] The early stages of the formal professionalization (and commercialization) of the sport have been ongoing for nearly 15 years. Rugby union is now a professional and global game in process and whatever happens in the next phase of the sport's development will undoubtedly have implications for the players and the national cultures they represent. Will the commodification of rugby union fuel a shift in we–I power ratios with celebrity players showing more desire for themselves (and loyalty to their club) rather than their 'home' country? Will players continue to try for their nation?

Notes

1 This chapter draws from Tuck and Maguire's (1999) paper entitled 'Making sense of global patriot games: Rugby players' perceptions of national identity politics' published in *Football Studies*, 2: 26–54.

2 The 'British Isles' is composed of England, Scotland, Ireland and Wales whereas 'the United Kingdom' includes England, Scotland, Wales and Northern Ireland and 'Great Britain' pertains to England, Scotland and Wales. 'British' identity is therefore a complex construct comprising national and supra-national identities. *World in Union* is a theme song for the Rugby World Cup which emphasizes, through a play on words, the international spirit of the game. Its opening lyrics – 'There's a dream, I feel, so rare, so real' – seem poignant here.

3 Habitus, a term often associated with the work of Pierre Bourdieu, is used here in its Eliasian sense. It refers to those dispositions which are internalized and deeply embedded in the subconscious.

4 National habitus codes that surround mediated sport have been explored using this Eliasian approach by, amongst others, Maguire and Poulton (1999), Poulton (2004), Tuck (2003b) and Woo Lee and Maguire (2009).

5 The history of the Gaelic Athletic Association (GAA) has been documented by Cronin (1999) and Sugden and Bairner (1993).

6 The 'Home' Unions refer to the governing bodies (or Rugby Unions) of England, Ireland, Scotland and Wales. These countries are collectively known within the British Isles as the Home Nations. The British and Irish Lions are a rugby union team who tour the southern hemisphere every four years and are composed of the best players from all four Home Unions. The existence (and increasing media profile) of a British rugby union team raises questions regarding the degree to which a British identity exists within the sport.

7 Twenty-six 'first team' players took part in the study which ran from 1995 to 1999. All the players in the sample participated in the 1995 World Cup. Several were 'dual nationals' – that is, 'migrant' players who hold dual nationality (through either the birthplace of a parent or grandparent, or through residency) and have the opportunity to play representative rugby for more than one nation. Pseudonyms are used here to preserve the players' anonymity.

8 The phrase 'ninety minute patriots' was coined in 1992 by Jim Sillars (an ex-Member of Parliament for the Scottish National Party) to describe the way in which the Scottish public only seemed to express their national identity at sporting events.

9 Rugby union has been likened to an expression of denied nationhood in Wales. The Welsh tradition in the sport and its relationship with Welsh culture and society has been well documented by Williams (1991) and Smith and Williams (1980). 'Cool Cymru' refers to a (post)modern Welsh cultural, sporting and political renaissance that began with the opening of the first Welsh parliament for 600 years in 1999.

10 *Jerusalem* is an English patriotic song based on the short poem *And did those feet in ancient time* by William Blake. It implies how the visit of Jesus created a heaven in England's 'green and pleasant land'.

11 The Scottish Rugby Union adopted *Flower of Scotland* as their 'official' anthem in 1990. This popular Scottish folk song replaced the more traditional 'national' anthem *God Save the Queen*. Interestingly, this new anthem was first heard when the English team visited Murrayfield.

12 *Ireland's Call* was commissioned by the Irish Rugby Football Union to ensure all the provinces of Ireland were represented standing 'shoulder to shoulder' in a 'unifying' anthem.

13 As the professionalization of rugby has unfolded, it is possible to reflect on two significant developments involving the Home Nations. First, with increased financial backing, there was a dramatic increase in the recruitment of foreign migrant labour to English club rugby. This movement has also led to an increase in the number of possible dual nationals. For example, in 2009, Riki Flutey, the New Zealand-born England centre, became only the second player to play both for and against the British and Irish Lions. Second, Europeanization processes have ensured the development and growth of the European Cup (inaugurated in 1995/6). The success of this pan-European club competition is likely to continue and will create even more fixtures for the region's top players. In addition, with a salary cap now in place in English club rugby, elite French clubs are starting to coax players away from the English Premiership.

Part V
Impacts of migration on sports and societies

15 The new international division of cultural labour and sport[1]

Toby Miller, David Rowe and Geoffrey Lawrence

You do the football, we'll do the beer.
(Budweiser slogan, 2006 Men's Football World Cup)

Under the Taliban, which supposedly withdrew from the world of states, Afghanistan affiliated with one of the most venerable and successful institutions of global civil society. Not long before the United States began military action there in 2001, the country became the 74th member of the International Cricket Council (ICC). (The Taliban's decision to affiliate had been inspired by connections to Pakistan, where cricket is very popular. Those ties had been developed, with CIA encouragement during the previous two decades, following the Soviet invasion – which the US Government had furtively encouraged in order to generate a Vietnam equivalent to undermine the former Soviet republic.) Today, the headquarters of the Afghanistan Cricket Federation remain in Kabul, aided by Pakistan Cricket Board money and ICC encouragement, and there are more than 300 Afghan cricket clubs, with many players having learnt the game in Pakistan's refugee camps or under the sponsorship of foreign charity. In 2009, the national team qualified for one-day international status (Williams, 2001; 'Bowled over', 2005; Luke, 2009).

This anecdote references two things. First, it illustrates the relative autonomy of sport from politics. How else could a regime known to abjure links to colonial, neocolonial, capitalist and secular pastimes – rejecting even basic diplomacy – endorse a powerful (and Western-dominated) institution? Second, it illustrates that this relative autonomy is underpinned by politics; for Afghanistan's cricketing link derived from Cold-War surrogacy and post-colonial hangovers and was then stimulated by an invasion that toppled the regime. The anecdote's lesson is clear: that the globalization of sport through migrating players is equally about the appeal of sport and its imbrication with world capitalism.

In the English language, the principal academic writings on globalization and sport veer between figurational perspectives, deriving from the sociological theories and empirical studies of Norbert Elias (e.g. Maguire, 1999, 2005, 2008), and a blend of neo-Marxism, focusing on the division of labour and media ownership, and Foucauldianism, concentrating on subjectivity and governmentality. The latter animated our work in *Globalization and Sport* (Miller *et al.*, 2001; also see Miller,

2007, 2009). In this chapter, we begin with a summary of the political–economic argument from *Globalization and Sport*, namely that certain simultaneous, uneven, inter-connected processes characterize the present moment: globalization, governmentalization, Americanization, televisualization and commodification. They occur in the context of a New International Division of Cultural Labour (NICL). Hence the paradox stimulating and characterizing our project: that these processes operate in both complementary and contradictory ways. It is not appropriate to view globalization as a totalizing and homogenizing force: we provided ample evidence throughout *Globalization and Sport* that it is not. Yet, many components of globalization are common across sites, leading to the acceptance of certain laws, media norms and economic tendencies.

In this chapter, after explicating the NICL, we concentrate on how US professional sports and the *bourgeois* media utilize a global labour pool and audience to supplement an oversupplied local market. We conclude that, whilst the classic capitalist problem of overproduction is slowly eroding the sealed-off nature of US culture, the forces of protectionism continue to characterize US sport, precluding equal exchange.

The NICL derives from a reconceptualization of economic dependency theory that followed the inflationary chaos of the 1970s. Developing markets for labour and products, and the shift from the spatial sensitivities of electrics to the spatial *in*sensitivities of electronics, pushed First-World businesses beyond treating Third-World countries as suppliers of raw materials, viewing them instead as shadow-setters of the price of work, competing amongst themselves and with the First and Second Worlds for employment. That process broke up the prior division of the world into a small number of industrialized nations and a majority of underdeveloped ones, as production was split across continents. Fröbel *et al.* (1980) christened the phenomenon the New International Division of Labour (NIDL). The NIDL is not without its critics. Has flexible specialization superseded mass production, is there super-exploitation of workers in non-core regions and must political authoritarianism necessarily accompany corporate global expansion (Hill and Lee, 1994; Jenkins, 1994)? However, it is clear that post-Second World War capitalist growth has been premised on the exploitation of peasant, and more recently formerly state-socialist, nations in a manner that reconstitutes economic, social and cultural arrangements in favour of transnational capital (Rosset, 2006). The NIDL paradigm continues, therefore, to be deployed to great effect (Hoogvelt, 2001; McMichael, 2009).

The idea behind the NICL is that, just as manufacturing fled the First World, cultural production has also relocated. This is happening at the level of popular and high-culture texts, computer-aided design and manufacture, sales, marketing and information exchange (Freeman, 2000; Baldoz *et al.*, 2001). The NICL has been most dramatically applied to film and television production (Miller *et al.*, 2005). In sport, labour-market expansion and developments in global transportation and communications technology have diminished the need for co-location of management, labour and consumption. More than a decade ago, Bale and Maguire (1994) highlighted the growing Afro-Caribbean involvement in British football[2] and the presence in the United States of track and pool athletes from many nations, stimulated largely by college scholarship programmes. They reported the summer 'invasion' of cricketers from the Commonwealth of Nations to play in England's domestic competition, and commented on the lifestyles of élite golf, tennis, rugby union and rugby league players.

Today, football is the major site of international labour mobility. Players move in accordance with several factor endowments, beyond issues such as talent and money. There is a clear link between imperial history and job destination in the case of Latin Americans going to Spain, Portugal and Italy, or Africans playing in France, while cultural links draw Scandinavians to Britain (Giulianotti, 2002). A small labour aristocracy experiences genuine class mobility in financial terms, underpinned by a huge reserve army of labour and ancillary workers, each subject to various, and often quite severe, forms of exploitation. This tendency is so marked that it has given rise to a Professional Football Players' Observatory, which tracks the success and value of players, complete with an interactive online instrument to illustrate migration (see http://eurofootplayers.org).

The impact of the NICL is not restricted to cosmopolitan workers. It also generates new ways of transferring knowledge. Lash and Urry (1994) have argued that reflexive accumulation (the production of knowledge) combines with flexible specialization in the workplace to challenge orthodox notions of space and time.[3] Globally, mobile citizens are part of information flows. In turn, they influence those flows. In rendering problematic both space and time, globalization confuses identity – one effect of which is to question the meaning and efficacy of nationalism. Multicultural national sporting teams (e.g. England being represented by cricketers of Zimbabwean, South African, Caribbean, New Zealand/Aoetaroan, Indian, Peruvian, Italian, Scottish, Welsh and Australian birth or upbringing) blur the meaning of 'us' versus 'them', the traditional political and racial core of nationalist sentiment.

Since the very beginnings of codified sport in the late nineteenth century, marketing has been central. For example, the growth spurt of football in Britain in the 1890s and 1900s was closely connected to sponsorship from breweries. A century ago, Manchester United went into liquidation until it was bought and renamed by Manchester Breweries (Collins and Vamplew, 2002, pp. 46–7). So, in no sense would we argue for a halcyon period of romance when business and sport were separate spheres of civil society. The NICL opens up new domestic fronts in a dynamic of identification and commodification. The key is that the rise of global electronic media coverage, inter-twined with new forms of market-driven administration, has conditioned the relative autonomy of sport from the media, government and commerce. A turning point came with the emergence of global cricket contests that transcended nationally selected teams, starting in 1970, when South Africa was exiled from the world game because of *Apartheid*, and the brewing company Guinness sponsored a substitute tour of England by a global team (including white South Africans) (Collins and Vamplew, 2002, p. 60). A few years later there was a television takeover of world cricket from traditional authorities. The first of these phenomena signalled the prospect of transnational organization, commerce and identification. The second referenced the support given to cricket over many years by public broadcasters across much of the former British Empire, which excited the profit drives of less inventive commercial interests. In other words, once public broadcasters had created a viewing public, brokering the risk on public money, capital moved in to pick up a market that it had not shown the skill to initiate or cultivate (Miller, 1989). Similar stories could be told of basketball in the United States, which was stimulated by coverage on public TV in San Francisco.

Since the growth of sponsorship income and commercial control of sports that we traced in *Globalization and Sport*, a newly vigorous process of product placement has emerged. Not content with 30-second TV spots or arena signage, Adidas redesigned its football boot for the 2002 World Cup to achieve 'maximum on-field visibility' for television viewing. Regardless of the angle or the use of slow motion, the company's three-stripe logo would be visible every time one of the 150 players in the tournament who were paid to wear the 'Predator Mania' shoe was in-shot. Major stars were encouraged to don a champagne-coloured variety, which had been tested for maximum televisual impact (Kahn, 2002). Brewers routinely take advantage of ball-by-ball TV coverage of world cricket by claiming naming rights – such as the former Foster's Oval in England. Alcohol promotion is also highly visible in British football with, for example, Carling sponsoring its eponymous Cup and advertising on the shirts of Glasgow Celtic and Rangers, while Liverpool and Everton players wear, respectively, the brands of Carlsberg and Chang. Sales increases in the aftermath of these moves have been staggering, and the results have been similar for Anheuser-Busch in the United States (Collins and Vamplew, 2002, pp. 60–1, 63–4). In short, the NICL produces new publics in its restless search for spectators whose viewing and supporting labour will persuade the media to cover sports and sell the presence of these publics to advertisers. We shall address these worker and audience trends serially.

The US NICL and sport

At the top of certain sports, rates of pay for workers who compete internationally have combined with a deregulated world TV market to create labour cosmopolitans across football, ice hockey, swimming, basketball, track, cycling, baseball, golf, tennis and cricket. In keeping with other new professional diasporas, they migrate on a seasonal or permanent basis (Cohen, 1997, pp. 155–76). Secondary labour markets overseas also provide a place to test home-grown players – more than 130 National Football League (NFL) footballers in 1998 had played in League-sponsored competitions outside the United States. In terms of foreign-born NFL players, the numbers are few – under 2 per cent in 1970, rising to no more than 3 per cent over the next three decades. Canada has always been the largest supplier. In the 1999–2000 season, the League featured 50 overseas players from 23 states (Brown, 2005, p. 1121). By 2002, a wide assortment of nations had been represented (Table 15.1).

Of course, some of these players were born of US parents living abroad as part of the work of empire (such as soldiers quartered overseas) or were the children

Table 15.1 Birth places of NFL players (2002)

	Number of players
American Samoa	3
Argentina	2
Australia	1
Barbados	1
Cameroon	1
Canada	15
El Salvador	1
Germany	9
Ghana	1
Guyana	1
Iran	1
Ivory Coast	1
Jamaica	7
Japan	1
Liberia	1
Mexico	2
Netherlands	1
New Zealand/Aotearoa	2
Nigeria	2
Norway	1
Philippines	1
Poland	1
Russia	1
Sierra Leone	1
South Africa	2
Uganda	2
Virgin Islands	1
Zaire	3

Source: Data derived from NFL International (2002).

of economic migrants, rather than direct recruits to the NFL. But that does not discount their place within an international division of cultural labour.

Foreign recruiting by US sports is partially designed to circumvent the historic gains made by local athletes to secure income redistribution. Between 1974 and 1991, the proportion of revenue spent on Major League Baseball (MLB) players' salaries increased from 17.6 per cent to 42.9 per cent, because baseballers achieved free agency in 1975, following court and union action. From that time on, wealthy clubs could purchase the most desirable players, leaving the poorer clubs struggling. In 1999, the New York Yankees' payroll was US$85 million, whereas the Montréal Expos paid out just US$16 million. The two sides performed as those figures would suggest. These circumstances stimulated the desire to develop players outside the US college system in order to cut beginners' compensation. In 1970, fewer than 10 per cent of MLB players were born outside the United States; by 2003, almost one-fifth of MLB players were born beyond US borders (Marcano Guevara and Fidler, 1999, pp. 517–18; Brown, 2005, p. 1117). The 2009 season featured 229 players from 15 nations and territories, amounting to 28 per cent of the total roster (see http://mlb.com/news/press_releases/press_release.jsp?ymd=20090406&content_id=4139614&vkey=pr_mlb&fext=.jsp&c_id=mlb).

Most infamously, MLB teams set up baseball academies across Latin America in the 1980s. They search for young men (defined as 11+) who will sign up for much less than equivalently gifted players domiciled in the United States. Some US-based *hispanohablantes* also drop out of high school to join the Dominican amateur leagues, in the hope of being noticed by MLB representatives (Brown, 2002). Academy members are outside the US amateur draft's protection of wages and conditions – sporting corporations are uninterested in applying labour laws and conditions that protect their own executives! Teams discourage young boys from attending school and require them to avoid agents (whose bargaining skills have been so important in the domestic arena). The biggest source is the Dominican Republic, with Puerto Rico, Venezuela and Mexico of increasing importance. In the 2002 season, 89 Dominicans had Major League contracts, and 1,561 were playing in the Minors, accounting for almost 25 per cent of all pro-ballplayers in the United States. MLB teams have 30 baseball academies in the Republic, and the sport ranks among the top five national industries. Life in the academies is brutish and short, and there are many tragic stories of players destined for the equivalent of a wrecking yard if injuries or skill levels militate against their success. Rejected in their early twenties, they have totally unmarketable skills (Marcano Guevara and Fidler, 2002; Gmelch, 2006; Klein, 2006).

It is especially significant that these programmes are aimed at Third-World states. The First World has an entirely different type of aid, based on developing spectator interest in baseball rather than schooling stars (Japan, not the Dominican Republic, was the first place outside North America[4] to host an official MLB series, in 2000). When US-based players have sought to play off-season back home in Latin America, MLB has often blocked them, lest there develop an alternative baseball system. There was great irony and symbolic violence in baseball's nomination of March 2000 and 2001 as 'The Month of the Americas', in recognition of Latino contributions to the sport. As if in mocking preparation for this moment, *Sports Illustrated* offered a photo-essay of young boys in the Dominican Republic using makeshift equipment in the dirt, overlooked by satellite dishes bringing coverage of US games (Chass, 1998a, 1998b; Marcano Guevara and Fidler, 1999, pp. 512, 518; 'MLB honors Latin impact in 2000 with "Month of the Americas"', 1999; Winegardner, 1999; 'Leading off', 2000). Officially binational leagues, where teams themselves come from outside the United States, must comply with multiple legal systems. For example, North American pro leagues in baseball, basketball and hockey are all subject to Canadian as well as to US labour legislation (see Jarvis and Coleman, 1999, p. 347). This has not been a problem in practice for baseball in its dealings with Latin America, which is not surprising: the Monroe Doctrine lives on in licensing dismissive attitudes towards the legal framework of the region.

Aggressive recruiting activities are not restricted to pro sports. We've already mentioned efforts by US colleges to attract athletes who can heighten universities' national standing. The 'latter-day scramble for Africa', an unseemly search for track-and-field stars that started in the 1970s, resembled nineteenth-century imperial powers seeking new territory. In 1960, US colleges recruited 8 per cent of their athletes from Africa. By 1980, that proportion had reached 33 per cent of the campus total, spurred on by numerous Olympic successes by middle-distance runners from African nations. When these student-athletes came to the United States, they were frequently overworked to service boosterism, leaving town with devastated bodies that allowed no room for further success on behalf of their own countries (Bale, 1991, pp. 79, 74).

US professional sports have recently been forced to transcend the provincialism of domestic arenas and media outlets because of the classic capitalist problem of overproduction. Having saturated the domestic supply of good, cheap, obedient athletes and affluent consumers, the National Basketball Association (NBA) went overseas during the 1990s in search of cheap talent and likely customers, opening offices in Switzerland, Spain, Australia, Hong Kong and Mexico. Whereas three international players were drafted into the NBA for the 1993–4 season, opening rosters for 1999–2000 contained 37 from 25 countries, while in 2002–3, 69 players from 33 countries featured, including Argentina, Belize, Brazil, the Dominican Republic, Mexico, Spain and Venezuela, as well as Europe. They comprised almost 14 per cent of all NBA professionals. The 2008–9 season included 77 players from 33 nations ('Global player list grows', 1999; Jackson and Andrews, 1999, p. 34; Whitnell, 1999; NBA, 2002, 2009; Brown, 2005, p. 1119).

Of course, the corollary of this development is the disintegration of essentialist Yanqui shibboleths, notably that 'white men can't jump' (a position that was always already implausible, given the history of the high jump, pole vault and triple jump). With the growing presence of Latin, Asian and European players across the NBA, such assertions looked increasingly anachronistic. They finally tumbled to the floor in 2002, when the US national team was easily defeated on successive nights in the World Basketball Championship by Argentina and Yugoslavia – on a US court.[5] By that point, most lists of the 20 leading players in the NBA included a Yugoslavian (Peja Stojakovic), a Virgin Islander (Tim Duncan), a German (Dirk Nowitzki) and a Canadian (Steve Nash), while the best of the young included representatives from France (Tony Parker), Spain (Pau Gasol) and Turkey (Hedo Turkoglu) (Wilbon, 2002). In 2007, the NBA Finals were won by a team with backgrounds in four countries, against a team with backgrounds in one (the United States). That year, like the two previous ones, the Most Valuable Player (MVP) Award went to a foreigner. In 2001, the MVP in American League Baseball was Ichiro Suzuki from Japan and the National Hockey League scoring champion was Jarome Iginla, who was of Nigerian descent. Gasol was the NBA rookie of the year, and he was joined in the All-Rookie team by Parker and Russia's Andrei Kirilenko. The following season, the number one basketball draft pick was Yao Ming from the People's Republic of China, and 29 per cent of NBA draftees came from outside the United States (Coffey, 2002; Price, 2002b; Steele, 2002; Wells, 2008).

For its part, the Women's National Basketball Association (WNBA) *began* with use of the NICL, rather than turning to it once the domestic market in players and fans had become supersaturated, respectively, in quality and quantity. This was a means of immediately moving to a high standard of player ability and global spectator appeal. A total of 23 nations were represented by 46 players in the 2002 season, with 25 per cent of WNBA pros born outside the United States. The most powerful countries were Brazil and Australia. Five All-Stars were foreign nationals, from Australia (Lauren Jackson and Penny Taylor), Portugal (Ticha Penicheiro), Canada (Stacey Dales-Schuman) and Congo (Mwadi Mabika) (Orton, 2002). In 2005, 29 players came from 19 countries (see http://www.wnba.com/players/ international_roster.html). US discourses of racialization, which held that black people could play high-quality basketball and leap high while white people could not, were shown to be intensely local.

The NICL and audiences

The NICL is partly formed through the increased significance of the media in funding and disseminating sport. Emergent media forms have long harnessed themselves to strong, immediate, senses of 'being there' at sporting events of great moment – in the 1930s, by simulating actuality radio commentary on cricket matches in England for Australian audiences, and in the 1970s, through vivid satellite coverage of global mega sports events (Real, 1989, 1996; Rowe, 2004a, 2004b; Andrews, 2006). In the late 1990s, a CBS Internet affiliate offered US cricket fans ball-by-ball information on matches around the world ('SportsLine USA and CricInfo launch 1999 World Cup site', 1999), and one-day internationals involving South Asian teams were available on pay-per-view TV. By the 2006–7 and 2009 Ashes series, US residents were watching every ball online (unreliably in 2006, reliably in 2009, as services improved).

Football players and other athletes are effectively vended as screen actors by sports organizations to television broadcasters and advertisers. They may soon be more directly employed as TV talent by sports that will control the electronic distribution and display of competitions, in keeping with the vertical integration pioneered by companies like the International Marketing Group, which represents players and stages, promotes, markets, televises and secures advertising and sponsorship for sporting events (Barnett, 1990, p. 188; Rowe, 1995, p. 112). Given the cross-border capacity of satellite television and the Internet, we expect to see more sporting competitions shaped by technological and commercial reach, rather than by the boundaries of nation-states and their contained populations.

This does not mean, though, an end to national identification. In Ireland, Sky and CNN may beam foreign sports in, but RTE covers Gaelic games, and Setanta Sport (although its UK operation collapsed in 2009) provides worldwide coverage to the Irish diaspora, not to mention additional highlights on aeroplane programming (Cronin, 1999, p. 68). Diasporic spectatorship sees fans 'double-declutching' between their nations of origin and domicile, and between regions. Since 1994, 14 MLB teams have offered domestic Spanish-language broadcasts. New York City-based Dominicans have long congregated at a bar that provides simultaneous coverage of all games involving such prominent Major League batters from the Republic as Sammy Sosa and Manny Ramirez, whose Yanqui team affiliations were smoothly erased by their homeland in the eyes of such spectators. Bulgarian viewers of NTV tuned in to the WNBA to watch the Houston Comets' number one draft pick, expatriate Polina Tzekova, and dozens of reporters from Germany covered the 1999 NBA game between Seattle and Dallas, which featured their countrymen Nowitzki and Detlef Schrempf (Cooper, 1999; Dempsey, 1999; Marcano Guevara and Fidler, 1999; Whitnell, 1999).

Also consider the famous 1998 contest between the Anglo-American Mark McGwire and the Latino Sosa (who, as a child, had sold fruit and shone shoes on the streets of San Pedro de Macorís) to eclipse Roger Maris' single-season baseball home-run record. Their rivalry was consistently coded as a contest between a lost US homogeneity and a segmented nation, where the 'national pastime' was becoming, literally, a thing of the past (Juffer, 2002; also see Sobchak, 1997). Bairner (2001, p. 101) notes that:

> Afterward McGwire observed, 'I'm glad I've been associated with Sammy Sosa. It's been a great year for everyone. I'm absolutely exhausted. I don't think you can use your mind any more playing baseball. I've amazed myself that I've stayed in a tunnel for so long. It just proves to me I can overcome anything with the strength of my mind.' . . . Sosa's assessment of the season had been rather more cryptic but no less instructive. Speaking about his own personal achievement, he is on record as saying, 'My country is happy.' . . . He did not mean the United States.

The NBA's strategic use of Yao Ming and of other leading players to attract audiences in their countries of origin and in their diasporic contexts is a conspicuous example of global sport marketing (Rowe and Gilmour, 2008). The NFL's increasing reliance on a global marketplace has even produced 'collaborations' with rival codes: in 2002, FC Barcelona, the leading Catalan football club, signed a cross-promotional deal with the League. American football, a minor sport globally, gained from an association with a truly competitive sport, while Barcelona obtained a certain *entrée* to the United States. The Barcelona deal followed one struck by Manchester United with the Yankees, the only US sporting club with any real meaning across the globe following the demise of Michael Jordan (Buckley, 1999; 'NFL full of foreign-born players', 1999; NFL International, 1999; G. Solomon, 2002; Miller, 2004). These arrangements led to protests from sectors of the US media, a representative reaction being the *Village Voice*'s denunciation of football: 'Every four years the World Cup comes around, and with it a swarm of soccer nerds and bullies reminding us how backward and provincial we are for not appreciating soccer enough' (Barra, 2002).

There is also, of course, a brand of academia that celebrates a putative 'American exceptionalism'. This concept began as an attempt to explain why socialism had not taken greater hold in the United States. It has since turned into an excessive rhapsody to Yanqui world leadership, difference and sanctimony. So we find claims made – in all seriousness – that 'foreignness' can make a sport unpopular in the United States, and the media will not accept anything that is coded as 'other' (Brown, 2005). Wiser critics, such as Selassie (2002), connect such protectionist expressions to Cold-War scapegoating of immigrants, with the rejection of football in the 1940s and 1950s a rejection of difference, and there is ample evidence of equivalent ethnic marking in Anglo-settler societies elsewhere (Miller *et al.*, 2001).

Perhaps the most appalling instance of 'American exceptionalism' was provided by Reaganite Republican Jack Kemp. He famously derided football before Congress as a 'European socialist' sport by contrast with its 'democratic' US rival (quoted in Lexington, 2006). Similarly ethnocentric denunciations – predicated, of course, on letting Latinos and migrants know they're not 'American' – largely flow from the intemperate keystrokes and irate penmanship of angry white men. Frustrated at the prominence and popularity of the sport, they are desperate to attack its 'European . . . death and despair' (Webb, 2009).

But these are death-throes against the tide of history. By 2005, the United States had English- and Spanish-language TV networks dedicated to football, covering leagues in Britain, Germany, Asia, Africa, France, Spain, the Netherlands, Latin America – and the United States (men's and women's by 2009). In Los Angeles, 93,000 people turned up to watch a football match in 2009. Although, as noted above, Setanta television went bankrupt in Britain that year, Disney's ESPN bought up its rights to screen the English Premier League in the United Kingdom. In 2008, ESPN Star Sports, a joint Disney–News Corporation venture (Mickey-meets-Rupert), invested a billion US dollars over a decade in the new Twenty20 cricket world championships, while the Indian Premier League used a draft system whereby players were bid for as per the United States – but as established stars rather than rookies. Stars flocked from across the globe to sign up for unprecedented sums (Gibson, 2009; Hutton, 2009; Rowe and Gilmour, 2009). The clouds had grown heavy and thick around elderly, inadequate ways of understanding the US sporting market, via 'American exceptionalism'.

Time magazine's European business correspondent (Ledbetter, 2002) acknowledges the world-historical extent of cultural protectionism in the United States, which applies across the entertainment spectrum (Miller *et al.*, 2005). One might regard the level of protection in US sport as akin to socialism – a draft for *faux* students who have been trained for free in directly and indirectly state-subsidized universities; limits on salaries; revenue-sharing; stadiums paid for through taxation; exemptions from anti-trust legislation; and limits on cable competition (Ford, 2002). This is a planned, command, economy by any other name – one that works with the recognition that, in sport, firms need opponents in order to survive. Competition in sport is, therefore, unlike its role in other forms of capitalism, more an end than a means.

The early twenty-first century clearly shows that the protectionism of the US sports market has run into a domestic over-supply. Networks, cable and satellite companies, universities and municipal governments have begun to question the vast public subsidies given to the four major pro sports, and the nature and extent of their externalities. Expansion teams are under close scrutiny – Disney immediately looked to sell the 2002 'World' Series winners, the Anaheim Angels, which it had only bought as a means of 'relandscaping and reinvigorating' the location that housed Disneyland (Goldsmith, 2002). Morgan Stanley suggests that the major TV networks lost US$1.3 billion on sports between 2002 and 2006. The NFL's fortunes are in decline, with a decrease in TV ratings of 13 per cent in the five seasons to 2002. Disney dispatched *Monday Night Football* from ABC to ESPN in 2006 due to falling audience numbers, where it was a success at that much lower ratings threshold. In 2009, NBC was unable to sell all its advertising slots for the Super Bowl. Along the way, the working-class pretensions of these sports – especially powerful in the class claims made against football – have been eroded. In the five years from 1997, the proportion of NFL fans earning below US$30,000 decreased by over 7 per cent, while the proportion earning over US$100,000 increased by 30 per cent. In keeping with this gentrification, banks moved into the centre of US sports sponsorship, even as they were dealing with the public opprobrium resulting from their role in the Great Recession and subsequent reward of corporate welfare (Beyers, 2002; Hiestand, 2002; J. Solomon, 2002; Nunn and Rosentraub, 2003; Goetzl, 2008; 'Is it recession-proof?', 2009; 'Play on', 2009).

The response to this overproduction has been to stimulate overseas demand. The NFL subsidizes thousands of hours of television across the globe, invested forlornly in overseas teams via NFL Europe/Europa until it gave up in 2007, and offers exhibition games ('The world's fare?', 2002). The NBA's Commissioner euphemizes the drastic domestic overexpansion as a sign that '[t]he American sports market is mature', as he unveils plans to draw 50 per cent of the league's revenue from overseas (Hiestand, 2002). NBA TV began in 1999, and within ten years was available in 79 countries and territories (see http://www.nba.com/schedules/international_nba_tv_schedule.html and http://www.nba.com/FanNight). But those raw numbers do not disclose popularity so much as the dramatic need to fill up hours in recently deregulated televisual systems.

This movement from provincial protectionism to a NICL that addresses the crisis of domestic overproduction is the key to the future of US basketball, with white European stars an added 'advantage' via racialized marketing both internationally and at home. As the famous anti-racist black coach John Thompson has said, 'It's only economically smart' (quoted in Coffey, 2002). The NBA has legalized zone defence in order to diminish the boredom of US players backing opponents into the low post, favouring instead the skilled European jump shooter and hence enabling international rules to operate in a hitherto protected environment (Price, 2002a). Meanwhile, the stubbornly parochial, race-baiting world of the National Association for Stock Car Racing (NASCAR) has struggled, with logos dropping from vehicles like flies, and teams amalgamating to counter desperate financial straits ('Is it recession-proof?', 2009).

Conclusion

US sport has long been in a speculative bubble, analogous to the dot-com era's 'irrational exuberance' (Shiller, 2000) and the asset inflation that followed it. In barely a decade, overbidding for TV rights, fuelled by Rupert Murdoch's dual ambition of creating a global sporting television service while achieving hegemony in its foundational market, has turned broadcast sport from a prized commodity, to a valued loss leader, and finally into a contractual liability. As one commentator puts it, during the largest slump in spending on advertising since the Second World War and before the debt-driven crisis five years later, '[t]he US media market is glutted with more sports and entertainment properties than there is ad money to go round' (McCarthy, 2002, p. 27). This oversupply led to writedowns in the value of rights to TV sport paid by US media companies in the vicinity of US\$3 billion. Such hard-fought deals as NBC's contract for future Olympic Games are financial albatrosses around corporate necks (Chenoweth and O'Riordan, 2002). When rights are up for renegotiation, television's losses are passed onto sports. Competition for shrinking resources between owners, administrators, coaches, élite players and other factions of the sporting industries was not pretty in the early years of this century, and no less so in the post-2007 global financial crisis.

There is considerable debate about whether the sporting media are immune to recessions. Premium sports claim that their brand will protect them from reductions in TV rights and sponsorship revenue, while media companies confront balance sheets with reduced advertising and subscription revenue. Murdoch's News Corporation lost US\$5.4 billion in 2008–9, partly because of declining advertising revenue for regional cable sports networks and increased marketing and sports rights costs (such as NASCAR). Under these circumstances, smaller sports (including many Olympic and US college sports) and media companies vulnerable to the credit squeeze (like Setanta) are in jeopardy (Sherlock, 2008; Arango, 2009; News Corporation, 2009). The United States is not the only saturated media market seeking audiences through consumerist branding – clubs from the English Premier League and Spain's *La Liga* routinely tour Asia, sell overpriced merchandising made in Asian factories and undermine local football competitions (Rowe and Gilmour, 2008). But the most advanced and desperate manoeuvres are evident in the United States.

The sporting cartels of the United States are endeavouring, through the NICL, to avoid paying the price of their overproduction. Protectionism has consequently eased somewhat in terms of player origins and rules of the game, but major barriers remain to truly international exchange. Massive resources are dedicated to importing and exporting players and exporting tastes, but few to importing the latter. A case in point here, perhaps, is the Los Angeles Galaxy's US\$250 million hiring of leading English footballer David Beckham as a pivotal marketing figure for both domestic consumption and reexport to regions such as Australasia (Gilmour and Rowe, 2009). To return to our opening anecdote about Afghan cricket, relative autonomy and civil society depend on a shifting complex of politics and economics. That complex has long made the flow of sport between the United States and the rest of the world asymmetrical and exploitative. It is likely to remain so.

Notes

1 Thanks to Marie Leger, Daniel Mato, Kristina Riegert, Alan Tomlinson, Chris Young and the editors for their comments on earlier versions, and to Jim McKay, our co-author of an earlier paper (Miller *et al.*, 2003).
2 We use the word 'football' to describe Association Football, its referent for 96 per cent of the world's population.
3 Of course, some critics argue that this claim to a post-Fordist world is misguided (Hirst *et al.*, 2009).
4 In the field of US sports, 'North America' is, bizarrely, used in a way that excludes Mexico.
5 It should be noted that these championships had debuted in Brazil, half a century earlier. It beat the United States in the first contest (Brown, 2005, p. 1119).

16 Transnational athletes

Celebrities and migrant players in fútbol and hockey

Ricardo Trumper and Lloyd L. Wong

In the era of globalization the nation-state is seemingly declining. Supranational organizations, coupled with trade pacts, weaken laws to the benefit of transnational capital and effectively deregulate global movements of capital, goods and regulate people's mobility. There seems to be a re-shaping of the nation-state as the site of mediation between the local and the global. At the same time, states, classes and political movements seek the re-affirmation of the nation and of nationalism giving priority to national identities (Poole, 1999, p. 74). Sport plays a part in both undermining and strengthening today's nations and national identities. In this context we examine the cases of former celebrity transnational athletes in *fútbol* and hockey. Although we focus on ex-Chilean fútbol player Iván (Bam Bam) Zamorano and ex-Canadian hockey player Wayne Gretzky we also examine less prominent migrant sport workers in these sports.

On the surface, Zamorano and Gretzky were 'borderless athletes' (Chiba *et al.*, 2001) representing a new type of citizen who works and lives borderless and bordered lives. Yet, their lives show that, despite high incomes and migratory facilities, they were not immune to the allures of 'home'. Through these examples, we show that it is paradoxical that, in Chile, Zamorano represented and symbolized a new Chileanness and, in Canada, Gretzky is still a symbol of a 'true' Canadian. Both have conformed to accepted definitions of transnational citizens living in national and transnational spaces, athletes who navigate the complexity of the social relations at 'home' and abroad. These athletes embody transnational cultural and capitalist business practices while willingly serving as national cultural icons for the re-affirmation of national identities.

Zamorano emigrated from a small Chilean club to Switzerland in 1989 to play for modest St Gallen. He was then sold to Sevilla, a Spanish team, finding stardom in powerful Real Madrid, after which Internazionale de Milano then purchased his contract. In early 2001, Bam Bam was hired by América of Mexico. By 2003, like many other migrant Chilean players, he moved back to Chile to play for Colo Colo, retiring soon after. Gretzky first played in the National Hockey League (NHL) with the Edmonton Oilers. In his 21-year career, he played the first ten years in Canada and the last 11 in the United States. Upon retirement he has continued to live in the United States and has his principal residence in Arizona where until recently he was the head coach of the Phoenix Coyotes of the NHL.

Zamorano and Gretzky have engaged in practices that conform to definitions of transnationalism and deterritorialization including mixed commitments and allegiances. Transnationalism fundamentally transforms the relationship between 'place' of habitation and cultural practices, experiences and identities. Indeed, some scholars have argued that places are no longer the main supports of identity (Tomlinson, 1999) especially for highly mobile urban businesspersons and skilled workers in global cities. Several factors influence transnationalism, like microchip technology contributing to the dis-embedding of social relations and time–space compression promoting mobility and deterritorialization. Neo-liberalism causes individuals to lose ties with co-workers, neighbours and friends (Sennett, 1998), making the bonds with territory become more tenuous.

Indeed, some sport workers fit the definition of transmigrants. In Canada, star runners in the late twentieth century were born in the Caribbean, but ran for Canada. However, many more do not fit this definition. Maguire and Bale (1994, p. 2) include sports figures among the unrooted migrating professionals who have emerged from the transnationalization of capital since the mid-1970s. Barber (1992, pp. 54–5) places athletes among 'a new breed of men and women for whom religion, culture and nationality can seem only marginal elements in a working identity'. He is not just pointing to workers who move from place to place and job site to job site. He alludes to people who share a new culture. These migrants, with particular forms of capital, have been around for some time. But now transportation and communication technologies allow them to appear to 'live' in several places simultaneously. Yet, there are many professionals, including athletes, who keep their cultures without adopting a globalized one.

We argue that deterritorialization must be contextualized. Throughout the world, around 150 million people live outside of their countries of birth (Martin, 2001), many of them asylum seekers. Others are temporary workers with few citizenship rights. Guest workers in Germany, or agricultural labourers in Canada, show how borders and nation (and race) do matter. So, we problematize the notions of transnationalism and deterritorialization and global and transnational citizenship considering that there is just a small group of unrooted 'world citizens'. Moreover, Anderson (1992) argues that migrants' allegiances to the 'mother country' are exacerbated by distance. We wonder if this is not the case for migrant athletes. Some change allegiances, but many remain loyal to their countries of origin.

Transnational labour migration in sport

Political economy is still a useful perspective for examining sport labour migration. Sport labour migrants are flexible and part of an international division of labour within global capitalism. The pervasiveness of flexible transnational labour migration in sport, and its interconnectedness with global sport development, has been described by Maguire and Bale (1994) and Maguire (1999) and the economic commercialization of the sports of hockey and fútbol has necessitated the international migration of sport labour. Historically the process of sports labour migration began with colonialism and has continued after decolonization

(Darby, 2007a). Today's internationalization of labour markets is a stage in a historical process and corresponds to a particular economic, social, ideological and political time. The new international division of labour, which began in the 1970s, contains within it a division of sporting labour and encompasses uneven processes of globalization, governmentalization, Americanization, televisualization and commodification (Miller *et al.*, 2001, p. 4). For professional fútbol and ice hockey there have been significant increases in their commercialization as businesses since the 1980s. Players' salaries at the top tiers have risen dramatically, marketing and construction of consumer identities have been introduced and pay TV and the capital investment in teams have increased, all of which are integrally related to a liberalization of labour for the sports teams involved (Ammirante, 2006). Like Bairner (2007) we argue that 'bringing political economy back in' in the analysis of sport labour migration is constructive and valuable in light of the expansive commercialization of sport since the 1960s. Cultural globalization, particularly of the media, has meant that the commercialization of sport is facilitating the creation of a global sport industry that is marketed across cultures (Westerbeek and Smith, 2003). As the literature on transnationalism has shown, transnational resource inequalities of migrants often 'encapsulate the gross inequalities of the global economy' (Carling, 2008, p. 1467). As such, sport labour migration also needs to be viewed from a transnational lens. Sport worker migrants often straddle two countries with much movement back and forth.

Over the past several decades in ice hockey, there has been an international labour migration of European players to Canada and the United States. This migration occurs at both the junior and professional levels, and conversely, there has been an international migration of Canadian players to European countries (Genest, 1994; Maguire, 1999). On the other hand, fútbol is a transnationalized spectacle with a much longer history of players moving to play in other countries, selling their labour power and their physical capital throughout the world, far from their countries of birth and of citizenship. Mussolini's Italy attracted fútbol players with Italian surnames from Argentina to play for the Italian side in world competitions. The connections between Italian and South American fútbol migrants strengthened with the Fordist modernization of Italy after the war, although recently they have even strengthened further with the transformation of fútbol into a major spectacle and big business. Currently Italy and France attract fútbol immigrants as the needs of capital have transformed the nature of fútbol in their respective countries. Some of the clubs in Spain have depended on fútbol talent from other countries from early on. In the Franco era the immigration of players to big clubs, such as Real Madrid, was encouraged and financed. Now a team like Real Madrid relies primarily on migrant players. The 2009 team was coached by a Chilean, Manuel Pellegrini, and included two Portuguese, three Argentinians, two Brazilians, one Malian, two French, one Pole, one German, three Dutch and only eight Spaniards. The migration of fútbol players is not limited to these countries. Fútbolistas move from many countries in the European Union, Eastern Europe, Africa and Latin America to play in higher-paid Western Europe.

In general, numerous elite athletes are international migrants as sports became big business and a spectacle. Zamorano and Gretzky can be thought of as elite, global and borderless athletes, but we wonder if they represent and typify a new brand of person that is theorized under the rubric of transnationalism and deterritorialization. Perhaps closer to this type of person are Canadian-born ice hockey and fútbol players who now play for European national teams. For example, Owen Hargreaves, who was born in Canada, plays for Manchester United and England's national team. Although the Federation of International Football Associations (FIFA) is moving towards restricting these practices, many other national teams include foreign-born players.

Only on the surface do Zamorano and Gretzky seem to confirm the existence of such a new group of citizens. They were on global paths as migrant labour but were not typical international migrant fútbol or hockey players nor were they just merely professional athletes. From humble, modest backgrounds, they were superstar global athletes who circulated socially among the global elite and capitalist class. Zamorano and Gretzky were not only sport labour migrants but, as superstar athletes, they were and still are corporations in and of themselves, and they sold and sell themselves and their names commercially.

Gretzky remained in the United States upon retirement while Zamorano returned first to Latin America and then to Chile where he has become a media celebrity and a shrewd entrepreneur. Zamorano's decision to return to Chile represents the choices of a growing number of itinerant workers who are just-in-time temporary workers outside their countries of birth, sojourners who sometimes choose, but most often are forced, to return to their countries of origin. It is important to analyse how these two athletes, through their sports, were claimed by their nations of birth and how they have come to symbolize their nations despite their apparent transnationality.

Celebrity players

Fútbol – Iván Zamorano

Few Chileans would be recognizable by international audiences. However, for a number of years Bam Bam Zamorano played for and was recognized by audiences world-wide. As a player with Real Madrid, Internazionale and América, he was seen on television in many countries, including Spain, Italy, Mexico and Chile. Was he a deterritorialized transnational, or was he just another Chilean working outside Chile? Was his uniqueness with respect to other expatriate Chileans based on technology and his wealth? Were these differences what allowed him to take advantage of quick travel, instant telecommunications, and a business-created passion for the consumption of fútbol? Is Zamorano different from other Chilean players who play in big fútbol European or Latin American markets, or in smaller ones, like Guatemala, Indonesia or Uzbekistan?

For a while, it was difficult to ascertain where Zamorano really lived. He lived and worked in Chile, Switzerland, Spain, Italy and Mexico. He had homes in Milan, Switzerland, Seville and Madrid, held several passports and worked in Spain,

Italy and Mexico (Carcuro, 2000). There is no doubt Zamorano was dedicated to his profession, capable of selling his labour power in important market-oriented clubs, like Real Madrid and Internazionale de Milano. At the time of his decline, he was able to re-market himself to play for one million dollars a year for América in Mexico. He typified the ideal type, in a Weberian sense (Weber, 1947), of transnationalism. However, Zamorano's life seems to run counter to the ideal type of transnationalism. Irrespective of where he has lived, he has served as a hegemonic pillar in the reproduction of Chileanness.

He has been perceived as a Chilean and has perceived himself as a Chilean. More important, he has been a central element in the (re)making of the edifice of Chilean identity and also in the (re)construction of a Chilean patriotism that pervades all social groups.

In fact, for a Chilean, it would have been difficult to perceive Bam Bam when abroad as not Chilean. Many games he played in Europe were broadcast to Chilean television; the audiences for these games were larger than those for the Chilean competition. When Zamorano was playing in Europe, his actual location was ambiguous. When he played for Real Madrid or Internazionale he was still 'playing' in Chilean living rooms. It is ambiguity which made possible the Zamorano phenomenon. He played simultaneously in Chile and Europe, he was at once a performer and a fútbol player, and he played both for Real Madrid or Internazionale or América, and for Chile.

Moreover, when Zamorano was playing outside Chile he seemed to have commuted often. However, instead of reinforcing a global, rootless citizen, Zamorano's commuting, paradoxically, may have served to strengthen his national affiliation. How could he be perceived by Chileans to be non-Chilean when he was seen in Chile often? He was continually interviewed by Chilean television. He made physical appearances in Chile and was seen visiting his family. Journalists waited with expectation to see if he would vote in elections, and his engagement to a Chilean model was part of local celebrity life. While 'away', Zamorano launched a charitable foundation in Santiago; appeared on television programmes, at one time together with Chile's President; launched a line of clothing; and appeared in ads for a Spanish-owned telephone company operating in Chile. In fact, Zamorano reinforced his Chileanness by describing himself to be an ambassador for Chile (Carcuro, 2000, p. 131). He once declared:

> I believe the [Chilean] national team has given me the greatest satisfactions. I have shown the Chilean flag in every field in the world and I have always felt that I am a Chilean ambassador in each place I played.
>
> ('Ádios a "Bam Bam" Zamorano', 2003)

Zamorano's period as an international star player coincided with a time of unprecedented economic growth in Chile. It was a period when Chile was represented as a Jaguar, competitive, aggressive and successful, characteristics that meshed well with neo-liberalism, the system that has framed Chilean society since the 1970s. This Jaguar metaphor was enhanced by Zamorano's stardom, by the attention given to the national fútbol team that participated in the 1998 World Cup, a team that had Zamorano as captain, and by a bronze medal in football in the 2000 Olympic Games by a team that also had Zamorano as captain. Other sports figures also reinforced the neo-liberal discourse, notably tennis player Marcelo Ríos and fútbol star Marcelo Salas (Trumper and Tomic, 1999). But, Zamorano was the essential star to promote this view.

It was somewhat paradoxical that the discourse of success of neo-liberalism was linked to elite fútbol players playing outside Chile and, therefore, to the implied inability of the Chilean football clubs to retain them. Indeed, under different discursive deployments, these emigrations could have been taken rather as an indication of the dependent and peripheral status of a nation (Darby, 2001). Yet, in the discursive deployments of neo-liberalism, a number of athletes were represented as the models of the new spirit of the nation and of Chileans, the example and symbol of Chile.

In Chile, the Chilean athletes' success in the 'developed' world was construed not so much as the deterritorialization and transnationalism of the player or as forced economic emigration, but rather, as a marker of the reception of Chilean commodities abroad, like wine, fruit and salmon. Fútbolistas were not an exception (Arbena, 1994, pp. 104–5). Zamorano's life and triumphs outside Chile enhanced both his presence in Chile and Chilean nationalism, thus undermining concepts of transnational deterritorialization and globalism. But Zamorano is one of the very few Chilean athlete-workers to have reached stardom. The fate of the majority of Chilean players outside Chile tends to confirm that they share the characteristics of millions of other migrant temporary workers. They do not become deterritorialized global elites or global citizens, but rather, they are part of a temporary work force that provides just-in-time labour to capitalist enterprises, for which access to this form of labour is essential to keep competitive. Perhaps the difference with other temporary migrant workers is that fútbol players are more than labourers. They are also bodies bought and sold that, at times, may turn out to be good investments. Ironically, one of Zamorano's companies is Passball, a business that facilitates buying and selling bodies by 'representing' and managing fútbolistas.

Ice hockey – Wayne Gretzky

Wayne Gretzky was traded to the Los Angeles Kings in 1988 after winning four Stanley Cups with the Edmonton Oilers, a Canadian professional hockey team in the NHL. This trade included the selling of Gretzky for $15 million and three players in exchange. As in most professional sports this situation can be described as 'unfree' migrant labour where the 'unfreeness' means that there is a compulsion to provide labour to a specific employer and an inability to circulate freely in the labour market (Satzewich, 1990, p. 329). The sale of Gretzky from a Canadian to an American employer bound him, by the conditions of the NHL, to play hockey for his new employer. However, given the privileges and wealth of star professional hockey players in the NHL, it is clear that his degree of subordination, powerlessness and exploitation is incomparable to low-wage unfree migrant labourers. Overall, in his 21-year career as a professional hockey player, Gretzky played the first ten years in Canada and his final 11 years in the United States with the Los Angeles Kings, St. Louis Blues, and finally with the New York Rangers. It was during his time in the United States that Gretzky the businessperson took full flight and this has continued over the past decade since his retirement in 1999.

Since the mid-1990s Gretzky has been in the business of marketing and selling his celebrity status as the best hockey player in the world. His television commercials throughout the years have included endorsing the products of such companies as Budweiser, Folgers, Tylenol, Kodak, Goodyear, Johnson and Johnson, Canadian Imperial Bank of Commerce, TransAlta Energy Company, McDonald's and Ford. His recent commercials continue to support and uphold his iconic status in Canada and to continue to give Canadians a sense of his omnipresence in Canada while in actuality his presence is more symbolic than real. Gretzky also has public capital investments and evolving ownerships in various business enterprises. Over the decades these have included junior hockey teams, a professional football team in Canada, hockey stick companies, race horses, stamps, coins, collector sports cards, E-commerce companies and the Phoenix Coyotes of the NHL. He has dabbled in a line of fashionable clothing sold in Canada by the Bay department stores and recently in 2007 he has partnered with Creekside Estate Winery in the Niagara region of Canada promoting his '99' signature wine. In 2001 Gretzky became a minority owner and managing partner of the Phoenix Coyotes, an American NHL team where he was head coach from 2005 to 2009.

Gretzky's ambassadorship for the game of hockey and his charitable and philanthropic activities are intricately related to his business interests. Whenever there is a controversial issue that arises in the game of hockey, Gretzky, as the game's leading ambassador, is asked for his point of view by the media. Furthermore, it is common for celebrity athletes to establish foundations for charitable purposes while at the same time the name association enhances and promotes their personal trademarks. For example one of the current largest foundations is the Tiger Woods Foundation whose aim is to empower youth. Gretzky hosts an annual pro-Am golf tournament named the 'Ford Wayne Gretzky Classic' where the proceeds benefit the Wayne Gretzky Foundation where underprivileged children are given the chance to participate in minor hockey and to also see professional NHL games. Gretzky also operates a fantasy hockey camp for adults where the proceeds also go to his foundation. All of these business and charitable adventures have continued to provide Gretzky with a Canadian public identity that continues to ignore the border between Canada and the United States.

Representing hockey and the nation

The case of Gretzky is similar to that of Zamorano's in that he was an athlete who seemingly left his country of birth and possessed multiple allegiances. In contrast to Zamorano, Gretzky has not returned to his native country to live after retirement.

Many professional Canadian hockey players who live and play in the United States acquire US citizenship, and thus become dual American and Canadian citizens. It is assumed by those knowledgeable about financial and tax matters (Ingram, 1996) and media reporters (CTV.ca news staff, 2003) that Gretzky has dual Canadian–United States citizenship. While he has lived in the United States for two decades he is often in Canada either physically or virtually. Canadians do not consider him as an emigrant who left Canada. The United States–Canadian border continues to be, even in the post-9/11 era, very porous in terms of the movement of capital and, to some extent, labour. Thus Gretzky is perceived by Canadians to be a Canadian public personality. When Gretzky moved from Canada to the United States the situation was decried and grieved nationally (Jackson, 1994, pp. 438–41). He was very much in the Canadian public eye during his playing days in the United States and also since then through his involvement with the Phoenix Coyotes and also as executive director of Canada's men's Olympic hockey team. The penetration of these porous frontiers, via telecommunications technology such as cable and satellite television, continues to make Gretzky's presence felt in Canada.

What is important here is not so much Gretzky's current place of primary residence (Scottsdale, Arizona), or even his trekking back and forth from Canada and the United States to conduct business, or the porousness of the Canada–US border. After all, Canadian nationalism is a force in the Canadian political economy. What is important is that Gretzky had been reincarnated into a new packaged truth, that of a transnational capitalist who, like other transnationalized businesses, offers the example of Canadian world success. Transnationalism and deterritorialization in their purest forms exist today with financial capital and corporations. Other 'capitals' are still attached to people and people attached to nations, with their lives and identities remaining packaged into a national wrapping. The building of Canada as a country is to some extent tied to hockey, and Gretzky is a powerful part of this nation building. Thus Gretzky wraps himself in the Canadian flag during the Olympics through his association with Canada's national hockey team and also through his association with hockey – a sport that allegedly provides Canadians with a core value that transcends all other fault lines.

Ice hockey first emerged as an organized sport in Canada over a century ago and was considered as a reflection of Canadian society (Metcalfe, 1987, pp. 61–73). It is still quintessentially Canadian, an 'invented tradition', habitus, and an integral part of the imagined national culture and nationalism. Deeply embedded in this imagined national culture are myths, discourses and practices of ice hockey. One perpetuated myth is that ice hockey, as a sport, provides an opportunity for upward social mobility (Gruneau and Whitson, 1993, pp. 132–3), particularly for boys and men, since hockey provides a hyper-masculine vision of 'Canadianness' (Whitson and Gruneau, 2006, p. 3) and has a relationship with Canadian nationalism and masculinity (Robidoux and Trudel, 2006, p. 117). Furthermore, hockey teams that represent Canada in international tournaments symbolize the supposed uniqueness and character of the nation. Elite Canadian hockey players, who make up these teams, are celebrated as individuals with great skills in the game. However, what is also celebrated is the nation that produced them (Gruneau and Whitson, 1993, p. 247). So hockey has been a fundamental part of masculine nation building in Canada and has always been part of the politics of Canada's national identity. As hockey is intricately involved in the construction of Canadianness, so is Wayne Gretzky. As the best male player ever to play the game Gretzky is a representation of Canada and claimed by Canada because hockey is the nation's game.

By the summer of 1988, Gretzky was a Canadian superstar and celebrity hockey player with success as a player leading Team Canada in four international tournaments with wins in the Canada Cup, in 1984 and 1987, over Sweden and the Soviet Union. However, that summer was a very memorable one for Gretzky and for Canada. In July, he married Janet Jones, an American Hollywood actress, model and dancer. The wedding was a mega-event with 700 official guests, many of whom were celebrities and politicians; 200 credentialed media journalists; television network coverage; 10,000 uninvited guests in the streets outside the cathedral; and massive security provided by the police and fire departments (Gretzky and Reilly, 1990, p. 156). The Canadian media referred to this wedding as 'Canada's Royal Wedding'. This was ironic in post-colonial Canada who had repatriated her constitution from Britain only in 1981. Canada's national magazine, *Maclean's*, described the wedding as 'the union of a talented and gentlemanly sports hero who, for many Canadians, embodies some of the nation's most cherished values, and his glamorous American princess' (Redmond, 1993, p. 64).

However, less than one month after his wedding, Gretzky was sold to the Los Angeles Kings. This event shocked Canada, and when it was announced, television programming was interrupted all across North America to announce the trade, and local newspapers throughout Canada devoted their front pages to the news. Gretzky's marriage and trade must be contextualized in terms of the political economy of the NHL and an inter-related crisis in Canadian identity in 1988. Commercial spectator sport relies on expansion and growth of territories and markets to enhance capital accumulation (Kidd, 1979). The NHL is part of the 'major league' sports industry (Whitson and Gruneau, 1997) and has become a big business, undergoing increasing commercialization since its inception in the early 1900s. Thus, it is like many other commercial enterprises, in that it has a history of expansion, which in this case is the number of teams in the league, and of seeking new sources of revenue (Whitson, 1997). The pressure and plan for the NHL's sixth major expansion began in 1989 (Stein, 1997, p. 65), which was shortly after Gretzky's trade to the US Los Angeles Kings. Thus, the decade of the 1990s (1990–2000) saw the NHL expand from 21 teams to 30 teams, an increase of almost one-third, with Gretzky's marquee status spurring and facilitating this expansion mostly to the southern United States. As Jackson (1994, pp. 433–4; 2001, pp. 174–7) pointed out, Gretzky's marriage and trade were interwoven in public discourse with the Canada–US Free Trade Agreement, concern over the threat of the Americanization of Canada, and a crisis in Canadian identity and cultural uniqueness.

In contrast to Zamorano, whose migration and success outside of Chile were celebrated, Gretzky's departure from Canada was viewed in terms of death-like loss and mourning. Canadians viewed Gretzky's migration to the United States as different from the migration of thousands of other lesser-known Canadians who follow the same path. The migration of Canadian hockey players to the United States was, at the time, pervasive and still today the most common form of geographic mobility. More recently this migration has included many European destinations. Up until the past two decades, Canadian players dominated the NHL and comprised over 90 per cent of the players, but American teams have always comprised the majority of the teams in the modern era. In the 1950s and 1960s virtually all NHL players were Canadians. However, over the past 25 years, there has been a globalization of the nationalities of the players. In 1998, Canadians constituted 61 per cent of the players, and Europeans comprised 23 per cent and Americans 16 per cent (Houston, 1998, p. A26). By 2006 Canadians dropped to 53.6 per cent with Europeans increasing to 27.9 per cent and Americans increasing to 18.5 per cent (Haché, 2006, p. 1). So, at the time Gretzky was playing it was, and still is, not only common but also expected that most Canadians playing in the league would play for American-owned and US-based teams. In Gretzky's case, however, as a Canadian superstar athlete who represented and symbolized the nation, this migration was viewed as a loss for the nation. A Canadian sports columnist described this loss in an article in *Sports Illustrated* entitled 'A Nation in Mourning' (Taylor as cited in Redmond, 1993, p. 53). However, as the legitimation of free trade between the United States and Canada consolidated, the iconization of Gretzky continued in Canada throughout the 1990s. At an emotional and spiritual level, Canadians continued to feel Gretzky's presence, on the one hand, due to his widespread television exposure in Canada and, on the other hand, due to the perceived integration of markets, reinforcing the transnational bi-national character of the NHL. After his departure for the United States, Gretzky continued to represent the national team as he played for Team Canada in international tournaments which culminated at the 1998 Nagano Olympics.

In the 1990s the NHL expanded as Gretzky became instrumental in the selling of the game of hockey in the United States. His presence in the United States initiated and facilitated the expansion and reinvention of a new NHL over the past two decades to include many more American cities such as Anaheim, Columbus, Dallas, Denver, Fort Lauderdale, Minneapolis, Nashville, Phoenix, Raleigh and Tampa. Shortly after the major expansion of the NHL to many of these new American cities, a certain ironic twist of fate occurred for many Canadian hockey fans and Canadian-based teams. Gretzky's success in selling hockey in the United States made it more difficult for many Canadian teams to remain competitive (financially and on the ice), and this paved the way for the moving of two teams from Canadian cities (Quebec City and Winnipeg) to the United States.

It could be argued that Gretzky became, over his last 12 years of playing hockey in the United States, more American and less Canadian, at least with respect to his place of residence, business practices and family orientation. Most Canadians, however, are not cognizant of this due to Gretzky's national iconic status as he is thought of as Canadian: representing the nation and transcending hockey. Since his retirement Gretzky continues to be heavily involved in Canadian national hockey teams. He has been the men's executive director for the Canadian team at the World Hockey Championship in 2001 and the executive director of the Canadian men's national hockey team for the Winter Olympic Games (in Salt Lake City in 2002 and Turin in 2006) and serves as the advisor to the executive director for the Vancouver Olympics in 2010.

In Gretzky's retirement and induction into the Hockey Hall of Fame, Canadian tributes and adoration were illustrative of his cultural iconic status in Canada and his representation of the nation. In his last game, the words of the Canadian national anthem were altered to include a small tribute to Gretzky. In the anthem, sung by Bryan Adams, the second-to-last line was altered with the words 'We're going to miss you, Wayne Gretzky', and it should also be noted that in the American anthem, sung by John Amirante, the last line was also altered to 'O'er the land of Wayne Gretzky, and the home of the brave' (Podnieks, 1999, p. 129). Dryden (1999, p. 102), a former NHL player, lawyer and general manager of an NHL team, and currently a member of the Canadian parliament, wrote the following about hockey and Gretzky as a performer in Canada's national theatre:

> To get to the top in hockey you have to live a Canadian life, one of ice and snow, struggle and physical pain. Even if Wayne Gretzky never lives in Canada again, deep in his bones he is Canadian. With him, Canadians feel a bond. . . . He is the champion we all could have been . . . he is the face that Canadians would most like to present to the world.

A decade ago in Gretzky's induction into the Hockey Hall of Fame, the Canadian media portrayed him as Canada's kid ('Canada's kid is in the hall', 1999), demonstrating the continuing notion that Gretzky belongs to Canada. Other honours bestowed to Gretzky included Male Athlete of the Century in Canada and the All American Heroes Award in New York. As such, he is recognized on both sides of the border, but in the United States, he is only one celebrity athlete among many others, particularly where American football, baseball and basketball dominate. In Canada, Gretzky still has no peer. He received the Order of Canada award bestowed to him by the governor general of Canada in 1998. During Canada's 134th birthday celebration in Ottawa on 1st July 2001, the prime minister of Canada and the governor general, along with Wayne Gretzky, delivered Canada Day messages, although Gretzky's was via video so he was in Canada virtually. So, despite his lack of physical presence in Canada, Gretzky's public persona is one that many Canadians like to have of themselves, and this is what has contributed to his symbolization of Canada.

Migrant players

Fútbol: exporting Chilean migrant fútbol workers

Chilean professional fútbol has been neo-liberalized in the twenty-first century. Legislation has been passed to transform clubs into private companies traded in the stock exchange. Large Chilean clubs like Colo Colo and Universidad de Chile have become publicly traded companies with profit as their goal. In a country where income from audiences and television is low, many fútbol clubs depend on selling the contracts of players. The players, in turn, are represented by individuals and companies who profit. Zamorano is not the only one to do this; there are others, many legitimized by FIFA. For the players, better working and financial opportunities are often found outside Chile. The foreign clubs invest in these players to incorporate them into their teams or as holding investments.

The number of exported Chilean players is best visualized by the national team. While the team that played for Chile in the 1962 World Cup was drawn from local clubs, the national side in the eliminatory rounds for the 2010 World Cup was mostly drawn from foreign clubs. For example, in a match against Argentina, in 2008, only one player belonged to a Chilean club, two played in Argentina, one in Greece, two in Italy, four in Mexico, one in Portugal, one in Russia and one in Spain. In another eliminatory match, in 2009, the Chilean squad used three players who played for Chilean clubs while the rest originated from foreign clubs.

Chances are that these players, none of whom can be considered as a superstar, will eventually return to Chile. Historically, the few footballers who worked outside Chile eventually returned, even the best ones, like superstar Marcelo Salas. Although some of the expatriate Chilean footballers in Mexico have stayed in that country, the ones who do not return are few.

Reasons for athletes to migrate to work in foreign countries may include the search for new life experiences, bettering skills, improving status and better economic conditions and they may be perhaps divided into migrants, mercenaries, settlers, ambitionists, exiled, nomadic cosmopolitans and celebrity superstars (Maguire and Bale, 1994; Magee and Sugden, 2002; Maguire, 2004). However, Chilean expatriate fútbol players have mostly acted like temporary migrants, people who sell their labour power abroad, spurred by need, and then are quickly discarded when their labour is not needed. It is mainly lower salaries in Chile that push them to accept better-paid positions in other parts of the world. Once they stop playing for the clubs who hire them, they move to another club, often in another country, or they return to Chile to play in local clubs, or to retire. Their internationalization is similar to other temporary migrant workers who experience precarious work. Indeed, there may be a few transnational athletes, mostly superstars, who draw high salaries, and have a choice of where to live. But there are also a large number of temporary migrant footballers originating in peripheral and semi-peripheral countries who sell their labour power precariously and who return home after more or less short stints abroad.

Most of the present crop of Chilean fútbol players abroad belong to the last category. Their impact on Chile is different to the imprint left by Zamorano in the 1990s. In part this is due to the social, political and economic conditions of the country in the twenty-first century. The triumphal discourse of growth and development that emphasized the qualities of the Chilean neo-liberal model in the 1990s, where the image of Zamorano juxtaposed images of the country as a

Jaguar, has given place to disenchantment, individualism, consumerism and the triumph of spectacle over substance. Some of the fútbolistas in the first decade of the 2000s are part of this system, often the focus of scandals on television and gossip papers, scandals even involving the national team. In the twenty-first century the players are a metaphor for a nation with a tired neo-liberal model characterized by flashy consumption, great economic disparities, and a disenchanted youth. Some of these players reinforce the growing criminalization of the Chilean poor from where many originate, as they spend time partying instead of following a disciplined professional life. The lacklustre participation of Chileans in foreign clubs also reinforces the sense of lack of direction for the nation. Players frequently end up in secondary teams or secondary markets, some sit on the bench as replacements, others are sold to other clubs, and most return to Chile when their careers are over or when they have little options abroad. Even the recent qualification of the Chilean side to the 2010 World Cup in South Africa, after ten years, has been met with a sort of national disbelief and pinned on the disciplining and acumen of the Argentinian coach that was hired by the Chilean association to take charge of an unruly group.

Hockey: exporting Canadian ice hockey players to Europe

Professional Canadian ice hockey players are part of a global migration pattern to various countries in the world but most significantly to the United States and Europe. Professional teams in the United States and Europe are numerous where in the latter there is a hierarchy with the higher-level leagues in Sweden, Czech Republic, Slovakia, Switzerland, Germany, Russia and Finland and the lower-level leagues in Britain, Hungary, Netherlands, Romania, Lithuania and Belgium (Elliott and Maguire, 2008a, p. 164, figure 1).

In contrast to the NHL the recruitment and entry point into European professional ice hockey teams is based more on social networks, rather than through professional agents, and this is due, in part, to the lower salaries for professional players in Europe. Elliott and Maguire (2008a) show that it is more the social networks of friends and key contact persons, such as coaches, rather than direct third-party agents, who facilitate recruitment. These transnational networks across the Atlantic demonstrated the interdependence of the key actors in the recruitment process and these processes are similar to highly skilled migrants in other professions.

The number of Canadian players in Europe has been steadily increasing over the past 40 years. In 1970 there were approximately 70 players and by the late 1980s there were approximately 1,500 (Genest, 1994, p. 113) which constituted about twice the number of Canadians who were playing in the NHL at the time. In the past two decades these numbers have increased to a current level of approximately 3,000 according to estimates by Genest (VMC, n.d.) and they now represent approximately five times the number of Canadians playing in the NHL in 2005–6 (Haché, 2006). In a recent study of Britain's Elite Ice Hockey League, Elliott and Maguire (2008a, p. 165) found that of the 120 players in the 2004–5 season over half of them were Canadians. Maguire's data for the 1994–5 season showed that Canada was the largest exporter of ice hockey players (35 per cent of all players) in the global ice hockey circuit. At the other end Germany (36 per cent), Russia and former Soviet Republics (12 per cent) and Great Britain (11 per cent) were the largest importers of ice hockey players (1996, pp. 341, 342). Moreover, of the countries that imported specifically Canadian players, Germany and Great Britain were the largest at 31 per cent and 25 per cent, respectively (Maguire, 1996, p. 343).

Beyond the numbers Maguire (1996) provided pioneering theoretical analysis for Canadian ice hockey migrants in Europe with a particular focus on their experiences in British ice hockey. He examined their participation in British ice hockey subculture and issues of labour rights. He situated Canadian players in a preliminary typology of sport labour migration arguing that they exemplify all five types of migrants (pioneers, settlers, returnees, mercenaries and nomadic cosmopolitans) (Maguire, 1996, p. 340).

In contrast to the Chilean fútbol case, none of the Canadian players in Europe simultaneously play for Canada's national teams at the World Championships or Olympic Games. A few of them who have dual Canadian and European citizenships play for their European national team. Thus playing in European professional hockey leagues is a clear second or third choice for Canadian ice hockey players and is usually a second choice for star European ice hockey players as well. Undoubtedly Canada continues to be the core locale for the production of ice hockey labour (Elliott and Maguire, 2008a, p. 163). When highly skilled Canadian players are unable to play in the NHL they may play in the next tier below called the American Hockey League whose teams are affiliated with the NHL teams. Other highly skilled Canadian-born players often migrate to Europe to play where they can make a comfortable living while extremely talented European hockey stars gravitate to the NHL due to vast differences in salaries between the professional European teams and NHL teams. Recent figures from the NHL for the 2008–9 season indicate that of the 974 active players 244 of them, or 25 per cent, were from Europe (Cincotta, 2009). For Europeans playing in the NHL there are issues of adaptation to Canadian and American cultures but given the widespread use of English their integration is usually facilitated. Arguably the adjustment of Canadians playing in Europe is more difficult than it is for Europeans playing in North America due to the Canadians' reluctance to learn European languages and to adjust culturally (Cantelon, 2006, p. 232). Many of these Canadians remain temporary workers in European teams, returning to Canada in the off-season. The following summary provides a personal glimpse of a current Canadian player in Europe and his global migrant trails.

Adam Stefishen, a left winger for the Edinburgh Capitals in Scotland, was born in Vancouver, Canada, in 1982. He played junior hockey in the Canadian Western Hockey League with the Prince George Cougars in 2000–1. Then he played a season in the national league in Austria before returning to North America to play in the middle-tier professional East Coast Hockey League for several seasons before he went on to play in LNAH in Quebec and the minor professional Central Hockey League in the United States. After this stint he went back over the Atlantic to begin his current stint with Edinburgh of the Elite UK league where he has played over the past two seasons from 2007 to 2009. Stefishen brings to the Elite league a physical component where in his first season he had 289 penalty minutes and where the director of hockey operations for the Edinburgh team revealed that Stefishen had suitors from other teams in the league and that he was worried that the Edinburgh Capitals would lose him (European Hockey, n.d.). Stefishen is reported to be a fan favourite by a blogger (Peron, 2008).

Conclusion

Both Zamorano and Gretzky are international performers, celebrities, athletes and businesspersons whose 'space of flows' is transnational. Each has achieved a position that allows them to compress time and space in ways that few can. In this sense, it is ironic that Zamorano's and Gretzky's transnationality serve as both instruments to contradictory phenomena, strengthening of discourses of globalization and hardening of national identities and nationalism expressed through a sense of belonging to national communities.

Zamorano and Gretzky, as performers and businessmen, have existed in a seemingly virtual space, contributing to notions of porous borders and ease of travel. Yet, much of the permeability of the frontiers in this new era has been for goods and capital. The people who cross them and reside in more than one country are few, often thanks to their economic, physical or cultural capital. For ordinary people the task is challenging. Unlike Gretzky, for many Canadians, despite NAFTA, to live in the United States legally is not easy. Although NAFTA has eased restrictions for Canadians, in 1996 there were 120,000 Canadians illegally in the United States (Immigration and Naturalization Service, 1997). By 2005 this figure had grown exponentially (Passel, 2006, p. 4). These illegal immigrants cannot be considered transnational. Although Zamorano can travel abroad easily, many Chileans have trouble travelling to Europe, Canada or the United States. Emigration to those countries is even harder. Yet, Zamorano and Gretzky are metaphors for a globalized neo-liberalism. They represent what does not exist for ordinary labourers: free movement.

The essence of neo-liberal capitalism is to restrict labour mobility (Chomsky, 1995). Labour shortages are solved with just-in-time temporary migrant workers. A globalized reserve army of labour ready to move and willing to accept restrictions to their rights is key for global capitalism. The temporary migrants, guest workers and illegal immigrants work in segregated labour markets that vary according to the importing countries, specific labour markets and exporting nation. It is racialized, gendered and classed, even for transnational celebrity athletes. Many athletes remain temporary migrants, an international athletic reserve army of labour fed by global inequalities. Ironically, celebrity athletes like Gretzky and Zamorano inspire national pride, and strengthen the existing concepts of nation. They are symbols for their nations of birth, helping to reproduce and make them strong while limiting the impact of the discourses of globalization that promise human mobility and global citizenship.

17 Out of Africa

The exodus of elite African football talent to Europe[1]

Paul Darby

As a reflection of the acceleration of globalisation in the latter part of the twentieth and the opening years of the twenty-first centuries, transcontinental migration of playing talent has increasingly come to characterise football across the world. Nowhere is this more apparent than in the dramatic expansion in the numbers of Africans who earn their living in the European football market (Poli, 2006b).[2] The pace and pervasiveness of this process has recently heralded a debate, of increasingly acrimonious proportions, in both the media and football's corridors of power. The normative view of African player migration, at least in European football circles, is that exposure to Europe's elite leagues contributes to the development of the African game and its footballers and as such should be allowed to continue unfettered. Others though vehemently disagree and compare the loss of Africa's football resources to Europe with broader colonial and neo-colonial exploitation of the developing world by the developed. This view was expressed most explicitly by the president of the Fédération Internationale de Football Association (FIFA), Sepp Blatter, who described those European clubs involved in the trade of African playing talent as 'neo-colonialists' involved in 'social and economic rape' (Blatter, 2003). Analyses of the causes, consequences and possible legacies of this process have also begun to feature in the growing literature on sports labour migration. Although the key academic studies of African player migration to Europe have adopted a more considered position than football administrators, there has been general agreement that this practice is ultimately extractive and one that has involved varying degrees of neo-colonial impoverishment of African football and exploitation of African players (Darby, 2000, 2006, 2007a, 2009; Lanfranchi and Taylor, 2001; Poli, 2002, 2005, 2006a, 2006b; Bale, 2004; Darby *et al.*, 2007). The purpose of this chapter is not to retread this ground, although attention is paid in the conclusion to signposting ways in which theorising on African football labour migration might be advanced. Rather, this essay will concentrate on locating the transit of African footballers to Europe in its historical context, accounting for the changing patterns that have characterised these migrations and identifying those factors that have contributed to the development of this process from the colonial period through to the current day.

The colonial origins of the European trade in African football talent

The recruitment of African players by professional European clubs extends back to the beginning of the twentieth century. The geographical patterning of this process in this era clearly reveals that African colonies were recognised by Europeans as being rich in natural resources, raw materials and cheap labour not just in the economic sense but also in relation to football. Indeed, in many senses the recruitment of African players by European clubs was reflective of the broader economic imperialism of the time in that it involved the mining, refinement and export of raw materials, in this case football talent, for consumption on the European market. It should come as no surprise that the football clubs of those countries that had a significant imperial presence in Africa were the main beneficiaries of the export of African talent. This was particularly the case in France and players from the *motherland*'s North African territories were visible in the French professional game from its inception in 1932. Indeed, by 1938 there were more than 140 Africans playing in the French first and second divisions and between 1945 and 1962 almost 120 North Africans played in the French professional game (Murray, 1995; Lanfranchi and Taylor, 2001). Beyond the domestic game, the French national team also benefited from the naturalisation of African talent, a process that began with Moroccan-born Larbi Ben Barek who won 17 caps for his 'adopted' country during the late 1930s and 1940s (African Soccer, 1992–3). This trend has of course continued well beyond the collapse of French colonialism and France's recent successes in the international game has been attributable in no small measure to players born in Africa. The case of Africans playing in French football says much about the strength of the link between football migration from Africa to Europe and broader socio-economic processes associated with colonialism. Indeed, the expropriation of African players to play their domestic and international football in France during the colonial period can clearly be interpreted as an extension of France's policy of *Gallicalisation* or the assimilation of the local population into the citizenship of the motherland (Albertini, 1992).

The role of colonial ties in facilitating the migration of African football talent to Europe is also apparent when we consider the history of the game in Portugal. The influx of Africans into domestic Portuguese football can be traced back to the late colonial era. In this period a number of prominent clubs such as Sporting Lisbon, Benfica and Porto established links with clubs in Portugal's African territories and established scouting networks designed to source, refine and ultimately export talented players to Portuguese football (Armstrong, 2004). The impact of Mozambique-born Lucas Figuereido 'Matateu', who finished top scorer in the Portuguese league in 1953 and 1955 while playing for Belenenses, was crucial in this regard and his success encouraged more clubs to actively seek out African recruits (Lanfranchi and Taylor, 2001). Bela Guttmann, the veteran Hungarian coach of Benfica, was a strong proponent of this colonial resource and he was particularly pro-active in drawing on the rich pool of talent that it provided in his pursuit of domestic and European honours. This is evidenced by the fact that four of the team that brought Benfica its first European Cup success in 1961 hailed from Africa. These included the centre forward, Jose Aguas, the goalkeeper, Costa Pereira, and inside forwards, Joaquim Santana and Mario Coluna. Most of these players also played in Benfica's three other European Cup Final appearances in the first half of the 1960s.

The Portuguese national team also benefited from African-born football talent in the colonial period. The 'Indigenous People's Rule' introduced by the Portuguese dictator Antonio Salazar which gifted 'assimilated' status for culturally 'Europeanised' Africans from Portugal's colonial territories allowed a number of exceptional players from Africa to represent Portugal in international competition. For example, Matateu won his first cap for Portugal in 1952 before going on to represent the national team 27 times while Sporting Lisbon's Mozambique-born recruit Hilario was capped 40 times (Lanfranchi and Taylor, 2001). The most prominent African-born player to represent Portugal though was undoubtedly Eusebio da Silva Ferreira, known globally as Eusebio. Eusebio was signed by Benfica in 1961 and was making a significant contribution to their success in Portuguese and European football.[3] He was also naturalised soon after he signed for the club and went on to form the focal point of the Portuguese national team in this period. Indeed, had it not been for his contribution at the 1966 World Cup where he finished top scorer, Portugal would probably not have finished the tournament in third place, their highest ever ranking in the competition. The same can be said for Eusebio's fellow Mozambique-born Portuguese international, Mario Coluna, who was also a key part of the Portugal national team at that tournament. While he did not receive the same level of international acclaim as his compatriot, Coluna's 57 appearances for Portugal were central to the status of the Portuguese national team in the 1960s (Darby, 2007a).

The post-colonial era

The collapse of colonial rule in Africa did little to restrict the migration of African players to Europe, and by the 1970s there was a steady flow of African football talent to France and Belgium (Broere and Van der Drift, 1997). For example, migrant players from the former French colonies such as the Malian Salif Keita, Jules Bocande from Senegal, the Algerian Rabah Madjer and the Cameroonian duo Roger Milla and Antoine Bell all became household names in France while the Belgian club, Anderlecht, began its tradition of actively recruiting African talent during the 1960s and 1970s. A shared colonial history was clearly significant in determining the countries where French, Belgian and Portuguese clubs sought to recruit African football talent in this period but it had also been central in the decisions of African migrant players regarding the leagues that they aspired to play in. Indeed, the opportunity of playing in a country where there were likely to be fewer linguistic and cultural barriers and where players had more opportunities to mix with compatriots in broader social settings was paramount in this regard.

By the early 1980s African talent began crossing European borders in even greater numbers. This trend accelerated significantly in the 1990s and by the mid-point of the decade there were an estimated 350 Africans playing first or second division football in Europe (Gleeson, 1996). At the start of the new millennium this figure had more than doubled (Ricci, 2000). As in the immediate post-colonial period, colonial history continued to be a key determinant in shaping the geography of this process. A few correlations based on data from the 1999–2000 season exemplify this point. Of the 118 Africans who played their football in Portugal in this season, 69 per cent hailed from the former Portuguese colonies of Angola, Mozambique, Cape Verde and Guinea-Bissau. This trend is also evident when we consider the country of origin of the 163 Africans playing in French football at this time with 59 per cent being nationals from the former French territories of Senegal, Cameroon, the Ivory Coast, Algeria and Mali. Furthermore, Africans from those regions of the Congo that were once under Belgian rule also constituted the largest grouping of African migrants, approximately 31 per cent, within Belgian football (Ricci, 2000).

These figures from those countries that have historically been the three main importers of African football talent highlight the extent to which they continue to draw on colonial linkages to source cheap but highly skilled football labour. The use and expansion of such networks by recruiting European clubs has been strongly criticised as a form of neo-imperialism by those with responsibility for safeguarding the interests of African football. For example, Issa Hayatou, the President of the Confédération Africaine de Football (CAF), described the trade in African players by using the type of language routinely found in discourse on imperialism and neo-imperialism:

> After the flight of brains Africa is confronted with the muscle exodus. The rich countries import the raw material – talent – and they often send to the continent their less valuable technicians. The inequality of the exchange teams is indisputable. It creates a situation of dependence and . . . the pauperisation of some clubs . . . and national championships.
>
> (CAF, 1998)

Running parallel to this neo-colonial pattern of migration has been a much more diffuse and seemingly random movement of African players to a range of leagues throughout Europe and beyond. For example, at the African Cup of Nations in 2002, the 16 qualifying teams included players from no less than 26 non-African leagues (Boniface, 2001). This highlights the fact that the range of countries over which African players are distributed includes many that did not have colonial links with the continent. Thus, colonial and neo-colonial linkages offer only a partial explanation of a complex process which has not only accelerated exponentially since the early 1990s but has also taken on features not previously seen in the history of Africa's football exodus. A fuller explanation of football migration patterns between Europe and Africa must therefore move beyond colonial or neo-colonial models and take into account a range of other factors specific to football's global political economy.

The dynamics of 'supply' and 'demand' between African and European football

The growing profile and status of African national teams in the international arena since the mid-1980s has undoubtedly been one of the most significant factors in the increasingly rapid flow of Africans to the European game. This development was closely linked to radical transformation in the political economy of FIFA and world football, heralded by the election of the Brazilian João Havelange as the world body's President in 1974. Havelange's election brought about dramatic change in FIFA's mission and resulted in an increase in political, financial and technical support for football in the third world (Darby, 2002). A by-product of this was the allocation of more places at the World Cup Finals for African teams and a concomitant improvement in performances from African qualifiers from the 1982 edition onwards (Darby, 2005). The profile that this allowed the African game to acquire in the international arena was augmented by excellent performances from African teams at the under-20 and under-17 level world youth championships which were introduced by Havelange's FIFA in 1977 and 1985, respectively. These developments began to challenge the traditional stereotype of African players as merely 'natural footballers' who relied on their instincts, speed and skill but lacked the tactical maturity, discipline and organisation to compete effectively on the international stage or in the European game (Lanfranchi and Taylor, 2001; Bale, 2004). In doing so, African successes at world senior and youth levels effectively showcased the potential of African talent to European clubs and created the 'demand' for African players in Europe. The Bosman ruling and the loosening of the quota system in European football in the mid-1990s which had previously restricted the number of players from outside the European Union that clubs could sign ensured that the demand for African talent was further extended as the century drew to a close.

The specific conditions that gave rise to the 'supply' side of this migratory equation were undoubtedly rooted in the fragile political economy of African football *vis-à-vis* the economic strength of the European club game. Largely on the back of the revenue generated by the Union of European Football Associations (UEFA) Champions League and the sale of media rights, clubs in Europe's top-level leagues, particularly in England, Germany, Spain, Italy and France, have been in a position to offer the type of salaries that simply do not exist elsewhere in the football world, and least of all in Africa (King, 2003; Poli, 2006a). This explains the attraction of European football, but what was it about the African game that made, and continues to make, the 'lure' of Europe so irresistible for African players? An analysis of the economics and administrative culture of football in Africa's two primary player-exporting 'zones', North Africa and those coastal nations in the sub-Saharan west of the continent (Bale, 2004), allows us to answer this question.

In parts of North Africa, particularly Morocco, Tunisia and Egypt, there exists in some clubs the type of professional infrastructures that can provide the sort of salaries that encourage players to remain at home, at least in the early part of their careers. Some clubs such as Al Alhy in Egypt and Esperance in Tunisia have slowly built up the professional foundations that have allowed them to not only hold on to their most talented players for longer but also buy and retain players from other African countries. Other clubs, such as Arab Contractors in Egypt, have relied on investment from the corporate sector and have been able to do likewise, albeit with less long-term security (Guesdet, 2002). Despite these varying levels of professionalism in North Africa there are still significant differentials in the finances that the region's most successful professional clubs and European teams, even those playing outside the elite level, have at their disposal for player salaries. For example, the annual operating budgets of the two Moroccan clubs Raja Casablanca and Widal, generally recognised as being amongst the wealthiest clubs on the continent, represent only one-third of that of some of the smallest teams in the French first division (Tshimanga, 2001), while the wage gap between professional clubs in North Africa and their counterparts in France can be as large as twenty to one (De Brie, 2001).

These stark statistics represent one of the key reasons for the migration of significant numbers of North Africans to professional leagues in Europe and beyond. However, these financial disparities and the 'push' factor that they generate are magnified in the coastal nations of the sub-Saharan west of Africa where the precarious socio-economic and political climate has wreaked havoc on domestic football infrastructures and has severely restricted any potential for setting up well-organised professional clubs and leagues. The vast majority of clubs here operate without significant corporate or individual sponsorship and few have been able to offer the sort of contracts that afford players the regular, guaranteed salaries and labour protection found in Europe or, for that matter, parts of North Africa. Whilst broader issues such as extreme poverty, political instability and the debilitating legacy of colonialism have undoubtedly featured amongst the problems afflicting football here, there are other ingredients, specific to sub-Saharan football's administrative culture and economic structure, that have prevented clubs from raising the type of funds that might allow them to retain players.

Internal administrative malaise, or what the respected Tunisian journalist Mahjoub (1992, p. 38) referred to as a 'culture of mediocrity', has long been one of the key constraining factors in the development of African football and has, by implication, had a negative impact on the extent to which clubs have been able to persuade young talent to stay in their domestic leagues. The endemic corruption that invariably characterises the administration of the game in sub-Saharan Africa has done little to ameliorate this problem and has made the creation of the sort of professional infrastructures that might restrict the talent exodus virtually impossible to achieve (Sugden and Tomlinson, 1998). Government interference in football has also compounded this problem. In the aftermath of independence, newly constituted African governments provided financial subsidies for the game and thus argued that they were entitled to play a central role in its running. However, since the economic crisis of the 1980s and subsequent structural adjustment programmes, the levels of funding provided for the game by African governments has diminished dramatically. For example, the budget of Cameroon's

Ministry of Youth and Sports in 1970 accounted for 5.58 per cent of the country's national budget but by 1996 it had been reduced to a mere 0.06 per cent (Keimbou, 2004). This has led to a situation whereby African governments, eager to accrue the political capital that comes with success in international sporting competition, have concentrated what limited finances there are for football on the national team (Keimbou, 2004). This focus on and interference in the management of the national team on the part of sub-Saharan African sports ministries has not only weakened the domestic game but has also often undermined the work of national football federations (Darby, 2002). The fact that most pitches and stadia are owned by the government and are managed either by the Ministry of Sports or by local government administrators and therefore cannot be used by clubs to generate revenue presents further difficulties for the development of professional infrastructures for African football (Mahjoub, 1997).

This analysis of the political economy of football in those regions that export the highest number of players to Europe highlights the stark choice that young African footballers with aspirations to make a career from the game are confronted with. There is little in the way of infrastructure, professionalism or the possibility of a good salary to encourage them to remain in their home nations and eschew the potential of earning the almost unimaginable riches, by African standards at least, that the European game offers (Darby and Solberg, 2010). It would be difficult, if not impossible, to be critical of the choice that the majority of Africa's most talented players have made in terms of where their best career options lie and for seeking to achieve their ambitions. Despite the successes, economic and sporting, of those players who have the ability and good fortune to 'make it' in the European game, there has, since the immediate post-colonial period, been a strong tradition of resistance within Africa against the transit of its football resources to Europe. More recently this resistance has featured on the political agendas of International Non-Governmental Organisations such as the United Nations as well as continental and international football governing bodies, leading to a lobby that sought some form of regulation.

Regulating the trade in African football talent

In the immediate aftermath of independence, the CAF as well as a number of African governments, conscious of the damaging impact that they believed the talent exodus could have for the development of the African game, introduced measures aimed at restricting the loss of their football resources. For example, CAF instituted a regulation in 1965 that prevented national teams from fielding more than two overseas-based players while the governments of Zaire, Mozambique, Mali and the Congo, amongst others, prohibited their players from migrating abroad. Ydnekatchew Tessema, President of CAF between 1972 and 1987, believed that such measures were necessary to prevent African countries remaining as 'eternal suppliers of raw materials to the premium countries' (cited in Mahjoub, 1997). However, beyond forceful political rhetoric, Tessema struggled to restrict the flow of football talent from Africa to Europe and he was effectively powerless to prevent players and clubs from accepting offers of contracts or trials from European clubs and talent speculators (Radnege, 1998). The inception of the African Champions League in 1997 by his successor, Issa Hayatou, did go some way towards creating the economic incentives necessary to encourage players to remain with some African clubs (Ahlstrom, 1997). However, this applied only to a handful of clubs who qualified for the competition and at best it served only to delay the migration of the most talented African players to financially stronger leagues.

In the 1990s and early 2000s, the deskilling of African football accelerated, partly as a consequence of the actions of increasing numbers of scouts, agents and talent speculators who recognised in the trade of African football labour an opportunity for personal financial gain. The work of Broere and Van der Drift (1997) is particularly revealing of the types of exploitation that characterised this period and their qualitative research with African players and agents demonstrates the ways that this occurred. For example, an interview with the Nigerian William Osundu revealed that he signed a contract with a Dutch agent that guaranteed his 'representative' 50 per cent of his future salary. In addition, their discussions with Jan van Tuijl, a Dutch adviser to the Football Association of Guinea and representative of a number of Guinean players in Europe at the time, highlighted that at least half of these players were being exploited by both their clubs and agents (Broere and Van der Drift, 1997). Other accounts reveal similar experiences of exploitation of African players who were recruited by Portuguese, Dutch and English clubs during the 1990s (Obayiuwana, 1996).

The case of the Ghanaian Nii Odartey Lamptey is perhaps the starkest case of the unscrupulous manner that the careers of young African players were increasingly being handled by European agents in this period. Shortly after Lamptey had starred for Ghana at the under-16 World Championships in 1989, he was recruited by Antonio Caliendo, an Italian agent, before he was transferred to the Belgian club, Anderlecht. Thereafter, Lamptey slowly realised that his inability to read or write had been ruthlessly exploited by Caliendo via the terms of the five-year contract that he had brokered with Anderlecht (interview with Lamptey, 11 February 2008). Although he made 38 appearances for the Ghanaian national team, by the time he reached 21 Lamptey's career quickly went into freefall and he ultimately failed to live up to the immense promise that had moved Pelé to proclaim that 'he is my natural successor' after he had watched him lead Ghana to victory at the under-17 World Championship in 1991 (Oliver, 2008). According to Otto Pfister, the German coach who managed that team, Lamptey's failure to reproduce on a consistent level was a consequence of the fact that he 'was treated like a piece of meat' by a whole series of middlemen who brokered subsequent loan and transfer deals during his career (interview with Pfister, 9 February 2008).

Although the trade in African football talent and the highly questionable practices therein were unlikely to elicit criticism from those within the European game who benefited most, the increasing exploitation of young African talent during the 1990s by unscrupulous agents and speculators raised concerns outside of the African continent. For example, Paul Carlier, founder of the pressure group Sport and Freedom in the early 1990s, began campaigning on behalf of the young African players who had been brought to Belgium by clubs and agents for trials and simply abandoned if unsuccessful. This group highlighted the fact that many of those who were not successful in securing contracts were often not returned home by those who had organised the trials and were left as illegal immigrants on the streets of Belgium. In some cases these migrants turned to child prostitution as their only means of survival (Krushelnycky, 1999; Donnelly and Petherick, 2004). While it is difficult to determine with complete accuracy the numbers involved in this sort of trafficking at any given point in time, in 1999 a Belgian senator and a former Olympian, Jean-Marie Dedecker, highlighted to the Belgian courts what he claimed were 442 incidents of illegal trading in Nigerian minors by Belgian clubs (Lindberg, 2006). Although the situation in Belgium improved with the passing of legislation in 1999 which prevented the more sinister features of the influx of aspiring African football talent, what effectively constituted child exploitation continued to characterise aspects of the European-driven trade in African players. The depth of the concern over this was perhaps best exemplified by the fact that the United Nations Commission on Human Rights initiated an investigation into the problems of young African players being effectively bought by agents and then taken to Northern European countries to be offered to clubs. The resulting report, published in 1999, concluded by making reference to the 'danger of effectively creating a modern day "slave trade" in young African footballers' (Bale, 2004, p. 240).

While Carlier's pressure group had been successful in introducing a degree of regulation in the export of African players to Belgium and the UN report had raised the profile of the more nefarious features of this process, the intervention of Sepp Blatter in the debate in the late 1990s was crucial. His criticism of the loss of Africa's football resources to Europe went beyond political rhetoric and he became the key driver in a set of transfer regulations, introduced in September 2001, which effectively prevented clubs from signing players under the age of 18. Interestingly, one of the key pillars of this move was a desire on the part of FIFA for the protection of minors. In addition, these regulations made provision for those clubs involved in the training and education of players between the ages of 12 and 23 to receive compensation from the buying club (FIFA, 2002). Blatter, a long-standing advocate of the African game,[4] clearly had Afro-European player migration in mind when introducing a set of regulations which were aimed not only at providing African clubs with more compensation than they were able to accrue in the past but also at curbing the most exploitative practices of talent speculators and European clubs. However, this is not to say that minors no longer feature in the trade in African footballers. Indeed, a new system of recruiting young talent through football academies in Africa has been gathering pace since the early to mid-1990s that both CAF and FIFA fear may allow European clubs to effectively circumvent the new transfer regulations and continue to procure the services of young African players for a minimal financial outlay.

Football academies in Africa

Academies and training schools which aim to source, refine and transfer young talent to Europe have long been part of the football landscape in Africa (Darby *et al.*, 2007). However, with the increasing *scramble* for Africa's finest football talent since the 1990s and the introduction of FIFA's new transfer regulations, these ventures have mushroomed across the continent. It is important to note that football academies in Africa are not uniform entities. Some are organised and run by African club sides or African national federations, and operate, on the surface at least, in a manner similar to those that exist in, for example, Europe. Others involve either a partnership between an existing academy and a European club or an arrangement whereby a European team takes a controlling interest in an African club and then either subsumes the team's existing youth structures or establishes new ones. There also exists an increasing number of private or corporate-sponsored academies which have well-established foundations and operate with the support and sponsorship of private individuals, usually former high-profile African players, national football federations or the corporate sector. Finally, there are also a plethora of non-affiliated, improvised academies, which are set up on an *ad hoc* basis and involve poorly qualified staff and lack proper facilities (Darby *et al.*, 2007).

It has been suggested that the establishment of the types of ventures outlined above, with the exception of those in the last category, makes a positive contribution to the development of African football and the lives of those aspiring footballers who pass through the academy system. This hypothesis, espoused by those involved in academies as managers, directors, owners or partners, typically argues that these facilities provide proper training and a co-ordinated and systematic approach to youth player development and in doing so contributes to the game at both local and international levels. Beyond the impact of academies on football it has also been suggested that it is possible for some academies to function in a more ethically responsible fashion and contribute to the broader 'development' of African society not least through the provision of academic and vocational education, life-skills and health-related training that 'students' might otherwise not receive and through the reinvestment or remitting of foreign-earned capital and expertise (from those players who progress from academies to Europe) in African economies (Manzo, 2007; Darby, 2009).

For others though, not least prominent officials within CAF, including its president, Issa Hayatou, these facilities are, in essence, nothing more than fronts for the systematic deskilling and exploitation of Africa's football resources and that they are increasingly being used by European clubs and agents as a way of circumventing FIFA's new transfer regulations. It is argued by CAF, for example, that academies contribute to the underdevelopment and impoverishment of the domestic African game because the focus is on refining local talent for export to Europe which reduces the quality of the domestic football product available for consumption in Africa (Mahjoub, 1997). In doing so, academies are part of a broader system of talent identification, recruitment and export that mitigates against the development of the type of professional or semi-professional leagues that might encourage local players to stay at home and make the game a more attractive and fulfilling product for local populations. This is a point forcefully made by Tataw who argues that the vast majority of academies in the continent are 'geared towards grooming and exporting youngsters to foreign clubs with the attendant results of leaving local clubs bereft of talent' (Tataw, 2001, p. 13). There is little question that European clubs, who enter into partnerships with African academies or, as in the case of Ajax, buy controlling stakes in African clubs,[5] are essentially creating nurseries that allow them to reserve African talent until it can be legally transferred to Europe. This arrangement may be more favourable than the previous system of talented young players being transferred to Europe at a very young age because it allows African youths to remain within their country of origin and family networks for longer and hence reduces the psychological and cultural problems associated with adjusting to foreign climes. However, the ultimate objective of these academies is to export African talent, thus strengthening European football at the expense of the African game.

Criticism of the impact of academies on the development of football in Africa has emanated from the highest echelons of the governance of the game. Both Sepp Blatter and Issa Hayatou have been particularly vociferous in this regard (Homewood, 2000). Concerns have also been expressed about the fate of those graduates who fail to secure a professional contract on completion of their academy training, a group whose number far exceeds those who actually go on to earn a living from the game. While many of the academies provide a general schooling and cater for the all-round development of the student, the majority concern themselves primarily with the provision of intensive football training. This emphasis on football combined with the dreams of young African players of 'making it' in Europe often leads to a disregard for academic or vocational training and when the vast majority leave the academy at the age of 18 with their aspirations of a professional contract unfulfilled their prospects are often bleak. This is a point encapsulated by Maradas:

> For every Arune Dindane who makes the leap from ASEC to Anderlecht in the Belgian top division, there are thousands of others investing millions of hours of practice – time that could be spent on school work or learning another trade – without even reaching the first hurdle. Only a handful out of each year's intake to the top schools will ever make a living from football. The rest are destined to be turned loose at 18 to fend for themselves.
>
> (Maradas, 2001, p. 8)

This problem is magnified when one considers those youths who sign up for the myriad non-affiliated, improvised academies throughout the continent. Few, if any, of these types of facilities concern themselves with preparing their students for a life outside of football and for those who are deemed to have the potential to at least earn a trial with a European club they are more vulnerable to exploitation and mistreatment by unscrupulous academy managers and agents.

New directions in theorising African football labour migration

In my early work on African football labour migration (Darby, 1997, 2000), I argued that the movement of Africa's elite football talent to Europe was intimately linked to globalisation and as such could be understood by drawing on elements of the considerable corpus of work that has sought to analyse the origins, nature, causes and consequences of this process. Given the North–South geography and power asymmetries that have historically characterised the out-migration of African football labour, a number of economistic, broadly Marxist perspectives of global development offered potential in facilitating a structural understanding of global football labour markets. Wallerstein's (1974, 1979) world system theory and Frank's (1969) contribution to dependency theory appeared particularly salient in this regard and these perspectives opened up a whole canon of analytical language that helped me to conceptualise the migration of African players to Europe. For example, I was able to argue that African clubs were in a position of *dependent* trading, that the domestic African game was *deskilled* and *impoverished*, that Europe's elite leagues were able to *dictate the terms* upon which the transfer of African players was conducted, that the trade mirrored broader *neo-colonial* relations and that the relationship between European and African actors in this process was *uneven*.

While this conceptual language facilitated an understanding of the transit of African football labour at a systemic level during the course of the twentieth century, the introduction of FIFA's new transfer regulations in 2001, discussed earlier, combined with some subsequent collaborative research on football academies in Africa (Darby *et al.*, 2007), began to raise questions about the extent to which notions of dependency or Wallerstein's model adequately captured the intricacies, complexities and nuances of how the process of talent identification, player development and export overseas currently plays out in the local exporting context. Motivated in part by a desire to examine whether aspects of the trade in African players offer the potential for challenging or recasting broader structural core–periphery power relations, I recently embarked on two research projects. The first, undertaken with a PhD student (Julian Ward), focuses on the experiences and migratory pathways of Africans in the English professional game while the second, a collaborative venture with Alan Klein, funded by the Economic and Social Research Council (RES-000-22-2617), compares and contrasts football academies in Ghana with baseball academies in the Dominican Republic. This latter project has most pertinence to the discussion here because, beyond representing the first in-depth empirically grounded analysis of the outflow of football players from one African country and the first cross-sport comparison of athletic labour migration, it seeks ways of moving beyond a framework that constrains us to think about this process solely in terms of a traditional core–periphery model.

While this project is in its early stages, the fieldwork conducted to date, some of which has been undertaken collaboratively, has begun to reveal that the movement of football players from Ghana to Europe and the transit of baseball talent from the Dominican Republic to the United States involve opportunities for resistance or at least counter-hegemonic tendencies in the exporting context. For example, Klein's ongoing fieldwork in the Dominican Republic has begun to reveal evidence of processes that challenge the contention that the transfer of Dominican baseball talent is one entirely controlled by Major League Baseball (MLB) interests. Klein (2006a) argues that the insertion of local brokers, or *'buscones'*, is particularly revealing of the extent to which local Dominican interests are being served through the trade in baseball talent and he concludes that baseball in the Dominican Republic is increasingly functioning as a neo-liberal exception. Similarly, my ongoing fieldwork in Ghana has begun to highlight complexities in the system of football player production and export that do not necessarily fit with traditional interpretations of South–North athletic migration which typically conceive of this process in terms of dependency, underdevelopment, impoverishment and exploitation. The recent and growing tendency for Ghanaians to insert themselves at various points in the trade in football labour as well as the emergence of more ethical approaches to establishing academies have been key here (Darby, 2009).

In order to conceptualise counter-hegemonic processes in baseball, Klein has begun to utilise a 'Global Commodity Chain' (GCC) model as well as what is deemed its theoretical successor, 'Global Value Chain' (GVC) analysis. Influenced by what I am seeing on the ground in Ghana and by my collaboration with Klein, I have begun to explore the value of GCC analysis as a way of making sense of the production and export of Ghanaian football labour. The GCC approach has its origins in world system theory and more specifically in the work of Hopkins and Wallerstein (1986) who defined commodity chains as 'a network of labour and production processes whose end result is a finished commodity' (p.159). In the mid-1990s, Gereffi and Korceniewicz (1994) took this basic premise and developed a specific approach for understanding global commodity chains across a range of global industries. It has since been applied to any number of industries giving rise to a vast literature. In short, the GCC and GVC approaches involve mapping out the processes involved in the production of commodities, including the process of adding value; identifying and accounting for the institutional context within which the chain operates, including the agents, agencies and policies that impact on the production process at a local, national and international level; examining the space or territory through which the chain operates; and finally, analysing the structures or relations of power between lead firms and other actors that determine how human, financial, technological and material resources are distributed and flow within the chain (Gereffi, 1994, 1996, 1999, 2001; Gereffi and Korceniewicz, 1994; Dicken *et al.*, 2001; Plahe, 2005).

What I propose doing with this approach in future analyses of football academies in Ghana, as well as comparative, collaborative work with Klein, is to conceive of the trade in Ghanaian football labour as a global commodity chain. This will allow me to frame football academies as an element or node of global labour and production processes in the football industry that ultimately result in the key commodity, athletic labour. As part of this analysis I intend to account for the institutional structures within which academies operate, locally and internationally, and map out the geography through which the commodity – football labour – moves. This approach will also allow me to focus on the issue of governance or relations of power within the chain. The value of drawing on the GCC framework to theorise African, and more specifically Ghanaian, football labour migration is threefold. First, using this approach does not necessitate a major paradigm shift from my previous work and allows me to continue to classify African football labour migration to Europe as an extractive process. Second, it will also allow for a clearer structural understanding of the full range of processes involved in the production and export of African football players. Finally, and perhaps most importantly, the focus of much of the GCC and GVC approaches on issues around governance will provide a framework that will allow for a consideration of the extent to which aspects of the production and export of Ghanaian football players can be viewed as challenging or recasting broader core–periphery power asymmetries that typify the global trade in athletic labour.

Notes

1 This chapter is based in large part on an article published in 2007: *WorkingUSA: The Journal of Labor and Society*, 10(4): 443–56.
2 According to statistics generated by Poli, in 78 professional and semi-professional leagues within UEFA's 52 member states, there were 1,156 African players present during the 2002/03 season. This constituted 18.6 per cent of all foreign players in these leagues.
3 By the time he retired from Benfica in 1975, he had led the club to seven domestic league titles, two national cup victories, the European Cup along with three other appearances in the final and had finished top scorer in the Portuguese league on four occasions.
4 There is a debate about whether Blatter's support for African football is rooted in political expediency or a genuine concern for the concerns and aspirations of the game on the continent.
5 In 1999 Ajax acquired a 51 per cent controlling stake in the Cape Town club, Cape Town Spurs, who were subsequently renamed Ajax Cape Town. This club currently plays in the South African Premier Soccer League and, while it contributes to the local game there, the club's best players invariably find their way to Ajax Amsterdam or other European clubs.

18 Touring, travelling and accelerated mobilities

Team and player mobilities in New Zealand rugby union

Camilla Obel and Terry Austrin

For the mythology of rugby union in New Zealand it is essential to locate the origins of the game in the people: in the community and the club. This is where the passion for the game was mobilised in the amateur period and we recognise the power of this passion to mobilise support for the contemporary game. However, we will suggest a more complex story of ordering designed to regulate the mobilities of teams and players. We will argue that the regulation of team and player mobilities has always been central to the configurations, of the national union and local clubs, that have sought to stabilise the game of rugby union in New Zealand. We will contrast the way in which this regulation operated in the amateur (1892–1995) and professional periods (1995 onward), and show how it has always sought to privilege the national team, the All Blacks, over the local clubs. Our point is that the generation of passion for the game of rugby union requires organisation.

We first review the work of Elias (1986) and Leifer (1995) on the importance of mobilities for the organisation of sport. We then show how a centralised pattern of regulation of team and player mobilities was crucial to the success of New Zealand rugby union in the amateur period. Lastly, we show how this success has been destabilised by the introduction of accelerated mobilities of players and teams in the professional period. One consequence of this destabilisation is the development of a local argument about professionalism and the future of rugby union in New Zealand. This local argument focuses on the increase in the numbers of players migrating from New Zealand to the Northern Hemisphere.

At stake in this argument is the question of how to organise a national game that is subject to the powerful pull-factor of 'core' economies and core rugby union leagues. In a situation in which wealthy clubs, embedded in media-sponsored professional sports leagues of the Northern Hemisphere, compete with the national rugby union (the New Zealand Rugby Football Union, hereafter the NZRU following the name change in 2002) in attracting the best available rugby union talent, should the flows of players be encouraged or blocked? For those predicting an inevitable demise of the local game, the consequence of unchecked migration will produce, at best, dependent development and, at worst, under-development of the game in New Zealand. They agree, with Bale (1991), that this 'brawn drain' creates a 'deskilling' effect on 'donor' countries. They also confirm the arguments of Maguire (1994a), and Maguire and Stead (1998a), that migration flows are part of a general process disrupting the association of national sports and national identities.

The argument is conducted in emotional registers that ascribe either condemnation or worth to players and coaches. In Romanos' (2002) account, the increasing mobility of professional players is described as movements of mercenaries. By contrast, Howitt and Haworth (2002) celebrate the new mobilities as positive features of an increasingly global rugby union market in which New Zealand 'pioneering' players and coaches make a significant contribution. We are not suggesting that we can resolve this debate but we will show how it works to constantly monitor the shifting organisation of the game.

Norbert Elias, Eric Leifer and the question of mobilities

Elias (1986) and Leifer (1995) provide accounts of amateur and professional sports that pay attention to the way in which team travel structures both the establishment of organised competitions and, in turn, the relationships between organisers, players and spectators. Elias (1986) argues that travel by teams is the critical factor provoking the transformation of local pastimes into national and international sports overseen by supervisory bodies. In his argument, travelling teams, operating across geographically distant locations, provoke the need for the establishment of uniform rules and autonomous administrative arrangements. In turn, these supervisory bodies take over effective control of the game. They become responsible for the co-ordination of all local clubs and the organisation of a national team.

This logic of travel and the autonomy of organisational development are presented with reference to cricket. With his characteristic 'eye' for social organisation, he notes: 'when it became customary to organize game-contests above the local level because cricket teams were travelling from one place to another, it was necessary to ensure uniformity of the game' (Elias, 1986, p. 39). For our purposes the significance of his argument is the recognition that the collective travel of teams between places promotes both rationalisation of the rules of the game and furthers local ties by providing for comparisons between teams representing places. We will show how this argument, one that emphasises the civilising function of sport, overlaps with one side of the local argument on rugby union in New Zealand.

The regulation of sports in Leifer's (1995) argument is concerned less with the rules of the game and more with offsetting the financial threats posed by fickle public identification with professional teams. For Leifer (1995), professional sports expand through three interlocking processes: team attachment to cities; the routinisation of travel, in the form of organised league competitions; and control over professional player mobility through the establishment of exceptional sports labour markets. He notes that 'the first professional sport teams roamed the countryside playing pieced-together local teams, billing nearly every match-up as a championship in order to attract crowds' (p. 27). These mobile, independent professional teams not only spread interest in games, and diffused new technologies of play, but were also the precursors for the establishment of the major sports leagues based on city teams. Following Elias (1986), Leifer views the development of professional leagues as 'a sort of culmination of the civilizing process' (1995, p. 26). In his account this development was controversial in so far as it threatened amateur teams that were integrally tied to pre-existing groups such as clubs, schools and workplaces. In this context, professional players were initially regarded as 'unsavoury mercenaries' (1995, p. 28).

Leifer (1995) also stresses the way in which team travel induces both uniformity above the level of the local and comparison between different local teams. In his argument team mobility is re-organised in the form of financially stable league competitions structured by the repetition of home and away games throughout a pre-determined season. This process of guaranteed repetition not only marks the novelty of leagues but also facilitates the preservation of teams attached to cities and the placing of constraints on individual player mobility between teams.

Elias' (1986) and Leifer's (1995) emphasis on the significance of team mobilities for reconfiguring local traditions and organising spectator sports is supplemented in the literature on sport and labour migration by accounts of the mobilities and motivations of individual athletes (Bale, 1991; Bale and Maguire, 1994; Wilson, 1994; Maguire and Stead, 1998a; Maguire, 1999; McGovern, 2000; Magee and Sugden, 2002; Maguire, 2004). For example, Maguire (1996) has drawn on Appadurai's (1990) 'ethnoscapes' to develop typologies of the motivations of both amateur and professional sports migrants. He documents types of mobility characteristic of pioneers, settlers, returnees, mercenaries and nomadic cosmopolitans. These typologies will be drawn upon to identify differences in the mobility patterns of the amateur and professional periods of the game.

Team and player mobility in the amateur game

Current arguments about the demise of the national game of rugby union in New Zealand draw on a popular narrative of the exceptional and superior nature of the game in New Zealand (Zavos, 2002). This narrative is closely tied to claims about both the national team and the national organisation of the game. Chris Laidlaw, rugby union columnist and former All Black, has referred to the All Black phenomenon as a *romance*. He notes of the national team: 'Like the Brazilians, the All Blacks enjoy a different kind of imagery from all their competitors. There is real romance' (Laidlaw, 2003).

At the core of this romance he claims there is an indefinable mystique which, according to Romanos, is increasingly at stake because of the loss of the All Black tour and the traditional rivalries – 'those tours were the lifeblood of international rugby' (2002, p. 76). Those tours, or, in our terms, mobility associated with the national team, were controlled by, and a condition for the success of, the NZRU. They were the key calendar events of international amateur rugby union.

The NZRU, a supervisory body in Elias' (1986) terms, was established in 1892. The proposal for the new body was first mooted, following disputes in the late

Table 18.1 Countries toured by NZ/All Black teams, 1892–1940

	Visits	%
Australia	16	45.7
Canada	3	8.6
England	3	8.6
France	2	5.7
Ireland	3	8.6
Scotland	2	5.7
South Africa	1	2.9
United States	2	5.7
Wales	3	8.6
Total	35	100.1

Source: Chester, R., Palenski, R., and McMillan, N. (1998) *The Encyclopaedia of New Zealand Rugby.*

1880s, as a solution to the problem of how to control and select a national team for international rugby union matches and tours (Richardson, 1995). Provincial administrators concerned to establish amateur rugby union as the national game supported the idea of a national union as the sole organiser of these tours. They promoted a national union as a safeguard against professionalism, leagues and, in addition, as a means to constrain individual player mobility (Coffey, 1987; Haynes, 1996). The success of their defence of amateurism and the retention of the link with the 'home countries' led to a routinisation of national team mobility referred to as 'touring'.[1]

References to this level of national organisation in an amateur sport places our argument between Elias' (1986) uniformity of the game and Leifer's (1995) securing of the financial stability of leagues. In this New Zealand version, the spread of the amateur game as the national game required more than Elias' (1986) uniformity of rules and less than Leifer's (1995) professional leagues. The critical problem faced by the NZRU was one of establishing centralised national control over both a national team and rival entrepreneurial moves to spread the game. The solution, assembled through trial and error, was the establishment of a national game in which the affairs of local teams were ordered into a hierarchy subordinated to a national team which came to be branded as the All Blacks: a name given to the national 1905–6 New Zealand touring team by the British press (Nauright, 1991).

Touring by the national All Black team and visits by overseas national and regional teams in the early part of the twentieth century was the key mechanism to securing the game's international spread, and its position as the national game in New Zealand. Three All Black teams toured Britain between the establishment of the NZRU and World War II (see Table 18.1); one All Black team toured South Africa in 1928 – a planned tour in 1940 was cancelled due to the war breaking out (Ryan, 2000); and 16 All Black teams toured Australia.

In return, Springbok teams toured New Zealand in 1921 and 1937 (see Table 18.2); British teams toured three times, while Australian teams toured 11 times.

Table 18.2 Combined national (and Australian state) teams touring in New Zealand, 1892–1940

	Visits	%
Anglo-Welsh	1	5.9
Australia	4	23.5
Fiji	1	5.9
Great Britain	2	11.8
NSW	6	35.3
Queensland	1	5.9
South Africa	2	11.8
Total	17	100.1

Source: Chester, R., Palenski, R., and McMillan, N. (1998) *The Encyclopaedia of New Zealand Rugby*.

Table 18.3 Countries toured by All Black teams, 1947–1995

	Visits	%
Argentina	3	3.2
Australia	18	19.6
Canada	6	6.5
England	11	12.0
Fiji	4	4.3
France	10	10.9
Ireland	7	7.6
Italy	3	3.2
Japan	1	1.1
Rhodesia	1	1.1
Romania	1	1.1
Scotland	8	8.7
South Africa	6	6.5
United States	3	3.2
Wales	10	10.9
Total	92	99.9

Source: Chester, R., Palenski, R., and McMillan, N. (1998) *The Encyclopaedia of New Zealand Rugby*.

In total, New Zealand national teams undertook 21 overseas tours to nine countries, while New Zealand hosted 17 touring teams representing seven countries between 1892 and World War II (Obel and Austrin, 2005). The successes of these tours, particularly those to Britain, have been elevated into mythological status (Phillips, 1987; Fougere, 1989; Ryan, 1993; Richardson, 1995; Romanos, 2002; Zavos, 2002).

After World War II, All Black tours increased in frequency with a further 92 until the end of the amateur period in 1995 (see Table 18.3). Romanos identifies the 1956 Springbok tour as 'perhaps the most significant' (2002, p. 77) in capturing the national imagination. The inbound tours to New Zealand were dominated

Table 18.4 National teams touring in New Zealand, 1947–1995

	Visits	%
Argentina	2	2.7
Australia	18	24.0
British Isles	7	9.3
Canada	1	1.3
Cook Islands	1	1.3
England	3	4.0
England B	1	1.3
Fiji	7	9.3
France	7	9.3
Ireland	2	2.7
Italy	1	1.3
Japan	1	1.3
Romania	2	2.7
Scotland	3	4.0
South Africa	4	5.3
Soviet Union	1	1.3
Tonga	5	6.7
Wales	2	2.7
Western Samoa	6	8.0
World XV	1	1.3
Total	75	99.8

Source: Chester, R., Palenski, R., and McMillan, N. (1998) *The Encyclopaedia of New Zealand Rugby*.

by the seven significant rugby union rivals of England, Wales, Scotland, Ireland, South Africa, Australia and France (62.7 per cent or 47 of 75 – see Table 18.4) (Obel and Austrin, 2005).

This practice of touring constituted both the national team, the All Blacks, and promoted the popular link between the nation and the single, male sport of rugby union. As a form of amateur international organisation it was also significant for the economic welfare of both the NZRU and provincial unions. All key provinces not only played the visiting national teams but also hosted the national team – 'every provincial team worth its salt felt able to take on a touring side' (Romanos, 2002, p. 76). As Romanos notes, 'to the average rugby fan, these were great times' (p. 78). Income from hosting the national and international teams helped provincial unions promote their teams to local fans, develop playing facilities and nurture their local clubs, thereby strengthening the game's popularity throughout the country. In this way, the rugby union park and the rugby union club became key institutions of both the provinces and the society.

Romanos (2002) views these developments from the 'bottom up'. From this viewpoint, club rugby union was 'the prime focus of the sport in New Zealand and a very important part of the social fabric of the country' (p. 115): regional identity and rivalry as well as national identity were forged out of club rugby union (p. 116). He argues: 'club rugby was not an imposition but a delight. They loved the football and thrived on the camaraderie' (p. 118). Legendary ex-All Black Colin Mead adds to this by emphasising the link between club and community: 'the footie club used to be the community meeting place in our district for everything from dog trials to a meeting of the women's division of the Federated Farmers' (p. 122).

In both Romanos and Mead's accounts (Romanos, 2002) local ties were cemented by team and player mobility. Local clubs raised money (white envelopes) for their All Blacks picked to tour (Howitt, 1989, p. 14; Romanos, 2002, p. 123) and All Blacks spent their Saturday nights in the club rooms performing normal club duties. Local ties were secured because player mobility was constrained through rules requiring players to be resident in their province and a member of a local club for at least three weeks prior to selection for their provincial team (NZRFU, 1994, p. 89). The few players who transferred between provincial unions within New Zealand officially did so because of work commitments and, later, increasingly to take advantage of educational opportunities. However, it was widely understood that this practice was a form of 'shamateurism' which produced a 'black market' in which players moved to a new province in return for money or a 'rugby job'. This pattern of limited mobility by mercenary players within the space of the nation was dependent on local sponsorship of clubs and did not provoke a tension between individual players and the national team.

For the most part this mobility of players in the amateur period was, as Maguire (1996, p. 337) points out, seasonal or transitory. Players from New Zealand also migrated internationally for reasons of educational and career advancement separate from the game of rugby union, as in the case of All Black Chris Laidlaw (Laidlaw, 1973) and more recently Anton Oliver (Turner, 1995). As cosmopolitan nomads, All Blacks Murray Mexted, Andy Haden and John Kirwan migrated on a seasonal basis in the 1980s (Haden, 1983, 1988; Misa, 1987; Howitt and Haworth, 2002, pp. 286, 288) and it was even claimed that Haden played for a club in Italy and England simultaneously (Palenski *et al.*, 1998, p. 81). These players were not excluded from All Black selection but others including Matthew Ridge, Frano Botica, John Schuster, Paul Simonsson, Darryl Halligan and Clarry and Brett Iti (Palenski *et al.*, 1998, p. 72) migrated, arguably as mercenaries and not in a transitory manner, to the rival professional code of rugby league, thereby preventing their return to the amateur code.

Professionalism and accelerated mobilities

The inauguration of the Rugby World Cup, in 1987, was the catalyst for professionalism. The new competition was watched by television audiences in 17 countries; the 1999 World Cup was watched in 214 countries; and the 2007 event reached an estimated four billion TV viewers in over 200 countries (International Rugby Board, 2009). The World Cup competition is supplemented by a televised transnational competition, the Super 12 (hereafter referred to as Super 19 following the expansion of the competition in 2009), operating across the Southern Hemisphere between teams based in New Zealand, Australia and South Africa.

This new mediated version of the professional game is premised upon the accelerated mobility of both teams and players (Paul, 2007a).

The four-yearly World Cup tournament is pivotal to both forms of mobility. The new competition repositions the status of touring to a testing ground for new players rather than showcasing the continued dominance of All Black teams. For Romanos (2002) this demeans both tours and the status of tests: 'Test results aren't as important now. The next World Cup is always just around the corner and the great increase in tests matches has very much devalued their currency' (p. 79). And the increase in the number of tests is significant. In 2008 the All Blacks played 15 'not so important' test matches, plus a game against Munster. This was the highest number ever recorded in a calendar year (Paul, 2007a). In the amateur period the maximum was approximately four in any one year.

The new competition has also generated acute anxieties about the risks not only of player migration but also to the status of New Zealand rugby union. Failure to win the World Cup since 1987 has provoked extensive argument on the merits of the organisation of the game and the next World Cup already threatens. Sean Fitzpatrick, former All Black captain, emphasises the key emotional components of these arguments:

> We cannot fail in 2011, not just because we're hosts or because of dented pride or some impending sense of disappointment as history repeats itself – but because of something altogether much more serious: to lose would be to announce to the world that the All Black jersey really is losing its magic.
>
> (Fitzpatrick, 2009b)

Fitzpatrick's appeal to history, magic and the jersey articulates the dilemma that the new 'test' of the World Cup has introduced.

The transnational Super 14 league competition grew out of independent tours undertaken by amateur provincial union teams in the 1980s. The initial aim of the league was to match the economic opportunities provided for players in both the expanded professional game of rugby league in Australia and the new global professional World Rugby Corporation competition (Hyde, 1995; Obel, 1998). The league, administered by the NZRU and its equivalents in Australia and South Africa, is a mobile transnational competition that requires teams (franchises rather than provincial teams which are guaranteed of their inclusion into the league) to travel between countries to play regular matches in a yearly programme. Just as the All Blacks travelled between countries on tours now this pattern of mobility is the norm for professional, franchised league teams. Encounters against overseas teams, once celebrated as a part of the national calendar, are a routine organising feature of the new league.

The national union controls the five franchised teams by contractual terms that subordinate their organisation to the purposes of securing the national team. Elite players benefit from the high salaries paid in the league but this 'sweetener' is supplemented with constraints on their mobility imposed by the national union acting as the agency contracting players and coaches. At the beginning of the professional period, in 1996, the national union contracted 140 players to participate in the new Super 14 competition. All players' contracts required them to be available for: the Super 14 competition; the National Provincial Championship for the provincial union they were affiliated to; and any other national representative team, including the New Zealand Sevens team and the New Zealand Maori team. Out of those 140 Super 14 contracted players, 35 players had their contracts supplemented with All Black contracts following national selection (Obel, 2001a).

The national union uses the franchised teams as 'training camps' for the national team. Week by week it is able to use software tracking to contrast and compare the performance of individual players. It also intervenes into the selection process of the franchises by retaining the right to decide whether to move a player from one Super 14 team to another. While the five Super 14 coaches initially select their desired franchise players from within their catchment areas (a new demarcation of the country into five areas overlaying the existing 27 provincial unions), the national union retains the right to decide where best to utilise the players in the five Super 14 teams. According to John Hart, All Black Coach (1996–9), such decisions are taken as a means to ensure that players are given maximum opportunity to gain playing experience (interview, 1998). In addition, players selected for the All Blacks have to be residents of New Zealand. Further constraints, to offset the threat of an international transfer market in the local game, include a player transfer system, approved by the Commerce Commission in 1997 (Rugby Union Players' Association v. Commerce Commission, 1997). These transfer regulations: limit unions to contract a maximum of five players from other unions in one year (including a maximum of one All Black and three Super 14 players); introduced a transfer fee system with maximum fees that unions can demand in return for releasing a player; and limit transfers to take place only during the month of November.

Despite this establishment of an exceptional labour market to secure the local game, commentators have pointed out several faults with its configuration of national team, super transnational franchises and provincial unions. These range from the impact of professionalism on club rugby union through to the continued exit of elite players to the Northern Hemisphere. Writing of the National Provincial Championship (NPC) and the pattern of dominance secured by bigger unions, Chris Laidlaw notes: 'All around the country, the same pattern is being repeated. Its trickle up; the brave new rugby economy, and its [sic] slowly strangling the life out of the little provinces' (Laidlaw, 2002).

Trickle up refers to the mobility of the talented players out of the more marginal provinces into the richer provinces. In this scenario, the players are no longer locals and this is made clear in the contracting of all Super 14 players to the NZRU.

The response to this 'withering away' of provincial rugby union has led to calls for innovation to reinvent the provincial rivalries of the amateur period. Echoing the sociological account of Fougere (1989), Fitzpatrick argues:

Our focus should be on getting the blood boiling at tribal level. That gives the All Black culture an environment within which it can flourish. Provincial rugby is where it has all happened for decades – 50,000 people at Eden Park roaring on their boys; Otago, Canterbury, Auckland, Waikato and Wellington and the others all vying for bragging rights; local heroes dominating; and a genuine link between players and supporters. I remember when North Harbour and Auckland wouldn't even countenance a joint Christmas party, let alone playing under one banner.

(Fitzpatrick, 2009a)

Fitzpatrick's (2009a) references are to the past, to the vitality of the provincial game played as a local game, rather than as a managed preparation for the national team. His analysis, strong on passion, lacks an account of how such passion is to be reinvented in the professional period. This is Leifer's (1995) problem but in his analysis the generation of such passion requires the manipulation of league competitions and city-based teams: there is no reference to national sports, the peculiar problem that New Zealand rugby union faces.

Matheson, editor of *NZ Rugby World*, identifies the external loss of players. In 2000, and following the All Black team's disappointing performance at the 1999 Rugby World Cup, he blamed the NZRU for the loss of players, highlighting the 'tiered' payment structure which has Super 14 players' payments at only a quarter of what an All Black player receives:

To the New Zealand Rugby Football Union the problem may seem small. But the truth is that rugby's player drain is an insidious blight on our game. We are losing talent hand over fist and the hole is getting bigger and blacker. What can we do; how long before our out-moded tier structure becomes a real tear structure?

(Matheson, 2000)

Similarly, in Romanos' (2002) account we find reference to the exodus of players overseas: 'Over the past ten or fifteen years, thousands of good players, some provincial and many just good, solid, senior club standard, have headed overseas' (p. 127). In 2007, again following the failure of the All Blacks in the World Cup, the All Black squad appeared to be haemorrhaging as several All Black players including Jerry Collins, Chris Jack, Carl Hayman, Troy Flavell, Ruben Thorne, Keith Robinson, Byron Kelleher and Luke McAllister left for the Northern Hemisphere.

More ironically it could be said that the establishment of professional rugby careers has resulted in a saturation of the domestic labour market in New Zealand. In turn, this has had the effect of pushing players towards professional opportunities in the Northern Hemisphere. In this version, contractual attempts to halt the out-flow of players need to be seen against the continuing disparity in the value of player contracts in New Zealand and other rugby union nations including England, France, Italy and Japan. Super 14 player contracts in New Zealand

Table 18.5 Status of New Zealand rugby union migrants, 1998–2002 ($n = 3,160$)

Migrant status	Players	%
Club	2,030	64.2
NPC	402	12.7
Pro age	200	6.3
N/A	192	6.1
Prov. Dev./B	170	5.4
Youth, School	75	2.3
Super 12	34	1.1
NZ Maori	18	0.6
All Black	15	0.5
Social	5	0.2
NZ Sevens	5	0.2
International (PI)	4	0.1
Black Fern, NPC	4	0.1
Coach	3	0.1
NZ Army	2	0.1
Rugby League	1	0
Total	3,160	100

Source: NZRU, Clearance Register, 1996–2002.

are worth less in financial terms than in Australia and South Africa and only the contracts of the most senior and high profile All Black players are comparable with the contracts players can negotiate in England and Japan. It is this disparity that continues to encourage players to leave New Zealand for better economic opportunities in the Northern Hemisphere.

An exceptional labour market constructed around possible selection for the All Blacks and success in the World Cup will always remain vulnerable to the very different 'super' clubs of the Northern Hemisphere. This vulnerability is not (yet) equated with an organised international transfer market and therefore patterns of migration are variable. Players currently migrate at different points in their career, matching several of Maguire's typologies (see Table 18.5): most of these migrants are arguably cosmopolitan nomads (including club, provincial (NPC) and younger developing players); others leave as mercenaries at the end of their Super 14 contracts or negotiate their release from existing contracts after assessing their chances for All Black selection as minimal and elect to migrate in search of greater financial opportunities with clubs in Europe or companies in Japan while their careers are still on a high.

The traditional home of rugby union, Britain, remains the predominant destinations of these New Zealand players (see Table 18.6). Between 1996 and 2002 England received the 'lion's share' of over 41 per cent (1,596) of New Zealand players, followed by Scotland (17 per cent or 667) and Wales (3 per cent or 129). Together, Ireland, the third largest 'recruiter' of New Zealand rugby union players (14 per cent or 547), and Britain were the destination of choice for over 75 per cent of migrants. While a not unsubstantial number of players return to New Zealand

Table 18.6 Top 12 national rugby unions importing New Zealand players and coaches, 1996–2002 (*n* = 3,844 out of a total of 3,935)

	Players	*%*
Australia	135	3.5
England	1,596	41.5
France	277	7.2
Ireland	547	14.2
Italy	201	5.2
Japan	95	2.5
Netherlands	45	1.2
Portugal	50	1.3
Scotland	667	17.3
Spain	61	1.6
United States	41	1.1
Wales	129	3.4
Total	3,844	100

Source: NZRU, Clearance Register, 1996–2002.

(e.g. between 1999 and 2002 a total of 468 players returned to New Zealand; one country alone, Scotland, accounted for 43 per cent of the returnees; see Table 18.7), today the fear is that players still at the height of their career choose to settle in Europe (Obel and Austrin, 2005). Overall, these figures indicate the difficulties associated with attempts to stabilise the game in the professional period but they do not support the claim that New Zealand players (and coaches) are part of an increasingly global ethnoscape. The new professional game has not (yet) meant an expansion of the game beyond its traditional amateur 'home'.

If New Zealand is becoming a donor country for Northern Hemisphere clubs, the Pacific Islands are becoming donor countries for world rugby union. The numbers are small but significant for smaller countries: between 1999 and 2002 18 players moved from Fiji, seven from Tonga, four from Papua New Guinea and two from Samoa to New Zealand (see Figure 18.1).

These moves into the New Zealand game were not off-set by a single New Zealand player moving the other way. More worrying for Pacific rugby union is the much greater player loss created by players' dual national status often as a result of a player's parents migrating to improve their family's opportunities or to unite with migrated family members. Players' increased eligibility status, enabling them to represent core rugby union nations, such as New Zealand, Australia and Japan, is off-set by the International Rugby Board (IRB) regulation to limit players' mobility to representing only one country in their career. As a result, a large number of players with Pacific ties and residency in New Zealand opt not to make themselves available for their Pacific national team in the hope of making the All Black team. This mobility and these career choices provide evidence of a 'deskilling' as Pacific countries operate as donor countries to

Table 18.1 'Origin' of rugby union players migrating to New Zealand, 1999–2002
(*n* = 468)

	Players	%
Australia	38	8.1
Canada	9	1.9
Denmark	1	0.2
England	29	6.2
Fiji	18	3.9
France	24	5.1
Germany	1	0.2
Hong Kong	2	0.4
Ireland	38	8.1
Italy	7	1.5
Japan	12	2.6
N/A	1	0.2
Netherlands	3	0.6
PNG	4	0.9
Portugal	1	0.2
Samoa	2	0.4
Scotland	202	43.2
South Africa	30	6.4
Spain	2	0.4
Tonga	7	1.5
United States	16	3.4
Wales	18	3.9
Zimbabwe	3	0.6
Total	468	99.9

Source: NZRU, Player Inward Register, 1999–2002.

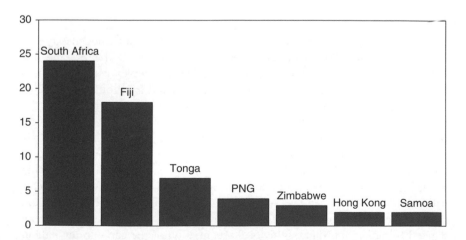

Figure 18.1 Net gain of rugby union players to New Zealand, 1999–2002

New Zealand, Australia and increasingly to the Northern Hemisphere (Obel and Austrin, 2005).

The most recent innovation to deal with the desire of elite players to move to the Northern Hemisphere has been the introduction of sabbaticals, another contractual device for securing the eligibility of players for the World Cup in 2011. Dan Carter, a key player for the All Blacks, was allowed to take a six-month cosmopolitan sojourn with the French club Perpignan before returning to New Zealand in June 2009. Carter's stated motive was wanting to test himself against the best in Europe but he was able to play only five games for the club before his campaign ended in injury. Nevertheless, Perpignan's signing of the international celebrity player led to increases in sales of season tickets, merchandising and sponsorship and is said to have been a shrewd investment (Rees, 2009). Celebrity status apart, the shift to sabbaticals has also opened up the argument on the need for the national union to relax the rule on overseas players playing for the national team. Fitzpatrick has argued that the national union no longer has a choice:

> We have to start selecting from the overseas players' base, simply because there are now so many of them and because we have to take care that we don't spiral into a culture of loss. Allowing those doors to open will also safeguard New Zealand player stocks better than sabbaticals.
>
> (Fitzpatrick, 2008)

This practice has not been introduced yet but 'opening the doors' to 'returnees' would transform the organisation of the game in New Zealand. The risk is that it would confirm New Zealand's status as a donor country for the Northern Hemisphere clubs and at the same time damage the credibility of the game in New Zealand.

Conclusion

Maguire and Bale have argued that sports migration 'is not a homogeneous experience' but reveals a 'highly differentiated political economy' (Maguire and Bale, 1994, p. 282). In our account we have highlighted complex configurations of organisational forms built on contractual regulation and the promotion of different types of mobilities of both teams *and* players. We have shown how the configurations of amateur and professional rugby union in New Zealand differed in respect of regulating the mobility and migration patterns of players; we have argued that the shift to professionalism, the focus of the current debates, has foregrounded Elias' (1986) and Leifer's (1995) arguments about the way in which sports organisations both nurture and attempt to regulate mobility through competitions and contracts; and we have highlighted that the new professional game in New Zealand, exemplified in the Rugby World Cup and the transnational Super 14 league, subordinates the local organisation of the game to the national team. We have described this arrangement as an exceptional labour market constructed in order to offset risks to the national team provoked by migration. We have ended with evidence that the management of this professional, contractual regime continues to give way to the desire of elite players to migrate.

Our emphasis has been on the organisation of the national game and within it the role of the national team, the All Blacks, rather than the motives of migrant players. The devices used to block the outflow of elite players are designed to facilitate the assembling of a national team; they are measures designed to protect the advantages secured by a small nation in the amateur period of the sport, prior to 1995. We have shown how the introduction of professionalism served to extend the national union's control over the sport and also how it exposed it to the power exercised by clubs operating in the larger economic markets of the Northern Hemisphere. This destabilising influence, which increases players' mobility rights and also benefits the wealthiest professional clubs in 'core' leagues, will always create problems for national sports organisations based outside of the core of wealthy clubs and leagues (Miller and Redhead, 1994; Maguire and Pearton, 2000b, 2000c). In the case of New Zealand rugby union, the ultimate threat of expanded migration is to undo the competitive balance of the rugby union cores of the North and South. Such a development would also be damaging for the organisation of the professional world game.

Note

1 While the 1908 All Gold's tour was the precursor for the establishment of rugby league in the Southern Hemisphere, international rugby league tours in the following decades were limited to national teams from Australia and the United Kingdom. More significantly for our argument, amateur rugby union touring involving national teams in Europe, South Africa and North and South America became a central feature of international amateur rugby union, while in rugby league it was the establishment of local league competitions that became the organising feature of the professional sport.

Future directions

Sporting mobilities, immobilities and moorings

Mark Falcous and Joseph Maguire

It is now over a decade and a half since the publication of *The Global Sports Arena* in 1994 – an initial marker in the formulation of the sports migration field. As *this* collection demonstrates, the research field has since burgeoned. It has grown in its breadth and now is constituted of scholars working in diverse locations drawing on a host of varied disciplinary resources. Yet it is critical that the field neither stagnates nor remains narrow. Most fundamentally, of course, it must go beyond the superficial and descriptive. Scholars must continue to strive for depth of insight and rigour and should be systematic in methods and theorizations. Research fields often develop in piecemeal ways – as researchers pursue apposite directions and seize readily available opportunities. At times the accessibility of data and pragmatic considerations dictate what is done and what is 'left for another day'. Researchers must work, however, to also fill in the gaps in the knowledge base, to challenge themselves to undertake the difficult, onerous and time-consuming work. Furthermore, the work must be relevant. It must be relevant, that is, to the wider issues of the day as they relate to issues of identity, social and environmental justice, regulatory structures, power struggles and exploitation. However, in seeking to be relevant, the danger is that researchers 'go native' and use knowledge about sport migration to assist the sports industrial complex – and the organizations and clubs located within it, to refine their exploitative practices and improve the 'bottom line'. While contributing both to fundamental and applied knowledge researchers need to maintain critical distance.

As new and complex issues continue to emerge, researchers will need to respond in kind with innovations in their approaches: paradigmatic, theoretical and methodological. Indeed, the issues, struggles and concerns surrounding the mobility of athletes in particular remain high profile within public discourse. For example, in September of 2009 the *Courier-Mail* (Brisbane) reported the Australian Immigration Minister announcing the relaxation of rules for elite athletes seeking citizenship. Specifically, the time migrating athletes would need to live in Australia was reduced from four years to two years; whilst residency stipulations were also relaxed (so transitory are some elite athletes that they rarely fulfilled 'normal' citizens' residency requirements of actually being present in the country). The changes were part of an attempt to increase the Australian 2010 Winter Olympic medal count. The face of the new legislation, Russian-born speed skater Tatiana Borodulina, who was seeking citizenship, was the subject of a struggle over her talents. The Australian chef de mission of the Winter Olympic team was quoted warily reporting: 'the Russians have tried to lure her back' (*Courier-Mail*, 1st September 2009, p. 7). Compare the struggle for Borodulina's talents with the case of six Australian rugby league players who a month earlier were ordered to leave Wales by the UK Border Agency (UKBA). The six were banned from re-entering the United Kingdom for the following ten years. Their Welsh club – the Celtic Crusaders – faced a £GBP60,000 fine as a result and the players were given two weeks to leave as their visas were deemed invalid. A UKBA statement read uncompromisingly: '. . . If they refuse to do so voluntarily, we will enforce their removal' (cited in BBC [18th August 2009]). The stark juxtaposition of these two cases reveals that within the global sports system – to borrow Naomi Klein's (2002) formulation – for some there are *fences*, for others *windows*. Such evocative and contrasting cases – alongside the host of issues and contexts that the contributors to this collection have sought to shed light upon – demonstrate both emerging issues and the widely varying responses and outcomes of global sports (im)mobilities.

As further evidence of these emerging complexities, in the lead up to the Beijing Olympic Games, Craig Reedie, a senior International Olympic Committee (IOC) and British Olympic Association (BOA) member, estimated that around 25 athletes had 'swapped nationality'. In particular – and widely conveyed in western media – some former East African runners opted to compete for several 'Gulf States' whose 'petrodollars', channelled into economic development and place promotion, are challenging the long-standing western-centric patterns of the global sporting system. There is, however, a certain irony in Reedie's observations as the BOA itself scours the globe for athletes to supplement British medal chances at the 2012 Olympic Games. Such trends – which we would anticipate to increase – will likely stimulate a reaction from governing bodies, athletes and citizens. The acceleration of such 'patriot games' also provides a challenge to the global cultural economy – particularly to nationalism as a key organizing principle of contemporary identities and sports systems. 'New' mobilities, in this sense, are challenging some of the long-standing 'moorings' of the global sporting system. Researchers need to conceptualize and interpret such emerging trends in innovative ways as they reflect the contested dynamism of global sport, tracing and analysing the structured processes that enable and constrain people's lives.

Whilst most sport-related work to date has emerged from within the migration paradigm – hence the term sports labour migration dominating in the literature – there is a need for scholars of sports to engage with the emerging 'new mobilities' paradigm (see Sheller and Urry, 2006).[1] This 'mobility turn', Hannam *et al.* (2006) boldly suggest, is said to be transforming the social sciences. Specifically, they note it as 'placing new issues on the table, but also transcending disciplinary boundaries and putting into question the fundamental "territorial" and sedentary precepts of twentieth-century social science' (pp. 1–2). There is a pressing need for sports scholars to respond to this agenda.

The emphasis on mobilities, as Sheller and Urry note, arises from critiques of existing approaches. Specifically, the paradigm challenges the way in which much social science research has been 'a-mobile', seeking to go beyond stability, meaning and place as basic units of research, instead emphasizing the mobilities that course through them. Yet the mobilities approach is not merely an acknowledgement of the (increasing) significance of movement and encounter but also arises from a critique of approaches to globalization which has emphasized freedom or liberation from space and place as inherent to 'new' global interconnectedness. Specifically, that is, it also departs from conceptualizations of *deterritorialization* that emphasize post-national 'fluidity' characterized by speed of movement of people, money, commodities, images and information. Specifically, the new paradigm seeks a balance between acknowledging freedom, communication and mobility with understanding concomitant material and institutional infrastructure that simultaneously limits as well as promotes mobility.

This approach, Sheller and Urry (2006) note, emphasizes how all mobilities 'entail specific often highly embedded and immobile infrastructures' (p. 210). This new mobilities paradigm then seeks to navigate a course between, on one hand, overly static, structuralist approaches and, on the other, overly agentic formulations. Yet while there may be promise in such new directions, new frameworks should not be followed blindly – a particular pertinent point given the 'faddish' nature of the social sciences. Perhaps, predictably, proponents of the new mobilities approach have neglected sport in their analyses so far. Scholars of sports, then, will want to critically explore how their own subject content may test, stretch and add new layers to these new paradigms. This collection evidences a sensitivity to the concept of 'mobilities' that is already evident in research, but there is much scope for further explorations.

With these conceptual and theoretical trajectories in mind, scholars must seek to explore and understand emerging sports-related flows and movements that, so far, have eluded the migration paradigm. For example, it was reported that organizers of the 2010 FIFA World Cup in South Africa hoped for up to 450,000 visitors during the month-long tournament (see Duval-Smith, 15th December 2009). However ambitious such figures may be, they represent significant, albeit temporary, flows of people that the traditional 'migration' paradigm has frequently overlooked. Such flows of sports tourists/consumers – however short-lived – raise numerous issues of cultural encounter, equity, environment, identity and economy. Future research agendas are charged with accounting for these accelerating trends and patterns as they emerge, the phenomena they reveal, the processes they are part of, and their impacts on lives. For example, whilst such tourists may be enjoying state of the art stadia, locals will continue to live without clean water and electricity in a deeply unequal South African society. Such is the inequity of the global system, of which sporting flows play their part. The privileged mobilities enjoyed by some are not disconnected from the immobilities of others.

Such lines of enquiry provide linkages with developments in the field of sports tourism research, elements of which have adopted and increasingly advanced a critical approach (e.g. see Higham and Hinch, 2009). The field then must work to include analyses of those who are *at leisure* as much as those who *labour*. Indeed, the (uneven) circulation of people is a key, indeed accelerating, feature of global sport processes laden with emerging questions. For example, consider the circulation of a small coterie of highly paid administrators of sporting 'mega events' such as Olympic Games and FIFA World Cups, who circulate from one event to the next deploying the same practices and models, and the fans who are privileged enough to follow their teams/players who are as equally as 'mobile' a phenomenon of the global sports process as athletes. Researchers need to find new and innovative ways to conceptualize and understand these sport-related mobilities.

A developing strength of the field – borne out in the contents of this collection – is geographical diversity. That is, it incorporates work from many parts of the globe. The chapters in this collection, for example, draw upon work located within (and indeed making connections between) Africa, Central America, South America, Japan, the Pacific, the Antipodes, Europe and North America. Furthermore, the research sheds light on the unique characteristics and circumstances of migrations as they are 'played out' across varied sporting contexts: association football, rugby union, basketball, baseball, ice hockey, snowboarding and yachting. Yet notwithstanding that geographical breadth, there is more work needed to shed light on diverse local and national contexts. In particular, more work is needed on non-western sport and body cultures and how the migration of western sport, in various zones of prestige and emulation, not only prompted resistance but also led to the destruction of traditional ludic cultures (Maguire, 2005). As is frequently the case, we need more research from non-western contexts *and* from non-western perspectives (and, indeed, non-western researchers). Such work has the capacity to add to, broaden and, indeed, challenge the existing stock of knowledge in ways that will bolster the field and further spell out some of the inconvenient truths about sport migration.

In a similar vein, whilst the emphasis has frequently been on mainstream, often professionalized elite performers and contexts, more work is needed to explore non-competitive sport and leisure sport mobilities. As some of the contributions in this collection attest, the tale told from these 'margins' is likely a very different one from that which emphasizes the (usually male) elite competitions that dominate public discourse. More research is needed to explore sports-related mobilities that occur beyond the gaze of media and frequently at the margins of public discourse. Such work will provide a useful corrective to the skewed nature of public discourse on sport *and* broaden the research field conceptually. We hope this collection has, in some small way, assisted in the process of signalling new directions of research while also providing a summation of what we already know.

Note

1 Sheller and Urry note that the new paradigm includes work from anthropology, cultural studies, geography, migration studies, science and technology studies, tourism and transport studies and sociology. For details of some of the characteristics, properties and implications of 'mobility turn' within the social sciences see Sheller and Urry (2006) and Hannam (2006).

References and bibliography

'Ádios a "Bam Bam" Zamorano' [Farewell 'Bam Bam' Zamorano], *El Siglo de Torreón. com.mex*, 19 July 2003. Online. Available HTTP: http://www.elsiglodetorreon.com. mx/noticia/40588.adios-a-8220-bam-bam-8221-zamorano.html (accessed 5 August 2009).

African Soccer (1992–3) 'Obituary. Death of a star: Larbi Ben Barek', *African Soccer*, 1(December–February): 22.

Agergaard, S. (2008) 'Elite athletes as migrants in Danish women's handball', *International Review for the Sociology of Sport*, 43: 5–19.

Agergaard, S. and Sørensen, J. K. (2009) 'The dream of social mobility: Ethnic minority players in Danish football clubs', *Soccer and Society*, 10(6): 766–80.

Ahlstrom, F. (1997) 'Interview with Issa Hayatou – President of CAF', *The Meridian Cup Report*, Nyon: UEFA Press Department, pp. 5–8.

Albertini, R. V. (1992) *European Colonial Rule, 1880–1940: The Impact of the West on India, Southeast Asia and Africa*, Oxford, UK: Clio Press.

Albrow, M. (1996) *The Global Age*, Stanford: Stanford University.

Aldskogius, H. (1993) *Leksand, Leksand, Leksand! En studie av is hockeyns betydelse for en bygd*, Hedemora, Sweden: Gidlunds Bokforlag.

Alexander, C. and Knowles, C. (eds) (2005) *Making Race Matter: Bodies, Space and Identity*, Basingstoke, UK: Palgrave Macmillan.

Alexander, S. (2001, December 10) 'Sir Peter Blake (obituary)', *The Independent*, p. 6. Online. Available HTTP: http://www.independent.co.uk/news/obituaries/sir-peter-blake-729572.html (accessed 22 July 2004).

Amit, V. (2000) 'Introduction: Constructing the field', in V. Amit (ed.), *Constructing the Field: Ethnographic Fieldwork in the Contemporary World*, Florence, Italy: Routledge.

Ammirante, J. (2006) 'Globalization in professional sport: Comparisons and contrasts between hockey and European football', in D. Whitson and R. Gruneau (eds), *Artificial Ice: Hockey, Culture and Commerce*, Peterborough, UK: Broadview Press.

Amnyos (2008) *Etude du financement public et privé du sport, Etude réalisée dans le cadre de la présidence française de l'Union européenne, Ministère de la Santé, de la Jeunesse, des Sports et de la Vie Associative et du Secrétariat d'Etat aux Sports* [Study on Public and Private Sport Financing, Study achieved for the Ministry for Health, Youth, Sports and Associative Life in the framework of the French Presidency of Europe], Paris.

Anae, M. (2002) 'Papalagi redefined: Toward a New Zealand-born Samoan identity', in P. Spickard, J. L. Rondilla, and D. H. Wright (eds), *Pacific Diaspora: Island Peoples in the United States and Across the Pacific*, Honolulu, HI: University of Hawai'i Press.

Anae, M. (2004) 'From kava to coffee: The "browning" of Auckland', in I. Carter, D. Craig, and S. Matthewman (eds), *Almighty Auckland?*, Palmerston North, New Zealand: Dunmore Press.

Anae, M. (2006, December 21) 'Samoans', *Te Ara: The Encyclopedia of New Zealand*, 21 September 2007. Online. Available HTTP: http://www.TeAra.govt.nz/NewZealanders/NewZealandPeoples/Samoans/en (accessed 7 October 2007).

Anderson, B. (1983) *Imagined Communities: Reflections on the Origin and Spread of Nationalism*, London, UK: Verso.

Anderson, B. (1992) 'The new world disorder', *New Left Review*, 193: 3–13.

Andersson, M. (2007) 'The relevance of the black Atlantic in contemporary sport: Racial imaginaries in Norway', *International Review for the Sociology of Sport*, 42: 65–81.

Andreff, M., Andreff, W., and Poupaux, S. (2008) 'Les déterminants économiques de la performance sportive: Prévision des médailles gagnées aux Jeux de Pékin' [Economic determinants of sport performance. Predicting medal wins at the Beijing Games], *Revue d'Economie Politique*, 118(2): 135–69.

Andreff, W. (2001) 'The correlation between economic underdevelopment and sport', *European Sport Management Quarterly*, 1(4): 251–79.

Andreff, W. (2002) 'FIFA regulation of international transfers and the Coubertobin tax: Enforcement, scope and return. A rejoinder to Bill Gerrard', *European Sport Management Quarterly*, 2(1): 57–63.

Andreff, W. (2004) 'The taxation of player moves from developing countries', in R. Fort and J. Fizel (eds), *International Sports Economics Comparisons*, Westport: Praeger.

Andreff, W. (2006a) 'International labour migration', in W. Andreff and S. Szymanski (eds), *Handbook on the Economics of Sport*, Cheltenham, UK: Edward Elgar.

Andreff, W. (2006b) 'Pistes de réflexion économique', in D. Oswald (ed.), *La nationalité dans le sport. Enjeux et problèmes*, Neuchâtel [Pathways to an economic analysis, in D. Oswald, ed., The Nationality (or Citizenship?) in Sport. Contentions and Issues], Switzerland: CIES, Université de Neuchâtel.

Andreff, W. (2007a) 'French football: A financial crisis rooted in weak governance', *Journal of Sports Economics*, 8(6): 652–61.

Andreff, W. (2007b) 'Governance issues in French professional football', in J. Garcia, S. Késenne, and P. Rodriguez (eds), *Governance and Competition in Professional Sports Leagues* (pp. 55–86), Oviedo: Editions of the Oviedo University.

Andreff, W. (2008) 'Globalisation of the sports economy', *Rivista di diritto ed Economia dello Sport*, 4(3): 13–32.

Andreff, W. (2009a) 'Equilibre compétitif et contrainte budgétaire dans une ligue de sport professionnel' [Competitive Balance and Budget Constraint in a Professional Sports League], *Revue Economique*, 60(3): 591–633.

Andreff, W. (2009b) 'Un club de football européen est-il une firme multinationale?', in J. Fontanel, L. Bensahel, and P. Chaix (eds), *Regards sur l'économie et le management du sport et des sportifs professionnels* [Is a European football club a multinational company?, in J. Fontanel etc., Outlook on Sports Economics and Management and Professional Sports], Paris: L'Harmattan.

Andreff, W. (2009c) 'Public and private sport financing in Europe: The impact of financial crisis', Eighty-Fourth Western Economic Association International Conference, Vancouver, 29 June–3 July.

Andreff, W. (2009d) 'Strengths and weaknesses in a global world: Are new members a booster or dead weight?', in F. Luengo (ed.), *The Role of Europe in the International Context: Visions from Central and Eastern Countries*, Madrid: Complutense University of Madrid.

Andreff, W. and Bourg, J.-F. (2006) 'Broadcasting rights and competition in European football', in C. Jeanrenaud and S. Késenne (eds), *The Economics of Sport and the Media*, Cheltenham, UK: Edward Elgar.

Andreff, W. and Poupaux, S. (2007) 'The institutional dimension of the sports economy in transition countries', in M. Parent and T. Slack (eds), *International Perspectives on the Management of Sport*, Amsterdam: Elsevier.

Andreff, W. and Staudohar, P. (2000) 'The evolving European model of professional sports finance', *Journal of Sports Economics*, 1(3): 257–76.

Andreff, W., Dutoya, J., and Montel, J. (2009a) 'Le modèle européen de financement du sport: quels risques?' [The European model of sport financing: which risks?], *Revue Juridique et Economique du Sport*, 90: 75–85.

Andreff, W., Dutoya, J., and Montel, J. (2009b) 'A European model of sports financing: Under threat?', *Play the Game*. Online. Available HTTP: http://www.playthegame.org/home.html.

Andrews, D. (1997) 'The (trans)national basketball association: American commodity-sign culture and global–local conjuncturalism', in A. Cvetkovich and D. Kellner (eds), *Articulating the Global and the Local*, Boulder, CO: Westview.

Andrews, D., Carrington, B., Jackson, S., and Mazur, J. (1996) 'Jordanscapes: A preliminary analysis of the global popular', *Sociology of Sport Journal*, 13: 428–57.

Andrews, D. L. (1991) 'Welsh indigenous! and British imperial? Welsh rugby, culture, and society 1890–1914', *Journal of Sport History*, 18: 335–49.

Andrews, D. L. (2006) *Sport–Commerce–Culture: Essays on Sport in Late Capitalist America*, New York: Peter Lang.

Ansari, H. (2004) 'Introduction: Racialization and sport', *Patterns of Prejudice*, 38: 209–12.

Anthias, F. (1998) 'Evaluating "diaspora": Beyond ethnicity?', *Sociology*, 32: 557–80.

Anthias, F. and Yuval-Davis, N. with Cain, H. (1992) *Racialized Boundaries: Race, Nation, Gender, Colour and Class and the Anti-racist Struggle*, London, UK: Routledge.

Appadurai, A. (1990) 'Disjuncture and difference in the global cultural economy', *Theory, Culture and Society*, 7: 295–310.

Appadurai, A. (1996) *Modernity at Large: Cultural Dimensions of Globalization*, Minneapolis, MN: University of Minnesota Press.

Apparicio, P. (2000) 'Les indices de ségrégation résidentielle: un outil intégré dans un système d'information géographique', *Cybergeo: European Journal of Geography*. Online. Available HTTP: http://www.cybergeo.eu/index12063.html (accessed 14 October 2009).

Arango, T. (2009, August 5) 'News Corporation posts a loss on MySpace charge', *New York Times*.

Arbena, J. L. (1994) 'Dimensions of international talent migration in Latin American sports', in J. Bale and J. Maguire (eds), *The Global Sports Arena: Athletic Talent Migration in an Interdependent World*, London, UK: Frank Cass.

Armstrong, G. (2004) 'The migration of the Black Panther: An interview with Eusebio of Mozambique and Portugal', in G. Armstrong and R. Giulianotti (eds), *Football in Africa: Conflict, Conciliation and Community*, Basingstoke, UK: Palgrave Macmillan.

'ARU wants to stop club pressure' (2003) *One Sport*, 23 September. Online. Available HTTP: http://oneworldcup.nzoom.com/story/223179.html (accessed 6 August 2008).

Avila, Ralph interview, 11/02/07.

Baccigaluppi, J., Mayugba, S., and Carnel, C. (2001) *Declaration of Independents: Snowboarding, Skateboarding and Music: An Intersection of Cultures*, San Francisco: Chronicle Books.

Back, L., Crabbe, T., and Solomos, J. (2001) 'Lions and black skins: Race, nation and local patriotism in football', in B. Carrington and I. McDonald (eds), *'Race', Sport and British Society*, London, UK: Routledge.

Bagguley, P. and Hussain, Y. (2005) 'Flying the flag for England? Citizenship, religion and cultural identity among British Pakistani Muslims', in T. Abbas (ed.), *Muslim Britain: Communities Under Pressure*, London, UK: Zed Books.

Bairner, A. (2001) *Sport, Nationalism, and Globalization: European and North American Perspectives*, Albany, NY: State University of New York Press.

Bairner, A. (2003) 'Political unionism and sporting nationalism: An examination of the relationship between sport and national identity within the Ulster Unionist tradition', *Identities: Global Studies in Power and Culture*, 10: 517–35.

Bairner, A. (2007) 'Back to basics: Class, social theory, and sport', *Sociology of Sport Journal*, 31: 20–36.

Baldoz, R., Koeber, C., and Kraft, P. (eds) (2001) *The Critical Study of Work: Labour, Technology, and Global Production*, Philadelphia, PA: Temple University Press.

Bale, J. (1980) *Sports Geography*, London, UK: Spon.

Bale, J. (1984) *Sport and Place: A Geography of Sport in England, Scotland and Wales*, London, UK: Crowood.

Bale, J. (1991) *The Brawn Drain: Foreign Student-Athletes in American Universities*, Urbana, IL: University of Illinois Press.

Bale, J. (1994) 'Out of Africa: The development of Kenyan athletics, talent migration and the global sports system', in J. Bale and J. Maguire (eds), *The Global Sports Arena: Athletic Talent Migration in an Interdependent World* (pp. 206–25), London, UK: Frank Cass.

Bale, J. (2003) *Sports Geography* (2nd edn), London, UK: Routledge.

Bale, J. (2004) 'Three geographies of Africa footballer migration: Patterns, problems and postcoloniality', in G. Armstrong and R. Giulianotti (eds), *Football in Africa: Conflict, Conciliation and Community*, Basingstoke, UK: Palgrave Macmillan.

Bale, J. and Maguire, J. (eds) (1994a) *The Global Sports Arena: Athletic Talent Migration in an Interdependent World*, London, UK: Frank Cass.

Bale, J. and Maguire, J. (1994b) 'Sports labour migration in the global arena', in J. Bale and J. Maguire (eds), *The Global Sports Arena: Athletic Talent Migration in an Interdependent World*, London, UK: Frank Cass.

Bale, J. and Sang, J. (1996) *Kenyan Running: Movement Change, Geography and Global Change*, London, UK: Frank Cass.

Ballara, A. (1986) *Proud to be White? A Survey of Pakeha Prejudice in New Zealand*, Auckland, New Zealand: Heinemann.

Balsom, D. (1985) 'The three Wales model', in J. Osmond (ed.), *The National Question Again*, Llandysul, UK: Gomer.

Barber, B. (1992) 'Jihad vs. McWorld', *The Atlantic Monthly*, 269: 53–65.

Barnett, S. (1990) *Games and Sets: The Changing Face of Sport on Television*, London, UK: British Film Institute.

Barney, R. K., Wenn, S. R., and Martyn, S. G. (2002) *Selling the Five Rings: The International Olympic Committee and the Rise of Olympic Commercialism*, Salt Lake City, UT: University of Utah Press.

Barr, M., Moran, C., and Wallace, E. (2006) *Snowboarding the World*, Bath, UK: Footprint.

Barra, A. (2002, July 9) 'Nil and void', *Village Voice*.

Barrientos, S., Dolan, C., and Tallontire, A. (2003) 'A gendered value chain approach to codes of conduct in African Horticulture', *World Development*, 31(9): 1511–26.

Bartus, L. (2000) *Varga Zoli Disszidal* [Zoli Varga Defects], Budapest: Gyomai Kner Nyomda Rt.

BBC (2009, August 18) 'Six Crusaders are to be deported'. Online. Available HTTP: http://news.bbc.co.uk/sport2/hi/rugby_league/super_league/celtic_crusaders/8207827.stm (accessed 7 December 2009).

BBC News (2006, November 11). Television broadcast. London, UK: BBC.

Beach, J. (2004) *Godzilla Takes the Bronx: The Inside Story of Hideki Matsui*, New York: Taylor.

Beamish, R. (1982) 'Sport and the logic of capitalism', in H. Cantelon and R. Gruneau (eds), *Sport, Culture and the Modern State*, Toronto, ON: University of Toronto Press.

Beamish, R. (1988) 'The political economy of professional sport', in J. Harvey and H. Cantelon (eds), *More than Just a Game: Essays in Canadian Sport Sociology*, Ottawa, ON: University of Ottawa Press.

Beaverstock, J. V. (1991) 'Skilled international migration: An analysis of the geography of international secondments within large accountancy firms', *Environment and Planning A*, 23: 1133–46.

Beaverstock, J. V. (1996) 'Subcontracting the accountant! Professional labour markets, migration, and organisational networks in the global accountancy industry', *Environment and Planning A*, 28: 303–26.

Beaverstock, J. V. (2004) '"Managing across borders": Knowledge management and expatriation in professional service legal firms', *Journal of Economic Geography*, 4: 157–79.

Beaverstock, J. V. (2005) 'Transnational elites in the city: British highly skilled inter-company transferees in New York City's financial district', *Journal of Ethnic and Migration Studies*, 31(2): 245–68.

Bedford, R. (2003) 'New Zealand: The politicization of immigration', *Migrant Information Source*. Online. Available HTTP: http://www.migrationinformation.org/Profiles/display.cfm?ID=86 (accessed 3 August 2009).

Bedford, R. (2005, Winter) 'A Kiwi conundrum', *Off Campus*, p. 14.

Bedford, R. D. (2001) *Reflections on the Overseas Spatial Odysseys of New Zealanders*, paper presented at the New Zealand Geographical Society and Institute of Australian Geographers Conference, Dunedin, New Zealand.

Belich, J. (2007, September 26) 'Globalization and the nation', *Keynote Address to the Concepts of Nationhood Symposium*, Wellington, New Zealand. Online. Available HTTP: http://www.mch.govt.nz/dominion/belich.html (accessed 10 January 2007).

Bell, A. (2004) '"Half-castes" and "White natives": The politics of Māori-Pākehā hybrid identities', in C. Bell and S. Matthewman (eds), *Cultural Studies in Aotearoa New Zealand: Identity, Space and Place*, South Melbourne, VIC: Oxford University Press.

Bernard, A. B. and Busse, M. R. (2004) 'Who wins the Olympic Games: Economic resources and medal totals', *Review of Economics and Statistics*, 86(1): 413–17.

Bernstein, A. and Blain, N. (2003) *Sport, Media and Culture: Global and Local Dimensions*, London, UK: Frank Cass.

Besson, R., Poli, R., and Ravenel, L. (2008) *Demographic Study of Footballers in Europe*, Neuchâtel, Switzerland: CIES.

Beyers, W. B. (2002) 'Culture, services and regional development', *Service Industries Journal*, 22(1): 4–34.

Beynon, J. and Dunkerly, D. (eds) (2000) *Globalization: The Reader*, London, UK: The Athlone Press.

BIHA (1994, March 25) 'BIHA anger at players union claims', *Ice Hockey News Review*.

BIHA (1995, December 18) 'BIHA inquiry into Wasps' roughhouse', *The Guardian*.

Billig, M. (1995) *Banal Nationalism*, London, UK: Sage.

Black, J. (1986) *The Dominican Republic: Politics and Development in an Unsovereign State*, Boston, MA: Allen and Unwin.

'Blake killed in Amazon shootout' (2001, December 7), *The Evening Post*, p. 1.

'Blake's death leaves Viaduct crowd in sombre mood' (2001, December 10) *The New Zealand Herald*. Online. Available HTTP: http://www.nzherald.co.nz/section/1/story. cfm?c_id=1andobjectid=232805 (accessed 5 November 2004).

Blatter, S. (2003) 'Soccer's greedy neo-colonialists', *Financial Times*, p. 19.

Block, D. (2005) *Multilingual Identities in a Global City: London Stories*, Basingstoke, UK: Palgrave Macmillan.

Bloom, W. (1990) *Personal Identity, National Identity and International Relations*, Cambridge, UK: Cambridge University Press.

Bocsák, M. and Imre, M. (2003) *Megelhetesi Foci* [Cost of Living in Football], Dabas, Hungary: Dabasi Nyomda Rt.

Boniface, P. (2001) *La Terre est Ronde Comme Un Ballon* [The Earth Is a Round Ball], Paris: Sueill.

Botelho, V. L. (1999) *International Migration and Transnationalism: An Empirical Account*, Research report 8, Danish Center for Demographic Research, SDU, Odense University.

Bourdieu, P. (1984) *Distinction: A Social Critique of the Judgement of Taste*, London, UK: Routledge.

Bourdieu, P. (1998) *State Nobility*, Cambridge, UK: Polity Press.

Bourke, A. (2003) 'The dream of being a professional soccer player: Insights on career development options of young Irish players', *Journal of Sport and Social Issues*, 27: 399–419.

'Bowled over' (2005, October 1), *Economist*, p. 40.

Brah, A. (1996) *Cartographies of Diaspora: Contesting Identities*, London, UK: Routledge.

Braziel, J. E. and Mannur, A. (eds) (2003) *Theorizing Diaspora: A Reader*, Oxford, UK: Blackwell.

Brettell, C. B. (2000) 'Theorizing migration in anthropology: The social construction of networks, identities, communities, and globalscapes', in C. B. Brettell and J. F. Hollifield (eds), *Migration Theory: Talking Across Disciplines*, London, UK: Routledge.

Brettell, C. B. and Hollifield, J. F. (eds) (2000) *Migration Theory: Talking Across Disciplines*, London, UK: Routledge.

Brisick, J. (2004) *Have Board, Will Travel: The Definitive History of Surf, Skate, and Snow*, New York: HarperCollins.

Brislin, T. (2003) 'Exotics, erotics and coconuts: Stereotypes of Pacific Islanders', in P. M. Lester and S. D. Ross (eds), *Images that Injure: Pictorial Stereotypes in the Media* (2nd edn), Westport, CT: Praeger.

Broere, M. and Van der Drift, R. (1997) *Football Africa!*, Oxford, UK: Worldview Publishing, pp. 83–5.

Bromberger, C. (1994) 'Foreign footballers, cultural dreams and community identity in some North-Western Mediterranean cities', in J. Bale and J. Maguire (eds), *The Global Sports Arena: Athletic Talent Migration in an Interdependent World*, London, UK: Frank Cass.

Brosnan, P., Rea, D., and Wilson, M. (1995) 'Labour market segmentation and the state: The New Zealand experience', *Cambridge Journal of Economics*, 19: 667–96.

'Brothers Johnson dropped by father' (1993, December 31), *Daily Telegraph*.

Brown, J. (2002, March 25) 'Diamonds in the rough', *Christian Science Monitor*.

Brown, S. F. (2005) 'Exceptionalist America: American sports fans' reaction to internationalization', *International Journal of the History of Sport*, 22(6): 1106–35.

Brubaker, R. (2005) 'The "diaspora" diaspora', *Ethnic and Racial Studies*, 28: 1–19.

Bruce, T. (2004, November 27) *(Re)writing Particular Forms of Nationalism Over the Dead Bodies of Sports Heroes: Possum Bourne and Sir Peter Blake as Exemplars of Pakeha Masculinity*, paper presented at the Sociological Association of Aotearoa New Zealand (SAANZ) Conference, Wellington, New Zealand.

Bruce, T. and Wheaton, B. (2009) 'Rethinking global sports migration and forms of trans-national, cosmopolitan and disaporic belonging: A case study of international yachts-man Sir Peter Blake', *Social Identities*, 15: 585–608.

Brus, A. and Trangbæk, E. (2003) 'Asserting the right to play: Women's football in Denmark', *Soccer and Society*, 4(23): 95–111.

Buckley, J., Jr (1999) 'Football is booming around the world'. Online. Available HTTP: http://www.nfl.com/international

Burawoy, M. (2000) 'Introduction: Reaching for the global', in M. Burawoy, J. A. Blum, S. George, Z. Gille, T. Gowan, L. Haney, M. Klawiter, S. H. Lopez, S. O. Riain, and M. Thayer (eds), *Global Ethnography: Forces, Connection, and Imaginations in a Postmodern World*, Berkeley, Los Angeles, CA: University of California Press.

Burawoy, M. (2001) 'Manufacturing the global', *Ethnography*, 2: 147–59.

Burawoy, M., Blum, J. A., George, S., Gille, Z., Gowan, T., Haney, L., Klawiter, M., Lopez, S. H., Riain, S. O., and Thayer, M. (eds) (2000) *Global Ethnography: Forces, Connection, and Imaginations in a Postmodern World*, Berkeley, Los Angeles, CA: University of California Press.

Burdsey, D. (2004) '"One of the lads"? Dual ethnicity and assimilated ethnicities in the careers of British Asian professional footballers', *Ethnic and Racial Studies*, 27: 757–79.

Burdsey, D. (2006) '"If I ever play football, Dad, can I play for England or India?" British Asians, sport and diasporic national identities', *Sociology*, 40: 11–28.

Burdsey, D. (2007) 'Role with the punches: The construction and representation of Amir Khan as a role model for multiethnic Britain', *The Sociological Review*, 55: 611–28.

Butler, E. (2005, December 4) 'Blue hue at the end of current black out', *The Observer*, 4 December, Sport, p. 12.

Butt, D. (2006, July/August) 'Essence', *New Zealand Snowboarding Magazine*, p. 16.

CAF (1998) 'The importance of football for the African countries', *CAF News*, 64: 37.

'Canada's kid is in the hall' (1999, November 23), *The Calgary Herald*, p. A1.

Canniford, R. (2005) 'Moving shadows: Suggestions for ethnography in globalized cul-tures', *Qualitative Market Research*, 8: 204–18.

Cantelon, H. (2006) 'Have skates will travel: Canada, international hockey and the chang-ing hockey labour market', in D. Whitson and R. Gruneau (eds), *Artificial Ice: Hockey, Culture and Commerce*, Peterborough, UK: Broadview Press.

Carcuro, P. (2000) *Zamorano: Caído del Cielo. Una Historia Como Para Ponerse de Pie* [Zamorano: As If Sent from Above. An Outstanding Story], Santiago, Chile: Aguilar Chilena.

Carling, J. (2008) 'The human dynamics of migrant transnationalism', *Ethnic and Racial Studies*, 31: 1452–77.

Carrington, B. (1986) 'Social mobility, ethnicity and sport', *British Journal of Education*, 7: 3–18.

Carrington, B. and McDonald, I. (2001) 'Introduction: "Race", sport and British society', in B. Carrington and I. McDonald (eds), *'Race', Sport and British Society*, London, UK: Routledge.

Carrington, B., Andrews, D., Jackson, S., and Mazur, Z. (2001) 'The global Jordanscape', in D. Andrews (ed.), *Michael Jordan, Inc.: Corporate Sport, Media Culture, and Late Modern America*, New York: State University of New York Press.

Castells, M. (2000) *The Rise of the Network Society: Volume I: The Information Age: Economy, Society and Culture* (2nd edn), Oxford, UK: Blackwell.

Castles, S. and Miller, M. J. (2003) *The Age of Migration* (3rd edn), Basingstoke, UK: Palgrave.

Chappell, R., Jones, R., and Burden, A. (1996) 'Racial participation and integration in English professional basketball 1977–1994', *Sociology of Sport Journal*, 13: 300–10.

Chass, M. (1998a, March 22) 'A new baseball strategy: Latin-American bargains', *New York Times*.

Chass, M. (1998b, March 23) 'Baseball's game of deception in the search for Latin talent', *New York Times*.

Chenoweth, N. and O'Riordan, B. (2002, June 4) 'The sick business of sport', *Australian Financial Review*.

Chester, J. (2004, March 23) 'Burton snowboards'. Online. Available HTTP: http://www.hoovers.com/burton-snowboards/–ID__51732/fre (accessed 10 March 2006).

Chiba, N. (2004) 'Pacific professional baseball leagues and migratory patterns and trends: 1995–1999', *Journal of Sport and Social Issues*, 28(2): 193–211.

Chiba, N., Ebihara, O., and Morino, S. (2001) 'Globalization, naturalization and identity: The case of borderless elite athletes in Japan', *International Review for the Sociology of Sport*, 36(2): 203–21.

Chomsky, N. (1995) 'Rollback II', *Z Magazine*, February: 20–31.

Cincotta, H. (2009) 'Alex Ovechkin leads new wave of Russian, European hockey stars'. Online. Available HTTP: http://www.ctv.ca/servlet/ArticleNews/story/CTVNews/10 48585693197_256/?hub=TopStories (accessed 1 August 2009).

Clifford, J. (1994) 'Diasporas', *Cultural Anthropology*, 9: 302–38.

Coffey, J. (1987) *Canterbury XIII: A Rugby League History*, Christchurch, New Zealand: Canterbury Rugby Football League.

Coffey, W. (2002, July 18) 'Global warming changes the NBA landscape', *New York Daily News*.

Cohen, R. (1997) *Global Diasporas: An Introduction*, Abingdon, Oxon, UK: Routledge.

Cohen, R. (1997) *Global Diasporas: An Introduction*, Seattle, WA: University of Washington Press.

Coleman, A. G. (2004) *Ski Style: Sport and Culture in the Rockies*, Kansas, KS: University Press of Kansas.

Collins, M. F. and Buller, J. R. (2003) 'Social exclusion from high-performance sport: Are all talented young sports people being given an equal opportunity of reaching the Olympic Podium?', *Journal of Sport and Social Issues*, 27: 420–42.

Collins, T. and Vamplew, W. (2002) *Mud, Sweat and Beers: A Cultural History of Sport and Alcohol*, Oxford, UK: Berg.

Community–Government Relationship Steering Group (2002, August) *He Waka Kotuia: Joining Together on a Shared Journey*, Wellington, New Zealand: Ministry of Social Policy.

Conradson, D. and Latham, A. (2005) 'Friendship, networks and transnationalism in a World City: Antipodean transmigrants in London', *Journal of Ethnic and Migration Studies*, 31(2): 287–305.

'Conway holds key' (1993, January 29), *The Guardian*.

Cooper, M. (1999, September 18) '2-TV béisbol: Ramirez and Sosa', *New York Times*.

Cornelissen, S. and Solberg, E. (2007) 'Sport mobility and circuits of power: The dynamics of football migration in Africa and the 2010 World Cup', *Politikon*, 34(3): 295–314.

Cosgrove, A. and Bruce, T. (2005) '"The way New Zealanders would like to see themselves": Reading White masculinity via media coverage of the death of Sir Peter Blake', *Sociology of Sport Journal*, 22: 336–55.

Crampton, R. (2004) 'Foreword', *The International Journal of the History of Sport*, 21: 672–80.

'Cranston now looking for cash' (1995, September 22), *Daily Telegraph*.

Crawford, G. (2002) 'Cultural tourists and cultural trends: Commercialization and the coming of the storm', *Culture, Sport, Society*, 5(1): 21–38.

Cromartie, W. and Whiting, R. (1991) *Slugging It Out in Japan: An American Major Leaguer in the Tokyo Outfield*, Tokyo, Japan: Kodansha International.

Cronin, M. (1997) 'Which nation? Which flag? Boxing and national identities in Ireland', *International Review for the Sociology of Sport*, 32(2): 131–46.

Cronin, M. (1999) *Sport and Nationalism in Ireland: Gaelic Games, Soccer and Irish Identity Since 1884*, Dublin, Ireland: Four Courts Press.

CTV.ca news staff (2003) 'Gretzky says he backs Bush on US–Iraq war'. Online. Available HTTP: http://www.ctv.ca/servlet/ArticleNews/story/CTVNews/1048585693197_256/?hub=TopStories (accessed 1 August 2009).

Darby, P. (2000) 'The new scramble for Africa: African football labour migration to Europe', *European Sports History Review*, 3: 217–44.

Darby, P. (2001) 'The new scramble for Africa: African football labour migration to Europe', in J. A. Mangan (ed.), *Europe, Sport, World: Shaping Global Societies*, London, UK: Frank Cass.

Darby, P. (2002) *Africa, Football and FIFA: Politics, Colonialism and Resistance*, Portland, OR: Frank Cass.

Darby, P. (2005) 'Africa and the World Cup: Politics, eurocentrism and resistance', *International Journal of the History of Sport*, 22: 881–903.

Darby, P. (2006) 'Migração Para Portugal de Jogadores de Futebol Africanos: Recurso Colonial e Neocolonial' [African Football Labour Migration to Portugal: Colonial and Neo-Colonial Resource], *Análise Social: Football Globalizido*, XLI(2): 417–33.

Darby, P. (2007a) 'African football labour migration to Portugal: Colonial and neo-colonial resource', *Soccer and Society*, 8: 495–509.

Darby, P. (2007b) 'The new scramble for Africa: African football labour migration to Europe', *European Sports History Review*, 3(2): 217–44.

Darby, P. (2009) 'Ghanaian football labour migration to Europe: Preliminary observations', in G. Walters and G. Rossi (eds), *Labour Market Migration in European Football: Key Issues and Challenges*, London, UK: Birkbeck Sport Business Centre (Research Paper Series).

Darby, P. and Hassan, D. (eds) (2008) *Emigrant Players: Sport and the Irish Diaspora*, London, UK: Routledge.

Darby, P. and Solberg, E. (2010) 'Differing trajectories: Football development and patterns of player migration in South Africa and Ghana', *Soccer and Society*, 11(1–2): 117–29.

Darby, P., Akindes, G., and Kirwin, M. (2007) 'Football academies and the migration of African football labor to Europe', *Journal of Sport and Social Issues*, 31(2): 143–61.

De Brie, C. (2001) 'L'Afrique Sous la Coupe du Football' [Africa Under the Football World Cup], *Le Monde Diplomatique*, February.

Deacon, J. (1995, October 9) 'Hockey's reversal of fortune', *Macleans*, pp. 62–6.

Deforges, L. (1997) 'Checking out the planet: Global representations/local identities and youth travel', in S. Tracey and G. Valentine (eds), *Cool Places: A Geography of Youth Culture*, London, UK: Routledge.

Delanty, G. (1995) *Inventing Europe: Idea, Identity, Reality*, New York: St Martin's Press.

Deloitte (2009) *Annual Review of Football Finance*, Manchester, UK: Deloitte.

Dempsey, J. (1999, June 14–20) 'WNBA games going global', *Variety*.

Dezalay, E. (1990) 'The big bang and the law: The internationalization and restructuration of the legal field', *Theory, Culture and Society*, 7: 279–93.

Dicken, P. (2007) *Global Shift: Mapping the Changing Contours of the World Economy* (5th edn), New York: Guilford Press.

Dicken, P., Kelly, P., Olds, K., and Yeung, H. W. (2001) 'Chains and networks. Territories and scales: Towards a relational framework for analysing the global economy', *Global Networks*, 1(2): 89–112.

Dietschy, P. (2006) 'Football players' migrations: A political stake', *Historical Social Research*, 31(1): 31–41.

Dolan, C. and Humphrey, J. (2000) 'Governance and trade in fresh vegetables', *Development Studies*, 37(2): 151.

Donnelly, P. and Petherick, L. (2004) 'Workers' playtime? Child labour at the extremes of the sporting spectrum', *Sport in Society*, 7(3): 301–21.

'Don't be Canadian, Dampier warns GB' (1992, March 18), *The Guardian*.

Donzel, J. (1999) *Rapport sur le recrutement, l'accueil et le suivi des jeunes étrangers (hors Union euro-péenne) dans les centres de formation de football professionnels en France* [Report on Recruiting, Hosting and Following Up Young Foreigners (From Outside the European Union) in Professional Football's Training Centres in France], Paris: Ministère de la Jeunesse et des Sports, 30 novembre.

'Dorion shines as Hawks' plan to look to the East goes West' (1994, January 4), *The Guardian*.

Dovenyi, Z. and Vukovich, G. (1994) 'Hungary and international migration', in H. Fassmann and R. Munz (eds), *European Migration in the Late Twentieth Century: Historical Patterns, Actual Trends and Social Implications*, Aldershot, UK: Edward Elgar.

Drackett, P. (1987) *Flashing Blades: The Story of British Ice Hockey*, Marlborough, UK: Crowood.

Dreifort, J. (ed.) (2001) *Baseball History from Outside the Lines*, Lincoln, NE: University of Nebraska Press.

Dryden, K. (1999) 'A Canadian cultural icon', in S. Dryden (ed.), *Total Gretzky: The Magic, the Legend, the Numbers*, Toronto, ON, Canada: McClelland and Stewart.

Dubey, J. P. (2000) *La libre circulation des sportifs en Europe*, Bern, Bruxelles: Stämpfli.

Duke, V. (1994) 'The flood from the east? Perestroika and the migration of sports talent from Eastern Europe', in J. Bale and J. Maguire (eds), *The Global Sport Arena: Athletic Talent Migration in an Independent World*, London, UK: Frank Cass.

Duncan, O. and Duncan, B. (1955) 'A methodological analysis of segregation indexes', *American Sociological Review*, 41: 210–17.

'Durham call in police for Little' (1994, October 25), *The Guardian*.

Duval-Smith (2009, December 15) 'South Africa's World Cup venues are "white elephants"', *The Independent* (London).

Dyreson, M. (2003) 'Globalizing the nation-making process: Modern sport in world history', *The International Journal of the History of Sport*, 20: 91–106.

Edgar, B., Doherty, J., and Meert, H. (2004) *Immigration and Homelessness in Europe*, Bristol, UK: Polity Press.

Edmond, R. (1997) *Representing the South Pacific: Colonial Discourse from Cook to Gauguin*, Cambridge, UK: Cambridge University Press.

Edmunds, J. and Turner, B. (2001) 'The re-invention of national identity', *Ethnicities*, 1: 83–108.

Eitle, T. M. and Eitle, D. J. (2002) 'Race, cultural capital, and the educational effects of participation in sports', *Sociology of Education*, 75: 123–46.

Elias, N. (1965/1994) 'Introduction: A theoretical essay on established and outsider rela-tions', in N. Elias and J. Scotson (eds), *The Established and Outsiders: A Sociological Enquiry into Community Problems*, London, UK: Frank Cass.

Elias, N. (1983) *The Court Society*, Oxford, UK: Basil Blackwell.

Elias, N. (1986) 'Introduction', in N. Elias and E. Dunning (eds), *Quest for Excitement: Sport and Leisure in the Civilizing Process*, London, UK: Basil Blackwell.

Elias, N. (1991) *The Society of Individuals*, Oxford, UK: Basil Blackwell.

Elias, N. (1994a) *Time: An Essay*, Oxford, UK: Basil Blackwell.

Elias, N. (1994b) *Mozart: Portrait of a Genius*, Oxford, UK: Polity.

Elias, N. (1996) *The Germans: Power Struggles and the Development of Habitus in the Nineteenth and Twentieth Centuries*, Cambridge, UK: Polity Press.

Elias, N. (1983) *The Court Society*, Oxford, UK: Basil Blackwell.

Elias, N. (1986) 'Introduction', in N. Elias and E. Dunning (eds), *Quest for Excitement: Sport and Leisure in the Civilizing Process* (pp. 19–62), London, UK: Basil Blackwell.

Elias, N. and Scotson, J. L. (1994) *The Established and the Outsiders: A Sociological Enquiry into Community Problems*, London, UK: Sage.

Eliasson, A. (2009) 'The European football market, globalization and mobility among players', *Soccer and Society*, 10(3): 386–97.

Elliott, R. and Maguire, J. (2008a) 'Getting caught in the net: Examining the recruitment of Canadian players in British professional ice hockey', *Journal of Sport and Social Issues*, 32(2): 158–76.

Elliott, R. and Maguire, J. (2008b) 'Thinking outside of the box: Exploring a conceptual synthesis for research in the area of athletic labor migration', *Sociology of Sport Journal*, 25(4): 482–97.

'European clubs pressured islanders players, coach says' (2006), *International Herald Tribune*. Online. Available HTTP: http://www.iht.com/bin/print.php?id=351947 (accessed 14 November 2006).

European Hockey (n.d.) 'Adam Stefishen (CAN) Profile'. Online. Available HTTP: http://www.eurohockey.net/players/show_player.cgi?serial=53461 (accessed 30 August 2009).

Eurostat (2009) 'GDP per inhabitant varied by one to six across the EU27 member states'. Online. Available HTTP: http://epp.eurostat.ec.europa.eu/cache/ITY_PUBLIC/2-25062009- BP/EN/2-25062009-BP-EN.PDF (accessed 3 July 2009).

'Fact sheet: Burton Snowboards' (2003). Online. Available HTTP: http://www.burton.com (accessed 12 February 2004).

Falcous, M. and Maguire, J. (2005) 'Globetrotters and local heroes? Labour migration, basketball and local identities', *Sociology of Sport Journal*, 2: 137–57.

Falcous, M. and Maguire, J. (2006) '"Imagining America": The NBA and local–global mediascapes', *International Review for the Sociology of Sport*, 41(1): 59–78.

'Fastest growing sports' (n.d.) Online. Available HTTP: http://www.xdream.co.uk/xchannel/xcha_main.html (accessed 14 March 2005).

Federation of Oceania Rugby Unions (2008) 'Federation of Oceania Rugby Unions: Tournaments home'. Online. Available HTTP: http://www.oceaniarugby.com/tournaments/tournaments_home.html (accessed 3 August 2009).

Fernandes, S. (2003) 'Fear of a Black nation: Local rappers, transnational crossings, and state power in contemporary Cuba', *Anthropological Quarterly*, 76: 575–608.

Field, M. (2003, August 1) 'Rugby blackbirders snatching island boys', *Pacific Magazine*, 1 August. Online. Available HTTP: http://www.pacificmagazine.net (accessed 28 October 2008).

FIFA (2002, January 16) 'Transfer regulations: Protecting the interests of players and clubs'. Online. Available HTTP: http://www.FIFA.com.

FIFA (2007) *Fourth FIFA Women's Football Symposium*. Online. Available HTTP: http://www.fifa.com/aboutfifa/developing/women/symposium/index.html (accessed 13 July 2009).

Fiske, J. (1992) 'The cultural economy of fandom', in L. Lewis (ed.), *The Adoring Audience: Fan Culture and Popular Media*, London, UK: Routledge.

Fitzpatrick, S. (2008, June 15) 'Time to select overseas players', *The New Zealand Herald*.

Fitzpatrick, S. (2009a, July 12) 'Cure for player drain lies in the provinces', *The New Zealand Herald*.

Fitzpatrick, S. (2009b, July 26) 'Winning best bet to call home leading players', *Sunday Star Times* (Auckland).

'Flyers floored by Szabo's walkout' (1995, January 10), *Daily Telegraph*.

Ford, N. and Brown, D. (2006) *Surfing and Social Theory*, London, UK: Routledge.

Ford, P. (2002, June 19) 'In business of sport, US one of less-free markets', *Christian Science Monitor*.

'Former All Blacks challenge IRB' (2002, January 14), *The Press*, p. 25.

Foucault, M. (1991) *Discipline and Punish: The Birth of the Prison*, New York: Vintage.

Fougere, G. (1989) 'Sport, culture and identity: The case of rugby football', in D. Novitz and B. Willmott (eds), *Culture and Identity in New Zealand*, Wellington, New Zealand: GP Books.

Fox, J. E. (2003) 'National identities on the move: Transylvanian Hungarian labour migrants in Hungary', *Journal of Ethnic Migration and Migration Studies*, 29: 449–66.

Fox, N. (2003) *Prophet or Traitor? The Jimmy Hogan Story*, Manchester, UK: The Parrs Wood Press.

'Frame inherits bleak scene' (1994, March 4), *Daily Telegraph*.

Frank, A. G. (1969) *Capitalism and Under-Development in Latin America*, New York: Monthly Review Press.

Freeman, C. (2000) *High Tech and High Heels in the Global Economy: Women, Work, and Pink-Collar Identities in the Caribbean*, Durham, NC: Duke University Press.

Frick, B. (2009) 'Globalization and factor mobility: The impact of the "Bosman-Ruling" on player migration in professional soccer', *Journal of Sports Economics*, 10: 88–106.

FRIDE (2002) *Seminar on Democratic Transition and Consolidation, 2001–2002: The Transition in Hungary*. Online. Available HTTP: http://www.fride.org/publication/375/seminar-on-democratic-transition-and-consolidation-2001–2002-the-transition-in-hungary (accessed 3 July 2009).

Fröbel, F., Heinrichs, J., and Kreye, O. (1980) *The New International Division of Labour: Structural Unemployment in Industrialised Countries and Industrialisation in Developing Countries*, trans. P. Burgess, Cambridge, UK: Cambridge University Press; Paris: Éditions de la Maison des Sciences de l'Homme.

Frohlick, S. (2005) '"That playfulness of White masculinity": Mediating masculinities and adventure at mountain film festivals', *Tourist Studies*, 5: 175–93.

Gallagher, B. (2005, November 28) 'New Zealand should ease their island raiding', *The Daily Telegraph*, p. 21.

Gamlen, A. (2005) 'The brain drain is dead, long live the New Zealand diaspora', working paper no. 10, Centre on Migration, Policy and Society, University of Oxford, UK. Online. Available HTTP: http://www.compas.ox.ac.uk/fileadmin/files/pdfs/Alan%20Gamlen%20WP0510.pdf (accessed 7 January 2009).

Gardiner, S. and Welch, R. (2000) '"Show me the money": Regulation of the migration of professional sportsmen in post-Bosman Europe', in A. Caiger and S. Gardiner (eds), *Professional Sport in the European Union: Regulation and Reregulation* (pp. 107–26), The Hague: T.M.C. Asser Press.

Gelder, K. and Thornton, S. (eds) (1997) *The Subcultures Reader*, London, UK: Routledge.

Genest, S. (1994) 'Skating on thin ice? The international migration of Canadian ice hockey players', in J. Bale and J. Maguire (eds), *The Global Sports Arena: Athletic Talent Migration in an Interdependent World*, London, UK: Frank Cass.

Gereffi, G. (1994) 'The organisation of buyer-driven global commodity chains: How U.S. retailers shape overseas production networks', in G. Gereffi and M. Korceniewicz (eds), *Commodity Chains and Global Capitalism*, Westport, CT: Praeger.

Gereffi, G. (1996) 'Global commodity chains: New forms of coordination and control among nations and firms in international industries', *Competition and Change*, 4: 427–39.

Gereffi, G. (1999) 'International trade and industrial upgrading in the apparel commodity chain', *Journal of International Economics*, 48(1): 37–70.

Gereffi, G. (2001) 'Shifting governance structures in global commodity chains, with special reference to the internet', *American Behavioral Scientist*, 44(10): 1617–37.

Gereffi, G. and Korceniewicz, M. (eds) (1994) *Commodity Chains and Global Capitalism*, Westport, CT: Praeger.

Gereffi, G., Humphreys, J., and Sturgeon, T. (2005) 'The governance of global value chains', *Review of International Political Economy*, 12(1): 78–104.

Gerrard, B. (2002) 'The muscle drain, Coubertobin-type taxes and the international transfer system', *European Sport Management Quarterly*, 2(1): 47–56.

Gibbon, P. (2003) 'Value chain governance, public regulation and entry barriers in the global fresh fruit and vegetable chain in the UK', *Development Policy Review*, 21(5): 615–25.

Gibson, O. (2009, January 22) 'Where will the big bucks go when the bubble bursts?', *The Guardian*.

Giddens, A. (1984) *The Constitution of Society*, Cambridge, UK: Polity Press.

Gilchrist, P. (2005) 'Local heroes and global stars', in L. Allison (ed.), *The Global Politics of Sport*, London, UK: Routledge.

Gille, Z. (2001) 'Critical ethnography in the time of globalization: Toward a new concept of site', *Critical Studies–Critical Methodologies*, 1: 319–34.

Gillett, J., White, P., and Young, K. (1995) 'The Prime Minister of Saturday night: Don Cherry, the CBC, and the cultural production of intolerance', in H. Holmes and D. Taras (eds), *Seeing Ourselves: Media, Power, and Policy in Canada* (2nd edn), Toronto, ON: Harcourt Brace.

Gilmour, C. and Rowe, D. (2009) 'When Becks came to Sydney: Multiple readings of a sport celebrity', *Soccer and Society*.

Gilroy, P. (1991) *'There Ain't No Black in the Union Jack': The Cultural Politics of Race and Nation*, Chicago: University of Chicago Press.

Gilroy, P. (1993) *The Black Atlantic: Modernity and Double Consciousness*, London, UK: Verso.

Gilroy, P. (2001) 'Preface', in B. Carrington and I. McDonald (eds), *'Race', Sport and British Society*, London, UK: Routledge.

Gilroy, P. (2005) *Postcolonial Melancholia*, New York: Columbia University Press.

Giulianotti, R. (2002) 'Soccer goes glocal', *Foreign Policy*, 131: 82–3.

Giulianotti, R. and Robertson, R. (2006) 'Glocalization, globalization and migration: The case of Scottish football supporters in North America', *International Sociology*, 21(2): 171–98.

Gleeson, M. (1996, January) '"The African invasion". Kick-off: African Cup of Nations 1996', *Fans Guide*, p. 106.

Glenn, J. K. (2003) 'EU enlargement', in M. Cini (ed.), *European Union Politics*, Oxford, UK: University of Oxford Press.

'Global player list grows' (1999) Online. Available HTTP: http://www.nba.com.

Gmelch, G. (ed.) (2006) *Baseball Without Borders: The International Pastime*, Lincoln, NE: University of Nebraska Press.

'Go global baseball: What's new and hot' (2009) Online. Available HTTP: http://goglobalbaseball.com (accessed 29 August 2009).

Goetzl, D. (2008, December 30) 'ESPN: "Monday night football" top '08 cable series', *MediaDailyNews*.

Goldsmith, J. (2002, November 13–14) 'Mouse house chief flies with angels', *Variety*.

Gorman, E. (2001, December 7) 'Giant among men in Red Socks', *The Times*, p. 3.

Goudsblom, J. (1977) *Sociology in the Balance: A Critical Essay*, Oxford, UK: Basil Blackwell.

Grainger, A. (2006) 'From immigrant to overstayer: Samoan identity, rugby, and the cultural politics of race and nation in Aotearoa/New Zealand', *Journal of Sport and Social Issues*, 30: 45–61.

Grečić, V. (1993) 'Migration from Eastern Europe: A challenge to the West', in R. King (ed.), *The New Geography of European Migrations*, London, UK: Belhaven Press.

Gregory, A. (2004) 'Pacific islands eye rugby's riches', *The New Zealand Herald*, 8 August. Online. Available HTTP: http://www.nzherald.co.nz/world/news/article.cfm?c_id=2andobjectid=3582760 (accessed 3 August 2009).

Gretzky, W. and Reilly, R. (1990) *Gretzky: An Autobiography*, Toronto, ON, Canada: HarperCollins.

Grønkjær, A. B. and Olesen, D. H. (2007) *Fodbold, Fair Play og forretning* [Football, Fair Play and Business], Århus, Denmark: Turbine forlaget.

Gruneau, R. and Whitson, D. (1993) *Hockey Night in Canada*, Toronto, ON, Canada: Garamond.

Guesdet, K. (2002, September 27) 'Le Sport Africain il y a 20, 25 ou 30 ans', *Radio France International*.

Guest, A. (2009) 'The diffusion of development-through-sport: Analysing the history and practice of the Olympic Movement's grassroots outreach to Africa', *Sport in Society*, 12(10): 1336–53.

'H2B visa information' (2009) Online. Available HTTP: http://www.outbreak-adventure.co.uk/recruitment/visa.php (accessed 17 August 2009).

Haché, A. (2006) 'Analysis of the NHL players by country of birth'. Online. Available HTTP: http://www.thephysicsofhockey.com/documents/country.pdf (accessed 15 August 2009).

Haden, A. (1983) *Boots 'n' All*, Auckland, New Zealand: Rugby Press.

Haden, A. (1988) *Lock, Stock 'n' Barrel*, Auckland, New Zealand: Rugby Press.

Hall, M. (2000) *The Away Game: The Inside Story of Australian Footballers in Europe*, Sydney, Australia: Harper Sports.

Hall, S. (1984) 'The narrative construction of reality', *Southern Review*, 17: 2–17.

Hall, S. (1990) 'Cultural identity and diaspora', in J. Rutherford (ed.), *Identity, Community, Culture, Difference*, London, UK: Lawrence and Wishart.

Hall, S. (1992) 'The question of cultural identity', in S. Hall, D. Held, and T. McGrew (eds), *Modernity and Its Futures*, Cambridge, UK: Polity.

Hall, S. (1997) 'The spectacle of the "other"', in S. Hall (ed.), *Representation: Cultural Representations and Signifying Practices*, London, UK: Sage.

Hall, S. (2001) *The Multicultural Question* (Pavis Papers in Social and Cultural Research No. 4), Milton Keynes, UK: Open University.

Hammond, M. (ed.) (1991–2003) *The European Football Yearbook*, Warley, UK: Sports Projects Limited.

Hammond, M. (ed.) (2005–2008) *The European Football Yearbook*, Essex, UK: M Press Limited.

'Hand strikes for the home-grown' (1995, December 4), *The Guardian*.

Hannam, K., Sheller, M., and Urry, J. (2006) 'Editorial: Mobilities, immobilities and moorings', *Mobilities*, 1(1): 1–22.

'Hard numbers' (2005, November), *Transworld Snowboarding*, p. 58.

Harris, C. (1998) 'Introduction – theorizing fandom: Fans, subculture and identity', in C. Harris and A. Alexander (eds), *Theorizing Fandom*, Cresskill, NJ: Hampton Press.

Harris, J. (2006) '(Re)presenting Wales: National identity and celebrity in the postmodern rugby world', *North American Journal of Welsh Studies*, 6: 1–13.

Harris, J. (2007) 'Doing gender on and off the pitch: The world of female football players', *Sociological Research Online*, 12(1).

Harris, J. (2008) 'Match day in Cardiff: (Re)imaging and (re)imagining the nation', *Journal of Sport and Tourism*, 13: 297–313.

Harvey, J. and Saint-Germain, M. (2001) 'Sporting goods trade, international division of labour, and the unequal hierarchy of nations', *Sociology of Sport Journal*, 18(2): 231–46.

Harvey, J., Rail, J., and Thibault, N. (1996) 'Globalization and sport: Sketching a theoretical model for empirical analyses', *Journal of Sport and Social Issues*, 20(3): 258–77.

Hasegawa, S. (2003) *Tekisha Seizon – Meja eno Chosen* (The Survival of the Fittest – The Challenge to the Major League), Tokyo, Japan: Gentou Sha.

Hassan, D. (2003) 'Rugby union, Irish nationalism and national identity in Northern Ireland', *Football Studies*, 6: 5–18.

Hau'ofa, E. (1993) 'Our sea of islands', in E. Waddell, V. Naidu, and E. Hau'ofa (eds), *A New Oceania: Rediscovering Our Sea of Islands*, Suva, Fiji: School of Social and Economic Development, University of South Pacific.

Haynes, J. (1996) *From All Blacks to All Golds: New Zealand's Rugby League Pioneers*, Christchurch, New Zealand: Ryan and Haynes.

Hebdige, D. (1996) 'Digging for Britain: An excavation in seven parts', in H. Baker, M. Diawara, and R. Lindeborg (eds), *Black British Cultural Studies: A Reader*, London, UK: University of Chicago Press.

Held, D. (2000) 'Regulating globalization? The reinvention of politics', *International Sociology*, 15(2): 394–408.

Held, D. and McGrew, A. G. (eds) (2000) *The Global Transformations Reader: An Introduction to the Globalisation Debate*, Cambridge, UK: Polity Press.

Held, D., McGrew, A., Goldblatt, D., and Perraton, J. (1999) *Global Transformations: Politics, Economics and Culture*, Cambridge, UK: Polity Press.

'Helping out Samoa' (2003, August 22), *The Press*, p. 8.

Hendry, J. (2003) 'An ethnographer in the global arena: Globography perhaps?', *Global Networks*, 3: 497–512.

Hewett, C. (2000) '"Grannygate" inquiry ends in whitewash', *The Independent*, 4 May. Online. Available HTTP: http://www.independent.co.uk/sport/rugby/rugby-union/grannygate-inquiry-ends-in-whitewash-636537.html (accessed 28 November 2008).

Hewett, C. (2005) 'Samoa's ferocity factory gears up for full production', *The Independent*, 24 November. Online. Available HTTP: http://www.independent.co.uk/sport/rugby/rugby-union/samoas-ferocity-factory-gears-up-for-full-production-516647.html (accessed 28 November 2008).

Hickman, M. J., Morgan, S., Walter, B., and Bradley, J. (2005) 'The limitations of whiteness and the boundaries of Englishness: Second-generation Irish identifications and positioning in multiethnic Britain', *Ethnicities*, 5: 160–82.

Hiestand, M. (2002, April 30) 'Spanning the globe', *USA Today*.

Higham, J. and Hinch, T. (2009) *Sport and Tourism, Globalization, Mobility and Identity*, Sydney, Australia: Elsevier.

Hill, R. and Lee, J. (1994) 'Japanese multinationals and East Asian development: The case of the automobile industry', in L. Sklair (ed.), *Capitalism and Development*, London, UK: Routledge.

Hinton, M. (2002, December 29) 'The year ahead – over to you Mitch', *Sunday Star-Times*.

Hirai, H. (1996) 'Baseball, Japanese', in D. Levinson and K. Christensen (eds), *Encyclopedia of World Sport* (vol. 1., pp. 80–4), Santa Barbara, CA: ABC-CLIO.

Hirai, H. (2001) 'Hideo Nomo: Pioneer or defector?', in D. Andrews and S. Jackson (eds), *Sport Stars* (pp. 187–200). London, UK: Routledge.

Hirst, P., Thompson, G., and Bromley, S. (2009) *Globalization in Question* (3rd edn), Cambridge, UK: Polity Press.

Hobsbawm, E. J. (1983) 'Mass producing traditions: Europe, 1870–1914', in E. J. Hobsbawm and T. O. Ranger (eds), *The Invention of Tradition*, Cambridge, UK: Cambridge University Press.

Hobsbawm, E. J. (1990) *Nations and Nationalism Since 1780: Programme, Myth, Reality*, Cambridge, UK: Cambridge University Press.

Hokowhitu, B. (2007) 'Māori sport: Pre-colonisation to today', in C. Collins and S. Jackson (eds), *Sport in Aotearoa/New Zealand Society* (2nd edn), Melbourne, Australia: Cengage Learning.

Holt, R. (1996) 'Contrasting nationalisms: Sport, militarism and the unitary state in Britain and France before 1914', in J. A. Mangan (ed.), *Tribal Identities: Nationalism, Europe, Sport*, London, UK: Frank Cass.

Homewood, B. (2000, January 25) 'FIFA President wants minimum transfer age', *Reuters News Service*.

Hoogvelt, A. (2001) *Globalization and the Postcolonial World: The New Political Economy of Development* (2nd edn), Houndmills, UK: Palgrave.

Hopkins, T. and Wallerstein, I. (1986) 'Commodity chains in the world economy prior to 1800', *Review*, X(1): 157–70.

Horak, R. (2003) 'Diaspora experience, music and hybrid cultures of young migrants in Vienna', in D. Muggleton and R. Weinzierl (eds), *The Post-Subcultures Reader*, Oxford, UK: Berg.

Horn, G. (2002) 'The transition in Hungary', in FRIDE, *Seminar on Democratic Transition and Consolidation, 2001–2002: The Transition in Hungary*. Online. Available HTTP: http://www.fride.org/publication/375/seminar-on-democratic-transition-and-consolidation-2001–2002-the-transition-in-hungary (accessed 3 July 2009).

Horne, J. with Bleakley, D. (2002) 'The development of football in Japan', in J. Horne and W. Manzenreiter (eds), *Japan, Korea and the 2002 World Cup* (pp. 89–105), London, UK: Routledge.

Houston, W. (1998, April 4) 'A game in crisis', *The Globe and Mail*, p. A26.

'How British is British?' (1994, March 26), *Ice Hockey News Review*.

'How others see us?' (1994, April 9), *Ice Hockey News Review*.

Howe, S. (1998) *(SICK) A Cultural History of Snowboarding*, New York: St. Martins Griffin.

Howitt, B. (1989, June 5) 'Clubs lose out', *Time International (New Zealand edition)*, 33: 14.

Howitt, B. and Haworth, D. (2002) *Rugby Nomads*, Auckland, New Zealand: HarperSports.

Hugo, G. (2006) 'An Australian diaspora?', *International Migration*, 44: 105–32.

Humphrey, J. and Schmitz, H. (2004) 'Governance in global value chains', in H. Schmitz (ed.), *Local Enterprises in the Global Economy* (pp. 133–65), London, UK: Edward Elgar.

Huq, R. (2003) 'Global youth cultures in localized spaces', in D. Muggleton and R. Weinzierl (eds), *The Post-Subcultures Reader*, Oxford, UK: Berg.

Hutton, P. (2009, January 13) '2009 promises to be more about consolidation in challenging economic ties', *Indiantelevision.com*.

Hyde, T. (1995) 'What's up with rugby?', *Metro*, December 1995, pp. 106–20.

'Iceman highlights Pacific plight' (2003), *One Sport*. Online. Available HTTP: http://one worldcup.nzoom.com (accessed 27 October 2003).

'Illegal import turmoil' (1995, October 7), *The Guardian*.

Immigration and Naturalization Service (1997) *Immigration Fact Sheet 1996 (October 1997)*. Online. Available HTTP: http://www. ins.usdoj.gov/graphics/aboutins/statistics/299. htm (accessed 2 December 2001).

Index of Economic Freedom (2009) 'Hungary'. Online. Available HTTP: http://www. heritage.org/index/Country/Hungary (accessed 3 July 2009).

Ingram, D. (1996) 'The Cen-TapedeCUS/Canadian Tax', *Investment and Immigration Newsletter*, 11 May. Online. Available HTTP: http://centa.com/centa/centapede/0596. html (accessed 22 November 2001).

International Rugby Board (2009) 'IRB organisation'. Online. Available HTTP: http:// www.irb.com/aboutirb/organisation/index.html (accessed 23 September 2009).

Interview with All Black Coach John Hart (1998).

'IRB admits club problem' (2003) *One Sport*, 30 September. Online. Available HTTP: http://oneworldcup.nzoom.com/story/224993.html (accessed 27 October 2003).

'IRB should pay players' (2003) *One Sport*, 25 September. Online. Available HTTP: http:// oneworldcup.nzoom.com/story/223667.html (accessed 27 October 2003).

Iredale, R. (1999) 'The need to import skilled personnel: Factors favouring and hindering its international mobility', *International Migration*, 37(1): 89–123.

Iredale, R. (2001) 'The migration of professionals: Theories and typologies', *International Migration*, 39(5): 7–26.

Iredale, R. and Appleyard, R. (eds) (2001) 'Introduction to the special issue on the international migration of the highly skilled', *International Migration*, 39(5): 3–6.

'Is it recession-proof?' (2009, February 14), *Economist*, p. 69.

Ishi, K. (2003) *Meja no Ryugi* (The style of the Major League), Tokyo: Bungei Shunju Limited.

Jackson, S. (1994) 'Gretzky, crisis and Canadian identity in 1988: Rearticulating the Americanization of culture debate', *Sociology of Sport Journal*, 11: 428–46.

Jackson, S. (2001) 'Gretzky nation: Canada, crisis and Americanization', in D. Andrews and S. Jackson (eds), *Sport Stars: The Cultural Politics of Sporting Celebrity*, New York: Routledge.

Jackson, S. (2004) 'Exorcizing the ghost: Donovan Bailey, Ben Johnson and the politics of Canadian identity', *Media, Culture and Society*, 26: 121–41.

Jackson, S. and Andrews, D. (1996) 'Excavating the (trans) national basketball association: Locating the global/local nexus of America's World and the World's America', *Australiasian Journal of American Studies*, 15: 57–64.

Jackson, S. and Andrews, D. (1999) 'Between and beyond the global and the local', *International Review for the Sociology of Sport*, 43(1): 31–42.

James, C. (2007, September 26) 'Are we there yet? Resetting and settling the settler society', presentation at the Concepts of Nationhood Symposium, Wellington, New Zealand. Online. Available HTTP: http://www.mch.govt.nz/dominion/colin-james.html (accessed 10 January 2007).

'Japan Samurai Bears' (2009) Online. Available HTTP: http://en.wikipedia.org/wiki/ Japan_Samurai_Bears (accessed 28 August 2009).

'Japanese baseball players in Major League Baseball' (2009) Online. Available HTTP: http://baseball.yahoo.co.jp/mlb/japanese/ (accessed 28 August 2009).

Jarvie, G. and Walker, G. (eds) (1994) *Scottish Sport in the Making of the Nation: Ninety Minute Patriots?*, London, UK: Leicester University Press.

Jarvis, R. M. and Coleman, P. (1999) *Sports Law: Cases and Materials*, St Paul, MN: West Group.

Jeffery, T. (2001, December 6) 'Yachting: Peter Blake: The world's greatest sailor', *Daily Telegraph*, p. 19. Online. Available HTTP: http://www.telegraph.co.uk/sport/3018258/Yachting-Peter-Blake-The-world's-greatest-sailor.html (accessed 22 July 2004).

Jenkins, R. (1994) 'Capitalist development in the NICs', in L. Sklair (ed.), *Capitalism and Development*, London, UK: Routledge.

'Join us brothers . . . Brit or import' (1994, February 12), *Ice Hockey News Review*.

'Jones hits NZRFU over "abuses"' (2003, July 2), *The New Zealand Herald*, p. C3.

Joseph, J. (2009, July 15–18) *(Trans)nationality and Diaspora: Creating Borderless Communities Through Cricket*, paper presented at the World Congress of Sociology of Sport, Utrecht, Holland.

Juffer, J. (2002) 'Who's the man? Sammy Sosa, Latinos, and televisual redefinitions of the "American" pastime', *Journal of Sport and Social Issues*, 26(4): 337–59.

Kahn, G. (2002, June 5) 'Adidas knows the whole world is watching cup', *Wall Street Journal*.

Kay, J. and Laberge, S. (2003) 'Oh say can you ski? Imperialistic construction of freedom in Warren Miller's Freeriders', in R. Rinehart and S. Sydnor (eds), *To the Extreme: Alternative Sports, Inside and Out*, New York: State University of New York.

Keimbou, K. (2004) *Afrique Francophone et Development du Sport: du Mythe a la Realite?* Paris: L'Harmattan.

Kelly, W. (2007) 'Is baseball a global sport? America's national pastime as global field and international sport', in R. Giulianotti and R. Robertson (eds), *Globalization and Sport*, Oxford, UK: Blackwell.

Kelly, W. (2009) 'Samurai baseball: The vicissitudes of a national sporting style', *International Journal of the History of Sport*, 26(3): 429–41.

Kenway, J. and McLeod, J. (2004) 'Bourdieu's reflexive sociology and "spaces of points of view": Whose reflexivity, which perspective?', *British Journal of Sociology of Education*, 25: 525–44.

Khadria, B. (2001) 'Shifting paradigms of globalization: The twenty-first century transition towards generics in skilled migration from India', *International Migration*, 39(5): 45–71.

Kidd, B. (1979) *The Political Economy of Sport*, Calgary, Canada: University of Calgary.

Kidd, B. (1981) 'Sport, dependency and the Canadian state', in M. Hart and S. Birrell (eds), *Sport in the Sociocultural Process*, Dubuque, IA: William C. Brown.

King, A. (1990) 'Architecture, capital and the globalization of culture', *Theory, Culture and Society*, 3: 397–411.

King, T. (2003) *The European Ritual: Football in the New Europe*, Aldershot, UK: Ashgate.

Kivinen, O., Mesikammen, J., and Metsa-Tokila, T. (2001) 'A case study in cultural diffusion: British ice hockey and American influences in Europe', *Culture, Sport, Society*, 4(1): 49–62.

Klein, A. (1988) 'American hegemony, Dominican resistance and baseball', *Dialectical Anthropology*, 13: 301–12.

Klein, A. (1989) 'Baseball as underdevelopment: The political-economy of sport in the Dominican Republic', *Sociology of Sport Journal*, 6: 95–112.

Klein, A. (1991a) 'Sport and culture as contested terrain: Americanization in the Caribbean', *Sociology of Sport Journal*, 8: 79–85.

Klein, A. (1991b) *Sugarball: The American Game, the Dominican Dream*, New Haven, CT: Yale University Press.

Klein, A. (1994) 'Trans-nationalism, labour migration and Latin American baseball', in J. Bale and J. Maguire (eds), *The Global Sports Arena: Athletic Talent Migration in an Interdependent World*, London, UK: Frank Cass.

Klein, A. (1995) 'Culture, politics and baseball in the Dominican Republic', *Latin American Perspectives*, 22(3): 111–30.

Klein, A. (1999) 'Coming of age in North America: The socialization of Dominican baseball players', in J. Coakley and P. Donnelly (eds), *Inside Sports* (pp. 96–104), London, UK: Routledge.

Klein, A. (2000) 'Latinizing Fenway Park: A cultural critique', *Sociology of Sport Journal*, 17(4): 403–22.

Klein, A. (2006a) *Growing the Game: The Globalization of Major League Baseball*, New Haven, CT: Yale University Press.

Klein, A. (2006b) 'The Dominican Republic', in A. Klein (ed.), *Growing the Game: Globalization and Major League Baseball* (pp. 94–142), New Haven, CT: Yale University Press.

Klein, A. (2007) 'Latinizing the national pastime', *International Journal of the History of Sport*, 24(2): 296–310.

Klein, A. (2008) 'Progressive ethnocentrism: Ideology and understanding in Dominican baseball', *Journal of Sport and Social Issues*, 32(2): 121–38.

Klein, A. Field notes: 10/04/06; 4/14/07; 5/22/09.

Klein, A. (n.d.) 'New pride, old prejudice: The second coming of Dominican baseball', manuscript.

Klein, N. (2002) *Fences and Windows: Dispatches from the Front Lines of the Globalisation Debate*, London, UK: Flamingo.

Knowles, C. (1999) 'Here and there: Doing transnational fieldwork', in V. Amit (ed.), *Constructing the Field: Ethnographic Fieldwork in the Contemporary World*, Florence, Italy: Routledge.

Knowles, C. (2005) 'Making whiteness: British lifestyle migrants in Hong Kong', in C. Alexander and C. Knowles (eds), *Making Race Matter*, London, UK: Palgrave.

Kobayashi, I. (2004) *Gappei Baikyaku Shinkisannyu Takaga Saredo Puroyakyu* [Merger, Sale and New Entry: Professional Baseball], Tokyo, Japan: Takarajimasha.

Komatsu, N. (2002) *Ichiro on Ichiro Interview Special Edition* (in Japanese), Tokyo: Shinchosha.

Krishnan, V., Schaeffel, P., and Warren, J. (1994) *The Challenge of Change: Pacific Island Communities in New Zealand, 1986–1993*, Wellington, New Zealand: New Zealand Institute for Social Research and Development Limited.

Krushelnycky, L. (1999, March 10) 'Belgium's football "Slave Trade"', *BBC News Online*.

Kudo, Y., Nogawa, H., and Kudo, Y. (2003) *Migration of Top Athletes and the Emergence of Sport Tourism*, paper presented at the Second World Congress for the Sociology of Sport, Koln, Germany.

Lago, U., Simmons, R., and Szymanski, S. (2006) 'The financial crisis in European football: An introduction', *Journal of Sports Economics*, 7(1): 3–12.

Laidlaw, C. (1973) *Mud in Your Eye: A Worm's Eye View of the Changing World of Rugby*, Wellington, New Zealand: Reed.

Laidlaw, C. (1999) *Rights of Passage: Beyond the New Zealand Identity Crisis*, Auckland, New Zealand: Hodder Moa Beckett.

Laidlaw, C. (2002, September 27) 'All downhill for NPC minnows as big boys step up', *The Press*.

Laidlaw, C. (2003, January 26) 'Better not to think about All Blacks losing mystique', *Sunday Star-Times*.

Lanfranchi, P. (1994) 'The migration of footballers: The case of France', in J. Bale and J. Maguire (eds), *The Global Sports Arena: Athletic Talent Migration in an Interdependent World* (pp. 63–77), London, UK: Frank Cass.

Lanfranchi, P. (2002) 'Football, cosmopolitisme et nationalisme', *Pouvoir*, 10: 15–25.

Lanfranchi, P. and Taylor, M. (2001) *Moving with the Ball: The Migration of Professional Footballers*, Oxford, UK: Berg.

Larner, W. (2007) 'Expatriate experts and globalising governmentalities: The New Zealand diaspora strategy', *Transactions of the Institute of British Geographers*, 32: 331–45.

Lash, S. and Urry, J. (1994) *Economies of Signs and Space*, London, UK: Sage.

'Leading off' (2000, February 14), *Sports Illustrated*.

Ledbetter, J. (2002, November 4) 'The culture blockade', *The Nation*.

Leifer, E. (1995) *Making the Majors: The Transformation of Team Sports in America*, Massachusetts, MA: Harvard University Press.

Lewis, M. (2008, April 1) 'New baggage charges sweep airline industry', *Transworld Business*. Online. Available HTTP: http://business.transworld.net/features/new-baggage-charges-sweeping-the-airline-industry/ (accessed 12 August 2009).

Lewis, M. (2009, April 20) 'March mountain lodgings dive 21.3 percent', *Transworld Business*. Online. Available HTTP: http://business.transworld.net/march-mountain-lodgings-dive-213-percent/ (accessed 12 August 2009).

Lexington (2006, June 10) 'The odd man out', *Economist*, p. 32.

Lie, J. (2001) 'Diasporic nationalism', *Cultural Studies–Critical Methodologies*, 1: 355–62.

Lindberg, K. (2006) 'The man who traced 442 soccer slaves', *Play the Game Magazine*, p. 3.

'List of Major League Baseball players from Japan' (2009, August 29) Online. Available HTTP: http://en.wikipedia.org/wiki/List_of_Japanese_players_in_Major_League_Baseball.

Logan, I. and Rees, P. (2006, July/August) 'When passion and pride no longer is enough', *Spasifik*, 15: 14–15.

Lord Stevens (2006, December) *Final Report into Premiership Transfers, Presented to Premiership Chairmen*, London, UK.

Loto, R., Hodgetts, D., Chamberlain, K., Nikora, L., Karapu, R., and Barmett, A. (2006) 'Pasifika in the news: The portrayal of Pacific peoples in the New Zealand press', *Journal of Community and Applied Social Psychology*, 16: 100–18.

Lowe, L. (1996) *Immigrant Acts*, Durham, NC: Duke University Press.

Luke, W. (2009, April 29) 'MCC at heart of Afghanistan's future', *Cricinfo*.

MacGregor, R. (1993) *Road Games: A Year in the Life of the NHL*, Toronto, ON: MacFarlane.

Macpherson, C. (1997) 'The Polynesian diaspora: New communities and new questions', in K. Sudo and S. Yoshida (eds), *Contemporary Migration in Oceania: Diaspora and Network*, Osaka, Japan: National Museum of Ethnology.

Madan, M. (2000) '"It's just not cricket!": World series cricket: Race, nation, and diasporic Indian identity', *Journal of Sport and Social Issues*, 24: 24–35.

Magee, J. and Sugden, J. (2002) '"The world at their feet": Professional football and international labour migration', *Journal of Sport and Social Issues*, 26: 421–37.

Maguire, J. (1988) 'The commercialization of English elite basketball 1972–1988: A figurational perspective', *International Review for the Sociology of Sport*, 23(4): 305–23.

Maguire, J. (1990) 'More than a sporting "touchdown": The making of American football in Britain 1982–1989', *Sociology of Sport Journal*, 7(3): 213–37.

Maguire, J. (1991a) 'Sport, racism and British society: A sociological study of England's élite male Afro/Caribbean soccer and rugby union players', in G. Jarvie (ed.), *Sport, Racism and Ethnicity*, London, UK: RoutledgeFalmer.

Maguire, J. (1991b) 'The media–sport production complex: The emergence of American sports in European culture', *European Journal of Communication*, 6(3): 315–36.

Maguire, J. (1993a) 'Globalization, sport development and the media/sport production complex', *Sports Science Review*, 2(1): 29–47.

Maguire, J. (1993b) 'Hired corporate guns? Elite sport migrants in the global arena', *Vrijetijd en Samenleving*, 10: 19–30.

Maguire, J. (1994a) 'Preliminary observations on globalisation and the migration of sport labour', *The Sociological Review*, 42(3): 452–80.

Maguire, J. (1994b) 'Sport, identity politics, and globalization: Diminishing contrasts and increasing varieties', *Sociology of Sport Journal*, 11: 398–427.

Maguire, J. (1994c) 'Globalization, sport and national identities: The empire strikes back?', *Society and Leisure*, 16: 293–323.

Maguire, J. (1994d) 'American labour migrants, globalization and the making of English basketball', in J. Bale and J. Maguire (eds), *The Global Sports Arena: Athletic Talent Migration in an Interdependent World* (pp. 226–55), London, UK: Frank Cass.

Maguire, J. (1996) 'Blade runners: Canadian migrants, ice hockey, and the global sports process', *Journal of Sport and Social Issues*, 23: 335–60.

Maguire, J. (1999) *Global Sport: Identities, Societies, Civilizations*, Cambridge, UK: Polity Press.

Maguire, J. (2004) 'Sport labor migration research revisited', *Journal of Sport and Social Issues*, 28: 477–82.

Maguire, J. (2005) *Power and Global Sport: Zones of Prestige, Emulation and Resistance*, London, UK: Routledge.

Maguire, J. (2006) 'Development through sport and the sports industrial complex: The case for human development in sports and exercise sciences', in Y. Auweele, C. Malcolm, and B. Meulders (eds), *Sport and Development*, Cape Town, South Africa: Iannoo Campus.

Maguire, J. (2008) '"Real politic" or "ethically based": Sport, globalization, migration and nation-state policies', *Sport in Society*, 11: 443–58.

Maguire, J. and Bale, J. (1994a) 'Introduction: Sports labour migration in the global arena', in J. Bale and J. Maguire (eds) *The Global Sports Arena: Athletic Talent Migration in an Interdependent World*, London, UK: Frank Cass.

Maguire, J. and Bale, J. (1994b) 'Postscript: An agenda for research on sports labour migration', in J. Bale and J. Maguire (eds), *The Global Sports Arena: Athletic Talent Migration in an Interdependent World* (pp. 281–4), London, UK: Frank Cass.

Maguire, J. and Bale, J. (1994c) 'Sport labour migration in the global arena', in J. Bale and J. Maguire (eds), *The Global Sports Arena: Athletic Talent Migration in an Interdependent World*, London, UK: Frank Cass.

Maguire, J. and Guttmann, A. (2009) 'Factors affecting migration', *Encyclopædia Britannica*. Online. Available HTTP: http://www.britannica.com/EBchecked/topic/561041/sports (accessed 2 October 2009).

Maguire, J. and Pearton, R. (2000a) 'Global sport and the migration patterns of France '98 World Cup finals players: Some preliminary observations', *Soccer and Society*, 1(1): 175–89.

Maguire, J. and Pearton, R. (2000b) 'Global sport and the migration patterns of France '98 World Cup finals players: Some preliminary observations', in J. Garland, D. Malcolm, and M. Rowe (eds), *The Future of Football: Challenges for the Twenty-First Century*, pp. 175–89.

Maguire, J. and Pearton, R. (2000c) 'The impact of elite labour migration on the identification, selection and development of European soccer players', *Journal of Sport Sciences*, 18: 759–69.

Maguire, J. and Poulton, E. (1999) 'European identity politics in Euro 96: Invented traditions and national habitus codes', *International Review for the Sociology of Sport*, 34: 17–29.

Maguire, J. and Stead, D. (1996) 'Far pavilions? Cricket migrants, foreign sojourns and contested identities', *International Review for the Sociology of Sport*, 31: 1–23.

Maguire, J. and Stead, D. (1998a) 'Border crossings: Soccer labour migration and the European Union', *International Review for the Sociology of Sport*, 33(1): 59–73.

Maguire, J. and Stead, D. (1998b) '"Cricket's global finishing school": The migration of overseas cricketers into English county cricket', *European Physical Education Review*, 4: 54–69.

Maguire, J. and Stead, D. (2005) '"Cricketers of the empire": Cash crops, mercenaries and symbols of sporting emancipation?', in J. Maguire (ed.), *Power and Global Sport*, London, UK: Routledge.

Maguire, J. and Tuck, J. (2005) 'National identity, rugby union and notions of Ireland and the "Irish"', *Irish Journal of Sociology*, 14: 86–109.

Maguire, J., Jarvie, G., Mansfield, L., and Bradley, J. (2002) *Sport Worlds: A Sociological Perspective*, Champaign, IL: Human Kinetics.

Mahjoub, F. (1992) 'Culture of mediocity', *African Soccer*, 1(January/February): 38.

Mahjoub, F. (1997) 'The exodus: A savage market', in F. Mahjoub (ed.), *Confédération Africaine de Football: 1957–1997* (pp. 132–5), Cairo, Egypt: Nubar Printing House.

'Major League Baseball statistics and history' (2009) Online. Available HTTP: http://www.baseball-reference.com (accessed 1 September 2009).

Malcolm, D. (2009) 'Malign or benign? English national identities and cricket', *Sport in Society*, 12: 613–28.

Manzo, K. (2007) 'Learning to kick: African soccer schools as carriers of development', *Impumelelo: The Interdisciplinary Electronic Journal of African Sports*, 2. Online. Available HTTP: http://www.ohio.edu/sportsafrica/journal/Volume2/learntokick.htm.

Maradas, E. (2001) 'Human traffic', *African Soccer*, 66, May: 8–9.

Marcano Guevara, A. J. and Fidler, D. P. (1999) 'The globalization of baseball: Major League Baseball and the mistreatment of Latin American baseball talent', *Indiana Journal of Global Legal Studies*, 6: 511–77.

Marcano Guevara, A. J. and Fidler, D. P. (2002) *Stealing Lives: The Globalization of Baseball and the Tragic Story of Alexis Quiroz*, Bloomington, IN: Indiana University Press.

Marcus, G. (1995) 'Ethnography in/of the world system: The emergence of multi-site ethnography', *Annual Review of Anthropology*, 24: 95–117.

Martin, S. (2001) 'Remittances as a development tool', *Economic Perspectives*, 6(3). Online. Available HTTP: http://usinfo.state.gov/journals/ ites/0901/ijee/toc.IItm (accessed 3 December 2001).

Massey, D. (1994) *Space, Place and Gender*, Cambridge, UK: Polity.

Massey, D. (2005) *For Space*, London, UK: Sage.

Matheson, J. (2000, October) '… And the walls came tumbling down', *NZ Rugby World*, pp. 22–32.

Mayeda, D. (1999) 'From model minority to economic threat', *Journal of Sport and Social Issues*, 23(2): 203–17.

McCarthy, M. (2002, January 31) 'Super Bowl, Olympics compete for gold', *USA Today*.

McCreanor, T. (2005) '"Sticks and stones may break my bones…": Talking Pakeha identities', in J. H. Liu, T. McCreanor, T. McIntosh, and T. Teaiwa (eds), *New Zealand Identities: Departures and Destinations*, Wellington, New Zealand: Victoria University Press.

McDonald, M., Mihara, T., and Hong, J.-B. (2001) 'Japanese spectator sport industry: Cultural changes creating new opportunities', *European Sport Management Quarterly*, 1(1): 39–60.

McGovern, P. (2000) 'The Irish brawn drain: English league clubs and Irish footballers, 1946–95', *British Journal of Sociology*, 51(3): 401–15.

McGovern, P. (2002) 'Globalization or internationalization? Foreign footballers in the English league, 1946–95', *Sociology*, 36(1): 23–42.

McKay, D. (2005) 'Migration and the sensuous geographies of re-emplacement in the Philippines', *Journal of Intercultural Studies*, 26: 75–91.

McMichael, P. (2009) 'Contemporary contradictions of the global development project: Geopolitics, global ecology and the "development climate"', *Third World Quarterly*, 30(1): 247–62.

Meltdown Report (2007, December) *The Nationality of Premier League Players and the Future of English Football*, London, UK: The Professional Footballers' Association, 20 pp.

Messner, M. (1990) 'When bodies are weapons: Masculinity and violence in sport', *International Review for the Sociology of Sport*, 25: 203–20.

Metcalfe, A. (1987) *Canada Learns to Play: The Emergence of Organized Sport, 1807–1914*, Toronto, ON, Canada: McClelland and Stewart.

Meusburger, P. (2001) 'The role of knowledge in the socio-economic transformation of Hungary in the 1990s', in P. Meusburger and H. Jons (eds), *Transformations in Hungary: Essays in Economy and Society*, New York: Physica-Verlag.

Meyer, J.-B. (2001) 'Network approach versus brain drain: Lessons from the diaspora', *International Migration*, 39(5): 91–110.

Miles, S. (2000) *Youth Lifestyles in a Changing World*, Buckingham, UK: Open University Press.

Miller, F. and Redhead, S. (1994) 'Do markets make footballers free?', in J. Bale and J. Maguire (eds), *The Global Sports Arena: Athletic Talent Migration in an Interdependent World*, London, UK: Frank Cass.

Miller, T. (1989) 'World Series sound and vision', *Meanjin*, 48: 591–6.

Miller, T. (2004) 'Manchester, USA?', in D. L. Andrews (ed.), *Manchester United: A Thematic Study* (pp. 241–8), Abingdon, Oxon, UK: Routledge.

Miller, T. (2007) 'Sport, medien und globalisierung', trans. M. Ludwig, in T. Schier (ed.), *Handbuch Medien, Kommunikation Und Sport* (pp. 167–78), Schondorf: Hofmann-Verlag.

Miller, T. (2009) 'Michel Foucault and the critique of sport', in B. Carrington and I. McDonald (eds), *Marxism, Cultural Studies and Sport* (pp. 181–94), London, UK: Routledge.

Miller, T., Lawrence, G., McKay, J., and Rowe, D. (2001) *Globalization and Sport: Playing the World*, London, UK: Sage.

Miller, T., Rowe, D., McKay, J., and Lawrence, G. (2003) 'The over-production of US sports and the new international division of cultural labor', *International Review for the Sociology of Sport*, 38(4): 427–40.

Miller, T., Govil, N., McMurria, J., Maxwell, R., and Wang, T. (2005) *Global Hollywood 2*, London, UK: British Film Institute/Berkeley: University of California Press.

Mintz, S. (1985) *Sweetness and Power: The Place of Sugar in Modern History*, New York: Penguin.

Misa, T. (1987, November) 'The Monday-to-Friday John Kirwan', *North and South*, pp. 52–61.

Mitchell, J. (2003) *Immigration and National Identity in 1970s New Zealand*, PhD dissertation, New Zealand: University of Otago.

'MLB honors Latin impact in 2000 with "Month of the Americas"'. Online. Available HTTP: http://www.majorleaguebaseball.com (accessed 10 November 1999).

'MLB players from Japan'. Online. Available HTTP: http://www.japaneseballplayers.com/en/ (accessed 1 September 2009).

'MLB players from Japan' (in Japanese). Online. Available HTTP: http://www.japanese ballplayers.com/jp/ (accessed 1 September 2009).

Molnar, G. (2005) 'Fighting global uncertainties: A case-study of the post-communist migrations of Hungarian professional footballers', unpublished PhD thesis, Loughborough University.

Molnar, G. (2006) 'Mapping migrations: Hungary related migrations of professional foot-ballers after the collapse of communism', *Soccer and Society*, 7: 463–85.

Molnar, G. (2007) 'Hungarian football: A socio-historical perspective', *Sport in History*, 27: 293–318.

Molnar, G. (2010) 'Re-discovering Hungarianness: The case of elite Hungarian footballers', in P. Dine and S. Crosson (eds), *Sport, Representation and Evolving Identities in Europe*, Witney, UK: Peter Lang.

Molnar, G. and Maguire, J. (2008) 'Hungarian footballers on the move: Issues of and observations on the first migratory phase', *Sport in Society*, 11: 74–89.

Moorhouse, H. F. (1999) 'The economic effects of the traditional transfer system in European professional football', *Football Studies*, 2(1): 90–105.

'More than just work permits to fuss about' (1993, December 25) *Ice Hockey News*.

Morgan, G. (2005, November 11) 'The real best team in the world?', *Western Mail*, p. 20.

Morgan, W. J. (1997) 'Sports and the making of national identities: A moral view', *Journal of the Philosophy of Sport*, 24: 1–20.

Muggleton, D. and Weinzierl, R. (eds) (2003) *The Post-Subcultures Reader*, Oxford, UK: Berg.

Muroi, M. (2009) *Kankoku Puro Yakyu Kansen Gaido and Senshu Meikan 2009* [The Korean Professional Baseball Guide and Players Directory 2009], Tokyo, Japan: Shogakukan.

Murray, B. (1995) *Football: A History of the World Game*, Aldershot, UK: Scolar Press.

Nairn, T. (1977) *The Break-Up of Britain: Crisis and Neo-Nationalism*, London, UK: NLB.

Nakamura, Y. K. (2005) 'The Samurai sword cuts both ways: A transnational analysis of Japanese and US media representations of Ichiro', *International Review for the Sociology of Sport*, 40(4): 467–80.

Nauright, J. (1991) 'Sport, manhood and empire: British responses to the New Zealand rugby tour of 1905', *The International Journal of the History of Sport*, 8(2): 239–55.

Nayak, A. (2003) *Race, Place and Globalization: Youth Cultures in a Changing World*, Oxford, UK: Berg.

Nayak, A. and Kehily, M. (2008) *Gender, Youth and Culture: Young Masculinities and Femininities*, Basingstoke, UK: Palgrave Macmillan.

NBA (2002) www.nba.com/esp.

NBA (2009) www.nba.com/global.

News Corporation (2009, August 5) '4th quarter fiscal 2009 earnings release'. Online Available HTTP: http://www.newscorp.com/news/index.html.

'NFL full of foreign-born players' (1999) www.nfl.com/international.

NFL International (1999) www.nfl.com/international.

NFL International (2002) ww2.nfl.com/international/foreignborn010822.html.

NGSA Newsletter (2001, November 12) 'Skiers/snowboarder profile continues to change', *NGSA Newsletter*, 3(21).

Nomo, H. (1995) *Boku no Torunedo Senki* (My Tornado Record), Tokyo: Shuueisha.

Noy, C. (2004) '"This trip really changed me": Backpackers' narratives of self-change', *Annals of Tourism Research*, 31: 78–102.

Nunn, S. and Rosentraub, M. S. (2003) 'Sports wars: Suburbs and center cities in a zero-sum game', in J. Lewis and T. Miller (eds), *Critical Cultural Policy Studies: A Reader*, Malden, MA: Blackwell.

NZRFU (1994) *Handbook*, Wellington, NZ: New Zealand Rugby Football Union, p. 89.

Obayiuwana, O. (1996) 'Passport to success?', *When Saturday Comes*, 109(March): 37–8.

Obel, C. (1998) 'Local and global publics: Shifting popularity in rugby union and in rugby league', in H. Perkins and G. Cushman (eds), *Time Out? Leisure, Recreation and Tourism in New Zealand and Australia*, Auckland, New Zealand: Longman.

Obel, C. (2001a) 'Unions, leagues and franchises: The social organisation of rugby union in New Zealand', unpublished PhD thesis, Sociology and Anthropology Department, University of Canterbury, UK.

Obel, C. (2001b) 'National responses to the migration of players and coaches in the sport of rugby union', in K. Eunha *et al.* (eds), *Proceedings of the 1st World Congress of Sociology of Sport* (pp. 533–42), Seoul, South Korea: Organizing Committee for the 1st World Congress of Sociology of Sport.

Obel, C. and Austrin, T. (2005) 'The end of "our national game"? Romance, mobilities and the politics of organisation', in G. Ryan (ed.), *Tackling Rugby Myths: Rugby and New Zealand Society 1854–2004*, Dunedin, New Zealand: Otago University Press.

Öberg, S. and Boubnova, H. (1993) 'Ethnicity, nationality and migration potentials in Eastern Europe', in R. King (ed.), *Mass Migration in Europe: The Legacy and the Future*, London, UK: Belhaven Press.

Olin, K. (1984) 'Attitudes towards professional foreign players in Finnish amateur basketball', *International Review for the Sociology of Sport*, 19(4): 273–82.

Oliver, B. (2008, February 3) 'Boy wonder's lost years', *The Observer*.

Orton, K. (2002, July 14) 'A modern league of nations', *Washington Post*.

Østergaard-Nielsen, E. (2003) 'Counting the cost: Denmark's changing migration policies', *International Journal of Urban and Regional Research*, 27(2): 448–54.

Pacific Baseball League (2004) *Blue Book*, Tokyo, Japan: Pacific Baseball League.

Pacific Baseball League (2005) *Blue Book*, Tokyo, Japan: Pacific Baseball League.

Pacific Baseball League (2006) *Blue Book*, Tokyo, Japan: Pacific Baseball League.

Pacific Baseball League (2007) *Blue Book*, Tokyo, Japan: Pacific Baseball League.

Pacific Baseball League (2008) *Blue Book*, Tokyo, Japan: Pacific Baseball League.

Pacific Baseball League (2009) *Blue Book*, Tokyo, Japan: Pacific Baseball League.

Palenski, R., Chester, R. H., and McMillan, N. A. C. (1998) *The Encyclopaedia of New Zealand Rugby* (3rd edn), Auckland, New Zealand: Hodder Moa Beckett.

Pareti, S. (2004, January 1) 'Rugby's Pacific paupers: Island players decry an exclusive club called the IRB', *Pacific Magazine*, 1 January. Online. Available HTTP: http://www. pacificmagazine.net (accessed 28 October 2008).

Passel, J. (2006) *The Size and Characteristics of the Unauthorized Migrant Population in the U.S.*, Washington, DC: Pew Hispanic Center. Online. Available HTTP: http://pewhispanic. org/files/reports/61.pdf (accessed 30 August 2009).

Paul, G. (2007a) *Black Obsession: The All Blacks' Quest for World Cup Success*, Auckland, New Zealand: Exisle Publishing.

Paul, G. (2007b) 'Pacifika players dominating ranks', *The New Zealand Herald*, 4 March. Online. Available HTTP: http://www.nzherald.co.nz/author/story.cfm?a_id=196andobjectid= 10426898 (accessed 5 March 2007).

Paul, G. (2007c) 'Releases worry for Pacific', *The New Zealand Herald*, 11 March. Online. Available HTTP: http://www.nzherald.co.nz/sport/news/article.cfm?c_id=4andobjectid= 10428168 (accessed 11 March 2007).

Pearson, D. (2006, July) *From Empire to Empire: Situating Citizenship in British Settler States*, paper presented at the International Sociological Association World Congress, Durban, South Africa.

Pearson, D. (2008) 'Reframing majoritarian national identities within an antipodean perspective', *Thesis Eleven*, 95: 48–57.

Pelly, D. (2001, December 11) 'Back injury may thwart Dalton', *Daily Telegraph*. Online. Available HTTP: http://www.telegraph.co.uk/sport/3018561/Yachting-Back-injury-may-thwart-Dalton.html (accessed 22 July 2004).

Pepperell, S. (2001, December 8) 'Blake's last adventure', *The Waikato Times*, p. 15.

Pérez, L. (1994) 'Between baseball and bullfighting: The quest for Cuban nationalism: 1868–1898', *Journal of American History*, 81(2): 417–531.

'Permit problems hit imports' (1993, December 11), *Ice Hockey News Review*.

Peron, P. (2008) 'Stefishen back for more'. Online. Available HTTP: http://hockey-fights.com/forum/showtopic.php?tid/511146/post/last/ (accessed 30 August 2009).

Phillips, J. (1987) *A Man's Country? The Image of the Pakeha Male – A History*, Auckland, New Zealand: Penguin Books.

Phillips, J. (2000) 'Epilogue: Sport and future Australasian culture', in J. A. Mangan and J. Nauright (eds), *Sport in Australasian Society: Past and Present* (pp. 323–32), London, UK: Frank Cass.

Pilkington, H. and Johnson, R. (2003) 'Peripheral youth: Relations of identity and power in global/local context', *European Journal of Cultural Studies*, 6: 259–83.

Plahe, J. (2005) *The Global Commodity Chain (GCC) Approach and the Organisational Transformation of Agriculture: A Look into the Increasing Power of Retailers and Branded Merchandisers*, Department of Management Working Paper Series, Monash University.

'Play on' (2009, May 30), *Economist*, p. 79.

'Please . . . can I help?' (1994, October 16), *Ice Hockey News Review*.

Podnieks, A. (1999) *The Great One: The Life and Times of Wayne Gretzky*, Toronto, ON: Doubleday Canada.

Poli, R. (2002) *Le Football en Cote d'Ivoire – Organisation Spatiale et Pratiques Urbaines*, Centre International d'Etudes du Sport, Universite de Neuchâtel.

Poli, R. (2004) 'Les footballeurs africains en Suisse. Victimes de discrimination salariale', *TANGRAM*, 15: 79–84.

Poli, R. (2005a) 'Football players' migration in Europe: A geo-economic approach to Africans' mobility', in J. Magee, A. Bainer, and A. Tomlinson (eds), *The Bountiful Game? Football Identities and Finances*, Aachen, Germany: Meyer and Meyer Sport.

Poli, R. (2005b) 'The football players' trade as a global commodity chain: Transnational networks from Africa to Europe', paper presented in the workshop on Social Networks of Traders and Managers in Africa, Iwalea-Haus, Bayreuth, 4 November 2005.

Poli, R. (2006a) 'Les politiques migratoires dans le football européen. Quotas et naturalisations dans une optique géopolitique', *Histoire et Sociétés*, 18–19: 46–61.

Poli, R. (2006b) 'Migrations and trade of African football players: Historic, geographical and cultural aspects', *Afrika Spectrum*, 41(3): 393–414.

Poli, R. (2006c) 'Africans' status in the European football players' labour market', *Soccer and Society*, 7(2–3): 278–91.

Poli, R. (2007a) 'Migrations de footballeurs et mondialisation: du système-monde aux réseaux sociaux', *Mappemonde*, 88. Online. Available HTTP: http://mappemonde.mgm.fr/num16/articles/art07401.html (accessed 10 October 2009).

Poli, R. (2007b) 'The denationalization of sport: De-ethnicization of the nation and identity deterritorialization', *Sport in Society*, 10: 646–61.

Poli, R. (2008) 'Production de footballeurs, réseaux marchands et mobilités professionnelles dans l'économie globale. Le cas des footballeurs africains en Europe', unpublished thesis, Université de Neuchâtel et de Franche-Comté.

Poli, R. and Dietschy, P. (2006) 'Le football africain entre immobilisme et extraversion', *Politique Africaine*, 102: 173–87.

Poli, R. and Ravanel, L. (2005a) 'Borders of "free" movement in European football. Towards the globalization of players' flows', *Espace-Populations-Societies*, 2: 293–303.

Poli, R. and Ravanel, L. (2005b) 'Les frontières de la « libre » circulation dans le football: européen. Vers une mondialisation des flux de joueurs?', *Espace Population Société*, 2: 293–303.

Poli, R. and Ravenel, L. (2006) *Annual Review of the European Football Players, The Professional Football Players Observatory*, CIES, University of Neuchâtel and ThéMA, University of Franche-Comté (every year since 2006).

Poli, R. and Ravenel, L. (2009) 'Competitive balance and internationalization of squads: Big-5 Leagues and Champions League (1960–2008)', unpublished research report, University of Neuchâtel and Franche-Comté.

Poli, R., Ravenel, L., and Besson, R. (2009) *Annual Review of the European Football Players' Labour Market*, Neuchâtel, Switzerland: CIES.

'Poll results: How many times have you snowboarded in a foreign country?' Online. Available HTTP: http://snowboard.colonies.com/Polls/PollResults.aspx?pollID=36andshouldShowPollResults=True (accessed 1 February 2006).

Ponte, S. (2003) *Quality Conventions and the Governance of Global Value Chains*, paper prepared for conference, Conventions et Institutions, Paris.

Ponting, J., McDonald, M., and Wearing, S. (2005) 'Deconstructing wonderland: Surfing tourism in the Mentawai Islands, Indonesia', *Society and Leisure*, 28: 141–62.

Poole, R. (1999) *Nation and Identity*, New York: Routledge.

Pooley, J. (1981) 'Ethnic soccer clubs in Milwaukee: A study in assimilation', in M. Hart and S. Birrell (eds), *Sport in the Socio-Cultural Process*, Dubuque, IA: Wm. C. Brown.

Potter, T. (2001, December 9) 'Messages urge Blake's team to keep dream alive', *The Sunday Star Times*, p. 2.

Poulton, E. (2004) 'Mediated patriot games: The construction and representation of national identities in the British television production of Euro '96', *International Review for the Sociology of Sport*, 39: 437–55.

Price, D. (2002a, May 3) 'Mavs, Kings globetrotting', *Star-Telegram*.

Price, D. (2002b, June 27) 'NBA goes global', *Star-Telegram*.

Pries, L. (ed.) (2001) *New Transnational Social Spaces: International Migration and Transnational Companies in the Early Twenty-First Century*, London, UK: Routledge.

'Pro Yakyu now'. Online. Available HTTP: http://www.japanesebaseball.com (accessed 1 September 2009).

Radnege, K. (1998) *The Complete Encyclopaedia of Football*, London, UK: Colour Library Direct.

'Raiwalui rejects Fiji appeal' (2003) *One Sport*, 30 September. Online. Available HTTP: http://oneworldcup.nzoom.com/story/224745.html (accessed 27 October 2008).

Real, M. (1989) *Super Media: A Cultural Studies Approach*, Newbury Park, CA: Sage.

Real, M. (1996) *Exploring Media Culture: A Guide*, Thousand Oaks, CA: Sage.

Reaves, J. (2002) *Taking in a Game: A History of Baseball in Asia*, Nebraska, NE: University of Nebraska Press.

Redmond, G. (1993) *Wayne Gretzky: The Great One*, Toronto, ON, Canada: ECW.

Rees, P. (2005) 'World rugby needs Pacific unions to be strong', *Heavensgame*. Online. Available HTTP: http://www.heavensgame.com/index.php?option=com_contentandtask=viewandid=603andItemid=86 (accessed 27 October 2008).

Rees, P. (2009, April 29) 'Toulon bank on £1m Jonny Wilkinson to have Carter effect', *The Guardian*.

Reis, M. (2004) 'Theorizing diaspora: Perspectives on "classical" and "contemporary" diaspora', *International Migration*, 42: 41–60.

Rhein, C. (1994) 'La ségrégation et ses mesures', in J. Brun and C. Rhein (eds), *La ségrégation dans la ville* (pp. 121–61), Paris: L'Harmattan.

Ricci, F. M. (2000) *African Football: Yearbook 2000* (3rd edn), Rome, Italy: Pro Sports.

Richards, T. with Blehm, E. (2003) *P3: Pipes, Parks, and Powder*, New York: HarperCollins.

Richardson, L. (1995) 'The invention of a national game: The struggle for control', *History Now*, 1: 1–8.

Rigauer, B. (1981 [1969]) *Sport and Work*, New York: Columbia University Press.

Rinehart, R. and Sydnor, S. (eds) (2003) *To the Extreme: Alternative Sports, Inside and Out*, New York: State University of New York.

Ritzer, G. (2004) *The McDonaldization of Society* (4th edn), Thousand Oaks, CA: Pine Forge Press.

'Rival plans for new leagues in Europe raise British hackles' (1995, January 27), *The Guardian*.

Roberts, S. (ed.) (1994) *The Ice Hockey Annual 1994–1995*, Hove, UK: Caldra.

Robertson, G., Mash, M., Tickner, L., Bird, J., Curtis, B., and Putnam, T. (1994) *Travellers' Tales: Narratives of Home and Displacement*, London, UK: Routledge.

Robertson, M. and Williams, M. (2004) *Young People, Leisure and Place: Cross-Cultural Perspectives*, New York: Nova Science Publishers.

Robertson, R. (1990) 'Mapping the global condition: Globalization as the central concept', *Theory, Culture and Society*, 7: 15–30.

Robidoux, M. and Trudel, P. (2006) 'Hockey Canada and the bodychecking debate in minor hockey', in D. Whitson and R. Gruneau (eds), *Artificial Ice: Hockey, Culture and Commerce*, Peterborough, UK: Broadview Press.

Robins, K. (1997) 'What in the world is going on?', in P. Du Gay (ed.), *Production of Culture / Cultures of Production*, London, UK: Sage.

Robinson, G. and Corbett, M. (2008, March 25) 'Japanese flock to major league sales pitch', *Financial Times*.

Romanos, J. (2002) *The Judas Game: The Betrayal of New Zealand Rugby*, Wellington, New Zealand: Darius Press.

Rosset, P. (2006) *Food is Different*, Nova Scotia, Canada: Fernwood Publishing.

Rowe, D. (1995) *Popular Cultures: Rock Music, Sport and the Politics of Pleasure*, London, UK: Sage.

Rowe, D. (2003) 'Sport and the repudiation of the global', *International Review for the Sociology of Sport*, 38: 281–94.

Rowe, D. (2004a) *Sport, Culture and the Media: The Unruly Trinity* (2nd edn), Buckingham, UK: Open University Press.

Rowe, D. (ed.) (2004b) *Critical Readings: Sport, Culture and the Media*, Maidenhead, UK: Open University Press.

Rowe, D. and Gilmour, C. (2008) 'Contemporary media sport: De- or re-Westernization?', *International Journal of Sport Communication*, 1(2): 177–94.

Rowe, D. and Gilmour, C. (2009) 'Global sport: Where Wembley Way meets Bollywood Boulevard', *Continuum*, 23(2): 171–82.

Ruck, R. (1991) *The Tropic of Baseball*, Westport, CT: Meckler.

'Rugby Union Players' Association v. Commerce Commission (no. 2)' (1997) *New Zealand Law Review*, 3: 301–29.

Ryan, G. (1993) *Forerunners of the All Blacks: The 1888–89 New Zealand Native Team in Britain, Australia and New Zealand*, Christchurch, New Zealand: Canterbury University Press.

Ryan, G. (2000) 'Anthropological football: Maori and the 1937 Springbok tour of New Zealand', *New Zealand Journal of History*, 34(1): 60–79.

Rydgren, J. (2004) 'Explaining the emergence of radical right-wing populist parties: The case of Denmark', *West European Politics*, 27(3): 474–502.

Salmon, J. (2005, June 19) 'All Black make-up leaves Islanders off colour', *The Observer*, Sport, p. 4.

Satzewich, V. (1990) 'Rethinking post-1945 migration to Canada: Towards a political economy of labour migration', *International Migration*, 28: 327–46.

Sayama, K. (1996) *Jappu Mikado no Nazo – Bei Puro Yakyu Nihonjin Dai Ichigo wo Ou* [The Mystery of 'Jap Mikado': First Japanese in American Professional Baseball], Tokyo, Japan: Bungei Shunju Limited.

Schrag, D. (2009) '"Flagging the nation" in international sport: A Chinese Olympics and a German World Cup', *International Journal of the History of Sport*, 26: 1084–104.

Scraton, S., Magee, J., and Caudwell, J. (eds) (2008) *Women, Football and Europe: Histories, Equity and Experience*, London, UK: Meyer and Meyer.

Selassie, H. (2002, June 4) 'Warming up to soccer', *Village Voice*.

'Select snow brands to show at ASR' (2004, December 2) *Transworld Business, Surf, Skate, Snow*. Online. Available HTTP: http://www.twsbiz.com (accessed 9 November 2005).

Sennett, R. (1998) *The Corrosion of Character*, New York: W.W. Norton & Company.

Sheller, M. and Urry, J. (2006) 'The new mobilities paradigm', *Environment and Planning A*, 38: 207–26.

Sherlock, M. (2008, November 19) 'Downturn could offer sporting opportunity', *Sport Business*.

Sherowski, J. (2004, April) 'Notes from the down-underground', *Transworld Snowboarding*, pp. 106–17.

Sherowski, J. (2005, January) 'What it means to be a snowboarder', *Transworld Snowboarding*, pp. 160–9.

Sherwin, B. (2002) *Ichiro – Meja wo Shinkan saseta Otoko* (Ichiro: The Man who Shook the MLB), Tokyo, Japan: Asahi Shinbun Sha.

Shiller, R. J. (2000) *Irrational Exuberance*, Princeton, NJ: Princeton University Press.

Silk, M. (2005) 'Sporting ethnography: Philosophy, methodology and reflection', in D. Andrews, D. Mason, and M. Silk (eds), *Qualitative Methods in Sports Studies*, Oxford, UK: Berg.

Silk, M. and Andrews, D. (2001) 'Beyond a boundary? Sport, transnational advertising, and the reimagining of national culture', *Journal of Sport and Social Issues*, 25(2): 180–201.

Silk, M. L., Andrews, D., and Cole, C. L. (eds) (2005) *Sport and Corporate Nationalisms*, Oxford, UK: Berg.

Singh, I. (2006, November 14) 'Lam prefers individual teams', *Fiji Times*, p. 30.

Skelton, T. and Valentine, G. (eds) (1998) *Cool Places: Geographies of Youth Cultures*, London, UK: Routledge.

'Ski tourism on the rise' (2007, August 14) Online. Available HTTP: http://news.holiday hypermarket.co.uk/Ski-Tourism-On-The-Rise-18244376.html (accessed 10 August 2009).

Skogvang, B. O. (2006) 'Elite football – A field of changes', PhD thesis, Norwegian School of Sport Sciences, Department of Cultural and Social Studies, Oslo.

Skogvang, B. O. (2008) 'African footballers in Europe', in S. Jackson and C. Hallinan (eds), *Social and Cultural Diversity in a Sporting World: Research in the Sociology of Sport* (vol. 5, pp. 33–50), Bingley, UK: Emerald Group Publishing Limited.

Slater, D. (2004) *Geopolitics and the Post-Colonial: Rethinking North–South Relations*, Malden, MA: Blackwell.

Slot, O. (2005, June 29) 'All Blacks thriving on power of four', *The Times*, Sport, p. 73.

Smith, A. D. (1991) *National Identity*, Harmondsworth, UK: Penguin.

Smith, A. D. (1995) *Nations and Nationalism in a Global Era*, London, UK: Polity Press.

Smith, D. and Williams, G. (1980) *Fields of Praise: The Official History of the Welsh Rugby Union 1881–1981*, Cardiff, UK: University of Wales Press.

Smith, Michael D. (1993) *Violence and Sport*, Toronto, ON: Butterworths.

Sobchak, V. (1997) 'Baseball in the post-American cinema, or life in the minor leagues', in A. Baker and T. Boyd (eds), *Out of Bounds: Sports, Media, and the Politics of Identity*, Bloomington, IN: Indiana University Press.

'Society for American Baseball Research'. Online. Available HTTP: http://www.sabr.org (accessed 30 August 2009).

Solomon, G. (2002, January 31) 'Barcelona, NFL agree to a 3-year partnership', *Washington Post*.

Solomon, J. (2002, April 21) 'The sports market is looking soggy', *New York Times*.

Solomos, J. (2003) *Race and Racism in Britain* (3rd edn), London, UK: Macmillan Press.

Souster, M. (2001, November 10) 'Tuigamala issues stark warning over future of Samoa', *The Times*.

Spoonley, P. (1990) 'Polynesian immigrant workers in New Zealand', in C. Moore, J. Leckie, and D. Munro (eds), *Labour in the South Pacific*, Townsville, Australia: James Cook University of North Queensland.

Spoonley, P., Bedford, R., and Macpherson, C. (2003) 'Divided loyalties and fractured sovereignty: Transnationalism and the nation-state in Aotearoa/New Zealand', *Journal of Ethnic and Migration Studies*, 29: 27–46.

'SportsLine USA and CricInfo launch 1999 World Cup site' (1999, May 13), *Business Wire*.

Spracklen, K. and Spracklen, C. (2008) 'Negotiations of being and becoming: Minority ethnic rugby league players in the Cathar Country of France', *International Review for the Sociology of Sport*, 43: 201–18.

Stalker, P. (2000) *Workers Without Frontiers: The Impact of Globalisation on International Migration*, Geneva: International Labour Office.

Stanely, K. (2001) *Cold Comfort: Young Separated Refugees in England*, London, UK: Save the Children.

Statistics New Zealand (2008) *QuickStats About Pacific Peoples: 2006 Census*, Wellington, New Zealand: Statistics New Zealand.

Stead, D. and Maguire, J. (1997) *The Northern Invaders: The Involvement and Experiences of Nordic/Scandinavian Players in English Elite Soccer*. Unpublished paper. Presented at the Second Annual Congress of the European College of Sport Science, Copenhagen, Denmark, 20–23 August.

Stead, D. and Maguire, J. (2000a) 'No boundaries to ambition – soccer labour migration and the case of Nordic/Scandinavian players in England', in J. Bangsbo (ed.), *Soccer and Science in an Interdisciplinary Perspective*, Copenhagen, Denmark: University of Copenhagen Press.

Stead, D. and Maguire, J. (2000b) '"Rite de passage" or passage to riches? The motivation and objectives of Nordic/Scandinavian players in English League Soccer', *Journal of Sport and Social Issues*, 24(1): 36–60.

Steele, D. (2002, May 3) 'It's finally a global game', *San Francisco Chronicle*.

Stein, G. (1997) *Power Plays: An Inside Look at the Big Business of the National Hockey League*, Toronto, ON, Canada: Birch Lane.

Stoller, P. (1997) 'Globalizing method: The problems of doing ethnography in transnational spaces', *Anthropology and Humanism*, 21: 81–94.

Sua'rez-Orozco, M. M. (2001) 'Global shifts: U.S. immigration and the cultural impact of demographic change. An address', in J. S. Little and R. K. Triest (eds), *Seismic Shifts: The Economic Impact of Demographic Change*, Boston, MA: Federal Reserve Bank of Boston.

Sugden, J. and Bairner, A. (1993) *Sport, Sectarianism and Society in a Divided Ireland*, Leicester, UK: Leicester University Press.

Sugden, J. and Tomlinson, A. (1998) *FIFA and the Contest for World Football: Who Rules the Peoples' Game?* Cambridge, UK: Polity Press.

Sugden, J. and Tomlinson, A. (2000) 'Football, ressentiment and resistance in the break-up of the former Soviet Union', *Culture, Sport, Society*, 3: 89–108.

Takahashi, Y. and Horne, J. (2004) 'Japanese football players and the sport talent migration business', in W. Manzenreiter and J. Horne (eds), *Football Goes East: The Business and Culture of the People's Game in East Asia* (pp. 69–86), London, UK: Routledge.

Takahashi, Y. and Horne, J. (2006) 'Moving with the bat and ball: Preliminary reflections on the movement of Japanese baseball labour', *International Review for the Sociology of Sport*, 41(1): 7–88.

Tataw, T. (2001) 'Human traffic: Cameroon', *African Soccer*, 66(May): 13.

Taylor, M. (2006) 'Global players? Football, migration and globalization, c. 1930–2000', *Historical Social Research*, 31(1): 7–30.

Taylor, M. and Lanfranchi, P. (2001) *Moving With the Ball: The Migration of Professional Footballers*, Oxford, UK: Berg.

'The global business of sports television' (2005, 17 October), *Güexpress*.

'The good . . . the bad . . . and the nuts' (1994, August 20), *Ice Hockey News Review*.

'The world's fare?' (2002, January 29), *Times-Picayune*.

Therborn, G. (2000) 'Globalisations: Dimensions, historical waves, regional effects, normative governance', *International Sociology*, 15: 151–70.

Théry, H. (2006) 'Futebol et hiérarchies urbaines au Brésil', *Mappemonde*, 81. Online. Available HTTP: http://mappemonde.mgm.fr/num9/articles/art06103.html (accessed 13 October).

Thorpe, H. (2006) 'Beyond "decorative sociology": Contextualizing female surf, skate and snow boarding', *Sociology of Sport Journal*, 23: 205–28.

Thorpe, H. (2007) 'Snowboarding', in D. Booth and H. Thorpe (eds), *Berkshire Encyclopedia of Extreme Sport*, Berkshire, UK: Great Barrington.

Thorpe, H. (2008a) 'Extreme sports in China', in F. Hong, D. Mackay, and K. Christensen (eds), *China Gold: China's Quest for Global Power and Olympic Glory*, Berkshire, UK: Great Barrington.

Thorpe, H. (2008b) 'Foucault, technologies of self, and the media: Discourses of femininity in snowboarding culture', *Journal of Sport and Social Issues*, 32: 199–229.

Thorpe, H. (2009a) 'Psychology of extreme sports', in T. Ryba, R. Schinke, and G. Tenenbaum (eds), *The Cultural Turn in Sport Psychology*, Morgantown, WV: Fitness Information Technology.

Thorpe, H. (2009b) 'Bourdieu, feminism and female physical culture: Gender reflexivity and the habitus–field complex', *Sociology of Sport Journal*, 26: 491–516.

Tiesler, N. C. and Coelho, J. N. (2007) 'The paradox of the Portuguese game: The omnipresence of football and the absence of spectators at matches', *Soccer and Society*, 8(4): 578–600.

Tilly, C. (1990) 'Transplanted networks', in V. Yans-McLaughlin (ed.), *Immigration Reconsidered: History, Sociology, and Politics*, Oxford, UK: Oxford University Press.

Tobin, J. (1978) 'A proposal for international monetary reform', *Eastern Economic Journal*, 4.

Tomlinson, J. (1999) *Globalization and Culture*, Cambridge, UK: Polity.

Trumper, R. and Tomic, P. (1999) 'Representing neoliberalism: Tennis, fútbol, and the Chilean Jaguar', *Race and Class*, 40(4): 45–63.

Tshimanga, B. E. (2001) *Le Commerce et la Traite des Footballeurs Africains et Sud-Américains en Europe* [The Trade and Trafficking of African and South American Footballers in Europe], Paris: L'Harmattan.

Tuck, J. (2003a) 'Making sense of emerald commotion: Rugby union, national identity and Ireland', *Identities: Global Studies in Power and Culture*, 10: 495–515.

Tuck, J. (2003b) 'The men in white: Reflections on rugby union, the media and Englishness', *International Review for the Sociology of Sport*, 38: 177–99.

Tuck, J. and Maguire, J. (1999) 'Making sense of global patriot games: Rugby players' perceptions of national identity politics', *Football Studies*, 2: 26–54.

Turner, B. (1995) *Anton Oliver Inside*, Auckland, New Zealand: Moa Hodder.

Turner, G. (1997) 'Media texts and messages', in S. Cunningham and G. Turner (eds), *The Media in Australia: Industries, Texts, Audiences* (2nd edn, pp. 381–93), St Leonards, NSW: Allen and Unwin.

Urry, J. (2003) *Global Complexity*, Cambridge, UK: Polity.

VMC – Virtual Museum of Canada (n.d.) *Overtime – How They See Us – France: Encounters with a Different Sport Culture*. Online. Available HTTP: http://www.virtualmuseum.ca/Exhibitions/Hockey/English/Seeus/seeus.html (accessed 15 August 2009).

Voas, D. and Williamson, P. (2000) 'The scale of dissimilarity: Concepts, measurement and an application to socio-economic variation across England and Wales', *Transactions of the Institute of British Geographers*, 25(4): 465–81.

Vogt, J. (1976) 'Wandering: Youth and travel behaviour', *Annals of Tourism Research*, 4: 25–41.

Voigt-Graf, C. (2005) 'The construction of transnational spaces by Indian migrants in Australia', *Journal of Ethnic and Migration Studies*, 31(2): 365–84.

Wallace, C. and Stola, D. (2001) 'Introduction: Patterns of migration in Central Europe', in C. Wallace and D. Stola (eds), *Patterns of Migration in Central Europe*, Basingstoke, UK: Palgrave.

Wallerstein, I. (1974) *The Modern World System*, New York: Academic Press.

Wallerstein, I. (1979) *The Capitalist World Economy*, Cambridge, UK: Cambridge University Press.

Wallerstein, I. (1984) *The Politics of the World Economy*, Cambridge, UK: Cambridge University Press.

Wallerstein, I. (2004) *World-System Analysis: An Introduction*, London, UK: Duke University Press.

Wallerstein, I. (2006) *Comprendre le monde: introduction à l'analyse des systèmes-monde*, Paris: La Découverte.

Waters, M. (1995) *Globalization*, London, UK: Routledge.

Webb, S. H. (2009, March 12) 'Soccer is ruining America', *Wall Street Journal*.

Weber, M. (1947) *The Theory of Social and Economic Organization*, New York: Oxford University Press.

Weigelt, Y. and Knanoh, K. (2006) 'Elegant and on the offense – women's football in Europe', *Football Science*, 3: 21–8.

Wells, S. (2008, April 7) 'Johnny Foreigner has taught US basketball a painful lesson', *The Guardian*.

Westcot, J. (2006, July/August) 'Onset', *New Zealand Snowboarding*, 18.

Westerbeek, H. and Smith, A. (2003) *Sport Business in the Global Marketplace*, New York: Palgrave Macmillan.

Westgate, M. H. (2009) 'Nothing quite like the Lions'. Online. Available HTTP: http://www.lionsrugby.com/news/8425.php (accessed 3 July 2009).

Whannel, G. (2002) *Media Sports Stars: Masculinities and Moralities*, London, UK: Routledge.

Wheaton, B. (2002) 'Babes on the beach, women in the surf: Researching gender, power and difference in the windsurfing culture', in J. Sugden and A. Tomlinson (eds), *Power Games: A Critical Sociology of Sport*, London, UK: Routledge.

Wheaton, B. (2004a) 'Selling out? The globalization and commercialization of lifestyle sports', in L. Allison (ed.), *The Global Politics of Sport: The Role of Global Institutions in Sport*, London, UK: Routledge.

Wheaton, B. (ed.) (2004b) *Understanding Lifestyle Sports: Consumption, Identity and Difference*, London, UK: Routledge.

Wheaton, B. and Tomlinson, A. (1998) 'The changing gender order in sport? The case of windsurfing subcultures', *Journal of Sport and Social Issues*, 22: 251–72.

White, A. (2004) 'Rugby union football in England: Civilizing processes and the de-institutionalization of amateurism', in E. Dunning, D. Malcolm, and I. Waddington (eds), *Sport Histories: Figurational Studies of the Development of Modern Sports*, London, UK: Routledge.

Whiting, R. (1977) *The Chrysanthemum and the Bat*, New York: Dodd, Mead and Co.

Whiting, R. (1989) *You Gotta Have Wa*, New York: Vintage.

Whiting, R. (1999) *Hi izuru kuni no 'Dorei Yakyu' Nikumareta Dairinin Dan Nomura no Tatakai* [Baseball Slavery in the Land of the Rising Sun], Tokyo, Japan: Bungei Shunju Ltd.

Whiting, R. (2004) *The Meaning of Ichiro: The New Wave from Japan and the Transformation of Our National Pastime*, New York: Warner.

Whiting, R. (2005) *The Samurai Way of Baseball: The New Wave from Japan and the Transformation of Our National Pastime*, New York: Warner.

Whitnell, I. (1999) 'International players impact the NBA'. Online. Available HTTP: http://www.nba.com

Whitson, D. (1997) 'Hockey and Canadian identities: From frozen rivers to revenue streams', in D. Taras and B. Rasporich (eds), *A Passion for Identity: An Introduction to Canadian Studies* (3rd edn), Scarborough, ON, Canada: ITP Nelson.

Whitson, D. and Gruneau, R. (1997) 'The (real) integrated circus: Political economy, popular culture, and "major league" sport', in W. Clement (ed.), *Understanding Canada: Building on the New Canadian Political Economy*, Montreal, QC, Canada: McGill-Queen's University Press.

Whitson, D. and Gruneau, R. (2006) 'Introduction', in D. Whitson and R. Gruneau (eds), *Artificial Ice: Hockey, Culture and Commerce*, Peterborough, UK: Broadview Press.

Widdicombe, S. and Wooffitt, R. (1995) *The Language of Youth Subcultures: Social Identity in Action*, London, UK: Harvester Wheatsheaf.

Wieting, S. and Polumbaum, J. (2001) 'Epilogue: The future of exchange between local culture and global trends', *Culture, Sport, Society*, 4(2): 237–54.

Wilbon, M. (2002, September 6) 'Basketball's new world order', *Washington Post*.

Wiles, J. (2008) 'Sense of home in a transnational social space: New Zealanders in London', *Global Networks*, 8: 116–37.

Williams, G. (1991) *1905 and All That: Essays on Rugby Football, Sport and Welsh Society*, Llandysul, UK: Gomer Press.

Williams, J. (2007) *A Beautiful Game: International Perspectives on Women's Football*, London, UK: Berg.

Williams, J. and Copes, H. (2005) '"How edge are you?" Constructing authentic identities and subcultural boundaries in straightedge internet forums', *Symbolic Interaction*, 28: 67–89.

Wilson, J. (1994) 'Management and labour', in *Sport, Society and the State: Playing by the Rules*, Detroit, MI: Wayne State University Press.

Winegardner, M. (1999, October 3) 'Los Naturales', *New York Times Magazine*.

Wise, M. and St John, W. (2003, January 10) 'Zealand cries betrayal as skipper races for Swiss', *The New York Times*. Online. Available HTTP: http://www.nytimes.com/2003/01/10/sports/yacht-racing-new-zealand-cries-betrayal-as-skipper-races-for-swiss.html (accessed 23 July 2004).

Wong, L. and Trumper, R. (2002) 'Global celebrity athletes and nationalism', *Journal of Sport and Social Issues*, 26: 168–94.

Woo Lee, J. and Maguire, J. (2009) 'Global festivals through a national prism: The global–national nexus in South Korean media coverage of the 2004 Athens Olympic Games', *International Review for the Sociology of Sport*, 44: 5–24.

Woodcock, T. and Ball, P. (1985) *Inside Soccer*, London, UK: Queen Anne Press.

Woollard, R. (2001, November 10) *Test Great Jones Calls for Rule Change as Decimated Samoa Face Irish*, Agence France Presse.

World Bank (2006, October 30) *Dominican Republic Poverty Assessment: Caribbean Country Management Unit*, World Bank.

Wren, K. (2001) 'Cultural racism: Something rotten in the State of Denmark', *Social and Cultural Geography*, 2(2): 141–62.

Wu, F. H. (2002) *Yellow: Race in America Beyond Black and White*, New York: Basic Books.

Yeoh, B. and Willis, K. (2005) 'Singaporean and British transmigrants in China and the cultural politics of "Contact Zones"', *Journal of Ethnic and Migration Studies*, 31(2): 269–85.

Young, K., White, P., and McTeer, W. (1994) 'Body talk: Male athletes reflect on sport, injury, and pain', *Sociology of Sport Journal*, 11: 175–94.

Zavos, S. (2002) *Ka Mate! Ka Mate!: New Zealand's Conquest of British Rugby*, Auckland, New Zealand: Viking.

Index

Contents

"We all know that we need to change our habits to protect the planet. This book really demonstrates how doing that can also be good for business. For small businesses operating on small budgets – every business practice needs to deliver value. This guide to 'Sustainable Growth' shows us how."

— Michelle Gamble, CEO
Marketing Angels www.marketingangels.com.au

"As much a valuable handbook on crucial environmental issues as a sustainable growth manual for small business, but certainly a comprehensive database which opens the door for SMEs that want to save money, reposition their brand and prepare for the 'beyond business as usual' era.

Dee has provided up to date information, relevant Australian and international examples and identified the importance of leadership and who is providing it.

'Sustainable Growth' explains how reducing resource use, managing waste, transport and buildings' systems and making smart energy choices will both manage your 'bottom line' and build your reputation with customers and suppliers."

— Rob Gell, environmental geographer and sustainability consultant
Director, World Wind Pty Ltd. www.worldwind.com.au

"Plain-talking and straight-shooting, Dee's book covers all the 'sustainability for SMEs' bases in an effortless, easy-to-read, manual-style format. Comprehensive, sensible and convincing, it's an inspirational book for any small business owner that thinks they don't have the time or expertise to become sustainable.

Throughout the book, Dee zeros in on the legislation, organisations, regulations, myths, technical terms and concepts that are specifically relevant to SME owners, which will no doubt see 'Sustainable Growth' get passed from business-owner to business-owner around the block."

— Kate Hennessy, Features writer
Nett Magazine www.nett.com.au

SMALL BUSINESS, Big Opportunity

SUSTAINABLE GROWTH

Jon Dee

Also by Sensis in this series:
Small Business, Big Opportunity
by Rob Hartnett
Published 2006

Small Business, Big Opportunity:
Winning the right customers through smart marketing and advertising
by Rob Hartnett and Karina Keisler
Published 2008 by Sensis Pty Ltd (Second edition)

Small Business, Big Opportunity: Sustainable Growth
by Jon Dee
Published 2010 by Sensis Pty Ltd

Small Business, Big Opportunity: Sustainable Growth
by Jon Dee
Published 2010 by Sensis Pty Ltd (Second edition)

Cover and text design/art direction: Kristian Parrott, OMG! Creative
Illustrations: Kristian Parrott, OMG! Creative
Photography: Cameron Murray Photography
Editor: Equilibrium OMG
Editor: Jillian Bowen
Printed and bound in Australia by Vega Press
Typeset in Optima 9pt/13pt by Jeremy Norgren, Velocity Graphics

ISBN 978-0-9807228-1-9

Published by Sensis
ABN 30 007 423 912
222 Lonsdale Street, Melbourne, Victoria 3000

Sensis commissioned Jon Dee to author this guide and is proud to present this free resource as part of its commitment to sustainable business practices.

Message from Bruce Akhurst

Chief Executive Officer, Sensis

Welcome to the second print run of *Small Business, Big Opportunity: Sustainable Growth*, a free resource for small and medium enterprises in Australia.

We first launched the *Sustainable Growth* book in May 2010 and distributed nearly all 50,000 copies in the first six months! We decided to print extra copies because we wanted to continue spreading the word about environmentally sustainable business practices. Also, the growth and prosperity of the SME sector is key to our success. By supporting this sector to operate more efficiently, we're investing in the long-term prosperity of new and existing customers.

At Sensis, we have been helping Australians find, buy and sell for more than 130 years through our Yellow Pages® and White Pages® directories, which generates significant economic value. Our products play a vital role in delivering customers to small businesses throughout Australia and as such play an important role in contributing to Australia's economic prosperity.

Today, Sensis' multichannel network spans across print, online, mobile, over the phone, and new devices including the iPhone, iPad, Android phone and Telstra's T-Hub®. Our content is available via search engines including Google™, Bing and Yahoo!, and information can be shared from online to mobile and social networking sites. Our network connects people with businesses, services, government departments, community organisations, individuals and local information, anywhere, anytime and in any way people choose.

In the same way we recognise the importance of connecting people with information, we also understand that sustainability needs to be at the heart of our corporate strategy, guiding our behaviour and daily operational decisions. This means how we do things at Sensis is just as important as what we do.

We're proud of our sustainability achievements, such as the carbon neutral certification of our Yellow Pages® and White Pages® print and online directories through the Australian Government's Greenhouse Friendly™ program.* The carbon emissions created through the production of our directory products from 1 February 2010 will be offset through accredited providers and projects in Australia.

We made environmental sustainability the topic of this book to help small businesses understand how to save resources and become more sustainable. *Sustainable Growth* follows the popular *Small Business, Big Opportunity* advertising and marketing editions we published in 2006 and 2008. We have proudly given away 130,000 copies to SMEs all over the country free of charge.

You can download both books online at www.about.sensis.com.au/small-business along with other useful resources for your business.

On behalf of us all at Sensis, I wish you every success with your business.

Kind regards,

Bruce Akhurst

Bruce Akhurst

---

*   The Greenhouse Friendly™ program transitioned to the National Carbon Offset Standard, Carbon Neutral Program on 1 July 2010.

Introduction from Jon Dee

Founder and Managing Director, Do Something!

Why should you read this book? After all, you're incredibly busy and your first priority is to look after your customers and your business' bottom line.

If that's what you're thinking, then this book is for you. It has been written to help Australian businesses, especially small and medium businesses, increase their efficiency and productivity. Caught up in daily management, most of us are too busy to explore the many ways we can do more with less. But consider this: in many cases, using fewer resources will save your business money. So you can help the environment, support your community and make more money all at the same time.

Business sustainability can:

- enhance operational efficiency
- improve productivity
- save you money.

It's not just about helping to create a sustainable environment; it's also about maintaining a sustainable business and a sustainable society. Businesses need to take into account the expectations, standards and laws of the communities in which they operate. As such, this book shows you that being a sustainable business is about building sustainable relationships with your employees, customers, business partners and communities.

The move to sustainability in business is gathering momentum across the world and Australian SMEs are discovering that companies already on the path to sustainability increasingly prefer to do business with other sustainable companies. That's why understanding sustainability has become a vital part of continuous business development.

This book is also about positioning your business for the future. The world is starting to put a price on carbon pollution and your customers will start to prefer doing business with companies that are sustainable. If you don't prepare and adjust for these changes, then the opportunities for your business could be severely undermined.

Your business has the potential to make a real and positive difference to the environment and at the same time enhance its bottom line. *Small Business, Big Opportunity: Sustainable Growth* shows you how. In many cases, the tips and strategies in this book do not require significant time, money or resource investment.

For the modern and efficient business it's not a case of having a successful company OR a healthy environment. In a truly sustainable world, you must have both.

Jon Dee

Understanding the bottom line

'It makes good business sense
to pay attention to the social and
environmental bottom line.'

1

Sustainability: a turning point for your business

Sustainability is defined as 'development that meets the needs of the present without compromising the ability of future generations to meet their own needs.'[1] Sustainability is simply ensuring that economic, environmental and social developments go hand in hand.

1   Report of the *World Commission On Environment And Development: Our Common Future,* The Brundtland Commission, United Nations, 1987

The three elements of sustainability

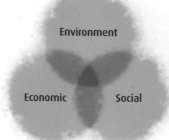

Being sustainable means taking into account the impact your business has on the environment and communities in which it operates. By paying attention to the social and environmental bottom line, you can run your business in a more efficient and effective way. This can have a positive impact on your financial bottom line and it makes good business sense.

Sustainability expert John Elkington coined the term 'triple bottom line' and argued that there should be three bottom lines:[2]

1. The 'profit' bottom line which is a measure of the traditional 'profit and loss' financial bottom line.

2. The 'people' bottom line which is a measure of how socially responsible a business has been.

3. The 'planet' bottom line which is a measure of how sustainable and environmentally responsible the business has been.

This book focuses mostly on helping businesses to understand environmental sustainability and how to adapt it to your business so you can start making changes and saving money by using fewer resources straight away.

All of us understand the basic concept of living within our means. If we spend more than we earn then at some point we hit the wall financially. However, when it comes to the environment and our use of its resources, the people of the world are not living within their means.

According to the Global Footprint Network, we currently use the equivalent of 1.4 planets to provide the resources we use and to absorb the waste we produce.[3] This is not sustainable. Using more resources than the planet can generate is called an 'ecological overshoot'.

---

2   *Cannibals With Forks: The Triple Bottom Line Of 21st Century Business.* John Elkington, Capstone, 1997

3   See www.footprintnetwork.org

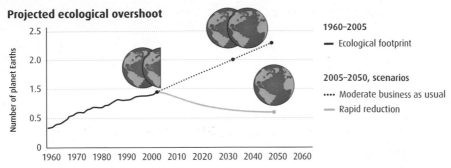

Projected ecological overshoot

1960–2005
— Ecological footprint

2005–2050, scenarios
•••• Moderate business as usual
— Rapid reduction

Source: Global Footprint Network[4]

Based on estimates from the United Nations on resource use and population, the Global Footprint Network predicts that between 2035 and 2050 we will reach the point where we need the equivalent of two planets to support us. If you ran your business the way humanity runs the planet, you'd go bust very quickly. Indeed, on its current trajectory, one could say that humanity is well on the way to environmental insolvency.

The fundamental issue is that as the world's population increases and consumerism continues to grow, the demand for the planet's limited resources will also increase.

In 1950, global population stood at 2.55 billion people. In 2010 it is more than 6.8 billion and by 2020 it is estimated that it will be 7.6 billion and will exceed 9 billion in 2050.[5]

World population growth since 1950

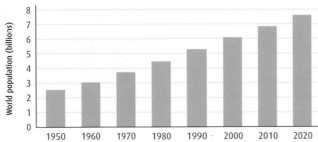

Source: US Bureau of the Census Total Midyear Population for the World.
See www.census.gov

4   See www.footprintnetwork.org
5   Total Midyear Population for the World. See www.census.gov (US Census Bureau)

The 1950s signalled the beginning of a consumer spending boom that started in the USA and quickly spread across the globe. This consumer-led boom generated major improvements in the quality of people's lives but it also changed the way we interacted with, and impacted on, the environment.

Case study: Sensis – Sustainability Strategy and Green Office Champions

The team at Sensis believe *how* they do business is just as important as what they do. They are committed to a sustainable future, which means they make decisions that consider the environment and community impact, as well as the cost. Sustainability is now integral to everything Sensis does.

Sensis introduced the Green Office program in 2003 to encourage employees across the country to make simple changes in the office to lessen the company's impact on the environment.

Green Office Champions around the business encourage their co-workers to 'Switch Off', 'Use Less' and 'Recycle'. They have implemented programs such as the 'Turn it off' campaign, where they undertook an audit of computer monitors after hours and left a small reward for people who had switched their monitors off. This campaign generated talk among employees the next day and provided an incentive for people to turn their monitors off at the end of the day. This not only saves Sensis money, it also reduces the company's environmental footprint.

Today, it means that the world is living on 'environmental credit'. At some point, future generations are going to have to pay a price for the over use of our natural resources. Indeed, our current use of oil could also lead to us running out of easily accessible fuel.

The number of vehicles purchased each year has increased from less than 10 million in the 1950s to more than 50 million in 2007.[6] At the same time, oil consumption has increased by tens of millions of barrels per day.[7] In addition to using up the world's limited supply of oil, this has led to increased exhaust emissions that harm humans and contribute to global warming.

This is the only planet we've got and as businesses, we can play a key role in making sustainable use of the resources that it gives us. A failure to do so is a failure of common business sense.

Sustainability and your business

Managing your business sustainably means managing it in a way that maximises the bottom line but optimises environmental, economic and social benefits for society as a whole.

The initiatives which sit under such a sustainability strategy are what many large businesses call 'corporate responsibility', 'corporate social responsibility' or 'corporate citizenship'. It's about businesses taking into account the needs and expectations of the environment and communities in which they operate.

Business is changing

A 2008 IBM worldwide survey[8] of senior executives highlights this business shift towards sustainability. 68 per cent of business respondents said they were implementing sustainability "as an opportunity and platform for growth" and more than 50 per cent said their companies' sustainability activities were giving them an advantage over their top competitors.

This is an extremely positive development. But for any such sustainability strategy to succeed, it also has to be backed and driven by the leaders of the business.

Despite this positive shift, nearly two-thirds of businesses questioned by IBM admitted they didn't fully understand their customers' concerns around sustainability. Understanding and responding to your customers on this issue is vital for your business relationships. As it currently stands, only 17 per cent of the IBM survey respondents said they really engaged and collaborated with customers regarding their sustainability activities.

6   See www.worldwatch.org
7   See www.earth-policy.org
8   *Attaining Sustainable Growth Through Corporate Social Responsibility,* IBM Institute for Business Value, IBM, 2008. See www.ibm.com/ibvcsrstudy

The report also highlighted the need to involve employees in any sustainability initiatives. A key reason for this is your customers will increasingly be asking your employees about the actions your business is taking for the community and the environment. Properly educated, your employees can be wonderful ambassadors for your business. However, the IBM survey showed that only 27 per cent of businesses engaged their employees on their sustainability initiatives.

KPMG's international survey about Corporate Social Responsibility reporting

In 2008, KPMG interviewed the 100 largest companies by revenue in 22 countries about their corporate social responsibility reporting. In total, 2200 companies were surveyed.

KPMG found that 80 per cent of the world's 250 largest companies now published CSR reports. This compared with only 45 per cent in Australia.

However, Australia's 2008 CSR reporting rate was nearly double that of 2005, showing real growth in this area of corporate accountability.

The main drivers for corporate social responsibility reporting were reported to be:

- ethical and economic considerations
- reputation or brand
- innovation and learning
- employee motivation.

In his introduction to the report, Lord Hastings, KPMG International's Head of Citizenship and Diversity stated that CSR reporting is now "becoming the norm instead of the exception within the world's largest companies."

KPMG in Australia has developed a good practice guide for companies and organisations who want to prepare such sustainability reports. Go to www.kpmg.com.au to download a copy.

What do Australians think about businesses and sustainability?

There is a large range of research and examples that shows Australians want companies to be sustainable and want products and services that are environmentally sound.

Australians are also sceptical; companies claiming to be sustainable need to be honest and open in their communication.

How big is the SME sector in Australia?[9]

According to the Australian Bureau of Statistics (ABS), the SME sector accounts for 73 per cent of trading businesses in Australia. It employs more than 4 million people or 42 per cent of total employed persons. These business entities are broken down as follows:

CATEGORY	EMPLOYEES	NUMBER
Micro-enterprises	0–4	1,699,277
Small firms	5–19	228,313
Medium-sized firms	20–199	78,304

It is estimated that SMEs contribute 46 per cent of the value of Australia's domestic production.

In 2008, Unilever Australia commissioned AMR Interactive Research and Newspoll to look at Australians' attitudes towards corporations and sustainability. It found:[10]

- 90% wanted Australian businesses to invest more in sustainable practices
- 72% thought companies had a broad responsibility to act responsibly
- 81% thought companies could still make a profit while being environmentally responsible and taking the welfare of their workers into consideration
- 64% thought companies needed to focus on sustainability to maintain their future profits

9   See www.abs.gov.au (ABS Sources: Cat. No. 8165.0, Cat. No.1321.0, Cat. No. 8155.0, Cat. No. 6202.0, Cat. No. 81550.0)

10   *Sustainable Australia?,* Unilever, AMR and Newspoll, 2009. See www.unilever.com.au

- 69% believed that businesses needed to prove their sustainability credentials in order to maintain future profits
- 75% believed there was a need for more sustainable products
- 37% said they were sceptical about the sustainability claims found on products
- 71% said they hadn't bought a certified or sustainable product because they hadn't noticed them.

The Net Balance / Australian Fieldwork Solutions (AFS) SME Sustainability Index

The Net Balance / AFS SME Sustainability Index was compiled from interviews with 800 decision makers from across 14 industries, with companies that employ five to 199 people.[11]

When asked which challenges they considered a major concern for their businesses, compliance and economic sustainability issues scored highest:

- maintaining revenues – 74%
- finding the right talent for your industry – 70%
- meeting government regulations – 55%.

However, the results also suggest that some Australian SMEs were not yet fully aware of the cost saving benefits that come from improving the efficiencies of their operations. 6 out of 10 SMEs did not consider energy efficiency a major concern when it came to saving money, yet this is one of the easier money-saving actions businesses can implement as part of their sustainability strategy.

There's an old saying that 'waste is another word for lost profit', yet only a third of SMEs had a major concern about managing their waste. And despite the extensive media coverage about the need for businesses to reduce their greenhouse emissions, only 25 per cent of SMEs said this was a major concern.

The survey did, however, uncover some positive indications. On the recruitment front, 26 per cent of organisations nationally said a 'sustainable image' helped them to recruit the best employee talent. The Index found that 'finding talent' ranked as one of the top priorities for SMEs with 70 per cent of companies surveyed saying it was a major concern for them.

11   See www.netbalance.com/reports/SME-Report.pdf

On a very positive note, 65 per cent of SME managers said they wanted to take action on climate change. Of particular note was that one-third of SMEs were not strongly concerned about climate change but were willing to act, with a further 32 per cent both concerned and willing to act.

The breakdown is shown in each quadrant below.

SME interest in sustainability

Source: Net Balance / AFS SME Sustainability Index[12]

The research showed there was a gap between perception and reality when it came to how SMEs saw themselves on environmental issues. Asked if their business was 'environmentally friendly', 72 per cent of those surveyed indicated that they were. However, the term 'environmentally friendly' is open to broad interpretation. When the actions they claimed to be undertaking were reviewed, less than 15 per cent were actually undertaking relevant activities that are sustainable enough to be considered environmentally friendly. Clearly there is still a long way to go.

According to the Index, those SMEs that had undertaken sustainability-related actions had experienced cost savings. Furthermore, 70 per cent of SMEs surveyed said they were moving forward on sustainability-related initiatives.

12   See www.netbalance.com/reports/SME-Report.pdf

Those who were experiencing success were very positive about the sustainability results that were being obtained. New business opportunities, manufacturing efficiencies, improved employee morale, cost savings and resource savings were just some of the benefits outlined by SMEs interviewed by AFS.

The Index showed that more than half of all SMEs were being influenced in some way to become more sustainable. The major influencers for SMEs were their internal cultures or promoters offering sustainable alternatives.

Sustainability adoption curve
Self-assessment – October 2009

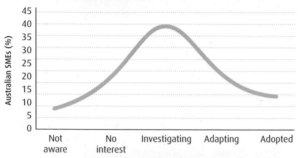

Source: Net Balance / AFS SME Sustainability Index[13]

The results also show more than one in five SMEs were being pressured directly by customers (including government procurement) to be more sustainable.

How will sustainability benefit my business?

Embracing environmentally sustainable practices in the workplace goes hand-in-hand with many benefits for SMEs:

- the public is behind the need for social and environmental change
- the public want change that is driven by government and businesses
- the public want to see leadership that brings about real and measurable change
- change represents new opportunities

13   See www.netbalance.com/reports/SME-Report.pdf

- change can be a driver for good
- change can create new jobs
- change encourages new ways of designing and manufacturing products
- change inspires innovation
- saving resources can also save you money.

It is reasonable for Australians to want the same lifestyle and opportunities they have right now, but, as the Unilever research noted earlier reveals, they want business to fix the problems caused by their current lifestyles. This is where the opportunity lies. Businesses that respond to this concern with a price-sensitive quality product or service that makes a difference will stand a better chance of getting a sale.

Case study: Toyota Prius – the petrol/electric hybrid car

Prior to the release of the Toyota Prius petrol/electric hybrid car, there was no real environmental alternative car that had mainstream appeal and potential.

Even though the Toyota Prius is more expensive than similar-sized cars, Toyota has sold more than 1.5 million of the vehicles worldwide and 13,000 in Australia since the car first went on sale in 2000.[14]

All companies need to look at the potential for change within their own organisation. Within the markets currently serviced by your business, what is your 'Prius equivalent' product or service that your business could offer that your competitors aren't? Companies who take such change seriously stand to improve their reputation and commercial opportunities from 'first-mover' status – particularly as the corporate sector increasingly moves towards a more sustainable way of operating.

14   Figures represent sales at January 2010

UNDERSTANDING THE BOTTOM LINE

Sustainability benefits for SMEs

1. **Contain costs**
    Being as efficient as possible in your use of energy and other resources reduces your overheads as well as input costs. By doing so, when the prices of those commodities go up, you are not as exposed to price fluctuations.

2. **Improve relationships with suppliers**
    Reducing the environmental and social impact of your supply chain is a joint journey that you undertake with your suppliers. When SMEs set out on this journey, they tend to build closer and more positive relationships with their suppliers.

3. **Attract and retain employees**
    Due to the education they've received at school, younger people tend to be far more aware and 'savvy' about social and environmental issues than older people in the workforce. If your business is serious about attracting and retaining the younger, socially aware employee, then they need to see your business is serious about sustainability.

Case study: Barb de Corti – investing in the environment with ENJO

In 1994, Barb de Corti set up a business distributing the ENJO fibre cloth that cleans with water only. She liked the chemical-free microfibre products so much she invested her life savings of $40,000 to become Australia's sole ENJO distributor.

Today, many homes use the product and the business turns over $100 million every year. With more than 1000 consultants directly selling the ENJO range, the business is generating sales from households who want to do something practical to help the environment.

4. **Reduce risk**

   Cost-cutting in the 1990s led to some companies being exposed as using overseas suppliers who used child labour, cheap labour or unfair working practices. Knowing where the goods and services in your supply chain are coming from is vital if you want to minimise threats to your corporate reputation.

   By minimising your use of energy and resources, your business doesn't just save money. You also reduce the risk of being caught out by price hikes or supply shortages.

5. **Increase market share**

   SMEs that are proactive on environmental and social issues are attractive to larger companies that have a sustainable procurement policy. If your business is supplying larger companies then there is significant potential in this space to 'go green' and benefit through increased market share.

   The general public is emotionally engaged on the issue of the environment. If your business can provide a good or service that is price compatible but has a lesser environmental impact than your competition, then you can potentially increase your market share.

How to boost your environmental performance

What makes for a high-performing organisation? In the past, such an organisation was defined solely by the success of its financial bottom line. But in today's world, a high-performing organisation is one that is:

- responsive to its customers' needs and wants
- responsive to the environment in which it operates
- resourceful in times of scarcity
- adaptable in times of change
- beneficial to others through its own prosperity.

On all these measures the small or medium business can be more than a match for a far larger corporation. Just as a small car can accelerate, turn, stop or reverse in much less time than a semi-trailer, the agility of a smaller business can make up for its lack of mass. These characteristics convey the SMEs' competitive advantage in a fast evolving business environment. They also demonstrate why SMEs are perfectly positioned to take advantage of the shift towards a more sustainable way of doing business.

Phases of sustainability

Sustainability is often described as a journey rather than a destination. The Queensland Government's Department of Environment and Resource Management[15] present this journey as a six-step 'sustainability evolution'.

Corporate sustainability evolution

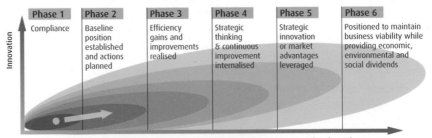

Source: Queensland Government, Department of Environment and Resource Management

The graph shows the path towards sustainability is also about continuous improvement.

Beginning the journey can introduce your business to a wide variety of productivity enhancements and new efficiencies. Cost savings can be identified from doing more with less, such as by being more efficient in your use of energy, water and other resources. New innovation and opportunities can arise through proper engagement of stakeholders and employees. In short, companies that embark on this journey can end up better positioned in the marketplace and future-proofed from a legislative and environmental perspective. Their business image can be enhanced and in the process, employees can also become more motivated and loyal.

Changing technology, new developments and legislation mean new opportunities and challenges will come up which will impact any plans your business puts in place. But remaining adaptable and responsive to a changing roadmap is vital if your business is to take full advantage of the potential of becoming a truly sustainable business.

15   See www.derm.qld.gov.au/environmental_management/sustainability

Sustainability: a risk-management approach

Bringing a risk-management approach to sustainability helps a business identify and prioritise what it should do. It also helps a business align sustainability actions with business goals and practices – it shows what is relevant to you and what you can control.

For example, the current government, consumer and business response to environmental concerns create the following risks that every business should consider:

- changing input costs (energy, water, waste, raw materials)
- tightening of environmental legislation and regulation
- customers wanting 'greener' products and services
- inability to meet the requirements set out by 'green' tenders
- revocation of regulatory licenses and permits.

Top tips to reduce the environmental risks and liabilities for SMEs[16]

1. Walk around your site with a fresh pair of eyes and try to identify things that 'don't seem responsible'. It's important that you address them before they address you.

2. Get an expert to undertake a risk assessment of your business to identify possible non-conformances or potential future liabilities.

3. Obtain licenses and consignment notes from your waste contractors.

4. Identify, record and monitor what legislation, permits or licenses apply to your business.

5. Identify, record and monitor other requirements to which your organisation subscribes. For example, do you have any contracts that require you to fulfil specific environmental criteria?

6. Ensure your contractors are environmentally responsible and compliant on your site.

16   Tips courtesy of Brett Miller, Senior E&S Consultant at Business SA. See www.business-sa.com

'Carbon dioxide and other greenhouse gases warm the surface of the planet naturally by trapping solar heat in the atmosphere.'

2

The hot issue of climate change

For some time, most people have accepted that climate change is real, is already happening and is the result of human activity and not just a natural occurrence.

As the CSIRO states, "...there are no known natural factors that can explain the observed warming."[17]

The cause is straightforward. Carbon dioxide and other greenhouse gases warm the surface of the planet naturally by trapping solar heat in the atmosphere. This is a good thing because it keeps our planet habitable. However, modern living – especially in developed and major developing countries – relies on using large amounts of fossil fuels such as coal, gas and oil. The resulting pollution and other activities create a dramatic and unsustainable increase in carbon emissions. All of this activity means we have dramatically increased the amount of carbon dioxide and other greenhouse gases in the Earth's atmosphere.

---

17   CSIRO *Climate questions, science facts.*
      See www.csiro.au/resources/climate-questions-science-facts.html

As a result, over the past century the global average temperature has risen 0.74 degrees Celsius. Average Australian temperatures have risen by around 0.9 degrees Celsius since 1950. This temperature rise appears small but small increases in temperature could lead to hotter days, more severe storms, droughts and fire and higher sea levels. This could threaten lives, industries and jobs, sustainable agricultural production, fresh water supplies and the survival of native species and ecosystems. The Intergovernmental Panel on Climate Change (IPCC) assessment is that an average global warming of 2 degrees or more above the pre-industrial level could result in dangerous and irreversible climate change with dramatic social, economic and environmental impacts.[18]

Left unchecked, this problem of global warming will only get worse. The potential impact on Australia's economy is significant – it will create both costs and opportunities for business.

Concern over climate change linked to human activities has existed for many years.

Long before Al Gore's 2006 Oscar® winning documentary *An Inconvenient Truth,* a 1958 documentary film called *The Unchained Goddess* featured a scientist talking about "… the release through factories and automobiles every year of more than 6 billion tonnes of carbon dioxide." This film referred to how "our atmosphere seems to be getting warmer," and calculations that a few degrees rise in the Earth's temperature "would melt the polar ice caps."[19]

That was 50 years ago and since then the science has become far stronger.

18   IPCC 4AR *Summary for Policymakers* Climate Change 2007: Synthesis Report, Intergovernmental Panel on Climate Change, November 2007
19   You can watch a clip of *The Unchained Goddess* at www.youtube.com

What are greenhouse gases?

The ability to sustain our way of life depends on the Sun's warmth being trapped by heat-trapping gases in our atmosphere. These greenhouse gases act like a blanket around the Earth. They trap the Sun's heat and cause the planet to stay at just the right temperature needed for us to sustain our habitat and the way we live.

Without these greenhouse gases, it's estimated the Earth's temperature would be about minus 18 degrees Celsius.

It is critical that your business has some understanding of greenhouse emissions and climate change because through laws, the supply chain, consumer demands and the price we pay for electricity, it will touch every business in Australia.

Unfortunately, too many of these heat-trapping gases have been released into the atmosphere over the past 200 years or so. Other activities such as deforestation (cutting down trees and not replacing them) also have an impact. As a result the world is retaining more heat. This is called the enhanced greenhouse effect.

It is critical that your business has some understanding of greenhouse emissions and climate change because through laws, the supply chain, consumer demands and the price we pay for electricity, it will touch every business in Australia.

Think of it as a bank; a greenhouse bank. For 200 years we've been depositing greenhouse emissions into this bank. Even if we were to stop creating greenhouse emissions tomorrow, we're going to be getting interest on those existing deposits for many years to come. That interest comes in the form of a warming planet.

Fortunately there are things we can do to help and it's not too late to make a difference. Our climate is changing but we have the time and opportunity to minimise that change. SMEs may feel they don't have enough impact to make a difference, but they do.

Which greenhouse gases are generated by human activity?

Most scientists agree that human-induced global warming is caused by atmospheric increases in the following heat-trapping greenhouse gases (also called carbon pollution):

Carbon dioxide (CO_2)

CO_2 is released through deforestation, the burning of vegetable matter and the combustion of fossil fuels such as oil (for transportation) and gas and coal (for energy generation). It is also a gas used in raw form in many production activities.

Methane (CH_4)

CH_4 is usually caused by the decomposition of landfill waste, the exhalation from cows, sheep and other ruminant animals, rice growing wetlands and fossil-fuel production.

Nitrous oxide (N_2O)

N_2O is a greenhouse gas that's generated by commercial and organic fertilisers, the combustion of fossil fuel, the production of nitric acid and the burning of biomass.

Perfluorocarbons (PFCs)

PFCs are by-products of uranium enrichment and the aluminium smelting process and are used in refrigerating units.

Hydrofluorocarbons (HFCs)

HFCs are used in fridges and the manufacturing of electrical equipment such as semiconductors.

Sulfur hexafluoride (SF_6)

SF_6 is mainly used to insulate high-voltage equipment.

When did it all start to change?

Our ability to have an impact on the climate began at the end of the late 18th century. This was the period when Britain experienced a significant transition from a manual labour and draft animal-based economy into one that utilised machine-based manufacturing.

In the process, a major transition in manufacturing, mining, transport and agriculture began that spread throughout the world. All-metal machine tools, canals, improved roads, railways and the introduction of coal-fired steam power fundamentally changed society over a period that became known as the Industrial Revolution. It was during this time humans started to create significant amounts of carbon dioxide pollution.

This was one of the by-products of using and burning coal as a source of energy. It was to have a cumulative impact on the global climate that has led to where we are today.

What about the last hundred years?

In the last century the global climate has been warming. On looking at this, scientists had to ascertain how much was caused by humans and how much was naturally occurring. Some of these increases could easily be explained by natural factors such as radiation outputs from the Sun and natural variations caused by volcanic eruptions.

The evidence linking climate change to human activity is now overwhelming. Developed countries use far more power and resources than they need to and the massive growth in emissions and resource use by developing countries like India and China could alone drive changes in the climate.

However, climate science is at a point where it can show that global temperature increases are caused by the activities of humans. Indeed, the U.S. Geological Survey states that 'human activities release more than 130 times the amount of CO_2 emitted by volcanoes.'[20]

20   See www.usgs.gov

The evidence linking climate change to human activity is now overwhelming. Developed countries use far more power and resources than they need to and the massive growth in emissions and resource use by developing countries like India and China could alone drive changes in the climate. This is why it's vital for the whole world to move in a unified way towards combating the problem.

Even though some people still question whether smoking causes cancer, the majority of us have accepted that it does. We all need to take a similar approach to climate change. The science is solid. The daily impacts of businesses and individuals is having a negative impact on the planet. The key thing is how do we balance that impact? We need to develop in a way that ensures we live sustainably on our planet, but we need to do so in a manner that underpins the viability and prosperity of our business operations.

The climate change caused by global warming will fundamentally affect the way all businesses operate in the future.

What impact will climate change have on Australian business?

The climate change caused by global warming will fundamentally affect the way all businesses operate in the future. Your decision to implement sustainable practices in your business now is a key building block on the path to dealing with this issue.

According to the futurist Dr Patrick Dixon, the debate about climate change could also be shaped by emotion just as much as by the science. His belief is that companies will go faster and further than government when it comes to combating the issue. As the ramifications of climate change begin to hit home, there's a high likelihood that consumer pressure will change every product and service sold. This is why now, more than ever, SMEs need to listen, learn and act.

Dixon argues we have known about the science of climate change since the 1950s. The difference today is that people are now emotionally engaged. As Dixon says, "Most children alive today will find their future lives are deeply affected by new patterns of disease, extreme weather patterns, and by strict controls on energy and carbon use. Future generations will judge us by how we respond (today)."[21]

21   See www.pdixon.blogspot.com and/or www.globalchange.com

These are key issues on which we must challenge ourselves as we move to deal with the problem of climate change. You need to consider how you will improve your financial bottom line while still taking into consideration the future wellbeing of tomorrow's Australians.

The physical risks of climate change are very real for Australian businesses. While climate change cannot be related to any single event, recent trends in extreme weather events show increasing numbers and severity.

For example, in 2006 when Cyclone Larry wiped out about 80 per cent of the Queensland banana crop, it hit the banana industry hard with losses amounting to hundreds of millions of dollars.[22] The knock-on impact was also felt by many SMEs in that region and consumers paid much higher prices for bananas for many months.

According to the re-insurance company Swiss Re, 2008 was one of the worst years in history, with natural catastrophes costing property insurers more than US$44 billion.

Storms caused the greatest number of claims. Industry experts have estimated those businesses in areas at risk of storms and floods due to climate change could see insurance premiums double.[23]

As the ramifications of climate change begin to hit home, there's a high likelihood that consumer pressure will change every product and service sold. This is why now, more than ever, SMEs need to listen, learn and act.

In a speech to the Lowy Institute in November 2009, then Australian Prime Minister Kevin Rudd said that estimates of increased storm surges and rising sea levels could put 700,000 business and residential properties at risk. Mr Rudd stated that the value of coastal property exposed to these risks was between $50 and $150 billion.[24]

In the longer term, businesses may find themselves unable to afford or obtain insurance because they are on a low-lying part of the Australian coast. Or they may not be able to get cover for facilities they own in a part of Asia that's at risk of flooding. These developments could well happen over time and they will have significant impacts on a wide range of businesses when they do.

---

22   'Cyclone devastates Australia's banana crop', *Sydney Morning Herald*, March 20, 2006
23   See http://business.timesonline.co.uk/tol/business/industry_sectors/banking_and_finance/article5949991.ece
24   *Distinguished Speaker Series*, The Hon Kevin Rudd MP, The Lowy Institute, Sydney, 6 November 2009

Upside for the business

Climate change and the responses to it present opportunities for business. For example, the Australian Government initiative to fund energy efficiency programs in homes created thousands of jobs.

The NSW Business Chamber identifies a number of ways businesses can benefit from climate change:[25]

1. Access to an increasing number of government grants that are available for businesses wishing to undertake eco-efficiency measures.

2. Potential to be a preferred supplier if your business can demonstrate it has reduced the environmental impact of its operations. If you start the shift now to becoming a more sustainably run business, then you might end up with a head start on your competitors.

3. Developing products and services that differentiate and set you apart from your competition (adopting early changes to your business practices).

4. Research and development on new ideas. Have you developed a solution for problems like flash floods, freak storms and increased wind speeds? Got an idea that reduces greenhouse emissions from other companies? If you can find ways that minimise the impact that climate change will have on the way we live our lives and run our businesses, then you could be part of a growing new business sector.

Preparing for change

While reducing greenhouse emissions may keep temperatures down and potentially avoid extremes of climate change, the overwhelming scientific consensus is that some degree of climate change is now unavoidable. In terms of timing, the predictions are that the weather and physical impacts may be beginning now and will become more noticeable over the next ten years.

The timing of regulatory and economic changes is similar. Many companies, governments and people around the world are already making decisions based on changes to the climate and the fact the world is looking to reduce carbon emissions. These changes will increase over time as governments legislate to reduce carbon emissions and provide incentives and transition plans for business. Companies will also seek to reduce the emissions in their own operations and those within their supply chain.

25   See www.nswbusinesschamber.com.au

Predicted climate change impacts across Australia forecast more extreme weather events (storms, floods, droughts etc) as well as changing patterns of temperature and rainfall (less rain and higher temperatures across Australia's south and south-east and more rain and higher temperatures across the central and northern coastal areas).

Many companies, governments and people around the world are already making decisions based on changes to the climate and the fact the world is looking to reduce carbon emissions.

Each of these areas of impact will raise different issues for businesses depending on what they do and where they operate but some key issues to consider are:

- physical impacts on buildings
- supply, transport and distribution interruption
- changing agricultural patterns
- insurance and emergency planning.

Regulatory and economic responses will be positive and negative – there will be increased costs, accounting and reporting requirements but there will also be new business opportunities and transition assistance (both in terms of financial assistance and information and advice). Some issues to consider are:

- changes to energy costs (electricity, gas, petrol, diesel)
- legal compliance with new laws
- accounting for your carbon emissions
- customer and supplier expectations
- opportunities for new business
- opportunities for assistance.

So what are you going to do about it?

Media coverage of environmental issues often focuses on natural disasters or negative impacts. Little coverage is given to the positive impact that environmental improvement can have on our businesses and society if we start to do something about it.

The response to climate change and higher energy prices will impact your business. But it is going to impact on all other SMEs too. Rather than look at this as a negative, why not turn your response to this into a competitive advantage?

It's a given that SMEs have to be sustainable from an economic standpoint. But it's also important for them to become sustainable in the way they interact with the environment and the communities in which they operate.

Think about the four key strategies for responding to climate change:

1. **Adaptation** – how can you change your practices and build resilience into your operation to adapt to the impacts of climate change?

2. **Mitigation** – how can you control your costs and contribute to solving the problem? How can you offset or reduce your carbon emissions?

3. **Research and development** – is there an area of your business where you can build extra capacity to manage the impacts of climate change, is there a new business opportunity to explore?

4. **Communication** – how do you learn more so that you are communicating effectively with your employees, customers and suppliers? Informed communication can underpin sound decision-making on this issue.

For more detailed information on climate change, what it means for various business sectors and the strategies needed to respond to it, go to Australia's CSIRO website: www.csiro.au

The bottom line

At the end of the day the move to combat climate change represents the biggest new business opportunity of the coming century. How your business reacts will decide your place in the low-carbon economy.

Case study: Sensis – Commitment to Climate Change

On 3 February 2010, Sensis launched its Commitment to Climate Change.

As part of the launch, Sensis announced that its Yellow Pages® and White Pages® print and online directories were certified carbon neutral through the Australian Government's Greenhouse Friendly™ program. This program has since transitioned to the National Carbon Offset Standard Carbon Neutral Program.

Sensis will achieve this by offsetting the carbon emissions of its directories through accredited projects and providers in Australia.

Sensis had a Life Cycle Assessment of its Yellow Pages® and White Pages® print and online directories undertaken so the full 'cradle to grave' impact of the directories could be understood. This enabled Sensis to identify opportunities to reduce its carbon emissions and play its part in tackling climate change.

Sensis also announced its target to reduce its operational greenhouse gas footprint by 5 per cent year-on-year. To help reach this target, Sensis has enabled video conferencing at 21 office locations, introduced 4 cylinder diesel cars into the Sensis fleet and is scoping new IT Purchasing Guidelines incorporating energy efficiency.

Sensis will measure and monitor these impacts annually through a detailed Emissions Monitoring Plan and report annually on its carbon footprint and detail improvements.

Go to www.about.sensis.com.au/sustainability for further information on Sensis' commitment to sustainability.

What is emission trading?

At the moment, polluters are able to release carbon pollution into the atmosphere at no financial cost. Emission trading is a program that puts a price on pollution to make it less attractive for polluters to pollute, and make it more attractive for polluters to invest in cleaner production. The idea is the more you pollute, the more you pay.

Under an Emissions Trading Scheme (ETS), a government adds up the pollution generated by top companies and divides it into emissions permits. If you're a leading company that pollutes 100,000 tonnes a year, then theoretically you would have to hold 100,000 emissions permits.

As an ETS puts a price on carbon that is polluted into the atmosphere, a company has an incentive to reduce its emissions if it's cheaper to do so than to buy credits. To ensure that such an ETS reduces the amount of carbon pollution emitted by the leading polluters, each year the government can simply reduce the number of emissions permits that they make available.

Emission trading is not new. Countries have used it in the past to reduce nitrous oxide and sulphur dioxide (which cause acid rain). Australia started one of the first carbon emissions trading schemes in the world when the NSW Government established the Greenhouse Gas Abatement Scheme in 2003. Twenty nine countries are also part of the European Union Emissions Trading Scheme that began in 2005.

Measuring your carbon footprint

When it comes to measuring the size of your business' carbon footprint, you need to measure the greenhouse emissions emitted by your overall operations.

For most SMEs, all you need to do is use a carbon calculator to calculate your carbon emissions. Go to http://calculator.futureclimate.com.au for a good calculator for this type of basic reporting.

However, some SMEs may want to follow the example of their major clients by measuring their direct and indirect Greenhouse Gas (GHG) emissions in far more detail. The www.ghgprotocol.org website has information on how to measure and report on Scope 1, 2 and 3 greenhouse emissions. Swinburne University also has a short course in carbon accounting. Go to www.swinburne.edu.au/ncs for more information.

There is much focus on using emission trading to address greenhouse gases (also called carbon pollution). This is important for business to understand because emission trading for carbon is now on a scale not seen before. Carbon is so inextricably linked to so many things we do that the price impact of any emission trading activity can touch all businesses and consumers.

How will such a scheme affect SMEs?

Emission trading is designed to directly affect large polluters, so SMEs are not required to directly participate in such a scheme – unless they choose to do so.

According to the NSW Business Chamber, the ETS implications for SMEs include:[26]

- increases in energy prices
- further government regulation – potentially covering energy efficiency and energy sources
- corporate regulation – if a major business affected by an ETS is a client of your company, you could face a requirement to be 'greener' in your business operations
- supply chain dynamics – raw materials may become more expensive and companies may demand that SME suppliers become more sustainable and accountable for their environmental impacts
- consumer demands – as consumer awareness and education increases, consumers may purchase products that are seen to be 'greener' than others.

However, by reducing your emissions and becoming more efficient in your use of resources (such as electricity and gas), SMEs can greatly minimise or potentially avoid the cost of an emissions trading scheme. In the energy chapter of this book, there are a range of tips that will show you how to save money and reduce your business' energy use.

How can SMEs reduce their greenhouse gas emissions?

According to the NSW Business Chamber and other bodies, there are a number of things SMEs can do straight away as part of their response to this issue:

1. Understand how much energy is used by your business and work out ways to reduce your consumption levels. It's worth recording your efforts and results in order to show evidence of your achievements in this area.

---

26   See www.nswbusinesschamber.com.au

2. Assess if your business is part of the supply chain of one of the 1000 or so companies required to report under the *National Greenhouse and Energy Reporting Act 2007* (NGER Act).[27]

3. Think about how your operations would be affected if your energy prices were to go up by 20 per cent or more. Plan for such an eventuality and you will be on the front foot in your response to how climate change and regulations will affect SMEs in your industry. While you're at it, how would you respond if the cost of your raw materials went up by 20 per cent?

4. Increasingly, government grants or assistance will be available to SMEs to help them in the transition to a low-carbon economy. Your company should be on the look out to take advantage of these funding opportunities. Industry groups can assist with this and a guide to grants is available to purchase from Equilibrium OMG at www.eqlomg.com.

5. Look for the 'greener' alternative. Look at your raw materials – are they as environmentally sourced as they could be? When you're buying products and services, ask to be shown the environmentally better option and compare it with what you're using now.

6. Assess how much your customers and stakeholders are motivated by climate change and environmental issues. You might find they have implemented environmental ideas your company could adapt. If they're environmentally inclined, engaging them on this issue is a good way of showing that you share their corporate values.

7. All companies use equipment that uses energy. Obtain a power meter and measure how much energy is used by the appliances your business uses. Understanding this goes a long way to reducing the daily energy use of these appliances or to buying more energy-efficient alternatives when you come to replace them.

27 *National Greenhouse and Energy Reporting Act 2007.* See www.climatechange.gov.au

Carbon offsets – what you need to know

A carbon offset is any activity that:

- removes greenhouse gases from the atmosphere
- captures greenhouse gases that would otherwise be discharged into the air
- avoids the generation of greenhouse gases in the first place.

What type of carbon offsets should you buy?

You should look to purchase carbon offsets that are accredited to a recognised standard. The Carbon Offset Watch initiative says the best available offsets are those that are accredited under the international Gold Standard and Clean Development Mechanism. These as well as those offsets listed as eligible under the National Carbon Offset Standard (NCOS).

What should you look out for?

Carbon Offset Watch recommends that companies get a documented guarantee from their offset retailer that they will 'retire' the offset from the market on your behalf. Alternatively, they should transfer the ownership of the carbon offset to your company so that you can retire it instead, which avoids the offset being used twice.

Carbon offsets can be listed in a register that tracks their ownership. When you buy an offset, this register can record that your offset has been removed from the market. This helps to ensure that it's not sold again.

The Australian Competition and Consumer Commission (ACCC) has developed guidance for consumers and industry on the Trade Practices Act implications of carbon offset claims. Go to www.accc.gov.au/content/index.phtml/itemId/807902 for more information.

The NCOS was introduced on 1 July 2010, following the closure of the Greenhouse Friendly™ program. The NCOS provides national consistency and consumer confidence in the voluntary carbon market. It provides guidance on what constitutes a genuine, additional voluntary carbon offset and sets minimum requirements for achieving 'carbon neutrality' for organisations and products.[28]

How can SMEs offset their greenhouse gas emissions?

No matter how much a business reduces its environmental impact, it will still produce greenhouse emissions. As these emissions contribute to man-made climate change, your company may want to consider carbon offsetting part or all of your emissions.

The basic concept behind a carbon offset is that if your company generates 10 tonnes of emissions, then you fund a project that reduces emissions in the atmosphere by the same 10 tonnes. This can be achieved by funding projects that:

■ reduce emissions – this can be achieved via energy efficiency projects that reduce energy use, by generating renewable energy or by capturing methane at landfills

■ sequester carbon from the atmosphere – this can be achieved by planting trees or by avoided deforestation.

It may be too expensive to offset all your emissions. If that is the case, as a starting point why not look to offset your business' car and air travel emissions?

---

28   See www.climatechange.gov.au/government/initiatives/national-carbon-offset-standard.aspx

Boosting your performance

'Sustainable procurement is when companies buy goods and services based on environmental and social, as well as financial aspects.'

3

Sustainable procurement: 'green up' for business growth

Sustainable procurement has enormous potential to profoundly affect the way SMEs do business.

Sustainable procurement is when companies buy goods and services based on environmental and social, as well as financial aspects. It covers everything from companies asking suppliers for information on the environmental management system (see Chapter 12) they have in place, right through to requesting details on the energy, water and carbon pollution associated with a specific product or service.

Many Australian companies have started to 'green up' their supply chain and the move is having significant ramifications for the SMEs who supply them.

In today's international economy, business processes tend to become standardised a lot faster than they used to, particularly in the area of environmental management and business sustainability. Many companies in the United States of America and Europe have well-established sustainability programs for suppliers and Australian companies are adopting these processes.

Retailers have been leaders in this area. Grocery and bulk discount operator Walmart is the single-largest private employer in the United States. In 2009 the company released a document outlining its desire 'to produce zero waste, to be supplied with 100 per cent renewable energy and to sell sustainable products.'

In July 2009, Walmart brought together 1500 of its suppliers and associates to announce plans to develop a worldwide Sustainable Product Index. As part of its desire to make 'sustainability sustainable', it announced a three-stage plan for the project.[29]

Walmart Sustainable Product Index

The following questions have been adapted from the Walmart Sustainable Product Index.[30]

Energy and climate – reducing energy costs and greenhouse gas emissions:

1. Have you measured your corporate greenhouse gas emissions?

2. What is your total annual greenhouse gas emissions reported in the most recent year measured?

3. Have you set publicly available greenhouse gas reduction targets? If yes, what are those targets?

Material efficiency – reducing waste and enhancing quality:

4. If measured, please report the total amount of solid waste (rubbish and recycling) generated from the facilities that produce your product(s) for the most recent year measured.

5. Have you set publicly available solid waste reduction targets? If yes, what are those targets?

6. If measured, please report total water use from facilities that produce your product(s) for the most recent year measured.

7. Have you set publicly available water-use reduction targets? If yes, what are those targets?

29   See www.walmartstores.com/sustainability
30   Reproduced and adapted with permission from Walmart

The first stage was a survey that was distributed to its 100,000 suppliers around the world. The questions were designed by Walmart with input from suppliers, government, academia, not-for-profits and others in the retail community, and were based around four key areas: energy and climate; material efficiency; natural resources; and people and community.

By establishing a Sustainable Product Index, Walmart aims to help its suppliers '... identify both cost savings and opportunities for new revenue.' Walmart believes this process represents a tremendous business opportunity for its company and its 100,000 suppliers.

Natural resources – producing high quality, responsibly sourced raw materials:

8. Have you established publicly available sustainability purchasing guidelines for your direct suppliers that address issues such as environmental compliance, employment practices and product/ingredient safety?

9. Have you obtained third-party certifications for any of the products that you sell?

People and community – ensuring responsible and ethical production

10. Do you know the location of 100% of the facilities that produce your product(s)?

11. Before beginning a business relationship with a manufacturing facility, do you evaluate the quality of, and capacity for, production?

12. Do you have a process for managing social compliance at the manufacturing level?

13. Do you work with your supply base to resolve issues found during social compliance evaluations and also document specific corrections and improvements?

14. Do you invest in community development activities in the markets you source from and/or operate within?

What does this mean for you? Being able to answer these questions is vital for any SME that doesn't want to miss out on an opportunity to work with a large company because it doesn't know its own environmental and social sustainability position.

Creating your own sustainable procurement system

The best place to start developing sustainable procurement processes is to ask yourself key questions and assess their relevance to the materials and services your business both purchases and sells:

1. Is there a more environmentally responsible version of the same product?

2. Does the product have any recycled content?

3. Is it made from sustainably derived materials? With regards to paper or furniture, is it certified as having come from sustainably-managed forests?

4. Is it energy-efficient? Do other versions of this product use less energy over time?

5. Can it be reused or refilled?

6. What has the manufacturer or supplier done to reduce the environmental impact of its products and services?

7. Does the manufacturer or supplier release any type of environmental reporting?

8. Has the supplier ever breached environmental regulations or used toxic ingredients in its manufacturing processes? You can search records at each state and territory environment protection agency or authority or look at the company's annual reports.

9. What has the manufacturer done to 'green up' the supply chain for its products?

10. Are they supplying products to any existing, well-known sustainable procurement scheme, such as ECO-Buy?

As you develop a better understanding of the specific elements of sustainable procurement which are applicable to your business, consideration and documentation of the following principles can form the basis of a good sustainable procurement policy.

Principle one – avoid unnecessary consumption:

1. Assess the need for making a new purchase. Consider alternatives such as refurbishment, reconditioning or purchasing a second-hand item.

2. Consider alternatives to acquisition, such as short-term hire or using a service provider.

Principle two – select products and services with the lowest environmental impact:

1. Analyse goods from a whole-of-life-cycle perspective. That means looking at everything that goes into making, distributing, selling and using a product or service as well as its end-of-life disposal. Factor in both the initial cost and also operational efficiency, expected life-span, reuse/recycling options at the end-of-life, and cost of disposal/replacement. The cheapest product is not always the most cost-effective option.

2. Look for evidence of environmental management. If a company is large enough it may have environmental certification. The most common is the International Organization for Standardization (ISO) 14000 series.[31]

3. Look for a credible eco-label, indicating the environmental claims are certified by an independent third-party (see the 'Know your eco-labels' section on page 44 for more information).

4. Give preference to products that are reusable, recyclable and/or contain recycled content. Collecting materials for recycling is one thing but your business is not truly recycling unless it's buying recycled-content products.

Principle three – support businesses to create a market for sustainable goods and services:

1. Encourage suppliers to measure and report their environmental management and actions.

2. Favour suppliers who are committed to design, production and operational processes that are more environmentally sustainable.

3. Look for suppliers who accept 'extended producer responsibility'. These suppliers will take responsibility for their product when you have finished with it.

4. Support suppliers who participate in government programs to improve environmental performance (such as the Australian National Packaging Covenant), voluntary reporting protocols (such as the Global Reporting Initiative), or industry groups promoting the uptake of sustainable business practices (such as Environment Business Australia).

31 See www.iso.org

Case study: Marks & Spencer – looking behind the label

In January 2006, UK department store Marks & Spencer launched Look Behind the Label (LBTL), a program to market the environmental and ethical benefits of its products. It was supported by an internal program to make sure products were as sustainable as possible and that marketing claims were true.

With 15 million UK customers a week, Marks & Spencer used the campaign to explain its position on environmental and social issues that mattered most to its customers. Marks & Spencer has a massive supply chain with 30,000 products sourced from 1900 suppliers who employ 100,000 people in 70 countries.

To provide an example of the impact of the campaign, Marks & Spencer worked with 70,000 producers in 12 countries to change 38 of its product lines to Fairtrade coffee and tea. Many of these businesses were SMEs. The switch to Fairtrade increased Marks & Spencer's sales and meant that £340,000 (about AU$690,000) in Fairtrade Premium went back to farmers to invest in their communities.

To communicate the change, Marks & Spencer launched an ad, backed up by real and measurable corporate change, which advised its customers: "Our coffee won't leave a bitter taste in your mouth. It's Fairtrade." You can find more information about communicating your business' commitment to sustainability in Chapter 13 of this book.

The positive reaction to LBTL provided confidence to develop a more ambitious aspirational set of aims which was launched in January 2007 as 'Plan A'. As part of the campaign, the company promotes the fact that 'there is no Plan B' when it comes to protecting the environment.

The Marks & Spencer approach to sustainability is now embedded within the company and with its suppliers. The results achieved by the company in 2008/09 include:

- 31% of the company's energy now comes from renewable sources, with the goal of being carbon neutral by 2012. Over a 12-month period they reduced carbon emissions by 18% and improved energy efficiency in stores by 10%

- in 2009, the company signed a deal to ultimately power all Marks & Spencer stores and offices in England, Wales and Scotland with renewable power

- packaging for one of its Easter Egg lines was reduced by 90% and pizza packaging was reduced by 62% (480 tonnes); non-glass food packaging was also reduced by 12%

- more than 8 million Fairtrade certified cotton garments were sold

- a recycling rate of 41% was achieved and in one year 125 million hangers were collected for reuse or recycling

- a healthier food range now makes up 30% of its total food offer

- fuel use in delivery fleets was reduced by more than 20%

- 50% of all wood used to build and fit out stores now comes from Forest Stewardship Council (FSC) sources

- the company is working with the environment group WWF to reduce the amount of water being used in product sourcing and production stages

- 44% of staff have been with Marks & Spencer for more than five years which is one of the lowest employee turnover rates in UK retail.

In March 2010, Marks & Spencer extended the 'Plan A' program to cover 180 sustainability commitments,[32] with the aim of becoming the world's most sustainable major retailer by 2015. The company also announced that 'Plan A' has helped save £50 million (about AU$82.5 million) in 2009/10.

How could your business achieve similar results, albeit on a smaller scale? Would your business be ready to react and engage in the same way if larger Australian companies you supply developed similar programs?

32   See http://plana.marksandspencer.com

Know your eco-labels

Not all green claims are the same and not all eco-labels are the same either. When looking for products and services, here are the eco-labels that you can definitely trust. Their use on a product indicates that it has been independently verified by a respected third party.

General products

The Good Environmental Choice (GEC) label certifies products that are environmentally preferable from a whole-of-life-cycle perspective compared to others in the same category. The GEC mark is awarded on independently audited and monitored criteria for environmental, quality and social performance. Go to www.geca.org.au for a list of GEC-accredited products.

Paper and wood products

The Forest Stewardship Council (FSC) symbol guarantees timber and wood products (including paper) are sourced from well-managed forests or verified recycled materials. Independent assessment is undertaken according to social and environmental standards agreed to by the FSC, which is an international coalition of timber buyers, traders and non-government organisations. For more information, visit www.fsc.org. You can also go to www.goodwoodguide.org.au to check out the Greenpeace Good Wood Guide.

Office equipment

Energy Star is the international standard for energy-efficient electronic equipment, including computers, printers, photocopiers, monitors, televisions, DVD players and audio equipment. The Energy Star label shows the equipment can automatically switch into energy-saving features such as 'sleep' mode when not in use and can also use less energy when in 'standby' mode. Go to www.energystar.gov.au for more information.

Energy-efficient appliances

The Energy Rating label is mandatory on appliances like refrigerators, freezers, clothes washers, clothes dryers, dishwashers and air conditioners. It is now also used on TV sets. Similar to the Water Rating label, it uses a star rating system to show you how efficient the product is.

The more stars means the more you'll save on electricity. The label also tells you the estimated annual energy consumption in kW/h through typical use. Go to www.energyrating.gov.au for more information.

Case study: Corporate Express & 'Pilot 'B2P'

In August 2010, a 'Pilot B2P' Galaxy study showed that 90 per cent of Australians think businesses should do more to make their products less damaging to the environment.

In response to this growing demand for 'greener' products, Corporate Express has published a sustainable procurement guide for Australian businesses. The 'Go Green Guide – for a Greener Workspace' features more than 1500 EarthSaver classified products that help Australian businesses to make more informed and sustainable choices. Corporate Express has also been active on the emissions reduction front. The company's second Sustainability Report issued in 2010 indicated that it had reduced its gross CO2 emissions by 20 per cent on the previous year.

One of the products featured in the guide is the new 'B2P' (Bottle to Pen) from Pilot Pens. Since its release, 1.7 million old PET bottles have been turned into Pilot 'B2P' pens around the world.[33]

Water-efficient appliances

The Water Efficiency Labelling and Standard (WELS) scheme is an Australian Government mandatory label for products like showerheads, tap equipment, toilets, urinals, washing machines and dishwashers. The label is similar to the energy-rating system for electrical appliances – more stars means it's more efficient. The label also gives an estimate of water consumption. Go to www.waterrating.gov.au for more information.

The Smart Approved WaterMark label is the sister scheme to WELS, certifying products and services that help to reduce outdoor water use. Go to www.smartwatermark.info for more information.

33   See www.ce.com.au and www.pilotpenaustralia.com.au for more information.

Sustainable agriculture

Fairtrade certification promotes more sustainable agriculture by paying a higher-than-market price to producers to ensure that minimum labour, environmental and social conditions are met. Fairtrade-labelled products are sourced directly from local co-operatives, putting more money in the pockets of growers. Go to www.fairtrade.com.au for more information.

Not all green claims are the same and not all eco-labels are the same either.

Rainforest Alliance certification primarily addresses ecosystem conservation and wildlife protection, though it also requires meeting minimum conditions for workers. Coffee bearing this logo is now being stocked in outlets all around Australia. Indeed, every coffee bean that McDonald's Australia use at McCafé® is sourced only from Rainforest Alliance Certified™ farms.[34] Go to www.rainforest-alliance.org for more information.

Travel and tourism

Green Globe is the worldwide benchmarking and certification program for the travel and tourism industry, including hotels, restaurants, resorts and vehicle rental companies. The certification process was developed in conjunction with the Co-operative Research Centre for Sustainable Tourism in Australia. Go to www.greenglobe.org for more information.

Sustainable fishing

The Marine Stewardship Council label certifies that seafood has been fished in a sustainable manner. The standard applies to wild-capture fisheries only, not to farmed fish. Go to www.msc.org for more information.

---

34   See www.mcdonalds.com.au/mccafe/rainforest-alliance

Responsible investment

The Responsible Investment Certification Program is run by the Responsible Investment Association Australasia. This certifies environmentally and socially responsible investment products and services. Go to www.responsibleinvestment.org for more information.

Organic food produce

There are seven certification organisations, each with its own logo, approved by the Australian Quarantine Inspection Service:[35]

- Australian Certified Organic: www.aco.net.au
- NASAA Certified Organic: www.nasaa.com.au
- The Organic Food Chain (OFC): www.organicfoodchain.com.au
- AUS-QUAL: www.ausqual.com.au
- Bio-Dynamic Research Institute: www.demeter.org.au
- Safe Food Production Queensland: www.safefood.qld.gov.au
- Tasmanian Organic-Dynamic Producers: www.tasorganicdynamic.com.au

In addition to these logos, there is also an Australian Government Certified mark to provide greater assurance for buyers of organic and biodynamic produce. Go to the website of the Organic Federation of Australia at www.ofa.org.au for more information. For small organic producers, you can also sign up with the BFA/OGA Small Producers Program. For membership enquiries, visit www.organicgrowers.org.au

Concentrate

Concentrated cleaning products help to reduce packaging waste and allow for better transport efficiencies. Another benefit of concentrated products is they take up less space in your storeroom.

Make sure your cleaning service or cleaning department only uses non-toxic and phosphate-free cleaning products. This can help to reduce the impact of cleaning products on the environment.

35   See www.daff.gov.au/aqis

Guides to buying green

ECO-Buy

ECO-Buy helps SMEs to 'green' their purchasing and makes it easier to integrate sustainable purchasing into daily business practices. Backed by nine years of experience, ECO-Buy aims to increase the use of green products and services. It has just launched a 'Sustainable Procurement Assessment Tool'. This useful tool helps companies to measure and assess their green purchasing programs and policy. Go to www.ecobuy.org.au for more information.

Good Environmental Choice Australia

This website details those products that have achieved certification with the Good Environmental Choice Label. It also gives useful tips and information about sustainable procurement. Go to www.geca.org.au for more information.

Ecospecifier

Ecospecifier Australasia offers an online knowledge base of more than 3500 eco-products, eco-materials, technologies and resources. It is particularly useful for those companies who want to source products for building and construction projects. Go to www.ecospecifier.org for more information.

Queensland Government Sustainable Procurement

The Queensland Government spent approximately $12 billion on goods, services and construction in 2007/2008. This website is designed to help agencies, suppliers and other interested parties to understand sustainable procurement. Go to the 'Sustainable Procurement' page at www.qgm.qld.gov.au for more information.

Green Purchasing in Australia

The Green Purchasing in Australia report is very useful for organisations who want to implement sustainable procurement into their business operations. Go to www.netbalance.com or www.ecobuy.org.au to download the report.

If suppliers offer you 'degradable' bags, these are not biodegradable (under the AS4736 standard). Indeed, degradable bags can contain metals that breakdown the bags into smaller fragments – such fragments are problematic for smaller animals.

If the sales person says their bag is biodegradable, ask for certification that proves the bag – and the printing on that bag – is compliant with the AS4736-2006 Australian standard for compostable bags.

Visit www.banthebag.com.au for more information about alternatives to plastic bags.

'Everything your business throws away
is something you've paid for – and you also
have to pay to have it carted away.'

4

Lifting the lid on waste and recycling

What you throw away is a good indicator of how efficient your business is. If you create lots of waste, then you're not operating as efficiently as you could. Reducing waste and recycling more will save you money.

Waste is lost profit

Everything your business throws away is something you've paid for – and you also have to pay to have it carted away.

But that's just the start of it. What is paid for in waste disposal and landfill represents a small percentage of the total cost of producing waste. The hidden waste costs include:

■ lost opportunities to convert waste materials into valuable finished products

■ the cost of resources, like energy, that go into the processes that created the waste

■ the costs of clean-up, storage and waste treatment before disposal

■ employee time spent on unproductive waste-management work.

Did you know?

According to MobileMuster, one tonne of mobile phone circuit boards can yield the same amount of precious metals as 110 tonnes of gold ore.[36]

Where to start: conducting a waste audit

You can't manage what you don't measure. A waste audit will help your business to understand the different types and volumes of waste you generate. An audit involves collecting all waste generated over a week then sorting it to determine composition and quantity. This will enable you to understand the effectiveness of your existing approach to waste minimisation.

The waste audit will also need to identify the key areas across your business where waste is being generated. This can include everything from paper to water, right through to raw materials and packaging. It is essential that you involve your employees in this process – ask them where waste is being generated and how they think this could be reduced.

Office – waste composition

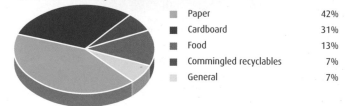

Paper	42%
Cardboard	31%
Food	13%
Commingled recyclables	7%
General	7%

Source: ecoBiz Queensland[37]

According to ecoBiz Queensland, one office worker can throw away up to a quarter of a tonne of materials every year. How much is your office throwing away?

---

36   See www.mobilemuster.com.au

37   *Eco-efficiency for small business.* See www.derm.qld.gov.au

Case study: Reducing waste and saving money

A good way to initiate a review of your waste and recycling practices is to form a waste committee. According to ecoBiz Queensland, one aged care facility in Brisbane achieved significant cost savings when it did the following:

Cardboard

Simply crushing its cardboard boxes enabled the facility to reduce the size of its recycling bins and how frequently they needed to be collected. This immediately saved them hundreds of dollars every month.

General recycling

Prior to the waste audit, the facility had no way of recycling newspapers, milk containers and steel cans. The acquisition of five new recycling wheelie bins led to monthly savings on general waste disposal costs.

Paper recycling

Recycling bins for office paper were placed near all printers, fax machines and photocopiers. This reduced the collections of general waste bins.

Clinical waste

The audit showed that some employees were placing normal waste in the clinical waste bins. Training employees to put standard waste into normal bins saved them money.

Organic waste

The facility was able to take its kitchen and garden waste to a nearby bioenergy facility that captures methane from organic waste and turns it into electricity.

Total saved

In addition to reducing the amount of waste going to landfill by many tonnes, the facility saved thousands of dollars in reduced waste costs. Helped along by the WasteWise Queensland program and the local recycling business, it was able to achieve a significant result for the environment and its bottom line.

Creating an action plan

After reviewing the tips in this book and listening to advice from your own employees, make up an action list of the measures that will reduce waste in your business.

The action plan should be designed and implemented in accordance with this waste hierarchy diagram:

Waste hierarchy guide

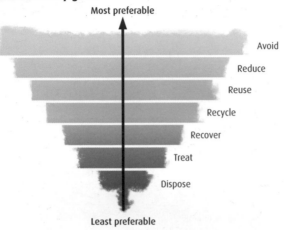

1. Avoid using goods and resources to maximise your savings.

2. Reduce the amount of goods and resources that you use.

3. Reuse products if you can, or sell your waste to a company that will reuse it in the manufacture of new products.

4. Recycle materials that you can no longer use.

5. Recover the valuable and useable components of what is thrown away (with the assistance of waste management and recycling companies if necessary).

6. Treat materials to ensure the potentially harmful impacts of waste materials is minimised (with the assistance of waste management and recycling companies if necessary).

7. Dispose only as a last option.

Reducing your resource use and saving money can be as simple as replacing bottled water in your office with filtered water or tap water. Using reusable mugs and buying coffee, tea and sugar in bulk can also save money and resources.

Recycling should not be the first option that you go with. It is always best to avoid, reduce and reuse materials before you recycle. If implemented correctly, a waste minimisation strategy based on these principles can realise significant efficiencies and savings for your business.

Recycling rules

There are some simple rules to follow when it comes to recycling in the workplace:

1. Make sure your business is recycling all that it can. Go to www.recyclingnearyou.com.au to find out everything that can be recycled in your local area.

2. Talk to your existing recycling contractor to see if they can provide your business with facilities to recycle more materials. For details on recycling companies in your area, use your Yellow Pages® *Book,* visit yellowpages.com.au online or on your mobile, or ask your local council waste officer for advice on recycling in your local community. Some companies can also help you to organise a recycling audit and service for your business. Such companies include Visy Recycling (1300 368 479 or email customerservice@visy.com.au), SITA Environmental Solutions (131335 or www.sita.com.au) and Veolia Environmental Services (02 8571 0000 or national@veolia.com.au).

3. Educate your employees about what can and cannot be recycled. Talk to them about the benefits of recycling and make it as easy as possible for them to play their part. Also talk to your cleaning service to make sure they are putting your recyclables into the right bin.

4. Don't put recyclables in plastic bags. Plastic bags are a major problem for recycling companies and can prevent the material inside from being recycled.

5.   Pyrex ovenproof glass, ceramic mugs and broken wine or drinking glasses should not be put in your recycling bins. Just 15g of ceramics or a small piece of ovenproof glass can stop a whole tonne of normal glass bottles from being recycled.[38] The reason why? They melt at a higher temperature and contaminate the glass making process.

6.   Take the lids off plastic bottles. The lid is made from a different plastic to the bottle – doing this also ensures there is no liquid left inside the bottle.

Where to go for waste and recycling advice and information

National

The Planet Ark and Sensis Recycling Near You service provides practical information on waste reduction. If you need further advice, contact your local council's waste management officer or the following entities for advice and information.

Recycling Near You (just enter in your postcode): www.RecyclingNearYou.com.au

Australian Government – Department of Sustainability, Environment, Water, Population and the Arts: www.environment.gov.au

Visy Recycling: www.visy.com.au

Australian Capital Territory

Department of the Environment, Climate Change, Energy and Water: www.environment.act.gov.au

Department of Territory and Municipal Services (waste section): www.tams.act.gov.au

New South Wales

Department of Environment, Climate Change and Water: www.environment.nsw.gov.au

NSW Business Chamber (sustainability toolkits): www.nswbusinesschamber.com.au

Northern Territory

Department of Natural Resources, Environment, The Arts and Sport: www.nt.gov.au/nreta

---

38   Planet Ark. See www.planetark.org

7. Sensitive or confidential documents can be shredded prior to recycling. Alternatively there are a number of waste disposal contractors who specialise in confidential document destruction and recycling.

8. If you have computers, furniture and office equipment that your business no longer needs, talk to local community groups and charities to see if they want them. You can also distribute them for nothing via your local Freecycle or Green Collect group. Go to www.freecycle.org or www.greencollect.com.au for further information.

Queensland

Department of Environment (including the ecoBiz small business program): www.derm.qld.gov.au

Chamber of Commerce and Industry Queensland: www.cciq.com.au

South Australia

Zero Waste SA: www.zerowaste.sa.gov.au

Business SA (go to the sustainable business development unit, in business services): www.business-sa.com

Tasmania

Department of Primary Industries, Parks, Water and Environment: www.environment.tas.gov.au

Victoria

Grow Me The Money: www.growmethemoney.com.au

Resource Smart: www.resourcesmart.vic.gov.au

Western Australia

Zero Waste WA: www.zerowastewa.com.au

Using the services of an accredited waste auditor can also be a very cost-effective approach to developing a waste plan, especially if you haven't done one before. Business-friendly organisations like Grow Me The Money and Business SA can help here.

9. Finally, it's not enough to put material out for recycling. People and businesses can play their part by buying products that are made from that recycled material. Examples include Dr Harry's Light and Easy Cat Litter, which is made from recycled Yellow Pages® and White Pages® *Books* or the SAFE and Earthwise toilet tissue. Thousands of tonnes of used office paper goes into making these toilet tissue brands every year.

Case study: Yellow Pages® and White Pages® – Directory Recycling program

In late 2009, Sensis® celebrated the 10th anniversary of its kerb-side recycling program. Yellow Pages® and White Pages® directory recycling rates have improved from 4 per cent in 1999 to 98 per cent recycled or reused in 2010.*

Sensis® manages the national directory recycling program with assistance from Visy Recycling.

The program now allows for old directories to be included with other paper recycling in most areas throughout Australia, for both residential and commercial services.

If your business has a Visy paper and cardboard recycling service, you can include your old directories in this service. If your business doesn't have a recycling service, you can or visit www.visy.com.au or call Visy Recycling on 1300 368 479.

Old directories are collected with other recyclables and then they're sorted and recycled by Visy Recycling into a range of recycled cardboard packaging products.

* Results exclude the proportion of respondents who indicated that they had not disposed of, recycled or reused their book.

Chapter 4 – Lifting the lid on waste and recycling

Recycling collaboration

In order to collect quantities that are attractive to a recycling service, small businesses can join with neighbouring businesses to form a 'recycling alliance'. In addition to reducing waste that goes to landfill, it could also potentially reduce your waste disposal and recycling costs.

In an industrial park, the recycling location could be a space that's supplied by park management. Or it could be that one of the businesses has enough space to act as a central recycling drop-off point for all the businesses around them. With a little bit of innovative thinking, this kind of approach is another way to recycle materials that would otherwise end up in landfill.

We're the best in the world

Australians are currently recycling more than two billion newspapers and magazines every year. With a recycling rate in 2009 of 78 per cent, we're the best newspaper and magazine recyclers in the world. Go to www.pneb.com.au for more information.

Reuse

There's an old saying that one person's junk is someone else's treasure. If you have leftover materials from your operations, you can place them on www.wasteexchange.net.au. This free national online database was established by the Victorian Waste Management Association and EPA Victoria. It enables businesses to list unwanted materials that other companies might find useful. If you're in manufacturing, there may be a raw material you use that another SME might currently be throwing out. Investigating this might lead to significant cost savings in your business.

Electronic and electrical waste

In 2005 an estimated 312,930 tonnes of electronic equipment was disposed of in Australia's landfills.[39]

Electronic waste, or e-waste, is the term given to redundant or discarded electronic or electrical equipment. This includes computers, mobile phones, televisions, video and DVD players, stereos, fax machines, photocopiers, printers, printer cartridges, batteries and peripheral devices that came with the equipment.

Mobiles: There are two solutions to this. One is to make your mobile phone last as long as possible, or to pass it on to other people. The other is to recycle your mobile via the MobileMuster recycling bins available in Telstra outlets. When you next decide to upgrade your mobile, put up a poster at work to collect other people's old phones. When you go to the shop to get your new phone, take them with you and put them in the recycling bin. Go to www.mobilemuster.com.au for all recycling locations. To arrange a one-off MobileMuster recycling push at your workplace, call 1800 249 113. Don't forget to remove the SIM cards and wipe the data off the phones.

Printer cartridges: It's easy for SMEs to recycle their old cartridges. You can do this through Cartridges 4 Planet Ark www.cartridges.planetark.org or at Cartridge World retail outlets.

Computers: SMEs can make their computers last longer by installing the maximum amount of RAM and using functions such as cloud computing, where applications and services are hosted by other organisations and accessed via the internet, thereby reducing the need for on-site computers and servers. See the IT section (chapter 11) of this book for other tips.

TV sets: A national recycling scheme is being established so keep old TVs stored until a local recycling service is in place.

Batteries: Companies like Cleanaway, SITA, MRI, Sony, Battery World and others all have rechargeable battery recycling services that your business can use.

Lighting: There are a number of recycling options available including temporary bins, prepaid collection boxes and even a Tube Terminator option for in-house crushing of collected lighting waste. Go to www.cmaecocycle.net for further information.

---

39   *Waste and recycling in Australia,* Hyder Consulting, November 2008.
      See www.environment.gov.au

Oil recycling

One litre of oil can contaminate more than one million litres of water. So if your business is using oil in any way, it's vital that you recycle it.

269 million litres of used oil was recycled by Australians in 2008–09.[40] While this has increased over the past five years, there is still more oil that could be recycled. Used oil, also called 'sump oil', can be recycled into industrial burner oil, mould oil, hydraulic oil, bitumen based products and can be used as an additive in manufactured products.

Go to www.oilrecycling.gov.au/safety-tips.html for tips on how to safely recycle your oil. For information about the national oil recycling program visit www.oilrecycling.gov.au; to find out your nearest oil recycling location, go to www.recyclingnearyou.com.au or talk to your local council recycling officer.

Plastic recycling

There is much confusion about which types of plastic can or can't be recycled. The numbers and arrows on the bottom of plastic bottles and on other plastic products are not recycling symbols; they identify the type of plastic the product is made from. However these symbols can be used to help determine whether that plastic can be put in your recycling bin. To find out which types of plastic can be recycled in your area, go to www.recyclingnearyou.com.au or contact your recycling contractor.

How does recycling help the environment?

Recycling doesn't just save resources. It also saves water, saves energy and reduces greenhouse emissions.

---

40   Department of the Environment, Water, Heritage and the Arts annual report 2008–09 – volume two. See www.environment.gov.au

Recycling one can or bottle at a time, you'd be forgiven for thinking that recycling doesn't add up to much. But when you consider how many businesses and households are now recycling, it all adds up. In a big way.

In 2006, the Australian Council of Recyclers estimated that commodities recycling helped to reduce Australia's CO_2 equivalent emissions by 8.8 million tonnes. It also saved 202 terajoules (TJ) of energy and 92 gigalitres (92 billion litres) of water. They also estimated that the equivalent of 3 million trees, 365,000 tonnes of sand, 4 million tonnes of iron ore and 1.6 million tonnes of bauxite were saved through Australia's commodity recycling activities.

How does recycling and waste management help the economy?

In 2006, the recycling industry directly employed 10,900 people and indirectly employed 27,700. Figures from the Australian Council of Recyclers also show that the industry contributed $11.5 billion to the economy.[41] When it comes to waste, more than 14,000 Australians were employed in 1092 public and private businesses.

In 2002–3, the Australian Bureau of Statistics estimated that waste management, excluding resource recovery, had an industry value of $1.3 billion. Showing how much the clout of small business adds up, 74 per cent of these waste businesses were small enterprises employing up to four people.[42]

How much do we waste?

In 2006–07, Australia generated 14.4 million tonnes of commercial and industrial waste. Of this, 6.4 million tonnes (44.5 per cent) was dumped in landfill and eight million tonnes was recycled (55.5 per cent).

Estimated breakdown of the commercial and industrial waste stream

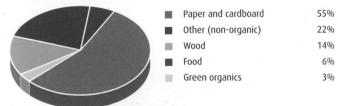

■	Paper and cardboard	55%
■	Other (non-organic)	22%
■	Wood	14%
■	Food	6%
■	Green organics	3%

Source: Hyder Consulting 2008

41   *Australian Recycling Values – A Net Benefits Assessment,* July 2008, Australian Council
      of Recyclers and Hyder Consulting
42   *Waste Management Services Australia,* ABS Report no. 86980. 2002–3

In 2006–7, Australia managed to recycle 8.5 million tonnes (54.5 per cent) of construction and demolition waste. But 7.1 million tonnes (45.5 per cent) still went to landfill. When it came to municipal waste, 4.6 million tonnes was recycled, while 7.3 million tonnes ended up in landfill.

From a waste-efficiency point of view, Australia is not doing as well as it could. In a single year we dumped an estimated 20.8 million tonnes of waste in landfill. That represents a major inefficiency in our usage of resources.

This situation is worsening. Between 2002–3 and 2006–7, Australia generated 52 per cent more commercial and industrial waste. If this trend continues, by 2020 Australia will generate 33.2 million tonnes of commercial and industrial waste every year.[43]

Every kilogram of that 33.2 million tonnes will represent a hit on the bottom line of Australia's businesses. Implementing a waste policy in your business will help to reduce this.

Case study: Rosedale Leather – composting initiative

With 120 employees processing 7000 hides a week, Rosedale Leather generated a lot of waste when they tanned hides to be used as leather car seats.

After implementing changes to make its tanning process more environmentally responsible, Rosedale Leather worked in partnership with EPA Victoria to see how they could convert what was previously described as prescribed industrial waste into a safe composting material.

The three individual waste products from Rosedale Leather are now composted with local green waste and meet all applicable Australian standards.

In addition to helping the environment, it's also helped the bottom line. By diverting its waste to compost instead of landfill, Rosedale Leather saved $140,000 in 2009.[44]

---

43   *A National Waste Policy: Managing Waste to 2020,* Department of the Environment, Water, Heritage and Arts, 2009

44   See www.cedaily.com.au

'When looked at in four key areas –
greening your fleet, supply chain, business
travel and encouraging employees –
there are opportunities for everyone.'

5

Get on board with sustainable transport

Transportation is vital for business. As with other energy-using activities, transportation offers lots of opportunities to save money and reduce pollution at the same time.

Considering and planning for alternative transport arrangements can also deliver productivity increases. The size of the benefit is limited only by the amount of transport you currently use and your commitment to reducing it. When looked at in four key areas – greening your fleet, your supply chain, business travel and encouraging employees – there are opportunities for everyone.

1. Greening your fleet

Buying and leasing

When it comes to making a greener vehicle choice there are some basic rules to follow:

- if your business owns or leases cars, you should undertake an annual review of usage to ensure you don't have too many vehicles

- you also need to assess whether your business is using the right type of vehicles; buying or leasing bigger and more expensive vehicles can seem attractive from a prestige point of view but the rising cost of fuel makes fuel-efficient models a better choice for the bottom line

- think about the most appropriate car for your needs; if you operate in an inner-city area, there are many advantages to having a smaller car – they're cheaper to buy, easier to park, use less fuel and therefore their emissions are a lot less.

What to buy?

Australians buy more than one million cars every year. Our passenger cars account for 8 per cent of our greenhouse emissions, putting 43.7 million tonnes of greenhouse gases into the atmosphere every year.[45] The transportation sector generates 78 million tonnes of greenhouse emissions every year. That equates to 14.6 per cent of our national emissions. The majority of that is from road transportation.[46]

If you operate your own delivery vehicles, try to group pick-ups into geographic zones when collecting or delivering goods. This will minimise the kilometres travelled by your vehicles, while at the same time reducing emissions and saving on fuel costs.

45   *Greener Motoring*, The Australian Automobile Association. See www.aaa.asn.au/documents/reports/2008/FACTA4_EcoDriving.pdf

46   DECC Australian National Greenhouse Accounts – National Greenhouse Gas Inventory, May 2009

The Green Vehicle Guide website at www.greenvehicleguide.gov.au can help your business to save thousands of dollars and reduce its environmental impact at the same time. It gives you information about cars sold in Australia and allows you to compare the car you're interested in with other cars in the same class. The comparisons include:

■ fuel type

■ fuel consumption on a litre per 100 kilometre basis

■ CO_2 emissions on a gram per kilometre basis

■ a greenhouse rating

■ an air pollution rating

■ overall star rating (combining the greenhouse and pollution ratings).

The site has a handy fuel calculator which can determine your annual fuel costs and total greenhouse gas emissions. An information kit is also available from the website which you can show to colleagues and management in your business. The site also lists the fuel efficiency details of older model cars if you're looking to buy a second-hand vehicle.

More tips

1. If you're wandering around a car yard, look out for the Fuel Consumption label on cars that you're interested in buying or leasing. This is on the front windscreen and details the fuel efficiency of the car and its greenhouse emissions performance.

2. Register with the Australasian Fleet Managers' Association Greener Motoring program at www.afma.net.au for detailed guidance on strategies to reduce fleet emissions and costs.

What to rent?

If you're travelling for work and need to hire a car, choosing a more environmentally friendly option will save you money and send a strong message to your professional network that your business walks the talk on environmental issues.

All car-rental companies offer fuel-efficient or hybrid cars. Some rental companies also offer carbon offsets for the cars that you hire. Others have made a public commitment to stock new-generation electric cars when they are released in Australia.

Renting a car is also a great way to 'try before you buy'. If you find a car that has rated well on the Green Vehicle Guide, why not rent it for the day to check that it's the right vehicle for your business?

Choosing the right tyres

When it comes to tyres, the issues of safety and performance are a priority for most people. However, not many people think about the efficiency of the tyres and the amount of fuel they use.

Research conducted by Michelin shows that tyres account for one tank of fuel out of every five.[47] So buying fuel-efficient tyres can save you money and help the environment.

Look for tyres with low rolling resistance and maximum efficiency. Properly maintained and inflated, such tyres can reduce your fuel bills by up to 4 per cent.

Also, make sure you pump up your fleet's tyres to the manufacturer's recommended levels each week. It may sound tedious, but it is safer and more fuel-efficient, and therefore greener.

SME transport innovation

Australian parts manufacturer Futuris has won a PACE Award from the American Society of Automotive Engineers for its enviroTUF™ carpet. The carpet for each car can use up to 100 recycled PET bottles. According to the judges, "Futuris is able to offer PET carpet at lower cost than nylon but with better appearance and feel. And it is 100 per cent recyclable."

47   See www.michelin.com

Efficient driving

If you have a large fleet and a large fuel bill, it often pays to send your employees on eco-driving courses that show them how to drive in a way that saves fuel.

Here are our top ten tips for eco-efficient driving:

1. Avoid hard accelerating and braking. According to TravelSMART, less aggressive driving can reduce fuel consumption by up to 30 per cent.[48] Driving your car too hard can also cause costly wear and tear on the engine, tyres, transmission and brakes.

2. Avoid areas and times of heavy traffic congestion to minimise 'stop-start' driving. Traffic interruptions account for about 40 per cent of average fuel consumption in city driving.[49]

3. Avoid short trips wherever possible and plan ahead to combine multiple errands.

4. Most vehicles do not need to be 'warmed up' except in very cold conditions and after long periods of non-use. Don't leave the motor running when the vehicle is stationary.

Driving your car too hard can also cause costly wear and tear on the engine, tyres, transmission and brakes.

---

5. Avoid high revs. Engines operate most efficiently when revving at about 1500 to 2500 rpm. In a manual transmission vehicle, shift up a gear as quickly as is practical. An automatic transmission will shift up a gear more rapidly if you ease back on the accelerator once the car has momentum.

6. Clear out clutter from boots and back seats. Every 50 kilograms of extra weight a typical car carries increases its fuel consumption by about 2 per cent.[50]

7. Minimise wind resistance. The faster you drive, the greater the wind resistance and fuel consumption. Remove roof racks and other external attachments when they are not needed. Open sunroofs and windows will also significantly increase fuel consumption at faster speeds.

48   See www.transport.vic.gov.au/travelsmart
49   Bureau of Infrastructure, Transport and Regional Economics
50   See www.racv.com.au

8. Air-conditioning can increase fuel consumption by 5–10% but it is more efficient than an open window at speeds of more than 80 km/h. While an air-conditioner does need to be used regularly, to avoid leaks and operation problems, avoid running it all the time. Use the vents instead.[51]

9. Keep tyres inflated to the highest recommended pressure. Under-inflated tyres can reduce fuel-efficiency. Optimum inflation will also increase tyre life and improve handling.

10. Keep your vehicle well-maintained for optimum performance. Have the engine serviced and wheel alignment checked according to the manufacturer's guidelines (usually every six months or 10,000km, whichever comes first). Also make sure to regularly check oil, coolant and other fluid levels.

Alternative fuels

Alternative fuels are far from new. According to HydrogenCarsNow, the first car designed in 1806 by Swiss Francois Isaac de Rivaz was fuelled by a hydrogen-oxygen mix. Rudolf Diesel designed his engine to run on peanut oil while the iconic Ford Model T was designed to run on either petrol or ethanol.

There are a number of alternative fuels available for cars in Australia. These include:

Biodiesel

Biodiesel is derived from dead animals and vegetable oils, including used cooking oil from restaurants and a number of plants such as canola and mustard seeds. It can potentially be used directly in any existing, unmodified diesel engine. It is now readily available across the country at B2 levels and many fleet operators are using B20, B50 and even B100 biodiesel.

LPG

Liquefied Petroleum Gas (LPG, LP Gas or Autogas) is synthesised from gases found in crude oil and natural gas fields and produced during the oil refining process. Australia is one of the biggest users of LPG on a per capita basis. It is our third most commonly used fuel, accounting for nearly 7 per cent of road transport fuel sales.[52]

---

51   See www.makecarsgreen.com/10-points.html
52   See www.ret.gov.au

Car-sharing services

Membership of a car-sharing service is a useful and cost-effective addition to promoting walking, cycling and public transport. Cheaper than taxis or rental cars, car-share services can free your business and employees from the expense of vehicle ownership. By joining a service, you get the use of a shared car fleet when needed, with vehicles based at a wide range of locations and accessible 24 hours a day.

Members pay for use according to the distance travelled and the length of time used – you can rent the car for as little as one hour, to as long as you like. Though most common in Sydney and Melbourne, car-sharing services are also starting to take off in other capital cities as higher housing density and traffic congestion makes driving and parking a chore. They're an ideal solution for SMEs looking to save money and reduce emissions.

Ethanol

Ethanol in Australia is currently derived from cereals, sugarcane, crop waste and the waste from flour production. It's a renewable fuel and is mainly added to petrol in blends of E5 to E10 which is now readily available in service stations around the country. E10 is completely safe for most vehicles produced from 1986 and of the cars produced in 2009, 99.44 per cent could take an ethanol blend. However, there are global concerns about the environmental impact of using land to make ethanol from crops like corn when it could be used for food production or forest eco-system preservation.

Electricity

Electric cars don't just reduce pollution in our cities. They're also fast. The first car to break the 100 km/h land speed record in 1899 was an electric car called La Jamais Contente. Hybrid cars that use petrol and electric motors have mainstreamed electric cars, with Toyota selling more than two million of them. Coming soon to the mainstream Australian car market are Extended Range Electric Vehicles (EREV) and a wide range of electric cars. The recharging times for electric cars continues to improve, so in coming years expect wider availability in the marketplace.

Case study: GoGet – a car-share service

As the owner of Meerkat Computer Services, Sven Knutsen is based in inner-city Sydney where car parking spaces are difficult to find.

At no cost, his business joined the GoGet Carshare service which has eight cars in permanent designated parking spots all within 10 minutes walk of his workplace. All he has to do is book a car on the website at www.goget.com.au and then pick it up. For him, using GoGet is sometimes faster than getting a taxi and it works out a lot cheaper.

Using a car-share service has helped to reduce transportation costs of getting Sven to and from clients. He gets to take all his equipment and tools with him and he can hire the car by the hour for as little or as long as he wants. Most important of all, using the service helps the environment, saves him money and he still gets to his clients on time.

SMEs in inner-city Sydney also use station wagons from car-share services to deliver supplies or use hire cars to go to meetings. Using a car-share scheme can be a cheaper way to give your business flexibility in your transportation requirements.

Flexicar has car-share vehicles available in both Sydney and Melbourne. Go to www.flexicar.com.au for further information.

The benefits of car-sharing services include:

- when a vehicle is not needed for frequent daily use, car-sharing alleviates the high fixed costs of ownership, such as registration and insurance (often amounting to thousands of dollars per year), as well as helping to reduce traffic and parking congestion
- many car-sharing fleets use the most modern, eco-efficient models

- research suggests that, because cars are expensive to own but relatively cheap to use, car ownership encourages more driving, even when other options would be as convenient or healthier; car sharing therefore promotes walking, cycling and using public transport, with car sharers driving a lot less than car owners.

2. Supply chain

A number of transportation companies such as Linfox are making real efforts to reduce the amount of fuel they use and their emissions. Is your current delivery company or courier service one of them?

Ask your delivery company about the actions they're taking to reduce their emissions and fuel use. Are they actively measuring the impact they have on the environment? Are they using fuel-efficient or alternative-powered vehicles? Are they driving in a more fuel-efficient way? If not, it is an opportunity to talk to them about 'greening' their performance.

3. Business travel

Here is a quick run-down of the key things to consider.

Telecommuting

Overseas governments are promoting telecommuting from home as a way of combating traffic congestion and air pollution. As Internet speeds soar, more Australian companies are also looking at this option. It doesn't suit every person or workplace – and it does require a workplace culture where output is rated more highly than the length of time a person is 'seen' to be doing their job.

The potential savings make it worth exploring. Workers save time and money on travel, while your business saves on real estate and parking costs. Businesses with employees that telecommute are expected to supply the equipment needed to enable them to work from home. This would include items such as a laptop, webcam and internet connection and the company would also contribute to the cost of electricity. This can often cost far less than having that person full time in the office.

Businesses that do have employees working from home should undertake a site inspection to ensure the office location meets all Occupational Health and Safety standards.

Go to www.lifehacker.com.au/tags/telecommuting/ for more information.

'Virtual' meetings

Remember the Yellow Pages® advertising slogan 'Let your fingers do the walking®'? Well, that's even truer these days. It's not called the information superhighway for nothing!

Online communication is revolutionising business by eliminating the need for employees to hit the road. While 'face time' is still important, there are many instances where meeting in person can be replaced by teleconferencing, web-conferencing or video-conferencing. All involve a fraction of the time, money and energy.

For more information, guides and tips on 'virtual' meetings, see www.telstraenterprise.com/conferencingcollaboration

The great thing about a webcam or video-conference meeting is that you get to see the person you're talking to, allowing you to pick up on their body language. If both parties have high speed internet, you can even have the video meeting in full screen mode on your computer or monitor – something that makes for very productive meetings.

Video-conferencing programs like Skype, iChat and Windows Messenger are free of charge – iChat also allows you to bring in people from multiple locations on video. But you do need to ensure that all parties taking part have good internet connections.

Commercial programs from companies like Adobe and Webex also allow all parties in the meeting to interact with documents as well. There are many tools out there that can help SMEs to be more productive and are far cheaper than a face-to-face meeting.

Air travel

The cost of air travel is not just financial. There's a big environmental cost as well. Air travel produces significantly more carbon emissions than other types of passenger transportation. Aircraft emissions have a greenhouse effect that's a number of times greater than road vehicle emissions. This is because they're released at higher altitude where they remain in the atmosphere for longer periods of time.

According to Qantas, a return trip to London from Sydney generates 3.8 tonnes of CO_2-e per passenger. Going the same distance in multiple short-haul flights produces even more emissions due to the amount of fuel burnt during each take off and landing.

By utilising video-conferencing, SMEs can save time and money by:

- avoiding the need for so many flights – flights between the capital cities can cost hundreds of dollars

- reducing the use of taxis – getting taxis to and from the airport can be expensive and there's often a big queue
- not driving to the airport means no airport parking costs
- the time wasted travelling to and from the airports at both ends is avoided.

Go to www.travelsmart.gov.au for more useful information about travel.

If you must travel, why not carbon offset your air flights? Qantas, Virgin and other airlines offer these offsets as part of the ticket buying process. It's as easy as ticking a box and best of all, it's very cheap to do. Offsetting your flights is a very economical way to make a real difference to your company's greenhouse emissions.

4. Encouraging employees

Walking and cycling – get on your bike

Many people already own a bike and in 2008, bicycles outsold cars with more than one million bikes sold.[53]

In today's busy world, many employees are working longer hours and don't always have the time to keep as fit as they should. There's a downside to this from a business perspective as unfit employees are not going to work to their optimum potential.

An easy way to get your employees fit and reduce your environmental footprint is to get them to ride to work. For those who don't own a bike, how can you make it easy for them to do so?

One Dutch company called Waterschap Veluwe gave a free pushbike to all employees who lived within 10 kilometres of its office. It put in place shower facilities, changing rooms and bike sheds and even offered employees an allowance for getting home on rainy days. As a result, 40 per cent of the employees cycle to work, making for a fitter and more emissions-friendly workplace.[54]

---

53   'Bicycle sales race ahead as city dwellers go green', *The Australian*, December 6, 2008
54   See www.travelsmart.gov.au

Walking to work

Why not encourage your employees to walk to work? A good time to start such a push is on the national Walk to Work day. Run by the Pedestrian Council of Australia, the scheme encourages businesses small and large to get their employees fitter and become more environmentally friendly in the way they travel to work. Go to www.walk.com.au for more information.

Research suggests that those who get in 30 minutes of physical activity five times a week significantly reduce their chance of developing a serious illness and they also improve their mental alertness. Fitter employees are better employees as they're healthier and less likely to take time off work. Investing in bike-friendly facilities and promoting incentives to encourage walking or cycling therefore makes good business sense.

Walking or travelling to work on public transport one day a week can cut a regular car commuter's weekly fuel use and greenhouse emissions by up to 20 per cent.

If your business is interested in becoming bike-friendly, it should:

- provide showers and lockers for cyclists
- ensure there's a secure, sheltered area to lock up bikes
- provide financial incentives, such as salary sacrificing so employees can purchase bike equipment or consider providing long-serving employees with a free bike as part of their overall package
- make walking and cycling part of a team-building exercise by involving your business' bike riders in charity fundraising events.

Case study: **Coles – ride to work initiative**

In 2009, the Coles headquarters in Melbourne created secure cage parking facilities for 120 pushbikes. In addition to providing an air pump for flat tyres, they also put in place 30 showers, clothes dryers and ironing boards. For people affected by rain and wind, they've even provided a hair straightener.

Case study: **Monash University – Bike Share Scheme**

In 2009, Monash University started a Bike Share Scheme at its Clayton campus. Seventy bikes made up of recycled parts have been made available for the scheme and each bike comes complete with a free helmet, lights and a 'shopping trolley' locking system. This makes it very easy for the students and employees to get around. Could your business do something similar for your employees?

For more information on these and other case studies, visit the TravelSmart Victoria website at www.travelsmart.gov.au

For information on creating a more bike-friendly workplace email bicyclevic@bv.com.au or go to www.bv.com.au and type in 'workplace'.

You can read the Australian Greenhouse office case study at www.travelsmart.gov.au/employers/cyclefriendly.html for more information on managing an employee bike fleet.

Go to www.tmr.qld.gov.au for information on setting up a workplace bike pool.

Public transport

If 50 people catch a bus or train that's potentially 50 fewer cars on the road. The environmental benefits are obvious. But let's face it, there's a reason people prefer cars: public transport isn't always convenient, and people's use of it depends very much on the frequency of services and travel times.

Create a workplace culture that actively encourages the use of public transport wherever possible:

- provide interest-free loans or let employees salary sacrifice the purchase of periodic travel passes
- provide easy access to public transport maps and timetables
- where possible provide some flexibility for those who might find it easier to start and finish work earlier or later, depending on available services
- consider giving regular public transport users Cabcharge vouchers as a fallback plan when they work late.

It's also important to promote the positive benefits of public transport to your employees:

- it's cheaper than driving a car to work
- coming to work on a bus or a train allows people time to read a book or a newspaper
- they don't have the stress of traffic jams, so there's a better chance they'll arrive at work happier.

Car pooling

If you've ever been stuck in peak-hour traffic, you might have noticed that the majority of cars only hold one person. Why not encourage your employees to share the commute to work by car pooling. It's better for the environment and it will save them money.

For a typical 6-cylinder family sedan doing the average number of kilometres, the estimated cost of owning and running it in NSW is up to $265 per week.

With car pooling, your employees can potentially halve their costs. This figure can be even higher if your employees go without their car altogether.[55]

---

55   See www.mynrma.com.au

Car pooling is probably the easiest 'sell' to get employees to reduce their transport eco-footprint. They still get the convenience of car travel but save on petrol costs, reduce pollution and greenhouse emissions and get to use the transit lane.

The basic rules of car pooling for your employees:

- they should agree upfront on the terms of their car pool arrangement and how they will share the costs

- they should never be late for the person picking them up

- they should not expect to stop off for milk on the way home!

To encourage car pooling:

- have a postcode coffee morning at work so people who live in similar postcodes can be introduced to each other and arrange to car pool; you might even extend this to include neighbouring businesses

- incentives can also play a key role in getting people to make the switch; offer a guaranteed car parking space for car pooling employees or offer them a free car tune up – for some companies the cost of tuning a car is far cheaper than having to supply a car parking space

- use an online car pooling service like www.thecarpool.com.au

- provide a fallback transport option so employees are never left stranded when plans go awry; if a car pool partner has to rush home because their child is sick at school, guarantee them a ride home – the UK chemist Boots does this and even though they have 7500 employees, this option is reportedly only required a few times a year.

Flexi-time

Flexi-time arrangements contribute to the morale of employees by giving them a greater sense of control over work-life balance and also support eco-efficient transport.

Commuting during morning and afternoon peak traffic is time-consuming and energy-intensive. Half of all travel on Australian roads occurs in congested traffic (moving at less than one-third of free-flowing speeds) or interrupted traffic (moving at less than half free-flowing speeds).

Analysis by the Australian Bureau of Infrastructure, Transport and Regional Economics indicates traffic interruptions account for about 40 per cent of all vehicle fuel consumption in major cities, contributing 17 per cent of total domestic transport greenhouse gas emissions. Yet as little as a 4 per cent change in traffic volume can mean the difference between free-flowing traffic and gridlock.[56] Whether employees drive, take the bus or ride a bike, flexi-time can help them avoid the crush and reduce travel times.

Case study: Linfox

Changing driving techniques has changed Linfox's bottom line. Linfox drivers undertook the 'Eco Drive' course* as part of a multi-pronged push to successfully reduce the company's carbon emissions by 28 per cent between 2007 – 2009.

Being gentle on the brakes, using the appropriate gear, driving steadily and keeping tyres fully inflated were just some of the techniques that reduced pollution and saved Linfox money. Go to www.linfox.com/environment.aspx for more information.

* See www.ecodesk.com

---

56   *Greenhouse Gas Emissions from Australian Transport: Base Case Projections to 2020,* – Bureau of Infrastructure, Transport and Regional Economics. See www.bitre.gov.au

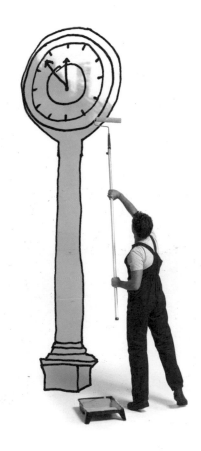

'Using less paper not only saves money, it can also reduce poor practices and inefficiencies that excessive paper use may create in your business.'

6

Reduce, reuse, recycle: easy steps to cut out paper waste

Whatever amount of paper you use, reducing it is a great place to start for any business wishing to save money.

Using less paper not only saves money, it can also reduce poor practices and inefficiencies that excessive paper use may create in your business.

Shifting your business away from paper and into electronic document management can bring about significant improvements in efficiency and productivity. Greater use of electronic documentation for writing, storage and distribution can benefit business and the environment – but it needs to be smart.

Just like paper, electronic devices have environmental impacts. The devices you use and how you use them is just like your choice of paper and how you use it – it has to be right for your organisation. If you think smart and take into account the wider range of costs and benefits involved with your paper and electronic documents, you will find opportunities for significant environmental and cost improvements.

What are the real financial costs of paper?

The primary cost of paper is buying the paper itself but secondary costs include:

- printing and copying
- postage and packing
- storage and disposal
- employee administration and time
- wasted office space and infrastructure.

Better management of the paper use in your business will help to reduce these hidden costs.

Reduce, reuse, recycle

Making paper uses up vast amounts of water, trees and energy. The whole process uses tens of millions of trees[57] per year and generates millions of tonnes[58] of greenhouse gases. Disposing of paper in landfill also generates a greenhouse gas called methane – averaged over a hundred year period, the global warming potential of methane is 25 times more potent[59] than the carbon pollution from car exhausts. With these environmental impacts in mind, remember the waste-reduction mantra:

- reduce your consumption of paper
- reuse the paper you consume
- recycle the paper you dispose of.

Getting started on a paper reduction campaign

1. Get support

Speak with your colleagues and get support and approval to develop a campaign for paper reduction.

2. Plan your campaign

Ask for volunteers or set up a working group, involving people from different parts of your business. Without champions and encouragement, people can easily fall back into bad habits – it's important to keep reminding everyone that every single wasted piece of paper adds up.

---

57   See www.worldwatch.org/node/5326

58   See www.savepaper.com.au

59   IPCC, 2007: *Climate Change 2007: The Physical Science Basis*. Contribution of Working Group I to the Fourth Assessment Report of the Intergovernmental Panel on Climate Change – www.ipcc.ch/ipccreports/ar4-wg1.htm

To establish a baseline for measuring the success of your campaign, conduct an assessment of how much paper you're currently using. The Paper-Less Print Logger Software at www.savepaper.com.au/software[60] will help you to do this by tracking your printing and is free of charge for businesses with less than five employees. Also examine the 'non-office' papers, such as tissues, that are used in your workplace.

Once you understand how much of what type of paper you use, you can then identify actions to reduce it.

3. Launch your campaign

Make sure everyone knows what you're trying to achieve and how much paper you're currently using.

Starting out, you need to set targets for paper reduction and provide practical advice on how people can achieve those goals.

4. Monitor your progress

As soon as you have success, make sure you communicate it positively and enthusiastically to all employees. It's about using the right sort of paper efficiently, only when you have to and taking responsibility for reusing or recycling the paper when you're finished with it.

First basic steps to smart paper use

1. Share documents electronically:
   - avoid sending faxes and posting letters – mail the documents electronically instead; if this sounds obvious, it's worth noting that Australian businesses still post 4.2 billion items ever year[61]
   - instead of printing multiple sets of paper documents, keep electronic files that employees can access
   - review and edit your files on screen rather than on paper
   - encourage suppliers and clients to send you mail and bills electronically
   - scan paper documents that come into your business and convert them to searchable PDF format; do the same with key documents in your filing cabinets

---

60   SavePaper.com.au is a campaign by the action group, Do Something. Jon Dee is the Founder and Managing Director of this not-for-profit organisation.

61   'Paper cut could hurt Australia Post's bottom line', *Australian Financial Review,* July 29, 2009

- set up a computer as a fax machine so that faxes can be easily converted into a searchable PDF format
- change your printed forms to electronic format; this reduces the need for employees to convert handwritten forms into database accessible information and your clients or customers can type information straight into an electronic form.

2. Don't print emails:
   - challenge yourself and your employees to minimise your printing of emails
   - for efficient retrieval, organise and save emails in an electronic folder system and train your employees to use a standardised e-filing system
   - if you have to print, to save paper you should only copy the essential content of an email and paste it into a word-processing document.

3. Think before you print or copy:
   - think whether you really need to print it at all
   - use the on-screen print-preview feature before printing
   - when printing a document, don't print the pages you don't need.

4. Printing:
   - as a first step, find out if your office equipment can do double-sided printing and copies and set it as the default option
   - use the blank sides of already used paper for draft printing.

5. Reduce business 'junk mail':
   - to save time and money, audit and update your mailing lists and remove 'not at this address' returns or companies that you no longer do business with
   - stop mailing people who have registered themselves on the 'do not mail' list; the Australian Direct Marketing Association can provide more information on compliance[62]
   - when companies send you unwanted mail, ask them to remove you from their lists
   - make it easy for recipients of mail you send to sign up for electronic versions

---

62   See www.adma.com.au

- remind employees periodically that unsubscribing from mailing lists is easier and more productive than wading through a large pile of letters each day and throwing half of them in the bin.

6. Test before copying big jobs:
   - doing this can prevent costly mistakes on a multiple copy job
   - if the machine doesn't have a sample button, run a sample copy before you run off multiple copies.

7. Don't print websites unnecessarily:
   - if you want to have a high quality copy of a web page, download the free Evernote software;[63] this includes a web clipper that enables you to create PDFs of a web page that you'd like to keep
   - if you must print a web page, look for a 'printer-friendly' option that will minimise paper use.

8. Print more words on each page:
   - reduce page numbers by using smaller fonts in larger documents
   - use thinner page margins and less line spacing to maximise the amount of space for text
   - choose a space-efficient font that gets more text on screen and on paper.

9. Save and re-use paper around the office:
   - place labels over old addresses and envelopes
   - flatten and store large boxes until they're needed again
   - collect and reuse one-sided paper by turning them into notepads.

10. Back up
    - organise a 'set and forget' daily back up system for all your business files and emails so you don't lose them if a computer crashes
    - you can even set up a system so it automatically backs up files as you change or create them

---

63   See www.evernote.com

- save revisions of important files, have more than one back up, watch your storage space, test your backups and make sure you store a copy of your critical data off site

- if there's a robbery, fire or flood, your data can disappear for good, so store a back up drive at home, in a safety deposit box or at a secure online back up service.

Non-office paper

Office paper isn't the only paper consumed in the workplace. Tissues, serviettes, napkins, hand towels, toilet paper, brochures, direct mail, invoicing and record keeping all add to paper use and potential waste. Here are some simple tips to reduce that waste:

1. Replace paper towels in kitchen areas with tea towels and wash cloths.

2. Replace paper cups with ceramic mugs. Australians use more than 400 million single-use cups every year. Over a lifetime of about 1000–3000 uses, ceramic mugs will produce far less solid waste and less air pollution than single-use cups.[64]

3. Replace paper towels in the bathroom with reusable roll towels. A hand dryer is also a better option environmentally and it reduces the amount of paper waste ending up in landfill. Where possible, use hand dryers that dry your hands quickly as these use less energy.

64   Report of the Starbucks Coffee Company/Alliance for Environmental Innovation Joint Task Force, 2000

Share it online

When it comes to sharing documents internally or with other organisations, you can share files online at your website, through free services such as www.evernote.com, or through low-cost services such as www.me.com and www.basecamphq.com

Companies like Redmap[65] also have software for SMEs that can handle this task for you.

What paper should I buy?

When it comes to paper purchasing, consider recycled-content paper and independently certified paper, such as Forest Stewardship Council (FSC) certified paper stock. See page 44 for more information.

Why buy recycled paper?

The best paper to buy from an environmental perspective is recycled paper. Recycled paper can use up to 50 per cent less energy in manufacture than virgin paper[66] and keeping waste paper out of landfill reduces greenhouse emissions – as the paper breaks down it gives off methane, which even the best managed landfills cannot capture all of. Each tonne of paper recycled can also save approximately 24 trees and uses up to 60 per cent less water.[67]

Further information

Within Australia, there is an excellent free resource called *Know Your Paper: A guide to purchasing recycled content office paper*. Published by the NSW Department of Environment, Climate Change and Water, each copy comes complete with printed samples of the different stocks available.

65   See www.redmap.com.au/SME
66   *Amcor Submission to State Sustainability Strategy NSW,* NSW DECC, 2002
67   *Know Your Paper: A guide to purchasing recycled content office paper.* NSW Department of Environment, Climate Change and Water, January 2009

Also available from the same department, is the *Know Your Printing Paper: A guide to purchasing recycled content printing paper for corporate stationery and promotional materials.*[68] Again, this comes complete with printed samples of the different available paper stocks.

Go to www.environment.nsw.gov.au to order or download these guides.

Accredited paper

If you want to buy paper that's not made from recycled material but is environmentally superior, check if it has independent third-party certification. The dominant schemes for paper (and other timber products) are the Forest Stewardship Council (FSC) and the Programme for the Enforcement of Forest Certification (PEFC).

Established in 81 countries, FSC is an international not-for-profit organisation that was founded in 1993 by environmentalists, social interest groups, retailers and the timber industry. It is supported by major conservation groups like WWF, Greenpeace and the Australian Conservation Foundation.

Want to search your handwritten notes?

If you're in a meeting and you write notes on a piece of paper, wouldn't it be nice if you could put your notes on a computer and search for key words in what you've written? There are now software applications that help you do just that. One example is Evernote[69] and its basic version is free.

You can also use your phone camera to take pictures of notes on whiteboards and restaurant napkins. Some software packages, such as Evernote, then enable you to send the picture to your account or desktop so you can file it away and search it as needed.

---

68 *Know Your Printing Paper: A guide to purchasing recycled content printing paper for corporate stationery and promotional materials.* NSW Department of Environment, Climate Change and Water, March 2009

69 See www.evernote.com

Chapter 6 – Reduce, reuse, recycle: easy steps to cut out paper waste

Benefits of digital versus paper filing systems

How much more efficient would your business be if all your company information was in one place and as easy to find as using an internet search engine?

Electronic data management is becoming easier to use and less expensive so SMEs have a genuine option to explore the business benefits that can be achieved when every Word and PDF document, every spreadsheet, every piece of paper and every email is efficiently stored and easily searchable.

Such systems are often called Electronic Data Management Systems or Electronic Data Management Software (which is a registered trademark brand) but they are all designed to streamline document management and turn paper files into electronic ones.

Other reasons to manage your documents electronically

1. Greater security and confidentiality

The filing cabinets in many companies are unlocked and people come and go as they please with the files. With electronic filing you can determine who sees which documents and what they can do with those documents.

2. Reduction in the cost of searching

Electronic filing is as easy to access as doing an internet search and rarely do your documents go missing.

3. Easier, cheaper and faster to share

Paper-based information is very difficult to share with multiple people without copying the document many times. Electronic documents can be securely shared and viewed by a number of people at the same time.

4. Frees up valuable floor space to make money

Many offices use large areas of valuable floor space to store paper in filing cabinets. This is space that could be freed up to generate income for the business, or next time you move, you won't need to rent so much space. According to Redmap, a 500GB hard disk can store the same number of black and white documents as hundreds of four drawer filing cabinets.

Maintain compliance

Businesses in Australia are required to keep records. These may include:

- financial records such as invoices, receipts, cheques and working papers – these may help you to comply with the *Corporations Act 2001* (Commonwealth)
- employee relationship records that help you to comply with various workplace relations laws.

These records need to be kept in a state where they are readily available. Failure to comply with record-keeping obligations may have serious consequences for businesses and their directors and officers, including fines and other penalties. You'll find that storing them electronically can often be a lot cheaper.

Given some records have to be kept for substantial periods of time (for example, seven years for financial records under the Corporations Act), it's worth your while looking at the cost that's involved in printing, filing and storing paper-based documents over that period of time. You'll find that storing them electronically can often be a lot cheaper.

Going further – going digital to reduce paper use

Electronic filing of your business documents can streamline your document handling and reduce paper use. Taking additional steps to use digital communications can provide further improvements and efficiencies.

Paper-free expense reports

Putting together expense reports can take time and involve lots of paperwork, such as tracking down receipts and diary entries. There is now software such as Mobile Receipt[70] that lets the user take a photo with their phone and the receipt is then put into a simple to use database that's instantly backed up online.

This software enables the creation of reports that are then emailed into your normal inbox. These come in PDF format complete with scans of the receipts themselves.

---

70 See www.miteksystems.com/oomph_mobilereceipt.asp

Billing and invoicing

Sending invoices via the post means people have to be employed in the printing, packing and disseminating of those invoices. In turn, these bills then have to be posted at a cost to the business. The alternative is an automated electronic billing system that can email your invoices. This is a faster and far more cost-effective system. A Life Cycle Assessment commissioned by Telstra in 2008 looked at all aspects of paper versus electronic billing and found that for every 1 million customers using electronic billing more than 19 million sheets of A4 paper were saved.[71]

Bills payable

Setting in place electronic billing from your suppliers will also save your suppliers' time and money, and it makes doing business with you easier.

Handwriting directly into your computer

If you prefer handwriting to typing, there are now computers and software to help you do that. Tablet PCs are useful as they enable you to write directly on the computer screen. There are also inexpensive plug-in devices from companies like WACOM that enable writing and drawing directly into your computer.

Tablet PCs contain software like Journal, OneNote or Evernote that enable easier storage and searching of your handwritten notes or drawings – making them easier to find in the future.

Electronic payments

Paying bills and wages with cheques is a time consuming and inefficient way to make payments. Why not set up your payments systems so that you only pay electronically? Regular payments can also be set up to be paid automatically.

71   *Online Billing Life Cycle Analysis,* prepared for Telstra by URS, April 2008

Email marketing

An alternative to direct-mail marketing is to develop email marketing campaigns that comply with the Spam Act. If you can compile the email addresses of customers, suppliers and others, software packages are available that can personalise your emails and monitor the response to your mailings.

The benefits of email marketing include:

- it's cheaper; no stamps, envelopes, packing, paper or printing are required
- you don't have the environmental cost of transporting your mail by trucks and delivery vehicles
- potentially better return on investment – in many cases you can also find out who opens, clicks and acts on your email promotions
- email marketing campaigns can be turned around faster than conventional paper-based direct mail campaigns.

It's essential to factor in the Spam Act when preparing an email marketing campaign. It prohibits the sending of unsolicited commercial electronic messages, such as email, unless you have the recipients' consent and the message includes an unsubscribe functionality, identifies the sender and includes accurate sender contact information.

Australia's e-marketing and internet industries have codes of practice to supplement the Spam Act. The codes explain the requirements of the Spam Act and provide procedures to enable organisations to comply with the Act and handle spam complaints. Go to the Australian Communications and Media Authority (ACMA) website[72] for further information.

For more information

If you want to see how other companies are reducing their use of paper, go to www.savepaper.com.au for tips and tools that will help your business to save paper and money.

72   See www.acma.gov.au

Case study: **Australian National Audit Office –**
saving money with electronic document storage

The Australian National Audit Office (ANAO) audits more than 300 government bodies. Until 2008 this audit process involved the collection of large numbers of paper documents from agencies. Its own paper bill was $70,000 and as its files had to be kept for ten years, its external file storage cost amounted to $120,000 per year.

In a move to electronically store documents and records, the ANAO introduced a Commonwealth-compliant Electronic Document and Records Management System (EDRMS) in 2008.

ANAO employees are now scanning paper files and gathering electronic documents from agencies and placing them as records in its EDRMS.

The key benefits include:

- employees no longer have to transport large suitcases of paper around during their audits – they now carry audit files electronically when they travel

- documents can now be shared easily between audit team members when they are on or offsite

- the number of records management employees has been reduced

- the ability to comprehensively search the EDRMS stored documents has provided positive assurances on the audit findings

- information and knowledge sharing has improved and there is now easier access to previous best practice examples of audit planning and work.

The current productivity benefit gained by this paper-reduction measure is estimated to be in the order of $1.3 million per year. The ANAO also estimates it will reduce its external file storage costs by 15 per cent per annum over the next six years.

The reduced paper use, manual handling and storage costs will also provide additional savings to the ANAO.

'The quickest and most
cost-effective way for your
business to save money
is to reduce unnecessary
energy use.'

7

Seeing the light: energy choices that save money and the environment

If you were going to read only one chapter in this book, then this would be the one.

Whatever type of business you operate, the one thing you have in common with other SMEs is that you use energy. Every time you turn on a plug or switch on a light, it doesn't just cost you money, the power you use creates greenhouse gas emissions.

When it comes to saving money and reducing those emissions, the quickest and most cost-effective solution for your business is to reduce unnecessary energy use. Yet despite energy efficiency being 'low-hanging fruit' that's ripe for the picking, it often goes unnoticed until it drops and hits someone on the head.

Why is this?

Consider the humble incandescent light bulb. An invention of the 19th century, it was made commercially practical by Thomas Edison in 1879. Very little cutting-edge technology from that time is still with us: the only place you'll find a phonograph or telegraph machine is in a museum. Yet the incandescent bulb blazed on as the most widely used form of lighting despite it being incredibly inefficient – it wastes up to 90-95 per cent of the energy that it uses (they give out more energy in the form of heat rather than light). You might even still be using some in your business or home.

So why should SMEs care? Apart from environmental considerations, the bottom line is that electricity isn't going to get any cheaper in the foreseeable future...

So why did they last so long? Well, incandescent bulbs sold well because they were cheap – so long as you ignored how much energy they used and how short a life they had.

Until recently, many SMEs looked at energy-saving light globes and incandescent bulbs and did their sums as to which type they'd buy. The cheapest, at first glance, appeared to be the incandescent bulb, but they weren't. Compared with an incandescent, an energy-saving globe can save up to $30 or more in energy and avoided costs over its lifetime. Although the energy-saving globes used only one-fifth of the energy and lasted eight to ten times longer, they looked less attractive because the upfront cost to buy them was significantly more.

The Australian Government phased out the sale of traditional incandescent globes at the beginning of November 2009. It is also progressively phasing out specialist incandescent globes as other viable replacement options become available.[73] It is estimated this ban will save the nation an estimated 30 terawatt hours of electricity and 28 million tonnes of greenhouse gas emissions between now and 2020 – equivalent to decommissioning a small coal-fired power station or taking half a million cars off the road. More importantly for the SME bottom-line, it is expected to save Australian individuals and businesses around $380 million a year by 2020 in reduced energy costs.[74]

---

73   See www.energyrating.gov.au
74   See www.environment.gov.au

After the US and Canada, Australia has the third most energy-intensive industrial sectors in the developed world. One reason is our high level of energy-intensive raw material production and mineral processing. Another is our relatively low energy prices – which means people don't worry too much about wasting energy.

Yet another – and perhaps the most entrenched problem – is that, like bulb-buying consumers, appreciating the most cost-effective options in your business requires you to gather information, do your sums and be committed enough to sweat the small stuff now for longer-term gain.

The bottom line

So why should SMEs care? Apart from environmental considerations, the bottom line is that electricity isn't going to get any cheaper in the foreseeable future, and commercial energy consumption is growing rapidly – by about 3.7 per cent a year.[75]

Inefficient energy use is probably costing you far more than you realise. Lighting and office machines, for example, don't just add to your energy bills directly but also indirectly through higher air-conditioning costs (where there is light there is heat, as the saying goes). Saving energy in one area can therefore deliver savings in another.

Commercial sector energy services 2004–05

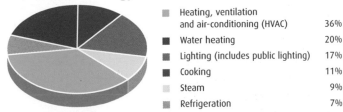

Heating, ventilation and air-conditioning (HVAC)	36%
Water heating	20%
Lighting (includes public lighting)	17%
Cooking	11%
Steam	9%
Refrigeration	7%

Source: Victorian Energy Efficiency Action Statement[76]

This chart shows the major areas of energy consumption (excluding transport) for the commercial sector. How things stack up for your workplace will, of course, depend entirely on the nature and location of your business: if you're running a café or restaurant, the kitchen will be your energy hot spot; if a deli, then probably refrigeration; if a design studio, computers and printers will feature more prominently.

75   See www.sustainability.vic.gov.au
76   Department of Sustainability and Environment, 2006. See www.sustainability.vic.gov.au

Tracking your use

Knowing where and how you're using and paying for energy within your business right now is your first step. You can then prioritise the actions you can take to cut energy use and save money. This may require research to find the best options for your business over the medium to longer term:

1. Review your energy bills (ideally over the past 24 months or so) to get an idea of how much you're using and paying. This will enable you to see how much your costs vary between summer and winter, and whether you are paying a high tariff for peak demand. If you're having difficulty working out how your bill is calculated, call your energy provider for assistance.

2. Record your energy use and cost in a spreadsheet. You can download a free software application developed by Sustainability Victoria called the Energy Smart Tracker.[77] This will assist you in monitoring your energy demand and associated greenhouse gases.

3. Buy a power meter to better understand the amount of electricity being used by your individual machines and appliances. These handy devices, usually costing around $100, plug in between the power point and the appliance and give a read-out of how much power is being drawn. By inputting the price of your electricity you can tell exactly how much an appliance is costing to run, in addition to the amount of greenhouse gases produced.

4. Calculate the carbon footprint of your business. A SME's carbon footprint is calculated when it measures the amount of greenhouse gas emissions emitted by its overall operations. You can input the different impacts of your business and get your carbon footprint by going to http://calculator.futureclimate.com.au and using the SME carbon calculator.

The key to energy efficiency is choosing options that you or others don't have to think too much about once they are implemented. The biggest difference you can make on this score is at the purchasing stage. As such, it pays to undertake a complete cost assessment of your appliances and fittings that accounts for their energy consumption and maintenance requirements.

Energy saving and your bottom line

Energy costs are one of the easiest things to reduce. With minimal expenditure and effort, many companies can reduce their energy bills by up to 20 per cent. This example from the UK Carbon Trust shows how a 20 per cent saving on your energy bill is equivalent to a five per cent increase in overall profits.

Turnover	$1,000,000
Profits before energy saving	$100,000
Cost of gas and electricity	$25,000
Potential energy saving (20 per cent of $25,000)	$5,000
Profit after energy saving	$105,000

Representing a 5 per cent increase in profits[78]

Keeping it simple

Creating a culture that promotes saving energy in your business is important, because employees tend to go with the flow of whatever is accepted practice. Signs, emails and leading by example can make a difference to keeping energy conservation 'in sight' and thus 'in mind'.

But human nature is hard to overcome. Any plan to reduce energy use that depends on constant vigilance, such as having people manually switch things off after use, is likely to fail – particularly if the onus is on people who don't see it as making all that much difference. This is also the case when the extra costs don't come out of their own pocket. This is one key reason why it makes sense to encourage your employees to also reduce their energy use at home. Habits undertaken to save money at home will, over time, be brought into the workplace in a way that can save your business money.

---

78   Adapted from the UK Carbon Trust. See www.carbontrust.co.uk

Energy performance contracts

Looking for a simple, low-risk way to maximise your energy-efficiency without the high up-front capital cost? Then an energy performance contract (EPC) might be the ideal solution for your business.

Energy performance contracting is well-established in the US, Canada and Europe and is increasingly being used in Australia. It involves contracting an energy service company (known as an ESCO) to provide a complete energy-efficiency service to your business.

The contractor starts by conducting an expert analysis of the potential energy-saving measures that can be made throughout your operations. They then make a proposal to your business to install, tune and maintain a range of cost-saving energy-efficiency measures.

The contractor guarantees you will achieve your energy and cost saving targets. This means the energy savings will pay back your initial investment, typically over a period of three to eight years, and improve the profitability of your business. The contractor is paid out of the energy savings, and if the project doesn't yield the promised energy or cost savings, the contractor pays the shortfall, not your business.

While your business may want to finance the energy-efficiency measures itself or through your bank, some energy service companies even arrange finance so that you don't have to outlay any capital. The savings from EPCs can be substantial.

All sounds too good to be true? Fortunately it isn't. The website of the Energy Efficiency Council has a free best practice guide on how to choose an ESCO, how to define the scope of the project and how to negotiate and implement an EPC. This guide is a must-read for any SME wishing to enter into an arrangement with an ESCO. The Energy Efficiency Council can also provide template EPC contract documents.

Go to the Energy Efficiency Council website at www.eec.org.au for more information about energy performance contracts, including whether or not an energy performance contract is suitable for your business.

Case study: Penrith City Council

Penrith City Council appointed Siemens for its energy performance contract. Siemens then delivered per year up to 167 per cent of guaranteed electricity savings and 171 per cent of guaranteed greenhouse gas reduction.

Over a three year period, Penrith City Council paid back its internal loan and saved more than $640,000 in electricity and water charges. In the process it also reduced its carbon emissions by more than 4000 tonnes – equivalent to supplying enough power for 850 energy-efficient houses.

Case study: State Library of NSW

With an energy performance contract that focused on lighting controls, heating, ventilation and air-conditioning upgrades and water savings, the State Library of NSW contracted with Energy Conservation Systems to achieve guaranteed savings of $104,000 per annum, total savings of $229,000 per annum and a reduction in CO_2 emissions of 988 tonnes per annum.

According to Jim Sinclair, Energy Manager for the State Library of NSW, "The Energy Performance Contract has allowed us to implement a range of improvements which will benefit the library and its users as well as save on energy bills. And the guaranteed savings mean there's no risk to Treasury, who provided the financing."[79]

79   See www.eec.org.au

Case study: De Bortoli Wines – smart use of resources

The NSW DECC's 'Sustainability Advantage' program has generated significant savings for hundreds of its corporate members, clubs and government bodies.

One member, De Bortoli Wines, managed to save money at its Bilbul winery in the Riverina by recycling all wastewater and significantly reducing energy use.

By removing sodium from all cleaning and production processes, the winery's wastewater is able to be used for irrigation. De Bortoli Wines now has a farm dedicated to the cropping of wastewater from which they generate grain and straw for sale.

By simplifying wastewater treatment through the introduction of a new low energy aeration system, the amount of energy used to treat wastewater was reduced by 90 per cent. This was equivalent to more than $180,000 in annual energy costs.

Taking advantage of the DECC Sustainability Advantage – Staff Engagement modules and the introduction of Lean and Visual Manufacturing Principles, De Bortoli Wines has also made major improvements to its manufacturing processes.

Examples of other savings include:

■ production-line efficiency improvements varying between 15% and 37%

■ reduction in non-conforming processes of 35%

■ customer complaints reduced by 40%.

The business' Operations Manager says these initiatives have a net benefit of more than $500,000 per annum and the programs deferred capital spending of $350,000 for large power supplies.[80]

80   See www.debortoli.com.au

What you need to know about heating, ventilation and air-conditioning

Heating, ventilation and air-conditioning (HVAC) accounts for about 70 per cent of energy use in the average Australian commercial building. HVAC was found to be the most significant cause of greenhouse gas emissions at approximately 63 per cent of total emissions.[81] Every degree of heating and cooling can increase energy consumption by up to 10 per cent. As such, increasing HVAC efficiencies has great potential to bring about significant financial savings for your business.

How much you can reduce your heating, cooling and ventilation costs depends on your building, its location and, of course, whether you own or lease your premises. In our chapter on building performance (chapter 9) we'll look at the bigger structural issues to do with HVAC. In this section, we'll focus on the simpler actions that can improve the performance of your existing systems. Things your business can do today include:

1. Adjust the temperature according to the season. Many workplaces set systems to a constant 20–24 degrees regardless of the weather and what people are wearing. Set the temperature a little higher during summer (24–27° Celsius) and lower (18–20° Celsius) in winter.

2. Turn off systems overnight and on weekends when the building is not occupied. If a few people are working during those times, consider having efficient portable heaters or air coolers available to keep the temperature comfortable.

3. Install Energy Star compliant programmable thermostats. These can cost between $25 to $100 but can cut HVAC costs by as much as 30%[82] by running your heating and cooling according to both temperature and whether the building is occupied. Set them to turn on your system just before people arrive to work and off just before they leave.

4. Don't waste energy by heating and cooling little-used areas. Block vents in areas that are unoccupied, and consider doing the same in areas that are used only for a short time, such as toilets and storerooms.

5. Use fans to increase the efficiency of central air-conditioning. The evaporative effect of air movement can mean people feel just as cool with the thermostat set 3–5° Celsius higher.

6. Open doors and windows can easily double heating and cooling energy costs. Keep them closed where possible and consider installing hydraulic door closers or thermal strip curtains in high-traffic areas.

81   *Australian Commercial Building Greenhouse Gas Emissions 1990–2010,* Australian Greenhouse Office 1999

82   Origin Energy, Energy Efficiency Fact Sheet: Heating, Ventilation and Air Conditioning

7. Poorly maintained HVAC equipment can add up to 10% to your energy bill.[83] Ensure it is regularly serviced in line with the manufacturer's recommendations and have condenser coils, evaporators and filters cleaned; valves and refrigerant levels checked, and leaks fixed.

8. Avoid peak demand periods. By adjusting workplace schedules and reducing energy use during peak demand periods, savings can be made on air-conditioning, lighting and other electricity use.

Water heating

Water heating is an energy-intensive process, whether it's running a laundry or doing something simple like boiling water for cups of tea.

Relative carbon dioxide emissions from different water heater types

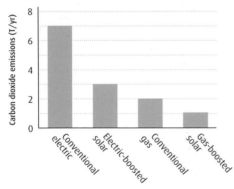

The graph shows the difference in greenhouse emissions produced by the main types of hot water systems. Although taken from a residential study, it's worth noting that higher emissions mean higher running costs. But your choice of hot water systems will often depend on whether you own your premises, so let's focus here on some more immediate strategies to improve water-heating efficiency:

1. According to UK magazine *Which?*,[84] on average it takes as much energy to boil a litre of water as it does to run a standard fridge for seven hours. Employees don't link the energy they use with the cost impact it has on your bottom line. The solution is to put up signs near your kettles that remind people to only boil

83 Origin Energy, Energy Efficiency Fact Sheet: Heating, Ventilation and Air Conditioning
84 See www.which.co.uk

the water they need. It's also worth reminding people to watch out for dripping hot water taps. Get input from employees on what other reminders could be put near your other hot water devices.

2. Hot water systems often overheat water and in doing so cost you money that you shouldn't be paying. If your system has an adjustable thermostat, set the temperature lower: while storage hot water systems should be set to at least 60° Celsius (to prevent the growth of micro-organisms that cause Legionnaires Disease) there is no need to go any higher than 65° Celsius; instantaneous hot water systems can be set at 50°Celsius.[85]

On average it takes as much energy to boil a litre of water as it does to run a standard fridge for seven hours.

---

3. Systems located a long distance from outlets waste energy through the transferral of heat to pipes. Even if you don't have any control over the location of your main hot water supply, you can insulate the hot water pipes to minimise heat loss. Insulating your storage tanks also helps to reduce heat loss.

4. Consider installing local instantaneous booster systems or urns in high-use areas like kitchens. These can be switched off when not in use, such as overnight.

5. If your business doesn't require hot water around the clock, turn off systems and pumps when they won't be used for an extended period, such as holiday seasons or even over long weekends.

6. Choose water-efficient fittings and appliances. Even an inexpensive device like a flow-stem valve can help to halve water use. Check the water-rating label that is mandatory on water fittings. When buying new appliances, like washing machines and dishwashers, you should also check the energy-rating label.

7. Choose units that meet the demand you place on them. A water heater with a high energy-efficiency rating that's too big for your needs could use more energy than a smaller unit with a lower rating.

---

85 Energy Efficiency Information Sheet: Hot Water, Australian Government Department of the Environment, Water, Heritage and the Arts

8. If you have shower facilities for employees, install water-efficient showerheads. The 3 star water-efficient showerheads can significantly reduce your use of water and save up to $100–$150 a year in water and heating costs. Given these showerheads cost anything from $30–$90, it's a sensible investment. Better still, a good 3 star rated showerhead can give your employees a shower that's just as good as the old water-guzzling type.

9. Ensure hot water heaters are properly maintained. Have them serviced according to the manufacturer's instructions to ensure they're running at optimum efficiency.

Combining energy-saving lighting with simple use-reduction strategies can potentially cut your lighting costs by half.

Lighting

Lighting accounts for just over 17 per cent of energy use and just over 20 per cent of greenhouse emissions from commercial buildings. The Australian Greenhouse Office estimated that simple measures could reduce those figures by 50–70 per cent.[86]

It is a common misconception that energy-efficient lights just aren't up to the job: "they're not as bright," "give off a 'cold' light," and "don't come in the same range of fittings and sizes as incandescent globes." While this was true a few years ago, it's no longer the case today. Energy-saving lights can now meet every purpose and every brightness level, lasting far longer and using a lot less electricity than old-fashioned globes.

For SMEs starting out on their eco-efficiency journey, combining energy-saving lighting with simple use-reduction strategies can potentially cut your lighting costs by half. Follow these tips to save money and the environment:

1. Make the most of natural light. Keep windows clean and clear of shading, and position workspaces to make the most of available light sources.

2. Choose light colours that reflect light for walls, ceilings and bench tops.

3. Replace inefficient incandescent and halogen lights with energy-efficient lighting. This can be a combination of fluorescent, compact fluorescent or LED. Beacon Lighting estimate that this could reduce lighting power use by up to 80 – 90 per cent. If your business already has fluorescent lighting, significant savings can also be made by utilising newer technologies. The common T8 linear fluorescent that's

86 *Australian Commercial Building Greenhouse Gas Emissions 1990–2010*, Australian Greenhouse Office 1999

used in huge quantities in offices and showrooms can now be swapped over to more efficient T5 models. This will save around 30 per cent in running costs. Improvements in reflector designs in fluorescent fittings mean that a one or two tube product could replace your current two or four tube product with no effect on lighting output.

4. Task lighting a small area such as a desk is far more efficient than lighting a whole area. Task lights can be combined with dimmable space lighting (dimmable, energy-saving CFLs are now available). This allows you to adjust the lighting in a room so that it meets everyone's needs, achieving the best outcome in terms of occupational health and safety, as well as maximising energy efficiency and cost savings.

5. Be green and clean. Keep fixtures clean and free of dust as that diminishes lighting effectiveness.

6. Turn lights off that aren't needed and place reminders near light switches.

7. Install movement activated sensors that will turn lights off automatically when no one is around. It makes sense to put these sensors in places like meeting rooms and toilets where the lights don't need to remain on all the time. The technology has now developed to the point where you can also use them throughout the whole office. In addition to this, there are daylight (photoelectric) sensors which can be connected to light fittings. If it's a bright day, the daylight sensor will dim the lighting to maintain a consistent light level. This light dimming results in power savings.

8. Businesses wanting to minimise their lighting bills should keep a close eye on developments surrounding LED lighting. This ultra-efficient lighting is a fast-moving sector where many new technologies and products are being brought to market.

Cooking

Cooking-related energy use obviously doesn't apply to every business. But even if you're not running a café or restaurant the general principles that apply to energy efficiency in the kitchen are really no different to any other work environment: it's all about using the right tools for the job, being smart about your work practices and keeping equipment well maintained so it operates at peak performance.

The benefit to your business is not just lower energy bills but also better performance. It's also about extending the lifespan of often very expensive equipment. Besides, you've got a kitchen at home, right? So these tips will help save energy there too:

1. Make the most of the energy you use. Limit the opening of oven doors. Keep lids on your pots and pans as much as you can. Use flat-bottom saucepans that match the size of hotplates to maximise heat transfer. Ensure energy isn't wasted by flames licking around the sides of pots.

2. Combine jobs. Use a saucepan with a stacking steamer to make the most of a single hotplate. Plan ahead to use a heated oven that can cook several dishes.

3. Use the most efficient implements. Smaller appliances can help to meet peak needs where large appliances, taking longer to heat up, would be underused. A microwave oven is far more efficient (and faster) than an oven, so use it to thaw frozen food.

4. Adopt energy-conscious cooking styles. Reducing heat after initial searing then cooking at moderate temperatures will preserve food quality and save energy. An oven can usually be turned off several minutes before food is fully cooked because the residual heat will complete the process.

Case study: La Porchetta – investing in new equipment and saving money

La Porchetta has more than 80 Italian restaurants around Australia. Each restaurant spends between $8000 and $15,000 per year on gas supplies. They have now identified a new gas powered oven that reduces this gas usage by a third. Better still, it cooks food faster.

Using this oven will save money, reduce gas-related emissions and get the food out quicker to hungry customers. This is the kind of win-win environmental development that all companies should be on the lookout for.

5. Clean, well-maintained equipment will work at peak efficiency. Ovens and other thermostat-controlled devices should be recalibrated about twice a year. Check that your oven and fridge seals are in good order, and hotplates and range hoods are free of grease and baked-in residue.

6. Move your fridge away from the wall and make sure there is at least an 80mm space on all sides of your fridge to allow air to circulate around the rear coils. Locate your fridge in a cool spot, ideally out of direct sunlight and away from the oven.

7. Always check the star rating labels and try to purchase the most efficient appliances with the highest ratings, to meet your needs.

8. Most important of all, understand the capabilities of your equipment and communicate energy-efficiency principles to your employees. Be patient, because ingrained habits take time to unlearn.

Office equipment

Energy-efficient machines and energy-saving practices can cut the cost and emissions associated with office equipment. Significant savings can be derived by switching these machines off outside of normal office hours.

Think about this: there are 168 hours in a week, but most offices are only used for 50 to 60 of those hours. That leaves 118 hours when the office is unoccupied. Anything left on at this time could consume up to twice the energy it would during occupied hours.

We'll consider the environmental impact of information technology later in the book (chapter 11) but for now here are some starting tips on how to save energy:

1. Leaving machines on, contrary to one strange urban myth, does not save more power than switching them off then on again. Apart from devices that need to be on, like fax machines, photocopiers and computer servers, most other machines likely to be unused within the half hour can be switched off.

2. In business hours, set computers to go into sleep mode when left idle for 10 minutes or more. A sleeping computer will use as little as 5% of full power. Sleep mode also saves screens from phosphor burn-in far more economically than screen savers, which save the screen but no energy.

3. Flat LED screens consume less energy than LCD screens, which in turn consume less power than bulky CRT monitors.

4. Laptop computers consume less electricity than desktop and tower CPUs. If your employees take work home or are often out of the office, think about equipping them with a laptop.

5. When buying new machines look for the Energy Star label, the international standard for energy-efficient electronic equipment. Energy Star-compliant machines can save significant amounts of energy when idle – which in the case of printers and fax machines is up to 95% of the time. When you purchase Energy Star-compliant equipment, make sure all the settings are turned on when you first set up the machine.

Placing posters around the office encouraging everyone to switch off unused equipment is a surprisingly easy way to save money.

---

6. A larger printer or photocopier shared by many people is generally more energy-efficient than several smaller machines used by a few. A larger machine is also more likely to have better features such as double-sided printing (the greatest source of carbon emissions from office machines is the embedded energy of consumables like paper and ink). But bigger isn't always better: ink-jet printers, for instance, can use up to 90% less energy than a small laser printer. Choose what meets your needs.

7. Many electronic devices are never truly off but in standby mode, drawing power 24 hours a day even though they might be used for a few hours, or even a few minutes (think of how long you might use a microwave oven, for instance). Install accessible power boards that can easily switch off such equipment at the power source. Placing posters around the office encouraging everyone to switch off unused equipment is a surprisingly easy way to save money.

8. Use computer system preferences, software or external timers on a power point to ensure that all designated machines will automatically be switched off at a set time. Be sure to provide instructions on overriding the software or timer when employees need to work out of normal hours.

9. Mobile phone rechargers and other transformers can be drawing electricity even when not connected to the devices they power. Encourage employees to plug them into a socket only when they need to. People can also save energy by recharging their mobile phones when driving.

10. Encourage employees to think about energy use and ways to do things more efficiently. It can be as simple as taking responsibility to turn off their computer and check other machines when they step out for lunch or go home. Or planning to do their printing job in one batch, since most energy in photocopiers and printers is used to heat the components that fuse the toner to paper. Getting team 'buy-in' to saving energy is crucial if you are to achieve optimum results.

Case study: Melbourne Airport – reducing environmental impact in the bathroom

If you've ever flown through Melbourne Airport, then you're one of the 25 million passengers who use the airport every year.[87]

Among the busiest places in the airport are the bathroom facilities. As part of its recent upgrade, a decision was made to install hand dryers.

The Dyson Airblade[tm] hand dryer was chosen because of the energy saving and environmental benefits offered by the unit. It dries your hands in 10 seconds instead of the 28 second average for normal dryers and it only uses 1 watt on standby instead of 3 watts. Over the lifetime of the dryers, the cost saving is estimated to be more than 85 per cent. In addition to saving trees and reducing the number of paper towels going to landfill, the dryers will potentially save 186,761 kg of CO_2 emissions and use 76.8 per cent less energy.[88]

---

87   See www.melbourneairport.com.au
88   *Green Purchasing in Australia*, by NetBalance Foundation for ecoBuy, 2009

Refrigeration

If you're in food processing, running a deli or managing a bar, refrigeration costs can be a big part of your energy bills. Even if you're an office-based business, simple low-cost practices can easily reduce refrigeration expenses by 15 per cent or more:

1. Check to make sure your cold-storage units aren't needlessly too cold. Refrigerators can optimally run at 3 to 4° Celsius and freezers at −15 to −18° Celsius. Use a thermometer to ensure your thermostats are working properly.[89]

2. Keep freezers frost-free because any ice build up greater than about 5mm in thickness will act an insulator, increasing energy consumption. Also periodically clean the condenser coils, as a build-up of dust will inhibit their operation.

3. Ensure equipment is properly maintained. Check that seals, hinges and catches are working to keep the units airtight. If motors are running continuously or making a strange noise, then call in a refrigeration mechanic.

4. While overfilling can decrease efficiency by inhibiting air circulation, so too can under-filling. A refrigerator works best when at least two-thirds full and a freezer when at least three-quarters full. The more empty space, the more energy goes into cooling air, which spills out when the door is opened. If you've got a half-empty fridge, fill it up with airtight containers of water. Distribute contents evenly for maximum cooling efficiency. You can fill the gaps in your freezers with scrunched up paper.

5. Position units out of direct sunlight and away from heat-producing equipment. Leave sufficient clearance space (generally at least 80mm) between the back and the wall, to allow good airflow around the condenser coils; insufficient ventilation reduces heat dispersal and can reduce energy efficiency by up to 15%.

6. If refrigeration is a big part of your business, it may make sense to replace old units with new energy-efficient models that can use up to half the energy and are therefore twice as cheap to run. Bear in mind the energy efficiency rating, size (smaller is cheaper) and whether the unit is self-defrosting; non-defrosting models will require a little more maintenance but will usually use less energy.

89   Energy Efficiency Fact Sheet: Refrigeration, Origin Energy

Steam systems

When we think of steam, many of us think of steam trains and a by-gone era. But steam systems are still prevalent, used for everything from driving turbines, heating, climate control, cooking and cleaning, and account for nine per cent of total energy use in the commercial sector.[90] Here are some tips for getting the best out of your steam system:

1. Have a qualified tradesperson regularly measure the temperature and pressure of your feed water and steam output, flow rate and fuel consumption to ensure your boiler is operating at maximum performance.

2. Boiler blowdown – to control solids in the boiler water, protecting surfaces from scaling or corrosion problems – is an important part of boiler maintenance. If done too infrequently you risk damage to the boiler but if done too frequently you waste energy. Get an expert assessment to determine what is optimum, based on the energy use and cost of blowdown compared with options to improve feed-in water quality.

3. Leaks in pipe sections, connections and steam traps that drain condensate can be a big cause of energy loss from steam systems. While big leaks may be easily seen and heard, ultrasonic leak detection by a trained technician will identify smaller leaks.

4. A key tip is to be resourceful with how you use your system. Questions to ask include:

   a) Could you use a smaller boiler?

   b) Could you lower the temperature of your steam supply?

   c) Is the efficiency of the system being maximised by locating the boiler as close as possible to where the steam is used?

   d) Is there any inappropriate use of the system, such as heating water?

   e) Could you use a more efficient fuel source such as natural gas or, better yet, waste heat from another piece of equipment?

---

90   Sustainability Victoria: *ResourceSmart Energy Efficiency Best Practice Guide: Steam, Hot Water and Process Heating*

Compressed air

Compressed air is often described as the fourth utility, after water, electricity and gas, powering everything from pneumatic hammers to drills and paint sprayers.

It is also the most expensive, accounting for about 10 per cent of all electrical energy consumed by business. With 73 per cent of the cost of a compressor due to energy use, significant cost savings can be made by improving energy efficiency.[91]

There are many easy and low-cost ways to improve energy efficiency: by fixing leaks, reducing intake air temperature, optimising pressure, optimising compressor operation and avoiding inappropriate use.

What is renewable energy and why should SMEs care?

Renewable energy is the term given to power that's generated from naturally renewing sources such as wind, sunlight, flowing water, 'hot rocks' and energy derived from plants and animal waste (generally called biomass).

When you sign up to use accredited renewable energy the electricity company looks at how much energy you use and then sources the equivalent amount from a renewable power generator. This renewable energy is not fed directly to your home or business, it is fed into the power grid, reducing overall greenhouse emissions.

After reducing your energy use (electricity, gas, petrol, diesel etc), one of the simplest things SMEs can do to be more sustainable is to use accredited renewable energy – called GreenPower.[92]

Case study: The ecoswitch®

Australian inventor Rod Sheppard came to the realisation that many computers and printers are left on because it's too difficult to turn them off at the plug. So he came up with the ecoswitch®. It's an extension switch that makes it far easier to turn off appliances at the plug. Leaving such devices in standby mode wastes electricity and money so the $20 device will pay for itself in a short period of time. Visit www.ecoswitch.com.au for more information.

91   See www.resourcesmart.vic.gov.au

92   The Australian Government has an official program called GreenPower that accredits genuine renewable energy providers. See www.greenpower.gov.au

Like to know more?

For more detailed advice about practical ways to improve energy-efficiency, check out these great online resources:

Energy and greenhouse management toolkit

Developed by Sustainability Victoria and EPA Victoria, this toolkit provides tools, case studies and very detailed guides on how to improve eco-efficiency and cut energy costs. Go to www.sustainability.vic.gov.au to find out more.

Energy ratings

A joint initiative of Commonwealth, State, and Territory government agencies, this site is a comprehensive guide to choosing energy-efficient appliances, including details on the standards that must be met by all products that carry an energy label or are regulated under the Minimum Energy Performance Standards protocol. Go to www.energyrating.gov.au to find out more.

The Energy Efficiency Council

The Energy Efficiency Council was formed in 2009 in order to bring energy-efficiency providers and clients together and to grow the market for energy-efficient products and services.

The EEC is well-known for its ability to provide advice and help on energy-efficiency services and products. Its members also provide a wide range of energy-efficiency products and services that include the identification and implementation of energy-efficiency projects at buildings and sites.

For more information, email info@eec.org.au, visit www.eec.org.au or call 03 8327 8422.

Like some other sustainability initiatives, purchasing GreenPower can cost more upfront than non-renewable energy but it delivers other benefits. For the nation and for the environment it reduces greenhouse emissions; for you it can assist in meeting environmental goals and gaining third-party accreditation; and for your customers and suppliers it shows you're serious about being more sustainable.

After reducing your energy use (electricity, gas, petrol, diesel etc), one of the simplest things SMEs can do to be more sustainable is to use accredited renewable energy – called GreenPower.

The Electricity Supply Association of Australia estimates that more than one-fifth of Australia's electricity is used by the commercial sector. More than 80 per cent of this energy comes from the burning of coal which contributes to global warming.

The benefits of using renewable energy are:

1. Positioning your business as one that is committed to environmentally sustainable practices with employees, customers, suppliers and the wider community.

2. Directly contributing to the reduction of Australia's carbon footprint. This could help to position your business to cope more easily with environmental performance requirements imposed now or in the future by regulators, lenders, insurers or investors.

3. Bringing greater focus to your energy-saving strategies, improving your potential to lower overall electricity costs.

4. Differentiating your company from competitors and potentially increasing your appeal to consumers and increasing sales – particularly among the 821,504 households currently purchasing GreenPower. You will also be among the 38,293 commercial customers who buy GreenPower.[93]

---

93 *National GreenPower Accreditation Program Status Report* Quarter 3: 1 July to 30 September 2009

GreenPower

The Australian Government runs a program called GreenPower which was launched in 1997 to provide independent accreditation of renewable energy production. The program undertakes publicly available independent auditing of energy retailers to make sure a company that sells accredited renewable energy products is investing in renewable energy.

There are about 130 accredited renewable energy products for business and residential users under GreenPower. You can also use GreenPower to run events.

GreenPower is available from most licensed electricity retailers, so obtaining it for your business is as simple as picking up the phone to an electricity company.

Go to www.greenpower.gov.au to learn more about renewable energy providers and renewable energy generally.

While GreenPower represents less than one per cent of electricity sales to commercial customers, this graphic shows the high level of growth that GreenPower has experienced in the commercial sector.

GreenPower sales growth 2004–08

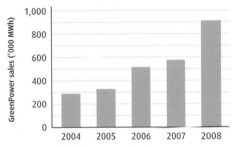

Source: Green Purchasing Australia Report 2008 – ECO-Buy and Net Balance Foundation[94]

Renewable energy fact sheets

What's the difference between solar photovoltaic power and solar thermal? Confused about hydro or geothermal power? If you want more information on renewable energy, go to www.cleanenergycouncil.org.au to check out the Clean Energy Council fact sheets.

94   See www.ecobuy.com.au

Renewable energy sources

Solar PV

Photovoltaic technology uses semi-conducting solar cells to transform solar photons into direct electric current. Although there is great potential for large-scale solar PV in Australia, its main current use is for decentralised power generation that utilises rooftop space to power individual buildings. Contact your local energy utility to see if any solar feed-in tariffs are available for your business.

Ocean power

Ocean energy can be tapped from a range of sources including marine currents, thermal layering and salt gradients, but the two sources being investigated for development in Australia are tides and waves. Compared to most other renewable energy sources, ocean power is relatively straightforward, easily scalable and has the advantage of being sited close to where most of the population is – in coastal areas.

Geothermal

Geothermal energy uses underground heat to power turbines. New Zealand generates electricity by tapping its abundant volcanic geysers and the International Energy Agency estimates geothermal energy could supply 5 per cent of global electricity by 2020. A number of companies are currently developing geothermal projects in Australia.

Biomass

Biomass power is primarily generated in two ways. Burning waste vegetative material (commonly done from sugar cane plantations and paper mills) is a renewable resource as is capturing and burning methane that's created by the breakdown of organic matter in rubbish tips or sewage treatment plants. Both are able to be used to generate energy onsite at production facilities or for power generation and feed-in to the electricity grid.

Solar thermal

Solar hot water systems are the main type of solar thermal technology currently being used in Australia. This technology has been in use since 1941 and is primarily used to heat household hot water. Other low-temperature solar thermal technologies are solar ponds and, for larger-scale electricity generation, solar chimneys. Solar thermal energy is emerging as a cost-competitive source of electrical power because it can be co-located with existing energy generation infrastructure. The International Energy Agency estimates that solar thermal generation costs will be on a par with coal-fired power stations by 2030.

Wind

Wind power is a tried and true technology. Small and medium farms have used hundreds of thousands of windmills over the years. With commercial power generation, bigger, taller and better-designed turbines have helped to significantly reduce the cost of wind generation over the past 15 years. Wind power has the potential to supply a significant percentage of Australia's electricity needs. It continues to play an important role in small-scale and local off-grid systems.

Hydro

Australia has about 100 hydro-electric power stations, which generate the bulk of Australia's current renewable energy. While some new projects are planned or being built, expansion is limited by a lack of waterways to dam. This is particularly so given the state of water flows in most of our river systems and the likelihood that climate change will reduce those flows even further. There is, however, scope for widespread use of mini-hydro power systems, like the South East Water Mini Hydro Project in Victoria. This is expected to generate enough electricity to power 165 homes.

'There are steps everyone can take
to be more efficient and use less water.'

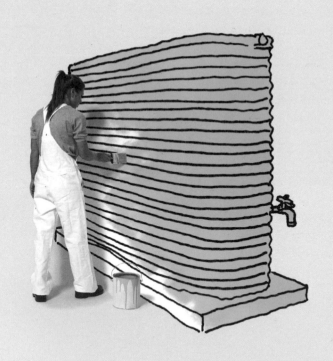

8

Splash out with water savings

Water is an important issue for us all. Even if your business doesn't use a lot of water it's likely to be facing some restriction on use and increase in cost.

If your business relies on water and operates in drought-affected areas, you would be acutely affected already.

The water problems Australia faces are predicted to worsen over coming decades. However, there are steps everyone can take to be more efficient and use less water to lessen the problem, while also maintaining business operations.

Your water use

Before you can better manage your water use, you need to understand it. Doing so requires some life-cycle thinking to look at all your direct and indirect water using activities.

Direct water use

1. Calculate your baseline use – that is, the total amount of water your business consumes. If you're not clear on how to do this, call your water utility for assistance.

2. Track variables such as seasonal differences, downtime or holidays, changes in employee numbers, number of customers, or differences in work undertaken.

3. Identify equipment and activities that use water. If you have high-demand areas consider sub-metering to better measure where and how your business uses water.

Indirect water use

Every good or service contains what is called 'embodied water'. This is a measure of the total water used in producing that good or service. For example, it is estimated that a kilogram of potatoes takes about 500 litres to produce; a kilogram of rice about 1550 litres; and a kilogram of beef 50,000–100,000 litres.[95] A typical ream of paper, weighing 2.5 kilograms, takes about 60 litres of water to make; while a vehicle weighing 1.5 tonnes uses about 71,000 litres in its manufacture.[96]

Mining, growing, processing, manufacturing, packaging, transporting, storage and waste disposal all consume water. SMEs that minimise consumption by reducing, reusing and recycling resources can help to save very large amounts of water. Recycling one tonne of paper, for example, can save up to 31,780 litres of water.[97] This saving may be out of sight and out of mind but the savings are significant all the same.

Your water saving strategy

A water-efficiency strategy for SMEs involves four key elements:

- the use of water-efficient appliances and fittings
- the capturing and reuse of waste water
- maintaining equipment at maximum operational efficiency
- educating and raising awareness about the need to minimise water use.

---

95   See www.clw.csiro.au/issues/water

96   'The Future of Water' in *Future Dilemmas: Options to 2050 for Australia's population, technology, resource and environmental*, CSIRO Sustainable Ecosystems, October 2002

97   See www.csiro.au/helix/sciencemail/activities/hand-madepaper.html

Using water-efficient appliances and fittings

The Water Efficiency Labelling Scheme (WELS) can tell you which products are more water-efficient than others. Devices receive a rating to a maximum of six stars. More stars means less water is used and there is an associated saving on water and energy costs.

The WELS scheme covers tap equipment, urinals, toilet equipment, showers, flow controllers, washing machines and dishwashers. Go to www.waterrating.gov.au for more information about the scheme.

The savings from buying water-efficient equipment can be significant:

■ toilet equipment accounts for 22% of the water saving from the WELS scheme; modern dual-flush toilets use only four litres of water – an old single flush toilet can use three times that amount

■ according to the WELS site, the average urinal uses about 2.2 litres per flush, whereas a water-efficient urinal will use 1.5 litres

■ a water-efficient dishwasher can use half the water of less efficient models.

Finding out more about water-efficient appliances

Check out www.waterrating.gov.au for the water-efficiency ratings of the 12,700 products that carry the WELS symbol.

The sister scheme to WELS for other water products and services is the Smart Approved WaterMark. More than 160 products now carry the Smart Approved WaterMark label. For more information, go to www.smartwatermark.org or call 02 9290 3322.

Visit www.greenplumbers.com.au to find a plumbing service that can advise on the most water-efficient products and appliances for your needs.

Capturing and reusing waste water

Your scope for doing this will depend on the nature of your business. It could be as simple as diverting water from bathroom basins to toilet cisterns in a small office. In larger companies, it could include a comprehensive wastewater management plan involving treatment and recycling where water is used an industrial input.

As these solutions, and the savings to be made, are very site-specific it is best to seek advice from a qualified plumber, your local water authority or a waste-management specialist.

Water systems that handle black and grey water can also be found at the www.smartwatermark.org website.

Maintain equipment

Improving the operational efficiency of equipment is one of the simplest ways to reduce water consumption. A study by Sydney Water found nearly a third (28 per cent) of water consumption in the average commercial building can be due to leaks.[98]

Solutions to the problem of leaks include:

- read water meters regularly to help detect leaks and to identify equipment that may be operating in error
- check the meter when no one is in the office or your plant is not running – if the meter is running ask your water authority to investigate
- conduct regular inspections of hot water systems, steam boilers and air-conditioning units, as well as pipes, hoses and connections
- put food dye in a toilet cistern overnight; if the water in the bowl is coloured in the morning, you have a cistern leak that needs to be fixed.

Educating and raising awareness

Effective training and communication is vital if you are to achieve your water-saving goals. Here are a few ideas to encourage water-conscious behaviour in your business:

1. Place signs on all water-using fixtures, explaining how much water they use and how to use them most efficiently, such as not running a dishwasher before it is full.

---

98   Sydney Water: *Best Practice Guidelines for water conservation in commercial office buildings and shopping centres*

Saving money on bottled water:

- Australians spend more than half a billion dollars a year on bottled water – SMEs can pay more for a litre of water than they do for a litre of petrol

- Westpac removed bottled water from its offices and branches and replaced it with filtered water – this is the better environmental option as it can save your business money and at the same time reduce the need to bottle and transport large drum bottled water and small single-use bottles; for more case studies on corporate bottled water reduction visit www.gotap.com.au

- in 2009, in a move that generated global headlines, all the small business retailers in the NSW town of Bundanoon banned single-use still bottled water; they now sell refillable bottles instead – their customers fill them up for free and the retailers make money on the refillable bottles

- according to DECC, it takes up to 200 millilitres of oil to produce, transport, refrigerate and dispose of one litre of bottled water.

2. Look out for leaks. Place posters around your business that give a phone number or email so people can report leaks in bathrooms, kitchens and other areas of your business. It makes sense to put these posters in the areas where water is being used.

3. Install shower timers to encourage shorter showers. Using a water-efficient shower and reducing shower durations from seven minutes to four minutes can save up to 30 litres or more per shower. As you're also reducing the amount of water you have to heat, the savings from this move can be significant.

4. Include water conservation in employee inductions and invite a representative from a municipal or state government water-efficiency program to address an employee seminar.

5. Use newsletters, email or pay-slip notifications to communicate water-saving tips, new measures and positive feedback on water saving reductions.

6. Promote your water-saving initiatives within the local community via media releases and the local newspaper. Such steps can enhance your business profile, raise your awareness with consumers and potential customers and generally raise awareness in the community. See chapter 13 for more information on communicating your committment to sustainability.

7. Provide opportunities for your employees and contractors to play a leadership role in water-saving initiatives. Make sure you provide a mechanism to acknowledge their contribution as well as incentives to encourage better outcomes.

Use newsletters, email or pay-slip notifications to communicate water-saving tips, new measures and positive feedback on water-saving reductions.

Getting assistance

Most water authorities and suppliers offer assistance to businesses to reduce their water usage and water bills.

They do this through a range of services such as site assessments to conduct a water efficiency appraisal and comprehensive reports providing your business with a water-saving plan.

Different authorities offer different options for these services – some provide initial advice for free and then either charge directly for more detailed work or offer pay-by-saving programs that charge a scheduled payment over time as your business reduces water use and costs.

Go to www.savewater.com.au/programs-and-events/savewater-efficiency-service for more information and to see if this service is available in your area.

Actions for your water strategy

Kitchens:

1. Install water-efficient dishwashers. A six-star rated model under the Water Efficiency Label Scheme (WELS) can use half the water of older models. Also avoid running dishwashers until they are fully loaded.

2. Use WELS-certified plumbing fixtures, such as low-flow and aerator devices on taps.

3. Replace wok stoves with waterless models. Traditional stoves use an average of 5500 litres of water a day in cooling and cleaning, costing thousands of dollars in water.[99] A waterless wok stove can pay for itself in about a year.

4. Turn off combi ovens when not in use.

5. Avoid the use of running water to wash or thaw produce.

6. Clean floors with brooms and mops, rather than hosing them down.

7. Use a water filter on taps instead of buying bottled water.

8. Put water aerators and flow restrictors on kitchen taps.

Bathroom areas

1. Use water-efficient plumbing fixtures. Flow control valves on taps reduce average flow from 12 litres to four litres or less a minute. Water-efficient showerheads can reduce flow from about 15 litres to nine litres or less a minute. The latest 4.5/3L dual-flush toilets use 30 to 60% less water than older models.

2. Install water-efficient urinals with infrared 'smart' flushing controls. One single inefficient urinal in a high-use location can use up to 700 litres of water a day. To cut water use to virtually nothing (besides cleaning) consider waterless urinals – though make sure you have piping that can cope with them as the undiluted ammonia in urine can corrode copper pipes.

3. Insulate hot water pipes and minimise the distance between hot water tanks and taps. This avoids running the tap to get hot water, thereby helping you to save money by reducing the energy needed to heat the water.

---

99   *The Waterless Wok Stove*, Sydney Water. See www.sydneywater.com.au

Waterless urinals

A bathroom with a waterless urinal system can save up to 150 kilolitres of water each year.[100]

Laundry areas:

1. Replace top-loading washing machines with water-efficient front-loading models. The best rated machines can use up to two-thirds less water than older models. Avoid running them until there is a full load.

2. Washing in cold water will also help to reduce the cost of heating the water – which in turn helps to reduce greenhouse emissions.

3. Ensure equipment such as boilers, pumps, chillers and water heaters are maintained to prevent water loss due to leaks, steam or condensation. Try to make sure that they are used according to actual loads and are shut down when not in use.

4. Install timers to turn off equipment when it's not in use.

5. Install a system to reuse water where the opportunity exists.

Plants and outdoor areas:

1. Choose water-efficient products, such as trigger nozzles on hoses, and service providers displaying the Smart Approved WaterMark. The label certifies products and services that help to reduce indoor and outdoor water use.[101]

2. Use native and drought-tolerant plants and replace ornamental or unused lawn areas with ground cover or a bush garden.

---

100   *Water Efficiency Guide: Office and Public Buildings,* Department of Environment and Heritage, October 2006

101   See www.smartwatermark.info

Case study: Caroma – saving water and money with the dual-flush toilet

How much water can efficiency measures save? Consider the case of the humble toilet. Prior to 1981 the standard toilet used about 12 litres of water per flush. Then Bruce Thompson, working for the Caroma company in Adelaide, developed a dual-flush design with a federal industry grant of $130,000.

A trial in South Australia found the dual-flush toilet, which used 11 litres for every full flush or 5.5 litres per half flush, saved 32,000 litres of water per household a year. Soon after, all states except NSW made the dual-flush toilet compulsory in new buildings.

In addition to stopping money from being flushed away, the dual-flush toilet is now exported to 30 countries around the world. It's another example of the business potential of environmental innovation.

About 75 per cent of toilets in Australian homes are now dual-flush and the water savings are an estimated 214 gigalitres a year. The Institute of Sustainable Futures at the University of Technology Sydney has estimated that replacing the remaining 3.1 million single-flush toilets with 4.5/3-litre dual-flush toilets would save a further 79 gigalitres of water a year.

Did you know?

We are sometimes not aware of the water our businesses waste. The Nursery and Garden Industry Australia's (NGIA) Best Practice Guidelines state that: "Water use efficiencies as low as 10 per cent are common in Australian nurseries."

3. Cover garden beds with mulch. This will reduce evaporative water loss from the soil by up to 70%.

4. Use timers and moisture sensors to avoid over-watering. Group plants with similar water requirements together (this is called hydro-zoning).

5. Minimise untreated run-off going straight down stormwater drains by routing drain pipes to ponds or bioswales (landscaped areas designed to remove silt and pollution from surface run-off water).

6. Use permeable pavers or paving designs that provide gaps for water to reach the Earth, where it can be filtered by the soil before entering the water table.

Be inspired

Want to see what other businesses are doing to reduce water use? Then visit www.savewater.com.au and check out the entries in the small business section of the Save Water! Awards.

The Dugine Native Plant Nursery won the 2009 awards by reducing its use of potable water by 100 per cent. They did this by switching to new rainwater tanks and bore water.

Go to www.savewater.com.au/how-to-save-water/in-business for tips on water saving in hospitality, food processing, nurseries, construction, textiles and manufacturing.

The Geelong Racing Club, a finalist in 2009, used 80 megalitres of water every year. From May 2008–9 it reduced its use of potable water by 69 per cent. This was achieved through rainwater tanks that were used for washing horses, a groundwater bore for maintenance of the sand track, the use of drought tolerant plants and mulch in its gardens. It also used a Siemens data logging system that alerted employees to water leaks.

How can your business reduce its water use?

Increased water costs for SMEs

According to the Water Services Association, which represents the companies who provide water to 15 million Australians, the cost of water is likely to rise by 50 to 100 per cent in the next few years.

There are no easy or cheap solutions. Except one – water efficiency.

As the price of water goes up, there will be good reasons to make your business water-efficient. That's because water efficiency:

- saves your business money – not just in direct supply charges but also through lower sewage and trade waste charges, as well as associated costs like water heating or pumping
- encourages better business practices – the discipline of measuring and managing water use contributes to overall business efficiencies
- demonstrates your commitment to being an environmentally and socially responsible business – both to customers and employees.

As with energy efficiency, water efficiency helps to protect the environment and your bottom line at the same time.

Did you know?

1. Just 3% of the world's water is fresh. Two-thirds of that is locked up in polar ice.

2. A slowly dripping tap or toilet can waste a couple of litres each hour – that's 15,000 to 20,000 litres a year.[102]

102   See www.savewater.com.au

How bad is the problem?

Australia's 'food bowl', the Murray-Darling Basin, which produces two-fifths of the nation's fruit, vegetables and grain production, is facing an ecological and economic crisis after a decade of drought. This pressure has been magnified by many more decades of unsustainable farming practices that have taken too much water from local rivers. The CSIRO estimates that warming temperatures have lowered rainfalls and these lower rainfalls have reduced surface flows across the basin's nearly two dozen river valleys by 40 per cent since 1950.

The once mighty Murray-Darling system, on which thousands of SMEs and about three million Australians depend directly for their water needs, is in danger due to lack of sufficient water flow.

Over the next two decades, the CSIRO predicts a warming climate will reduce rainfall further – by an average of 15 per cent in the catchment areas providing water to Australia's 10 largest cities.[103] At the same time the nation's population could grow from about 22 million people to 35 million by 2049, with the Australian Bureau of Statistics tipping Brisbane, Perth, Melbourne and Sydney as the cities experiencing the most growth. These cities and the SMEs within them have already grappled with shortfalls in water supplies. Such changes will only serve to undermine our water security even further.

Projected shortfall in Perth's water supply by 2060

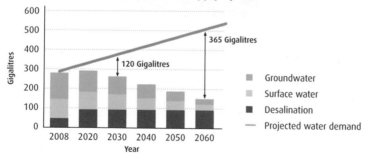

Source: CSIRO

This graph shows the scenario for Perth, where rainfall is predicted to drop 20 per cent in the next two decades. The underground aquifers which supply most of the city's water are facing increased stress. Australia's first large-scale desalination plant, costing $387 million, was opened in 2006, and now supplies about 17 per cent of the city's water. Although this plant

---

103 'Stormwater – helping to tackle Australia's water crisis' – *NOVA Science in the news* published by the Australian Academy of Science, June 2008

has already supplied more than 100 billion litres of water, the West Australian government has already announced the need for a second plant. This time, the total price tag for construction and integration with the water supply system is approaching $1 billion.

For more water information and tips, you can download a water efficiency guide from: www.environment.gov.au/settlements/publications/government/pubs/ water-efficiency-guide.pdf

Case study: the 321 Water Bottle – water innovation

People who travel a lot often end up spending a small fortune on bottled water. However, a group of Australian designers from a small business in Victoria have come up with an innovative water purification system that provides clean water for long journeys.

Designed by Gretha Oost, Paul Charlwood and Andrew Howley, the 321 Water Bottle is an inexpensive purifier for the health-conscious traveller. Working like a French-press coffee maker, the portable water filter is very simple to use. All the user has to do is fill the bottle with water from the nearest tap, slot in the filter and push it down. The filter is good for 100 uses (approximately 50 litres).

The 321 Water Bottle doesn't just filter water on the go; it also helps to reduce the use of single use plastic water bottles. And that doesn't just save the environment. With bottled water costing more per litre than petrol, it could save you money too.

It's a good example of a small business coming up with a money-making solution to an environmental problem.[104]

104   See www.321-water.com

'The business case for greener buildings is clear. While a sustainable building can cost more to refurbish or construct, it offers long-term operational savings...'

9

It's all around you: sustainable buildings and workspaces

Whether you work in an office, factory, café, news agency, pharmacy, florist or hairdresser, your workplace can be more sustainable and more productive.

The business case for greener buildings is clear. While a sustainable building can cost more to refurbish or construct, it offers long-term operational savings and evidence shows people who work in sustainable workplaces get sick less and are more productive.

The refurbishment of 500 Collins Street in Melbourne is a good example. The 30-year-old office tower was the first CBD commercial building to receive a Green Star rating for its refurbishment.[105] A study found that:

- greenhouse gas emissions were reduced by more than 1700 tonnes a year

- waste recycling rates increased from 13% to 42%

- average sick-leave days per employee fell by 39%

105   See www.greenerbuildings.com.au

- task productivity improved, with employees reporting better concentration and general well-being
- employees reported fewer cases of headaches, eye strain, colds and fatigue.

Green Star ratings system

Green Star is the Green Building Council of Australia's national, voluntary environmental rating system.

11 per cent of Australia's CBD commercial office buildings are now Green Star certified. This voluntary rating system evaluates and rates the environmental design and construction of commercial office buildings.

Its website provides a lot of useful tools, technical guides and calculators. Go to www.gbca.org.au/green-star to register your building project for Green Star certification.

Improving the environmental performance of your building or workspace therefore has multiple business benefits:

- it can significantly reduce the environmental impact of your business while also saving you money
- it can improve employee well-being and productivity, and can potentially reduce your occupational health and safety liabilities
- it can help to attract and retain talented employees
- it promotes your environmental credentials to customers and other stakeholders.

What makes a sustainable building?

It's a combination of factors. Rating schemes like the Green Building Council's Green Star system assess the following factors to determine a building's overall performance:

- management
- energy efficiency
- water efficiency
- indoor environment quality
- transport
- material selection
- land use and ecology
- innovation
- emissions.

As a SME, many of these factors can be considered when you're moving premises or looking at a refurbishment of your existing premises. But an effective environmental management plan can also improve the performance of your existing building.

From November 2010, owners of large commercial office buildings have been required to provide energy efficiency ratings when selling or leasing office space. According to the Department of Climate Change and Energy Efficiency, 'the aim of the scheme is to ensure that credible and meaningful energy efficiency information is given to prospective purchasers and lessees of large commercial office space.' The result is a scheme that makes it easier for companies to search out energy-efficient office space.[106]

---

106   See www.environment.gov.au/buildings

Building management for SMEs

You can conduct an environmental audit to better understand the performance of your workspace or building in the key areas of:

- lighting
- indoor air quality
- heating and air-conditioning
- water use
- waste generation.

NABERS

The National Australian Built Environment Rating System (NABERS) is the Federal Government's environmental rating system for existing buildings.

This scheme doesn't just help companies to save money by reducing their energy use and greenhouse gas emissions. It also enables them to see how well they're doing in managing the environmental performance of their building.

It does this by assessing a building's impact on a scale of one to five, with five being the best and one being the worst. This allows the building's environmental performance to be compared with others.

The NABERS website has an online calculator that helps SMEs to assess and compare their energy, water, waste and indoor environment performance. Go to www.nabers.com.au for further information.

If your business doesn't own its premises, then speaking with the facility manager, agent or owner is a good way to share the task. You could also look to negotiate a 'green lease'. Within such a lease the tenant and the building owner look at the ways in which they can reduce the environmental impact of the building. These initiatives are then included within the lease agreement. In some cases, the financial savings from efficiencies and reduced energy use can be shared between the tenant and the building owner.

The Green Lease Guide

The Investa Property Group has 17 buildings in the Sydney CBD that utilise green lease provisions. Together with a number of other organisations, it has drawn up a Green Lease Guide that sets out the ways in which a green lease can benefit businesses. It can be downloaded from the 'for business' sections of either www.resourcesmart.vic.gov.au or www.environment.nsw.gov.au

Ventilation and indoor air quality

We spend 90 per cent of our time indoors so air quality inside buildings is a major issue. However, many people are unaware that the quality of air inside buildings is often worse than the outside air. Indoor air doesn't just contain pollutants from outside, it also contains pollutants that are generated inside the building. These include emissions from photocopiers and printers, as well as the slow release of gas from carpets, paints and plastics.

There are a number of easy steps you can take to improve air quality in your building:

- ensure that all heating, ventilation and air-conditioning (HVAC) equipment is regularly cleaned and tested for contamination
- use low volatile organic compound (VOC) paints, sealants and adhesives
- have your indoor air quality tested and regularly monitor the level of carbon dioxide in areas where air is re-circulated
- open windows wherever possible and look for ventilation systems designed to maximise access to fresh air and that operate independently of your heating and air-conditioning systems.

Locating a green building professional

If you want to make your building more sustainable and you need help, the Green Star Accredited Professionals Directory at www.gbca.org.au is the best place to start. It contains a list of designers, architects, engineers, builders, project managers and other industry professionals who have shown a full understanding of the Green Star environmental rating system and the Green Star Office Design rating tool.

Material use

Studies show a clear link between health and the use of materials that contain synthetic chemicals. Wherever possible choose eco-friendly furniture, floor coverings and finishes made from natural, non-toxic materials. While such products may have a higher initial price, the overall cost can be lower as employees are healthier, have fewer sick days and can be more productive. Things to be aware of include:

1. Floor coverings, as these have the single greatest environmental impact of any fixed item, due to wear and tear. Look for durable flooring made from natural materials that can be reconditioned or recycled. Options include modular carpet, recycled tiling and timber and sustainably grown materials like bamboo.

2. Standard oil-based paints, adhesives and sealants that give off volatile organic compounds (VOCs). Choose natural or low-VOC paints and finishings.

3. Consult Good Environmental Choice's green procurement database at www.geca.org.au for the most environmentally preferable products.

www.yourbuilding.org

This Australian website contains useful advice and information on greener buildings. Run by the Property Council, the site also has a wide range of tips that are useful for SMEs wishing to make their building more sustainable.

Connection to nature

Proximity to nature aids health and wellbeing. Research by the University of Technology in Sydney indicate that plants improve indoor air quality and can remove volatile organic compounds (VOCs), that can cause sickness and lethargy. Its study found a mixture of plant species such as Peace Lily, Kentia Palm, Marginata and Devil's Ivy could achieve a complete removal of VOCs in 24 hours in a closed chamber with no ventilation, and a 10 to 20 per cent reduction in flow-through conditions.

Giving your employees a view of the outside world also makes a difference. Studies indicate that people who work near a window have lower levels of health complaints.

Green Building Fund

The Federal Government's Green Building Fund has been set up to reduce the energy used in the operation of existing commercial office buildings.

With $90 million of funding over five years, one of the two streams of funding targets owners of existing commercial office buildings. The fund will assist them to reduce energy consumption through the retro-fitting and retro-commissioning of these buildings. Grants of between $50,000 and $500,000 are available to cover up to 50 per cent of project costs.[107]

---

[107] For further information contact the AusIndustry hotline on 13 28 46
or email hotline@ausindustry.gov.au

Case study: Australian Ethical Investment – green building renovations on Trevor Pearcey House

For many SMEs, creating a green building will take place when you come to renovate your existing building. This is the case with the new head office of Australian Ethical Investment in Canberra.

The original two-storey building was over 20 years old when it was renovated into a 'green building'. Instead of a hi-tech renovation, a focus was placed on low-technology design principles that utilised passive systems and the reuse of materials.

From an energy-saving standpoint, the renovation used double-glazing windows, passive cooling and external insulation. Water-efficiency measures included the installation of rainwater tanks for use in toilet flushing and moisture sensors for use in garden irrigation.

According to the Greener Buildings website,[108] the renovation has achieved the following savings:

- a 75% decrease in greenhouse gas emissions
- a 75% reduction in water use
- 80% reduction in waste materials
- savings of $17,000 each year – or 52% – on energy costs.

After 12 months of operation, the building operates at 47 per cent less than the standard amount for a 5 Star NABERS Energy rated building. Greenhouse gas emissions have also fallen by around two-thirds.

The building was awarded a 6 Star Green Star rating, in the process showing that a modest renovation budget can achieve significant environmental and financial savings.

Many buildings that were built in the 1970s are now coming up for renovation. Go to http://tinyurl.com/yjhsbss for more information and advice specific to retrofitting old buildings.

108   See www.greenerbuildings.com.au

Self-sufficiency and overall efficiency

In addition to maximising energy and water conservation and minimising waste, a green building should also introduce measures that bring about a degree of self-sufficiency:

1. In the case of energy, this can be achieved through the installation of solar panels or wind turbines.

2. In the case of water, this can be achieved by collecting rainwater off the roof. After use in kitchen and bathroom basins, this water can then be recycled for toilet flushing or for use in cooling towers. It could even be used to water plants.

3. Establishing a green roof (that is, putting in soil and plants on your roof) can help to insulate the roof of your property.

CitySwitch – helping SMEs to green their offices

Many SMEs are unaware of their climate impact or the cost saving benefits of energy efficiency. To change this, Australia's local governments have partnered with businesses to create the CitySwitch Green Office program.

CitySwitch works with tenants to improve the energy efficiency of their offices. In addition to saving energy, the initiative also helps companies to save money and reduce the greenhouse emissions that are generated by their operations.

The program was initiated by local government following estimates that tenants can influence up to 50 per cent of the energy use in office buildings. At the time of publication, hundreds of tenancies utilising more than 1,100,000 sqm of office space have joined the CitySwitch program.[109]

---

109   See www.cityswitch.net.au

Emissions

Emissions related to a workspace and building can include air, light, noise and water pollution. Environmental management plans (see chapter 12) should include processes to identify and manage any such emissions so your space is as sustainable as possible.

Further information

Operating buildings on a more sustainable basis is vital if we are to realise the cost savings and environmental potential of greener buildings. To facilitate this, the Federal Government has released a guide to help building owners, managers and tenants operate Australia's buildings in a more sustainable manner.

The ESD Operations Guide for Owners, Managers and Tenants is available as a free download from: www.environment.gov.au/sustainability/government/publications/esd-operations-guide.html

The 'Waste Reduction in Office Buildings' guides for tenants and building managers are also available for free download from www.environment.nsw.gov.au/sustainbus/wastereductioninofficebuildings.htm

Insulation

Many SMEs do not have insulation in their factories or offices. With 60 per cent of Australian homes now insulated, the savings from insulation are well-documented:

- ceiling/roof insulation – up to 45%
- floor insulation – up to 5%
- wall insulation – up to 20%.

The Victorian Government has an insulation brochure that gives excellent advice on the different types of insulation available. It also contains advice on how to install it.[110]

---

110   See www.sustainability.vic.gov.au

Case study: The Green Building Council of Australia – greener refurbishment[111]

The Green Building Council of Australia (GBCA) is the key organisation behind the uptake of green building practices in Australia's property industry. Supported by both industry and government, the organisation has been highly effective in promoting sustainable buildings.

In addition to encouraging others to 'green up' their buildings, this small not-for-profit undertook a GreenHouse refurbishment of an 800m² space in Sydney's central CBD. The location was chosen as it had maximum daylight access and was situated close to public transport.

The GBCA took into account the waste hierarchy when planning its refurbishment. It went with an open-plan office and exposed ceilings in order to reduce the use of plasterboard and ceiling tiles. It reused some items from its previous office and the previous tenant. Café chairs and other furniture were also recycled and reupholstered to give them a fresh new look.

In July 2009, the GBCA GreenHouse achieved a 5 Star Green Star – Office Interiors v1.1 certified rating. The $1.3 million fit-out took less than five months to complete and came in on budget, showing such fit-outs are within the capabilities of other SMEs.

111   This overview has been sourced and adapted with permission from the Green Building Council of Australia case study at www.gbca.org.au/about/the-greenhouse

While most SMEs won't have a spare $1.3 million lying around to invest in a Green Star office fit-out, the GBCA environmental innovations can be treated like a green office 'wish list', so to speak. You may not be able to do everything but there are a number of great, cost-effective things you can introduce in your workplace to reduce your environmental footprint and save money for your business.

The refurbishment was a showcase for sustainable SME building initiatives and included the following environmental innovations:

Water saving

1. Dual-flush water-efficient cisterns were installed in the bathroom.

2. The GBCA also used 6 star water-efficient urinals that were controlled by motion detectors and used only 0.8 litres per flush. Other fit-outs of this size have also used waterless urinals.

3. To maximise efficiencies further, the bathroom taps are water-saving, spring loaded taps.

4. To minimise the use of potable water, toilets are connected to a grey water system.

5. All water and other material that goes into the dishwasher or down the sink (such as soap and food scraps), is pumped along a grey waste pipe and into a grey water collection tank. After all solid material is filtered out, the water is then used for flushing the toilets and urinals. The grey water is only released into the system when the tank level is high enough. At other times regular tap water is used.

Lighting

1. Energy-efficient lighting was used in the fit-out. To minimise lighting costs, the meeting room and boardroom lighting runs on a sensor system and the workstation lighting provides both task and ambient lighting within one system. Eventually all lights will be linked to a Dali automated system, providing maximum energy efficiency.

2. Light shelves are located along the east façade in window bays. The translucent materials are multipurpose, projecting diffused natural daylight into the space and reducing radiant heat.

3. Blinds were installed on all the perimeter windows to control light penetration, glare and heat. All window blinds are fully automated and controlled by a touch screen panel. Eventually, these blinds will be set on a timer, with manual override.

Air quality

1. CO_2 monitors are located in the GBCA meeting rooms and general office areas. These devices monitor the amount of CO_2, while sensors deliver higher levels of fresh air for occupant comfort.

2. A highly energy-efficient mechanical air-conditioning system was installed, delivering air through vents at floor level in workstation areas, window bays and through plenum wall boxes along the perimeter of the west and south areas of the office. This air is then vented out through return air ducts above the light shelves. Floor vents can be rotated to direct the flow of air to maximise worker comfort.

3. Living plants are supplied and maintained by a supplier. These act as bio-filters to convert CO_2 into oxygen. A functional and decorative living plant wall is also featured behind the reception area. As the plants grow they will also provide visual privacy.

4. All printers, photocopiers and computer racks are located in the utilities room. As such, all pollutants are contained and the area can be properly ventilated.

Waste minimisation and recycling

1. Waste bins have been provided for recycled paper and card, recycled plastic and appropriate food scraps which go to a worm farm. Small bins are used in the kitchen areas and large paper and plastic, glass, steel and aluminium recycling bins are in the utilities room.

2. Two worm farms are fed using food scraps generated by the GBCA employees. A worm can eat its own weight in food every day and the worm castings can be used on office plants.

3. Where possible, the GBCA chose to limit the installation of ceilings throughout the tenancy in order to avoid unnecessary use of materials (this leaves building services and cables exposed). An articulated plasterboard ceiling has been installed above workstations on the east façade to conceal the insulation and to optimise acoustics.

Furniture

1. Around 40% of the desk chairs are reused from the old GBCA office with the remainder being bought new to match the old chairs. The new chairs are all certified by Good Environmental Choice Australia (GECA).

2. Additional chairs were leased to the GBCA for use in the boardroom. In the future, these chairs can be returned and reused by other companies.

3. The boardroom tables have lockable castors, allowing them to be reconfigured according to the GBCA's meeting needs. This flexibility maximises their potential use and longevity.

4. The café/lounge area furniture includes a classic pre-loved 1950s designer lounge and table. Café chairs have been reused, with some being reupholstered to match the vibrant colour scheme of the office. The Australian designed and manufactured plywood stools are made of FSC-certified plywood and can be 'flat packed' for easy transportation. The dining table was reused from the GBCA's old office.

5. The workstation pin boards are made from recycled PET bottles and workstation storage units are all GECA certified.

Low toxicity

1. Where possible, all upholstery and curtain fabric is natural and low toxic.

2. The carpet has low VOC content and can be recycled. To avoid the use of carpet glue, the carpet tiles are held in place with adhesive stickers on the corners of each tile. The concrete floor has also been polished and sealed with water-based sealant.

3. All joinery, workstations and meeting tables are made from low formaldehyde (E0) board.

Go to www.gbca.org.au for more information about the GreenHouse refurbishment and the Green Building Council of Australia.

Greener Buildings

This comprehensive website provides a rundown of the benefits of green buildings. It has a range of case studies, tips on how to rate and improve building performance, questions to ask building owners and managers, and advice on green leasing.

The site is a collaboration between Victoria's Building Industry Consultative Council, state and federal environment departments and the Green Building Council of Australia.

Green building case studies can be found on this site at www.greenerbuildings.com.au/case-studies

Case study: Szencorp Building – Australia's first retrofitted building to achieve a 6 star Green Star rating

The Szencorp building in Melbourne was Australia's first retrofitted building to achieve a 6 Star Green Star rating.[112] The changes implemented in the building show the money saving and environmental potential of green buildings:

1. The building achieved 88% water savings compared to the industry average (as measured by the NABERS water rating of 2.5 Stars). Rainwater is combined with the grey water from showers and hand basins to flush the toilets. The toilets are dual flush and waterless urinals are used. Water-efficient taps and showerheads are also used throughout the building.

2. There was a 65% energy saving compared to the amount of energy used before the retrofit.

3. Waste was reduced by 54% when compared to the amount of waste generated by the average office worker.

4. Resource use is highly regulated and monitored. There are 59 individual meters to monitor energy use and the building is broken down into 21 occupancy zones. These zones are designed so the lights and air-conditioning only come on when needed.

5. The innovative waste minimisation and recycling infrastructure led to 76% of their waste being recycled.

6. 120% of emissions were offset by purchasing carbon credits from Climate Friendly.

7. The building utilises a solar hot water system and three solar PV arrays that generate approximately 20% of the building's electricity requirements.

8. There is insulation in the walls and roof as well as a double-glazed façade.

9. When the weather conditions allow, natural air ventilation supplements the air-conditioning system.

10. Bicycle parking, showers and lockers are available for occupants and visitors. A hybrid Prius is also available for employees' travel use.

112   See www.theszencorpbuilding.com

'The process of eco-design looks at the natural resources a product or process uses, the waste it creates and, equally as important, how the product or service is used and influences behaviour.'

10

Eco-design: the environmental impact at every stage of your product's life

Eco-design is about designing products and services in a way that minimises negative environmental impacts.

Eco-design does this by considering a product or a process from the point of view of its entire environmental impact – often described as 'from cradle to grave'. The process of eco-design looks at the natural resources a product or process uses, the waste it creates and, equally as important, how the product or service is used and influences behaviour.

When developing a product from scratch, ask yourself how it can be designed so that it uses fewer inputs and materials.

1. What materials will be used?

   a) Can you use recycled materials or materials that are made from renewable resources?

   b) Can they be sourced within Australia instead of from overseas?

   c) Can less toxic or less environmentally harmful materials be used?

   d) Can materials that use less energy to make be incorporated into the product?

   e) Are you buying your raw materials from the most environmentally and socially responsible source?

Inform yourself about the chemicals used in your business' products and processes.

A useful place to start is www.safersolutions.org.au which is an initiative of the Total Environment Centre. It provides a glossary of the major chemicals found in consumer products.

Wherever possible, use natural-based, non-toxic substitutes and make it a procurement policy to favour products and companies with a similar commitment.

2. Light-weighting

   a) How can the product be designed so it weighs less?

   b) Can it be reduced in size so that more units can be transported?

3. Leaner production

   a) How can the production process be tightened so it uses less energy, fewer raw materials, fewer processes and cleaner technology?

   b) Can this be done in a way that generates less waste and pollution?

4. Product distribution

   a) How can the product distribution process be streamlined?

   b) Can the packaging be made of recycled content or, at the very least,
      be easily recycled?

   c) How can the packaging itself be reduced?

   d) Is your product designed to maximise transport efficiencies? Furniture for example,
      can be flat packed, allowing for more products to be shipped in the same
      sized container.

   e) Is there a more environmentally efficient way of transporting your goods
      to your customers?

   f) Does your delivery company have vehicles that use alternative fuels? Do they use
      smaller delivery vehicles that offer a more fuel-efficient way of delivering your
      products? Do they use rail? Do they back load and maximise their loads?

5. Product efficiency

   a) Can the product be made to use less energy when it's switched on?

   b) Can it achieve energy efficiency standards that make it 'best in class'?

   c) Can the product be made so it uses no energy at all?

   d) Can it be constructed so it uses fewer secondary materials – for example,
      if it's a coffee filter, can it use reusable filters instead of single-use filters?

While some water carbonating units use electricity, the Sodastream carbonator
uses the energy from the carbonating gas cylinder. This means no electricity
is needed when it makes sparkling water. When the gas cylinder is empty,
customers have to return it to the retailer they got it from in order to buy a new
cylinder. This ensures that the old cylinder can be reused and refilled. This more
environmental approach is really working with the public. In the last year, sales of
Sodastream products in Australia have tripled. Visit www.sodastream.com.au for
more information.

6. Making it last

   a) So many products these days don't seem to last as long as they used to. Can your product be made to last as long as possible?

   b) Can it be made more reliable and easier to repair?

7. End-of-life

   a) Can the product be made so that it's far easier to recycle? Can you reuse any of the components of your product?

   b) If recycling facilities for your product are not easily available, can you extend your producer responsibility and take back your product for recycling?

   c) Can you help to ensure recycling markets for the materials within your products?

   d) Can you take back raw materials derived from the recycling of your products?

Testing from the German TÜV NORD agency indicates that 40 per cent of the mass of the new VW Golf is made from recycled materials. The majority of the car is also recyclable.

What is eco-efficiency and cleaner production?

Queensland Government agency ecoBiz defines 'eco-efficiency' and 'cleaner production' as being about saving money while improving environmental performance. This is also achieved through the use of fewer resources such as water, energy and raw materials and producing less waste overall.

For SMEs, it's about doing more with less. This involves coming up with production solutions that don't necessarily follow the 'business as usual' model. The World Business Council for Sustainable Development (WBCSD) and ecoBiz outline the seven elements of eco-efficiency as:[113]

- reducing material intensity (making more goods with fewer inputs)
- reducing energy consumption (making more goods with less energy)
- reducing the dispersion of toxic substances (making more goods but with less toxic waste)
- enhancing recyclability of materials (making the goods more recyclable)
- maximising sustainable use of renewables (using renewable energy or making goods out of materials that won't run out)
- extending product durability (making goods that last)
- increasing service intensity (meeting demand with a service and not with goods).

The 'What is Eco-design?' website is a complete online guide to sustainable design for industrial, fashion, graphic and textile designers.

Backed by the Victorian Government and Design Victoria, the project has been developed by the Centre for Design at RMIT University, WSP Environmental and leading industry experts. This highly recommended website has a range of tools and reference guides that provide SMEs with practical eco-design information that can be used in business operations.

For more information visit:

- What is Eco-design?: www.designvic.com/whatisecodesign
- RMIT Centre for Design: www.rmit.edu.au/cfd
- Society for Responsible Design: www.green.net.au

---

113   Adapted from: WBCSD, 2000, eco-efficiency, ecoBiz Queensland, 2008, Fact Sheet, Introduction to ecoBiz. See: www.derm.qld.gov.au/ecobiz

Case study: InterfaceFLOR – redesigning business

The story of how Ray Anderson 'redesigned' InterfaceFLOR is one that is told by many sustainability professionals.

Back in 1994, as the CEO of InterfaceFLOR, Anderson oversaw a carpet company that generated air and water pollution and many tonnes of waste. It's safe to say the company, like many others back then, did not enjoy a good environmental reputation.

What set Anderson apart is how he went about fundamentally changing the very basis of how InterfaceFLOR did business. He realised that businesses needed to use the Earth's natural resources in a more sustainable way. Under his leadership, the company generated new patents and invented innovative machines. It used new materials and created different manufacturing processes. The results showed the potential of making a business more sustainable in the way it did business.

Between 1994 and 2009, InterfaceFLOR claims to have:

- cut greenhouse gas emissions by 82%

- cut fossil fuel consumption by 60%

- cut waste by 66%

- cut water use by 75%

- increased sales by 66%, doubled earnings and raised profit margins.

To ensure even greater results, the company's Mission Zero™ is an initiative to eliminate InterfaceFLOR's negative environmental impacts by 2020.

The way in which Anderson achieved his results is set out in the book *Confessions of a Radical Industrialist*. It's a must-read for SMEs who want to see how practical ideas can be implemented in a way that boosts environmental performance and the bottom line.[114]

114   See www.interfaceflor.com.au

'From the office desk to the shop counter, the factory floor to out on the road, digital technology has become indispensable in virtually every aspect of business.'

11

Get connected with sustainable IT and business devices

Business use of information technology (IT) and electronic devices has helped Australia's economic growth and delivered significant productivity improvements.

SMEs in particular have benefited from these technology improvements. They've made accounting and record keeping easier and helped us to run factories more efficiently. They've smoothed out payroll responsibilities and generally enabled better communication with customers and suppliers.

From the office desk to the shop counter, the factory floor to out on the road, digital technology has become indispensable in virtually every aspect of business.

The gains have of course come at a price – not just the price of the new devices but also the environmental impact of those products, the energy needed to run them and the end-of-life disposal.

But by giving some additional consideration to the use and implementation of their IT, SMEs can actually make environmental improvements and even get more bang for their buck.

Making a difference

Reducing the environmental impact of your IT simply requires a more detailed understanding of the big environmental footprint behind the equipment, followed by an ability to communicate those details to the people who count in your business.

There are four key things to think about:

1. When buying new equipment, consider the environmental impacts of how it is manufactured, its energy requirements and the estimated length of its functioning life.

2. When using equipment, pay attention to energy efficiency by activating power-saving features and turning off machines not in use.

3. Get the most out of your investment in IT by using hardware and software to its fullest potential. This can help to streamline other business processes and operations and help to lower your overall environmental footprint.

4. Dispose of unwanted equipment responsibly by seeking out opportunities for reuse and recycling.

The environmental savings that come from paying attention to these key principles include lower use of raw materials, fewer greenhouse gas emissions, fewer hazardous by-products and less toxic waste. The business savings include:

- lower energy costs including additional savings on air-conditioning and maintenance
- longer lifespan for your equipment, reducing the capital cost of replacements
- increased productivity.

How to save money with your computer[115]

A computer left on 24 hours a day, 365 days a year will cost your business approximately $135 per annum.[116]

By switching off your computers at the end of a working day, you can easily reduce that usage to 10 hours per day, five days a week. If you do that then you can reduce the running cost to $40 per year. That's a saving of $95 per computer.

The table below gives you an indication of the potential savings for your business:

NUMBER OF COMPUTERS	POTENTIAL SAVINGS PER ANNUM
1	$95
5	$475
10	$950
15	$1425
20	$1900

Switching off all your other machines such as photocopiers and printers will result in additional savings.

115   *Eco-efficiency for small business.* See www.derm.qld.gov.au
116   Based on an energy tariff of $0.155/kWh

Purchasing

Sometimes the most business-friendly and environmentally responsible purchase is not to purchase at all. Always ask yourself whether you really need a new device. It's nice to have the latest but don't be swayed by the flashy marketing; sometimes the advertised improvements in performance don't mean much in reality. Do your research.

Consider good-quality second-hand or just-superseded equipment. Last year's top-of-the-range model from a respected brand might have more life left in it and be more efficient than the latest budget-priced offering that looks better on paper. Cheap PCs, for instance, often scrimp on components like power supplies, whereas higher quality power supplies can be far more efficient in converting incoming electricity for use.

If you're thinking about buying new equipment, consider the following tips first:

1. Explore options for upgrading existing equipment before investing in a new model. For example, getting extra RAM is likely to be cheaper than buying a new computer, so check out that option first.

2. When you do buy new equipment, invest in models that are designed to be upgraded, from manufacturers who also offer extended warranties. You should aim to get five years of service rather than the corporate standard of two or three years.

3. Consider switching over to laptops. Using a laptop computer rather than a desktop PC and monitor can reduce energy consumption by up to 80%. They also have the additional benefit of being portable, so your employees can use them when on the road or working from home.

4. In a bigger office, a network of 'thin clients' (a stripped-down PC that has low power needs) connected to a central server doing most of the processing and storage can be the most economical and efficient option. However, you should always check that the total power consumption of the thin clients combined with the servers and disk drives required to support them is lower than standard PCs.

5. If you are looking at the prospect of multiple servers, blade servers (in which many components are removed, with services such as power provided by the enclosure) will take up less space and use less power than a stack of standalone servers.

6. What goes for purchasing equipment also goes for services. Take responsibility for your environmental impact along the supply chain by choosing service providers who are committed to environmental performance. There are various internet service providers and web hosting companies that now use green energy in their operations.

Energy Star compliance reduces the amount of energy used by a product by either automatically switching it into 'sleep' mode when it's not being used and/or reducing the amount of power used when in 'standby' mode.

Donating your old computers to charity

If you want to donate your old computers to charity or a local school, it's worth checking first whether they have a use for them. For example, if you drop off your computers at a charity drop off zone without checking first, the charity may end up having to pay for the disposal of your computers.

The Our Community organisation has a web page which lists charities that accept old computers for recycling or refurbishment.[117]

Infoxchange Australia's GreenPC initiative enables people on low incomes to access technology and seeks to reduce the environmental impact of outdated technology by prolonging its lifespan and usability. The organisation refurbishes used computers and provides them to low-income communities, individuals and community organisations.[118]

When donating your old computers to charities, make sure you delete sensitive company data or personal data first. Software is available that guarantees the secure deletion of such information.

117   See www.ourcommunity.com.au
118   See www.greenpc.com.au

For a comprehensive assessment of desktop computers and notebooks, check out the Electronic Product Environmental Assessment Tool (EPEAT), an international rating standard developed with funding from the US Environmental Protection Agency to help IT purchasers. EPEAT evaluates environmental performance against 23 required criteria and 28 optional criteria, including a category for energy conservation. Go to www.epeat.net for more information.

For electronics equipment other than computers, Greenpeace's Guide to Green Electronics offers an assessment of the overall environmental performance of well known brands. Go to www.greenpeace.org to read the guide.

Another useful resource is the Silicon Valley Toxics Coalition website at www.svtc.org. It has lots of interesting information on environmental impacts, the performance of computer companies in material use and responsibility for end-of-life management.

Download and save

Depending on the scope of your operations, it is probably worth buying software to measure and manage your computer's energy-saving functions. Ask your IT supplier or service consultant for advice. In the meantime, here are a few handy applications that you can try out.

Watch Over Energy

For Windows 95, 98, ME, 2000, XP and NT systems, this free program manages your computer monitor's stand-by mode and helps to track your energy savings. The developers suggest it can reduce your monitor's energy costs by at least 20 per cent. Go to www.watchoverenergy.com to download a copy.

Shutdown Vaccine

For PC networks, this shareware software can automate power-related tasks such as shutting down all workstations at a particular time. Go to http://shutdown-vaccine.smartcode.com/info.html to download a copy.

Saving power

1. Switch computers off whenever possible. Left on day and night, every day for a year, as happens in some offices – a big energy inefficient desktop computer can use up to 850 kilowatts of electricity and generate up to 900 kg of carbon emissions.[119] Switching off a computer at the end of the working day can cut its electricity use to less than 250 kilowatts with comparable carbon and cost savings. Another simple way to save money is to encourage your employees to turn off their computers even when they are going to a meeting or to lunch. You can also buy far more energy-efficient computers.

2. What goes for computers goes for screens. There is no need to worry that turning it off and on will shorten its life. Even doing so five times a day will only increase the frequency of faults after 20 years (and it probably won't last that long anyway).

Greentrac

For Windows and Mac computers, Greentrac enables businesses to automate the power management of all their computers. It can shutdown, hibernate or put computers into standby mode. It also gives real-time energy feedback to employees in a way that encourages them to take personal responsibility for reducing their computer's energy waste. The company behind Greentrac is an Australian SME and they state that users of its software typically reduce PC energy consumption by 50–65 per cent. Go to www.greentrac.com for more information.

EZ Wizard

For Windows 2000 and Windows XP systems, this free application provides a simple point and click interface for monitoring power management. Go to www.energystar.gov to download a copy.

Sleep Monitor for Mac

This one isn't free, but you can trial it for 30 days. It charts a Mac's power use, showing how long it has been in use, asleep and switched off. Go to www.dssw.co.uk/sleepmonitor to download a copy.

---

119   'Computers' energy costs', *Choice Magazine*, May 2008. Based on NSW energy emissions using Energy Australia's energy calculator

3. Disable all screen savers. Most systems now have the option under power settings to turn the display off automatically after a nominated period of time. Turning off the display delivers significantly greater power savings than a screen saver even though the screen may look the same.

4. Power-saving features, even on Energy Star qualified computers, are not automatically activated. Go into system preferences and set them to put the screen and hard drive to sleep after 10 minutes of inactivity. Sleep mode will reduce energy consumption to as little as 5% of full power and save some screens from phosphor burn-in.

5. Some systems still never go off completely but into standby mode. To ensure they are drawing zero power, turn them off at the power point. This will maximise your financial savings.

6. Place IT equipment in locations that facilitate cost-effective cooling. The electricity used by internal cooling fans can be a significant part of total power consumption, so avoid placing gear like servers in unventilated cupboards or next to other heat-producing machines.

7. Go to the Energy Star website www.energystar.gov.au for more information about standby power and detailed guides on how to enable energy-saving features on Windows, Unix and Mac systems.

Getting the most out of your IT systems

There are very few businesses these days that can afford to ignore the potential gains of information and communications technology – or the potential losses from getting left behind.

Can there be an environmental upside to having to keep up with rapid advances in technology? The answer is yes. Enabling a customer to order and pay online, for instance, avoids them having to travel to your premises. Other strategies your business can start capitalising on include:

1. Virtualise your IT system. Transferring application and storage needs from individual workstations to a centralised server enables the most efficient use of overall storage capacity and processing power.

2. 'Cloud computing' is the term for extending virtualisation beyond your office by using web-based applications and services. It can be as simple as web-based email or more comprehensive, like storing all your data on a remote server. These strategies not only reduce hardware and energy needs, they also make it easy to share information between teams.

3. Virtualise your office. Once you liberate information from individual computers, why not liberate employees from their desks? Telecommuting is seen by governments overseas as a key strategy for reducing traffic congestion and travel-related carbon emissions. It can also help you reduce your need for expensive office space.

4. Although many companies no longer use faxes, those who do can have them sent directly to a PC, saving on printing and making them easier to store and forward as well.

5. Many overseas companies see the uptake of teleconferencing, web-conferencing and video-conferencing as a key strategy for reducing business-related carbon emissions from travel. It also has the benefit of significantly reducing travel costs while improving day-to-day communications with customers and stakeholders.

6. For SMEs, the advantages of video meetings are significant. While it's good to get out of the office, all that time getting to meetings and waiting for others to show up is money down the drain. Check out the federal government's e-strategy guide at www.e-strategyguide.gov.au for tips on the lowest cost options. Though pitched at not-for-profit organisations, the information is equally useful for SMEs.

One Australian SME has devised software that helps you to measure and offset the carbon emission impact of your computer(s). The Little Green Genie software monitors when your computer is switched on and also takes into account the environmental impact of producing your computer.

Go to www.zerocarboncomputing.com for more information and to download a copy.

Why should you properly recycle your e-waste?

Making sure your equipment only goes to proper recycling companies is important. It's vital to ensure your equipment does not end up in developing countries where it can be recycled inappropriately. The Silicon Valley Toxics Coalition breaks down the ingredients of e-waste as follows:

Lead: used in older monitors as well as in soldering on circuit boards. Exposure can cause brain damage, nerve damage, blood disorders, kidney damage and developmental damage to unborn babies. Acute exposure can cause vomiting, diarrhoea, convulsions, coma or death.

Mercury: used in flat-panel displays, LCD screens, switches and printed wiring boards as well as in some batteries. High levels of exposure through ingestion or inhalation can cause central nervous system and kidney damage.

Polyvinyl chloride (PVC): used in printed circuit boards and components such as connectors, plastic covers and cables. When burnt it releases highly carcinogenic dioxins. Combinations of plastics that are difficult to separate and recycle are also used in printed circuit boards and in components such as connectors, plastic covers and cables.

Cadmium: used in chip resistors, infrared detectors, semiconductors, older cathode ray tubes and some plastics. It concentrates in the body and can cause kidney and bone damage. It's also a known carcinogenic.

Brominated flame retardants (BFRs): used in plastic casings and released when electronics are dumped or incinerated. BFRs bio-accumulate in organisms and along the food chain. Minute doses of BFRs can impair attention, learning, memory and behaviour. They are also probable endocrine disruptors.

Barium: used in the front panel of CRT monitors to protect users from radiation. Short-term exposure can cause brain swelling, muscle weakness and damage to the heart, liver and spleen.

Beryllium: used on motherboards and connectors. Is a known human carcinogen (can cause cancer).

Hexavalent chromium: used for corrosion protection of untreated and galvanised steel plates and hardener for steel housing. It can cause DNA damage and asthmatic bronchitis.

Disposal

Of the more than 3 million computers sold in Australia each year, business purchases account for half of these. The sad fact is that after a few years most of them are likely to end up being dumped in landfill or stockpiled. Use your purchasing power to buy the most environmentally sound option and ensure your business is not contributing to the problem.

1. Select brands from manufacturers that minimise use of toxic materials, enable component recycling and take back equipment at the end-of-life to ensure it is recycled rather than sent to landfill.

2. If you're leasing your equipment, make sure the leasing company will guarantee to take back the equipment for verifiable refurbishment or recycling.

3. If you have old machines not covered by take-back guarantees, check out www.recyclingnearyou.com.au to for other recycling options in your area. It's worth visiting this site on a regular basis as legislation to bring about national recycling schemes for e-waste is currently in the pipeline.

4. For mobile phones, contact MobileMuster[120] or the Mobile Phone Recycling Program[121] to organise a workplace collection.

5. Recycle printer cartridges through Cartridges 4 Planet Ark[122] or you can have them refilled at locations such as Cartridge World.

The real cost of IT

In 2008, IBM conducted a global survey of 1100 executives working in companies employing 50 to 500 people (in manufacturing, financial services, retail, health care, hospitality, IT and professional services). About one in three estimated that IT accounted for 10 to 50 per cent of their total energy costs and about one in every four – outside of professional and IT services – had no idea how much IT was adding to their energy costs.

The International Energy Agency warns that our love of electronic equipment is a major stumbling block to curbing greenhouse gas emissions and limiting the effect of global warming. Its research indicates global ICT-related energy consumption will double by about 2020 and triple by 2030 – to 1700 Terawatt hours, equivalent to the total amount of energy now used by the American and Japanese residential sector.

---

120 See www.mobilemuster.com.au
121 See www.mobilephonerecycling.com.au
122 See www.cartridges.planetark.org

Other environmental costs

But that's only one aspect of the environmental problem. Research by the United Nations University in Tokyo indicates that electronic devices are very resource-intensive to manufacture.

Then there is the problem of waste. Electronic equipment becomes obsolete faster than just about anything else you can buy. Processing power doubles about every two years, and software developers quickly work out how to use that power to create even more sophisticated applications, which then become the standard, leaving older machines looking like museum pieces.

To give you an idea of how far we've come, the first digital computer, completed in 1946, cost US$500,000, (about AU$638,000), weighed about 25 tonnes and took up 63 square metres. Today, the equivalent computing power can be delivered in a chip smaller than your fingernail.

What we do with superseded electronic equipment is one of the biggest environmental headaches we face, because electronic equipment can contain materials that pose a hazard if they're not recycled and recovered.

Green IT help

The Australian Information Industry Association has an excellent free Green IT eBook that helps businesses to develop environmentally responsible IT systems and practices.
Go to www.aiia.com.au/greenit to download a copy.

Case study: Queensland Government Chief Procurement Office – smart IT decisions

The Queensland Government Chief Procurement Office manages purchasing arrangements for agencies, state hospitals, state schools, government-owned corporations and statutory authorities.

According to the 2009 Green Purchasing Australia Report, it implemented a whole-of-government arrangement for desktop PCs, portable computers and servers.

As a result, the Queensland Government's fleet of desktop PCs now has lower operating costs due to the improved energy-efficiency of the machines. This delivered significant financial savings and environmental benefits to the Queensland Government.

Compared with normal computers, these energy-efficient machines cost an extra $30–$50 each. However, the payback period to recover this cost was only 12 months. Over the estimated three-year life of each machine, the savings from reduced energy consumption will be about $60 per unit.

The scale of the computer order was such that the Queensland Government will save an estimated $6 million dollars in reduced energy costs.

Environmentally, this purchase will also result in savings of approximately 2.2 million tonnes of CO_2 emissions per year. In addition to reviewing the energy-efficiency of these computers, the government also took into account hazardous substances, packaging and product take back.

For more information, check out the 2009 Green Purchasing Australia Report. Go to www.ecobuy.com.au to download a copy.

'An environmental management system provides an objective assessment of your environmental impact and what your business is doing to address it.'

12

Bringing it together with an environmental management system

Every business has an impact on the environment. As discussed in this book, managing that impact in a proactive way can have benefits for your bottom line.

An environmental management system (EMS) documents and systemises your business' approach to managing its environmental impact.

Such a system will provide an objective assessment of your environmental impact and what your business is doing to address it. This can be done in such a way that anyone who reads your EMS can clearly understand what you're doing to manage your environmental issues.

The amount of work required to do this depends on the level of environmental impact and environmental risk your business has – that is, the impact it has now and what could happen if something went wrong in the future. Obviously a high-impact and high-risk business may need a very formal and accredited EMS but a low-impact and low-risk business can easily implement its own EMS.

Stage one: how to start an EMS

Management commitment

Senior management needs to commit to understanding the environmental impact of your business and for someone to be given the time and authority to start the EMS.

Review your environmental impact

A baseline assessment looking at your operations, products and/or services will identify the energy, water, waste, discharges, materials, chemicals and other impacts associated with your business. This enables you to assess the level of overall environmental impact and risk and therefore determine the level of sophistication needed in your EMS, as well as priorities for environmental improvement.

Establish key performance indicators (KPIs)

A set of KPIs should be established so your business can measure and monitor its environmental impact. If you own a café, for example, an indicator may be energy, water and waste per 1000 meals served. If you are an office-based consultant, it may be the amount of energy, water and waste per employee or per square metre of office space.

Environmental policy

Write up a policy that documents your commitment to reducing the environmental impact of your business. This environmental policy can be communicated to employees, customers, suppliers and others.

Employee training

If you have employees, consider appropriate training to make them aware of your EMS and their role in it.

Action plan

The baseline assessment and indicators will provide ideas for where improvements can be made. Documenting the ideas and then assessing which are able to be done in the short, medium or long term will provide a checklist that can then be regularly reviewed, progress checked and, where necessary, have new ideas added.

Getting help

There is a range of assistance to help SMEs develop and implement an EMS.

Consultants, government and industry groups all have someone who will be able to help you with your EMS.

In each state and territory, your environment department or environment protection agency will have guides or people to help you (see 'Resources and tools', page 195).

Most industry groups also have guides and can offer assistance to help SMEs develop an EMS. While some require you to become a member to get the advice, some provide initial assistance for free. Grow Me The Money[123] and Business SA[124] can also provide very useful tools and help.

Your specific industry group may also have more tailored assistance – whether it's the Real Estate Institute of Australia, Australian Newsagents' Federation, Cabinet Makers Association, National Independent Retailers Association or the Pharmacy Guild of Australia, to name just a few, there is industry support for almost every type of business.

The Environmental Consultants Association in Western Australia has a guide to engaging environmental consultants. Go to www.eca.org.au for further information.

123   See www.growmethemoney.com.au
124   See www.business-sa.com

Writing an environment policy

This is a document that sets out your business' commitment to operate in a way that minimises your impact on the environment. When you have reduced your environmental footprint, your business can operate more efficiently which positively impacts your financial bottom line.

Environment policies don't have to be long-winded documents. If possible, you should write your policy up as a single A4 document that can be framed and put into your reception area.

The environmental policy needs to contain the following:

1. The clearly stated aims and objectives of your policy and that your business will operate within the boundaries of all applicable environmental legislation.

2. A commitment to regularly review and improve the environmental impact and performance of the business. You may want to state that you will also review the environmental impact of your contractors and suppliers.

3. Your business will seek to reduce its waste and emissions as well as its use of energy, resources and supplies. This could be linked to a statement about your business' commitment to running a more sustainable operation.

4. If there are specific environmental impacts associated with your business such as packaging or water usage, then include a reference to these in the policy.

5. It should state that your employees have accepted and will abide by the policy. Spell out how your business will educate and train its employees on environmental issues so they have increased awareness about how their actions at work affect the environment.

6. The policy should be endorsed by senior management and at the very least should be formally signed by the owner, managing director or environment manager.

If you have a major client that has an environmental policy, you may want to make sure that your policies are aligned.

Your environment policy should be a key part of your business strategy. As such, you should print your environmental policy on letterhead or design it so people see that it's a formal business document.

Business SA also recommends that you include your business' mission statement, so the policy explains what your organisation does and why your business is committed to being environmentally and socially sustainable.

Business SA is very proactive in dealing with SME-related environmental issues. Its website has a range of useful environmental information and it publishes a 'how to' guide to environmental management that SMEs will find particularly useful. Go to www.business-sa.com for more information.

Stage two – ensuring legal compliance

Companies need to understand the environmental legislation that they have to comply with.

The environmental protection authority or agency in each state and territory is a good place to start. Their websites or information lines will be able to quickly identify whether your business needs an environmental permit, as well as any general laws that you may need to be aware of (see 'Resources and tools', page 195).

Companies also need to identify other environmental requirements that relate to customer contracts, as well as industry standards, codes of practice, corporate environmental policies and any other agreement that they've entered that has environment-related clauses.

Ongoing compliance

If you identify legal compliance issues, your EMS should then include processes to ensure and demonstrate ongoing compliance. The simplest way to do this is to write a register of legal obligations into your EMS documentation and include a checkbox to track reviews and updates. Specific activities in your action plan can also ensure ongoing compliance – such as allocating responsibility to a person to review and update laws by a particular date each year.

Employee training

If it is relevant to your business, ongoing employee training should include legal compliance.

Stage three – developing the EMS and setting targets and objectives

To finalise your EMS simply bring together all the elements already discussed in this chapter. Your EMS will be complete when you document, review and communicate the EMS with key stakeholders. Issues to consider are:

1. Finalising targets and goals – are there any more goals and targets that can be included?

2. Allocating responsibility – who is responsible for managing the EMS?

3. Key impacts – have you developed a register of energy, water, waste and other impacts?

4. Avoiding pollution – if your business has the potential to cause environmental pollution, it should plan to minimise this risk. In the event of such pollution taking place, who in your company will implement and oversee an emergency response plan?

5. Monitoring the EMS – there are a number of issues to consider:

   a) How will the EMS be monitored and kept up to date?

   b) Who will oversee the record-keeping relevant to your EMS?

   c) Who will monitor your CO_2 emissions?

   d) Who will oversee and measure the financial expenditure involved in implementing your EMS and any financial savings that arise from that expenditure?

   e) What corrective action will your company take if the EMS fails to deliver environmental improvements and financial savings?

6. Public communication – should you communicate your environmental commitment and EMS to employees, customers, and suppliers?

7. Environmental report – think about when you want to start writing an annual environmental report to track your environmental performance.

8. Review and update – what is your plan for a regular review and update of your EMS? Have you considered whether independent verification and auditing may be of value?

9. Establish a baseline – your company also needs to establish a baseline from which you can measure your progress. For example, "Since 2008, Smith Resources has reduced its energy usage by 15%", allows others to evaluate you and it enables you to measure your progress.

KPIs to include in environmental reports and your EMS:

1. How much energy was used? You can get this information from your energy and fuel bills.

2. How much water was used? You can get this information from your water bills.

3. It needs to detail your transport impact – this includes air and ground transport related to your daily operations, as well as the impact of your employees getting to work.

4. How much packaging, cardboard and paper were used?

5. How much office equipment and consumables were used?

6. How much waste was generated? Your waste contractor can help you with this, or your company can monitor this on its own (this is particularly relevant if you manufacture products where waste is generated or raw materials are left unused by the production process).

7. How much waste was recycled? Your recycling company can help you with this or you may be able to monitor this on your own.

8. What solvents, refrigerants, VOCs and chemicals were used? All need to be included. How many greenhouse emissions – also called carbon emissions – were generated by your overall operations? This can be done by using a carbon calculator or by bringing in a consultant[125] who can do this for you.

---

125 The ECA has a guide to engaging environmental consultants. See www.eca.org.au

Independent accreditation and ISO 14001

With an increasing number of companies setting up sustainable procurement policies, a well-documented and implemented EMS will stand your business in good stead. Many companies have also gone one step further and had their EMS independently certified. The best known of these independent certifications is ISO 14001.

While for most SMEs just having an EMS will be satisfactory, if your business is supplying or working with major companies, it is worth examining ISO 14001 certification of your EMS. This may be even more important if you have competitors that are certified to ISO 14001 or if you have customers who have requested independent verification of your environmental processes and claims.

ISO 14001

ISO 14001 is a standard for environmental management systems that is published by the International Organization for Standardization. The ISO 14001 standard helps companies to improve their environmental performance and reduce their impact on the environment.

It's the most important environmental standard in the world and any sized business can seek ISO 14001 certification. To do so, however, you need an external auditor to verify that your EMS conforms to the requirements of the ISO 14001 standard.

This external audit and certification is one of the key benefits of ISO 14001, as it shows your customers and stakeholders that you operate to high standards of environmental management.

Go to www.iso.org for more information.

Engaging others

'Any sustainability plan must involve communication. It's a key part of your sustainability journey.'

13

Tell someone who cares: communicate your commitment to sustainability

It is critical for a business to communicate its commitment to sustainability.

Customers, employees, suppliers and partners need to know what you're doing so they can contribute to your goals and benefit from your improved performance.

According to the United Nations Environment Program (UNEP) and Futerra Sustainability (Futerra) consultants, for communication regarding sustainability to work, it needs to:

- be practical
- be targeted
- raise awareness
- change attitudes
- change behaviour.

UNEP and Futerra advise that you need to:

1. **Set objectives** – set out exactly what it is that you want to achieve. If you want to reduce energy use by 5%, then say so clearly and succinctly.

2. **Define your approach** – decide your approach, know your audience and then target it with messages that will resonate. You also need to decide how long the campaign will run.

3. **Develop your message** – decide your core messages and develop them to ensure they will emotionally engage and connect with your audience.

4. **Decide the channels of communication** – exactly how are you going to reach people? You need to decide the most appropriate methods to communicate to them. A water-saving campaign, for example, could best be served by water-saving posters near sinks and taps and on the backs of toilet doors.

5. **Provide a mechanism for feedback** – if you're putting up water-saving posters, tell people who to call if they spot a leaking tap.

6. **Decide who will manage and implement the campaign** – if someone calls to report a leaking tap, they need to be able to talk with someone who then organises to fix the tap.

7. **Measure the results** – think of what you need to measure. Is it awareness, behavioural change, reductions in energy usage? Whatever it is, prior to commencing any campaign, make sure you know the baseline by which you can measure the improvements that result from that initiative.

8. **Report and evaluate** – any communication campaign needs to report and evaluate the results. This allows for continuous improvement should you wish to run the campaign on an ongoing basis.

Use positive, targeted messages tailored to your audience and test it with people in your personal network. If it doesn't work with them, then it's highly unlikely to work on your employees.

When communication is carried out well and in an integrated manner, it can bring about significant change. Any sustainability plan your business has must therefore involve communication – it's a key part of your business' sustainability journey.

Talking to customers

Sensis has decades of experience helping SMEs to effectively communicate with their customers. Research has shown that the most effective Yellow Pages® ads focus on the needs of the customer and tell them:

- what your business does
- what benefits your business provides potential customers
- why potential customers should choose you.

Telling people about your environmentally sustainable business initiatives, no matter how big or small, is a great way to open your business up to customers who make their purchasing decisions based on the sustainability credentials of a business. So make sure you're telling your employees and customers alike about all the great stuff you're doing.

Appropriately and accurately tailored sustainability messages can give you an edge when talking to customers.

Businesses with a limited advertising and marketing budget should also consider where to invest their money in order to best communicate to customers and potential customers.

The best way to ensure your business and its environmental credentials have maximum exposure among potential customers is to spread your advertising and marketing budget across multiple active information sources.

Active information sources include:

- directories
- classifieds
- websites
- search engines
- mobiles
- newspapers.

For example, if your business' advertisement is featured in a print directory, on mobile and also online – you've got more chance of engaging a potential customer than if your advertisement is only featured in one of those sources.

Avoid 'greenwash'

'Greenwash' is the term used when a business makes environmental claims about a product which, on closer examination, don't stack up.

Many cases of 'greenwash' may be the result of ignorance or sloppiness rather than malicious intent.

SMEs making 'green' claims about their products need to keep up with developments in this area. The Australian Competition and Consumer Commission (ACCC) has released a guide titled *Green Marketing and the Trade Practices Act* to help businesses understand what claims are permissible.[126]

A study undertaken in 2007 by Terrachoice Environmental Marketing found that the major problems with 'greenwashing' were:

■ no proof being available with regards to the claim

■ vagueness about the benefit of the claim

■ irrelevance of the claim

■ fibbing about the benefit of the product.

Companies that deliberately mislead consumers can face criminal prosecution and significant fines. This, however, has not put companies off making green claims.

According to the consumer group Choice, there has been a significant increase in the use of green claims on product labels. Choice's view is that many claims are not supported by evidence, are irrelevant or are poorly explained.[127] This risk here, of course, is that such claims leave consumers confused.

Choice found 630 green claims in a stocktake of just 185 non-food supermarket items. These products included garbage bags, tissues, cleaners, detergents and toilet paper.

The issue is being closely monitored by the media and SMEs need to be aware that customers are becoming more educated about the issue of environmental claims. Given the heightened level of concern about 'greenwash' by the ACCC and a range of not-for-profit organisations, it pays to err on the side of caution when marketing your business' environmental initiatives.

---

126 *Green Marketing and the Trade Practices Act*, ACCC, 2008. See www.accc.gov.au
127 See www.choice.com.au/greenwatch

The Environmental Claims in Advertising and Marketing Code

In 2009, the advertising industry introduced a new code of practice to help ensure companies are able to back up their environmental claims.

The aim of the Environmental Claims in Advertising and Marketing Code is:

"To ensure advertisers and marketers develop and maintain rigorous standards when making Environmental Claims in Advertising and Marketing Communications and to increase consumer confidence to the benefit of the environment, consumers and industry."

The Australian Association of National Advertisers (AANA) noted consumer confidence can be undermined by generalised claims such as 'natural', 'biodegradable' and 'environmentally friendly'. Scott McClellan, chief executive of the AANA said, "Advertisers should be encouraged to develop and promote environmentally sustainable products." However, he stated that the claims must be "credible and legitimate."

Under the new code, if a consumer makes a complaint to the Advertising Standards Bureau, the advertiser should be able to substantiate its claims in a timely manner.

ACCC checklist for marketers

In a media release from 2007, the ACCC stated that "in light of the growing number of complaints, the ACCC is taking a closer look at a number of the green claims being made at the moment, and all businesses need to ensure they are not misleading their customers with such claims."

If you are going to make environmental claims on your products or in your advertising, you should note the following points from the ACCC:[128]

1. Avoid using terms like 'safe' and 'friendly' and unqualified pictures or graphics. At best they are unhelpful and encourage scepticism; at worst they are misleading.

2. Spell out exactly what is beneficial about a product in plain language that consumers can understand.

3. Link the environmental benefit to a specific part of the product or its production process, such as extraction, transportation, manufacture, use, packaging or disposal.

4. Make sure any claims you make about your product can be substantiated. Think about how you would answer a query regarding the environmental benefits you are claiming about your product. For example, which scientific authority could you use to justify the basis of your claim?

Entering awards

Entering your business in awards programs can be a very rewarding process and a great way to communicate your business' sustainability achievements.

While preparing award submissions can take some time, the end result is a thorough overview of your business' achievements. This will allow you to identify the areas you're doing really well in, and also where the opportunities for improvement are.

Awards programs can also provide excellent networking opportunities, positive exposure in the media and reputational benefits.

Some of the well known business awards with environmental sustainability categories in Australia include:

■ Banksia Environmental Awards: www.banksiafdn.com

128   See www.accc.gov.au

- Telstra Business Awards, Yellow Pages® Social Responsibility award category: www.telstrabusinessawards.com

- United Nations Association of Australia (UNAA) World Environment Day Awards: www.unaavictoria.org.au/pages/awards-program/world-environment-day-awards.php

- Premier's Sustainability Awards (VIC): www.sustainabilityawards.vic.gov.au

The Green Cred Checklist[129]

The NSW based environment group Total Environment Centre has developed a Green Cred Checklist which contains the top ten questions marketers need to answer prior to making green claims about their products or services.

Motivation and knowledge

1. **Motive**

   Why are we making this green claim or taking a corporate position on environment or sustainability?

2. **Knowledge**

   Are we adequately informed or skilled up to understand relevant environmental issues before making claims?

Telling the whole story

3. **Truth**

   Telling the truth is obviously vital, as is clarity, but are you using the truth in the right way?

continued overleaf ...

---

129 The checklist is reproduced courtesy of the Total Environment Centre. Its use cannot be taken to imply any endorsement of a product or its marketing by Total Environment Centre. A full breakdown of these questions is available. See www.tec.org.au

4. **Materiality**

Building on truth, is what we're claiming material? That is, does it really matter, or is it inconsequential?

5. **Full disclosure**

Material omissions are a problem too, so are you sure everything significant is on the table?

Executing well

6. **Life cycle**

Are we looking at everything along the whole value chain and life cycle, or is something we should know invisible to us?

7. **Self control**

Are we sure we're not getting carried away by over-enthusiasm or our aspiration, or even by commercial rivalry?

8. **Core words**

Do we really understand the meaning of core words that are being used in our claims, and are we protecting their integrity?

9. **Proof points**

Are we backing up our claims with specific proof points that are accessible to the target audience?

Don't be afraid to ask for assistance

10. **Help**

If we can't answer all of the points in this checklist with confidence, who can help us to get it right?

Resources and tools

'There are many government and
business-led resources that can help SMEs
on their sustainability journey.'

Further resources

There are many government and business-led resources that can help SMEs on their sustainability journey. Here are some of the best web resources in Australia.

Although this is a state-by-state list, many of these resources are not state-specific. Indeed, Grow Me The Money from Victoria and Business SA from South Australia offer direct help to SMEs in other states and are highly recommended.

National

Business.Gov.Au
www.business.gov.au

**Department of Sustainability,
Environment, Water, Population
and Communities**
www.environment.gov.au

The National SME Project
www.thehub.ethics.org.au

Green Capital
www.greencapital.org.au

Good Business Register
www.goodbusinessregister.com.au

New South Wales

Sustainable business
www.environment.nsw.gov.au/
sustainbus

Business Treading Lightly
www.btl.net.au

Sustainability Toolkit
www.nswbusinesschamber.com.au

It's a Living Thing
www.livingthing.net.au

Energy Smart Toolbox
www.energysmart.com.au

West Australia

Being Green In Business
www.smallbusiness.wa.gov.au

Energy Smart Directory
www.energysmartdirectory.com

Northen Territory

Greening the Territory
www.greeningnt.nt.gov.au

ecoBiz NT
www.ecobiznt.nt.gov.au

Further resources

Victoria

Grow Me The Money
www.growmethemoney.com.au

Carbon Down
www.carbondown.com.au

Carbon Compass
www.carboncompass.com.au

Resource Smart for Businesses
www.resourcesmart.vic.gov.au

**Department of Sustainability
and Environment**
www.dse.vic.gov.au

**Energy and Greenhouse
Management Toolkit**
www.sustainability.vic.gov.au

Life Cycle Management
www.epa.vic.gov.au/lifecycle

South Australia

Business Sustainability Alliance
www.southaustralia.biz

**Business SA – Sustainable Business
Development Unit**
www.business-sa.com

**EPA/Business SA – Small Business
Environmental Management
Solutions guide**
www.epa.sa.gov.au/business

Australian Capital Territory

ACTSmart for Your Business
www.environment.act.gov.au/actsmart/
your_business

Tasmania

Earn Your Stars
www.earnyourstars.tas.gov.au

Sustainable Business and Industry
www.epa.tas.gov.au

Queensland

**ecoBiz Queensland and
Business Sustainability**
www.derm.qld.gov.au

'Don't know the difference between global warming and the greenhouse effect? Check out our definitions here.'

Glossary

At the end of this chapter are the sources of information for the following definitions.

ACF

Australian Conservation Foundation (environment group).

Alternative energy (also called renewable energy)

Energy derived from non-traditional sources such as solar, hydroelectric, wind, wave, geothermal and biomass (as opposed to traditional sources of coal, gas and oil).

Anaerobic digestion

A biological process that produces a gas composed of methane (CH_4) and carbon dioxide (CO_2), sometimes known as biogas. These gases are produced from organic wastes such as livestock manure, sewage, green waste and food waste and can be used to generate energy.

Anthropogenic

Literally meaning human-made. Often used when discussing climate change and global warming, it is usually used when referring to the increased emissions of greenhouse gases caused by human activity.

Biodegradable

Refers to materials that can be broken down by bacteria or other decomposers. Paper and organic wastes such as green waste, food waste and animal manure are biodegradable.

Bioenergy/bioenergy facility

Bioenergy is renewable energy that's created when biological material is converted into energy (see biomass and biofuels). This energy can take the form of electricity or heat. Bioenergy facilities include landfill gas capture (where the gas is burnt and either creates heat or is taken a step further and used to generate electricity) and sites that burn wood waste or agricultural waste (such as paper mills, sawmills and sugar plantations).

Biofuel

Gas or liquid fuels that are made from plant or animal material. Such material includes wood, wood waste, agricultural waste, sludge waste, waste alcohol, municipal solid waste, abattoir waste and other organic matters. Biofuel includes landfill gas, ethanol and biodiesel.

Biodiversity

Short for biological diversity, it refers to the vastness and variability of all living things across terrestrial, marine and other aquatic ecosystems as well as the ecological systems of which they are part. It also includes diversity within species, between species and in ecosystems.

Biomass

Materials that are biological in origin, including organic material (both living and dead) from above and below ground. This can include trees, crops, grasses, tree litter, roots, animals and animal waste.

Biomass energy

This is energy that's produced by combusting biomass materials such as wood – also called alternative energy and sometimes renewable energy. The carbon dioxide emitted from burning biomass does not increase total atmospheric carbon dioxide if this consumption is done on a sustainable basis – that is, where plantations and re-growth forests take up as much carbon dioxide as is released from the burning of the biomass.

Bioswales

Landscaped areas that are designed to remove pollution and silt from run-off surface water before the water is released into waterways or the stormwater system. Sometimes referred to as bio-filters, the areas are commonly filled with plants or gravel or any other medium that traps pollutants while allowing the water to slowly course through the system.

Black water

Waste water from toilets and urinals. Also called foul water or sewage, it refers to any water containing faecal matter or urine, but is distinct from grey water (see grey water).

Brundtland Commission

See the World Commission on Environment and Development.

Carbon dioxide (CO_2)

CO_2 is a small component of the Earth's atmosphere but it's also the planet's most important greenhouse gas. CO_2 is released through deforestation, the burning of vegetable matter and the combustion of fossil fuels such as oil (for transportation) and gas and coal (for energy generation). It is also a gas used in raw form in many production activities. It is a greenhouse gas that traps radiation and contributes to the potential for global warming.

Carbon dioxide equivalent (CO_2-e)

A measure used to compare the emissions of various different greenhouse gases based upon their global warming potential (see global warming potential).

Carbon neutral

Carbon neutrality occurs when the total amount of carbon emissions from any given activity is neutralised by other measures. For example, if a business or household purchases 100 per cent renewable energy GreenPower for electricity use, their electricity use is carbon neutral. All activities using transport, producing goods, offices, events, etc – can be managed in a carbon-neutral fashion.

Carbon offsets

After you generate greenhouse emissions, a carbon offset takes place when you reduce emissions elsewhere by the same amount. This can be achieved by funding projects that reduce emissions (by reducing energy use, generating renewable energy and capturing methane) or by sequestering carbon from the atmosphere (via tree planting or avoided deforestation).

Carbon sequestration

Refers to processes that store carbon. For example, trees and plants absorb carbon dioxide, release the oxygen and store the carbon.

Carbon sink

Carbon reservoirs and conditions that take in and store more carbon (for example, carbon sequestration) than they release. Carbon sinks can serve to partially offset greenhouse gas emissions. Forests and oceans are large carbon sinks.

Carcinogen

A carcinogen is a substance or radiation that can cause or exacerbate cancer. Common examples of carcinogens are asbestos, certain dioxins (see dioxin) and tobacco smoke.

CFLs (Compact fluorescent lamps)

Compact fluorescent lamps or CFLs are also called energy-saving lights. They are fluorescent lights that use less energy and last longer than the incandescent light globes they're designed to replace. Typically they last 6 to 10 times longer than incandescent bulbs and use up to 80 per cent less energy.

Cleaner production

Cleaner production is when you make the same amount of products or services in a way that minimises waste, prevents pollution, and reduces the use of energy, water and material resources (see also eco-efficiency).

Climate

The average weather taken over a period of 20 to 30 years for a particular region. Climate is not the same as weather but it is the average pattern of weather for a particular region. Weather describes the short-term state of the atmosphere.

Climate change

Climate change is a natural occurrence, however human-caused pollution of greenhouse gases has accelerated the scale and pace of change well beyond natural changes.

The Climate Institute

An independent think tank focused on climate research, education and communication.

Cloud computing

Cloud computing is the general term for computing services and/or software that is delivered and hosted over the internet so that the need for on-site infrastructure (such as computers, software or servers) is reduced.

Coal

Coal is a non-renewable resource because it cannot be replenished in a human time frame. It is formed from plant and animal matter that has been transformed over millions of years. Australia has abundant amounts of brown and black coal and in 2009 coal was used to produce 80 per cent of Australia's electricity. Coal generally causes more greenhouse pollution per unit of electricity than any other fuel.

Cogeneration

Cogeneration is when you generate two forms of energy from the one fuel source. For example, paper mills and sugar cane operations in Australia commonly burn biomass to boil water and generate electricity on-site but have leftover steam that can be captured and used in their industrial processes. Cogeneration is often referred to as heat and power systems.

Commingled materials

Commingled materials is what you get when people put all of their different recyclables such as glass, plastic and metal into the one bin. Commingled recyclable materials require sorting and separating after collection before they can be recycled. This sorting and separating takes place at a Material Recovery Facility (MRF).

Deforestation

Deforestation refers to logging practices where trees are removed and not replaced. This is often the result of forested lands being transformed to non-forest uses. Deforestation is one of the major causes of the enhanced greenhouse effect for two reasons. Firstly, the burning or decomposition of the wood releases carbon dioxide into the atmosphere. Secondly, once they're logged, the trees are no longer removing carbon dioxide from the atmosphere.

Dioxin

Highly toxic chemical compounds that can cause human health problems and which are highly persistent in the environment. They are emitted to the air through fuel and waste emissions, including motor vehicle exhaust fumes, burning fuels (like wood, coal or oil), chlorine bleaching, some manufacturing processes and garbage incineration. It is a general term used to cover a wide family of chemicals.

Eco-efficiency

Producing the same number of goods and services while reducing environmental and ecological impacts. This includes reducing materials and resource use, energy, water and waste through the whole lifecycle of a product or service (see also cleaner production).

Eco label

This term refers to any labelling or logo system that conveys to consumers that the product or service benefits the environment or minimises negative environmental effects. Examples of eco labels include Good Environmental Choice Australia, Fairtrade and the Forest Stewardship Council (FSC). Eco label systems operate in a number of ways – independently by not-for-profit groups, by Government, by industry associations and by individual companies.

Ecological footprint

The size and environmental impact of the energy, water, waste and resources associated with an individual, business, community or other entity. This is often expressed as the area of land required to produce the resources consumed by a person, entity or activity.

Ecosystem

The system of plant, animal, fungal, and microorganism communities and their associated non-living environment interacting as an ecological unit. Ecosystems have no fixed boundaries; instead their parameters are set by the scientific, management or policy question being examined. Depending on the purpose of analysis, a single lake, a watershed, or an entire region could be considered an ecosystem.

Electronic waste/e-waste

Electronic or e-waste generally refers to any sort of electrical equipment that is no longer wanted – computers, televisions, DVD and VHS players, printers, mobile phones, kitchen appliances etc. It is an environmental concern because many of these products contain contaminants as well as valuable materials that can be recovered.

Emission inventory

A record of air pollutants emitted into or from a particular area over a period of time. It can refer to emissions associated with a business, community, State, country or the Earth.

Emissions

The release of a substance (usually a gas when referring to the subject of climate change) into the atmosphere.

Energy efficiency

Is about using less energy to perform the same action. For example, energy-saving light globes use 80 per cent less electricity than incandescent light globes.

Enhanced greenhouse effect

The concept that the natural greenhouse effect has been enhanced by increased emissions of greenhouse gases caused by human activity. This increased concentration of greenhouse gases traps more infrared radiation, thereby exerting a warming influence on the climate.

Environmental management systems (EMS)

A systemised approach to identifying and managing a company's environmental impacts.

Environmental stewardship

The responsibility for preserving environmental quality shared by all those whose actions affect the environment.

Fossil fuels

Fossil fuels come in three major forms – coal, oil, and natural gas. Because fossil fuels are a finite resource and cannot be replenished once they are extracted and burned, they are not considered renewable.

Geothermal energy

Heat transferred from the Earth's core to underground deposits of dry steam, wet steam, hot water, or rocks lying under the Earth's surface. This energy can be used to generate renewable power.

Global Reporting Initiative (GRI)

The most widely used framework around the world for companies and other organisations that want to assess and report on sustainability performance and commitments.

Global warming

The progressive gradual rise in average temperatures of the Earth's near-surface air and oceans. Global warming has occurred in the distant past as the result of natural influences, however the term is used today to refer to the warming predicted to occur as a result of increased emissions of greenhouse gases caused by human activity.

Global Warming Potential (GWP)

The index used to translate the impacts of different greenhouse gas emissions into a common measure. Global Warming Potential (GWP) is calculated as the ratio of the impact that would result from 1 kilogram of a particular greenhouse gas to that from 1 kilogram of carbon dioxide over a period of time (usually 100 years). For example, the GWP of methane is 25 times more potent a greenhouse gas over 100 years than carbon dioxide.

Greenhouse effect

The Earth's ability to sustain a temperature conducive to life depends on the natural 'greenhouse effect'. This is where the Sun's heat is trapped by heat-trapping greenhouse gases in our atmosphere. These greenhouse gases act like a blanket around the Earth. Without this 'greenhouse effect', the planet's average surface temperature would be about minus 18 degrees Celsius. The global warming attributed to the increased level of greenhouse gases is called the 'enhanced greenhouse effect'.

Greenhouse gas

Any atmospheric gas that contributes to the greenhouse effect. The main greenhouse gases are water vapour, carbon dioxide, methane, nitrous oxide, ozone and chlorofluorocarbons.

Green roof

Green roofs reduce rooftop and building temperatures. Also known as rooftop gardens, green roofs are planted over existing roof structures and consist of a waterproof, root-safe membrane that is covered by a drainage system, lightweight growing medium, and plants.

GreenPower

Electricity generated from renewable energy sources such as wind, solar, mini hydro and biomass. GreenPower is a government-certified scheme to promote the expansion of these types of renewable energy. When you pay extra for GreenPower, the Government ensures that this money is invested in renewable energy. 100 per cent GreenPower is the best option, but lower-cost 10 per cent GreenPower is also available. Regardless of the amount of GreenPower that you buy, it all helps to boost the renewable energy sector.

Greenwashing

The process by which a company publicly and misleadingly exaggerates or embellishes the environmental attributes of its operations or its products.

Green building

A process of design and construction that employs techniques to minimise adverse environmental impacts and reduce the energy consumption of a building, while contributing to the health and productivity of its occupants.

Grey water

Wastewater from washing processes such as dishwashing, laundry, showers, baths and hand basins. It is also called sullage. Grey water can often be treated on-site (in both houses or businesses) for re-use on gardens or for flushing toilets. It is not fit for human consumption, but can be if it is treated.

Hybrid car

A hybrid car is a vehicle that uses two or more sources of power – the most common being a combination of petrol and electric power. Petrol/electric cars use a traditional combustion engine as the main engine and an electric motor that helps to reduce emissions or provide extra power. Most hybrids do not need to be plugged in – the energy generated during deceleration or braking is captured and stored in a battery. Some hybrid cars can use half the fuel of a equivalent-sized vehicle.

Hydro electricity

Electrical energy produced by falling or flowing water.

Hydrofluorocarbons (HFCs)

HFCs are used in fridges and the manufacturing of semiconductors. Depending on the type of HFC used, these can be 140–11,700 times more potent a greenhouse gas than CO_2.

HVAC

Stands for Heating Ventilation and Air Conditioning.

Intergovernmental Panel on Climate Change (IPCC)

When it comes to the science of climate change, the IPCC is looked to as the main international advisory body to the world's governments. The IPCC organised the development of internationally accepted methods for conducting national greenhouse gas emission accounting and inventories. The IPCC is a United Nations entity and draws upon thousands of the world's scientists as expert reviewers and authors and assesses information in the scientific and technical literature related to the issue of climate change.

ISO 14001

The international standard for companies seeking to certify their environmental management system.

Joule

The international unit for the measurement of energy is the joule (J). As the joule is a rather small unit, a prefix is usually added to form a unit of a more convenient magnitude. For example, kilo (1000 times) is combined to joule to form kilojoule (kJ). Natural gas consumption is usually measured in megajoules (MJ), where 1 MJ = 1,000,000 J. On large accounts it may be measured in gigajoules (GJ), where 1 GJ = 1,000,000,000 J.

Kyoto protocol

An international agreement adopted at the United Nations Framework Convention on Climate Change (UNFCCC) in Kyoto, Japan in December 1997. It sets legally binding targets and timetables for cutting the greenhouse gas emissions of industrialised countries which have accepted it.

LEDs

Stands for light emitting diode – they are small and compact light sources that are very bright and energy-efficient. They are used in a range of applications such as indicators on cars and traffic signals and increasingly for text and video displays and light bulbs.

Life cycle assessment (LCA)

A technique to assess the total environmental impacts associated with a product, process or service. This is achieved by completing and analysing a detailed inventory of energy and material inputs and environmental releases.

The term 'life cycle' refers to the notion that a fair, holistic assessment requires the assessment of raw material production, manufacture, distribution, use and disposal including all intervening transportation steps necessary or caused by the product's existence. The sum of all those steps – or phases – is the life cycle of the product. The concept also can be used to optimise the environmental performance of a single product (eco-design) or to optimise the environmental performance of a company.

Methane (CH_4)

Methane is a very significant greenhouse gas. Averaged over a hundred year period, the global warming potential of methane is 25 times more potent than CO_2.[130] CH_4 is usually caused by the decomposition of landfill waste; exhalation from cows, sheep and other ruminant animals; rice growing, wetlands and fossil fuel production. As the world warms, there is also great potential for significant amounts of methane to be emitted by melting tundra.

Natural gas

Underground gas consisting of 50 to 90 per cent methane (CH_4) and small amounts of heavier gaseous hydrocarbon compounds such as propane (C_3H_8) and butane (C_4H_{10}).

130   IPCC, 2007: *Climate Change 2007: The Physical Science Basis*. Contribution of Working Group I to the Fourth Assessment Report of the Intergovernmental Panel on Climate Change – www.ipcc-wg1.unibe.ce

Natural resource

Raw materials or energy supplied by nature and its processes (for example: water, minerals, plants). Trees are a natural resource used to make paper, and sunlight is a natural resource that can be used to heat homes.

Nitrous oxide (N_2O)

N_2O is the result of commercial and organic fertilisers, the combustion of fossil fuel, the production of nitric acid and the burning of biomass. As a greenhouse gas, it's 310 times more potent than CO_2.

NGO

Non-governmental organisation (environment groups and community groups are NGOs).

Organic food

Organic food is produced without using most conventional pesticides; fertilisers made with synthetic ingredients or sewage sludge; bioengineering; or ionising radiation. Organic meat, poultry, eggs, and dairy products come from animals that are given no antibiotics or growth hormones.

Perfluorocarbons (PFCs)

PFCs are by-products of uranium enrichment and the aluminium smelting process and are used in refrigerating units. Depending on the type of PFC used, as a greenhouse gas these can be 6500 to 9200 times more potent than CO_2.

PET

Polyethylene terephthalate. A clear and tough polymer that's used to make plastic products – it is commonly used for drinks bottles, food packaging and fabrics.

Phosphor burn-in

Also called screen burn, it is where a computer or television screen is damaged and disfigured by an image being permanently visible on the screen due to the fact that is was left static and visible for too long. Putting a computer into sleep mode or turning it off, is a way to stop burn-in.

Photovoltaic (PV)

A system that converts sunlight directly into electricity using cells made of silicon or other conductive materials.

Pollution

A change in the physical, chemical, or biological characteristics of the air, water, or soil that can affect the health, survival, or activities of humans in an unwanted way. The term can also be expanded to include harmful effects on all forms of life.

Post-consumer

Materials recovered and recycled after use by consumers. For example, many newspapers contain some post-consumer recycled content. Office paper that is turned into toilet paper is a post-consumer raw material.

Pre-consumer

Materials recovered, salvaged and recycled for reuse from an industrial or manufacturing process. Paper manufacturers sometimes use offcuts from the paper making process and add this pre-consumer 'waste' into new paper.

Radiation

Energy that is transmitted or radiated in the form of electromagnetic waves or particles that release energy when they're absorbed by an object.

Radiation has differing characteristics depending upon the wavelength. Because the radiation from the Sun is relatively energetic, it has a short wavelength (ultra-violet, visible, and near infrared) while energy radiated from the Earth's surface and the atmosphere has a longer wavelength (for example, infrared radiation) because the Earth is cooler than the Sun.

Recycling

Collecting, reprocessing and re-using a resource to make a new product.

Renewable energy

Energy obtained from sources that are essentially inexhaustible, unlike, for example, fossil fuels, of which there is a finite supply. Renewable sources of energy include waste, geothermal, wind, wave and solar energy.

Renewable Energy Certificate (REC)

Renewable Energy Certificates are credits for electricity generated from renewable sources. They are able to be bought, sold and generally used in processes for proving the validity of renewable energy production and for compliance with state or national laws.

Renewable resource

Naturally occurring raw material that comes from a limitless source such as the Sun and wind or a renewable resource like trees.

Resource recovery

The process of obtaining matter or energy from discarded materials. Recycling is resource recovery, as is waste to energy.

Retrofitting

The application of conservation, efficiency, or renewable-energy technologies to existing structures.

Solar energy

Direct radiant energy from the Sun.

Stormwater

Stormwater discharges are generated by rain and runoff from land, pavements, building rooftops and other surfaces. Stormwater runoff accumulates pollutants such as oil and grease, chemicals, nutrients, metals and bacteria as it travels across land.

Sulfur hexafluoride (SF_6)

SF_6 is mainly used to insulate high-voltage equipment. It is also used in cable-cooling systems. As a greenhouse gas, it is 22,800 times more potent than CO_2. It is the most potent greenhouse gas.

Sulfur oxides (SOx)

Sulfur oxides are significant air pollutants generated by the combustion of fossil fuels but also from natural sources such as volcanoes. Power plants burning high-sulfur coal or heating oil are generally the main sources of anthropogenic sulfur dioxide emissions worldwide, followed by industrial boilers and nonferrous metal smelters.

Sustainability

Any process or condition that can be maintained indefinitely without interruption, weakening, or loss of valued qualities.

Sustainable agriculture

Farming systems that are capable of maintaining their productivity and usefulness indefinitely. Such systems satisfy human food and fibre needs while maintaining the natural resource base and making efficient use of non-renewable resources.

Sustainable development

Development that meets the needs of the present without compromising the ability of future generations to meet their own needs.

Sustainable procurement

Also called green procurement, this is a concept whereby a spending or investment decision doesn't just consider price and quality. It also takes into consideration the environmental and social impact of a product or service.

Volatile organic compound (VOC)

Organic compounds that evaporate readily into the atmosphere at normal temperatures. Volatile organic compounds (VOCs) contribute significantly to photochemical smog production and certain health problems.

Waste hierarchy (also called waste management hierarchy)

Sometimes referred to as 'reduce, reuse, recycle'. The waste hierarchy promotes the management of waste in the following order: firstly avoidance, then reuse, recycling, recovery of energy, treatment, containment, and finally disposal.

Watt

In the International System of Units, the Watt is a derived unit of power. It is the number of joules used per second. That is 1 W = 1 J/s. This unit is also used in greater magnitudes such as kilowatts (kW), where 1 kW = 1 kJ/s = 1000 J/s; and megawatts (MW).

Electricity consumption is measured in units of watt-hours (Wh), or more typically, kilowatt-hours (kWh) and megawatt-hours (MWh), where 1 MWh = 1000 kWh. 1 kWh means 1 kW of power being used for 1 hour.

WELS

Stands for the Water Efficiency Labelling and Standards Scheme. It is an Australian Government run scheme that requires a range of water-using devices (such as dishwashers, clothes washers and shower nozzles) to be assessed and labelled for their water efficiency. The label is star rating based – the more stars means more water efficiency.

World Commission on Environment and Development (WCED)

The World Commission on Environment and Development is also known as the Brundtland Commission, from its chairperson Gro Harlem Brundtland. The WCED was commissioned by the United Nations General Assembly in 1983 to report on the global environment to the year 2000 and beyond and to propose strategies for sustainable development. The Commission published a report in 1987 entitled *Our Common Future* that addressed the issue and provided the most cited definition of the term sustainable development: 'Development that meets the needs of the present without compromising the ability of future generations to meet their own needs.' An Australian edition titled *A Sustainable Future for Australia* was published in 1990.

The information in this glossary is from a wide range of sources including:

- Australian Bureau of Meteorology: www.bom.gov.au
- Australian Government Department of Sustainability, Environment, Water, Population and Communities: www.environment.gov.au
- Australian Government Department of Climate Change and Energy Efficiency: www.climatechange.gov.au
- *Cannibals With Forks: The Triple Bottom Line of 21st Century Business,* John Elkington, Capstone, 1997
- *Environmental Decision-making,* Ronnie Harding, Federation Press, 1998
- GreenFacts: www.greenfacts.org
- *Leading Change Toward Sustainability,* Bob Doppelt, Greenleaf, 2003
- Sustainability Victoria: www.sustainability.vic.gov.au

"Doing more with less makes your business operate more efficiently and helps your bottom line."

– Jon Dee

About the author

Jon Dee is the Founder and Managing Director of Do Something. He was also the NSW Australian of the Year for 2010. Since 1992, he has been one of Australia's most influential figures on environmental issues, inspiring millions of Australians to make positive environmental change.

He founded National Tree Day with Olivia Newton-John, an event for which 2 million Australian volunteers have planted 15 million native trees and shrubs. In 1991, he founded Planet Ark together with his close friend Pat Cash. Through his role with Planet Ark, Jon was a driving force behind a number of groundbreaking environmental campaigns. He instigated National Recycling Week, the National Recycling Hotline and www.recyclingnearyou.com.au which is used by more than one million Australians every year.

He has spearheaded the media campaign to phase out plastic bags and co-founded the 'plastic bag-free towns' push in Coles Bay, Tasmania. Jon was also the official spokesperson for the Australian DVD release of *An Inconvenient Truth*.

Jon also initiated the successful lobbying campaign for Australia's three-year phase-out of incandescent light globes, a move that will save Australians hundreds of millions of dollars. Other countries are now following Australia's lead in phasing out the use of such globes.

In addition to producing and directing more than 350 environmental TV and radio ads, Jon was the founder of *World Environment News*, one of the world's leading environmental news services. He also co-organised the bottled water ban in Bundanoon, NSW that created headlines around the world.

Jon is in strong demand here and overseas as a corporate speaker. Companies who have hired Jon to speak to them include Hewlett-Packard, Commonwealth Bank, McDonald's, ANZ, Toyota, NAB, BMW, Foster's Group and many others.

Through his work with the Do Something organisation, Jon is currently running a number of campaigns to bring about positive social and environmental change. To find out more, visit www.dosomething.net.au, www.jondee.com. You can also follow Jon on Twitter via www.twitter.com/JonDeeOz

Acknowledgements

Jon would like to acknowledge and thank Tim Wallace, Leanne Dee, Liz Durnan, Jessica Langmead, Jill Riseley and Sensis for their help and assistance with this book. He would also like to thank OMG! Creative and Equilibrium OMG for their work.

About the author

About Sensis

To obtain another copy of this book, visit www.about.sensis.com.au

Sensis is Telstra's advertising business and Australia's leading directories information resource. Sensis delivers innovative and integrated local search and digital marketing solutions via print, online, voice, mobile, landline and new devices including the iPhone, iPad, Android phone and Telstra's T-Hub®. Our content can be found via search engines including Google™, Bing and Yahoo!, and information can be shared from online to mobile and social networking sites. This network connects Australians with information anywhere, anytime and in any way people choose. Sensis' powerful, multi-channel portfolio provides an unparalleled local information source, helping Australians find, buy and sell.

Yellow Pages®

For more than 80 years, Yellow Pages® has been connecting Australian buyers and sellers more than any other business. Today, with just one Yellow Pages® listing, your business details could be found across our network of products including print, online, over the phone, mobile and satellite navigation products. Yellow Pages® advertisers' business address details can also be searched for on search engines such as Google™,[131] Yahoo7! and Bing, as well as on online mapping sites such as Google Maps™, Whereis® and Bing Maps. Through this network approach, Yellow Pages® is putting advertisers in front of more people that are looking to buy.

www.yellowpages.com.au
www.yellowadvertising.com.au
13 23 78

White Pages®

The White Pages® is Australia's most reliable source of contact information and has been connecting Australian communities for almost 130 years. It is where Australians turn for contact details for people, businesses, government and community organisations. Today, the White Pages® is available across a network of products including print, online, mobile and voice directories. Each month, more than half the Australian adult population use the White Pages® Network,[132] with six out of ten people who search White Pages® directory and/or whitepages.com.au looking for a business of which they are not an existing customer.[133]

www.whitepages.com.au
www.whywhitepages.com.au
1800 810 211

Sensis Digital Media™

Sensis Digital Media™ commercialises the digital media assets of Telstra, Sensis and leading third party sites. They do this by combining their progressive digital products, a highly targeted network and industry leading experts to make it easy for advertisers to meet their goals.

www.sensisdigitalmedia.com.au
1300 734 477

131   Google is a trademark of Google Inc.

132   Roy Morgan Single Source Australia, 14 years and over, monthly average. January 2008 – December 2008. White Pages® Network includes White Pages® directory, whitepages.com. au, sensis.com.au, Telstra Directory Assistance, Call Connect (12456) and 1234. Call Connect (12456) is available to most Telstra customers. 1234 is available to most Telstra customers except where preselected to another carrier for long distance calls.

133   Independent research of 18-64 year olds by TNS in metropolitan directory markets in Melbourne, Sydney, Brisbane, Adelaide and Perth, January 2006 – December 2007.

1234™

1234™ is a premium voice information service that provides a whole range of information such as what's on in your city, the latest sports results, movie session times, street directions, as well as phone numbers and a connection service. The 1234™ business draws on the comprehensive Yellow Pages® and White Pages® databases to provide millions of Australians with information about businesses, people and locations.

www.1234.com.au

13 23 78

Citysearch®

Citysearch.com.au is an online and mobile entertainment and lifestyle destination that keeps Australians up to date with what's on in each Australian capital city across key entertainment categories. These include restaurants, bars, music, movies, TV, the arts and major events. Citysearch® helps people make informed and inspired decisions about where to spend their time and money by delivering rich content and local expertise via a dedicated editorial team, local writers, expert bloggers and useful tools. You'll find business listings, user reviews, and videos nationwide. Citysearch® content including user comments and votes can also be shared on social networks like Facebook, via the online and mobile sites or the free Citysearch® iPhone app.

www.citysearch.com.au

13 24 89

Whereis®

Whereis® is a leading provider of digital maps and content for Australia and New Zealand. Whereis® digital maps and content have enormous reach across Australia via popular website www.Whereis.com, Whereis® *Mobile*, GPS offerings in portable and in car navigation devices and specialist phone applications for iPhone and other GPS enabled phones via Whereis® Navigator. Whereis.com receives more than 4 million visits every month.[134]

A key ingredient to Whereis®' unique offering is the rich content of the Yellow Pages® and White Pages® databases. Yellow Pages® listings are found among the 600,000-plus points of interest available on Whereis® maps. This means when Australians search for a business or an address on a map, they are drawing on information from one of the most comprehensive databases in Australia.

134   Omniture Site Catalyst – average site visits: December 2009 – February 2010

The www.whereismaps.com website provides rich information to consumers interested in GPS and navigation. It promotes maps as a key element in these products while also giving consumers the opportunity to buy map updates for their in-car, portable and mobile GPS devices.

www.whereis.com
www.whereismaps.com
1800 819 471

Sensis Data Solutions

Sensis® Data Solutions delivers data quality, directory search and verification, and location intelligence solutions to businesses and government. Our solutions are based on Sensis' range of information sources including the White Pages® and Yellow Pages® directories and Whereis® mapping data. Our solutions are designed to enhance a business' sales and marketing activities and improve operational efficiencies.

www.sensisdata.com.au
1800 033 807

Sustainability at Sensis

We believe how we do business is just as important as what we do. At Sensis, our Sustainability Strategy is about supporting the needs of current and future generations, today and tomorrow. It's being ethical, sustainable and accountable with all our stakeholders in everything we do. We look to achieve this goal by minimising the environmental impacts of our products and making a positive contribution to the communities in which we operate.

The Yellow Pages® and White Pages® print and online directories were certified carbon neutral through the Australian Government's Greenhouse Friendly™ program in February 2010. Sensis will offset the carbon emissions of its directories through Greenhouse Friendly™ accredited providers and projects in Australia. Sensis also announced its target to reduce operational carbon emissions by 5 per cent year-on-year.

www.about.sensis.com.au/sustainability
sustainability@sensis.com.au

About this book

Design

This book has been designed by OMG! Creative, which has developed extensive skills in creating and executing communications strategies for brands that incorporate sustainability as part of their brand DNA.

OMG! Creative was the first advertising agency to gain the Greenhouse Challenge Plus accreditation. In addition to undertaking sustainable practices in its business, OMG! Creative offset all remaining greenhouse emissions through government-approved certificates.

The agency ensured all aspects of the creation and production of the book from design concept through to the manuscript approval process, printing and the selection of business partners had minimal impact on the environment.

Technical Editing

The content and facts in this book have been reviewed and edited by Equilibrium OMG, a specialist sustainability management and consulting company. Equilibrium OMG offers strategies, management and tools to improve your sustainability and help you grow your business. The personnel of Equilibrium OMG have more than 30 years collective experience in environmental management and sustainability and bring together practical services and products that support improved performance, profitability and reputation.

Paper

This publication has been printed on ecoStar, which is manufactured from 100% post consumer recycled paper in a process chlorine free environment under the ISO 14001 environmental management system. The fibre source has been independently certified by the Forest Stewardship Council (FSC) and greenhouse gas emissions have been reduced to net zero through carbon offsetting certified by the CarbonNeutral Company. The carbon emissions of the manufacturing process for ecoStar have been measured and offset through the CarbonNeutral Company. The assessment/audit of the greenhouse gas emissions has been undertaken by the Edinburgh Centre for Carbon Management (ECCM), an independent third party in accordance with the WBCSD-WRI GHG Protocol and the emissions have been reduced to net zero through internal change and/or externally through carbon offsetting by the CarbonNeutral Company in accordance with the requirements of the CarbonNeutral Protocol for the stated activity. www.raleighpaper.com.au www.eccm.uk.com www.carbonneutral.com

Printing

This book has been printed by Vega Press using soy and vegetable based inks on a printing press that operates alcohol free with closed loop water recycling systems. Vega Press is committed to continual environmental improvement through its ISO 14001:2004 Environmental Management Systems certification and has implemented water, energy and waste minimisation systems across its production processes. Vega Press has taken action to reduce and report on its carbon emissions in accordance with ISO 14064-1:2006 and was the first Australian Business certified to this Standard (2008-2009). Emissions that are not able to be avoided are offset by purchasing carbon offsets from the Carbon Reduction Institute®. All offsets purchased meet or exceed the criteria set by the Kyoto Protocol and are independently audited by a third party. Vega Press has Forest Stewardship Council Chain of Custody Certification and works with paper suppliers and others in the supply chain to ensure the best possible environmental outcome when choosing materials and recycling waste. In 2010 Vega Press won the Victorian Premier's Sustainability Award, multiple environmental awards in the local community and was a finalist in the national Banksia Environmental Awards.
www.vega.com.au

Index

Index